2015 Index of
Economic Freedom

CONTRIBUTORS

Ambassador Terry Miller is Director of the Center for Trade and Economics and the Center for Data Analysis, of the Institute for Economic Freedom and Opportunity, and the Mark A. Kolokotrones Fellow in Economic Freedom, at The Heritage Foundation.

Anthony B. Kim is Senior Policy Analyst in the Center for Trade and Economics.

Senator Jim DeMint is President of The Heritage Foundation.

James M. Roberts is Research Fellow for Economic Freedom and Growth in the Center for Trade and Economics.

Bryan Riley is Jay Van Andel Senior Analyst in Trade Policy in the Center for Trade and Economics.

Ryan Olson is Research Associate in the Center for Trade and Economics.

Paul A. Gigot is Editor of *The Wall Street Journal* Editorial Page.

Stephen Moore is Chief Economist at The Heritage Foundation.

Joel Griffith is Research Associate for the Chief Economist at The Heritage Foundation.

Antonio Nucifora, PhD, is the former Lead Economist for Tunisia at the World Bank.

Erik Churchill is a political analyst and consultant at the World Bank.

Bob Rijkers, PhD, is an economist in the Research Department at the World Bank.

Nicolas D. Loris is the Herbert and Joyce Morgan Fellow and Senior Analyst in the Thomas A. Roe Institute for Economic Policy Studies of the Institute for Economic Freedom and Opportunity.

2015 Index of Economic Freedom

Ambassador Terry Miller
Anthony B. Kim

with James M. Roberts, Bryan Riley, and Ryan Olson

The **Heritage Foundation**   THE WALL STREET JOURNAL.

The Heritage Foundation
214 Massachusetts Avenue, NE
Washington, DC 20002
(202) 546-4400
heritage.org

The Wall Street Journal
Dow Jones & Company, Inc.
200 Liberty Street
New York, NY 10281
(212) 416-2000
www.wsj.com

Cover image © thinkstockphotos.com
ISBN: 978-0-89195-287-9
ISSN: 1095-7308

Contents

Foreword

In his famous 1980 book and TV series *Free to Choose*, the incomparable Milton Friedman held forth with the backdrop of Hong Kong harbor on the miracle of the then-British colony. He called it "the modern exemplar of free markets and limited government."

He was surely right, as I learned when I lived in Hong Kong in 1979 and again through much of the 1980s. The pile of rocks had prospered under the "positive non-interventionism" of its wise British rulers, and it has continued to do so since it became a Special Administrative Region under light Chinese control in 1997. With that happy legacy, Hong Kong has also remained at the top of the annual *Index of Economic Freedom*.

The question raised this year is how long its premier status will last. Singapore, another city-state dependent largely on human capital, has been inching closer to Hong Kong and now is essentially tied.

More ominously, doubts have increased this year about Hong Kong's rule of law as protests broke out over Beijing's control of future elections in the territory. Pro-democracy students took to the streets, gaining global headlines but little movement from Beijing or its yes-men in the Hong Kong government. Supporters of democracy were harassed, notably media baron Jimmy Lai, a chief funder of the democracy movement whose home was raided by Hong Kong's anti-corruption agency that previously had a reputation for incorruptibility. That raid and others looked to be motivated by politics.

This matters for economic as much as for political freedom because the rule of law is essential to property rights and a free society. Liberty has prospered in Hong Kong in part because contracts have been protected by the British legal tradition. If the law in the future can be bent to political ends, then individual workers and business investors will eventually get the message that they too are vulnerable to threats, harassment, and perhaps expropriation if they get on the wrong side of the Chinese Communist Party.

Some will argue that economic freedom can exist without political freedom, and perhaps that is true for a time. But eventually, the need for political control compromises the rule of law and the freedom to make economic choices.

This is what could now be happening in Hong Kong, and it is why the city's democracy protestors deserve the world's support. They are fighting to protect their way of life as much as they are for the right to elect a chief executive. This is why we at *The Wall Street Journal* have devoted so much coverage to Hong Kong's democratic uprising. In 2014, Hong Kong has been on freedom's front lines.

Hong Kong's struggle is also a reminder that economic liberty is not guaranteed, and the wealth of nations can rise and fall with surprising rapidity. The "Executive Highlights" in this year's *Index* contrast some of the gainers and losers in what is the eternal battle by men and women to determine their own fate. It is heartening to see progress in parts of Africa, long ignored as hopeless in the West, but dispiriting to see setbacks in Europe, original home of the Enlightenment and capitalism.

America, my home, is having its own struggles. Its precipitous decline in the *Index* in the wake of the financial panic of 2008 and the rise of the Obama Administration seems to have been arrested. The election of a Republican Congress in November 2014 gives some new hope for a revival, but that will require the rise of a new generation of leaders willing to relearn the old lessons about freedom and prosperity that Milton Friedman taught us through the example of Hong Kong. So here we go, back to the barricades.

Paul A. Gigot
Editorial Page Editor
The Wall Street Journal
November 2014

Preface

As I write this in November 2014, people around the world are celebrating the 25th anniversary of the fall of the Berlin Wall. This *Index* was inspired in many ways by the heroic events that took place in Europe a quarter of a century ago, and it was only shortly thereafter that we began, in connection with *The Wall Street Journal*, to record the march of freedom around the world.

The unraveling of the Soviet Union and the liberation of Eastern Europe represent a great triumph for freedom and economic advancement. People who once lived in fear and poverty have experienced a rebirth of productivity and dramatic economic modernization. Countries that once lagged badly have emerged from the shadows of repression to join as equals in freedom those who in the past they could view only dimly through an iron curtain.

The lesson is clear: The human spirit is the real wellspring of economic prosperity. That spirit is at its most inspired when it is unleashed from the chains in which it has been bound.

Still, as events in countries like Georgia, Ukraine, and Russia show, the fight for freedom requires perpetual vigilance against the inroads of enemies both external and internal. False starts toward economic freedom have been seen in places like China, where a burst of economic reform 30 years ago lifted millions out of poverty but where economic momentum is flagging as reform has stalled. The collapse of countries like Zimbabwe and Venezuela, where dictatorial rule has destroyed lives and prospects for the future, is a vivid reminder that freedoms hard won may be easily lost. In my own country, the United States, economic freedom has not advanced in recent years. We are performing far below potential as a result. In the Middle East, a burst of revolutionary fervor is driving change toward ends as yet unknown.

Perhaps the most critical lesson for these tumultuous times is that the proven superiority of the free-market system and the value of economic liberty must be steadfastly reiterated, particularly in times of trouble. The data we present in the *Index of Economic Freedom* are a good foundation for that discussion.

In addition to its country analysis and rankings, the 2015 *Index* contains three informative chapters that explore topics of particular relevance to today's policy debates.

- In Chapter 3, Steve Moore, Chief Economist at The Heritage Foundation, and his co-author, Joel Griffith, undertake comparative analysis of selected countries in various regions, highlighting ways in which the rule of law, efficient regulatory structures, open markets, and a commitment to lower taxes promote greater prosperity.

- In Chapter 4, the *Index* takes a closer look at the causes and prospects for the Arab Spring. Presenting a detailed case study on Tunisia, three World Bank economists analyze the harm inflicted by cronyism and underscore the urgent need for inclusive policies that provide opportunities for all Tunisians to ensure a successful economic and political transition.

- In Chapter 5, Nick Loris, a researcher focusing on energy, environmental, and regulatory issues as the Herbert and Joyce Morgan Fellow at The Heritage Foundation, assesses the critical linkages between economic freedom, energy, and development.

Like its predecessors, the 2015 *Index* provides ample evidence that dynamic economic gains can be achieved by advancing freedom. Countries that are gaining freedom enjoy higher economic growth, greater gains in employment, higher incomes, better health, cleaner environments, and a host of other benefits. Those that are not are, on average, lagging behind and, in the worst cases, remain stuck in stagnation and poverty. Such failures are inexcusable. Most important, they are preventable.

We cannot, of course, know what the future will bring as the *Index of Economic Freedom* advances into its third decade. Nonetheless, it is encouraging to know that economic freedom is still on the march. As the *Index* has shown in case after case, nations that find the political will and wisdom to advance economic freedom will be best positioned to see their citizens prosper in the years ahead.

Jim DeMint, President
The Heritage Foundation
November 2014

Acknowledgments

The *Index of Economic Freedom* is a product of intense collaboration with people and organizations around the world. While it is impossible to mention all of those who have contributed to our success, we wish to express our gratitude to the myriad individuals serving with various international organizations, research institutions, U.S. government agencies, foreign embassies, and other organizations who provide the data used in the *Index*. Assistance from them is vital and greatly appreciated.

The Heritage Foundation's Center for Trade and Economics (CTE) leads the *Index* production effort. The CTE team of James Roberts, Bryan Riley, and Ryan Olson shared with us the responsibility for grading the 10 components of economic freedom. CTE interns Fan Mo, Tori Whiting, Ashley Wright, Bridget Mudd, Elizabeth Allen, Andy Marguiles, Preston Turner, and Charlotte Howson contributed substantial research.

Various Heritage Foundation foreign policy experts who provided country backgrounds informed by their regional and country expertise include Lisa Curtis, Bruce Klingner, Bill Wilson, and Director Walter Lohman of the Asian Studies Center; Luke Coffey and Daniel Kochis of the Margaret Thatcher Center for Freedom; and Charlotte Florance, James Phillips, and Ana Quintana of the Douglas and Sarah Allison Center for Foreign and National Security Policy.

The *Index of Economic Freedom* is a substantial publication that is brought to print each year by an incredibly talented team of editors and production specialists. We wish to express our deepest appreciation to Senior Editor Richard Odermatt, who is responsible for final review of the completed text, and Senior Copy Editor William T. Poole, who bears the primary responsibility for perfecting the language we employ, as well as Therese Pennefather, Deputy Director of Research Editing, and Senior Data Graphics Editor John Fleming. Creative Director Melissa Bluey and Jay Simon, Publication Production Specialist, were responsible for the design and layout of the book.

The availability of the entire *Index* and its database online at www.heritage.org/index has greatly expanded the publication's reach and accessibility over the past years. The transposition to the Web each year would not be possible without the expertise of Director of Marketing

Technology Tim McGovern and his team, including Roger Spurzem, Maria Sousa, Isabel Isidro, Jeph Christoff, Joe Perez, Catherine Dugyon, and former Heritage staffer Jim Lawruk.

Jack Spencer, Vice President for the Institute for Economic Freedom and Opportunity, and Dr. James Carafano, Vice President for the Kathryn and Shelby Cullom Davis Institute for National Security and Foreign Policy, provide substantial help and advice in connection with many aspects of *Index* production and marketing. We are also grateful for the contributions to our work over the past year of Derrick Morgan, former Vice President for the Institute for Economic Freedom and Opportunity.

Senator Jim DeMint, President of The Heritage Foundation, and Phil Truluck, Executive Vice President of The Heritage Foundation, have been enthusiastic supporters and great sources of encouragement in producing this annual publication. The ongoing support from Group Vice Presidents David Addington, Ed Corrigan, John Fogarty, and Geoff Lysaught; Vice Presidents Becky Norton Dunlop, John Von Kannon, Wesley Denton, and Matt Streit; and Chief of Staff Bret Bernhardt is sincerely appreciated.

We also wish to acknowledge our enduring debt to Chairman Thomas A. Saunders III and the Heritage Board of Trustees, and particularly to Ambassador J. William Middendorf II, who originally encouraged us to undertake such a study of global economic freedom. We remain deeply indebted to Dr. Edwin J. Feulner, Founder and former President of The Heritage Foundation, and Heritage Distinguished Fellow Dr. Kim R. Holmes, who was a founding editor of the *Index*. Without their vision and insight, this project could never have become a reality and achieved such success over the past 21 years.

Very special thanks also go to Paul Gigot and Mary Anastasia O'Grady at *The Wall Street Journal*, whose partnership and support we truly cherish.

Ambassador Terry Miller
Anthony B. Kim
November 2014

Executive Highlights

The results of the 2015 *Index of Economic Freedom* confirm that the significant rebound in world economic freedom reported in the 2014 *Index* was no fluke. While the growth in economic freedom has slowed over the past year, the global average economic freedom score has nonetheless reached its highest level ever.

This 21st edition of the *Index* analyzes economic policy developments in 186 countries and territories since the second half of 2013. Economies in six regions have been graded and ranked on 10 aspects of economic freedom that evaluate the rule of law, the intrusiveness and size of government, regulatory efficiency, and the openness of markets.

HIGHLIGHTS FROM THE 2015 *INDEX*

- Despite the continuing challenges that confront the world economy, the global average economic freedom score has improved over the past year by one-tenth of a point, reaching a record 60.4 (on a 0-to-100 scale) in the 2015 *Index*. Although the rate of advancement has slowed in comparison to last year's near record 0.7-point increase, the world average has now reached a level a full point higher than

that recorded in the aftermath of the financial crisis and recession, thus regaining all of the ground that had been lost.

- On a worldwide basis, the increase in economic freedom was driven by improvements in trade freedom, monetary freedom, and freedom from corruption, for which global ratings have advanced by close to one point or more on average.

- Average scores for most other economic freedoms, including business freedom, property rights, labor freedom, and financial freedom, registered small declines. More troubling were declines in the *Index* measures related to assessing government size. With a score drop of 1.0 point, the control of government spending recorded the biggest deterioration, reflecting a continuation of countercyclical or interventionist stimulus policies in some countries.

- 101 countries, the majority of which are less developed or emerging economies, showed advances in economic freedom over the past year; 37 countries, including Taiwan, Lithuania, Georgia, Colombia, Israel, Cabo Verde, Montenegro, and Côte d'Ivoire, achieved their highest economic freedom scores ever in the 2015 *Index*.

- While five countries (Singapore, Finland, Mexico, Madagascar, and Suriname) recorded no score change, declines in economic freedom were registered in 72 countries in the 2015 *Index*; 11 countries, including Venezuela, Equatorial Guinea, Argentina, Bolivia, Algeria, Greece, and El Salvador, recorded their lowest economic freedom scores ever.

- Sub-Saharan Africa is home to six of the 10 biggest score improvements. São Tomé and Príncipe, Democratic Republic of Congo, Togo, Senegal, Burundi, and Zimbabwe all recorded score gains of two points or more. Five countries in Europe (Slovenia, Ukraine, Armenia, Greece, and Turkey) were among those registering the worst score declines.

- Average levels of economic freedom advanced in half of the six *Index* regions. Sub-Saharan Africa (led by São Tomé and Príncipe and Democratic Republic of Congo) and the Asia–Pacific region (led by Maldives and the Philippines) each showed an average score improvement of 0.3 point, and Middle East/North Africa countries (led by Israel and Morocco) gained 0.1 point on average. While average economic freedom for the South and Central America/Caribbean region stayed the same as last year, Europe and North America registered slight declines of 0.1 point and 0.2 point, respectively.

- Three northern European economies (Estonia, Lithuania, and Latvia—the so-called Baltic Tigers) are on the move toward greater economic freedom. Overcoming severe recessions following the global financial turmoil, these countries have maintained their openness to global markets and competition, further reformed their economies, and shrunk the size of their governments. Each has advanced economic freedom and moved up in the global rankings every year since 2012.

- The United States continues to be only the 12th-freest economy, seemingly stuck in the ranks of the "mostly free," the second-tier economic freedom category into which the U.S. dropped in 2010. However, the downward spiral in U.S. economic freedom over the previous seven years has come to a halt. In the 2015 *Index*, the U.S. has recorded modest score gains in six of the 10 economic freedoms and an overall score increase of seven-tenths of a point. On the other hand, the U.S. score for business freedom has plunged below 90, the lowest level since 2006.

Countries with higher levels of economic freedom continue to outperform others in reducing poverty, achieving greater prosperity, and ensuring broader progress in many dimensions of social and human development.

- The intensity of poverty in countries whose economies are considered mostly free or moderately free is only about one-fourth the level found in countries that are rated less free.

- Despite varying degrees of economic freedom across the regions around the globe, the positive relationship between economic freedom and prosperity is unequivocally consistent within the regions: Per capita incomes are much higher in countries that are economically free.

- Not surprisingly, overall human development also thrives in an environment that is economically free. Economic freedom is about more than a business environment in which entrepreneurship and prosperity can flourish. Higher economic freedom induces greater overall human development in such key areas as life expectancy, literacy, education, and the standard of living.

- There is a robust relationship between improving economic freedom and achieving higher per capita economic growth. Whether long-term (20 years), medium-term (10 years), or short-term (five years), the relationship between changes in economic freedom and changes in economic growth is consistently positive. As economies gain economic freedom and thus achieve dynamic growth, individuals and companies are empowered to build businesses, create jobs, and generate greater innovation for their communities and societies.

THE GLOBAL ECONOMIC FREEDOM RANKINGS

- Hong Kong has maintained its status as the world's freest economy, a distinction that it has achieved for 21 consecutive years. However, the gap between that territory and Singapore, the second-freest economy, has almost vanished. Hong Kong's economic freedom score declined by half a point, with an erosion of the rule of law reflecting an increased level of perceived corruption.

- Along with Hong Kong and Singapore, New Zealand, Australia, and Switzerland are the only economies considered "free" with economic freedom scores above 80 on the 0-to-100 *Index* grading scale. New Zealand moved up two slots and reclaimed third place in the rankings as a result of committed efforts to cut government spending. Canada remains the world's sixth-freest economy for the fifth year in a row.

- Chile (seventh) and Mauritius (10th), two reform-minded developing economies, continue to rank among the world's 10 freest economies. Both have demonstrated persistent commitment to the rule of law, limited government, regulatory efficiency, and open markets.

- Moving up three slots, Estonia has become the world's eighth-freest economy. The small Baltic nation has rejoined the world's 10 freest economies for the first time since 2007, overtaking Denmark (11th), Ireland (ninth), and Mauritius.

- The *Index* rankings just below the top 10 underwent considerable reshuffling. Taiwan and Lithuania, benefitting from uninterrupted score improvements since 2009, have recorded their highest economic freedom scores ever, jumping to 14th and 15th places, respectively, and surpassing Sweden, Finland, Germany, Luxembourg, the Netherlands, and Bahrain.

- The so-called BRICS economies (Brazil, Russia, India, China, and South Africa) showed little progress in economic freedom. Scores for India and Brazil actually declined. South Africa recorded a modest improvement to remain in the ranks of the "moderately free," but the other BRICS countries continue to be considered "mostly unfree."

2015 *Index of Economic Freedom* World Rankings

World Rank	Country	Overall Score	Change from 2014	Property Rights	Freedom from Corruption	Fiscal Freedom	Government Spending	Business Freedom	Labor Freedom	Monetary Freedom	Trade Freedom	Investment Freedom	Financial Freedom
1	Hong Kong	89.6	-0.5	90	75.0	93.2	89.7	100.0	95.9	81.8	90.0	90	90
2	Singapore	89.4	0.0	90	86.0	91.2	93.8	96.9	96.9	83.7	90.0	85	80
3	New Zealand	82.1	0.9	95	91.0	70.4	43.0	95.5	91.4	87.6	86.8	80	80
4	Australia	81.4	-0.6	90	81.0	63.7	61.8	94.1	81.6	85.3	86.4	80	90
5	Switzerland	80.5	-1.1	90	85.0	70.3	65.1	78.1	75.3	86.3	90.0	85	80
6	Canada	79.1	-1.1	90	81.0	79.9	48.3	89.0	76.1	77.9	88.4	80	80
7	Chile	78.5	-0.2	90	71.0	76.5	83.3	69.3	67.0	85.6	82.0	90	70
8	Estonia	76.8	0.9	90	68.0	80.6	53.2	81.5	58.7	77.6	88.0	90	80
9	Ireland	76.6	0.4	85	72.0	73.6	45.6	82.1	76.2	83.9	88.0	90	70
10	Mauritius	76.4	-0.1	65	52.0	91.9	87.4	78.0	68.2	77.6	88.4	85	70
11	Denmark	76.3	0.2	95	91.0	39.6	1.8	97.4	92.1	87.6	88.0	90	80
12	United States	76.2	0.7	80	73.0	66.2	51.8	88.8	98.5	76.6	87.0	70	70
13	United Kingdom	75.8	0.9	90	76.0	62.9	30.3	91.1	75.6	74.4	88.0	90	80
14	Taiwan	75.1	1.2	70	61.0	80.4	87.1	92.4	55.2	83.3	86.4	75	60
15	Lithuania	74.7	1.7	60	57.0	92.9	61.3	84.9	62.0	81.2	88.0	80	80
16	Germany	73.8	0.4	90	78.0	60.8	40.1	88.2	51.2	81.5	88.0	90	70
17	The Netherlands	73.7	-0.5	90	83.0	51.8	23.8	84.3	66.3	79.8	88.0	90	80
18	Bahrain	73.4	-1.7	60	48.0	99.9	73.1	72.5	83.1	74.2	78.6	65	80
19	Finland	73.4	0.0	90	89.0	66.4	3.6	92.6	54.8	79.9	88.0	90	80
20	Japan	73.3	0.9	80	74.0	68.7	47.1	84.1	90.2	86.7	82.6	70	50
21	Luxembourg	73.2	-1.0	90	80.0	62.3	42.2	71.3	42.1	80.7	88.0	95	80
22	Georgia	73.0	0.4	40	49.0	87.2	73.8	88.6	79.9	82.7	88.6	80	60
23	Sweden	72.7	-0.4	90	89.0	43.0	19.2	87.9	54.0	85.5	88.0	90	80
24	Czech Republic	72.5	0.3	75	48.0	81.5	40.6	68.2	82.9	81.2	88.0	80	80
25	United Arab Emirates	72.4	1.0	55	69.0	99.5	85.8	74.7	83.8	83.8	82.4	40	50
26	Iceland	72.0	-0.4	90	78.0	72.0	32.6	90.5	62.2	77.0	88.0	70	60
27	Norway	71.8	0.9	90	86.0	52.1	43.8	92.1	48.2	81.7	89.4	75	60
28	Colombia	71.7	1.0	50	36.0	80.3	76.0	81.5	81.7	80.1	81.2	80	70
29	South Korea	71.5	0.3	75	55.0	72.5	67.9	89.7	51.1	81.6	72.6	70	80
30	Austria	71.2	-1.2	90	69.0	50.1	19.8	78.0	76.7	80.3	88.0	90	70
31	Malaysia	70.8	1.2	55	50.0	84.4	74.0	93.5	75.7	80.8	80.0	55	60
32	Qatar	70.8	-0.4	70	68.0	99.7	71.9	70.5	71.2	79.7	81.8	45	50
33	Israel	70.5	2.1	75	61.0	61.9	47.8	72.4	67.1	81.6	88.6	80	70
34	Macau	70.3	-1.0	60	49.7	71.8	91.8	60.0	50.0	74.9	90.0	85	70
35	Saint Lucia	70.2	-0.5	70	71.0	77.7	65.8	75.6	79.8	85.5	72.0	65	40
36	Botswana	69.8	-2.2	70	64.0	79.5	61.9	66.8	70.0	73.9	72.2	70	70

2015 *Index of Economic Freedom* World Rankings

World Rank	Country	Overall Score	Change from 2014	Property Rights	Freedom from Corruption	Fiscal Freedom	Government Spending	Business Freedom	Labor Freedom	Monetary Freedom	Trade Freedom	Investment Freedom	Financial Freedom
37	Latvia	69.7	1.0	50	53.0	84.4	59.2	82.1	61.5	83.8	88.0	85	50
38	Jordan	69.3	0.1	60	45.0	93.7	70.7	59.1	74.4	80.6	79.6	70	60
39	Brunei	68.9	-0.1	35	60.0	87.0	63.6	68.3	96.9	76.6	81.8	70	50
40	Belgium	68.8	-1.1	80	75.0	43.6	10.2	90.7	63.7	81.7	88.0	85	70
41	The Bahamas	68.7	-1.1	70	71.0	97.8	83.2	68.9	75.3	78.8	52.2	30	60
42	Poland	68.6	1.6	60	60.0	82.1	47.1	67.3	60.4	81.3	88.0	70	70
43	Uruguay	68.6	-0.7	70	73.0	77.1	65.1	72.6	64.3	71.6	81.8	80	30
44	Saint Vincent and the Grenadines	68.0	1.0	70	62.0	73.3	75.3	70.8	78.2	82.3	68.4	60	40
45	Cyprus	67.9	0.3	70	63.0	79.5	36.7	79.5	59.6	82.7	88.0	70	50
46	Barbados	67.9	-0.4	80	75.0	73.8	42.1	71.6	69.2	78.2	63.8	65	60
47	Peru	67.7	0.3	40	38.0	78.6	88.5	67.7	63.4	83.9	87.0	70	60
48	Jamaica	67.7	1.0	40	38.0	81.5	73.2	85.9	76.5	71.4	75.0	85	50
49	Spain	67.6	0.4	70	59.0	53.1	39.8	77.5	52.6	81.3	88.0	85	70
50	Slovak Republic	67.2	0.8	50	47.0	80.8	55.1	69.6	56.5	75.5	88.0	80	70
51	Costa Rica	67.2	0.3	50	53.0	80.0	89.9	64.5	54.6	75.8	83.8	70	50
52	Armenia	67.1	-1.8	20	36.0	84.4	82.8	82.7	64.3	70.6	85.4	75	70
53	Macedonia	67.1	-1.5	35	44.0	91.4	65.6	79.2	70.7	79.0	86.2	60	60
54	Hungary	66.8	-0.2	55	54.0	78.7	25.9	74.5	67.7	79.2	88.0	75	70
55	Bulgaria	66.8	1.1	30	41.0	91.0	64.5	68.5	76.6	83.2	88.0	65	60
56	Oman	66.7	-0.7	55	47.0	98.5	44.2	68.4	76.1	76.2	76.8	65	60
57	Romania	66.6	1.1	40	43.0	86.9	62.3	69.8	68.6	77.3	88.0	80	50
58	Malta	66.5	0.1	75	56.0	63.1	44.4	61.0	55.6	81.8	88.0	80	60
59	Mexico	66.4	-0.4	50	34.0	77.8	78.0	71.5	59.9	77.6	85.6	70	60
60	Cabo Verde	66.4	0.3	75	58.0	78.3	67.9	61.8	42.1	81.0	69.6	70	60
61	Dominica	66.1	0.9	60	58.0	73.6	61.5	71.6	68.7	89.5	72.8	75	30
62	El Salvador	65.7	-0.5	35	38.0	79.4	85.5	53.3	53.3	82.5	85.2	75	70
63	Albania	65.7	-1.2	30	31.0	87.2	76.1	70.6	52.9	80.8	87.8	70	70
64	Portugal	65.3	1.8	70	62.0	61.1	28.8	87.5	42.9	82.8	88.0	70	60
65	Rwanda	64.8	0.1	30	53.0	80.2	79.2	59.5	84.5	76.0	80.8	65	40
66	Montenegro	64.7	1.1	40	44.0	92.6	36.7	77.1	77.5	79.7	84.8	65	50
67	Trinidad and Tobago	64.1	1.4	50	38.0	79.0	69.3	65.3	76.6	74.3	78.6	60	50
68	Panama	64.1	0.7	30	35.0	84.5	78.8	71.5	41.5	76.4	78.4	75	70
69	Kazakhstan	63.3	-0.4	25	26.0	93.2	85.0	73.7	87.0	74.6	79.0	40	50
70	Turkey	63.2	-1.7	45	50.0	76.1	57.6	61.0	50.2	72.4	84.6	75	60
71	Ghana	63.0	-1.2	50	46.0	84.6	70.8	62.5	56.9	69.2	64.8	65	60

2015 *Index of Economic Freedom* World Rankings

World Rank	Country	Overall Score	Change from 2014	Property Rights	Freedom from Corruption	Fiscal Freedom	Government Spending	Business Freedom	Labor Freedom	Monetary Freedom	Trade Freedom	Investment Freedom	Financial Freedom
72	South Africa	62.6	0.1	50	42.0	69.5	68.2	73.0	61.6	74.9	76.6	50	60
73	France	62.5	-1.0	80	71.0	47.5	2.5	80.2	43.5	77.5	83.0	70	70
74	Kuwait	62.5	0.2	45	43.0	97.7	61.1	58.6	64.2	74.0	76.2	55	50
75	Thailand	62.4	-0.9	40	35.0	81.5	81.4	72.5	63.5	69.9	75.4	45	60
76	The Philippines	62.2	2.1	30	36.0	79.1	89.3	55.3	58.2	78.8	75.4	60	60
77	Saudi Arabia	62.1	-0.1	40	46.0	99.7	61.9	65.8	72.7	68.4	76.4	40	50
78	Samoa	61.9	0.8	60	38.0	80.2	46.5	73.6	78.4	81.2	75.8	55	30
79	Madagascar	61.7	0.0	45	28.0	90.9	94.7	62.3	45.1	79.2	71.8	50	50
80	Italy	61.7	0.8	55	43.0	54.2	23.2	71.9	55.4	81.2	88.0	85	60
81	Croatia	61.5	1.1	40	48.0	74.9	46.5	55.8	42.8	80.0	87.2	80	60
82	Kyrgyz Republic	61.3	0.2	20	24.0	93.6	53.2	73.7	85.0	73.8	80.2	60	50
83	Paraguay	61.1	-0.9	30	24.0	96.0	81.9	58.4	26.3	78.3	81.4	75	60
84	Vanuatu	61.1	1.6	40	33.5	97.2	83.8	51.5	46.4	82.9	75.4	60	40
85	Azerbaijan	61.0	-0.3	20	28.0	88.1	59.7	74.5	79.1	79.8	76.0	55	50
86	Dominican Republic	61.0	-0.3	30	29.0	84.1	87.1	53.5	57.5	76.0	77.8	75	40
87	Guatemala	60.4	-0.8	20	29.0	79.6	94.1	54.7	50.6	76.8	84.6	65	50
88	Slovenia	60.3	-2.4	60	57.0	58.1	0.0	81.2	57.1	81.3	88.0	70	50
89	Morocco	60.1	1.8	40	37.0	70.9	61.0	68.8	33.4	81.9	78.2	70	60
90	Serbia	60.0	0.6	45	42.0	82.4	27.1	57.8	70.4	72.2	78.2	75	50
91	Swaziland	59.9	-1.3	40	39.0	76.4	68.6	60.5	69.3	73.9	76.0	55	40
92	Uganda	59.7	-0.2	25	26.0	73.3	89.0	43.3	87.5	76.3	76.6	60	40
93	Namibia	59.6	0.2	30	48.0	66.7	56.0	64.3	90.9	74.3	71.2	55	40
94	Lebanon	59.3	-0.1	20	28.0	91.3	70.6	54.7	60.7	72.0	75.8	60	60
95	Tonga	59.3	1.1	20	28.6	87.2	79.0	74.1	92.1	73.5	78.4	40	20
96	Mongolia	59.2	0.3	30	38.0	83.9	35.6	68.2	82.7	69.2	74.8	50	60
97	Bosnia and Herzegovina	59.0	0.6	20	42.0	82.9	27.3	53.5	63.4	84.0	87.2	70	60
98	Fiji	59.0	0.3	25	22.3	81.3	74.6	63.2	75.2	78.3	70.2	50	50
99	Benin	58.8	1.7	30	36.0	68.3	86.7	55.2	53.2	79.9	58.4	70	50
100	Zambia	58.7	-1.7	30	38.0	71.9	78.0	68.2	46.0	73.2	76.8	55	50
101	Sri Lanka	58.6	-1.4	35	37.0	85.0	88.4	72.5	58.7	68.2	71.6	30	40
102	Burkina Faso	58.6	-0.3	25	38.0	82.4	79.8	49.6	57.8	80.0	68.2	65	40
103	Côte d'Ivoire	58.5	0.8	35	27.0	77.7	82.4	65.4	46.0	75.0	71.4	55	50
104	Gabon	58.3	0.5	40	34.0	77.5	74.6	57.9	64.3	78.4	61.0	55	40
105	Indonesia	58.1	-0.4	30	32.0	83.3	88.3	49.3	48.7	74.9	74.8	40	60
106	Senegal	57.8	2.4	40	41.0	71.3	74.6	54.6	39.5	83.0	74.0	60	40
107	Tunisia	57.7	0.4	40	41.0	74.3	70.8	81.2	69.1	74.8	61.2	35	30

2015 *Index of Economic Freedom* World Rankings

World Rank	Country	Overall Score	Change from 2014	Property Rights	Freedom from Corruption	Fiscal Freedom	Government Spending	Business Freedom	Labor Freedom	Monetary Freedom	Trade Freedom	Investment Freedom	Financial Freedom
108	Nicaragua	57.6	-0.8	10	28.0	78.4	76.6	58.0	56.7	67.8	85.4	65	50
109	Tanzania	57.5	-0.3	30	33.0	79.9	79.3	45.0	61.4	69.7	67.0	60	50
110	Cambodia	57.5	0.1	25	20.0	90.5	87.5	29.2	62.2	78.7	72.2	60	50
111	Moldova	57.5	0.2	40	35.0	85.1	51.8	66.8	40.6	76.1	79.8	50	50
112	Djibouti	57.5	1.6	25	36.0	81.2	57.1	55.4	66.6	78.9	54.8	70	50
113	The Gambia	57.5	-2.0	25	28.0	75.4	73.4	55.7	66.7	70.8	65.0	65	50
114	Seychelles	57.5	1.3	50	54.0	79.8	59.4	67.7	63.9	76.0	44.0	50	30
115	Bhutan	57.4	0.7	60	63.0	82.6	60.1	61.9	81.1	66.0	49.4	20	30
116	Honduras	57.4	0.3	30	26.0	84.9	78.7	53.2	28.0	75.4	77.6	60	60
117	Belize	56.8	0.1	30	6.7	82.4	78.3	59.1	61.8	79.3	70.4	50	50
118	Brazil	56.6	-0.3	50	42.0	68.4	50.9	53.6	52.1	69.4	69.6	50	60
119	Mali	56.4	0.9	25	28.0	69.6	89.2	47.2	50.7	81.1	73.2	60	40
120	Nigeria	55.6	1.3	30	25.0	85.2	76.1	48.3	77.7	70.4	63.8	40	40
121	Pakistan	55.6	0.4	30	28.0	77.7	86.1	65.6	42.1	71.2	65.6	50	40
122	Kenya	55.6	-1.5	30	27.0	78.0	72.1	47.9	63.8	72.8	64.0	50	50
123	Guyana	55.5	-0.2	25	27.0	68.7	70.8	63.8	74.5	78.4	72.0	45	30
124	Egypt	55.2	2.3	20	32.0	85.8	68.0	65.4	53.6	67.4	70.0	50	40
125	Mozambique	54.8	-0.2	30	30.0	75.2	66.5	60.9	37.9	82.0	75.4	40	50
126	Malawi	54.8	-0.6	40	37.0	78.5	49.0	49.1	63.1	53.8	72.2	55	50
127	Niger	54.6	-0.5	30	34.0	76.6	83.6	39.2	40.9	81.3	65.6	55	40
128	India	54.6	-1.1	55	36.0	79.4	78.3	43.3	48.7	65.3	64.6	35	40
129	Suriname	54.2	0.0	35	36.0	69.3	73.8	42.2	81.9	77.2	66.2	30	30
130	Greece	54.0	-1.7	40	40.0	64.2	0.0	73.3	51.6	77.8	83.0	60	50
131	Bangladesh	53.9	-0.2	20	27.0	72.7	92.0	62.2	63.7	67.7	59.0	45	30
132	Burundi	53.7	2.3	20	21.0	73.5	61.3	61.4	68.1	69.8	72.2	60	30
133	Yemen	53.7	-1.8	30	18.0	91.5	59.9	54.0	57.1	68.5	77.6	50	30
134	Maldives	53.4	2.4	25	21.9	95.5	50.6	85.8	73.4	74.1	47.8	30	30
135	Mauritania	53.3	0.1	25	30.0	80.2	59.8	50.5	52.1	76.6	69.0	50	40
136	São Tomé and Príncipe	53.3	4.5	25	42.0	87.8	41.4	65.1	45.8	70.7	75.2	50	30
137	Papua New Guinea	53.1	-0.8	20	25.0	66.9	68.7	53.5	74.5	72.7	85.0	35	30
138	Togo	53.0	3.1	30	29.0	69.7	78.1	51.9	43.4	80.4	67.8	50	30
139	China	52.7	0.2	20	40.0	69.7	81.5	52.1	63.0	74.2	71.8	25	30
140	Tajikistan	52.7	0.7	20	22.0	92.1	81.9	65.4	46.4	69.6	74.6	25	30
141	Liberia	52.7	0.3	25	38.0	83.0	69.9	60.1	43.9	72.7	74.4	40	20
142	Comoros	52.1	0.7	30	28.0	64.5	78.8	47.3	52.0	77.9	73.0	40	30
143	Russia	52.1	0.2	20	28.0	86.1	57.8	76.3	58.9	63.9	75.0	25	30

2015 *Index of Economic Freedom* World Rankings

World Rank	Country	Overall Score	Change from 2014	Property Rights	Freedom from Corruption	Fiscal Freedom	Government Spending	Business Freedom	Labor Freedom	Monetary Freedom	Trade Freedom	Investment Freedom	Financial Freedom
144	Guinea	52.1	-1.4	15	24.0	68.1	79.5	51.6	74.4	66.7	61.2	40	40
145	Guinea-Bissau	52.0	0.7	20	19.0	89.1	88.0	39.6	61.7	77.5	65.4	30	30
146	Cameroon	51.9	-0.7	25	25.0	71.7	87.8	41.6	47.8	75.6	59.6	35	50
147	Sierra Leone	51.7	1.2	10	30.0	80.8	87.5	53.4	41.6	68.5	70.2	55	20
148	Vietnam	51.7	0.9	15	31.0	79.1	77.1	61.5	62.9	66.8	78.6	15	30
149	Ethiopia	51.5	1.5	30	33.0	77.4	91.4	55.9	56.4	66.1	64.4	20	20
150	Laos	51.4	0.2	15	26.0	86.2	86.8	59.5	57.1	74.5	58.6	30	20
151	Haiti	51.3	2.4	10	19.0	80.3	76.2	43.1	63.7	73.5	77.6	40	30
152	Nepal	51.3	1.2	30	31.0	85.6	88.9	65.7	44.3	70.5	61.8	5	30
153	Belarus	49.8	-0.3	20	29.0	86.4	54.7	72.0	80.1	44.5	81.0	20	10
154	Micronesia	49.6	-0.2	30	30.0	93.2	0.0	51.0	79.1	76.9	81.0	25	30
155	Lesotho	49.6	0.1	35	49.0	68.5	0.0	54.7	63.9	75.2	64.6	45	40
156	Ecuador	49.2	1.2	15	35.0	79.1	51.0	51.4	51.3	68.2	71.4	30	40
157	Algeria	48.9	-1.9	30	36.0	80.0	38.7	66.6	50.5	71.2	60.8	25	30
158	Angola	47.9	0.2	15	23.0	84.5	50.1	47.4	43.2	65.4	70.2	40	40
159	Solomon Islands	47.0	0.8	30	25.0	61.1	25.7	67.7	68.6	74.3	73.0	15	30
160	Uzbekistan	47.0	0.5	15	17.0	90.2	67.3	73.1	64.2	63.5	69.8	0	10
161	Burma	46.9	0.4	10	21.0	86.9	77.9	28.7	79.3	66.1	74.2	15	10
162	Ukraine	46.9	-2.4	20	25.0	78.7	28.0	59.3	48.2	78.6	85.8	15	30
163	Bolivia	46.8	-1.6	10	34.0	86.8	60.9	53.7	25.5	69.7	77.6	10	40
164	Kiribati	46.4	0.1	30	29.2	73.0	0.0	56.8	83.9	80.6	55.4	25	30
165	Chad	45.9	1.4	20	19.0	46.2	83.6	27.1	47.7	75.6	55.2	45	40
166	Central African Republic	45.9	-0.8	15	25.0	65.0	92.0	27.2	37.5	69.6	52.4	45	30
167	Timor-Leste	45.5	2.3	20	30.0	64.7	0.0	59.8	72.0	68.7	79.6	40	20
168	Congo, Dem. Rep.	45.0	4.4	10	22.0	72.9	85.7	42.8	38.4	75.1	63.0	20	20
169	Argentina	44.1	-0.5	15	34.0	66.8	41.2	52.8	43.3	59.6	68.8	30	30
170	Congo, Republic of	42.7	-1.0	10	22.0	67.4	60.7	36.8	36.0	71.6	62.4	30	30
171	Iran	41.8	1.5	10	25.0	81.2	93.0	57.0	51.3	48.7	41.4	0	10
172	Turkmenistan	41.4	-0.8	5	17.0	94.0	93.5	30.0	20.0	64.2	80.0	0	10
173	Equatorial Guinea	40.4	-4.0	10	19.0	75.4	31.4	37.5	33.5	78.3	53.8	35	30
174	Eritrea	38.9	0.4	10	20.0	57.0	71.8	18.2	65.5	57.8	69.2	0	20
175	Zimbabwe	37.6	2.1	10	21.0	66.6	74.2	37.1	23.7	75.4	58.4	0	10
176	Venezuela	34.3	-2.0	5	20.0	75.0	52.0	41.6	24.2	42.8	62.8	0	20
177	Cuba	29.6	0.9	10	46.0	61.8	0.0	20.0	20.0	64.8	63.8	0	10
178	North Korea	1.3	0.3	5	8.0	0.0	0.0	0.0	0.0	0.0	0.0	0	0
N/A	Afghanistan	N/A	N/A	N/A	8.0	91.7	81.2	61.4	67.5	72.6	N/A	55	N/A

2015 *Index of Economic Freedom* World Rankings

World Rank	Country	Overall Score	Change from 2014	Property Rights	Freedom from Corruption	Fiscal Freedom	Government Spending	Business Freedom	Labor Freedom	Monetary Freedom	Trade Freedom	Investment Freedom	Financial Freedom
N/A	Iraq	N/A	N/A	N/A	16.0	N/A	43.8	57.7	74.4	73.6	N/A	N/A	N/A
N/A	Kosovo	N/A	N/A	30	33.0	N/A	73.9	66.8	72.1	74.9	N/A	65	N/A
N/A	Libya	N/A	N/A	10	15.0	95.0	37.5	46.8	66.7	71.4	80.0	5	N/A
N/A	Liechtenstein	N/A	N/A	N/A	N/A	N/A	N/A	N/A	N/A	N/A	90.0	85	80
N/A	Somalia	N/A	N/A	N/A	8.0	N/A	N/A	N/A	N/A	N/A	N/A	N/A	N/A
N/A	Sudan	N/A	N/A	N/A	11.0	86.4	94.5	49.0	43.8	52.8	55.6	15	N/A
N/A	Syria	N/A	N/A	10	17.0	N/A	N/A	57.3	49.1	N/A	N/A	0	20

Chapter 1

Principles of Economic Freedom

Ambassador Terry Miller and Anthony B. Kim

[A] society that puts freedom first will, as a happy by-product, end up with both greater freedom and greater equality. Though a by-product of freedom, greater equality is not an accident. A free society releases the energies and abilities of people to pursue their own objectives. It prevents some people from arbitrarily suppressing others.

—Milton and Rose Friedman[1]

In an economically free society, each person controls the fruits of his or her own labor and initiative. Individuals are empowered—indeed, entitled—to pursue their dreams by means of their own free choice.

In an economically free society, individuals succeed or fail based on their individual effort and ability. The institutions of a free and open market society do not discriminate either against or in favor of individuals based on their race, ethnic background, gender, class, family connections, or any other factor unrelated to

individual merit. Government decision-making is characterized by openness and transparency, which illuminates the shadows where discrimination might flourish and promotes equal opportunity for all.

In an economically free society, the power of economic decision-making is widely dispersed, and the allocation of resources for production and consumption is on the basis of open competition so that every individual or firm gets a fair chance to succeed.

These three fundamental principles of economic freedom—empowerment of the individual, non-discrimination, and open competition—underpin every measurement and policy idea presented in the *Index of Economic Freedom*.

ECONOMIC FREEDOM: THE ROLE OF GOVERNMENT

As Friedrich Hayek once observed, "To be controlled in our economic pursuits means to be controlled in everything."[2] Hayek's keen insights into economic freedom are based on the moral truth that each person is, as a matter of natural right, a free and responsible being with inalienable dignity and fundamental liberties that righteous and effective political systems should regard as unassailable. Governments that are just, according to the U.S. Declaration of Independence, are instituted precisely to secure these rights.

Any discussion of economic freedom thus has at its heart reflection on the critical relationship between individuals and the government. In general, state action or government control that interferes with individual autonomy limits economic freedom.

However, the goal of economic freedom is not simply an absence of government coercion or constraint, but the creation and maintenance of a mutual sense of liberty for all. As individuals enjoy the blessings of economic freedom, they in turn have a responsibility to respect the economic rights and freedoms of others within the rule of law. Governments are instituted to ensure basic protections against the ravages of nature or the predations of one citizen against another. Positive economic rights such as property and contracts are given societal as well as individual defense against the destructive tendencies of others.

A comprehensive view of economic freedom should encompass all liberties and rights of production, distribution, or consumption of goods and services. The highest forms of economic freedom should provide an absolute right of property ownership; full freedom of movement for labor, capital, and goods; and an absolute absence of coercion or constraint of economic activity beyond that which is necessary for the protection and maintenance of liberty itself. An economically free society encourages the handling of economic decisions in a decentralized fashion. Individuals are free to work, produce, consume, and invest in any way they choose under the even-handed application of laws, with their economic freedoms at once both protected and respected by the state.

Some government action is necessary for the citizens of a nation to defend themselves, promote the peaceful evolution of civil society,
and enjoy the fruits of their labor. For example, citizens are taxed to provide revenue for public safety, the protection of property, and the common defense. Other goods—what economists call "public goods"—may be supplied more efficiently by government than through private means. Some public goods, such as the maintenance of a police force to protect property rights, a monetary authority to maintain a sound currency, and an impartial judiciary to enforce contracts among parties, are themselves vital ingredients of an economically free society. When government action rises beyond the minimal necessary level, however, it leads inevitably and quickly to the loss of freedom—and the first freedom affected is often economic freedom.[3]

Throughout history, governments have imposed a wide array of constraints on economic activity. Such constraints, though sometimes imposed in the name of equality or some other noble societal purpose, are in reality imposed most often for the benefit of societal elites or special interests, and they come with a high cost to society as a whole. By substituting political judgments for those of the marketplace, government diverts entrepreneurial resources and energy from productive activities to rent-seeking, the quest for economically unearned benefits. The result is lower productivity, economic stagnation, and declining prosperity.

Government provision of goods and services beyond those that are clearly considered public goods also imposes a separate constraint on economic activity, crowding out private-sector activity and usurping resources that otherwise might have been available for private investment or consumption. Constraining economic choice distorts and diminishes the production, distribution, and consumption of goods and services (including, of course, labor services). The wealth of a nation inevitably declines as a result.

MEASURING ECONOMIC FREEDOM

The *Index of Economic Freedom* takes a broad and comprehensive view of economic freedom, measuring country performance in 10 separate areas. Some of the aspects of economic freedom that are evaluated are concerned with a country's interactions with the rest of the world—for example, the extent of an economy's openness to global investment or trade. Most, however, focus on policies within a country, assessing the liberty of individuals to use their labor or finances without undue restraint and government interference.

Each of the measured aspects of economic freedom plays a vital role in developing and sustaining personal and national prosperity. All are complementary in their impact, however, and progress in one area is often likely to reinforce or even inspire progress in another. Similarly, repressed economic freedom in one area—respect for property rights, for example—may make it much more difficult to achieve high levels of freedom in other categories.

The 10 measured aspects of economic freedom may be grouped into four broad categories:

- **Rule of law** (property rights, freedom from corruption);
- **Government size** (fiscal freedom, government spending);
- **Regulatory efficiency** (business freedom, labor freedom, monetary freedom); and
- **Market openness** (trade freedom, investment freedom, financial freedom).

Rule of Law

Property Rights. The ability to accumulate private property and wealth is understood to be a central motivating force for workers and investors in a market economy. The recognition of private property rights and an effective rule of law to protect them are vital features of a fully functioning market economy. Secure property rights give citizens the confidence to undertake entrepreneurial activity, save their income, and make long-term plans because they know that their income, savings, and property (both real and intellectual) are safe from unfair expropriation or theft.

The protection of private property requires an autonomous and accountable judicial system that is available to all equally and without discrimination. The independence, transparency, and effectiveness of the judicial system have proven to be key determinants of a country's prospects for long-term economic growth. Such a system is also vital to the maintenance of peace and security and the protection of human rights.

A key aspect of property rights protection is the enforcement of contracts. The voluntary undertaking of contractual obligations is the foundation of the market system and the basis for economic specialization, gains from commercial exchange, and trade among nations. Even-handed government enforcement of private contracts is essential to ensuring equity and integrity in the marketplace.

Freedom from Corruption. In the context of economic freedom, corruption can best be understood as the failure of integrity in the economic system, a distortion by which individuals or special-interest groups are able to gain at the expense of the whole. Often a direct result of the government's concentration of economic or political power, corruption manifests itself in many forms such as bribery, extortion, nepotism, cronyism, patronage, embezzlement, and graft.

Corruption can infect all parts of an economy in systematic ways. There is a direct relationship between the extent of government intervention in economic activity and the prevalence of corruption. In particular, excessive and redundant government regulations provide opportunities for bribery or graft. In addition, government regulations or restrictions in one area may create informal markets in another. For example, by imposing numerous burdensome barriers on conducting business, including regulatory red tape and high transaction costs, a government can incentivize bribery and encourage illegitimate market interactions.

Ensuring transparency is crucial to dealing effectively with corruption. Openness in regulatory procedures and processes can promote equitable treatment and greater efficiency.

Government Size

Fiscal Freedom. Fiscal freedom is a direct measure of the extent to which government permits individuals and businesses to keep and manage their income and wealth for their own benefit and use. A government can impose fiscal burdens on economic activity through taxation, but it also does so when it incurs public debt that ultimately must be paid off through taxation.

The marginal tax rate confronting an individual is, in effect, the government's cut of the profit from that individual's next unit of work or engagement in a new entrepreneurial venture; whatever remains after the tax is the individual's actual reward for the effort. Therefore, the higher the government's cut, the lower the individual's reward—and the lower the incentive to undertake the work at all. Higher tax rates interfere with the ability of individuals and firms to pursue their goals in the marketplace and thereby reduce overall private-sector activity.

While individual and corporate income tax rates are important to economic freedom, they are not a comprehensive measure of the tax burden. Governments impose many other indirect taxes, including payroll, sales, and excise taxes, as well as tariffs and the value-added tax (VAT). In the *Index of Economic Freedom*, the burden of these taxes is captured by measuring the overall tax burden from all forms of taxation as a percentage of total GDP.

Government Spending. The cost of excessive government is a central issue in economic freedom, both in terms of generating revenue (see fiscal freedom) and in terms of spending. Government spending comes in many forms. Some government spending—for example, to provide infrastructure, fund research, or improve human capital—may be considered investments. Government also spends on public goods, the benefits of which accrue broadly to society in ways that markets cannot price appropriately.

All government spending that must eventually be financed by higher taxation, however, entails an opportunity cost. This cost is the value of the private consumption or investment that would have occurred had the resources involved been left in the private sector.

Excessive government spending runs a great risk of crowding out private economic activity. Even if an economy achieves faster growth through more government spending, such economic expansion tends to be only temporary, distorting the market allocation of resources

and private investment incentives. Even worse, a government's insulation from market discipline often leads to bureaucracy, lower productivity, inefficiency, and mounting public debt that imposes an even greater burden on future generations.

As many economies have experienced in recent years, high levels of public debt accumulated through irresponsible government spending undermine economic freedom and prevent dynamic entrepreneurial growth.

Regulatory Efficiency

Business Freedom. Business freedom is about an individual's right to establish and run an enterprise without undue interference from the state. Burdensome and redundant regulations are the most common barriers to the free conduct of entrepreneurial activity.

By increasing the costs of production, regulations can make it difficult for entrepreneurs to succeed in the marketplace. Although many regulations hinder business productivity and profitability, the most inhibiting to entrepreneurship are those that are associated with licensing new businesses.

In some countries, as well as many states in the United States, the procedure for obtaining a business license can be as simple as mailing in a registration form with a minimal fee. In Hong Kong, for example, obtaining a business license requires filling out a single form, and the process can be completed in a few hours. In other economies, such as India and parts of South America, the process of obtaining a business license can take much longer, involving endless trips to government offices and repeated encounters with officious and sometimes corrupt bureaucrats.

Once a business is open, government regulation may interfere with the normal decision-making or price-setting process. Interestingly, two countries with the same set of regulations can impose different regulatory burdens. If one country applies its regulations evenly and transparently, this can lower the regulatory burden by facilitating long-term business planning. If the other applies regulations inconsistently, it raises the regulatory burden by creating an unpredictable business environment. Rigid and onerous bankruptcy procedures are also distortionary, providing a disincentive for entrepreneurs to start businesses in the first place.

Labor Freedom. The ability of individuals to work as much as they want and wherever they want is a key component of economic freedom. By the same token, the ability of businesses to contract freely for labor and dismiss redundant workers when they are no longer needed is essential to enhancing productivity and sustaining overall economic growth. The core principle of any market is free, voluntary exchange. That is just as true in the labor market as it is in the market for goods.

State intervention generates the same problems in the labor market that it produces in any other market. Government regulations take a variety of forms, including wage controls, restrictions on hiring and firing, and other constraints. In many countries, unions play an important role in regulating labor freedom and, depending on the nature of their activity, may be either a force for greater freedom or an impediment to the efficient functioning of labor markets.

Onerous labor laws penalize businesses and workers alike. Rigid labor regulations prevent employers and employees from freely negotiating changes in terms and conditions of work, resulting often in a chronic mismatch of labor supply and demand. In general, the greater the degree of labor freedom, the lower the rate of unemployment in an economy.

Monetary Freedom. Monetary freedom requires a stable currency and market-determined prices. Whether acting as entrepreneurs or as consumers, free people need a steady and reliable currency as a medium of exchange, unit of account, and store of value. Without monetary freedom, it is difficult to create long-term value or amass capital.

The value of a country's currency can be influenced significantly by the monetary policy of its government. With a monetary policy that endeavors to fight inflation, maintain price stability, and preserve the nation's wealth, people can rely on market prices for the foreseeable future. Investments, savings, and other longer-term plans can be made more confidently. An inflationary policy, by contrast, confiscates wealth like an invisible tax and also distorts prices, misallocates resources, and raises the cost of doing business.

There is no single accepted theory of the right monetary policy for a free society. At one time, the gold standard enjoyed widespread support. What characterizes almost all monetary theories today, however, is support for low inflation and an independent central bank. There is also widespread recognition that price controls corrupt market efficiency and lead to shortages or surpluses.

Market Openness

Trade Freedom. Trade freedom reflects an economy's openness to the flow of goods and services from around the world and the citizen's ability to interact freely as buyer or seller in the international marketplace. Trade restrictions can manifest themselves in the form of tariffs, export taxes, trade quotas, or outright trade bans. However, trade restrictions also appear in more subtle ways, particularly in the form of regulatory barriers.

The degree to which government hinders the free flow of foreign commerce has a direct bearing on the ability of individuals to pursue their economic goals and maximize their productivity and well-being. Tariffs, for example, directly increase the prices that local consumers pay for foreign imports, but they also distort production incentives for local producers, causing them to produce either a good in which they lack a comparative advantage or more of a protected good than is economically efficient. This impedes overall economic efficiency and growth.

In many cases, trade limitations also put advanced-technology products and services beyond the reach of local entrepreneurs, limiting their own productive development.

Investment Freedom. A free and open investment environment provides maximum entrepreneurial opportunities and incentives for expanded economic activity, greater productivity, and job creation. The benefits of such an environment flow not only to the individual companies that take the entrepreneurial risk in expectation of greater return, but also to society as a whole. An effective investment framework will be characterized by transparency and equity, supporting all types of firms rather than just large or strategically important companies, and will encourage rather than discourage innovation and competition.

Restrictions on the movement of capital, both domestic and international, undermine the efficient allocation of resources and reduce productivity, distorting economic decision-making. Restrictions on cross-border investment can limit both inflows and outflows of capital, thereby shrinking markets and reducing opportunities for growth.

In an environment in which individuals and companies are free to choose where and how to invest, capital will flow to its best use: to the sectors and activities where it is most needed and the returns are greatest. State action to redirect the flow of capital and limit choice is an imposition on the freedom of both the investor and the person seeking capital. The more restrictions a country imposes on investment, the lower its level of entrepreneurial activity.

Financial Freedom. An accessible and efficiently functioning formal financial system ensures the availability of diversified savings, credit, payment, and investment services to individuals. By expanding financing opportunities and promoting entrepreneurship, an open banking environment encourages competition in order to provide the most efficient financial intermediation between households and firms as well as between investors and entrepreneurs.

Through a process driven by supply and demand, markets provide real-time information on prices and immediate discipline for those who have made bad decisions. This process depends on transparency in the market and the integrity of the information being made available. A prudent and effective regulatory system, through disclosure requirements and independent auditing, ensures both.

Increasingly, the central role played by banks is being complemented by other financial services that offer alternative means for raising capital or diversifying risk. As with the banking system, the useful role for government in regulating these institutions lies in ensuring transparency and integrity and promoting disclosure of assets, liabilities, and risks.

Banking and financial regulation by the state that goes beyond the assurance of transparency and honesty in financial markets can impede efficiency, increase the costs of financing entrepreneurial activity, and limit competition. If the government intervenes in the stock market, for instance, it contravenes the choices of millions of individuals by interfering with the pricing of capital—the most critical function of a market economy. Equity markets measure on a continual basis the expected profits and losses in publicly held companies. This measurement is essential in allocating capital resources to their highest-valued uses and thereby satisfying consumers' most urgent requirements.

ECONOMIC FREEDOM: AN END IN ITSELF, A MEANS FOR PROGRESS

As a vital element of human dignity, autonomy, and personal empowerment, economic freedom is valuable as an end itself. But just as important is the fact that economic freedom is the key to achieving the broad-based economic dynamism that ensures lasting inclusive growth and increased prosperity for society as a whole. As Hayek foresaw decades ago, "the guiding principle in any attempt to create a world of free men must be this: a policy of freedom for the individual is the only truly progressive policy."[4]

As editions of this *Index* have documented over the past two decades, the link between economic freedom and long-term development is clear and strong. Countries that allow their citizens more economic freedom reach higher incomes and better standards of life. People in economically free societies live longer. They have better health. They are able to be better stewards of the environment, and they push forward the frontiers of human achievement in science and technology through greater innovation.

ENDNOTES

1. Milton Friedman and Rose D. Friedman, *Free to Choose: A Personal Statement* (New York: Harcourt Brace Jovanovich, 1979).

2. Friedrich A. Hayek, *The Road to Serfdom* (Chicago: University of Chicago Press, 1944).

3. "The property which every man has in his own labor, as it is the original foundation of all other property, so it is the most sacred and inviolable." Adam Smith, *An Inquiry into the Nature and Causes of the Wealth of Nations* (New York: The Modern Library, 1937), pp. 121–122; first published in 1776.

4. Hayek, *The Road to Serfdom*.

Chapter 2

Why Economic Freedom Matters

Ambassador Terry Miller and Anthony B. Kim

Since its inception in 1995, the *Index of Economic Freedom* has chronicled hundreds of examples of government policy changes that have enhanced economic freedom, thereby promoting human progress and greater prosperity. As the *Index* has catalogued, nations with higher degrees of economic freedom prosper because they capitalize more fully on the ability of the free-market system not only to generate, but also to reinforce dynamic growth through efficient resource allocation, value creation, and innovation. Policies that promote freedom, whether through improvements in the rule of law, the promotion of competition and openness, or suitable restraints on the size and economic reach of government, turn out in practice to offer and advance practical solutions to a wide range of economic and social challenges that face the world's societies.

The findings of the 2015 *Index* once again demonstrate the strongly positive linkages between economic freedom and various dimensions of human development. Many of the linkages are straightforward: Higher taxes, for example, reduce investment and hurt job growth. Others, such as the impact on economic growth from the promotion of property rights or the maintenance of a stable monetary system, are more intricate, multidimensional, and nonlinear.

Even in these cases, however, the evidence is strong that adherence to the principles of economic freedom is an unmatched strategy for promoting solutions to human problems and advancing overall well-being. No alternative systems—and many have been tried—come close to the record of free-market capitalism in promoting growth and improving the human condition.

ECONOMIC FREEDOM: ADVANCING OPPORTUNITY

Today's successful economies are not necessarily geographically large or richly blessed with natural resources. Many economies have managed to expand opportunities for their citizens by enhancing their economic dynamism. In general, the overarching objective of economic policies

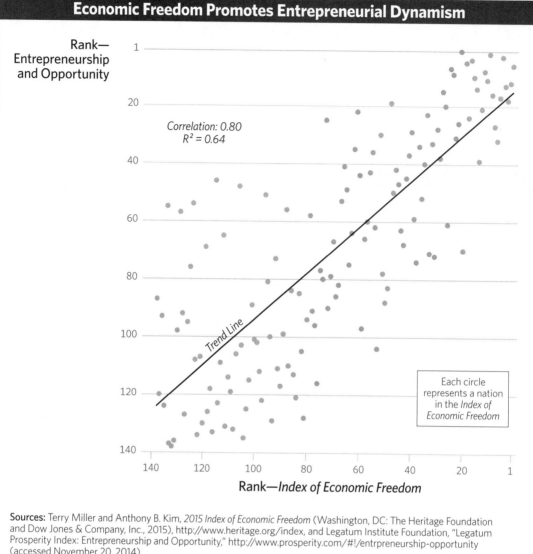

Economic Freedom Promotes Entrepreneurial Dynamism

Rank—
Entrepreneurship
and Opportunity

Correlation: 0.80
$R^2 = 0.64$

Trend Line

Each circle
represents a nation
in the *Index of
Economic Freedom*

Rank—*Index of Economic Freedom*

Sources: Terry Miller and Anthony B. Kim, *2015 Index of Economic Freedom* (Washington, DC: The Heritage Foundation and Dow Jones & Company, Inc., 2015), http://www.heritage.org/index, and Legatum Institute Foundation, "Legatum Prosperity Index: Entrepreneurship and Opportunity," http://www.prosperity.com/#!/entrpreneurship-opportunity (accessed November 20, 2014).

Chart 1 ☎ heritage.org

must be to create an environment that provides the most opportunity for the widest range of activities that can lead to increased prosperity.

The *Index* results have shown that sustaining such economic dynamism is achievable only when governments adopt economic policies that empower individuals and firms with more choices, encouraging greater entrepreneurship.

It is noteworthy that despite recent policy missteps by many countries in responding to the global economic slowdown, which amounted to a political assault on capitalism in some places,

the free-market system is not on the verge of breakdown. In fact, as the negative impact of regulatory and spending mistakes has become apparent, a greater number of people around the world seem to be realizing that the economic damage inflicted by the heavy hand of government—subpar growth, deteriorating entrepreneurial environments, and lower employment growth—is not inevitable, but rather the result of bad policy choices.

Even as the free market has been under challenge in countries such as Venezuela, Bolivia,

GDP per Capita (Purchasing Power Parity)

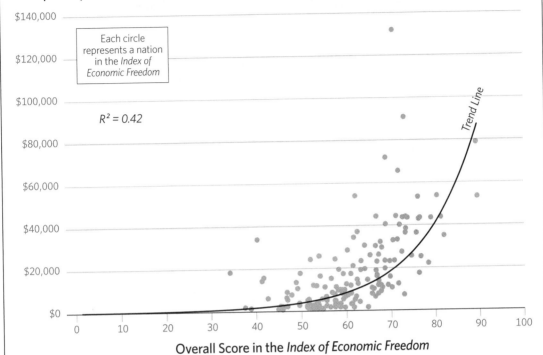

$R^2 = 0.42$

Each circle represents a nation in the *Index of Economic Freedom*

Trend Line

Overall Score in the *Index of Economic Freedom*

GDP per Capita (Purchasing Power Parity)

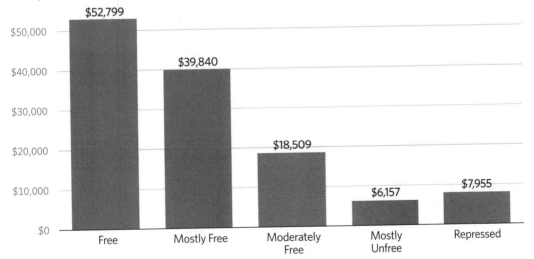

$52,799	$39,840	$18,509	$6,157	$7,955
Free	Mostly Free	Moderately Free	Mostly Unfree	Repressed

Category in the *Index of Economic Freedom*

Sources: Terry Miller and Anthony B. Kim, *2015 Index of Economic Freedom* (Washington, DC: The Heritage Foundation and Dow Jones & Company, Inc., 2015), http://www.heritage.org/index; and International Monetary Fund, World Economic Outlook Databases, http://www.imf.org/external/ns/cs.aspx?id=28 (accessed November 19, 2014).

Chart 2 ☎ heritage.org

As Economic Freedom Rises, the Global Economy Expands and Poverty Falls

Average Score in the
Index of Economic Freedom

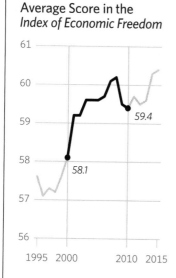

Global GDP, in Trillions
of 2005 U.S. Dollars

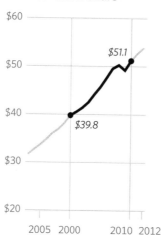

Percent of Global
Population in Poverty

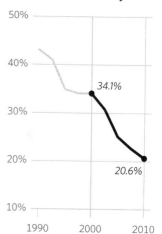

Sources: Terry Miller and Anthony B. Kim, *2015 Index of Economic Freedom* (Washington, DC: The Heritage Foundation and Dow Jones & Company, Inc., 2015), http://www.heritage.org/index; The World Bank, World Development Indicators Online, http://databank.worldbank.org/data/views/variableSelection/selectvariables.aspx?source=world-development-indicators (accessed November 20, 2014); and The World Bank, PovcalNet, http://iresearch.worldbank.org/PovcalNet/index.htm?1 (accessed November 20, 2014). Some figures have been interpolated.

Chart 3 ☎ heritage.org

Russia, and even the United States, many other governments around the world have acknowledged its superiority. Decades of evidence, some presented in the pages of this *Index*, are hard for even the most ideological governments to ignore. Not only does the free-market system remain viable, but many of its core features, such as private property rights, openness to trade and investment, and fiscal discipline, have entrenched themselves as the policy standard, any deviation from which requires strong justification.

ECONOMIC FREEDOM: PROMOTING PROSPERITY

In many respects, economic freedom is merely shorthand for an openness to entrepreneurial activity that increases opportunity for individuals to succeed in their endeavors. Chart 1 shows the close correspondence between economic freedom and entrepreneurial opportunity as measured by the Entrepreneurship and Opportunity sub-index of the Legatum Prosperity Index, which "measures a coun-

try's entrepreneurial environment, its promotion of innovative activity, and the evenness of opportunity."

Given such a strong relationship, it should be apparent that a government's most effective stimulus activity will not be to increase its own spending or increase layers of regulation, both of which reduce economic freedom. The best results are likely to be achieved instead through policy reforms that improve the incentives that drive entrepreneurial activity, creating more opportunities for greater economic dynamism.

Equally notable are the fundamental benefits that stem from the strong positive relationship between economic freedom and levels of per capita income. For countries achieving scores in the *Index* that reflect even moderate levels of economic freedom (60 or above), the relationship between economic freedom and per capita GDP is highly significant.

As indicated in Chart 2, countries moving up the economic freedom scale show increasingly high levels of average income. Economies rated

Advancing Economic Freedom Leads to Higher Economic Growth

Average Annual Growth in Real Per Capita GDP

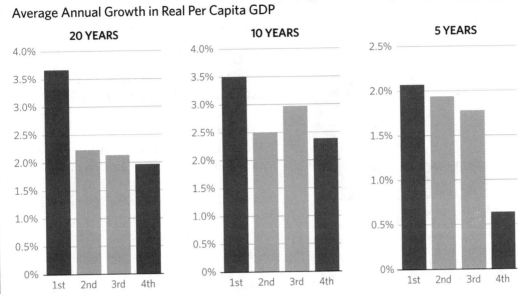

Change in Economic Freedom Score, by Quartile
(1st—most improvement, 4th—least)

Sources: Terry Miller and Anthony B. Kim, *2015 Index of Economic Freedom* (Washington, DC: The Heritage Foundation and Dow Jones & Company, Inc., 2015), http://www.heritage.org/index, and The World Bank, World Development Indicators Online, http://databank.worldbank.org/data/views/variableSelection/selectvariables.aspx?source=world-development-indicators (accessed November 20, 2014). Changes in economic freedom score have been calculated as the annual compound growth rate.

Chart 4 ☎ heritage.org

"free" or "mostly free" in the 2015 *Index* enjoy incomes that are over twice the average levels in all other countries and more than five times higher than the incomes of "repressed" economies.

ECONOMIC FREEDOM: ANTIDOTE TO POVERTY

By a great many measures, the past two decades during which the *Index* has been charting the advance of economic freedom have been the most prosperous in the history of humankind. Those countries that have adopted some version of free-market capitalism, with economies supported by efficient regulations and open to the free flow of goods, services, and capital, have participated in an era of globalization and economic integration in which solutions to many of the world's development problems have taken hold and generated real improvements in living standards.

The free-market system that is rooted in the principles of economic freedom has fueled unprecedented economic growth around the world. As Chart 3 illustrates, as the global economy has moved toward greater economic freedom over the past two decades, real world GDP has increased by about 70 percent, and the global poverty rate has been cut in half, lifting hundreds of millions of people out of poverty.

Greater economic freedom has had a positive impact not just on the number of people in poverty, but also on the intensity of the poverty still experienced by some. Poverty intensity as measured by the United Nations Development Programme's Multidimensional Poverty Index, which assesses the nature and intensity of deprivation at the individual level in education, health outcomes, and standard of living, is much lower on average in countries with higher levels of eco-

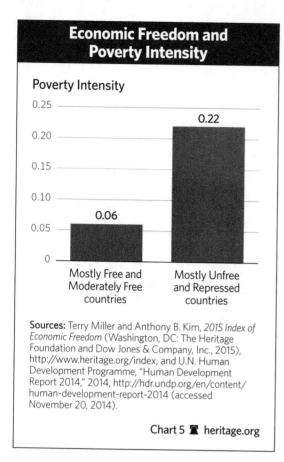

Economic Freedom and Poverty Intensity

Poverty Intensity

- 0.25
- 0.20 — 0.22
- 0.15
- 0.10
- 0.05 — 0.06
- 0

| Mostly Free and Moderately Free countries | Mostly Unfree and Repressed countries |

Sources: Terry Miller and Anthony B. Kim, *2015 Index of Economic Freedom* (Washington, DC: The Heritage Foundation and Dow Jones & Company, Inc., 2015), http://www.heritage.org/index, and U.N. Human Development Programme, "Human Development Report 2014," 2014, http://hdr.undp.org/en/content/human-development-report-2014 (accessed November 20, 2014).

Chart 5 ☎ heritage.org

nomic freedom. Chart 5 shows that the intensity of poverty in countries whose economies are considered mostly free or moderately free is only about one-fourth the level in countries that are rated less free.

The key driver of poverty reduction is dynamic and resilient economic growth that creates jobs. Not surprisingly, one of the most important goals of economic policy in almost every country in the world has thus been to increase the rate of economic growth.

As Chart 4 demonstrates, there is a robust relationship between improving economic freedom and achieving higher per capita economic growth. Whether long-term (20 years), medium-term (10 years), or short-term (five years), the relationship between changes in economic freedom and changes in economic growth is consistently positive.

Undeniably, countries moving toward greater economic freedom tend to achieve higher rates of per capita GDP growth over time. Whether in the short term or over the long run, the average annu-

al per capita economic growth rates of countries that have grown economic freedom the most are at least 50 percent higher than those of countries where freedom has stagnated or slowed.

ECONOMIC FREEDOM: SOCIETAL DEVELOPMENT AND DEMOCRATIC PROGRESS

Growing economic freedom is unequivocally about more than financial success. Achieving greater overall prosperity that goes beyond materialistic and monetary dimensions of well-being is equally important. The societal benefits of economic freedom extend far beyond higher incomes or reductions in poverty. Countries with higher levels of economic freedom enjoy higher levels of overall human development as measured by the United Nations Human Development Index, which measures life expectancy, literacy, education, and the standard of living in countries worldwide. As Chart 6 shows, governments that choose policies that increase economic freedom are placing their societies on the pathway to more education opportunities, better health care, and higher standards of living for their citizens.

In some countries, government policies and actions concerning the environment have become more intrusive and economically distortionary. Many governments have pushed programs to tax carbon emissions and increase taxes on gasoline, organized non-transparent and sometimes corrupt exchanges for the buying and selling of carbon emissions, and provided subsidies for "clean" energy to politically favored firms. Such policies impose a huge direct cost on society, and they also retard economic growth—and all for uncertain environmental benefits.

Interestingly, the same free-market principles that have proven to be the key to economic success have also proven to deliver environmental success. Around the world, economic freedom has been shown to increase countries' capacity for innovation and thus to improve overall environmental performance.

The positive link between economic freedom and higher levels of innovation ensures greater economic dynamism in coping with various developmental challenges, and the most remarkable improvements in clean energy use and energy efficiency over the past decades have occurred not as a result of government regulation, but rather because of advances in technology and trade. A virtuous cycle of investment, innovation (including in greener technologies), and dynamic economic growth has flourished where governments have trusted market forces and competition to spur efficiency. (See Chart 7.)

Greater economic freedom can also provide more fertile ground for effective and democratic governance. Debate over the direction of causality between economic freedom and democracy has become more controversial in recent years because of the multifaceted interaction between the two. Undoubtedly, achieving greater political freedom through well-functioning democracy is a messy and often excruciating process.

However, the positive relationship between economic freedom and democratic governance is undeniable. (See Chart 8.) By empowering people to exercise greater control of their daily lives, economic freedom ultimately nurtures political reform by making it possible for individuals to gain the economic resources necessary to challenge entrenched interests and compete for political power, thereby encouraging the creation of more pluralistic societies.

Pursuit of greater economic freedom is thus an important stepping-stone to democracy. It empowers the poor and builds the middle class. It is a philosophy that encourages entrepreneurship and disperses economic power and decision-making throughout society.

ECONOMIC FREEDOM: THE KEY TO UPWARD MOBILITY AND GREATER SOCIAL PROGRESS

The massive improvements in global indicators of income and quality of life largely reflect a paradigm shift in the debate over how societies should be structured to achieve the most optimal outcome. Over the past two decades, this debate has largely been won by capitalism. However, fears that the immediate benefits of capitalism are fading has brought to the forefront concerns about economic mobility and economic freedom.

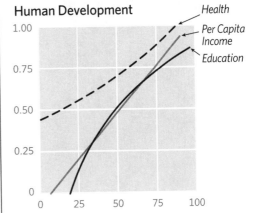

Greater Freedom Means Greater Performance by Several Measures

Human Development

Health
Per Capita Income
Education

Overall Score in the *Index of Economic Freedom*

Sources: Terry Miller and Anthony B. Kim, *2015 Index of Economic Freedom* (Washington, DC: The Heritage Foundation and Dow Jones & Company, Inc., 2015), http://www.heritage.org/index, and U.N. Human Development Programme, International Human Development Indicators, http://hdr.undp.org/en/statistics/ (accessed November 20, 2014). Human Development values have been converted to a 0–1 scale.

Chart 6 ☎ heritage.org

At the heart of ensuring upward economic mobility is the task of advancing economic freedom so that dynamic and inclusive growth can meaningfully occur for ordinary people in a free society. Milton and Rose Friedman made a keen observation on the critically intertwined relationship between freedom and mobility:

> [S]o long as freedom is maintained, it prevents ... positions of privilege from becoming institutionalized. Freedom means diversity, but also mobility. It preserves the opportunity for today's disadvantaged to become tomorrow's privileged and, in the process enables almost everyone, from top to bottom, to enjoy a fuller and richer life.[1]

Economic freedom is critical to generating the broader-based economic growth that brings more opportunities for a greater number of people to work, produce, and save. In other words, ensuring greater economic freedom is

Economic Freedom, Innovation, and the Environment

Innovation Capacity

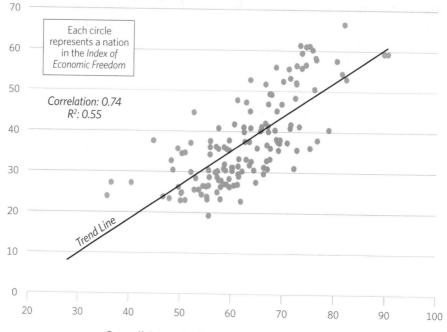

Each circle represents a nation in the *Index of Economic Freedom*

Correlation: 0.74
R^2: 0.55

Trend Line

Overall Score in the *Index of Economic Freedom*

Environmental Performance Index

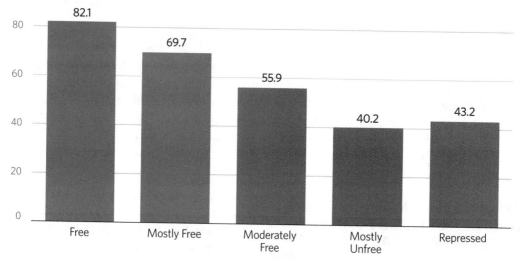

82.1
69.7
55.9
40.2
43.2

Free | Mostly Free | Moderately Free | Mostly Unfree | Repressed

Category in the *Index of Economic Freedom*

Sources: Terry Miller and Anthony B. Kim, *2015 Index of Economic Freedom* (Washington, DC: The Heritage Foundation and Dow Jones & Company, Inc., 2015), http://www.heritage.org/index; and Cornell University, INSEAD, and World Intellectual Property Organization, *The Global Innovation Index 2013: The Local Dynamics of Innovation* (Geneva: World Intellectual Property Organization, 2013), http://www.globalinnovationindex.org/content.aspx?page=gii-full-report-2013 (accessed November 20, 2014); and Yale University, "2014 Environmental Performance Index," http://epi.yale.edu/epi (accessed November 20, 2014).

Chart 7 ☎ heritage.org

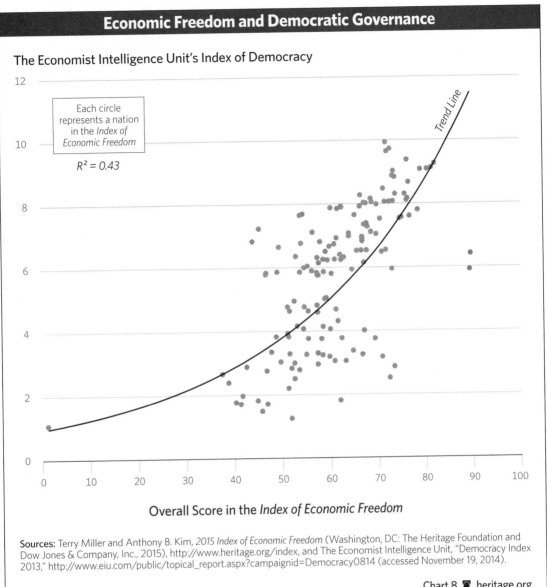

Economic Freedom and Democratic Governance

The Economist Intelligence Unit's Index of Democracy

Each circle represents a nation in the *Index of Economic Freedom*

$R^2 = 0.43$

Trend Line

Overall Score in the *Index of Economic Freedom*

Sources: Terry Miller and Anthony B. Kim, *2015 Index of Economic Freedom* (Washington, DC: The Heritage Foundation and Dow Jones & Company, Inc., 2015), http://www.heritage.org/index, and The Economist Intelligence Unit, "Democracy Index 2013," http://www.eiu.com/public/topical_report.aspx?campaignid=Democracy0814 (accessed November 19, 2014).

Chart 8 ☎ heritage.org

directly related to preserving and enhancing dynamic upward mobility.

Also notable is that although some naysayers claim that economic and social progress has been limited in recent years as incomes in some countries have become more unequal as a result of economic freedom, the evidence does not support this contention. Instead, societies based on economic freedom are the ones that have demonstrated the strongest social progress.

As shown in Chart 9, countries that largely embrace economic freedom provide the envi-

ronments that are most conducive to social progress.[2] Countries that improve their competitiveness and open their societies to new ideas, products, and innovations have largely achieved the high levels of social progress that their citizens demand. It is not massive redistributions of wealth or government dictates on income levels that produce the most positive social outcomes. Instead, mobility and progress require lower barriers to entry, freedom to engage with the world, and less government intrusion.

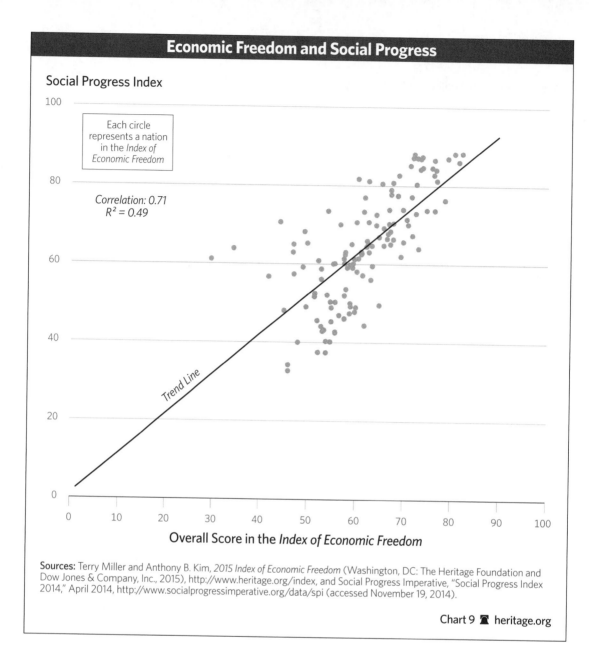

Economic Freedom and Social Progress

Social Progress Index

Each circle represents a nation in the *Index of Economic Freedom*

Correlation: 0.71
$R^2 = 0.49$

Trend Line

Overall Score in the *Index of Economic Freedom*

Sources: Terry Miller and Anthony B. Kim, *2015 Index of Economic Freedom* (Washington, DC: The Heritage Foundation and Dow Jones & Company, Inc., 2015), http://www.heritage.org/index, and Social Progress Imperative, "Social Progress Index 2014," April 2014, http://www.socialprogressimperative.org/data/spi (accessed November 19, 2014).

Chart 9 ☎ heritage.org

STAYING ON COURSE

The 21st edition of the *Index of Economic Freedom* shows economic freedom once again on the rise, reaching the highest point in the *Index*'s 21-year history. Behind this record are stories of human progress and the achievements of countries and their citizens—literally billions of people around the world whose lives have measurably improved.

It is no coincidence that the increase of economic liberty over the past decades has coincided with a massive reduction in worldwide poverty, disease, and hunger. The link between economic freedom and development is clear and strong. People in economically free societies live longer. They have better health. They are able to be better stewards of the environment, and they push forward the frontiers of human achievement in science and technology through greater innovation.

A recurring theme of human history has been resilience and revival. The country profiles in the 2015 *Index of Economic Freedom* include many examples of countries that have accelerated their economic and social progress in the face of difficult challenges and a sometimes harsh international environment. Their successes can be emulated by others. The *Index of Economic Freedom* charts not just one path to development, but as many as the ingenuity of humans can produce when they are free to experiment and innovate.

The principles of economic freedom are a sure guide, but only a guide. What truly will matter are the creative solutions to pressing world problems that are certain to flow from people who are, in the words of Milton and Rose Friedman, "free to choose."

ENDNOTES

1. Milton Friedman and Rose D. Friedman, *Free to Choose: A Personal Statement* (New York: Harcourt Brace Jovanovich, 1979).

2. The Social Progress Index defines social progress as the capacity of a society to meet the basic human needs of its citizens, establish the building blocks that allow citizens and communities to enhance and sustain the quality of their lives, and create the conditions for all individuals to reach their full potential.

Chapter 3

The Freedom Path to Economic Growth: A Comparative Analysis of Country Performance

Stephen Moore and Joel Griffith

For 21 years, the *Index of Economic Freedom* has provided an indispensable road map for countries that aspire to greater economic dynamism and prosperity. The rules are not complicated. As the *Index* has revealed, lasting prosperity is a result of a persistent commitment to low tax rates, a stable currency, limited government, strong private property rights, openness to global trade and financial flows, and sensible regulation. Together, these factors empower the individual and induce dynamic entrepreneurial activity.

The supply-side economics model, which focuses on ways to increase the production of goods and services rather than on maintaining high levels of demand, was popularized in the United States by President Ronald Reagan more than 30 years ago. It is now a primary operating principle of countries around the world. A key part of the supply-side model is careful attention to the potentially stifling nature of taxes, and tax cuts are often the preferred policy prescription for economic woes. Despite occasional howls of protest over "tax cuts for the rich," much of the world has taken note of the impressive and sustained rates of economic growth that typically follow such cuts, and tax rates have come down worldwide.

One of the taxes that have perhaps the largest impact on a nation's ability to compete in global markets is the corporate tax. The reason, of course, is that tax's large impact on the flow of investment. In this age of information and technology, borders do not matter much anymore for businesses. The world has become one massive shopping market for capital. Nations are in a contest to climb past each other in a race up the ladder of economic growth.

The impact of non-competitive corporate tax rates can be debilitating. For example, the U.S.'s effective statutory rate is now a full 50 percent higher than the average of its international competitors. Businesses are adapting by relocating overseas or through structural changes such as corporate inversion, in which companies legally reincorporate in a foreign country that has lower tax rates.

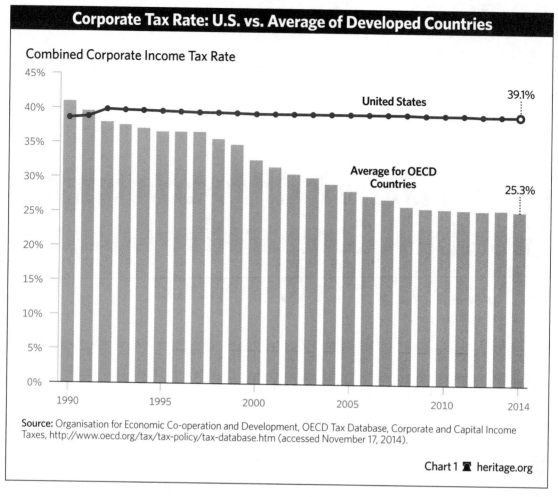

Corporate Tax Rate: U.S. vs. Average of Developed Countries

Combined Corporate Income Tax Rate

United States — 39.1%

Average for OECD Countries — 25.3%

Source: Organisation for Economic Co-operation and Development, OECD Tax Database, Corporate and Capital Income Taxes, http://www.oecd.org/tax/tax-policy/tax-database.htm (accessed November 17, 2014).

Chart 1 ☎ heritage.org

The *Index of Economic Freedom* has shown that commitment to lower taxation is one of the key components of a country's effort to create a virtuous cycle of entrepreneurship, growth, and lasting prosperity for its citizens. A recent study by the Organisation for Economic Co-operation and Development examines why some countries are becoming more prosperous than others and concludes that "corporate taxes are found to be most harmful for growth, followed by personal income taxes, and then consumption taxes."[1] The OECD study finds, not surprisingly, that investment rates fall when corporate tax rates rise and that the most profitable and most rapidly expanding companies tend to be those that are the most sensitive to corporate tax rates. High corporate tax rates are also self-defeating because they produce little if any revenue.

But taxes are not all that matters. The rule of law, efficient regulatory structures, and open markets are vital to achieving greater prosperity. Over the lifetime of the *Index*, some politicians have evidently been listening and taking action. Others have not. The resulting disparities of living standards among countries are not just happenstance.

This essay provides three types of comparisons:

- We look at some dramatic differences between outcomes in neighboring countries that have pursued vastly different economic policies;
- We compare the economic results since the collapse of the Soviet Union in 1991 between a leading free market–embracing Baltic country and a less liberty-minded nation; and
- We explain that the interrelation between economic policy and outcomes is evidenced by the "laboratories of democracy" in the 50 United States.

NEIGHBORING COUNTRIES: SO CLOSE BUT SO FAR AWAY

In 2014, a book co-authored by one of us, *An Inquiry into the Nature and Causes of the Wealth of States*,[2] explored numerous instances in which individual U.S. states located close to one another achieved vastly different economic outcomes. Many of these disparate outcomes were linked to distinct state policies pursued by the state governments. To summarize, states with higher taxes, more restrictive regulations, and onerous labor restrictions often realized lower rates of job creation and economic growth.

Likewise, nations may share a common border and sometimes even the same language but implement vastly different economic policies. In countries where tax rates have been ratcheted down, sensible monetary policies are pursued by the central bank, and the free flow of capital is encouraged, economies have prospered; but where politicians attempt to seize the wealth of those with capital, co-opt the central banks to meet political ends, and engage in protectionism, citizens—particularly those aspiring to the middle class—are harmed.

The following case studies highlight how nations with similar cultural, geographic, or demographic conditions but different levels of economic freedom often realize far different outcomes.

CHILE VS. ARGENTINA

Chile. Chile's post-war history has been characterized by the struggle for greater freedom, with the right emphasizing economic freedom and the left emphasizing political freedom. In one of the more felicitous outcomes anywhere in the world during this period, both sides have succeeded: Chile now has robust democratic institutions and a strong commitment to human rights as well as one of the freest economies in the world.

Over the decades, Chile has undertaken a series of free-market reforms, including privatizing various government-run entities such as the telecommunications, power, and water sectors.[3] Chile also privatized the bankrupt social security system, granting citizens control of their personal retirement funds.[4] The nation also welcomed foreign trade and investment and abandoned various price-control schemes.[5] Through these reforms, Chile's per capita gross domestic product (GDP) has been growing at an average annual rate of 3.6 percent[6] over the past 38 years, and Chile has moved from being a debtor nation to being a creditor nation.

Today, mining, which is one of the pillars of Chile's economy, accounts for 57.3 percent of its total exports (by value) and 11.1 percent of GDP[7] and absorbs about one-third of foreign direct investment in Chile.[8] But Chile's mining sector was not always this prosperous. Throughout the 1970s, Marxist President Salvador Allende sought and obtained constitutional changes that gave the state "absolute, exclusive, inalienable, and imprescriptible"[9] ownership of production. This effectively paralyzed the entire sector.

Not until approval of the new 1980 constitution and the subsequent Constitutional Mining Law were traditional private property rights restored. The current prosperity is a result of these guarantees.[10] In the words of Jose Pinera, Secretary of Mining in Chile during these reforms, "The positive effects of the law began to show themselves in the form of increased exploration and production activity from the moment its approval was announced."[11] In other words, capital investment is spurred once investors are assured profits and successful projects are safe from state confiscation.

Furthermore, in stark contrast to Argentina (and other Latin American countries), Chile's healthy investment environment attracts foreign investment. According to the World Bank's Business Environment Snapshots, "Chile is one of the most open countries to foreign equity ownership, as measured by the Investing Across Sectors indicators."[12] A foreign limited liability company (LLC) can be established in less than a month.[13]

Minister of the Presidency Cristián Larroulet expressed his pleasure that Chile "has benefited from the presence of large local institutional investors—mainly private pension funds—which are sophisticated investors that continuously invest in the local market. As a result, high-qualified human capital and a solid regulatory framework are already in place."[14]

The decades-long respect for property rights has incentivized investing and fostered trust in financial institutions. With the Socialists currently back in control, all of this could be undone, but Chile has forged a remarkable record under both the left and the right in advancing and protecting hard-won freedoms, both political and economic. With Chile well on its way to becoming the first developed economy in Latin America, one can only hope that such political wisdom continues to prevail.

Argentina. Contrast Chile's remarkable success with the situation in Argentina, once Latin America's richest country. Argentina now ranks 169th out of 178 countries included in the *Index* and 27th out of 29 countries in the South and Central America/Caribbean region. Continuing to be mired in a climate of economic repression, Argentina has recorded its lowest economic freedom score ever in the 2015 *Index*.

The erosion of freedom is creating havoc. Cristina Fernández de Kirchner's government in Buenos Aires "bullies and nationalises businesses, and pressures the central bank to use international reserves for debt payments."[15]

For example, on April 16, 2012, Kirchner introduced a bill, overwhelmingly approved by both houses of Congress, that partially renationalized YPF, the nation's largest energy firm.[16] This followed the discovery by the company just months before of nearly 1 billion barrels of oil in one of its fields.[17] No wonder that the country is on track to remain dependent on foreign suppliers for energy even though the nation possesses the world's third largest deposits of shale gas, and no wonder that investors are hesitant to risk capital in such an environment.

Furthermore, in Argentina, politicians—regional governors—have sway over the operations of private businesses. The authority wielded by elected officials to set prices, mandate production, and engage in other corporate governance is in many ways similar to expropriation. Value is destroyed and profits diminished, although title of the wrangled entity remains in private hands. We have seen this before in Argentina during the socialist Peronist years, and the middle class suffered.

The recent $100 billion national debt default, a wave of nationalizations, and strict capital controls are deterring foreign investment, but Argentina's bureaucrats seem not to mind. Minister of Economy and Production Roberto Lavagna boasted that "Argentina isn't interested in luring speculative investors.... It generates bubbles that when they are reverted can produce a negative impact, especially for the poorest people."[18]

Economic results clearly show the repercussions of these policies. Consider R.R. Donnelly & Sons, a Chicago company that just shuttered the doors of its factory in Argentina. This printing plant employed up to 400 people for more than two decades. Yet, according to the company, "rising labor costs, inflation, materials price increases, devaluation, inability to pay debts as they become due, and other issues" forced the closure.[19]

Despite a population more than twice as large as Chile's, Argentina has barely attracted even a third the level of Chile's net foreign direct investment. Inflation in Argentina has run at more than three times that of Chile. Both taxes and government spending as a fraction of the economy are nearly twice the level of Chile's. In 2012, Argentina's 1.9 percent GDP growth greatly underperformed Chile's 5.5 percent boom.[20]

In fact, after years of Kirchner's steel grip, Argentina's economy is now smaller than Brazil's, Mexico's, and Colombia's.[21] This is quite a fall from grace for the Keynesian experiment considering that just 20 years ago, Argentina's economy was nearly five times that of Colombia's.[22]

This plunge in economic standing worsened as the government officially devalued the peso early in 2014. In combination with the flooding of the markets with newly created currency, future investment is chased away, and prices leap higher.

CHINA VS. HONG KONG AND TAIWAN

China. China ranks a dismal 139th worldwide in economic freedom and 30th out of 42 counties in the Asia–Pacific region. Some have touted China's model of state-guided capitalism as one to be followed.

China has enjoyed annual growth of nearly 9 percent over the past five years, and in the years since liberalization in the late 1970s, per capita income and real GDP have grown exponentially. However, economic freedom in China has advanced only sporadically since then, and problems long unaddressed are becoming impossible to ignore. In particular, the Chinese leadership still maintains inordinate control of the levers of economic power, including finance and investment, and has concentrated its development efforts on seizing market share in existing international markets rather than on developing new products and markets to advance world economic growth.

China's focus on technological imitation rather than innovation may have brought short-term, low-cost prosperity relative to 50 years ago, but unless the economy is freed from such state-imposed self-limitations, the nation will continue to lag behind its free-market competitors. A glance at production levels of state-owned vs. non-state-owned industrial firms illustrates this. Since 2008, non-state-owned industrial firms have enjoyed expansion rates that are twice as high as those of state-owned firms.[23]

Even after modest privatization, state-owned-enterprises (SOEs) still play an enormous role in China. Currently, SOEs exist in a broad range of sectors, including banking, aviation, petroleum, electricity, shipping, and machinery.[24] More than 150,000 enterprises are included in this list.[25] In the past, this has represented an enormous slice of the national economy, at times exceeding 30 percent of nationwide industrial and business revenue.[26] In 2013, these enterprises were worth $5.7 trillion,[27] more than half the size of China's official $9.4 trillion GDP.

Despite this dampening of authentic entrepreneurialism, certain market reforms have enabled robust economic growth. Tax reductions, for example, are an underappreciated part of the decades-long progress. In 1978, then Chinese leader Deng Xiaoping unleashed a series of free market–based economic reforms, including the legalization of privately owned farms (which caused a near doubling of food output above what the Communist state-owned farms produced); the establishment of coastal economic enterprise zones; new opportunities for foreign investment; and the privatization of state-owned enterprises.[28] Although sporadic and limited, these market reforms, enhanced by China's participation in the global trading system, have lifted more than half a billion people out of abject poverty—one of the great economic triumphs in human history.

Yet the errant political idea that bureaucrats are actually capable of centrally planning a large modern economy has held overall development far below potential and kept hundreds of millions of Chinese citizens in poverty. Furthermore, the concentration of power in the hands of central planners and away from local leadership has created environmental mayhem nationally. With growth rates falling, the pressures of unemployment are likely to increase, and with no legitimate democratic outlet for expression of the population's concerns, political and economic stability is a constant concern for the government.

Just think of the prosperity that could have resulted if the mainland Chinese had truly embraced economic and political freedom. But we don't have to imagine it. All we need do is look at Hong Kong and Taiwan.

Hong Kong. Hong Kong follows an ancient common-law tradition handed down from the English that "everything which is not forbidden is allowed." It is no surprise that it is ranked number one globally for economic freedom. Hong Kong also must surely be considered one of the great economic triumphs in human history.

This is a very inconvenient place for mercantilists. How, therefore, does one explain its prosperity? After all, as Milton Friedman reminded us in *Free to Choose*, this is a tiny port island with relatively few natural resources, the highest population density of virtually any nation except for Singapore and tiny Monaco, and no military power.

Hong Kong has never implemented the Maoist one-child policy of Communist China. Given its constricted geographical confines and limited natural resources, a Malthusian would have

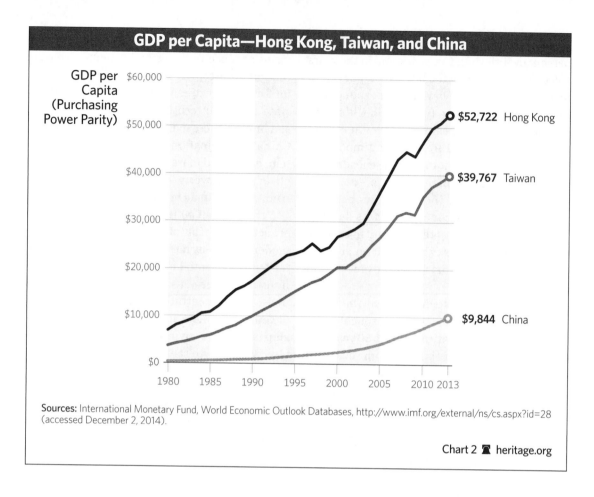

GDP per Capita—Hong Kong, Taiwan, and China

GDP per Capita (Purchasing Power Parity)

- $52,722 Hong Kong
- $39,767 Taiwan
- $9,844 China

Sources: International Monetary Fund, World Economic Outlook Databases, http://www.imf.org/external/ns/cs.aspx?id=28 (accessed December 2, 2014).

Chart 2 ☎ heritage.org

predicted more human misery after decades of unchecked population growth than one finds in the poorest province of India or village of Africa. Yet the contrary is true: Hong Kong's per capita GDP exploded by more than $45,000 from 1980 to 2013. The mainland's GDP grew under $300 yearly during that same period, to around $9,800 in 2013. In terms of GDP per capita adjusted for purchasing power parity, the average Hong Kong resident had a standard of living more than five times higher than the average mainlander.

By meeting the demands of individual consumers and companies across the globe rather than the dictates of state bureaucrats, Hong Kong has attained prosperity. Skeptics say, "Well, that's only because Westerners—Brits and Americans—invested so much there." Which begs the question: Why did they invest there? Hong Kong is the most economically free country on the planet. It has long had a 15 percent flat individual income tax; it is a free trade mecca; government

spending is low; regulations on small businesses are light; education is largely private; capital moves freely in and out, unhindered.

For many decades after it adopted a flat tax in 1947, Hong Kong enjoyed the benefits of a competitively low tax rate with no tax on dividends or capital gains or money earned outside of the island. Hong Kong has also embraced free trade, which explains why it has evolved into a capitalist paradise brimming with entrepreneurial spirit. The tax code is about 200 pages, compared to over 70,000 pages for the U.S. tax code.[29]

Over several decades, Hong Kong has evolved into one of the richest places on Earth despite its tiny land mass and no natural resources. The only mystery is why it took nearly half a century for the rest of the world to start copying the Hong Kong model.

Taiwan. In the wake of the Chinese Communist revolution, the remnants of the previous Chinese government were confined to the island of Taiwan, which operates for all practical purposes as an independent nation. Although Taiwan shares a common cultural and historic tradition with mainland China just 110 miles away, its economic system is far different from Beijing's.

Prudent macroeconomic policy within a stable legal and monetary environment has been the key to Taiwan's continuing success in achieving rising levels of economic freedom over the past two decades. A sustained commitment to structural reforms and openness to global commerce have enabled the country to advance far into the ranks of the "mostly free." Recording uninterrupted years of growth in economic freedom since 2009, Taiwan has achieved its highest score ever in the 2015 *Index*.

Starting a company in Taiwan takes just three steps, and property rights are generally protected. Business owners know that the judiciary exists to enforce contractual rights.[30]

Taiwan illustrates the benefits of free trade. During the past 40-plus years, foreign trade has been the core driver of Taiwan's economy as total annual trade increased nearly eightyfold from under $4 billion USD in 1971 to $300 billion in 2013.[31] Taiwan also illustrates the dynamism of comparative advantage in conjunction with economic freedom: Export composition has evolved from predominantly agricultural commodities to more than 98 percent industrial goods.[32]

The importance of tax cuts, particularly for businesses and investments, is demonstrated by Taiwan's response to the global economic downturn of 2008–2009. The negative growth of 2009 was Taiwan's first recession in 10 years.[33] In the midst of the turmoil, Taiwan slashed its corporate income tax from 25 percent to 17 percent in 2009.[34] The next year, it enjoyed a GDP boom of more than 10 percent—its most rapid growth in more than 30 years.[35]

BOTSWANA VS. ZIMBABWE

Botswana. Botswana ranks high on the freedom index at 36th globally and 2nd in Sub-Saharan Africa. Several factors enable Botswana to be an oasis of prosperity in a neighborhood of uncertainty and turmoil. These include taxation of individual income at no more than 25 percent,

declining government spending, political stability, and the lowest level of judicial corruption on the entire continent.[36]

Botswana also has a relatively high per capita income at over $16,000. This is higher than some European countries and by world standards makes it an upper-middle-class country. The past 10 years have seen an influx of foreign capital and growing privatization of many industries, and with this has followed growth, making Botswana one of the most prosperous countries in Africa. On a continent riddled with poverty, other countries would be wise to take note.[37]

Corporations are selecting Botswana for their international headquarters. The prestigious list includes Laurelton Diamonds (a Tiffany & Co. subsidiary); HJ Heinz; Hewlett-Packard; Barclays Bank; and the South African Development Community (SADC).[38] Certainly, the rejection of corruption in Botswana helps to attract foreign investment and employers. In 2013, Transparency International ranked Botswana the least corrupt African country.[39]

Botswana has also harnessed the power of free markets to conserve endangered species and wildlife areas. Revenue from increased tourism and sustainable hunting expeditions is protecting the nation's natural beauty while also spurring business growth.

Moreover, Botswana has advanced a type of government austerity that works. Unlike Western European "austerity," which fails to reduce government spending significantly and increases taxes, Botswana has cut both spending and taxes as a percentage of GDP.

Zimbabwe. Located due east of Botswana in the southern part of Africa is Zimbabwe. Despite some progress, Zimbabwe remains one of the least free economies in the world. President Robert Mugabe oversees a corrupt and inefficient government that is rife with graft and nepotism. The labor market is one of the most restricted in the world, and business licensing forces most workers to seek employment in the informal sector. The violent seizure of land has upset investor confidence in a once-vibrant agricultural sector.

Robert Mugabe has been in power since 1980, first as prime minister and then as president. For years, the government engaged in monetary mischief, printing such copious amounts of currency that inflation hit 79,600,000,000 percent in November 2008 with an average daily inflation rate of 98 percent a day. This fiscal malpractice, combined with lack of property rights, deters domestic and foreign investment.

Under the guise of racial equality and concern for the poor, the government has seized swaths of land belonging to white farmers. For those who pursue entrepreneurship, opening a business takes three months, during which you will need to go through nine different procedures and spend on average 140 percent of average gross per capita income. Protectionism is rampant, and foreign investment in numerous industries is severely restricted.[40]

Unemployment in Zimbabwe is estimated to be as high as 95 percent, with per capita GDP at only $600 per person. These alarming statistics, combined with the lack of foreign investment and economic growth, make Zimbabwe an economic nightmare.[41] Ironically, the neighboring country of Botswana, with almost identical geographic, demographic, and natural resources, is flourishing.

If Zimbabweans ever wish to lift themselves from poverty, all they need do is look next door to Botswana.

ISRAEL VS. LEBANON

Israel. Israel re-emerged as an independent nation in 1948. Since then, it has become known as the "start-up nation." Israel ranks 33rd for economic freedom globally and 4th in the Middle East/North Africa region. Registering the 10th largest score increase in the 2015 *Index*, Israel has achieved its highest score ever.

This tiny country in the Middle East has absorbed millions of impoverished immigrants from Eastern Europe, the Middle East, and Africa, yet its economy has boomed. Immigrants who fled often-repressive nations have transformed the desert into a start-up nation. Business incubators dot the landscape, and technological output is among the highest in the world. In fact, the number of Israeli companies trading on the Nasdaq totals 40 with more IPOs to come in 2015.[42]

Israel has welcomed foreign investment into these start-ups, embraced foreign expertise in governmental development, and sought foreign capital for its burgeoning energy sector.

Established with a socialist bent, Israel has been deregulating industry and allowing privatization and competition to grow in areas once dominated by state monopoly. Israel now has a booming technology sector with start-ups such as Consumer Physics and Reduxio, which raised $4 million and $12 million, respectively, in the past year. As home to between 4,000 and 5,000 start-ups, Israel is second only to Silicon Valley in technology innovation.[43]

Perhaps Israel best exemplifies what the late Julian Simon taught: "The ultimate resource is people—skilled, spirited, and hopeful people who will exert their wills and imaginations for their own benefit as well as in a spirit of faith and social concern. Inevitably they will benefit not only themselves but the rest of us as well."[44]

Despite the constant threat of war with hostile neighbors, terrorist activity, and diplomatic hurdles, Israel continues to advance. The ability of smaller political groups to obtain proportional representation in the Israeli parliament provides a robustness to Israel's democracy; the necessity to build coalitions has allowed economic reform to move forward. The entire world is better off as a result.

Lebanon. Although Israel and Lebanon share similar climate, geography, and cuisine, these two neighbors are far different in matters of economics. Lebanon ranks 94th globally and 10th in the region for economic freedom. In fact, the situation has deteriorated in recent years, and Lebanon's economy is now classified as "mostly unfree." This has come about as a result of a turbulent political situation influenced by radical ideology that is geared toward state control and socialism.

Recent years' decline in economic freedom has weakened an already fragile structural and institutional environment. Entrepreneurs are suffocated by restrictive business and labor regulations that inhibit business formation and the development of a dynamic private sector. Prevalent corruption has undermined the basic political institutions of society. Although the banking sector is relatively well-developed, Lebanon's economy remains more closed to trade and investment than those of many of its regional peers.

With a paramilitary terrorist and political force (Hezbollah) lodged within its borders, government instability is only exacerbated. Conflict with Syria and Israel, along with a rapid succession of leadership, has deterred those with capital from making longer-term investments. Furthermore, confidence that the courts will fairly adjudicate matters is low. Even the judiciary is heavily influenced by political interests. In 2013, per capita income was just half the level of Israel's.

ESTONIA VS. UKRAINE

Estonia. Following the dissolution of the Soviet Union in 1991, some countries chose to cling to centrally planned economic models. The Baltic republics of Estonia, Latvia, and Lithuania, however, threw off the shackles of statism and embraced free-market reform, implementing a dramatic policy turnaround. An economic boom ensued.

While the socialist instinct may be to demand that the rich "pay their fair share," those who are truly dedicated to expansion of the middle class and eradication of poverty understand that resisting the urge to confiscate private wealth results in more jobs and even more government revenue. Even former Communists are grasping this concept.

Mart Laar, former Prime Minister of Estonia, was the first politician to bring the flat tax to Eastern Europe. Mr. Laar told one of the authors in 2007 that when he first pushed the flat tax, the major opponents were not Estonian citizens, "who love the flat tax," but the economists and other wise men of government "both inside and outside of this tiny country. Almost all of the smartest minds told me 'We cannot have a flat tax. It is untested. It will not work. It will cause budget deficits.'"[45]

Mr. Laar, however, remembered the virtues of the flat tax in Milton Friedman's classic book *Free to Choose* and insisted that the plan would

work. In 1994, he heroically and wisely ignored the economic pundits and snapped in place one of the world's first flat taxes at 23 percent. Since then, Estonia has had one of the most rapid growth spurts of any nation, and adoption of the flat tax has been widely heralded as a cornerstone of its prosperity. In the 13 years immediately following adoption, GDP dipped below 4.5 percent only once (–0.3 percent in 1999). From 1995–2015, average annual GDP growth was 4.76 percent, and real per capita GDP jumped more than 150 percent.[46]

Estonia has become both a technology and angel investor hub. Technology such as Skype was developed there, and the nation welcomes foreign investment: In 2012, more than 80 percent of venture capital originated from outside investors.[47]

Yet Estonia's pro-market environment, created by a commitment to restrained government spending and low taxes, has not escaped criticism. Paul Krugman, for example, has blasted the nation as "the poster child for austerity defenders."[48]

The facts, however, speak loudly. Since 1993, real per capita GDP in Estonia has jumped more than 150 percent. In dollar terms, this represents an increase in income of more than $7,000 per person.[49]

Ukraine. Contrast Estonia's remarkable income growth with the situation in Ukraine, where income has grown only about 15 percent since 1993, a paltry $700 per person. Why the disparity? More than two decades since the collapse of the Soviet Union, Ukraine remains dedicated to many of the same policies and practices that held back its development during the Communist period.

According to the 2008–2009 Business Environment and Enterprise Performance Survey (BEEPS), almost all companies in Ukraine complain about high tax rates and corruption.[50] Ukraine was ranked 144th out of 177 countries in Transparency International's 2013 Corruption Perceptions Index.[51] The need to escape high taxes and regulation has led to a shadow economy that is equivalent to 44 percent of Ukraine's economic output.[52]

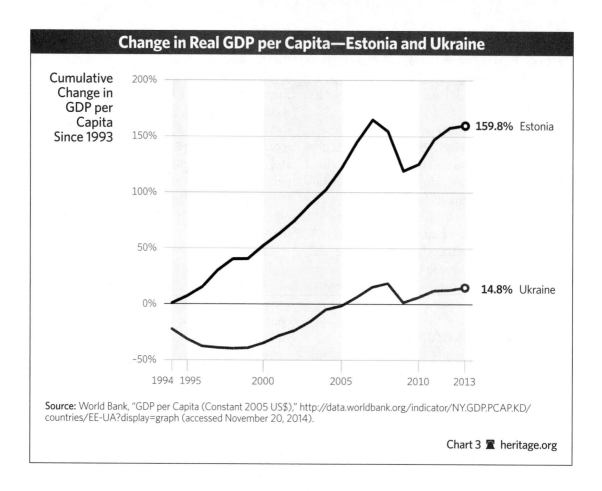

Change in Real GDP per Capita—Estonia and Ukraine

Cumulative Change in GDP per Capita Since 1993

159.8% Estonia

14.8% Ukraine

Source: World Bank, "GDP per Capita (Constant 2005 US$)," http://data.worldbank.org/indicator/NY.GDP.PCAP.KD/countries/EE-UA?display=graph (accessed November 20, 2014).

Chart 3 ☎ heritage.org

Ukrainian politicians use energy subsidies as a way to curry favor with the public, but by subsidizing up to 75 percent of the actual cost of natural gas, the nation also discourages domestic energy development. In fact, *The Economist* reports that "domestic production has slumped by two-thirds since the 1970s."[53]

In addition, the people that benefit from these subsidies actually are harmed by them. Jobs that would have been created from a booming energy sector fail to materialize. More important, lack of an affordable, abundant supply of energy gas results in Ukraine's not being as competitive in the manufacturing sector. In a European continent becoming ever more integrated, Ukraine places itself at a disadvantage with these policies.

Because of such policy mistakes, Ukraine ranks last in economic freedom in Europe and remains one of the poorest of the former Soviet republics.

U.S. EXPERIENCE UNDERSCORES BIG GOVERNMENT'S THREAT TO GROWTH

Every day in America the 50 states compete against each other for people, jobs, investment capital, and overall prosperity. This interstate competition is economically healthy because it forces governors and legislators to adopt fiscal and regulatory policies that maximize job opportunities and prosperity for their citizens.

State governments have generally divided into two competing camps, which we call "the red state model" and the "blue state model." This has raised the stakes in this interstate competition. The conservative red state model is predicated on low tax rates, right-to-work laws, light regulation, and pro-energy development policies. This policy strategy is now common in most of the southern states and the more rural and mountain states.

The liberal blue state model is found predominantly in the Northeast and in California,

Illinois, Minnesota, and (until recently) Michigan and Ohio. The blue states have doubled down on policies that include high levels of government spending, high income tax rates on the rich, generous welfare benefits, forced union requirements, super-minimum wage laws, and restrictions on oil and gas drilling.

Perhaps the area in which we can see the effect of these competing models most clearly is tax policy. California, Connecticut, Hawaii, Illinois, Minnesota, New York, and Oregon have raised their income tax rates on "the rich" since 2008.[54] In four of these states, the combined state and local income tax rates now exceed 10 percent.[55] Meanwhile, the red states of Arizona, Arkansas,[56] Kansas,[57] Missouri,[58] North Carolina,[59] Oklahoma,[60] and Idaho[61] have cut their tax rates. As a result, the income tax differential between blue and red states has widened for businesses and upper-income families.

Similarly, red states like Oklahoma, Texas, and North Dakota have embraced the oil and gas drilling revolution in America. Blue states like New York, Vermont, Illinois, and California have resisted it. Blue states have raised their minimum wages; red states generally have not.

A thorough examination of interstate migration, economic performance, and job growth shows that these divergent policy choices have a noticeable impact on growth. For example:

- The nine states with zero income tax gained an average of 3.7 percent population from domestic in-migration from 2003–2013, while the highest-income tax states lost an average of 2.0 percent population. Overall, population growth on an equally weighted basis from 2003–2013 was twice as high in the low-income tax states.[62] The flow of families from high-tax to low-tax states is unmistakable.[63]
- The jobs growth rate in the zero income tax states was more than two times higher than that of the high-income tax states on an equally weighted basis.[64] Businesses like Toyota are more likely to set up operations in low-tax states. This kind of business relocation to low-tax states is happening routinely and even accelerating.[65]

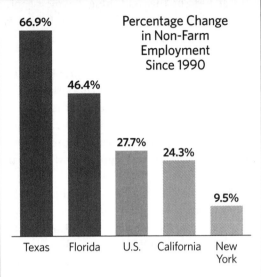

Employment Growth in Four Large States

Percentage Change in Non-Farm Employment Since 1990

- Texas: 66.9%
- Florida: 46.4%
- U.S.: 27.7%
- California: 24.3%
- New York: 9.5%

Source: U.S. Department of Labor, Bureau of Labor Statistics, "State and Metro Area Employment, Hours, and Earnings," http://www.bls.gov/sae/ (accessed November 17, 2014).

Chart 4 ☎ heritage.org

- Among the four largest states, from 1990–September 2014, the jobs growth rate in red states Florida (46 percent) and Texas (65 percent) was more than double the jobs growth of blue states California (24 percent) and New York (9 percent).
- Personal income has grown about 15 percent faster in the no-income tax states than it has in the highest-income tax states over the past decade.
- The right-to-work states enjoyed a jobs growth rate more than three times that of the forced union states. Jobs growth was 6.8 percent in right-to-work states and only 1.9 percent in non–right-to-work states.[66] With respect to the effect of right-to-work laws, the same picture comes into sharp focus. A right-to-work law does not prohibit a union, but rather empowers individual workers with the right to choose whether to join the union (and pay dues for political purposes) or not. As of January 1, 2013, 23 states were right to work and 27 were forced union.[67]

Interstate competition for jobs, people, and capital is a positive force that helps to discipline politicians to do the right thing. Yet many politicians and pundits pretend that taxes, labor laws, indebtedness, and heavy regulation do not affect economic growth.

Growth is not a zero sum game: More jobs, higher incomes, and expanded opportunity benefit *all* residents without regard to their income or status. And as states get richer, they are able to provide higher-quality public services—and will need fewer services—for things like welfare and crime prevention.

What would happen if every country were to adopt the pro-growth policies embraced by such states as Texas, Florida, and North Dakota? The entire globe would benefit from rising living standards and expanded opportunity. Billions of those who are now mired in poverty would benefit the most.

CONCLUSION

Twenty-one years ago, when the first edition of the *Index of Economic Freedom* was published, the supply-side idea of the Laffer Curve—that high tax rates reduce growth and can even reduce revenues—was still highly controversial and disregarded among the political class and even trained economists. Today, however, more nations around the globe are embracing the idea.

Few had predicted the rapid change with which Eastern Europe would embrace freedom or the notable extent to which many developing countries in other parts of the world would pursue free-market reforms that advance economic freedom. We have seen hundreds of millions of people advance rapidly from poverty and subsistence living to modern comforts. Experiences of individual nations have acted as laboratories to evaluate performance under a myriad of policy conditions.

Over the past 21 years, the *Index of Economic Freedom* has gathered ample evidence to track the performance of countries implementing to varying degrees the precepts of economic freedom and the resulting levels of their economic success. The comparisons presented in this chapter highlight the opportunity for prosperity that is inherent in giving people the freedom to choose.

Much has been accomplished, and much remains to be done. In charting the freedom path to economic growth, the challenge of advancing economic freedom is the challenge of pursuing sustained prosperity. Those countries that have been brave enough to accept the challenge have reaped great rewards and, in doing so, have set a powerful example for others to follow.

ENDNOTES

1. Åsa Johansson, Christopher Heady, Jens Arnold, Bert Brys, and Laura Vartia, "Tax and Economic Growth," Organisation for Economic Co-operation and Development, Economics Department *Working Paper* No. 620, July 2008, http://www.olis.oecd.org/olis/2008doc.nsf/LinkTo/NT00003502/$FILE/JT03248896.PDF (accessed November 17, 2014).

2. Arthur B. Laffer, Stephen Moore, Rex. A. Sinquefield, and Travis H. Brown, *An Inquiry into the Nature and Causes of the Wealth of States* (Hoboken, NJ: John Wiley & Sons, 2014).

3. Editorial, "Catalysts of Chile's Economic Revolution," *Orange County Register*, December 28, 2009, updated August 21, 2013, http://www.ocregister.com/articles/chile-225801-economic-free.html (accessed November 17, 2014).

4. Ibid.

5. Ibid.

6. World Bank, "Data: Indicators," http://data.worldbank.org/indicator (accessed November 17, 2014).

7. Central Bank of Chile, "Base de Datos Estadísticos," http://si3.bcentral.cl/Siete/secure/cuadros/arboles.aspx (accessed November 17, 2014).

8. Meredith Simpson, Enrique Aravena, and James Deverell, "The Future of Mining in Chile," CSIRO, June 2014, p. 5, http://www.csiro.au/~/media/CSIROau/Outcomes/Mineral%20Resources/Chile%20Centre%20of%20Excellence/AV_The%20Future%20of%20Mining%20in%20Chile-WEB.pdf (accessed November 17, 2014).

9. Jose Pinera, "Wealth Through Ownership: Creating Property Rights in Chilean Mining," *Cato Journal*, Vol. 24, Issue 3 (Fall 2004), pp. 295–301, http://object.cato.org/sites/cato.org/files/serials/files/cato-journal/2004/11/cj24n3-7.pdf (accessed on November 17, 2014).

10. Ibid.

11. Ibid.

12. World Bank, "Country Snapshot–Chile," Business Environment Snapshots, http://rru.worldbank.org/BESnapshots/Chile/default.aspx (accessed November 17, 2014).

13. Ibid.

14. Cristián Larroulet, "Chile's Path to Development," *World Commerce Review*, June 2013, http://www.worldcommercereview.com/publications/article_pdf/713 (accessed November 17, 2014),

15. Michael Boskin, "Why Does Chile Prosper While Neighbouring Argentina Flounders?" *The Guardian*, November 22, 2013, http://www.theguardian.com/business/economics-blog/2013/nov/22/chile-prosper-argentina-flounders (accessed November 17, 2014).

16. Marcela Valente, "Renationalized YPF Aims to Bring Self-Sufficiency in Oil and Gas," Inter Press Service News Agency, May 4, 2012, http://www.ipsnews.net/2012/05/renationalised-ypf-aims-to-bring-self-sufficiency-in-oil-and-gas/ (accessed November 17, 2014).

17. "Repsol YPF Announces 'Major Finding in Its History,'" *20 Minutos*, August 11, 2011, http://www.20minutos.es/noticia/1212601/5/ypf-repsol/descubre-petroleo/argentina/ (accessed November 17, 2014).

18. "Argentine Peso, Bonds, Stocks Drop on Investment Restrictions," Bloomberg, June 26, 2014, http://www.bloomberg.com/apps/news?pid=newsarchive&sid=am8_rxzm4dZU (accessed November 17, 2014).

19. "From Deadbeat to Despot," *The Wall Street Journal*, September 3, 2014. http://online.wsj.com/articles/from-deadbeat-to-despot-1409608642 (accessed on November 17, 2014).

20. Terry Miller, Anthony B. Kim, and Kim R. Holmes, *2014 Index of Economic Freedom* (Washington: The Heritage Foundation and Dow Jones & Company, Inc., 2013), Website, "Explore the Data," http://www.heritage.org/index/explore?view=by-variables (accessed November 17, 2014).

21. Darcy Crowe and Taos Turner, "Devaluation Hurts Argentina's Regional Standing," *The Wall Street Journal*, February 27, 2014, http://online.wsj.com/articles/SB10001424052702304899704579389501040961442 (accessed November 17, 2014).

22. World Bank, "Data: Indicators," http://data.worldbank.org/indicator (accessed November 17, 2014).

23. Nicolas Lardy, "China's Rise Is a Credit to Private Enterprise Not State Control," *The Financial Times*, September 13, 2014, http://www.ft.com/intl/cms/s/0/b14e3d58-38f6-11e4-a53b-00144feabdc0.html#axzz3JJ2TNqUH (accessed November 17, 2014).

24. State-owned Assets Supervision and Administration Commission of the State Council (SASAC), People's Republic of China, Website, http://www.sasac.gov.cn/n2963340/n2971121/n4956567/4956583.html (accessed November 17, 2014).

25. "Fixing China Inc," *The Economist*, August 30, 2014, http://www.economist.com/news/china/21614240-reform-state-companies-back-agenda-fixing-china-inc (accessed November 17, 2014).

26. "China Focus: China Pledges Further Reforms for State-dominated Sectors," Xinhua, October 24, 2012, http://news.xinhuanet.com/english/indepth/2012-10/24/c_131928023.htm (accessed November 17, 2014).

27. "China's Major SOEs Report Assets Growth," *Shanghai Daily*, July 27, 2014, http://www.shanghaidaily.com/business/Chinas-major-SOEs-report-assets-growth/shdaily.shtml (accessed November 17, 2014).

28. Justin Yifu Lin, "Rural Reforms and Agricultural Productivity Growth in China," UCLA *Working Paper* No. 576, December 1989, http://www.econ.ucla.edu/workingpapers/wp576.pdf (accessed November 17, 2014).

29. Institute for Research on the Economics of Taxation, "The Tax System of Hong Kong," *Policy Bulletin* No. 95, December 28, 2010, http://iret.org/pub/BLTN-95.PDF (accessed November 17, 2014).

30. U.S. Department of State, Bureau of Economic and Business Affairs, "2012 Investment Climate Statement—Taiwan," June, 2012, http://www.state.gov/e/eb/rls/othr/ics/2012/191245.htm (accessed November 17, 2014).

31. Taiwan Bureau of Foreign Trade, National Statistics Database, http://ebas1.ebas.gov.tw/pxweb/Dialog/statfile1L.asp (accessed November 17, 2014).

32. Ibid.

33. Ibid.

34. KPMG, "Corporate Tax Rates Table," http://www.kpmg.com/global/en/services/tax/tax-tools-and-resources/pages/corporate-tax-rates-table.aspx (accessed November 17, 2014).

35. Taiwan Bureau of Foreign Trade, National Statistics Database.

36. U.S. Department of State, Bureau of Economic and Business Affairs, "2014 Investment Climate Statement—Botswana," June 2014, http://www.state.gov/e/eb/rls/othr/ics/2014/226918.htm (accessed November 17, 2014).

37. Ibid.

38. Nake M. Kamrany and Jennifer Gray, "Botswana: An African Model for Progress and Prosperity," *The World Post*, http://www.huffingtonpost.com/nake-m-kamrany/botswana-economic-growth_b_2069226.html (accessed November 17, 2014).

39. Transparency International, Corruption Perceptions Index 2013, http://www.transparency.org/cpi2013/results (accessed November 17, 2014).

40. World Bank Group, "Ease of Doing Business in Zimbabwe," *Doing Business 2015*, http://www.doingbusiness.org/data/exploreeconomies/zimbabwe/ (accessed November 17, 2014).

41. U.S. Central Intelligence Agency, "Zimbabwe," *The World Factbook*, last updated June 20, 2014, https://www.cia.gov/library/publications/the-world-factbook/geos/zi.html (accessed November 17, 2014).

42. Ari Rabinovitch, "Nasdaq Expects Increase in IPOs from Israeli Firms," Reuters, May 11, 2014, http://www.reuters.com/article/2014/05/11/us-nasdaq-israel-idUSBREA4A04320140511 (accessed November 17, 2014).

43. Julie Bort, "The 20 Hottest Startups from Israel in 2014," *Business Insider*, June 15, 2014, http://www.businessinsider.com/20-hottest-startups-from-israel-2014-6?op=1 (accessed November 17, 2014).

44. Julian Simon, *The Ultimate Resource 2* (Princeton, NJ: Princeton University Press, 1998), p. xxxviii.

45. Stephen Moore, "The World Discovers the Laffer Curve," Chapter 4 in Terry Miller and Kim R. Holmes, *2009 Index of Economic Freedom* (Washington: The Heritage Foundation and Dow Jones & Company, Inc., 2009), p. 38, http://thf_media.s3.amazonaws.com/index/pdf/2009/Index2009_Chapter4.pdf.

46. World Bank, "Data: Indicators," http://data.worldbank.org/indicator (accessed November 17, 2014).

47. L. S. Tallinn, "Estonia's Technology Cluster; Not Only Skype," *The Economist*, July 11, 2013, http://www.economist.com/blogs/schumpeter/2013/07/estonias-technology-cluster (accessed November 17, 2014).

48. Paul Krugman, "Estonian Rhapsody," *The New York Times*, June 6, 2012, http://krugman.blogs.nytimes.com/2012/06/06/estonian-rhapsdoy/?_r=0 (accessed November 17, 2014).

49. World Bank, "Data," http://data.worldbank.org/ (accessed November 17, 2014).

50. Pekka Sutela, "The Underachiever: Ukraine's Economy Since 1991," Carnegie Endowment For International Peace, March 9, 2012, http://carnegieendowment.org/2012/03/09/underachiever-ukraine-s-economy-since-1991# (accessed November 17, 2014).

51. BBC News Business, "Ukraine Economy: How Bad Is the Mess, and Can It Be Fixed?" May 1, 2014, http://www.bbc.com/news/world-europe-26767864 (accessed November 17, 2014).

52. Igor Vinnychuck and Serhii Ziukov, "Shadow Economy in the Ukraine: Modeling and Analysis," *Business Systems and Economics*, Vol. 3, No. 2 (2013), https://www3.mruni.eu/ojs/business-systems-and-economics/article/view/1474/1420 (November 17, 2014).

53. C. W. London, "Why Is Ukraine's Economy in Such a Mess?" *The Economist*, May 5, 2014, http://www.economist.com/blogs/freeexchange/2014/03/ukraine-and-russia (accessed November 17, 2014).

54. Tax Foundation, "State Individual Income Tax Rates Data Series, 2000–2014," April 1, 2013, http://taxfoundation.org/article/state-individual-income-tax-rates (accessed November 17, 2014).

55. Arthur B. Laffer, Stephen Moore, and Jonathan Williams, *Rich States, Poor States, ALEC–Laffer State Economic Competitiveness Index,* 7th Edition, American Legislative Exchange Council, 2014, pp. 74 and 101, http://alec.org/docs/RSPS_7th_Edition.pdf (accessed November 17, 2014).

56. Jonathan Williams and Ben Wilterdink, "State Tax Cut Roundup: 2013 Legislative Session," American Legislative Exchange Council, November 2013, http://www.alec.org/wp-content/uploads/2013-TaxCutRoundup.pdf (accessed November 17, 2014).

57. Tax Foundation, "State Individual Income Tax Rates Data Series, 2000–2014."

58. Virginia Young, "Missouri Legislature Overrides Nixon's Tax Cut Veto," *St. Louis Post-Dispatch,* May 7, 2014, http://www.stltoday.com/news/local/govt-and-politics/missouri-legislature-overrides-nixon-s-tax-cut-veto/article_b4e9cc7f-8283-5dd6-ac9d-bb7b2abb0f06.html (accessed November 17, 2014).

59. Tax Foundation, "State Individual Income Tax Rates Data Series, 2000–2014."

60. Ibid.

61. Ibid.

62. Laffer, Moore, and Williams, *Rich States, Poor States*, Table 6, p. 39.

63. Laffer, Moore, Sinquefield, and Brown, *An Inquiry Into the Nature and Causes of the Wealth of States*, Table 3.1, pp. 57–58.

64. Laffer, Moore. and Williams, *Rich States, Poor States*, Table 6, p. 39.

65. Laffer, Moore, Sinquefield, and Brown, *An Inquiry Into the Nature and Causes of the Wealth of States*, Table 3.1, pp. 57–58.

66. Ibid.

67. Michigan became a right-to-work state in March 2013.

Chapter 4

Cronyism, Corruption, and the Arab Spring: The Case of Tunisia

Antonio Nucifora, PhD, Erik Churchill, and Bob Rijkers, PhD[1]

Editor's Note: *Since 2011, the countries of the Middle East and North Africa have experienced a period of economic and political turmoil—the Arab Spring—that holds both great promise and great risk. Such a widespread uprising against autocratic rule will have many diverse causes. What began as a protest by a street vendor against, in part, excessive economic regulation in Tunisia has become a wide-ranging movement challenging entrenched political, economic, cultural, and religious interests across an entire region. An empirical study presented in the 2012* Index *by Dr. Nahid Anaraki used the techniques of econometric analysis to demonstrate that the motivation for violence in the region is likely to be less about conflict between Islam and Western values and more about revenge against corrupt regimes. This chapter deepens that analysis, looking specifically at the role that cronyism and corruption played in the Tunisian uprising while identifying ongoing problems that must still be addressed if Tunisia is to achieve the full flowering of economic freedom and broad-based development that benefits everyone, not just a politically connected elite.*

The Tunisian Revolution took the world by surprise in January 2011 and unleashed expectations of a transition toward liberal Western-style democracy in the Arab World. Much progress has been made in Tunisia over the past three years on the political front. A new constitution was adopted with a large consensus in January 2014, and the first democratic parliamentary and presidential elections under the new constitution were held in October–November 2014.

Nevertheless, deep-rooted deficiencies of the socioeconomic system have not yet been tackled. This system, characterized by privileges and cronyism at the expense of competition and performance, is at the root of the Arab Spring and still needs to change if the future of the Tunisian transition is to be secured.[2]

Tunisia's economy was one of the best-performing in the region before 2011. Rapid poverty reduction was accompanied by significant

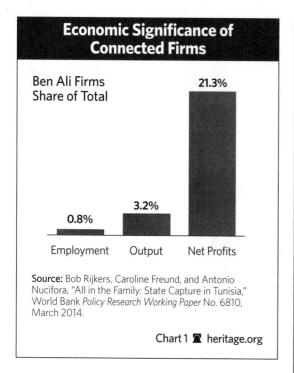

Economic Significance of Connected Firms

Ben Ali Firms Share of Total

- Employment: 0.8%
- Output: 3.2%
- Net Profits: 21.3%

Source: Bob Rijkers, Caroline Freund, and Antonio Nucifora, "All in the Family: State Capture in Tunisia," World Bank *Policy Research Working Paper* No. 6810, March 2014.

Chart 1 ☎ heritage.org

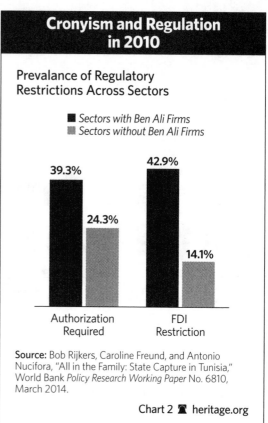

Cronyism and Regulation in 2010

Prevalance of Regulatory Restrictions Across Sectors

- ■ Sectors with Ben Ali Firms
- ■ Sectors without Ben Ali Firms

Authorization Required:
- 39.3%
- 24.3%

FDI Restriction:
- 42.9%
- 14.1%

Source: Bob Rijkers, Caroline Freund, and Antonio Nucifora, "All in the Family: State Capture in Tunisia," World Bank *Policy Research Working Paper* No. 6810, March 2014.

Chart 2 ☎ heritage.org

improvements in the main human development indicators. On the basis of these achievements, Tunisia was heralded as a role model for other developing countries by the International Monetary Fund and the World Bank. Similarly, the World Economic Forum repeatedly ranked Tunisia as the most competitive economy in Africa.

As the revolution made clear, however, beyond the shiny façade often presented by the former regime, the Tunisian socioeconomic model was (and remains) deeply deficient. Unemployment has remained high, especially among young graduates, and regional disparities have persisted. At the root of these disappointing economic outcomes lies a policy infrastructure put in place during the presidency of Zine al-Abidine Ben Ali (April 1989–January 2011), which results in privileges for an elite few at the expense of those who lack significant political connections.[3]

Achieving stability in the region will require transitioning to an open economic system that brings greater economic opportunity.[4] The key policy challenge, therefore, is to identify instruments that will ensure that such a transition is orderly, swift, and sustainable.

CRONYISM, CORRUPTION, AND SOCIAL EXCLUSION IN TUNISIA

Tunisia's economic development model has been predicated on an active role for the state since the 1960s. This model initially accelerated growth and rapid poverty reduction.[5] However, interventionism became increasingly directed by the country's elite for their own benefit. Over the past decade, extensive corruption and abuses were associated with the activities of the cronies and family of former president Ben Ali.[6] Pervasive barriers to competition allowed underperforming firms to survive in spite of low productivity and created opportunities for rent-seeking by cronies of the regime. This evolution of Tunisia's economy into a system of rents and privileges is at the root of its failure.

It is notoriously difficult to demonstrate clearly the impact of cronyism and predation on firms' growth and characteristics because access to relevant data is usually difficult.[7] In Tunisia, we were able to use information on 220 firms confiscated from President Ben Ali

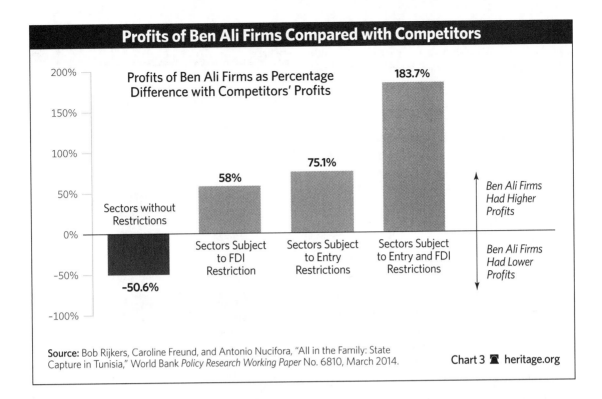

Profits of Ben Ali Firms Compared with Competitors

Profits of Ben Ali Firms as Percentage Difference with Competitors' Profits

- Sectors without Restrictions: **−50.6%**
- Sectors Subject to FDI Restriction: **58%**
- Sectors Subject to Entry Restrictions: **75.1%**
- Sectors Subject to Entry and FDI Restrictions: **183.7%**

Ben Ali Firms Had Higher Profits

Ben Ali Firms Had Lower Profits

Source: Bob Rijkers, Caroline Freund, and Antonio Nucifora, "All in the Family: State Capture in Tunisia," World Bank *Policy Research Working Paper* No. 6810, March 2014.

Chart 3 ☎ heritage.org

and his extended family (a total of 114 people) in the aftermath of the 2011 revolution and to compare their performance to that of all other firms in Tunisia.[8]

Firms confiscated from President Ben Ali's extended family were important from an aggregate economic point of view. Although they account for less than 1 percent of all jobs, they pocketed a striking 21.3 percent of all net private-sector profits in Tunisia, equivalent to US$233 million in 2010, corresponding to over 0.5 percent of GDP. (See Chart 1.) Considering that we identify only firms with direct links to the Ben Ali family as opposed to all firms with cultivated connections, this number is probably best interpreted as a lower bound on the importance of political connections.

How could connected firms make so much money? The firms confiscated from President Ben Ali's family were concentrated in sectors where profit margins are quite high and close relations with government counterparts is an important determinant of profitability, notably in the real estate and enterprise services sectors (59 firms); personnel services (20); transport (16); wholesale trade (15); automobile trade (11);

construction (nine); financial services (eight); the food industry (seven); hotels and restaurants (seven); media activities (five).

Specifically, our analysis found that confiscated firms are more likely to operate in sectors subject to entry regulation. Approximately 40 percent of Ben Ali firms were in sectors subject to authorizations and restrictions on foreign direct investment (FDI).[9] By comparison, authorization requirements apply to only 24 percent of all sectors in which Ben Ali firms are not present, while FDI restrictions apply to approximately 14 percent of sectors that are free of Ben Ali firms.[10] (See Chart 2.) Thus, regulatory restrictions and connected firms go hand-in-hand.

The superior performance of Ben Ali firms is especially marked in densely regulated sectors (at the five-digit sector level). Restrictions on entry into these sectors were associated with greater market share and greater profits for the firms owned by Ben Ali's extended family, who had privileged access. Ben Ali firms are especially more profitable than their peers in sectors that are subject to authorization and FDI restrictions; these regulations thus appear disproportionately to assist the profitability of Ben Ali firms. In sectors that are not subject to these restrictions, Ben Ali firms make significantly less profit than their competitors, which countermands the idea that Ben Ali family members were innately better entrepreneurs. (See Chart 3.)

Legislative changes introducing new entry restrictions were plausibly due to manipulation by the Ben Ali clan.[11] First, the prevalence of FDI restrictions and authorization requirements was significantly higher in sectors in which Ben Ali firms were present when the Investment Incentives Code was approved in December 1993. Second, over time, new restrictions were introduced at a higher frequency in sectors in which Ben Ali firms had set up shop.[12] Sectors in which Ben Ali firms are active are two times more likely to be subjected to new authorization requirements than sectors in which they are not and five times more likely to be subjected to new FDI restrictions.[13] (See Chart 4.) In sum, if existing regulations did not suffice to secure lucrative business deals, Ben Ali would use executive powers to change the legislation in his favor.

Tunisia's investment policies thus did not serve only their purported objectives of creating jobs and stimulating investment. Instead, regulations often served the personal interests of those in power at the expense of providing fair opportunities to the vast majority of Tunisian entrepreneurs who lacked political connections.

Is Tunisia an isolated case? Unfortunately not: Our findings are consistent with a large body of literature showing that countries with more extensive business entry regulations tend to grow more slowly and to have higher levels of corruption.[14] Across the globe, corruption and burdensome business regulation go hand-in-hand. (See Chart 5.)

In sum, our results substantiate that state interventions and barriers to competition created ample opportunities for rents extraction by cronies, severely hampering the performance of the private sector in Tunisia. While we have focused on authorizations and restrictions on FDI, several other policy instruments were also used to gain unfair competitive advantage and extract rents, notably through the discretionary enforcement of regulations (e.g., in tax

Prevalence of New Regulations by Presence of Ben Ali Firms

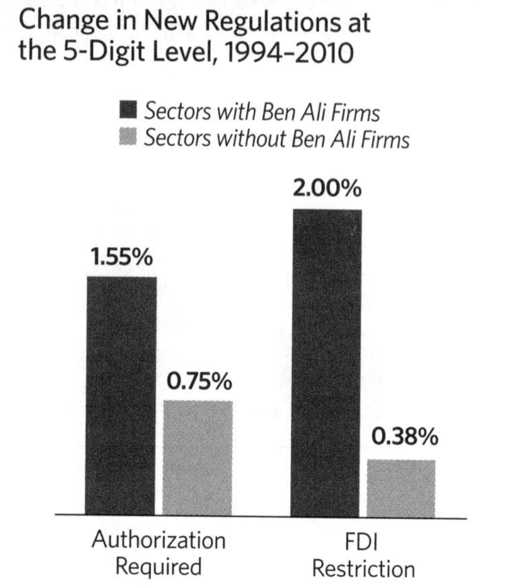

Change in New Regulations at the 5-Digit Level, 1994–2010

■ Sectors with Ben Ali Firms
▨ Sectors without Ben Ali Firms

Authorization Required: 1.55% / 0.75%
FDI Restriction: 2.00% / 0.38%

Source: Bob Rijkers, Caroline Freund, and Antonio Nucifora, "All in the Family: State Capture in Tunisia," World Bank *Policy Research Working Paper* No. 6810, March 2014.

Chart 4 ☎ heritage.org

administration, custom duties, and public procurement) and the (ab)use of public assets and public enterprises (including public banks).[15] All of these practices undermine competition by favoring better-connected firms and those who practice corruption.

The inefficiencies and distortions resulting from this system of rents extraction obstruct the development of a dynamic economic environment—which is at the root of the economic stagnation of Tunisia.[16] Few new firms are created, and productive firms do not grow, as they face unfair competition by crony firms.[17] The emergence and expansion of innovative dynamic firms is hampered by the expensive and low-quality goods and services they need to pay to crony firms. As a result, Tunisian entrepreneurs are competitive only in labor-intensive low-skill tasks, investment has been lacking, and unemployment has been rampant. Most of the jobs created were in low-value-added activities and mostly in the informal sector, offering low wages and no job security. Such jobs certainly do

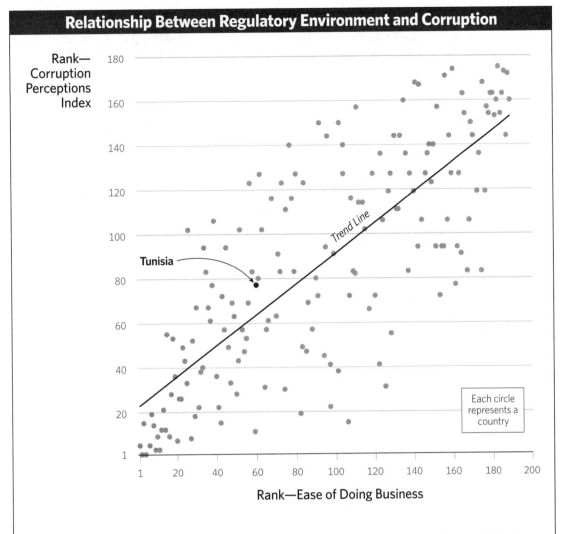

Relationship Between Regulatory Environment and Corruption

Rank—Corruption Perceptions Index

Tunisia

Trend Line

Each circle represents a country

Rank—Ease of Doing Business

Sources: World Bank, "Doing Business: Economy Rankings," http://www.doingbusiness.org/rankings (accessed November 17, 2014), and Transparency International, "Corruption Perceptions Index 2013," http://www.transparency.org/cpi2013 (accessed November 17, 2014).

Chart 5 ☎ heritage.org

not meet the aspirations of the growing number of graduates.

Tunisia's rents-prone economic system is not only inefficient, but also highly inequitable. That such a small group of 114 entrepreneurs could appropriate such a large share of Tunisia's wealth creation illustrates how corruption has been synonymous with social exclusion. Inequality of opportunity characterizes Tunisia today, as the current institutional infrastructure creates an "insider-outsider" culture. Even if the interventionist policies were introduced originally to foster the country's development,

they have been captured in practice for rents extraction and privileges by those who are close to those in power. The resulting inequality was a fundamental cause of the revolution and, since the economic model has not yet been changed, remains a latent source of instability in the Tunisian transition.

LESSONS FROM THE EXPERIENCE OF OTHER DEMOCRATIC TRANSITIONS

Successful transitions are often associated with rapid reforms, though historically, a country that undertakes a democratic transition has only a 30 percent probability of succeeding.[18] A democracy is more likely to be established when per capita GDP is high and increasing;[19] income distribution is equal (low Gini coefficient or low ratio of incomes of top-to-bottom quintile); populations are small; urbanization is advanced; people are educated; gender equality in primary education is high; natural resources are limited; there is no ethnic division; the transition is not conducted by a military regime; democratic states are present in the region (the "contagion effect");[20] the time to election is minimal; the regime is not a presidential regime or not dominated completely and permanently by one political force; and the country has a parliamentary system.

There is some consensus that rapid democratic transition occurs primarily when several fundamentals are in place: per capita GDP is high,[21] the middle class is large, urbanization is advanced, the percentage of people receiving primary school educations is high, gender equality in primary education is high, a military force is present before the transition, there is a previous attempt at democratization, democratic states are present in the region, and natural resources are limited. Further, although there is no empirical evidence from historical data, some scholars have noted that a democratic transition, especially in middle-income capitalist countries, might occur following years of declining growth and/or increasing inflation,[22] as was the case for Latin American countries during the period of hyperinflation in the 1980s and the Asian financial crisis in 1997.

Unlike many other Arab Spring countries, which have seen their transitions fail, Tunisia has many of these fundamentals. Some of these, such as high rates of urbanization and a large middle class, Tunisia possessed before its uprisings. Others are the outcomes of choices Tunisia has made since the revolution, such as the decision to opt for a parliamentary rather than presidential system. Together, they imply that the country has a high likelihood of successfully completing its democratic transition despite the risk of backsliding that is inherent in virtually all democratic transitions.

MOVING FROM A CLOSED SOCIOECONOMIC SYSTEM TO ONE THAT IS OPEN TO ALL CITIZENS

How can Tunisia move from a closed socioeconomic system to an open one? Since the Ben Ali regime limited access to political and economic functions in order to generate rents, we can turn to the limited access order (LAO) framework for guidance.[23] The framework is premised on the idea that power is tied to organizations and not to the individual and that rents-sharing is the process by which a dominant coalition reaches an equilibrium that allows economic activities to continue to generate rents.

Tunisia during the Ben Ali era could be characterized as a basic LAO with strong elements of predation. Few players were part of the dominant elite, which comprised the "ruling" family, the security forces, the administration, the media, civil society organizations, and business firms that allied with the political elite (or at least stayed out of politics). All other groups were marginalized or actively suppressed. In such a setting, the LAO framework offers guidance on how organizations in societies arrive at elite bargains—formal or informal agreements—to divide the available opportunities for rents extraction and profit making in the economy.

The LAO framework predicts that countries will not transition easily from limited access orders, in which rent-seeking dominates, to an open access order, which characterizes most liberal democracies. By limiting access to economic activity and resources, the LAO creates rents that help to maintain the equilibrium. Thus, there will be strong incentives for rent-seeking to continue, albeit with some changes in the cast of organizations in the dominant coalition. In other words, even if countries hold fair elections, they will not soon become open democracies, but they may mature in the range of institutions and organizations that are allowed to participate in broader decision making.

Of course, advancing the principles of economic freedom—empowerment of the individual, non-discrimination, and open competition—can weaken the rent-creation system that holds the LAO together. These changes, whether in the form of revolution or of reform, therefore threaten the basis of order and hold the risk of violence. Similarly, attempts to remove corruption, install a functioning rule of law, and institute democracy with competitive parties can also destabilize an LAO and generate broad resistance. Groups that benefit directly from market distortions, such as those reaping monopoly profits or receiving services at subsidized prices, will resist the reforms.[24]

It may be argued that although the revolution disrupted this equilibrium and empowered a new coalition, even after the departure of Ben Ali, most of the organizations supporting him have retained their interests and political importance. Consequently, they are likely to continue to play a role in shaping the evolving political arrangements in spite of facing increased competition among a wider set of elites, which now represent some segments of the population that had no voice or participation before.

Several political realities in Tunisia during the past four years are consistent with this characterization. New political actors have become central to negotiations about control of the economy, while interests of the previous regime have continued to play a major role. Two examples demonstrate this rebalancing.

First, when the Ennahda party, a previously banned political party, was elected to lead a coalition government (2011–2013), its term in office was marked more by bargaining and negotiation with political adversaries and interest groups than by changes in the status quo. Patronage in the form of civil service and state-owned enterprise recruitment continued, and legislation meant to change the Ben Ali–era economic policy infrastructure largely stalled.

Second, the General Union of Tunisian Workers (known by its French acronym UGTT), which had played an important role in Tunisia's independence but was eventually coopted by the state, became a balance against both government and private-sector initiatives that threatened its interests. During the transition period, the UGTT first led protests and then negotiations, which eventually resulted in the Ennahda government's handing over power to a technocratic government. As part of these negotiations, which included political, union, and business interests, the Ennahda government agreed to postpone plans to exclude former regime officials from running for office.

While the post-revolutionary political order included new interest groups in the form of the Ennahda party and the UGTT, these groups did not overturn the existing order, but rather added to its ranks. Moreover, the October 2014 parliamentary elections saw the return of many of these former regime officials to the political sphere.

During Tunisia's transitional period, reforms that might challenge the existing elite bargain have been either extremely slow to develop or rejected by those who continue to hold considerable leverage. These efforts have not only stymied controversial legislation, such as the aforementioned political exclusion law. They have also prevented reforms in less controversial areas such as the Investment Incentives Code, which was the basis for much of Ben Ali's rent-seeking.

Institutionally, extra-governmental dialogues, including both the National Dialogue negotiations[25] and protest movements, have provided a means for otherwise unreformed institutional structures to deal with newly competing interests. While this has served as a way for the country to avoid winner-take-all outcomes, it has come at the expense of the democratic process (i.e., decisions by legislative bodies) and has resulted in outcomes that have failed to fulfill the expectations of revolutionaries who fought largely against these elites.

While the return of former regime elements has been cast by some as a sign of failure of the revolution, the LAO framework suggests that elections will only gradually become an arena for competition among power groups. They serve to test the relative ability of competing organizations to mobilize supporters.

Meanwhile, achieving stability will require creating institutions that avoid winner-take-all outcomes. International experience shows that sustained improvements in LAOs and moves toward open access have happened in incremental steps rather than giant leaps. Historically, incremental steps that have led to increased openness have included greater predictability in the elite bargain. Notably, experience has shown the importance of building institutions that can underpin predictable resolution of conflict between elites (i.e., to enforce the rule of law for elites). As these elite-oriented rule-of-law institutions become stronger over time, they provide a platform to move from privileges for the elite to a level playing field for all citizens.

In Tunisia, several new institutions, in the form of the new, relatively liberal constitution or various laws such as those governing freedom of association or access to information, may form the basis for greater competition among a wider cross-section of society. Granting citizens access to information will enable independent analysis of the beneficiaries of existing policies, which will also increase the pressure for policy changes. Nevertheless, the LAO framework emphasizes that trying to go straight from revolution to an open access order has often led to disruption and more fragility.[26]

What is yet more difficult to measure, given the extent of elite capture that continues to prevail, is whether incremental progress is taking place in the aggregate. While certain institutional reforms appear objectively to be steps forward, these have been counterbalanced by economic decision making that has remained exclusive and unequal. Even the task of creating a workable limited access order will not be easy—as we see in many other post–Arab Spring countries.

THE WAY FORWARD: OPENING ECONOMIC OPPORTUNITY TO ALL TUNISIANS

Tunisia has made enormous progress in its democratic transition, and historical experience from other countries suggests that it has the key ingredients required to succeed. The challenge is to move from a fairly closed socioeconomic system, which privileges its elites and is at the root of the revolution, to a more open system for the benefit of all Tunisians.

This requires changing the policy infrastructure inherited from the Ben Ali era, which perpetuates social exclusion and invites corruption. The system of laws and regulations that allowed the family to capture such a large share of the country's wealth remains largely in place, maintaining the opportunities for firms to earn rents through cronyism and corruption. These regulations perpetuate social exclusion, as unconnected Tunisians have very limited economic opportunities.

Without such changes, there is a risk that instead of reforming the policy infrastructure, Tunisia's elites will collaborate just enough to share the spoils, albeit with a slightly different group of vested interests. In lieu of reforms that would level the playing field, the economic system would remain closed in favor of a small, though slightly expanded, minority of elites. Under this scenario, markets would remain closed off from competition, regulatory policy would remain subject to discretion, and decision making would be opaque.

Opening the economic system will require political determination, since fierce resistance can be expected from those who are at risk of losing rents and privileges. Moving too rapidly will likely create tension and instability, which could undermine the process. Moving too timidly, however, will fuel the frustration expressed by the marginalized groups in society.

Empowering strong independent governance institutions that enforce the rule of law on elites and vested interest groups will accelerate the change process. Enforcing citizens' right of access to information, as well as transparency and accountability in the government, is also critical in order to arrive at a stable democracy, both in Tunisia and everywhere else.

ENDNOTES

1. The findings, interpretations, and conclusions expressed in this paper are entirely those of the authors. They do not represent the views of the World Bank, its affiliated organizations, or the Executive Directors of the World Bank or the governments they represent.

2. World Bank, *From Privilege to Competition: Unlocking Private-Led Growth in the Middle East and North Africa*, MENA Flagship Development Report, 2009; World Bank, *The Unfinished Revolution: Bringing Opportunity, Good Jobs and Greater Wealth to All Tunisians*, Development Policy Review Report No. 86179-TN, May 2014; World Bank, *From Jobs to Privileges: Unleashing the Employment Potential of the Middle East and North Africa*, Report No. 88879-MNA, June 2014.

3. Bob Rijkers, Caroline Freund, and Antonio Nucifora, *All in the Family: State Capture in Tunisia*, World Bank *Policy Research Working Paper* No. 6810, March 2014; World Bank, *The Unfinished Revolution*. One of the words heard most frequently from young people demonstrating in Tunisia in early 2011 was "dignity." This highlighted that social and economic problems went beyond the narrow dimension of material poverty. It was first and foremost about exclusion and lack of access to opportunities and participation in the economy.

4. Adeel Malik and Bassem Awadallah, "The Economics of the Arab Spring," *World Development*, Vol. 45 (May 2013), pp. 296–313.

5. Institut National de la Statistique, African Development Bank, and World Bank, *Mesure de la pauvreté, des inégalités et de la polarisation en Tunisie* (Tunis: Institut National de la Statistique, November 2012); World Bank, *The Unfinished Revolution*.

6. Béatrice Hibou, *Surveiller et Réformer: Economie Politique de la Servitude Volontaire en Tunisie* (Paris: La Découverte, 2006).

7. Raymond Fisman, "Estimating the Value of Political Connections," *American Economic Review*, Vol. 91, No. 4 (September 2001), pp. 1095–1102; Thomas Ferguson and Hans-Joachim Voth, "Betting on Hitler—The Value of Political Connections in Nazi Germany," *Quarterly Journal of Economics*, Vol. 123, Issue 1 (February 2008), pp. 101–137.

8. Rijkers, Freund, and Nucifora, *All in the Family: State Capture in Tunisia*. In line with the Decree Law No. 2011-13 of February 2011, the government confiscated the assets of a list of 114 people, mostly close relatives of Ben Ali. Among the assets that were seized were over 400 enterprises (some of them abroad);

550 properties; 48 boats and yachts; 40 stock portfolios; and 367 bank accounts. The confiscation commission estimates that the total value of these assets combined is approximately US$13 billion, or more than one-quarter of Tunisian GDP in 2011.

9. Entry authorizations and restrictions on domestic and foreign investors remain the prevalent feature of the business environment in Tunisia. At present, these barriers exist through several pieces of legislation, notably the Investment Incentives Code; the Commerce Code; many of the sectoral legislations regulating services sectors (notably telecommunications, health, education, and professional services); and the Competition Law.

10. If we focus on firms engaged in activities covered by the investment code, we observe that in 2010, roughly two-thirds (64 percent) of all confiscated firms are in sectors in which firms require an "authorization" to operate. Similarly, two-thirds of confiscated firms (64 percent) are active in sectors in which foreign-owned firms are not allowed to operate. These shares are much higher than those for non-connected firms, which are 45 percent and 36 percent, respectively.

11. To attempt to shed light on this question, we assemble a database documenting all changes in the investment code during 1994 and 2010 and assess whether revisions in the code are more likely when Ben Ali firms are undertaking a particular activity. During 1994 and 2010, 22 decrees were signed by Ben Ali introducing new authorization requirements in 45 different sectors and new FDI restrictions in 28 sectors.

12. While statistical power is limited due to the relatively small number of observations on both connected firms and regulatory changes, we document a few instances of striking simultaneity between regulatory changes and deployment of business activities by clan members. For example, Decree No. 96-1234 issued in 1996 amended the investment code by introducing authorization requirements for firms engaging in the handling and transfer of goods in ports, as well as the towing and rescue of ships. The decree also introduced restrictions on FDI for firms involved in the transport of red meat. That same year, Med Afif Chiboub, uncle of Ben Ali's son-in-law Mohammed Slim Chiboub, established *La Méditérranéene pour le Commerce, le Transport et la Consignation*, a shipping and logistics company focused on the transport of refrigerated products. As another example, the establishment of Carthage Cement by Belhassen

Trabelsi, the brother of the president's second wife, followed on the heels of Decree No. 2007-2311 stipulating the need for government authorization for firms producing cement.

13. Rijkers, Freund, and Nucifora, *All in the Family: State Capture in Tunisia*. Each year 1.6 percent of all sectors in which Ben Ali firms are active are subjected to new authorization requirements, whereas only 0.8 percent of sectors in which Ben Ali firms are not present are subjected to new authorization requirements. For FDI restrictions, the difference is even larger with 2 percent of sectors in which Ben Ali firms are active being subjected to new FDI restrictions each year, compared to 0.4 percent of sectors without Ben Ali firms.

14. Simeon Djankov, Rafael La Porta, Florencio Lopez-De-Silanes, and Andrei Shleifer, "The Regulation of Entry," *The Quarterly Journal of Economics*, Vol. 117, Issue 1 (February 2002), pp. 1–37.

15. The 2011 report of the Tunisian Anticorruption Commission highlighted that the areas that had been the most at risk during the Ben Ali regime were real estate, agricultural land, state-owned enterprises, public procurement and concessions awards, large public investments projects, privatization, information technology, financial and banking sectors, customs and taxation, and justice. The Organisation for Economic Co-operation and Development (OECD) carried out an assessment of corruption risks in Tunisia and found similar problems. The results of a parallel qualitative survey that we carried out in Tunisia in 2012 broadly confirm this diagnosis. See Hamouda Chekir and Claude Menard, "Barriers to Private Firms Dynamism in Tunisia: A Qualitative Approach," Internal Mimeo, World Bank, October 2012.

16. Rijkers, Freund, and Nucifora, *All in the Family: State Capture in Tunisia*.

17. Bob Rijkers, Hassen Arrouri, Caroline Freund, and Antonio Nucifora, *Which Firms Create the Most Jobs in Developing Countries? Evidence from Tunisia*, World Bank *Policy Research Working Paper* No. 7068, October 2014.

18. Caroline Freund and Mélise Jaud, "Democratic Transitions: Successful, Gradual, and Failed," World Bank, Office of the Chief Economist, Middle East and North Africa Region, September 2012.

19. Adam Przeworski and Fernando Limongi also note that a democracy is unlikely not to last when per capita GDP is above $6,000. Adam Przeworski and Fernando Fernando Limongi, "Modernization: Theories and Facts," *World Politics*, Vol. 49, No. 2 (January 1997), pp. 155–183.

20. Abraham Lowenthal, *Exporting Democracy: Themes and Issues* (Baltimore: Johns Hopkins University Press, 1991).

21. Seymour Martin Lipset, "Some Social Requisites of Democracy: Economic Development and Political Legitimacy," *American Political Science Review*, Vol. 53, Issue 1 (March 1959), pp. 69–105.

22. Stephan Haggard and Robert R. Kaufman, "The Political Economy of Democratic Transitions," *Comparative Politics*, Vol. 29, No. 3 (April 1997), pp. 263–283.

23. Douglass C. North, John Joseph Wallis, Steven B. Webb, and Barry R. Weingast, *Limited Access Orders in the Developing World: A New Approach to the Problems of Development*, World Bank *Policy Research Working Paper* No. 4359, September 2007.

24. Ibid.

25. In the fall of 2013, a severe political impasse was resolved when the governing coalition and the opposition engaged in a National Dialogue process that was brokered by key civil society organizations. The dialogue focused on the constitutional and electoral timetables, as well as on the opposition's proposition to replace the government with a nonpartisan, technocratic government to oversee the final year of the transition until new elections would be held.

26. North, Wallis, Webb, and Weingast, *Limited Access Orders in the Developing World*.

Chapter 5

Economic Freedom, Energy, and Development

Nicolas D. Loris

Access to dependable energy is an essential requirement for development, underpinning our ability to produce goods and services more efficiently, communicate more easily, and trade with other parts of the world. Moreover, energy markets are becoming increasingly more international, and the energy sector evolves dynamically as technological, economic, and political environments change.

It is common these days to talk about an energy revolution, by which many politicians and commentators mean a government-planned and government-subsidized switch from conventional fuels to renewable forms of energy. But all forms of renewable energy continue to account for a very small percentage of world energy production. The real revolution, unforeseen and unplanned by any government but nonetheless bringing energy and opportunity to billions around the world, is a market-driven technological revolution in exploration and exploitation that has seen investment in energy supply more than double since 2000.[1] Whether it is through

conventional energy supplies or renewables, the world's energy needs will be met best through free markets.

Governments of all stripes regulate the energy sector with measures ranging from outright state ownership or the direct government management of prices or supply to the more general maintenance of a system of laws and property rights. The energy sector is uniquely prone to government intervention because of energy's unique connection to an economy.

While the exact relationship between energy consumption and gross domestic product (GDP) can vary, it is clear that energy is a key ingredient in a nation's economic growth.[2] Consequently, many governments have sought to control energy supply, manipulate demand, and limit competition through feed-in tariffs, preferential tax treatment, renewable energy quotas, regulatory structures, trade barriers, targeted stimulus investments, and other such market manipulations that artificially increase access to and perhaps lower the price of politically preferred energy or, conversely, decrease access and increase price of other energy sources.

Both experience and data show that policies designed to engineer energy markets through state interference hamper economic growth rather than stimulate it. Conversely, both experience and data show that whether a country is rich in natural resources or deprived of them, policies that sustain the four pillars of economic freedom—rule of law, limited government, regulatory efficiency, and open markets—are more successful not only in stimulating economic growth and innovation, but also in using energy more efficiently.

ECONOMIC FREEDOM AND ACCESS TO ENERGY

There are 1.3 billion people around the world without access to reliable electricity. More than 2.5 billion people use biomass for cooking, meaning that they cook their food and heat their homes with animal waste, leaves, wood, and charcoal.[3] Without access to reliable, affordable energy—something the developed world has enjoyed for a century or more—these people have little chance to improve their lives.

Economic and technological realities make conventional coal, nuclear, oil, hydroelectric, and natural gas the most affordable and reliable energy-dense sources of power. For example, Tanzania is hoping to switch increasingly from environmentally destructive charcoal to natural gas, and it recently built infrastructure to deliver offshore natural gas to the homes of Dar es Salaam.[4] While renewable sources like solar and wind may one day play a larger role, they cannot be relied on for the far-reaching or baseload power that fuels economies and reaches the average citizen.

Regrettably, too many special interests are pursuing political and environmental agendas that interfere with the effort to meet basic energy needs in developing countries. When Greenpeace India installed a solar micro-grid in Dharnai, an Indian village surviving without electricity since 1981, the villagers had one message for them: "Hamen nakli nahin, asli bijli chahiye (We do not want artificial energy, give us the

real one)." Young villagers carried signs demanding the "real source of energy" and "not the fake solar powered" one.[5]

In fact, the environmental concerns that drive such projects, while admirable in theory, are sadly misdirected when they hold back development. Arguably, advances in traditional energy production and use are the single most important factor in achieving the societal wealth that enables advances in health, pollution control, and higher standards of living.

Improved Efficiency and Environment. As economies develop and become richer, they also tend to be more capable of adopting greater energy efficiency through innovation. Both small and large innovations that improve energy efficiency add up to big savings for businesses as well as families, and the accumulation of these innovations and efficiency improvements can dramatically enhance a country's energy use per dollar of GDP.

As shown in Chart 1, economically freer countries tend to consume energy more efficiently. Granted, there are unfree countries that have both extremely low electrification and high rates of energy efficiency, but on average, free and mostly free countries use energy more efficiently than do mostly unfree and repressed economies.

Economically freer countries also enjoy cleaner environments and greater environmental sustainability. Freer economies have access to more products and technologies that make our lives healthier and the environment cleaner. For instance, the availability of simple products like soaps, cleaners, and detergents makes our homes dramatically cleaner and healthier. The development of sanitation systems and availability of garbage collection greatly reduce many types of diseases and reduce toxins in the air and water. As a country grows economically, it increases the financial ability of its citizens and businesses to care for the environment and reduce pollutants emitted from industrial growth.

One measure of different countries' environmental status is the Yale Center for Environmental Law and Policy's Environmental Performance Index (EPI), a joint project of the Yale Center for Environmental Law and Policy (YCELP) at

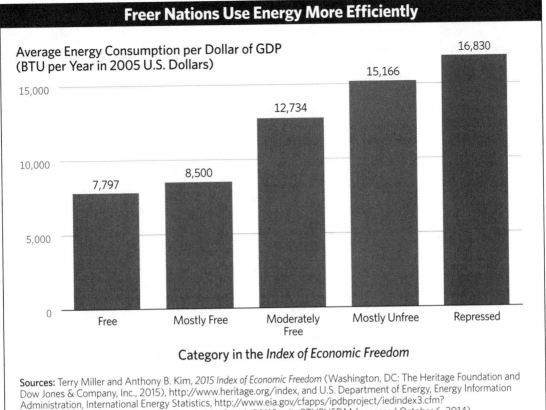

Freer Nations Use Energy More Efficiently

Average Energy Consumption per Dollar of GDP
(BTU per Year in 2005 U.S. Dollars)

Category	Value
Free	7,797
Mostly Free	8,500
Moderately Free	12,734
Mostly Unfree	15,166
Repressed	16,830

Category in the *Index of Economic Freedom*

Sources: Terry Miller and Anthony B. Kim, *2015 Index of Economic Freedom* (Washington, DC: The Heritage Foundation and Dow Jones & Company, Inc., 2015), http://www.heritage.org/index, and U.S. Department of Energy, Energy Information Administration, International Energy Statistics, http://www.eia.gov/cfapps/ipdbproject/iedindex3.cfm?tid=92&pid=46&aid=2&cid=regions&syid=2011&eyid=2011&unit=BTUPUSDM (accessed October 6, 2014).

Chart 1 ☎ heritage.org

Yale University and the Center for International Earth Science Information Network (CIESIN) at Columbia University. The EPI ranks countries based on a number of environmental indicators including agriculture, health impacts, air quality, biodiversity, climate, water and sanitation, and other measures.[6] It provides comprehensive analysis and important measurements of 178 countries' environmental performance.[7]

As it turns out, there is a highly positive correlation between a country's environmental performance as measured by the EPI and its economic freedom. (See Chart 2). The EPI is not without its faults; for example, the index places unwarranted and subjective weight on carbon emissions and climate change relative to more basic environmental measures. But even with the index's bias toward government command-and-control environmental regulation, it is striking that countries with greater economic freedom achieve the best results in protecting the environment.

The principles driving economic freedom and their importance to environmental improvements are unmistakable. Private property rights incentivize owners to take care of their belongings rather than abuse the land and water. As the economist's adage notes, "Nobody washes a rental car."

A sound rule of law ensures that polluters cannot violate the rights of others without accounting for externalities or providing just compensation for any damage inflicted. Free trade promotes competition and creates opportunities for businesses to adopt newer and more innovative technologies. When countries increase their economic prosperity by advancing economic freedom, their capacity to increase overall well-being and protect the environment also increases.

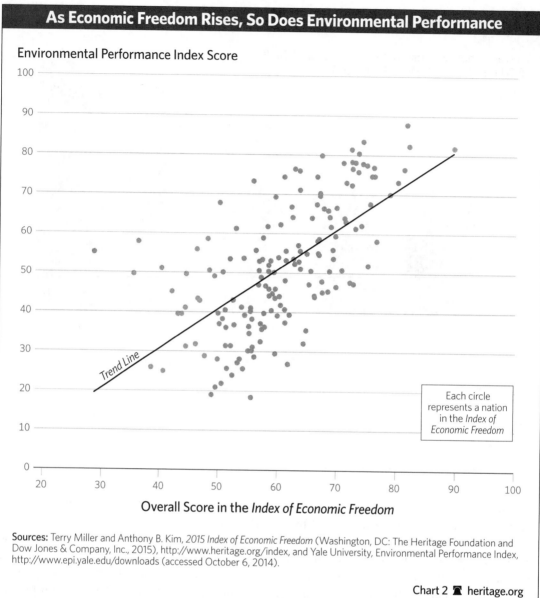

As Economic Freedom Rises, So Does Environmental Performance

Environmental Performance Index Score

Trend Line

Each circle represents a nation in the *Index of Economic Freedom*

Overall Score in the *Index of Economic Freedom*

Sources: Terry Miller and Anthony B. Kim, *2015 Index of Economic Freedom* (Washington, DC: The Heritage Foundation and Dow Jones & Company, Inc., 2015), http://www.heritage.org/index, and Yale University, Environmental Performance Index, http://www.epi.yale.edu/downloads (accessed October 6, 2014).

Chart 2 ☎ heritage.org

BENEFICIAL ENERGY POLICIES EMANATING FROM ECONOMIC LIBERTY

Many of the benefits the United States and other countries are experiencing from energy production stem from factors that promote economic freedom. Policies that open access to markets and secure private property rights broadly expand energy development opportunities and economic gains. Even some countries with centralized autocratic governments and weak legal foundations are implementing the necessary

free-market reforms to encourage investment and energy development.

Private Ownership with Clearly Defined and Enforced Property Rights. The United States is now the world's largest producer of oil and natural gas and, as a result, is reaping the tremendous economic benefits that such large-scale production generates. This success emerged organically from innovation in the private marketplace to unlock energy resources formerly thought inaccessible rather than from any specific government policy to promote these technologies and processes.

Oil and gas production is booming in some regions of the U.S., while the rate of production in others has slowed or even decreased. The divergent trajectories in production primarily boil down to one word: ownership. Much of the growth is occurring on private and state-owned lands, while oil and gas output on federally owned or controlled lands has been in decline.[8] In fact, because of U.S. government ownership and control, the U.S. is the only nation to prohibit energy exploration in a majority of its territorial waters.

The government of Canada, one of the world's economically freest countries and most successful energy producers, also upholds the strong enforcement of property rights when it comes to mineral and resources extraction.[9] Chile, one of the world's 10 freest economies according to the *Index of Economic Freedom,* is well known for its free-market reforms for water use, which include secure private property rights and private investments in hydroelectric power.[10]

Although land use laws are exceedingly complex in different regions of the world, the fact remains that delineated and enforceable property rights along with decentralized land management will be essential for rural energy and economic development in places like Latin America, sub-Saharan Africa, and South Asia. Progress has been made in decentralizing land management and changing land use laws in countries like Burkina Faso, Kenya, Malawi, Mozambique, Rwanda, and Zambia.[11]

Decentralizing and privatizing land use rights is a step in the right direction, but true reform will occur when the legal structure and rule of law protect those changes. Botswana and Cabo Verde, for example, have made enforceable reforms under which landowners' rights are truly protected.[12]

By contrast, in many countries around the world, not only are land and mineral resources state-owned, but entire supply chains of energy production are partially or fully state-owned or controlled. Fully or partially state-owned oil companies in Saudi Arabia, Brazil, Iran, China, Venezuela, Norway, Russia, and many other countries control much of the production and distribution of oil and gas. The problems inherent in government ownership extend far beyond the mere holding of title to the land.

Government-controlled energy enterprises still respond to the profit motive in order to bring money into the government's coffers and often can attain high rates of production. However, because they do not have to make appropriate decisions in a true market environment, state-owned oil and gas companies suffer from economic inefficiencies, reduced foreign investment, higher rates of pollution, wasteful spending, less technological innovation, and aging infrastructure. Further, by relying on oil companies' profits to fund other sectors of the economy, governments divert resources that otherwise would be available to invest in new energy technologies or potential new areas of energy exploration and development.[13]

Venezuela, for example, over the past several decades has poured billions of dollars in oil profits into social and military programs, leaving the country with out-of-date, inefficient infrastructure and gaps in energy investment.[14] As a result of former President Hugo Chávez's attempt to nationalize Venezuela's entire oil industry, oil production fell 30 percent, state-owned company PDVSA was underfunded to invest in infrastructure, and foreign investment practically vanished.[15]

Similarly, state-owned Petrobras in Brazil is facing massive delays and cost overruns because of failure to keep up with increasing domestic energy demand.[16] Exacerbating the problem, the Brazilian government sets the price for gasoline, artificially stimulating demand, hampering competitiveness, and reducing investment, which cannot respond to the proper price signals.[17]

Declines in Iran's oil recovery rate and serious losses in efficiency and investment stem from an increasingly meddlesome government that exercises nearly complete control of that sector of the economy.[18] Nigeria is another resource-rich nation that is plagued by restrictions on private investment as well as stringent regulations and fiscal stipulations for the oil industry.[19]

This is not to say that private-sector investments do not experience cost overruns or delays.

Many times, however, those obstacles can be traced to burdensome government regulations. The marked decline in the U.S. nuclear industry, even in the midst of significant international growth, is a clear case in point. Private businesses have the knowledge and expertise to respond to market signals and succeed or fail by taking risks with their own resources. Government intervention, no matter the form, interferes with that process.

Open Markets. Opening markets to domestic private investment and foreign investment is crucial to developing energy resources and increasing economic growth. The countries where private actors own the mineral rights and reap the rewards from risk-taking typically have more efficient, economically competitive outcomes than do countries where the proceeds from energy production funnel back to the government or to corrupt special interests allied with the government. Opening markets to encourage foreign investment will not automatically eliminate the political corruption that is prevalent within the governments of many countries, but access to foreign capital will result in more competition, expanded energy supplies, more jobs, and higher standards of living for more people.

While many countries are already enjoying the economic benefits that flow from open energy markets, others are recognizing the need for change. Underinvestment and serious inefficiencies in Mexico's government-run energy sector, for example, have led to wasteful, out-of-date infrastructure and the underdevelopment of energy supplies. Unlike its North American neighbors, Mexico has largely been detached from the energy boom in oil and natural gas created by new technology. From 2000 to 2012, the world's major oil-producing countries increased their proven reserves; during the same period, Mexico's proven reserves fell 50 percent.[20]

In recent years, however, Mexico has adopted a series of reforms that should open up investment for oil and gas production, refineries, power plants, and pipelines and enable it to upgrade existing energy infrastructure. Changes include ending the monopoly held by state-owned Pemex, kept in place since 1938, and allowing private companies to compete in the energy sector. As a direct result, the U.S. Energy Information Administration now projects that Mexico's oil production will stop its 10-year decline, level off, and eventually begin growing again.[21] An open, resource-rich Mexico is an extremely attractive new market for foreign investors, and reform of the power market will upgrade the country's energy infrastructure and provide both increased energy supplies and more economic opportunity.

Mexico is far from the only country implementing market-oriented reforms. India has signed civil commercial nuclear agreements with the United States and Australia, under which nuclear technologies can be traded freely and safely to bring electricity to energy-starved Indians. South African President Jacob Zuma is calling for more competitive pricing and encouraging foreign investment through increased private-sector participation.[22] The United States' Anadarko, Italy's ENI, and India's Jindal Steel and Power are investing directly in Mozambique's wealth of coal and natural gas, and the doubling of foreign direct investment has sparked steady economic growth for the country.[23]

Open markets can also foster the exploration and development of new and more efficient energy technologies. Innovation and increased access to energy spurred by competition have the ultimate effect of reducing energy costs. As energy becomes more affordable, both the expense of operating businesses and the cost of products decrease, benefiting consumers.

THE EROSION OF ECONOMIC LIBERTY AND HARMFUL ENERGY POLICIES

Many of the problems associated with accessing, producing, and consuming energy in countries around the world are a direct result of government intervention and policies that undermine economic liberty. Even in the freest economies, the energy sector is uniquely prone to government intervention. Governments have sought to control energy supply, manipulate demand, and limit competition. However, both experience and data show that policies seeking to engineer energy markets end up hampering economic growth rather than stimulating it.

Government Subsidies. Using the political process to support the production or consumption of one energy source or technology over another misallocates labor and capital, wastes taxpayer dollars, and perpetuates stagnation among the very technologies that governments want to promote. Government support that targets one group or industry artificially props up that market and suppresses the real price signals that drive efficiency.

Rather than increase competition, a special endorsement from the government gives one technology an unfair price advantage over others. Further, subsidies reduce the incentive for that technology to become cost-competitive and encourage dependence on the preferential treatment that a government subsidy represents. Energy sources that need subsidies from the government are those that cannot compete economically without them. If a project makes economic sense, however, investments will occur without government subsidies.

For example, policies in climate-conscious Europe have attempted to engineer energy supplies around heavily subsidized renewable sources like wind and solar while driving up the costs of conventional fuels in order to cap or reduce carbon dioxide emissions. Western Europe, often touted as the model to follow when it comes to energy policy, is suffering serious economic consequences because of this subsidizing of expensive, intermittent energy sources.

Europe's energy policies are not success stories; they are cautionary tales. For instance, between 2000 and 2010, Germany spent over $100 billion subsidizing solar and wind power. The result has been a higher tax burden, costlier electricity forced into the grid, and an unsustainable market propped up only by the government's support.[24] Even worse, electricity has become a luxury for more Germans who are unable to afford to heat their homes.[25] Consequently, German lawmakers have voted to scale back the government's "green" subsidies. Although Germany is maintaining an aggressive renewable policy

with subsidies, the new law reduces the amount and availability of subsidies and opens the energy market to more competition.[26]

Spain has suffered a similar fate. According to an Institute for Energy Research report:

> Spain's feed-in tariffs have created a "rate deficit" amounting to $41 billion (about $850 per Spaniard) as of February 2014. This deficit exists between the price that utilities are obligated to pay for renewable energy and the price that they are allowed to pass on to consumers, creating the impetus for **high electricity prices** and **high taxes** to fund the gap.[27]

Denmark has experienced similarly poor results from the government's spending on renewable projects.[28]

Although Germany, Spain, and Denmark have relatively high levels of economic freedom overall, their governments' energy policies, which are often driven by politically charged environmental agendas rather than by market realities, are characteristic of less free economies and are undoubtedly holding back economic growth.

Excessive Regulation and Energy Taxes. Much of the world's demand for energy is met by carbon-emitting conventional fuels; in fact, nearly 80 percent is met by coal, oil, and natural gas, and that situation is expected to continue at least for the next several decades.[29] Out of concern that man-made carbon dioxide emissions will result in catastrophic warming, many countries and sub-national jurisdictions have implemented or are planning carbon reduction policies.

The European Union, New Zealand, South Korea, Australia, and provinces in Canada each have their own carbon-emission trading schemes.[30] France, Costa Rica, Ireland, the United Kingdom, Switzerland, Sweden, Norway, Finland, Iceland, Denmark, and Japan all impose carbon taxes,[31] and South Africa plans to implement a carbon tax of its own.[32] Other countries such as Brazil, Chile, and Thailand have considered their own carbon-restricting plans, and the United States Environmental Protection Agency is attempting to regulate carbon emissions from motor vehicles and both new and existing power plants.

Carbon dioxide (CO_2) and other greenhouse gas (GHG) emissions do not have direct adverse health impacts. In fact, CO_2 is critical to enhancing plant growth and improving ecosystems, providing a number of agricultural and broad human health benefits. Countries around the world are implementing schemes to reduce CO_2 because, it is claimed, its contribution to global warming negatively affects human health and the environment. While a near-universal consensus exists among climatologists that man-made emissions have some warming effect, a large community of scientists have serious reservations about the rate of warming, the magnitude of climate change induced by GHG emissions, and the ability of climate models to predict conditions several centuries into the future.

More important, no matter what one believes regarding climate change, one thing is clear: Collectively, the proposed carbon-emissions reduction policies will cost billions of dollars in higher taxes[33] and trillions of dollars in lost economic opportunity while likely having little if any noticeable impact on global temperatures.[34] When energy prices are artificially increased, higher costs reverberate throughout the global economy as affected industries pass these costs onto consumers. Simply put, consumers are constrained to consume less as producers are forced to raise prices. This results in lower incomes, fewer jobs, and lost economic output.

Recognizing the high costs that a carbon tax was imposing on its citizens and businesses to achieve insignificant climate benefits, Australia abolished the tax in July 2014.[35] No doubt other countries are watching the Australian about-face with significant interest.

Carbon regulations and taxes are merely one example of how governments impose stringent regulations on the energy industry that achieve little in the way of meaningful environmental benefit. Many governments impose controls on exploration, exploitation, and trade in oil and natural gas.

Restrictions on Trade. With a wealth of natural resources and a recent surge in domestic energy production, the United States should be in a position to gain significant economic benefits by exporting energy. Rather than treating energy like other goods traded freely around the world, however, America bans exports of crude oil and places needless restrictions on the exporting of other energy sources and technologies.[36] It even hampers imports, as shown by its failure to approve construction of the Keystone XL pipeline that would facilitate imports of crude oil from Canada.

In other cases, governments have resorted to restrictions on energy trade in pursuit of strategic or tactical advantages. The government of Venezuela, for example, has subsidized oil exports to Cuba, other nations of the Caribbean and Central America, and even the United States in pursuit of political support for its foreign policy goals. Russia, by contrast, has restricted or threatened to restrict the flow of natural gas to European countries to mute their objections to its expansionist policies in Ukraine and Georgia.

The most famous case of the attempted use of energy export controls for strategic advantage is probably the 1973 Arab oil embargo enforced by the Organization of Petroleum Exporting Countries (OPEC) against the United States and others who were supporting Israel in the so-called Yom Kippur War. The result was a quadrupling of oil prices and a global recession. The link between government actions that reduce the availability of energy and economic growth could not have been demonstrated more vividly.

ENERGY: AN ESSENTIAL BUILDING BLOCK FOR AN IMPROVED STANDARD OF LIVING

Energy is a key building block for economic opportunity. Energy policies rooted in the principles of economic freedom lead to increased production, improved access, and greater prosperity, while governments that deviate from those principles are likely to doom their citizens to lives of energy scarcity, thereby curtailing economic growth, environmental progress, health, and longevity.

It is clear from the data that one need not choose between energy availability and cleaner environments. With technological advances and high rates of economic growth, societies can have both. But it is the freer economies—those that encourage competition and private ownership—that do the best job of providing the efficient, reliable, and clean energy that every society needs for a prosperous future.

ENDNOTES

1. International Energy Agency, *World Energy Investment Outlook*, 2014, http://www.iea.org/publications/freepublications/publication/weio2014.pdf.

2. See, for example, Ross McKitrick and Elmira Aliakbari, *Energy Abundance and Economic Growth: International and Canadian Evidence*, Fraser Institute, May 2014, http://www.fraserinstitute.org/uploadedFiles/fraser-ca/Content/research-news/research/publications/energy-abundance-and-economic-growth.pdf.

3. International Energy Agency, "World Energy Outlook," Energy Access Database, http://www.worldenergyoutlook.org/resources/energydevelopment/energyaccessdatabase/.

4. Deutsche Welle, "Tanzanian Natural Gas Comes Ashore," August 19, 2014, http://www.dw.de/tanzanian-natural-gas-comes-ashore/a-17862556.

5. Giridhar Jha, "Bihar Village Clamours for Real Electricity," India Today, August 6, 2014, http://indiatoday.intoday.in/story/bihar-village-dharnai-nitish-kumar-clamours-for-real-electricity/1/375733.html.

6. Yale Center for Environmental Law and Policy and Center for International Earth Science Information Network at Columbia University, 2014 Environmental Performance Index, "Our Methods," http://epi.yale.edu/our-methods.

7. Ibid.

8. Marc Humphries, "U.S. Crude Oil and Natural Gas Production in Federal and Non-Federal Areas," Congressional Research Service *Report for Congress*, March 7, 2013, http://energycommerce.house.gov/sites/republicans.energycommerce.house.gov/files/20130228CRSreport.pdf.

9. Doug Black, "A Canadian Energy Strategy Framework Summary," in *A Canadian Energy Strategy Framework: A Guide to Building Canada's Future as a Global Energy Leader*, Energy Policy Institute of Canada, August 2012, http://www.canadasenergy.ca/wp-content/uploads/2012/08/Final-Document-Aug-1.pdf.

10. Carl Bauer, "Market Approaches to Water Allocation: Lessons from Latin America," *Journal of Contemporary Water Research & Education*, Issue 144 (March 2010), pp. 44–49, http://www.ucowr.org/issue-144/market-approaches-to-water-allocation-lessons-from-latin-america.

11. William J. Garvelink, "Land Tenure, Property Rights, and Rural Economic Development in Africa," Center for Strategic and International Studies *Critical Questions*, February 17, 2012, http://csis.org/publication/land-tenure-property-rights-and-rural-economic-development-africa.

12. Daron Acemoglu, Simon Johnson, and James A. Robinson, "An African Success Story: Botswana," July 11, 2011, http://www.colby.edu/economics/faculty/jmlong/ec479/ajr.pdf, and Global Property Guide, "Property Rights Index—Cape Verde Compared to Continent," http://www.globalpropertyguide.com/Africa/Cape-Verde/property-rights-index.

13. David Victor, David R. Hults, and Mark C. Thurber, eds., *Oil and Governance: State-Owned Enterprises and the World Energy Supply*, (Cambridge, UK: Cambridge University Press, 2014), http://www.cambridge.org/us/academic/subjects/politics-international-relations/political-economy/oil-and-governance-state-owned-enterprises-and-world-energy-supply.

14. Cesar J. Alvarez and Stephanie Hanson, "Venezuela's Oil-based Economy," Council on Foreign Relations *Backgrounder*, updated February 9, 2009, www.cfr.org/world/venezuelas-oil-based-economy/p12089.

15. Jim Jelter, "Why Oil Prices Dipped on Chavez's Death," *The Wall Street Journal*, MarketWatch, March 5, 2013, http://blogs.marketwatch.com/thetell/2013/03/05/why-oil-prices-dipped-on-chavezs-death/.

16. Fabiola Moura, "Energy Losses Expose Petrobras Fuel Distortion: Corporate Brazil," Bloomberg, November 23, 2012, http://www.bloomberg.com/news/2012-11-23/energy-losses-expose-petrobras-fuel-distortion-corporate-brazil.html.

17. Christian Gómez, Jr., "Brazil's Energy Agenda: The Way Forward," Americas Society/Council of the Americas Energy Action Group *Working Paper*, September 2013, http://www.as-coa.org/sites/default/files/Brazils%20Energy%20Agenda.pdf.

18. U.S. Energy Information Administration, "Country Analysis Brief: Iran," last updated July 22, 2014, http://www.eia.gov/countries/analysisbriefs/Iran/iran.pdf.

19. KPMG, "Oil and Gas in Africa: Africa's Reserves, Potential and Prospects," 2013, http://www.kpmg.com/Africa/en/IssuesAndInsights/Articles-Publications/Documents/Oil%20and%20Gas%20in%20Africa.pdf.

20. Eduardo León, Iván Martén, Raul Livas, and Marcelo Mereles, "The Promise of Mexico's Energy Reform," Boston Consulting Group and EnergeA, April 2014, http://structura.com.mx/-/downloads/ThePromiseofMexicosEnergyReforms.pdf.

21. U.S. Energy Information Administration, "Energy Reform Could Increase Mexico's Long-term Oil Production by 75%," Today in Energy, August 25, 2014, http://www.eia.gov/todayinenergy/detail.cfm?id=17691.

22. Free Market Foundation Energy Policy Unit, "South Africa Has an Energy Plan—It Just Needs to Implement It," June 30, 2014, http://www.esi-africa.com/south-africa-has-an-energy-plan-it-just-needs-to-implement-it/.

23. Enerdata, Mozambique Energy Market, "Emerging Opportunities for Investors," January 21, 2014, http://www.enerdata.net/enerdatauk/press-and-publication/energy-features/mozambique-ressources-coal-and-natural-gas.php.

24. Rheinisch-Westfälisches Institut für Wirtschaftsforschung, *Economic Impacts from the Promotion of Renewable Energies: The German Experience*, Final Report, October 2009, http://instituteforenergyresearch.org/media/germany/Germany_Study_-_FINAL.pdf.

25. Spiegel Online International, "Germany's Energy Poverty: How Electricity Became a Luxury Good," September 4, 2013, http://www.spiegel.de/international/germany/high-costs-and-errors-of-german-transition-to-renewable-energy-a-920288.html.

26. Stefan Nicola, "German Lawmakers Vote to Reduce Renewable-Energy Subsidies," Bloomberg News, June 27, 2014, http://www.businessweek.com/news/2014-06-27/german-lawmakers-back-new-clean-energy-law-to-reduce-subsidies.

27. Institute for Energy Research, "Spain's Green Energy Experiment: A Cautionary Tale," 2014, http://instituteforenergyresearch.org/wp-content/uploads/2014/08/Renewables-in-Spain.pdf (emphasis in original).

28. CEPOS (Center for Politiske Studier), "Wind Energy Policy: The Case of Denmark," September 2009, http://www.cepos.dk/fileadmin/user_upload/Arkiv/PDF/Wind_energy_-_the_case_of_Denmark.pdf.

29. U.S. Energy Information Administration, *International Energy Outlook 2014*, September 2014, http://www.eia.gov/forecasts/ieo/pdf/0484(2014).pdf.

30. European Commission, Climate Action, "The EU Emissions Trading System (EU ETS)," http://ec.europa.eu/clima/policies/ets/index_en.htm.

31. World Bank, "Putting a Price on Carbon with a Tax," http://www.worldbank.org/content/dam/Worldbank/document/SDN/background-note_carbon-tax.pdf.

32. World Bank, "State & Trends Report Charts Global Growth of Carbon Pricing," May 28, 2014, http://www.worldbank.org/en/news/feature/2014/05/28/state-trends-report-tracks-global-growth-carbon-pricing.

33. Risa Maeda, "Japan's New Carbon Tax to Cost Utilities $1billion Annually," Reuters, October 10, 2012, http://www.reuters.com/article/2012/10/10/us-energy-japan-tax-idUSBRE8990G520121010.

34. Nicolas D. Loris, Kevin D. Dayaratna, and David W. Kreutzer, "EPA Power Plant Regulations: A Backdoor Energy Tax," Heritage Foundation *Backgrounder* No 2863, December 5, 2013, http://www.heritage.org/research/reports/2013/12/epa-power-plant-regulations-a-backdoor-energy-tax.

35. Australian Government, Department of the Environment, "Repealing the Carbon Tax," 2014, http://www.environment.gov.au/climate-change/repealing-carbon-tax.

36. Nicolas D. Loris, "Energy Exports Promote Prosperity and Bolster National Security," Heritage Foundation *Backgrounder* No 2931, July 23, 2014, http://www.heritage.org/research/reports/2014/07/energy-exports-promote-prosperity-and-bolster-national-security.

Chapter 6

Global and Regional Trends in Economic Freedom

Ambassador Terry Miller and Anthony B. Kim

The 2015 *Index of Economic Freedom* assesses economic policy developments in 186 economies in six regions around the world. The *Index* grades and ranks economies based on their performance in 10 key policy areas affecting overall economic freedom, which are grouped into categories that evaluate the rule of law, respect for the principle of limited government, regulatory efficiency, and the domestic and international openness of markets. The 2015 *Index*, the 21st annual edition, evaluates economic conditions and policy developments between July 1, 2013, and June 30, 2014.

GLOBAL PROGRESS IN ECONOMIC FREEDOM

The 2015 *Index* judges the world economy as a whole to be "moderately free." Average economic freedom has increased for the third year in a row. Although the pace of advancement has slowed sharply in comparison to last year's 0.7-point improvement, economic freedom has still advanced by 0.1 point to 60.4 in the 2015 *Index*.

That represents a 2.8-point overall improvement from the inception of the *Index* in 1995. (See Chart 1.)

Of the 178 economies graded in the 2015 *Index*, only five have sustained very high freedom scores of 80 or more, putting them in the ranks of the economically "free." The next 30 countries have been rated as "mostly free" economies recording scores between 70 and 80. With scores of 60 to 70, 55 countries have earned scores that place them in the "moderately free" category. Thus, a total of 90 economies, or about 50 percent of all nations and territories graded in the 2015 *Index*, provide institutional environments in which individuals and private enterprises benefit from at least a moderate degree of economic freedom in the pursuit of greater prosperity and success.

On the opposite side of the spectrum, nearly half of the remaining countries graded in the *Index*—88 economies—have registered economic freedom scores below 60. Of those, 62 economies are considered "mostly unfree" (scores of 50–60), and 26 are clearly "repressed" (below 50).

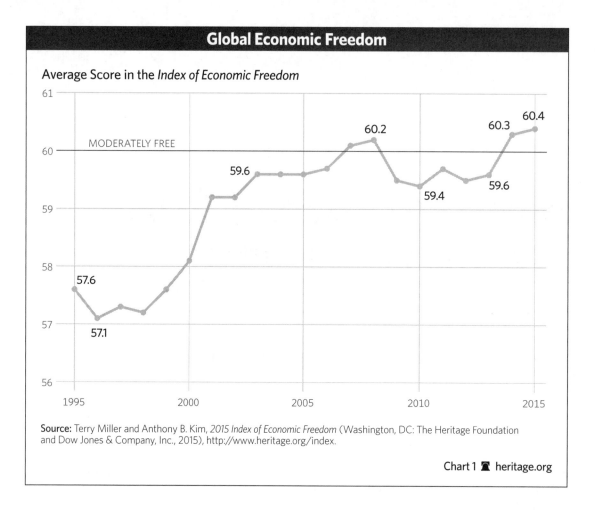

Global Economic Freedom

Average Score in the *Index of Economic Freedom*

MODERATELY FREE

57.6

57.1

59.6

60.2

59.4

60.3

59.6

60.4

Source: Terry Miller and Anthony B. Kim, *2015 Index of Economic Freedom* (Washington, DC: The Heritage Foundation and Dow Jones & Company, Inc., 2015), http://www.heritage.org/index.

Chart 1 ☎ heritage.org

Despite the global progress recorded over the 21-year history of the *Index*, the number of people living without economic freedom remains disturbingly high: 4.5 billion, or about 65 percent of the world's population. More than half of these people live in just two countries, China and India, where advancement toward greater economic freedom has been both limited and uneven. In the two most populous economies, structural reforms in a few key sectors have sometimes boosted growth, but the governments have failed to institutionalize open environments that promote broad-based and sustained improvements in the economic well-being of the population as a whole.

As shown in "The Ten Economic Freedoms: A Global Look" on the next page, on a worldwide basis, this year's increase in economic freedom has been driven by improvements in trade freedom, monetary freedom, and freedom from corruption, for which global ratings have advanced

by close to one point or more on average. Average scores for most other economic freedoms, including business freedom, property rights, labor freedom, investment freedom, and financial freedom, have registered small declines.

The loss of economic freedom was most pronounced in the area of respect for limited government. A score drop of 1.0 point in the category measuring control of government spending reflects the continuation of countercyclical or interventionist stimulus policies in some countries, though there is scant evidence that such policies are boosting growth or restoring employment.

GAINS AND LOSSES

In the 2015 *Index*, 101 countries, the majority of which are less developed or emerging economies, showed advances in economic freedom over the past year. Remarkably, 37 countries, including Taiwan, Lithuania, Georgia, Colom-

The 10 Economic Freedoms: A Global Look

Score Changes

RULE OF LAW		GOVERNMENT SIZE		REGULATORY EFFICIENCY		OPEN MARKETS	
Property Rights	-0.9	Fiscal Freedom	+0.1	Business Freedom	-0.8	Trade Freedom	+0.6
Freedom from Corruption	+1.6	Government Spending	-1.0	Labor Freedom	-0.3	Investment Freedom	-0.7
				Monetary Freedom	+0.8	Financial Freedom	-0.4

RULE OF LAW

Property Rights 42.2
Freedom from Corruption 41.9

The world average score for property rights has declined since last year, with 28 countries' scores deteriorating. In many countries, the judiciary has become more vulnerable to political interference. Despite some improvement, the average score for freedom from corruption still lags behind scores for other components of economic freedom. Populations in some countries have engaged in demonstrations calling for greater transparency and accountability.

GOVERNMENT SIZE

Fiscal Freedom 77.4
Government Spending 61.7

The average top individual income tax rate for all countries is about 28 percent, and the average top corporate tax rate is 24.1 percent. The average overall tax burden corresponds to around 23 percent of gross domestic product. The average level of government spending is equal to 34.7 percent of GDP. The average level of gross public debt for countries covered in the *Index* is equivalent to slightly over 50 percent of GDP.

REGULATORY EFFICIENCY

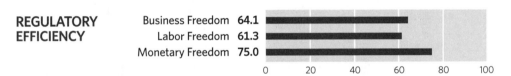

Business Freedom 64.1
Labor Freedom 61.3
Monetary Freedom 75.0

Many countries continue to implement regulatory reforms, although developed countries have generally lagged behind developing countries. Globally, starting a business takes seven procedures and 22 days, while licensing requirements consume over five months on average. For the world as a whole, burdensome labor codes stifle job growth. Monetary freedom registered a continued improvement as a result of generally low inflationary pressures.

OPEN MARKETS

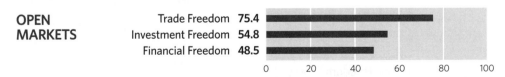

Trade Freedom 75.4
Investment Freedom 54.8
Financial Freedom 48.5

The average trade freedom score continues to improve. The average investment freedom score remains essentially unchanged. Many countries' investment policies remain geared toward sectoral investment promotion rather than general market openness. Despite some progress, the global financial system remains under continuing strain and uncertainty. Overall, global financial freedom has recorded a slight decline since last year.

Economic Freedom: Regional Variations (Regional Average)

Regional Ranking	North America (73.9)	Middle East / North Africa (61.6)	South and Central America / Caribbean (59.7)	Asia-Pacific (58.8)	Europe (67)	Sub-Saharan Africa (54.9)
1	Canada	Bahrain	Chile	Hong Kong	Switzerland	Mauritius
2	United States	United Arab Emirates	Colombia	Singapore	Estonia	Botswana
3	Mexico	Qatar	Saint Lucia	New Zealand	Ireland	Cabo Verde
4		Israel	Bahamas, The	Australia	Denmark	Rwanda
5		Jordan	Uruguay	Taiwan	United Kingdom	Ghana
6		Oman	Saint Vincent and the Grenadines	Japan	Lithuania	South Africa
7		Kuwait	Barbados	South Korea	Germany	Madagascar
8		Saudi Arabia	Peru	Malaysia	Netherlands	Swaziland
9		Morocco	Jamaica	Macau	Finland	Uganda
10		Lebanon	Costa Rica	Brunei	Luxembourg	Namibia
11		Tunisia	Dominica	Kazakhstan	Georgia	Benin
12		Egypt	El Salvador	Thailand	Sweden	Zambia
13		Yemen	Trinidad and Tobago	Philippines, The	Czech Republic	Burkina Faso
14		Algeria	Panama	Samoa	Iceland	Côte d'Ivoire
15		Iran	Paraguay	Kyrgyz Republic	Norway	Gabon
16			Dominican Republic	Vanuatu	Austria	Senegal
17			Guatemala	Azerbaijan	Latvia	Tanzania
18			Nicaragua	Tonga	Belgium	Djibouti
19			Honduras	Mongolia	Poland	Gambia, The
20			Belize	Fiji	Cyprus	Seychelles
21			Brazil	Sri Lanka	Spain	Mali
22			Guyana	Indonesia	Slovak Republic	Nigeria
23			Suriname	Cambodia	Armenia	Kenya
24			Haiti	Bhutan	Macedonia	Mozambique
25			Ecuador	Pakistan	Hungary	Malawi
26			Bolivia	India	Bulgaria	Niger
27			Argentina	Bangladesh	Romania	Burundi
28			Venezuela	Maldives	Malta	Mauritania
29			Cuba	Papua New Guinea	Albania	São Tomé and Príncipe
30				China	Portugal	Togo
31				Tajikistan	Montenegro	Liberia
32				Vietnam	Turkey	Comoros
33				Laos	France	Guinea
34				Nepal	Italy	Guinea-Bissau
35				Micronesia	Croatia	Cameroon
36				Solomon Islands	Slovenia	Sierra Leone
37				Uzbekistan	Serbia	Ethiopia
38				Burma	Bosnia and Herzegovina	Lesotho
39				Kiribati	Moldova	Angola
40				Timor-Leste	Greece	Chad
41				Turkmenistan	Russia	Central African Republic
42				North Korea	Belarus	Congo, Dem. Rep.
43					Ukraine	Congo, Republic of
44						Equatorial Guinea
45						Eritrea
46						Zimbabwe

Economic Freedom Scores

- ■ 80–100 Free
- ■ 70–79.9 Mostly Free
- ■ 60–69.9 Moderately Free
- ☐ 50–59.9 Mostly Unfree
- ☐ 0–49.9 Repressed

One-Year Freedom Score Change

Region	Index Year 2014	Index Year 2015	One-Year Change
Sub-Saharan Africa	54.6	54.9	+0.3
Asia–Pacific	58.5	58.8	+0.3
Middle East and North Africa	61.5	61.6	+0.1
South and Central America/Caribbean	59.7	59.7	No change
Europe	67.1	67.0	-0.1
North America	74.1	73.9	-0.2

Source: Terry Miller and Anthony B. Kim, *2015 Index of Economic Freedom* (Washington, DC: The Heritage Foundation and Dow Jones & Company, Inc., 2015), http://www.heritage.org/index.

Chart 2 ☎ heritage.org

bia, Israel, Cabo Verde, Montenegro, and Côte d'Ivoire, achieved their highest economic freedom scores ever in the 2015 *Index*.

While four countries (Singapore, Finland, Madagascar, and Suriname) recorded no score change, declines in economic freedom have occurred in 73 countries. Eleven countries, including Venezuela, Equatorial Guinea, Argentina, Bolivia, Algeria, Greece, and El Salvador, recorded their lowest economic freedom scores ever.

Sub-Saharan Africa is home to six of the 10 most improved countries. São Tomé and Príncipe, Democratic Republic of Congo, Togo, Senegal, Burundi, and Zimbabwe all recorded score gains of two points or more. On the other hand, Europe has the most countries (Slovenia, Ukraine, Armenia, and Greece) recording serious declines, followed by Sub-Saharan Africa (Equatorial Guinea, Botswana, and the Gambia) and Middle East/North Africa (Algeria and Yemen).

Score improvements in eight countries, all of which are developing or emerging economies, were significant enough to merit upgrades in their economic freedom status in the *Index*. Notably, Israel and Malaysia have joined the ranks of the "mostly free," in Israel's case for the first time ever and in Malaysia's case regaining a level of economic freedom it had not experienced since 1996. Three developing countries (Morocco, Serbia, and Vanuatu) have advanced into the ranks of the "moderately free." Three others (Haiti, São Tomé and Príncipe, and Togo) have escaped the status of economically "repressed."

Fourteen countries, including Angola, Poland, South Korea, Taiwan, and the United Arab Emirates, have achieved uninterrupted growth in economic freedom over the past five years. Seven of the 14, all developing countries, have recorded notable cumulative score gains of over five points: Zimbabwe, Burma, Comoros, Seychelles, Liberia, the Philippines, and Guinea–Bissau.

Competition for the top spot in the *Index* rankings has intensified. The 2015 *Index* has recorded a number of noticeable realignments and achievements within the top 20 global economic freedom rankings.

- Hong Kong has maintained its status as the world's freest economy, a distinction that it has achieved for 21 consecutive years. However, the gap between that territory and Singapore, the second-freest economy, has almost vanished. Hong Kong's economic freedom score declined by 0.5 point, with an erosion of the rule of law reflecting an increased level of perceived corruption.
- Along with Hong Kong and Singapore, New Zealand, Australia, and Switzerland are the only economies considered "free" with economic freedom scores above 80 on the 0-to-100 *Index* grading scale. New Zealand moved up two slots and reclaimed third place in the rankings as a result of committed efforts to cut government spending. Canada remains the world's sixth-freest economy for the fifth year in a row.

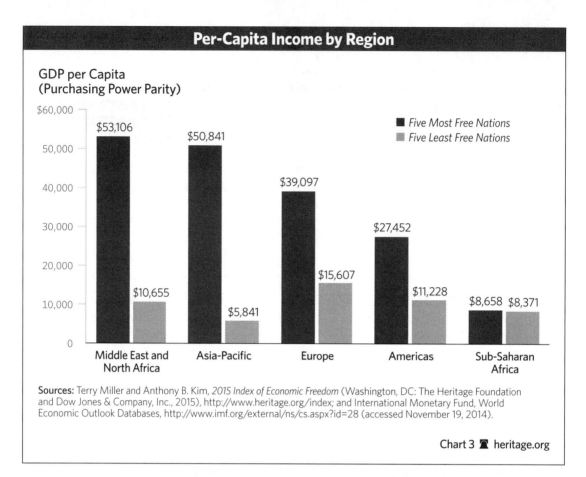

Per-Capita Income by Region

GDP per Capita
(Purchasing Power Parity)

- Five Most Free Nations
- Five Least Free Nations

Region	Five Most Free Nations	Five Least Free Nations
Middle East and North Africa	$53,106	$10,655
Asia-Pacific	$50,841	$5,841
Europe	$39,097	$15,607
Americas	$27,452	$11,228
Sub-Saharan Africa	$8,658	$8,371

Sources: Terry Miller and Anthony B. Kim, *2015 Index of Economic Freedom* (Washington, DC: The Heritage Foundation and Dow Jones & Company, Inc., 2015), http://www.heritage.org/index; and International Monetary Fund, World Economic Outlook Databases, http://www.imf.org/external/ns/cs.aspx?id=28 (accessed November 19, 2014).

Chart 3 ☎ heritage.org

- Chile (seventh) and Mauritius (10th), two reform-minded developing economies, continue to rank among the world's 10 freest economies. Both have demonstrated persistent commitment to the rule of law, limited government, regulatory efficiency, and open markets.
- Moving up three slots, Estonia has become the world's eighth-freest economy. The small Baltic nation has rejoined the world's 10 freest economies for the first time since 2007, overtaking Denmark (11th), Ireland (ninth), and Mauritius.
- The United States continues to be only the 12th-freest economy, seemingly stuck in the ranks of the "mostly free," the second-tier economic freedom category into which the U.S. dropped in 2010.
- Taiwan and Lithuania, benefitting from uninterrupted score improvements since 2009, have recorded their highest economic freedom scores ever, advancing to 14th and 15th places, respectively, and surpassing Sweden, Finland, Germany, Luxembourg, the Netherlands, and Bahrain.

REGIONAL TRENDS IN ECONOMIC FREEDOM

In the 2015 *Index*, each of the six regions continues to be represented by at least one country that ranks among the top 20 freest economies. However, as shown in Chart 2, average levels of economic freedom advanced in only half of the regions.

Sub-Saharan Africa (led by São Tomé and Príncipe and Democratic Republic of Congo) and the Asia–Pacific region (led by Maldives and the Philippines) each showed an average score improvement of 0.3 point, and Middle East/North Africa countries (led by Israel and Morocco) gained 0.1 point on average. While average economic freedom for the South and Central America/Caribbean region stayed the same as last year, Europe and North America registered slight declines of 0.1 and 0.2 point, respectively.

Among the six regions, average levels of economic freedom vary widely. North America and Europe continue to record the highest average

Comparing Regional Average Scores with the Global Average

Above or Equal to Global Average   Below Global Average

	North America	Europe	Middle East/ North Africa	South and Central America/ Caribbean	Asia-Pacific	Sub-Saharan Africa	GLOBAL AVERAGE
Overall	73.9	67.0	61.6	59.7	58.8	54.9	**60.4**
Property Rights	73.3	59.9	39.4	39.0	38.0	30.1	**42.2**
Freedom from Corruption	62.7	57.0	38.4	41.1	37.6	32.5	**41.9**
Fiscal Freedom	74.6	71.7	88.8	78.4	80.2	75.6	**77.4**
Government Spending	59.4	40.5	62.3	69.3	66.7	72.2	**61.7**
Business Freedom	83.1	76.6	64.0	60.3	65.4	52.2	**64.1**
Labor Freedom	78.2	61.9	64.4	57.5	67.3	55.2	**61.3**
Monetary Freedom	77.3	78.8	73.4	74.9	73.2	73.7	**75.0**
Trade Freedom	87.0	86.7	74.1	74.8	72.8	67.2	**75.4**
Investment Freedom	73.3	74.1	44.4	55.3	44.1	48.4	**54.8**
Financial Freedom	70.0	63.2	45.3	46.6	43.1	40.2	**48.5**

Source: Terry Miller and Anthony B. Kim, *2015 Index of Economic Freedom* (Washington, DC: The Heritage Foundation and Dow Jones & Company, Inc., 2015), http://www.heritage.org/index.

Table 1 ☎ heritage.org

economic freedom scores among the regions: 73.9 and 67, respectively. Despite the ongoing economic and political turmoil in a number of countries in the Middle East and North Africa, the region as a whole still achieved an average economic freedom score slightly above 60 due to high ratings of economic freedom in Bahrain, the United Arab Emirates, and Qatar, reinforced by improved scores in Egypt, Israel, and Moroc-co. Average economic freedom scores in the South and Central America/Caribbean region, the Asia–Pacific region, and Sub-Saharan Africa continue to be below 60.

Despite varying degrees of economic freedom across the regions, the fundamental relationship between economic freedom and prosperity is readily apparent worldwide. Chart 3 shows that, no matter the region, per capita

Economic Freedom in North American Countries

World Rank	Regional Rank	Country	Overall Score	Change from 2014	Property Rights	Freedom from Corruption	Fiscal Freedom	Government Spending	Business Freedom	Labor Freedom	Monetary Freedom	Trade Freedom	Investment Freedom	Financial Freedom
6	1	Canada	79.1	-1.1	90	81.0	79.9	48.3	89.0	76.1	77.9	88.4	80	80
12	2	United States	76.2	0.7	80	73.0	66.2	51.8	88.8	98.5	76.6	87.0	70	70
59	3	Mexico	66.4	-0.4	50	34.0	77.8	78.0	71.5	59.9	77.6	85.6	70	60

Table 2 ☎ heritage.org

North America

Economic Freedom Scores

- ■ 80-100 Free
- ■ 70-79.9 Mostly Free
- ▨ 60-69.9 Moderately Free
- ☐ 50-59.9 Mostly Unfree
- ☐ 0-49.9 Repressed
- ▨ Not Ranked

Source: Terry Miller and Anthony B. Kim, *2015 Index of Economic Freedom* (Washington, DC: The Heritage Foundation and Dow Jones & Company, Inc., 2015), http://www.heritage.org/index.

Map 1 ☎ heritage.org

income levels are consistently higher in countries that are economically freer.

The diversity of the world's peoples and cultures implies that there will be many paths to economic development and prosperity. The whole idea of economic freedom is to empower people with more opportunity to choose for themselves how to pursue and fulfill their dreams, subject only to the basic rule of law and honest competition from others. The patterns of economic freedom across the six *Index* regions are, not surprisingly, unique. They reflect the culture and history of each nation and the individuals that inhabit them, not to mention circumstances of geography or endowments of natural resources.

There is no single answer to the particular challenges of development that we face. One thing, however, is sure: Governments that respect and promote economic freedom provide the best environment for experimentation, innovation, and progress, and it is through these that humankind grows in prosperity and well-being.

NORTH AMERICA

The North America region has two "mostly free" economies (Canada and the U.S.) and one "moderately free" economy (Mexico). Canada has led the region in economic freedom since 2010.

Overall, average economic freedom in the region has registered a slight decline (0.2 point) since last year, with a small improvement in the

Economic Freedom in European Countries

World Rank	Regional Rank	Country	Overall Score	Change from 2014	Property Rights	Freedom from Corruption	Fiscal Freedom	Government Spending	Business Freedom	Labor Freedom	Monetary Freedom	Trade Freedom	Investment Freedom	Financial Freedom
5	1	Switzerland	80.5	-1.1	90	85.0	70.3	65.1	78.1	75.3	86.3	90.0	85	80
8	2	Estonia	76.8	0.9	90	68.0	80.6	53.2	81.5	58.7	77.6	88.0	90	80
9	3	Ireland	76.6	0.4	85	72.0	73.6	45.6	82.1	76.2	83.9	88.0	90	70
11	4	Denmark	76.3	0.2	95	91.0	39.6	1.8	97.4	92.1	87.6	88.0	90	80
13	5	United Kingdom	75.8	0.9	90	76.0	62.9	30.3	91.1	75.6	74.4	88.0	90	80
15	6	Lithuania	74.7	1.7	60	57.0	92.9	61.3	84.9	62.0	81.2	88.0	80	80
16	7	Germany	73.8	0.4	90	78.0	60.8	40.1	88.2	51.2	81.5	88.0	90	70
17	8	The Netherlands	73.7	-0.5	90	83.0	51.8	23.8	84.3	66.3	79.8	88.0	90	80
19	9	Finland	73.4	0.0	90	89.0	66.4	3.6	92.6	54.8	79.9	88.0	90	80
21	10	Luxembourg	73.2	-1.0	90	80.0	62.3	42.2	71.3	42.1	80.7	88.0	95	80
22	11	Georgia	73.0	0.4	40	49.0	87.2	73.8	88.6	79.9	82.7	88.6	80	60
23	12	Sweden	72.7	-0.4	90	89.0	43.0	19.2	87.9	54.0	85.5	88.0	90	80
24	13	Czech Republic	72.5	0.3	75	48.0	81.5	40.6	68.2	82.9	81.2	88.0	80	80
26	14	Iceland	72.0	-0.4	90	78.0	72.0	32.6	90.5	62.2	77.0	88.0	70	60
27	15	Norway	71.8	0.9	90	86.0	52.1	43.8	92.1	48.2	81.7	89.4	75	60
30	16	Austria	71.2	-1.2	90	69.0	50.1	19.8	78.0	76.7	80.3	88.0	90	70
37	17	Latvia	69.7	1.0	50	53.0	84.4	59.2	82.1	61.5	83.8	88.0	85	50
40	18	Belgium	68.8	-1.1	80	75.0	43.6	10.2	90.7	63.7	81.7	88.0	85	70
42	19	Poland	68.6	1.6	60	60.0	82.1	47.1	67.3	60.4	81.3	88.0	70	70
45	20	Cyprus	67.9	0.3	70	63.0	79.5	36.7	79.5	59.6	82.7	88.0	70	50
49	21	Spain	67.6	0.4	70	59.0	53.1	39.8	77.5	52.6	81.3	88.0	85	70
50	22	Slovak Republic	67.2	0.8	50	47.0	80.8	55.1	69.6	56.5	75.5	88.0	80	70

(continued on next page)

United States outweighed by declines in Canada and Mexico. The downward spiral in U.S. economic freedom over the previous seven years has come to a halt. In the 2015 *Index*, the U.S. recorded modest score gains in six of the 10 economic freedoms; however, its score for business freedom has plunged below 90, the lowest level since 2006.

The North American Free Trade Agreement remains the linchpin of massive trade and investment flows in the North America region. This increasing integration is reflected in converging scores for trade freedom and investment freedom in the region. In 1995, when the first edition of the *Index* measured these freedoms, the score differences between the United States and Mexico were over 10 points. Over the past two decades, the trade and investment freedom margins have narrowed to less than three points.

EUROPE

The Europe region includes 43 countries graded by the *Index*, the most of any region. Switzerland continues to be the only "free" economy in the region, with a score of 80.5. Nine of the world's 20

World Rank	Regional Rank	Country	Overall Score	Change from 2014	Property Rights	Freedom from Corruption	Fiscal Freedom	Government Spending	Business Freedom	Labor Freedom	Monetary Freedom	Trade Freedom	Investment Freedom	Financial Freedom
52	23	Armenia	67.1	-1.8	20	36.0	84.4	82.8	82.7	64.3	70.6	85.4	75	70
53	24	Macedonia	67.1	-1.5	35	44.0	91.4	65.6	79.2	70.7	79.0	86.2	60	60
54	25	Hungary	66.8	-0.2	55	54.0	78.7	25.9	74.5	67.7	79.2	88.0	75	70
55	26	Bulgaria	66.8	1.1	30	41.0	91.0	64.5	68.5	76.6	83.2	88.0	65	60
57	27	Romania	66.6	1.1	40	43.0	86.9	62.3	69.8	68.6	77.3	88.0	80	50
58	28	Malta	66.5	0.1	75	56.0	63.1	44.4	61.0	55.6	81.8	88.0	80	60
63	29	Albania	65.7	-1.2	30	31.0	87.2	76.1	70.6	52.9	80.8	87.8	70	70
64	30	Portugal	65.3	1.8	70	62.0	61.1	28.8	87.5	42.9	82.8	88.0	70	60
66	31	Montenegro	64.7	1.1	40	44.0	92.6	36.7	77.1	77.5	79.7	84.8	65	50
70	32	Turkey	63.2	-1.7	45	50.0	76.1	57.6	61.0	50.2	72.4	84.6	75	60
73	33	France	62.5	-1.0	80	71.0	47.5	2.5	80.2	43.5	77.5	83.0	70	70
80	34	Italy	61.7	0.8	55	43.0	54.2	23.2	71.9	55.4	81.2	88.0	85	60
81	35	Croatia	61.5	1.1	40	48.0	74.9	46.5	55.8	42.8	80.0	87.2	80	60
88	36	Slovenia	60.3	-2.4	60	57.0	58.1	0.0	81.2	57.1	81.3	88.0	70	50
90	37	Serbia	60.0	0.6	45	42.0	82.4	27.1	57.8	70.4	72.2	78.2	75	50
97	38	Bosnia and Herzegovina	59.0	0.6	20	42.0	82.9	27.3	53.5	63.4	84.0	87.2	70	60
111	39	Moldova	57.5	0.2	40	35.0	85.1	51.8	66.8	40.6	76.1	79.8	50	50
130	40	Greece	54.0	-1.7	40	40.0	64.2	0.0	73.3	51.6	77.8	83.0	60	50
143	41	Russia	52.1	0.2	20	28.0	86.1	57.8	76.3	58.9	63.9	75.0	25	30
153	42	Belarus	49.8	-0.3	20	29.0	86.4	54.7	72.0	80.1	44.5	81.0	20	10
162	43	Ukraine	46.9	-2.4	20	25.0	78.7	28.0	59.3	48.2	78.6	85.8	15	30
N/A	N/A	Kosovo	N/A	N/A	30	33.0	N/A	73.9	66.8	72.1	74.9	N/A	65	N/A
N/A	N/A	Liechtenstein	N/A	N/A	N/A	N/A	N/A	N/A	N/A	N/A	N/A	90.0	85	80

Table 3 ☎ heritage.org

freest countries are in Europe, and the vast majority of the region's countries are considered at least "moderately free." Europe has three "mostly unfree" economies (Moldova, Greece, and Russia) and two "repressed" economies (Ukraine and Belarus).

Taken as a whole, the Europe region still struggles with a variety of policy barriers to dynamic economic expansion, such as overly protective and costly labor regulations, higher tax burdens, various market distortionary subsidies, and continuing problems in public finance management resulting from years of expansion of the public sector.

The result has been stagnant economic growth, which has exacerbated the burden of fiscal deficits and mounting debt. In many countries of the region, decisive policy action is needed to cut spending. Where such actions have been taken, progress is apparent. Three Baltic economies (Estonia, Lithuania, and Latvia) are on the move toward greater economic freedom. Overcoming severe recessions

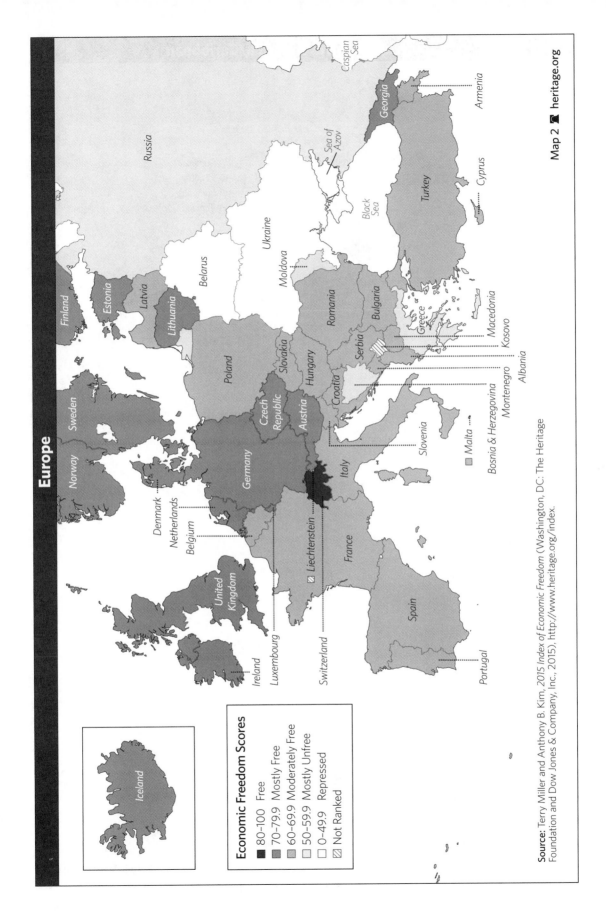

Europe

Economic Freedom Scores

- ■ 80–100 Free
- ■ 70–79.9 Mostly Free
- ■ 60–69.9 Moderately Free
- ■ 50–59.9 Mostly Unfree
- □ 0–49.9 Repressed
- ▨ Not Ranked

Source: Terry Miller and Anthony B. Kim, *2015 Index of Economic Freedom* (Washington, DC: The Heritage Foundation and Dow Jones & Company, Inc., 2015). http://www.heritage.org/index.

Map 2 🏠 heritage.org

South and Central America/Caribbean

The Bahamas
Cuba
Haiti
Dominican Republic
Belize
Honduras
Jamaica
Guatemala
El Salvador
Nicaragua
Costa Rica
Panama
Colombia
Ecuador
Venezuela
Guyana
Suriname
Dominica
St. Lucia
Barbados
Trinidad & Tobago
St. Vincent & The Grenadines
Peru
Brazil
Bolivia
Paraguay
Chile
Argentina
Uruguay

Economic Freedom Scores

- 80–100 Free
- 70–79.9 Mostly Free
- 60–69.9 Moderately Free
- 50–59.9 Mostly Unfree
- 0–49.9 Repressed
- Not Ranked

Note: French Guiana not depicted because it is French territory.

Source: Terry Miller and Anthony B. Kim, *2015 Index of Economic Freedom* (Washington, DC: The Heritage Foundation and Dow Jones & Company, Inc., 2015), http://www.heritage.org/index.

Map 3 ☎ heritage.org

Economic Freedom in South and Central America / Caribbean Countries

World Rank	Regional Rank	Country	Overall Score	Change from 2014	Property Rights	Freedom from Corruption	Fiscal Freedom	Government Spending	Business Freedom	Labor Freedom	Monetary Freedom	Trade Freedom	Investment Freedom	Financial Freedom
7	1	Chile	78.5	-0.2	90	71.0	76.5	83.3	69.3	67.0	85.6	82.0	90	70
28	2	Colombia	71.7	1.0	50	36.0	80.3	76.0	81.5	81.7	80.1	81.2	80	70
35	3	Saint Lucia	70.2	-0.5	70	71.0	77.7	65.8	75.6	79.8	85.5	72.0	65	40
41	4	The Bahamas	68.7	-1.1	70	71.0	97.8	83.2	68.9	75.3	78.8	52.2	30	60
43	5	Uruguay	68.6	-0.7	70	73.0	77.1	65.1	72.6	64.3	71.6	81.8	80	30
44	6	Saint Vincent and the Grenadines	68.0	1.0	70	62.0	73.3	75.3	70.8	78.2	82.3	68.4	60	40
46	7	Barbados	67.9	-0.4	80	75.0	73.8	42.1	71.6	69.2	78.2	63.8	65	60
47	8	Peru	67.7	0.3	40	38.0	78.6	88.5	67.7	63.4	83.9	87.0	70	60
48	9	Jamaica	67.7	1.0	40	38.0	81.5	73.2	85.9	76.5	71.4	75.0	85	50
51	10	Costa Rica	67.2	0.3	50	53.0	80.0	89.9	64.5	54.6	75.8	83.8	70	50
61	11	Dominica	66.1	0.9	60	58.0	73.6	61.5	71.6	68.7	89.5	72.8	75	30
62	12	El Salvador	65.7	-0.5	35	38.0	79.4	85.5	53.3	53.3	82.5	85.2	75	70
67	13	Trinidad and Tobago	64.1	1.4	50	38.0	79.0	69.3	65.3	76.6	74.3	78.6	60	50
68	14	Panama	64.1	0.7	30	35.0	84.5	78.8	71.5	41.5	76.4	78.4	75	70

(continued on next page)

following the global financial turmoil, these young free-market democracies have sustained their openness to global markets and competition, pursued regulatory reform, and shrunk the size of their governments. Each has moved up in the *Index* rankings every year since 2012, outperforming many older members of the European Union such as Spain, Portugal, France, and Italy.

SOUTH AND CENTRAL AMERICA/ CARIBBEAN

In the South and Central America/Caribbean region, 29 countries are distributed throughout the rankings in a more bell-shaped way than is found among the countries of any other region. All but eight countries have received an economic freedom score between 50 and 70 in the 2015 *Index*, and 14 countries fall in the middle economic freedom category of "moderately free." There is no "free" economy, but three "mostly free" economies (Chile, Colombia, and Saint Lucia) lead the region. Recording its highest score ever in the 2015 *Index*, Colombia has solidified its ranking as the second freest in the region. Although Haiti has moved out of the ranks of the "repressed," five countries (Cuba, Venezuela, Argentina, Bolivia, and Ecuador) persist with poor policy choices that trap their citizens in the lowest category of economic freedom.

Although countries in the region demonstrate a high degree of economic and political diversity, the stark reality in common across the region is that economies are underperforming and stagnating due to the lack or even loss of economic freedom. The foundations of well-functioning free-market democracy remain fragile in the South and Cen-

Economic Freedom in South and
Central America / Caribbean Countries (continued)

World Rank	Regional Rank	Country	Overall Score	Change from 2014	Property Rights	Freedom from Corruption	Fiscal Freedom	Government Spending	Business Freedom	Labor Freedom	Monetary Freedom	Trade Freedom	Investment Freedom	Financial Freedom
83	15	Paraguay	61.1	-0.9	30	24.0	96.0	81.9	58.4	26.3	78.3	81.4	75	60
86	16	Dominican Republic	61.0	-0.3	30	29.0	84.1	87.1	53.5	57.5	76.0	77.8	75	40
87	17	Guatemala	60.4	-0.8	20	29.0	79.6	94.1	54.7	50.6	76.8	84.6	65	50
108	18	Nicaragua	57.6	-0.8	10	28.0	78.4	76.6	58.0	56.7	67.8	85.4	65	50
116	19	Honduras	57.4	0.3	30	26.0	84.9	78.7	53.2	28.0	75.4	77.6	60	60
117	20	Belize	56.8	0.1	30	6.7	82.4	78.3	59.1	61.8	79.3	70.4	50	50
118	21	Brazil	56.6	-0.3	50	42.0	68.4	50.9	53.6	52.1	69.4	69.6	50	60
123	22	Guyana	55.5	-0.2	25	27.0	68.7	70.8	63.8	74.5	78.4	72.0	45	30
129	23	Suriname	54.2	0.0	35	36.0	69.3	73.8	42.2	81.9	77.2	66.2	30	30
151	24	Haiti	51.3	2.4	10	19.0	80.3	76.2	43.1	63.7	73.5	77.6	40	30
156	25	Ecuador	49.2	1.2	15	35.0	79.1	51.0	51.4	51.3	68.2	71.4	30	40
163	26	Bolivia	46.8	-1.6	10	34.0	86.8	60.9	53.7	25.5	69.7	77.6	10	40
169	27	Argentina	44.1	-0.5	15	34.0	66.8	41.2	52.8	43.3	59.6	68.8	30	30
176	28	Venezuela	34.3	-2.0	5	20.0	75.0	52.0	41.6	24.2	42.8	62.8	0	20
177	29	Cuba	29.6	0.9	10	46.0	61.8	0.0	20.0	20.0	64.8	63.8	0	10

Table 4 ☎ heritage.org

tral America/Caribbean region. With widespread corruption and the weak protection of property rights aggravating systemic shortcomings such as regulatory inefficiency and monetary instability caused by various market distortions, the region as a whole has become increasingly vulnerable to competing deceptive models of governance based on cronyism and populism.

Over the past year, economic freedom in the South and Central America/Caribbean region has improved in 13 countries while declining in 15. Suriname scored the same as the previous year. The erosion of economic freedom in populous countries such as Brazil and Argentina is particularly troubling, exacerbating poverty and increasing the challenge of fostering broad-based sustainable growth in the future.

MIDDLE EAST/NORTH AFRICA

The Middle East/North Africa region continues to be a critical global hot spot for economic, political, and security vulnerabilities. The majority of the Middle East/North Africa region's 15 economies graded by the *Index* continue to be only "moderately free" or "mostly unfree," with Algeria and Iran considered "repressed." Algeria, Yemen, and Bahrain recorded three of the 10 largest score declines in the 2015 *Index*, while Egypt and Israel were among the best in improving economic freedom this year.

Since early 2011, many countries in the region have been undergoing socioeconomic upheaval, with outcomes far from certain. The lives of many ordinary people in the region have yet to

2015 Index of Economic Freedom

Middle East/North Africa

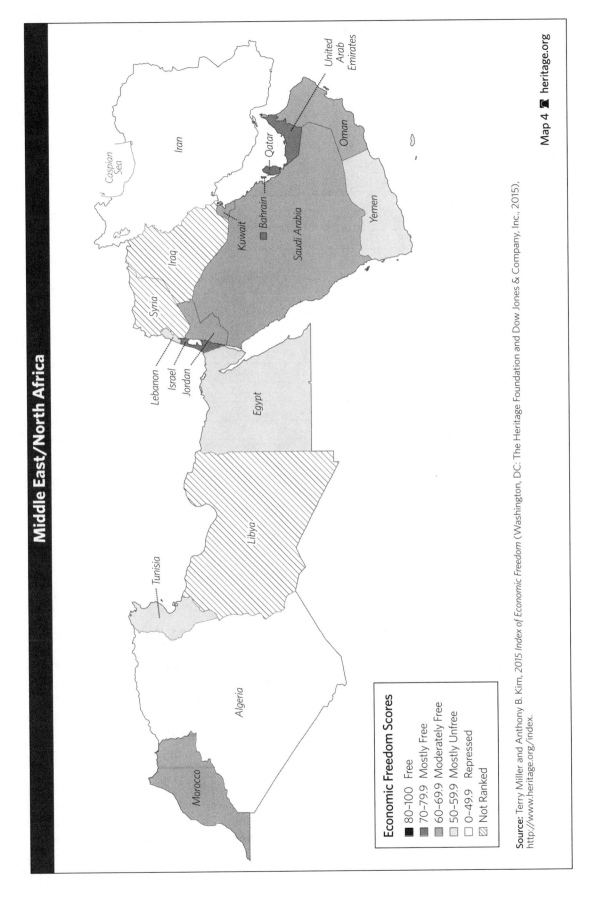

Economic Freedom Scores

- ■ 80-100 Free
- ■ 70-79.9 Mostly Free
- ■ 60-69.9 Moderately Free
- ☐ 50-59.9 Mostly Unfree
- ☐ 0-49.9 Repressed
- ☐ Not Ranked
- ▨ [hatched pattern]

Source: Terry Miller and Anthony B. Kim, *2015 Index of Economic Freedom* (Washington, DC: The Heritage Foundation and Dow Jones & Company, Inc., 2015), http://www.heritage.org/index.

Map 4 ☎ heritage.org

Economic Freedom in Middle East/North African Countries

World Rank	Regional Rank	Country	Overall Score	Change from 2014	Property Rights	Freedom from Corruption	Fiscal Freedom	Government Spending	Business Freedom	Labor Freedom	Monetary Freedom	Trade Freedom	Investment Freedom	Financial Freedom
18	1	Bahrain	73.4	-1.7	60	48.0	99.9	73.1	72.5	83.1	74.2	78.6	65	80
25	2	United Arab Emirates	72.4	1.0	55	69.0	99.5	85.8	74.7	83.8	83.8	82.4	40	50
32	3	Qatar	70.8	-0.4	70	68.0	99.7	71.9	70.5	71.2	79.7	81.8	45	50
33	4	Israel	70.5	2.1	75	61.0	61.9	47.8	72.4	67.1	81.6	88.6	80	70
38	5	Jordan	69.3	0.1	60	45.0	93.7	70.7	59.1	74.4	80.6	79.6	70	60
56	6	Oman	66.7	-0.7	55	47.0	98.5	44.2	68.4	76.1	76.2	76.8	65	60
74	7	Kuwait	62.5	0.2	45	43.0	97.7	61.1	58.6	64.2	74.0	76.2	55	50
77	8	Saudi Arabia	62.1	-0.1	40	46.0	99.7	61.9	65.8	72.7	68.4	76.4	40	50
89	9	Morocco	60.1	1.8	40	37.0	70.9	61.0	68.8	33.4	81.9	78.2	70	60
94	10	Lebanon	59.3	-0.1	20	28.0	91.3	70.6	54.7	60.7	72.0	75.8	60	60
107	11	Tunisia	57.7	0.4	40	41.0	74.3	70.8	81.2	69.1	74.8	61.2	35	30
124	12	Egypt	55.2	2.3	20	32.0	85.8	68.0	65.4	53.6	67.4	70.0	50	40
133	13	Yemen	53.7	-1.8	30	18.0	91.5	59.9	54.0	57.1	68.5	77.6	50	30
157	14	Algeria	48.9	-1.9	30	36.0	80.0	38.7	66.6	50.5	71.2	60.8	25	30
171	15	Iran	41.8	1.5	10	25.0	81.2	93.0	57.0	51.3	48.7	41.4	0	10
N/A	N/A	Iraq	N/A	N/A	N/A	16.0	N/A	43.8	57.7	74.4	73.6	N/A	N/A	N/A
N/A	N/A	Libya	N/A	N/A	10	15.0	95.0	37.5	46.8	66.7	71.4	80.0	5	N/A
N/A	N/A	Syria	N/A	N/A	10	17.0	N/A	N/A	57.3	49.1	N/A	N/A	0	20

Table 5 ☎ heritage.org

change for the better. Of the Arab Spring economies, Tunisia and Egypt have shown the most encouraging results over the past year. However, Yemen and Bahrain continue to be on downward paths in terms of economic freedom, and grading of economic freedom for Iraq, Libya, and Syria remains suspended because of ongoing violence and unrest.

Structural and institutional problems abound throughout the region, and private-sector growth continues to lag far behind levels needed to provide adequate jobs for growing populations. Taken as a whole, the Middle East/North Africa region's lack of job opportunities continues to be a serious problem, particularly for younger members of the labor force whose average unemployment rate is close to 25 percent.

Undoubtedly, mounting economic problems will not be solved simply by holding elections or allowing greater expressions of dissent. Existing policies and practices continue to restrict economic freedom. Over the past year, business freedom, the lack of which contributed to igniting Arab Spring protests, has declined in 11 of the 18 countries in the region. Equally troublesome is that costly subsidies on energy and food, which place a considerable burden on budgets and stand in the way of sound sustainable economic development, are still on the rise as many governments in the region continue to rely on lavish subsides to quell social and political unrest.

Asia and the Pacific

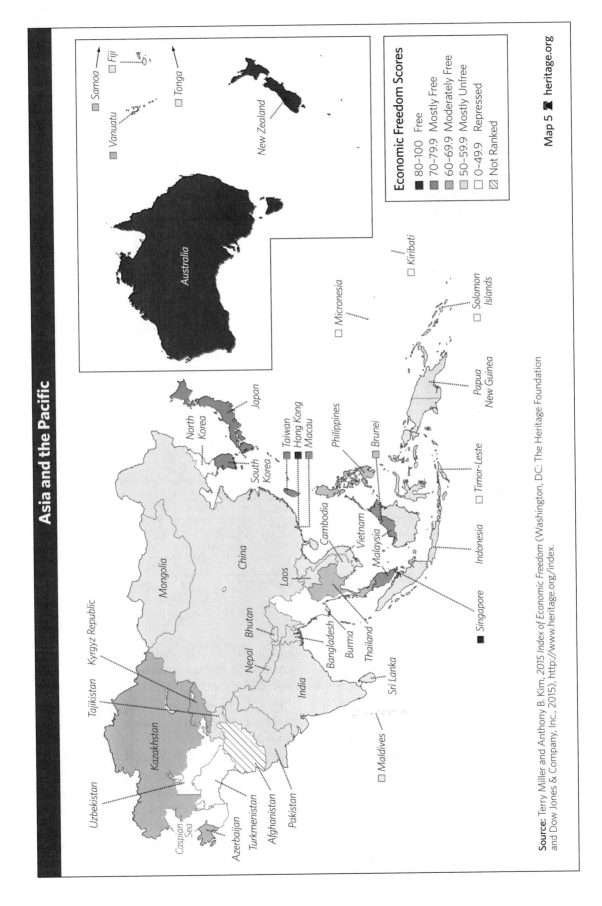

Economic Freedom Scores

- **80–100** Free
- **70–79.9** Mostly Free
- **60–69.9** Moderately Free
- **50–59.9** Mostly Unfree
- **0–49.9** Repressed
- Not Ranked

Map 5 ☎ heritage.org

Source: Terry Miller and Anthony B. Kim, *2015 Index of Economic Freedom* (Washington, DC: The Heritage Foundation and Dow Jones & Company, Inc., 2015), http://www.heritage.org/index.

Economic Freedom in Asia-Pacific Countries

World Rank	Regional Rank	Country	Overall Score	Change from 2014	Property Rights	Freedom from Corruption	Fiscal Freedom	Government Spending	Business Freedom	Labor Freedom	Monetary Freedom	Trade Freedom	Investment Freedom	Financial Freedom
1	1	Hong Kong	89.6	-0.5	90	75.0	93.2	89.7	100.0	95.9	81.8	90.0	90	90
2	2	Singapore	89.4	0.0	90	86.0	91.2	93.8	96.9	96.9	83.7	90.0	85	80
3	3	New Zealand	82.1	0.9	95	91.0	70.4	43.0	95.5	91.4	87.6	86.8	80	80
4	4	Australia	81.4	-0.6	90	81.0	63.7	61.8	94.1	81.6	85.3	86.4	80	90
14	5	Taiwan	75.1	1.2	70	61.0	80.4	87.1	92.4	55.2	83.3	86.4	75	60
20	6	Japan	73.3	0.9	80	74.0	68.7	47.1	84.1	90.2	86.7	82.6	70	50
29	7	South Korea	71.5	0.3	75	55.0	72.5	67.9	89.7	51.1	81.6	72.6	70	80
31	8	Malaysia	70.8	1.2	55	50.0	84.4	74.0	93.5	75.7	80.8	80.0	55	60
34	9	Macau	70.3	-1.0	60	49.7	71.8	91.8	60.0	50.0	74.9	90.0	85	70
39	10	Brunei	68.9	-0.1	35	60.0	87.0	63.6	68.3	96.9	76.6	81.8	70	50
69	11	Kazakhstan	63.3	-0.4	25	26.0	93.2	85.0	73.7	87.0	74.6	79.0	40	50
75	12	Thailand	62.4	-0.9	40	35.0	81.5	81.4	72.5	63.5	69.9	75.4	45	60
76	13	The Philippines	62.2	2.1	30	36.0	79.1	89.3	55.3	58.2	78.8	75.4	60	60
78	14	Samoa	61.9	0.8	60	38.0	80.2	46.5	73.6	78.4	81.2	75.8	55	30
82	15	Kyrgyz Republic	61.3	0.2	20	24.0	93.6	53.2	73.7	85.0	73.8	80.2	60	50
84	16	Vanuatu	61.1	1.6	40	33.5	97.2	83.8	51.5	46.4	82.9	75.4	60	40
85	17	Azerbaijan	61.0	-0.3	20	28.0	88.1	59.7	74.5	79.1	79.8	76.0	55	50
95	18	Tonga	59.3	1.1	20	28.6	87.2	79.0	74.1	92.1	73.5	78.4	40	20
96	19	Mongolia	59.2	0.3	30	38.0	83.9	35.6	68.2	82.7	69.2	74.8	50	60
98	20	Fiji	59.0	0.3	25	22.3	81.3	74.6	63.2	75.2	78.3	70.2	50	50
101	21	Sri Lanka	58.6	-1.4	35	37.0	85.0	88.4	72.5	58.7	68.2	71.6	30	40
105	22	Indonesia	58.1	-0.4	30	32.0	83.3	88.3	49.3	48.7	74.9	74.8	40	60

(continued on next page)

ASIA-PACIFIC

For two years in a row, the Asia–Pacific region has outperformed the other five regions in terms of advancing economic freedom. Since 2013, the region as a whole has recorded a cumulative score gain of close to 1.5 points. The Asia–Pacific area continues to have by far the largest number of the world's "free" economies. Hong Kong, Singapore, New Zealand, and Australia lead the *Index*. Nonetheless, the region is marked by sharp disparities in levels of economic freedom, with six of the world's 20 freest economies but also seven of the 20 least free countries. Over 60 percent of the 41 countries in the Asia–Pacific region score between 40 and 60 on the economic freedom scale, remaining either "mostly unfree" or "repressed."

Despite the stark divergences, the region on the whole continues to demonstrate an impressive degree of economic resilience and dynamism. Asia is home to the world's largest economies and a number of fast-growing emerging economies. As indicated by the region's high level of trade freedom, Asia–Pacific economies have been capitalizing on the freer flow of goods and services both around the world and within the region. Facilitating vibrant commercial engagement beyond borders and ampli-

Economic Freedom in Asia-Pacific Countries (continued)

World Rank	Regional Rank	Country	Overall Score	Change from 2014	Property Rights	Freedom from Corruption	Fiscal Freedom	Government Spending	Business Freedom	Labor Freedom	Monetary Freedom	Trade Freedom	Investment Freedom	Financial Freedom
110	23	Cambodia	57.5	0.1	25	20.0	90.5	87.5	29.2	62.2	78.7	72.2	60	50
115	24	Bhutan	57.4	0.7	60	63.0	82.6	60.1	61.9	81.1	66.0	49.4	20	30
121	25	Pakistan	55.6	0.4	30	28.0	77.7	86.1	65.6	42.1	71.2	65.6	50	40
128	26	India	54.6	-1.1	55	36.0	79.4	78.3	43.3	48.7	65.3	64.6	35	40
131	27	Bangladesh	53.9	-0.2	20	27.0	72.7	92.0	62.2	63.7	67.7	59.0	45	30
134	28	Maldives	53.4	2.4	25	21.9	95.5	50.6	85.8	73.4	74.1	47.8	30	30
137	29	Papua New Guinea	53.1	-0.8	20	25.0	66.9	68.7	53.5	74.5	72.7	85.0	35	30
139	30	China	52.7	0.2	20	40.0	69.7	81.5	52.1	63.0	74.2	71.8	25	30
140	31	Tajikistan	52.7	0.7	20	22.0	92.1	81.9	65.4	46.4	69.6	74.6	25	30
148	32	Vietnam	51.7	0.9	15	31.0	79.1	77.1	61.5	62.9	66.8	78.6	15	30
150	33	Laos	51.4	0.2	15	26.0	86.2	86.8	59.5	57.1	74.5	58.6	30	20
152	34	Nepal	51.3	1.2	30	31.0	85.6	88.9	65.7	44.3	70.5	61.8	5	30
154	35	Micronesia	49.6	-0.2	30	30.0	93.2	0.0	51.0	79.1	76.9	81.0	25	30
159	36	Solomon Islands	47.0	0.8	30	25.0	61.1	25.7	67.7	68.6	74.3	73.0	15	30
160	37	Uzbekistan	47.0	0.5	15	17.0	90.2	67.3	73.1	64.2	63.5	69.8	0	10
161	38	Burma	46.9	0.4	10	21.0	86.9	77.9	28.7	79.3	66.1	74.2	15	10
164	39	Kiribati	46.4	0.1	30	29.2	73.0	0.0	56.8	83.9	80.6	55.4	25	30
167	40	Timor-Leste	45.5	2.3	20	30.0	64.7	0.0	59.8	72.0	68.7	79.6	40	20
172	41	Turkmenistan	41.4	-0.8	5	17.0	94.0	93.5	30.0	20.0	64.2	80.0	0	10
178	42	North Korea	1.3	0.3	5	8.0	0.0	0.0	0.0	0.0	0.0	0.0	0	0
N/A	N/A	Afghanistan	N/A	N/A	N/A	8.0	91.7	81.2	61.4	67.5	72.6	N/A	55	N/A

Table 6 ☎ heritage.org

fying economic development, trade agreements have proliferated in the Asia–Pacific region over the past decade. There are now some 40 completed intraregional trade agreements and over 100 agreements with countries outside the region.

In the 2015 *Index*, the Asia–Pacific region has recorded some notable changes in economic freedom. The scores of 27 countries have improved, and those of 14 have worsened. Of those that have improved, seven countries, including Taiwan, Vietnam, and Laos, have achieved their highest economic freedom score ever in the 2015 *Index*. Four countries (Taiwan, South Korea, the Philip-

pines, and Burma) have achieved five consecutive years of advancing economic freedom.

On the other hand, Hong Kong's economic freedom score has tumbled to the territory's second lowest rating since 2007. Although Hong Kong continues strongly to maintain the features of an economically free society, the city's waning institutional uniqueness has placed it at a critical crossroads. The current failure to deliver promised meaningful electoral reform has galvanized greater pro-democracy sentiments in Hong Kong and undermined trust and confidence in the government.

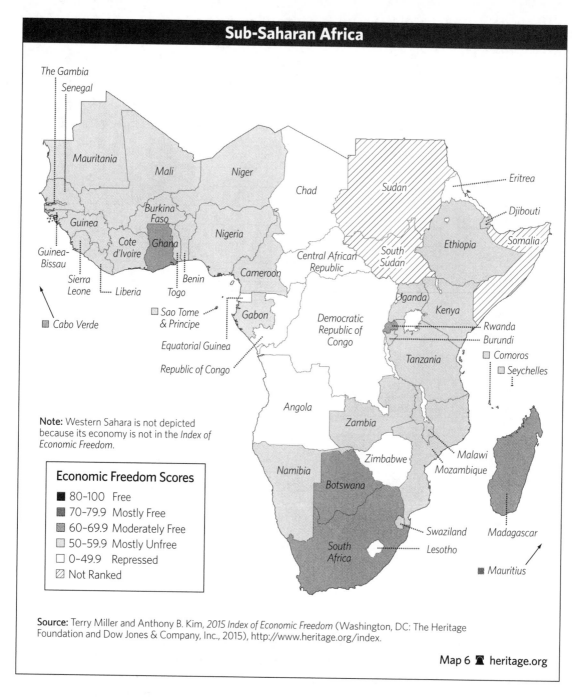

Sub-Saharan Africa

Note: Western Sahara is not depicted because its economy is not in the *Index of Economic Freedom*.

Economic Freedom Scores

- 80–100 Free
- 70–79.9 Mostly Free
- 60–69.9 Moderately Free
- 50–59.9 Mostly Unfree
- 0–49.9 Repressed
- Not Ranked

Source: Terry Miller and Anthony B. Kim, *2015 Index of Economic Freedom* (Washington, DC: The Heritage Foundation and Dow Jones & Company, Inc., 2015), http://www.heritage.org/index.

Map 6 ☎ heritage.org

SUB-SAHARAN AFRICA

Unlike other regions that have a more diverse and a wider range of economic freedom scores, Sub-Saharan Africa continues to show variations only within the lower bands of economic freedom. There is no "free" economy in the region, and Mauritius continues to lead the region as a "moderately free" economy. A majority of 46 nations are ranked either "mostly unfree" or "repressed." In fact, nine of the world's 26 "repressed" economies are in Sub-Saharan Africa.

Nevertheless, together with the Asia–Pacific region, Sub-Saharan African has experienced the most widespread increases in economic freedom over the past year. In the 2015 *Index*, economic freedom has advanced in 59 percent of the economies of the Sub-Saharan Africa

Economic Freedom in Sub-Saharan Africa Countries

World Rank	Regional Rank	Country	Overall Score	Change from 2014	Property Rights	Freedom from Corruption	Fiscal Freedom	Government Spending	Business Freedom	Labor Freedom	Monetary Freedom	Trade Freedom	Investment Freedom	Financial Freedom
10	1	Mauritius	76.4	-0.1	65	52.0	91.9	87.4	78.0	68.2	77.6	88.4	85	70
36	2	Botswana	69.8	-2.2	70	64.0	79.5	61.9	66.8	70.0	73.9	72.2	70	70
60	3	Cabo Verde	66.4	0.3	75	58.0	78.3	67.9	61.8	42.1	81.0	69.6	70	60
65	4	Rwanda	64.8	0.1	30	53.0	80.2	79.2	59.5	84.5	76.0	80.8	65	40
71	5	Ghana	63.0	-1.2	50	46.0	84.6	70.8	62.5	56.9	69.2	64.8	65	60
72	6	South Africa	62.6	0.1	50	42.0	69.5	68.2	73.0	61.6	74.9	76.6	50	60
79	7	Madagascar	61.7	0.0	45	28.0	90.9	94.7	62.3	45.1	79.2	71.8	50	50
91	8	Swaziland	59.9	-1.3	40	39.0	76.4	68.6	60.5	69.3	73.9	76.0	55	40
92	9	Uganda	59.7	-0.2	25	26.0	73.3	89.0	43.3	87.5	76.3	76.6	60	40
93	10	Namibia	59.6	0.2	30	48.0	66.7	56.0	64.3	90.9	74.3	71.2	55	40
99	11	Benin	58.8	1.7	30	36.0	68.3	86.7	55.2	53.2	79.9	58.4	70	50
100	12	Zambia	58.7	-1.7	30	38.0	71.9	78.0	68.2	46.0	73.2	76.8	55	50
102	13	Burkina Faso	58.6	-0.3	25	38.0	82.4	79.8	49.6	57.8	80.0	68.2	65	40
103	14	Côte d'Ivoire	58.5	0.8	35	27.0	77.7	82.4	65.4	46.0	75.0	71.4	55	50
104	15	Gabon	58.3	0.5	40	34.0	77.5	74.6	57.9	64.3	78.4	61.0	55	40
106	16	Senegal	57.8	2.4	40	41.0	71.3	74.6	54.6	39.5	83.0	74.0	60	40
109	17	Tanzania	57.5	-0.3	30	33.0	79.9	79.3	45.0	61.4	69.7	67.0	60	50
112	18	Djibouti	57.5	1.6	25	36.0	81.2	57.1	55.4	66.6	78.9	54.8	70	50
113	19	The Gambia	57.5	-2.0	25	28.0	75.4	73.4	55.7	66.7	70.8	65.0	65	50
114	20	Seychelles	57.5	1.3	50	54.0	79.8	59.4	67.7	63.9	76.0	44.0	50	30
119	21	Mali	56.4	0.9	25	28.0	69.6	89.2	47.2	50.7	81.1	73.2	60	40
120	22	Nigeria	55.6	1.3	30	25.0	85.2	76.1	48.3	77.7	70.4	63.8	40	40
122	23	Kenya	55.6	-1.5	30	27.0	78.0	72.1	47.9	63.8	72.8	64.0	50	50
125	24	Mozambique	54.8	-0.2	30	30.0	75.2	66.5	60.9	37.9	82.0	75.4	40	50
126	25	Malawi	54.8	-0.6	40	37.0	78.5	49.0	49.1	63.1	53.8	72.2	55	50

(continued on next page)

region. Most impressively, six of the top 10 largest score improvements in the 2015 *Index* have occurred in countries in this region. São Tomé and Príncipe, Democratic Republic of Congo, Togo, Senegal, Burundi, and Zimbabwe have all recorded score gains of two points or more. Liberia and Sierra Leone, two post-conflict countries currently confronting challenges of containing Ebola, have continued to move up from the ranks of the economically "repressed." Also encouraging is that six countries in the region, including Angola, Comoros, Guinea–Bissau, and Seychelles, have registered sustained growth in economic freedom throughout the past five years.

Many countries in the region have substantial growth momentum. The positive economic results achieved through advancing economic freedom

World Rank	Regional Rank	Country	Overall Score	Change from 2014	Property Rights	Freedom from Corruption	Fiscal Freedom	Government Spending	Business Freedom	Labor Freedom	Monetary Freedom	Trade Freedom	Investment Freedom	Financial Freedom
127	26	Niger	54.6	-0.5	30	34.0	76.6	83.6	39.2	40.9	81.3	65.6	55	40
132	27	Burundi	53.7	2.3	20	21.0	73.5	61.3	61.4	68.1	69.8	72.2	60	30
135	28	Mauritania	53.3	0.1	25	30.0	80.2	59.8	50.5	52.1	76.6	69.0	50	40
136	29	São Tomé and Príncipe	53.3	4.5	25	42.0	87.8	41.4	65.1	45.8	70.7	75.2	50	30
138	30	Togo	53.0	3.1	30	29.0	69.7	78.1	51.9	43.4	80.4	67.8	50	30
141	31	Liberia	52.7	0.3	25	38.0	83.0	69.9	60.1	43.9	72.7	74.4	40	20
142	32	Comoros	52.1	0.7	30	28.0	64.5	78.8	47.3	52.0	77.9	73.0	40	30
144	33	Guinea	52.1	-1.4	15	24.0	68.1	79.5	51.6	74.4	66.7	61.2	40	40
145	34	Guinea-Bissau	52.0	0.7	20	19.0	89.1	88.0	39.6	61.7	77.5	65.4	30	30
146	35	Cameroon	51.9	-0.7	25	25.0	71.7	87.8	41.6	47.8	75.6	59.6	35	50
147	36	Sierra Leone	51.7	1.2	10	30.0	80.8	87.5	53.4	41.6	68.5	70.2	55	20
149	37	Ethiopia	51.5	1.5	30	33.0	77.4	91.4	55.9	56.4	66.1	64.4	20	20
155	38	Lesotho	49.6	0.1	35	49.0	68.5	0.0	54.7	63.9	75.2	64.6	45	40
158	39	Angola	47.9	0.2	15	23.0	84.5	50.1	47.4	43.2	65.4	70.2	40	40
165	40	Chad	45.9	1.4	20	19.0	46.2	83.6	27.1	47.7	75.6	55.2	45	40
166	41	Central African Republic	45.9	-0.8	15	25.0	65.0	92.0	27.2	37.5	69.6	52.4	45	30
168	42	Congo, Dem. Rep.	45.0	4.4	10	22.0	72.9	85.7	42.8	38.4	75.1	63.0	20	20
170	43	Congo, Republic of	42.7	-1.0	10	22.0	67.4	60.7	36.8	36.0	71.6	62.4	30	30
173	44	Equatorial Guinea	40.4	-4.0	10	19.0	75.4	31.4	37.5	33.5	78.3	53.8	35	30
174	45	Eritrea	38.9	0.4	10	20.0	57.0	71.8	18.2	65.5	57.8	69.2	0	20
175	46	Zimbabwe	37.6	2.1	10	21.0	66.6	74.2	37.1	23.7	75.4	58.4	0	10
N/A	N/A	Somalia	N/A	N/A	N/A	8.0	N/A	N/A	N/A	N/A	N/A	N/A	N/A	N/A
N/A	N/A	Sudan	N/A	N/A	N/A	11.0	86.4	94.5	49.0	43.8	52.8	55.6	15	N/A

Table 7 ☎ heritage.org

have created valuable impetus for additional institutional reforms that are needed to ensure long-term economic development. However, the region as a whole continues to underperform in following through on policy changes that will help the emergence of a more dynamic private sector.

Despite sustained high growth over the past decade, structural transformation remains patchy in many African countries. Limited diversification has resulted in less broad-based growth, with exports often concentrated in sectors with little scope for sustained productivity increases. More critically, uneven economic playing fields, exacerbated by the weak rule of law, continue to leave those who lack connections with only limited prospects for a brighter future. It remains to be seen whether the region's political leaders have the political will to undertake the fundamental economic reforms that are needed to translate narratives of "Africa Rising" into reality.

Chapter 7

The Countries

This chapter reports data on economic freedom for each of the countries included in the 2015 *Index of Economic Freedom*, the 21st annual edition. Of the 186 countries included in the 2015 *Index*, 178 are fully scored and ranked. Because of insufficient data, Afghanistan, Iraq, Kosovo, Libya, Somalia, Sudan, Syria, and Liechtenstein are covered without numerical grading.

For analytical understanding and presentational clarity, the 10 economic freedoms are grouped into four broad categories of economic freedom:

- **Rule of law** (property rights, freedom from corruption);
- **Government size** (fiscal freedom, government spending);
- **Regulatory efficiency** (business freedom, labor freedom, monetary freedom); and
- **Market openness** (trade freedom, investment freedom, financial freedom).

Ranked countries are given a score ranging from 0 to 100 on each of the 10 components of economic freedom, and these scores are then averaged (using equal weights) to compute the country's final economic freedom score. In addition to the scores, the country pages include in each case a brief introduction describing the economic strengths and weaknesses and the political and economic background influencing a country's performance, as well as a statistical profile documenting the country's main economic indicators.

To assure objectivity and reliability within each of the 10 components on which the countries are graded, every effort has been made to use the same data source consistently for all countries; when data are unavailable from the primary source, secondary sources are used. (For details, see Appendix, "Methodology.")

DEFINING THE "QUICK FACTS"

Each country page includes "Quick Facts" with nine different categories of information. Unless otherwise indicated, the data in each country's profile are for 2013 (the year for which the most recent data are widely available) and in current 2013 U.S. dollars (also the most recent available). The few cases in which no reliable statistical data were available are indicated by "n/a." Definitions and sources for each category of information are as follows.

Population: 2013 data from World Bank, *World Development Indicators Online 2014*. For some countries, other sources include the country's statistical agency and/or central bank.

GDP: Gross domestic product—total production of goods and services—adjusted to reflect purchasing power parity (PPP). The primary source for GDP data is World Bank, *World Development Indicators Online 2014*. The major secondary source is International Monetary Fund, *World Economic Outlook Database, 2014*. Other sources include a country's statistical agency and/or central bank.

GDP growth rate: The annual percentage growth rate of real GDP derived from constant national currency units. Annual percent changes are year-on-year. The primary source is International Monetary Fund, *World Economic Outlook Database, 2014*. Secondary sources include World Bank, *World Development Indicators Online 2014*; Economist Intelligence Unit, *Data Tool*; Asian Development Bank, *Asian Development Outlook 2014*; and a country's statistical agency and/or central bank.

GDP five-year compound annual growth: The compound average growth rate measured over a specified period of time. The compound annual growth rate is measured using data from 2008 to 2013, based on real GDP expressed in constant national currency units. It is calculated by taking the nth root of the total percentage growth rate, where n is the number of years in the period being considered. The primary source is International Monetary Fund, *World Economic Outlook Database, 2014*. Secondary sources are World Bank, *World Development Indicators Online 2014*, and Asian Development Bank, *Asian Development Outlook 2014*.

GDP per capita: Gross domestic product (adjusted for PPP) divided by total population. The sources for these data are World Bank, *World Development Indicators Online 2014*; International Monetary Fund, *World Economic Outlook Database, 2014*; U.S. Central Intelligence Agency, *The World Factbook 2014*; and a country's statistical agency and/or central bank.

Unemployment rate: A measure of the portion of the workforce that is not employed but is actively seeking work. Data are from International Labour Organization, *Global Employment Trends 2014*.

Inflation: The annual percent change in consumer prices as measured for 2013 (or the most recent available year). The primary source for 2013 data is International Monetary Fund, *World Economic Outlook Database, 2014*. Secondary sources are Economist Intelligence Unit, *Data Tool*; Asian Development Bank, *Asian Development Outlook 2014*; and a country's statistical agency and/or central bank.

Foreign direct investment (FDI) inward flow: The total annual inward flow of FDI in current 2013 U.S. dollars, reported in millions. FDI flows are defined as investments that acquire a lasting management interest (10 percent or more of voting stock) in a local enterprise by an investor operating in another country. Such investment is the sum of equity capital, reinvestment of earnings, other long-term capital, and short-term capital as shown in the balance of payments and both short-term and long-term international loans. Data are from United Nations Conference on Trade and Development, *World Investment Report 2014*.

Public debt: Gross government debt as a percentage of GDP, which indicates the cumulative total of all government borrowings less repayments that are denominated in a country's currency. Public debt is different from external debt, which reflects the foreign currency liabilities of both the private and public sectors and must be financed out of foreign exchange earnings. The primary sources for 2013 data are International Monetary Fund, *World Economic Outlook Database, 2014*; International Monetary Fund, *Article IV Staff Reports*, 2011–2014; and a country's statistical agency. The data source for U.S. public debt is United States Office of Management and Budget. Concerning the U.S. data, gross debt includes both publicly held debt (bonds and Treasury bills held by foreigners, corporations, individual citizens, investment vehicles, etc.) and intragovernmental debt such as Social Security trust funds.

COMMONLY USED ACRONYMS

CARICOM: Caribbean Community and Common Market, composed of Antigua and Barbuda, the Bahamas, Barbados, Belize, Dominica, Grenada, Guyana, Haiti, Jamaica, Montserrat, Saint Lucia, Saint Kitts and Nevis, Saint Vincent and the Grenadines, Suriname, and Trinidad and Tobago.

CEMAC: Central African Economic and Monetary Community, which includes Cameroon, the Central African Republic, Chad, the Republic of Congo, Equatorial Guinea, and Gabon.

EU: European Union, consisting of Austria, Belgium, Bulgaria, Cyprus, Croatia, the Czech Republic, Denmark, Estonia, Finland, France, Germany, Greece, Hungary, Ireland, Italy, Latvia, Lithuania, Luxembourg, Malta, the Netherlands, Poland, Portugal, Romania, Slovakia, Slovenia, Spain, Sweden, and the United Kingdom.

IMF: International Monetary Fund, established in 1945 to help stabilize countries during crises; now includes 188 member countries.

OECD: Organisation for Economic Co-operation and Development, an international organization of developed countries, founded in 1948; now includes 34 member countries.

SACU: Southern African Customs Union, consisting of Botswana, Lesotho, Namibia, South Africa, and Swaziland.

WTO: World Trade Organization, founded in 1995 as the central organization dealing with the rules of trade between nations and based on signed agreements among member countries. As of September 2014, there were 160 member economies.

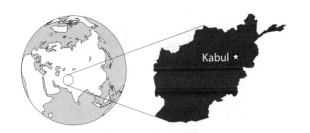

AFGHANISTAN

Kabul ★

Economic Freedom Score

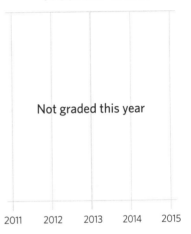

50
25   75
Least
free 0 ──────── 100 Most free

This economy is not graded

A fghanistan's economic freedom could not be fully assessed in the 2015 *Index of Economic Freedom* because of a lack of sufficient comparable data. This assessment is based on the limited information available from government and international sources. Afghanistan will receive an economic freedom score and ranking in future editions as more data become available.

While undergoing substantial political, economic, and social transformation over the past decade, Afghanistan has achieved rapid yet volatile economic growth. The construction and agricultural sectors have been the key contributors to economic expansion, which has averaged around 10 percent over the past five years. There have been noticeable improvements in such areas as health, education, and microfinance, but dependence on high levels of foreign aid continues.

The economy still lacks the overall institutional capacity to enhance productivity and promote self-sustaining growth. Although some progress has been made in developing the private sector, it remains small and informal, and there is little impetus for more vibrant entrepreneurial activity. Political uncertainty and security challenges undermine the rule of law and continue to be formidable.

BACKGROUND: Ashraf Ghani Ahmadzai is Afghanistan's new president following a hotly contested election marred by allegations of vote-rigging. After three months of political wrangling between run-off candidates Ghani and former Afghan Foreign Minister Abdullah Abdullah, the two agreed to form a unity government. The terms of the agreement call for President Ghani, who won the election according to Afghanistan's Independent Election Commission, to share power with Abdullah, who was named Chief Executive Officer. Ghani's signing of the Bilateral Security Agreement with the U.S. shortly after his assumption of power opens the way for the U.S. to leave a non-combat presence of 9,800 troops in the country. Taliban insurgents continue to attack Afghan security forces and civilians. Afghanistan's economy remains hobbled by poor infrastructure, insurgency, and corruption. The agricultural sector depends heavily on cultivation of the opium poppy.

Freedom Trend

Not graded this year

2011   2012   2013   2014   2015

Country Comparisons

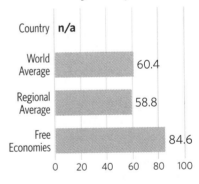

Country	n/a
World Average	60.4
Regional Average	58.8
Free Economies	84.6

0   20   40   60   80   100

Quick Facts

Population: 30.6 million
GDP (PPP): $35.1 billion
3.6% growth in 2013
5-year compound annual growth 10.5%
$1,150 per capita
Unemployment: 8.5%
Inflation (CPI): 7.4%
FDI Inflow: $69.3 million
Public Debt: 6.1% of GDP

2013 data unless otherwise noted.
Data compiled as of September 2014.

How Do We Measure Economic Freedom?
See page 475 for an explanation of the methodology
or visit the *Index* Web site at *heritage.org/index*.

THE TEN ECONOMIC FREEDOMS

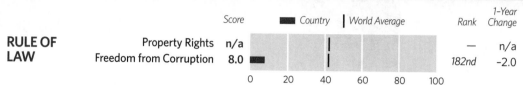

		Score	■ Country	│ World Average	Rank	1-Year Change
RULE OF LAW	Property Rights	n/a			—	n/a
	Freedom from Corruption	8.0			182nd	-2.0

In 2015, as foreign troops prepare to withdraw, the government is still challenged by serious corruption, heavy and persistent drug trafficking, and weak institutional capacity. Afghanistan's judicial system is severely underdeveloped. Protection of property rights is weak. The lack of property registries or a land-titling database leads to title disputes, and an estimated 80 percent of land is held and transferred informally.

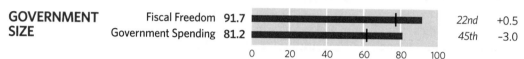

		Score		Rank	1-Year Change
GOVERNMENT SIZE	Fiscal Freedom	91.7		22nd	+0.5
	Government Spending	81.2		45th	-3.0

Despite efforts to improve the system, governance and security issues impede tax collection. The revenue that is collected comes from corporate and individual income taxes of 20 percent. Sales taxes also contribute to fiscal receipts. Expenditures have been rising and currently equal about 25 percent of the domestic economy. Future fiscal health may depend on the extent of donor contributions.

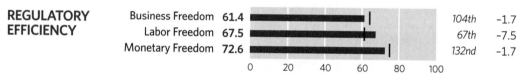

		Score		Rank	1-Year Change
REGULATORY EFFICIENCY	Business Freedom	61.4		104th	-1.7
	Labor Freedom	67.5		67th	-7.5
	Monetary Freedom	72.6		132nd	-1.7

The entrepreneurial environment still holds back private production and investment. Processes for establishing businesses and obtaining licenses have been relatively streamlined, but other structural barriers persist. The presence of a large informal economy continues to dampen development of a functioning labor market. The government has very limited influence on monetary policy.

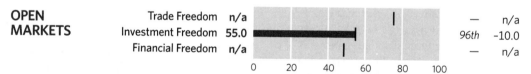

		Score		Rank	1-Year Change
OPEN MARKETS	Trade Freedom	n/a		—	n/a
	Investment Freedom	55.0		96th	-10.0
	Financial Freedom	n/a		—	n/a

Afghanistan has a 6.8 percent average tariff rate. Complex customs procedures deter imports. The constitution prohibits discrimination against foreign investors, but foreign ownership of land is not allowed. The underdeveloped financial sector remains dominated by banking. There are 17 commercial banks and three state banks, but scarce access to financing hinders private-sector growth.

Long-Term Score Change: n/a

RULE OF LAW		GOVERNMENT SIZE		REGULATORY EFFICIENCY		OPEN MARKETS	
Property Rights	n/a	Fiscal Freedom	n/a	Business Freedom	n/a	Trade Freedom	n/a
Freedom from Corruption	n/a	Government Spending	n/a	Labor Freedom	n/a	Investment Freedom	n/a
				Monetary Freedom	n/a	Financial Freedom	n/a

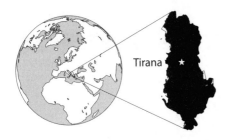

Tirana

ALBANIA

Economic Freedom Score

Least free 0   100 Most free

65.7

Albania's economic freedom score is 65.7, making its economy the 63rd freest in the 2015 *Index*. Its overall score has decreased by 1.2 points, with notable declines in business freedom, fiscal freedom, and investment freedom. Albania is ranked 29th among the 43 countries in the Europe region, and its overall score is above the world average.

Over the past five years, Albania has advanced its economic freedom score by 1.7 points. With score increases in six of the 10 economic freedoms, including trade freedom and the management of public spending, it has fluctuated within the category of "moderately free." However, in the 2015 *Index*, the upward trend of economic freedom in Albania has reversed.

The Albanian economy is mostly in private hands, but the state continues to control key enterprises, particularly in the energy sector. Although foreign direct investment has increased in recent years, overall levels still remain among the lowest in the region. Deeper structural reforms to diversify the economy and improve labor market flexibility remain critical for more broad-based economic development. Property rights and freedom from corruption are weak, and government interference and regulatory control continue to limit dynamic investment and overall economic efficiency.

BACKGROUND: Socialist Edi Rama was elected prime minister in June 2013, defeating conservative eight-year incumbent Sali Berisha. Rama campaigned on a promise to secure European Union candidacy status within a year. Albania achieved full membership in NATO in April 2009 and continues to make a small contribution to the NATO-led mission in Afghanistan. Albania has received significant foreign direct investment to fund development of its oil and natural gas resources. Its transportation and energy infrastructure remain poor by European standards. Corruption is an impediment to growth. The economy is dominated by agriculture, which employs about half of the workforce, and services, including tourism.

Freedom Trend

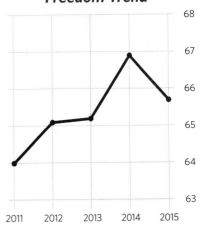

Country Comparisons

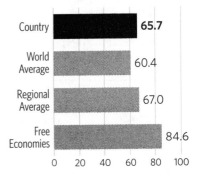

Quick Facts

Population: 2.8 million
GDP (PPP): $26.5 billion
0.7% growth in 2013
5-year compound annual growth 2.4%
$9,506 per capita
Unemployment: 16.1%
Inflation (CPI): 1.9%
FDI Inflow: $1.2 billion
Public Debt: 70.5% of GDP

2013 data unless otherwise noted.
Data compiled as of September 2014.

How Do We Measure Economic Freedom?
See page 475 for an explanation of the methodology
or visit the *Index* Web site at *heritage.org/index*.

THE TEN ECONOMIC FREEDOMS

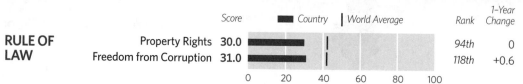

		Score		Rank	1-Year Change
RULE OF LAW	Property Rights	30.0		94th	0
	Freedom from Corruption	31.0		118th	+0.6

In 2014, Albania became an EU candidate country on the condition that it make further progress in reforming the judiciary and law enforcement to combat deeply rooted corruption and organized crime, especially human trafficking, fraudulent documents, and money laundering. Judges sometimes face threats and physical violence. Protection of intellectual and real property rights is weak, particularly for land tenure.

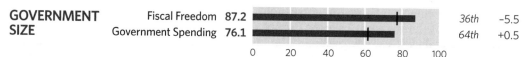

		Score		Rank	1-Year Change
GOVERNMENT SIZE	Fiscal Freedom	87.2		36th	−5.5
	Government Spending	76.1		64th	+0.5

The government has raised its top marginal individual and corporate income tax rates. The top individual income tax rate is now 23 percent, and the top corporate tax rate is 15 percent. Overall tax receipts remain stagnant at around 23 percent of gross domestic product. Public expenditures amount to 28.2 percent of the domestic economy, and public debt is equal to around 70 percent of domestic income.

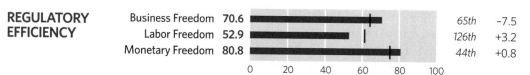

		Score		Rank	1-Year Change
REGULATORY EFFICIENCY	Business Freedom	70.6		65th	−7.5
	Labor Freedom	52.9		126th	+3.2
	Monetary Freedom	80.8		44th	+0.8

Despite recent reforms, the inefficient business environment still impedes broader economic development. On average, launching a business requires five procedures, but obtaining necessary permits can take over 200 days. In the absence of a well-functioning labor market, informal labor activity persists. Price controls and government subsidies distort domestic prices for electricity, water, agricultural products, and railroad transportation.

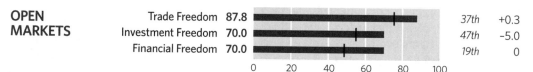

		Score		Rank	1-Year Change
OPEN MARKETS	Trade Freedom	87.8		37th	+0.3
	Investment Freedom	70.0		47th	−5.0
	Financial Freedom	70.0		19th	0

Albania has a 1.1 percent average tariff rate, and there are few non-tariff barriers. Promotion of foreign investment is a stated goal, but there are limits on foreign ownership of agricultural land. Banks account for over 90 percent of total financial-sector assets. Although the banking system remains relatively well capitalized, nonperforming loans have risen to over 20 percent of all loans.

Long-Term Score Change (since 1995)

RULE OF LAW		GOVERNMENT SIZE		REGULATORY EFFICIENCY		OPEN MARKETS	
Property Rights	−20.0	Fiscal Freedom	+5.5	Business Freedom	+0.6	Trade Freedom	+28.8
Freedom from Corruption	+21.0	Government Spending	+41.8	Labor Freedom	+3.9	Investment Freedom	0
				Monetary Freedom	+58.7	Financial Freedom	+20.0

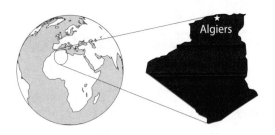

ALGERIA

Algeria's economic freedom score is 48.9, making its economy the 157th freest in the 2015 *Index*. Its overall score is 1.9 points lower than last year due to considerable declines in investment freedom and the management of government spending that outweigh improvements in freedom from corruption and monetary freedom. Algeria is ranked 14th among the 15 countries in the Middle East/North Africa region, and its score remains lower than both the regional and world averages.

Algeria's economy has been on a declining path of economic freedom over the past five years. Having registered the seventh-largest overall score decline in the 2015 *Index*, the economy is now rated "repressed." Public spending, bolstered by the hydrocarbon sector, has been expanding in recent years, undermining fiscal governance.

As policies to sustain regulatory efficiency and open markets have been neglected or even reversed, the economy has become more dependent on the state-dominated energy sector. Tariff and non-tariff barriers, coupled with burdensome business and investment regulations, continue to hamper development of a more dynamic private sector and interfere with much-needed diversification of the economic base.

BACKGROUND: President Abdelaziz Bouteflika won a fourth term in April 2014 despite rarely appearing in public after a 2013 stroke. After the "Arab Spring" protests swept Tunisia and Libya, the government introduced some political reforms, including an end to state-of-emergency restrictions on civil liberties that had lasted almost two decades. The socialist model adopted after independence from France in 1962 has hindered development. Formal-sector unemployment remains persistently high, and there is a housing shortage. Algeria is the world's sixth-largest exporter of natural gas and has the world's 10th-largest natural gas reserves and 16th-largest oil reserves. The government began a five-year, $286 billion program to modernize infrastructure in 2010 and appears to be trying to attract foreign and domestic private investment and to diversify the economy.

Economic Freedom Score

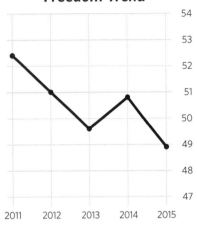

Freedom Trend

Country Comparisons

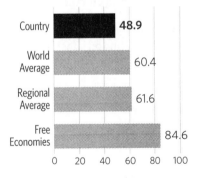

Quick Facts

Population: 37.9 million
GDP (PPP): $285.5 billion
2.7% growth in 2013
5-year compound annual growth 2.8%
$7,534 per capita
Unemployment: 9.8%
Inflation (CPI): 3.3%
FDI Inflow: $1.7 billion
Public Debt: 9.2% of GDP

2013 data unless otherwise noted.
Data compiled as of September 2014.

THE TEN ECONOMIC FREEDOMS

		Score		Rank	1-Year Change
RULE OF LAW	Property Rights	30.0		94th	0
	Freedom from Corruption	36.0		95th	+7.3

In 2014, the government introduced constitutional revisions that appear to be pro-democratic, but few expect improvements in the generally weak, slow, and opaque judicial system. High levels of corruption plague Algeria's business and public sectors, especially the energy sector. An estimated one-half of all economic transactions occur in the informal sector. Most real property remains in government hands.

		Score		Rank	1-Year Change
GOVERNMENT SIZE	Fiscal Freedom	80.0		83rd	−0.5
	Government Spending	38.7		154th	−12.3

Algeria's modest tax revenue amounts to around 12 percent of GDP. Individual income and corporate tax rates remain unchanged at 35 percent and 25 percent, respectively. Companies involved in tourism and mining pay reduced rates. Other taxes include a value-added tax. Government expenditures equal 45.2 percent of the domestic economy, and public debt is below 10 percent of gross domestic product.

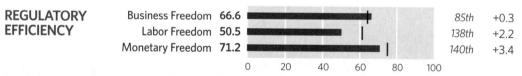

		Score		Rank	1-Year Change
REGULATORY EFFICIENCY	Business Freedom	66.6		85th	+0.3
	Labor Freedom	50.5		138th	+2.2
	Monetary Freedom	71.2		140th	+3.4

Despite some enhancement of the business environment, significant bureaucratic impediments to entrepreneurial activity and economic diversification persist. The labor market remains rigid, contributing to a high youth unemployment rate. Generous but unsustainable state spending on subsidies for food and fuel, price ceilings, and redistribution schemes to control prices have been used to stave off political unrest.

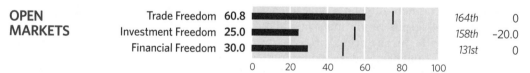

		Score		Rank	1-Year Change
OPEN MARKETS	Trade Freedom	60.8		164th	0
	Investment Freedom	25.0		158th	−20.0
	Financial Freedom	30.0		131st	0

Algeria has an 8.6 percent average tariff rate. Imports of medical equipment and used earth-moving equipment are restricted. The government screens foreign investment, and regulatory barriers discourage some investors. The financial system remains subject to government interference. State-owned banks provide over 80 percent of loans. The degree of financial intermediation remains low.

Long-Term Score Change (since 1995)

RULE OF LAW		GOVERNMENT SIZE		REGULATORY EFFICIENCY		OPEN MARKETS	
Property Rights	−20.0	Fiscal Freedom	+31.2	Business Freedom	−3.4	Trade Freedom	+6.6
Freedom from Corruption	−14.0	Government Spending	−30.8	Labor Freedom	−5.4	Investment Freedom	−25.0
				Monetary Freedom	+12.0	Financial Freedom	−20.0

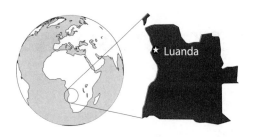

ANGOLA

Economic Freedom Score

47.9

Angola's economic freedom score is 47.9, making its economy the 158th freest in the 2015 *Index*. Its overall score has improved by 0.2 point, reflecting improvements in freedom from corruption, labor freedom, and monetary freedom that were largely offset by deteriorations in the control of government spending and fiscal freedom. Angola is ranked 39th out of 46 countries in the Sub-Saharan Africa region, and its score remains far below world and regional averages.

Over the past five years, Angola has advanced its economic freedom by 1.7 points. It has recorded an overall improvement each year since 2011, with gains in six of the 10 economic freedoms, including business freedom, investment freedom, and freedom from corruption.

Nonetheless, significant corruption and a lack of judicial independence because of political interference continue to undermine the foundations for economic progress. The government is highly dependent on oil and diamond revenues and plays an overly dominant role in the economy, undermining efficiency. Monopolies and quasi-monopolies are common in the most important sectors of the economy.

BACKGROUND: José Eduardo dos Santos has ruled Angola for more than three decades. His Popular Movement for the Liberation of Angola (MPLA) won parliamentary elections in August 2012, only the second such elections since the end of the 27-year civil war in 2002. Angola is Africa's second-largest oil producer, with much of its proven reserves concentrated in Cabinda province, a region plagued by a separatist conflict. Nevertheless, oil production has nearly doubled from 800,000 barrels a day in 2001 to over 1.4 million barrels a day in 2014. In 2014, a French oil company invested $16 billion in an offshore project. Angola also has natural gas, diamonds, hydroelectric potential, and rich agricultural land. Nonetheless, most Angolans remain poor and dependent on subsistence farming.

Freedom Trend

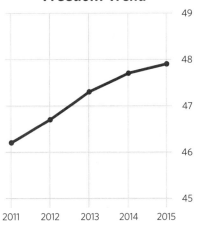

Country Comparisons

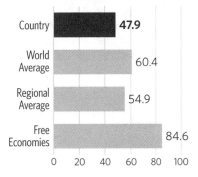

Quick Facts

Population: 20.8 million
GDP (PPP): $130.1 billion
4.1% growth in 2013
5-year compound annual growth 3.8%
$6,247 per capita
Unemployment: 8.4%
Inflation (CPI): 8.8%
FDI Inflow: –$4.3 billion
Public Debt: 26.6% of GDP

2013 data unless otherwise noted.
Data compiled as of September 2014.

How Do We Measure Economic Freedom?
See page 475 for an explanation of the methodology
or visit the *Index* Web site at *heritage.org/index*.

THE TEN ECONOMIC FREEDOMS

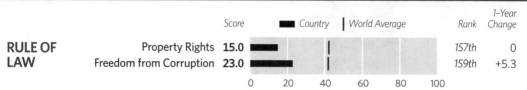

		Score	■ Country	│ World Average	Rank	1-Year Change
RULE OF LAW	Property Rights	15.0			157th	0
	Freedom from Corruption	23.0			159th	+5.3

Money-laundering legislation was passed in 2014, but government corruption and patronage remain endemic, especially in the extractive sectors. Bribery often underpins business activity. Although courts occasionally rule against the government, the judiciary is subject to extensive political influence, particularly from the executive. Property registration fees can be prohibitively expensive. Overall, protection of property rights is weak.

		Score			Rank	Change
GOVERNMENT SIZE	Fiscal Freedom	84.5			52nd	-3.2
	Government Spending	50.1			133rd	-5.2

The individual income tax rate is 17 percent, and the corporate tax rate is 35 percent. Other taxes include fuel and consumption taxes. Tax revenue is equal to 5.6 percent of gross domestic product. Government expenditures are 40.8 percent of domestic income, and public debt has fallen to less than 30 percent of the economy.

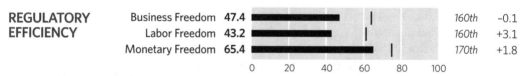

		Score			Rank	Change
REGULATORY EFFICIENCY	Business Freedom	47.4			160th	-0.1
	Labor Freedom	43.2			160th	+3.1
	Monetary Freedom	65.4			170th	+1.8

Despite the recent implementation of more streamlined business start-up procedures, burdensome regulations still hinder private-sector development. The regulatory system lacks transparency and clarity, and regulations are enforced inconsistently. The formal labor market is underdeveloped. Price controls are pervasive in many sectors, and energy subsidies amounting to 4 percent of GDP are the highest in the region.

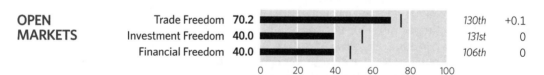

		Score			Rank	Change
OPEN MARKETS	Trade Freedom	70.2			130th	+0.1
	Investment Freedom	40.0			131st	0
	Financial Freedom	40.0			106th	0

Angola has a 7.4 percent average tariff rate. The government procurement process favors domestic companies. Most land is owned by the state, and investment in several sectors is restricted. The underdeveloped financial system has only a limited role in the economy, hampering private entrepreneurial growth. The banking sector, dominated by commercial banks, continues to evolve. There is no stock exchange.

Long-Term Score Change (since 1995)

RULE OF LAW		GOVERNMENT SIZE		REGULATORY EFFICIENCY		OPEN MARKETS	
Property Rights	-15.0	Fiscal Freedom	+22.9	Business Freedom	+7.4	Trade Freedom	+45.2
Freedom from Corruption	-7.0	Government Spending	+50.1	Labor Freedom	-1.7	Investment Freedom	+10.0
				Monetary Freedom	+65.4	Financial Freedom	+10.0

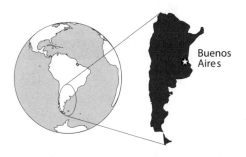

Buenos Aires

ARGENTINA

Economic Freedom Score

50

25　　75

Least free　0

Most free　100

44.1

Argentina's economic freedom score is 44.1, making its economy the 169th freest in the 2015 *Index*. Its overall score has decreased by 0.5 point due to declines in five of the 10 economic freedoms, including the management of government spending, labor freedom, and business freedom. Argentina ranks 27th out of 29 countries in the South and Central America/Caribbean region, and its overall score remains far below the regional and world averages.

Argentina continues to be mired in a climate of economic repression. Severely hampered by state interference, the formal economy grows increasingly stagnant as informal economic activity expands. Monetary stability is particularly weak, and there are price controls on almost all goods and services. Government interference in the financial sector further distorts price levels.

Over the past five years, Argentina's economic freedom score has dropped by over 7 points, plunging the economy into the "repressed" category. Considerable losses have occurred in eight of the 10 economic freedoms, most notably in government spending, investment freedom, business freedom, and property rights. In the 2015 *Index*, Argentina has recorded its lowest economic freedom score ever.

BACKGROUND: Argentina will elect a new president in October 2015. President Cristina Fernandez de Kirchner, elected in 2007 and re-elected in 2011, is constitutionally barred from seeking a third term. Argentina's investment profile has been badly damaged by monetary and fiscal mismanagement, rising protectionism, and expropriations. The 2001 debt default remains a stumbling block. A U.S. court decision in favor of holdouts who did not accept previous restructuring offers sent the country into default again in 2014. Economic growth has plummeted, and the poverty rate has increased. Capital controls have aggravated capital flight, and the economy has dropped from third-largest to fourth-largest in Latin America. Argentina continues to claim possession of the Falkland Islands despite a vote by residents to remain under British rule.

Freedom Trend

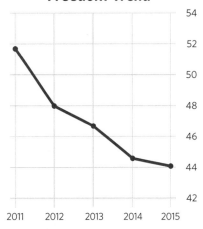

Country Comparisons

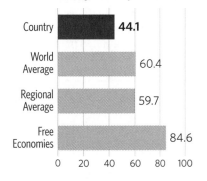

Country	44.1
World Average	60.4
Regional Average	59.7
Free Economies	84.6

0　20　40　60　80　100

Quick Facts

Population: 41.5 million
GDP (PPP): $777.9 billion
4.3% growth in 2013
5-year compound annual growth 4.9%
$18,749 per capita
Unemployment: 7.3%
Inflation (CPI): 10.6%
FDI Inflow: $9.1 billion
Public Debt: 46.9% of GDP

2013 data unless otherwise noted.
Data compiled as of September 2014.

How Do We Measure Economic Freedom?
See page 475 for an explanation of the methodology or visit the *Index* Web site at *heritage.org/index*.

THE TEN ECONOMIC FREEDOMS

		Score		Rank	1-Year Change
RULE OF LAW	Property Rights	15.0		157th	0
	Freedom from Corruption	34.0		107th	+4.5

Corruption plagues Argentine society, and scandals are common. In June 2014, Vice President Amado Boudou was charged with bribery and conduct incompatible with public office. The justice system is afflicted by scores of tenured but incompetent and corrupt judges. The lower courts are highly politicized, and the relatively independent Supreme Court has received heightened pressure from the government.

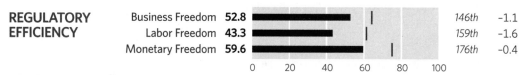

		Score		Rank	1-Year Change
GOVERNMENT SIZE	Fiscal Freedom	66.8		151st	+3.3
	Government Spending	41.2		150th	-8.7

Argentina's individual and corporate income tax rates are 35 percent. Other taxes include a value-added tax, a wealth tax, and a tax on financial transactions. The tax burden is 29.5 percent of gross domestic product. Government spending amounts to over 40 percent of GDP, and public debt is about half of the size of the domestic economy. The government is in technical default because of restructured bond payments.

		Score		Rank	1-Year Change
REGULATORY EFFICIENCY	Business Freedom	52.8		146th	-1.1
	Labor Freedom	43.3		159th	-1.6
	Monetary Freedom	59.6		176th	-0.4

Government regulation has increased, undermining efficiency and productivity growth. Establishing a new business is cumbersome, and obtaining necessary permits is costly. Reforms of the rigid labor market have long been stalled. The government underreports official inflation statistics; regulates prices of electricity, water, gasoline, and hundreds of other products; and pressures companies to fix prices and wages.

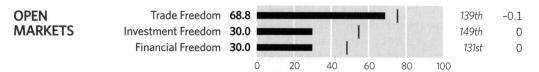

		Score		Rank	1-Year Change
OPEN MARKETS	Trade Freedom	68.8		139th	-0.1
	Investment Freedom	30.0		149th	0
	Financial Freedom	30.0		131st	0

Argentina has a 5.6 percent tariff rate. Non-tariff barriers include import licensing and an official "import substitution" policy. Foreign investment in some sectors of the economy is regulated. The government exercises considerable control of financial activities. Argentina's largest bank, which is state-owned and the sole financial institution in some areas, has been known to allocate credit based on political expediency.

Long-Term Score Change (since 1995)

RULE OF LAW		GOVERNMENT SIZE		REGULATORY EFFICIENCY		OPEN MARKETS	
Property Rights	-55.0	Fiscal Freedom	-13.9	Business Freedom	-32.2	Trade Freedom	+10.4
Freedom from Corruption	-16.0	Government Spending	-45.4	Labor Freedom	-0.6	Investment Freedom	-40.0
				Monetary Freedom	-1.5	Financial Freedom	-20.0

ARMENIA

Economic Freedom Score

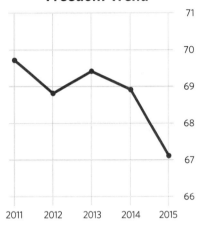

Least free 0

Most free 100

25 50 75

67.1

World Rank: 52   **Regional Rank: 23**

Armenia's economic freedom score is 67.1, making its economy the 52nd freest in the 2015 *Index*. Its overall score has declined by 1.8 points from last year, reflecting considerable deterioration in property rights, labor freedom, and monetary freedom. This decline was the eighth-largest in the 2015 *Index*. Armenia is ranked 23rd among the 43 countries in the Europe region, and its score puts it above the world and regional averages.

Armenia's transition to a more dynamic and market-oriented economy has been facilitated by openness to global commerce and by regulatory reforms designed to encourage entrepreneurial activity. However, continued efforts, particularly to strengthen the independence of the judiciary and eradicate corruption, are needed to ensure progress in long-term economic development.

Although Armenia performs relatively well in most categories compared to world averages, the historical gains are not fully institutionalized, and the country's economic freedom has been on a five-year downward path. This decline has taken place across six of the 10 economic freedoms, most notably in labor freedom, freedom from corruption, and monetary freedom.

BACKGROUND: President Serzh Sargsyan of the center-right Republican Party won a second five-year term in 2013. A cease-fire in Armenia's 24-year dispute with Azerbaijan over the Nagorno–Karabakh region has been in effect since 1994, but minor hostilities continue. The economy relies on manufacturing, services, remittances, and agriculture. Armenia announced in September 2013 that it was suspending an association agreement with the European Union and would seek membership in the Russian-backed Eurasian Economic Union. The eurozone financial crisis and the sluggish Russian economy are drags on growth, and unemployment is high. The government relies heavily on loans from the World Bank, the International Monetary Fund, the Asian Development Bank, and Russia. Armenia is running a modest budget deficit.

Freedom Trend

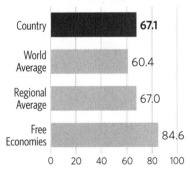

Country Comparisons

Country	**67.1**
World Average	60.4
Regional Average	67.0
Free Economies	84.6

0 20 40 60 80 100

Quick Facts

Population: 3.3 million
GDP (PPP): $20.4 billion
3.2% growth in 2013
5-year compound annual growth 0.3%
$6,191 per capita
Unemployment: 16.0%
Inflation (CPI): 5.8%
FDI Inflow: $370.0 million
Public Debt: 41.9% of GDP

2013 data unless otherwise noted.
Data compiled as of September 2014.

How Do We Measure Economic Freedom?
See page 475 for an explanation of the methodology
or visit the *Index* Web site at *heritage.org/index*.

THE TEN ECONOMIC FREEDOMS

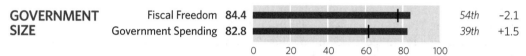

	Score	Rank	1-Year Change
RULE OF LAW			
Property Rights	20.0	138th	−10.0
Freedom from Corruption	36.0	95th	+9.3

In 2014, the president dismissed several well-known reformers and formed a new cabinet including officials who alledgedly have grown wealthy from their government connections. For example, the finance minister has long been subject to media allegations of corruption. The judicial system, hobbled by corruption, impedes the enforcement of contracts. Scores for rule of law are below average.

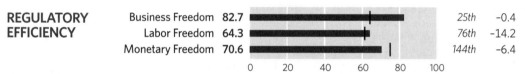

	Score	Rank	1-Year Change
GOVERNMENT SIZE			
Fiscal Freedom	84.4	54th	−2.1
Government Spending	82.8	39th	+1.5

Armenia's individual income tax rate is 26 percent, and its corporate tax rate is 20 percent. Other taxes include a value-added tax and an excise tax. The overall tax burden equals 22 percent of the domestic economy. Government expenditures equal about 24 percent of gross domestic income, and public debt reached a level equal to about 42 percent of the domestic economy in the most recent year.

	Score	Rank	1-Year Change
REGULATORY EFFICIENCY			
Business Freedom	82.7	25th	−0.4
Labor Freedom	64.3	76th	−14.2
Monetary Freedom	70.6	144th	−6.4

Several business reforms have been implemented in recent years. The minimum capital requirement for establishing a business has been eliminated, licensing requirements have been reduced, and the bankruptcy procedure has been modernized. The non-salary cost of labor is moderate, but the informal labor market is sizable. Increased government subsidies distort prices in such sectors as public transportation, electricity, and gas.

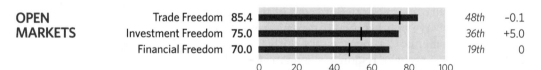

	Score	Rank	1-Year Change
OPEN MARKETS			
Trade Freedom	85.4	48th	−0.1
Investment Freedom	75.0	36th	+5.0
Financial Freedom	70.0	19th	0

Armenia has a 2.3 percent average tariff rate. Non-tariff barriers are low, but there are some bureaucratic barriers to trade and foreign investment. Land ownership is generally limited to domestic investors. The state no longer has a stake in any bank, but the banking sector, which accounts for over 90 percent of total financial-sector assets, still struggles to provide adequate long-term credit or sophisticated financial services.

Long-Term Score Change (since 1996)

RULE OF LAW		GOVERNMENT SIZE		REGULATORY EFFICIENCY		OPEN MARKETS	
Property Rights	−30.0	Fiscal Freedom	+8.6	Business Freedom	+27.7	Trade Freedom	+16.4
Freedom from Corruption	−14.0	Government Spending	+82.8	Labor Freedom	+2.2	Investment Freedom	+45.0
				Monetary Freedom	+70.6	Financial Freedom	+20.0

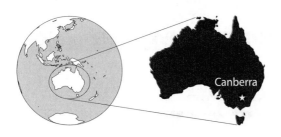

AUSTRALIA

Economic Freedom Score

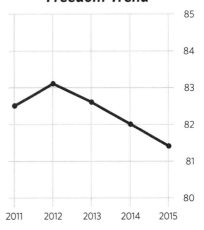

Least free 0 ... 100 Most free

81.4

World Rank: 4   **Regional Rank: 4**

Australia's economic freedom score is 81.4, making its economy the 4th freest in the 2015 *Index*. Its overall score is 0.6 point lower than last year, with gains in monetary freedom and labor freedom outweighed by declines in investment freedom, freedom from corruption, and the control of government spending. Australia is ranked 4th out of 42 countries in the Asia–Pacific region.

Australia's strong commitment to economic freedom has resulted in a policy framework that has facilitated economic dynamism and resilience. Although overall economic freedom has declined slightly over the past five years, the Australian economy performs remarkably well in many of the 10 economic freedoms. Regulatory efficiency remains firmly institutionalized, and well-established open-market policies sustain flexibility, competitiveness, and large flows of trade and investment. In 2014, Australia became the first developed country to repeal a carbon-emissions tax.

Banking regulations are sensible, and lending practices have been relatively prudent. Monetary stability is well maintained, with inflationary pressures under control. A well-functioning independent judiciary ensures strong protection of property rights, and corruption has been minimal.

BACKGROUND: Since the early 1980s, successive governments have deregulated financial and labor markets and reduced trade barriers. In September 2013, Liberal Party leader Tony Abbott was elected prime minister following his coalition's victory in national elections. Australia is one of the Asia–Pacific's wealthiest nations and has enjoyed more than two decades of economic expansion. Australia emerged from the global recession relatively unscathed, but stimulus spending by the previous Labor government generated a fiscal deficit. Australia is internationally competitive in services, technologies, and high-value-added manufactured goods. Mining and agriculture are important sources of exports.

Freedom Trend

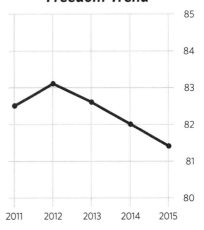

Country Comparisons

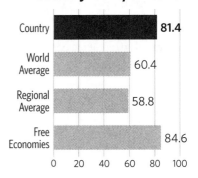

Country	81.4
World Average	60.4
Regional Average	58.8
Free Economies	84.6

0 20 40 60 80 100

Quick Facts

Population: 23.2 million
GDP (PPP): $999.6 billion
2.4% growth in 2013
5-year compound annual growth 2.5%
$43,073 per capita
Unemployment: 5.6%
Inflation (CPI): 2.5%
FDI Inflow: $49.8 billion
Public Debt: 28.8% of GDP

2013 data unless otherwise noted.
Data compiled as of September 2014.

How Do We Measure Economic Freedom?
See page 475 for an explanation of the methodology or visit the *Index* Web site at *heritage.org/index*.

THE TEN ECONOMIC FREEDOMS

		Score	■ Country	World Average	Rank	1-Year Change

RULE OF LAW

	Score	Rank	1-Year Change
Property Rights	90.0	3rd	0
Freedom from Corruption	81.0	9th	−6.7

Australia has a stable political environment with well-established and transparent political processes, a strong legal system, and a professional bureaucracy. Anti-corruption measures are generally effective in discouraging bribery of public officials. Australia's judicial system operates independently and impartially. Property rights are secure, and enforcement of contracts is reliable. Expropriation is highly unusual.

GOVERNMENT SIZE

	Score	Rank	1-Year Change
Fiscal Freedom	63.7	160th	−0.5
Government Spending	61.8	105th	−0.8

The top individual income tax rate is 45 percent, and the top corporate tax rate is 30 percent. Other taxes include a value-added tax and a capital gains tax. Total tax revenues equal about 27 percent of the domestic economy. A controversial carbon tax has been repealed. Government expenditures equal 35.7 percent of the economy, and public debt is equivalent to less than 30 percent of GDP.

REGULATORY EFFICIENCY

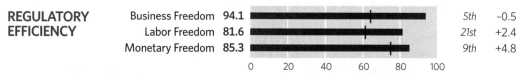

	Score	Rank	1-Year Change
Business Freedom	94.1	5th	−0.5
Labor Freedom	81.6	21st	+2.4
Monetary Freedom	85.3	9th	+4.8

Start-up companies enjoy great flexibility under licensing and other regulatory frameworks. It takes only one procedure to start a business, and no minimum capital is required. Flexible labor regulations facilitate a dynamic labor market, increasing overall productivity. In 2014, the government lifted price controls on electricity to encourage market-based production of power.

OPEN MARKETS

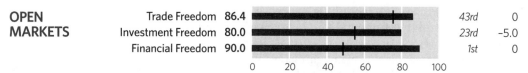

	Score	Rank	1-Year Change
Trade Freedom	86.4	43rd	0
Investment Freedom	80.0	23rd	−5.0
Financial Freedom	90.0	1st	0

Australia has a 1.8 percent average tariff rate, and non-tariff barriers are low. Large-scale foreign investments are subject to review. In 2013, the government rejected a takeover of Australia's GrainCorp by the U.S. firm Archer Daniels Midland. The well-developed financial sector offers a wide range of financing instruments. The banking system has remained stable, and all banks are privately owned.

Long-Term Score Change (since 1995)

RULE OF LAW		GOVERNMENT SIZE		REGULATORY EFFICIENCY		OPEN MARKETS	
Property Rights	0	Fiscal Freedom	+4.1	Business Freedom	+24.1	Trade Freedom	+9.4
Freedom from Corruption	+11.0	Government Spending	+7.9	Labor Freedom	−4.2	Investment Freedom	+10.0
				Monetary Freedom	−1.4	Financial Freedom	0

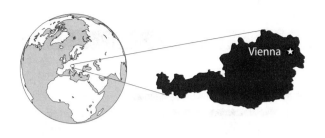

Vienna ★

AUSTRIA

Economic Freedom Score

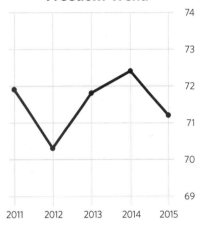

| Least free | 0 | 25 | 50 | 75 | 100 | Most free |

71.2

World Rank: 30   **Regional Rank: 16**

Austria's economic freedom score is 71.2, making its economy the 30th freest in the 2015 *Index*. Its score is 1.2 points worse than last year, with declines in freedom from corruption, labor freedom, and the management of government spending outweighing improvements in business freedom and monetary freedom. Austria is ranked 16th out of 43 countries in the Europe region, and its overall score is well above the regional and world averages.

Despite considerable strains over the past five years, Austria has maintained much of its economic stability and dynamism. Continued strong protection of the rule of law and the foundations of economic freedom is reflected in high scores in property rights and freedom from corruption, but these strengths are not matched by a commitment to limited government. Public spending has been expanding, generating great budgetary pressure.

Counterbalancing excessive government spending and weak fiscal freedom, the transparent and competitive business environment has promoted a thriving entrepreneurial private sector. The banking system has regained much of its characteristic efficiency and competitiveness after being roiled by the global economic crisis.

BACKGROUND: The coalition of the center-left Social Democratic Party and the center-right Austrian People's Party, led by Social Democrat Chancellor Werner Faymann, lost seats in September 2013 but retained a governing majority. Eurosceptic parties made gains. Austria's economy has been relatively resilient through the eurozone crisis, outperforming the economies of many other EU members, and unemployment is the lowest in the eurozone. Yet GDP growth has been modest, and government debt is growing. The government has gradually relinquished control of formerly nationalized oil, gas, steel, and engineering companies and has deregulated telecommunications and electricity. Austria has large service and industrial sectors and a small, highly developed agricultural sector.

Freedom Trend

	74
	73
	72
	71
	70
	69
2011 2012 2013 2014 2015	

Country Comparisons

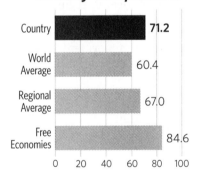

Country	71.2
World Average	60.4
Regional Average	67.0
Free Economies	84.6

0   20   40   60   80   100

Quick Facts

Population: 8.5 million
GDP (PPP): $361.4 billion
0.4% growth in 2013
5-year compound annual growth 0.4%
$42,597 per capita
Unemployment: 4.8%
Inflation (CPI): 2.1%
FDI Inflow: $11.1 billion
Public Debt: 74.2% of GDP

2013 data unless otherwise noted.
Data compiled as of September 2014.

How Do We Measure Economic Freedom?
See page 475 for an explanation of the methodology
or visit the *Index* Web site at *heritage.org/index*.

THE TEN ECONOMIC FREEDOMS

		Score		Rank	1-Year Change
RULE OF LAW	Property Rights	90.0		3rd	0
	Freedom from Corruption	69.0		26th	-6.5

Corruption is relatively rare, and cases are routinely reported in the media. Enforcement is improving but still somewhat haphazard, and legal proceedings in corruption cases are slow. The independent judiciary provides an effective means for protecting property and contractual rights of nationals and foreigners. The land registry, overhauled in 2012, is a reliable and accessible system for recording interests in property.

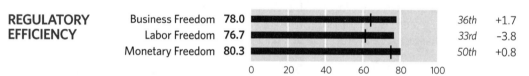

		Score		Rank	1-Year Change
GOVERNMENT SIZE	Fiscal Freedom	50.1		175th	-0.9
	Government Spending	19.8		170th	-3.7

Austria's top individual income tax rate is 50 percent, and its top corporate tax rate is 25 percent. Other taxes include a value-added tax and a tax on real estate transfers. The tax burden equals 43.2 percent of the economy. Government expenditures amount to over 50 percent of gross domestic product, and public debt has remained steady at 74 percent of domestic income.

		Score		Rank	1-Year Change
REGULATORY EFFICIENCY	Business Freedom	78.0		36th	+1.7
	Labor Freedom	76.7		33rd	-3.8
	Monetary Freedom	80.3		50th	+0.8

Austria's overall regulatory framework has been marked by transparency and efficiency, encouraging business innovation and productivity, but the absence of major regulatory reforms has eroded overall competitiveness. With no minimum wage, relatively flexible regulations facilitate employment growth. A high degree of state ownership and regulation remains in the electricity generation and transmission sectors.

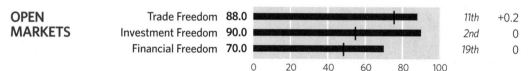

		Score		Rank	1-Year Change
OPEN MARKETS	Trade Freedom	88.0		11th	+0.2
	Investment Freedom	90.0		2nd	0
	Financial Freedom	70.0		19th	0

EU members have a 1.0 percent average tariff rate. Although some non-tariff barriers exist, the EU is relatively open to external trade. Austria is open to most investment, but the regulatory system is complicated. There are no controls on currency transfers, access to foreign exchange, or repatriation of profits. The modern and competitive banking sector provides a wide range of financial services.

Long-Term Score Change (since 1995)

RULE OF LAW		GOVERNMENT SIZE		REGULATORY EFFICIENCY		OPEN MARKETS	
Property Rights	0	Fiscal Freedom	+3.8	Business Freedom	+8.0	Trade Freedom	+7.0
Freedom from Corruption	-21.0	Government Spending	+10.2	Labor Freedom	+3.1	Investment Freedom	+20.0
				Monetary Freedom	-2.6	Financial Freedom	-20.0

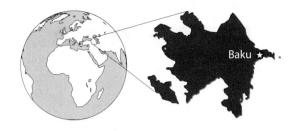

AZERBAIJAN

Economic Freedom Score

61.0

A zerbaijan's economic freedom score is 61.0, making its economy the 85th freest in the 2015 *Index*. Its overall score is 0.3 point lower than last year, reflecting declines in the management of public finance, investment freedom, and trade freedom that outweigh improvements in freedom from corruption and regulatory efficiency. Azerbaijan is ranked 17th out of 41 countries in the Asia–Pacific region, and its overall score is above the regional and global averages.

Azerbaijan's gains in economic freedom over the past five years have moved it into the "moderately free" category. Wide-ranging reforms have resulted in limited progress in regulatory efficiency and economic diversification, improving the overall macroeconomic and entrepreneurial environments. Tax reforms and continued openness to global trade and investment have aided Azerbaijan's gradual transition to a more market-based system.

Nonetheless, substantial challenges remain, particularly in implementing deeper systemic and social reforms to strengthen the foundations of economic freedom. Property rights and freedom from corruption remain fragile, and burdensome regulatory requirements continue to undermine the emergence of a more dynamic private sector and long-term economic development.

BACKGROUND: President Ilham Aliyev was elected to a third term in 2013 amid evidence of massive electoral fraud. His father, Heydar, ruled Azerbaijan first as a Soviet republic and later as an independent country until his death in 2003, when his son succeeded him. An upsurge in violence in 2014 between Armenian and Azerbaijani forces nullified progress in peace talks regarding their dispute over the Nagorno–Karabakh region, which has cost tens of thousands of lives and the loss of about a fifth of Azerbaijan's territory. Falling oil production is expected to be partially offset by natural gas exports. In 2015, construction will begin on the Trans-Anatolian Natural Gas Pipeline to export Azeri gas through Turkey and ease Europe's energy dependence on Russia. Negotiations for accession to the World Trade Organization began in 2002.

Freedom Trend

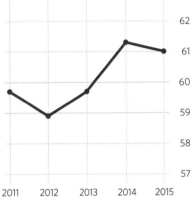

Country Comparisons

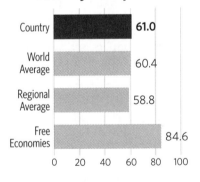

Quick Facts

Population: 9.3 million
GDP (PPP): $102.8 billion
5.8% growth in 2013
5-year compound annual growth 4.4%
$11,044 per capita
Unemployment: 5.5%
Inflation (CPI): 2.4%
FDI Inflow: $2.6 billion
Public Debt: 13.8% of GDP

2013 data unless otherwise noted.
Data compiled as of September 2014.

How Do We Measure Economic Freedom?
See page 475 for an explanation of the methodology
or visit the *Index* Web site at *heritage.org/index.*

THE TEN ECONOMIC FREEDOMS

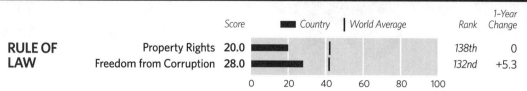

		Score	■ Country | World Average	Rank	1-Year Change
RULE OF LAW	Property Rights	20.0		138th	0
	Freedom from Corruption	28.0		132nd	+5.3

Corruption is widespread, and wealth from oil and gas exports creates growing opportunities for graft. The judiciary is corrupt, inefficient, and largely subservient to the president and ruling party. Government officials are rarely held accountable for corruption. In general, respect for property rights has plummeted. The state appears able to seize any property it wishes, and ordinary citizens have little recourse.

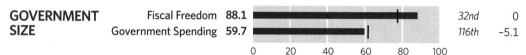

		Score		Rank	1-Year Change
GOVERNMENT SIZE	Fiscal Freedom	88.1		32nd	0
	Government Spending	59.7		116th	−5.1

Azerbaijan's top individual income tax rate is 25 percent, and its top corporate tax rate is 20 percent. Other taxes include a value-added tax and a property tax. The overall tax burden is equal to about 13 percent of gross domestic product. Government expenditures, supported in part by oil revenue, equal 36.7 percent of domestic income. Government debt amounts to less than 15 percent of the domestic economy.

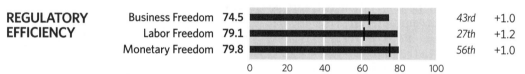

		Score		Rank	1-Year Change
REGULATORY EFFICIENCY	Business Freedom	74.5		43rd	+1.0
	Labor Freedom	79.1		27th	+1.2
	Monetary Freedom	79.8		56th	+1.0

The business start-up process has been streamlined, but licensing requirements remain time-consuming and bureaucratic. Although relatively flexible employment regulations have been put in place, enforcement has been uneven in practice. Price controls are in effect for most energy products, and monopolies, limits on imports, and agricultural subsidies also cause distortions in domestic prices.

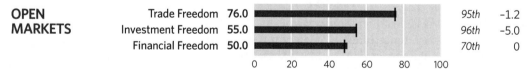

		Score		Rank	1-Year Change
OPEN MARKETS	Trade Freedom	76.0		95th	−1.2
	Investment Freedom	55.0		96th	−5.0
	Financial Freedom	50.0		70th	0

Azerbaijan's average tariff rate is 4.5 percent. Although the country is working to improve its customs procedures, its relatively inefficient regulatory and legal systems can deter trade and investment. Banks hold about 95 percent of total financial-sector assets. Azerbaijan's financial penetration rate remains one of the lowest in the region. Capital markets are dominated by government securities.

Long-Term Score Change (since 1996)

RULE OF LAW		GOVERNMENT SIZE		REGULATORY EFFICIENCY		OPEN MARKETS	
Property Rights	−10.0	Fiscal Freedom	+41.8	Business Freedom	+34.5	Trade Freedom	+21.0
Freedom from Corruption	+18.0	Government Spending	+10.9	Labor Freedom	+14.3	Investment Freedom	+45.0
				Monetary Freedom	+79.8	Financial Freedom	+20.0

THE BAHAMAS

Nassau

Economic Freedom Score

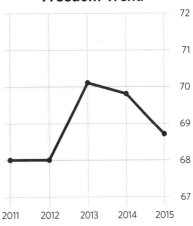

50

25   75

Least free 0   100 Most free

68.7

The Bahamas' economic freedom score is 68.7, making its economy the 41st freest in the 2015 *Index*. Its overall score has decreased by 1.1 points, with notable declines in financial freedom and labor freedom offsetting improvements in freedom from corruption and monetary freedom. The Bahamas' overall score continues to be higher than the regional and world averages, and its economy is the 4th freest out of 29 countries in the South and Central America/Caribbean region.

Over the past half-decade, economic freedom in the Bahamas has improved by 0.7 point despite score declines in the past two years. Gains in economic freedom have been led by strong improvements in freedom from corruption and trade freedom, which have advanced by 16 and 10 points, respectively. More modest improvements have occurred in monetary and fiscal freedoms.

Despite some improvement, corruption remains a problem, and regulatory inefficiency continues to hold back the economic dynamism that should result from the competitive financial sector and a tax regime with no personal or corporate income tax. Ultimately, it is the government's ability to promote more broad-based reforms that will determine the prospects for a long-term and diversified economic expansion.

BACKGROUND: In 2012, Prime Minister Perry Christie and his Progressive Liberal Party won a five-year term. The Bahamian economy centers on tourism, international banking, investment management, and financial services, with tourism accounting for more than 60 percent of GDP. While accession to the World Trade Organization would be a positive step, politicians and the private sector are locked in a dispute about how to replace the revenues that would be lost. Due to its geographic location just 50 miles off the coast of Florida, the country is a major transshipment point for illegal drugs, particularly shipments to the U.S. and Europe, and is used for smuggling illegal migrants into the U.S.

Freedom Trend

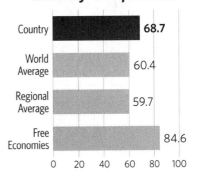

72

71

70

69

68

67

2011   2012   2013   2014   2015

Country Comparisons

Country   **68.7**

World Average   60.4

Regional Average   59.7

Free Economies   84.6

0   20   40   60   80   100

Quick Facts

Population: 0.4 million
GDP (PPP): $11.4 billion
1.9% growth in 2013
5-year compound annual growth 0.4%
$32,036 per capita
Unemployment: 13.6%
Inflation (CPI): 0.3%
FDI Inflow: $1.1 billion
Public Debt: 56.3% of GDP

2013 data unless otherwise noted.
Data compiled as of September 2014.

THE TEN ECONOMIC FREEDOMS

		Score	■ Country | World Average	Rank	1-Year Change
RULE OF LAW	Property Rights	70.0		30th	0
	Freedom from Corruption	71.0		22nd	+4.4

Corruption remains a problem at all levels of government and may be exacerbated by a reported increase in cocaine transshipment through the Bahamas in 2014. Ongoing concerns include money laundering and allegedly extensive nepotism, cronyism, and favoritism in government. The largely well-functioning legal system, based on British common law, is independent, but the judicial process tends to be very slow. Property registration is difficult and time-consuming.

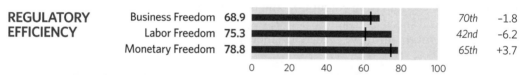

		Score		Rank	1-Year Change
GOVERNMENT SIZE	Fiscal Freedom	97.8		6th	+0.5
	Government Spending	83.2		38th	-0.9

The Bahamas imposes no individual or corporate income taxes and has one of the world's lowest tax burdens. Government revenue, which equals 15 percent of the domestic economy, is reliant on tariffs and national insurance, property, and stamp taxes. Government spending has reached 23.7 percent of gross domestic product, and public debt amounts to 56 percent of domestic income.

		Score		Rank	1-Year Change
REGULATORY EFFICIENCY	Business Freedom	68.9		70th	-1.8
	Labor Freedom	75.3		42nd	-6.2
	Monetary Freedom	78.8		65th	+3.7

The overall regulatory environment is efficient and facilitates business formation, although no major reforms have been implemented in recent years. The labor market is relatively flexible, but enforcement of the labor codes remains ineffective. The government influences domestic prices for such "breadbasket" items as medicines, gasoline, and petroleum gas and subsidizes state-owned corporations.

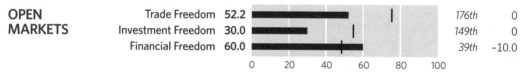

		Score		Rank	1-Year Change
OPEN MARKETS	Trade Freedom	52.2		176th	0
	Investment Freedom	30.0		149th	0
	Financial Freedom	60.0		39th	-10.0

The average tariff rate is 18.9 percent, and tariffs are a major source of government revenue. Some agricultural imports are restricted. New foreign investment is subject to a lengthy review process. The financial sector, the second most important contributor to the economy, is fairly competitive. However, nonperforming loans have increased to around 14 percent of total bank lending.

Long-Term Score Change (since 1995)

RULE OF LAW		GOVERNMENT SIZE		REGULATORY EFFICIENCY		OPEN MARKETS	
Property Rights	-20.0	Fiscal Freedom	+0.1	Business Freedom	-31.1	Trade Freedom	+33.2
Freedom from Corruption	+1.0	Government Spending	-3.7	Labor Freedom	-4.7	Investment Freedom	0
				Monetary Freedom	-3.8	Financial Freedom	-10.0

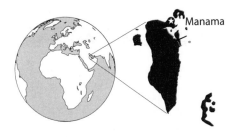
Manama

BAHRAIN

Economic Freedom Score

Least free 0 — Most free 100

73.4

Bahrain's economic freedom score is 73.4, making its economy the 18th freest in the 2015 *Index*. Its overall score has decreased by 1.7 points due to declines in investment freedom, monetary freedom, and business freedom. Bahrain continues to be the freest economy in the Middle East/North Africa region, and its economic freedom score is well above the world average.

Over the past five years, Bahrain's economic freedom score has declined by 4.3 points, with a particularly sharp drop following civil unrest in 2011. In the 2015 *Index*, the kingdom registered the 10th largest score decline. Renewed efforts to enhance the foundations of economic freedom through firm institutionalization of property rights and greater transparency remain critical to ensuring long-term economic development and a successful transition to a more open society.

The recent disappointing trend in economic freedom, however, masks significant score gains since 1995 when Bahrain was first graded in the *Index*. Impressive long-term improvements in financial, investment, and labor freedoms have helped the kingdom transform itself into a competitive trade and financial hub that leads the region in many areas.

BACKGROUND: Bahrain gained independence in 1971 and became a constitutional monarchy in 2002. In 2011, Shia activists launched a campaign demanding a new constitution and greater political power. When modest concessions and efforts at dialogue failed to stem the demonstrations, King Hamad authorized a crackdown that was subsequently supported by the regional Gulf Cooperation Council security forces. The government has sought to ease tensions through a national dialogue led by the crown prince and by introducing several law enforcement, intelligence, and judicial reforms. Efforts have been made to reduce dependence on declining oil reserves by encouraging investment in non-energy sectors. Home to many multinational firms that do business in the region, Bahrain has a modern communications and transportation infrastructure, a cosmopolitan outlook, and a free trade agreement with the U.S.

Freedom Trend

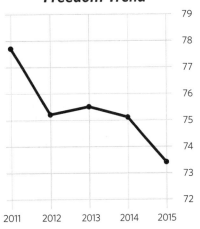

Country Comparisons

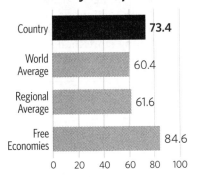

Country	73.4
World Average	60.4
Regional Average	61.6
Free Economies	84.6

Quick Facts

Population: 1.2 million
GDP (PPP): $40.6 billion
4.9% growth in 2013
5-year compound annual growth 3.4%
$34,584 per capita
Unemployment: 7.4%
Inflation (CPI): 3.3%
FDI Inflow: $988.8 million
Public Debt: 43.9% of GDP

How Do We Measure Economic Freedom?
See page 475 for an explanation of the methodology
or visit the *Index* Web site at *heritage.org/index*.

*2013 data unless otherwise noted.
Data compiled as of September 2014.*

THE TEN ECONOMIC FREEDOMS

		Score		Rank	1-Year Change
RULE OF LAW	Property Rights	60.0		41st	0
	Freedom from Corruption	48.0		57th	-1.4

Bahrain's long-serving prime minister, uncle of the king, approved legislation in 2014 to fight corruption and prevent the misuse of public money. Critics view the new laws as an effort to blunt a renewed, high-profile anti-corruption drive initiated by the crown prince in late 2013. The legal system adequately protects and facilitates acquisition and disposition of property rights. Expropriation is infrequent, and private property is secure.

		Score		Rank	1-Year Change
GOVERNMENT SIZE	Fiscal Freedom	99.9		1st	0
	Government Spending	73.1		77th	+1.7

Bahrain has no tax on individual income. Most businesses are exempt from taxation, but oil companies must pay a 46 percent income tax. Other taxes include a stamp tax and a tax on property purchases. Overall tax revenue amounts to less than 4 percent of gross domestic product. Government expenditures equal about 30 percent of the domestic economy, and public debt is equivalent to about 44 percent of GDP.

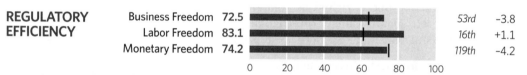

		Score		Rank	1-Year Change
REGULATORY EFFICIENCY	Business Freedom	72.5		53rd	-3.8
	Labor Freedom	83.1		16th	+1.1
	Monetary Freedom	74.2		119th	-4.2

Bahrain's commercial law system is relatively straightforward, but the regulatory environment lacks coordination and efficient enforcement of regulations. Following labor reforms in recent years, labor market flexibility has been relatively well maintained. Bahrain's subsidy programs, consuming more than 10 percent of GDP, cover natural gas for industrial users, food items, water, and electricity.

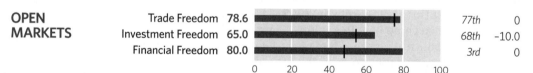

		Score		Rank	1-Year Change
OPEN MARKETS	Trade Freedom	78.6		77th	0
	Investment Freedom	65.0		68th	-10.0
	Financial Freedom	80.0		3rd	0

Bahrain has a 5.7 percent average tariff rate. Government procurement policies can favor domestic companies. Foreign investment in several sectors is restricted. Bahrain's more than 400 banks and financial institutions account for over a quarter of GDP. Foreign and domestic investors have access to a wide range of financial services. Capitalization of the banking system remains high, and nonperforming loans are declining.

Long-Term Score Change (since 1995)

RULE OF LAW		GOVERNMENT SIZE		REGULATORY EFFICIENCY		OPEN MARKETS	
Property Rights	0	Fiscal Freedom	+0.5	Business Freedom	-27.5	Trade Freedom	+0.2
Freedom from Corruption	-22.0	Government Spending	+1.4	Labor Freedom	+43.1	Investment Freedom	+15.0
				Monetary Freedom	-12.5	Financial Freedom	+10.0

Dhaka

BANGLADESH

Economic Freedom Score

25   50   75

Least free 0   100 Most free

53.9

Bangladesh's economic freedom score is 53.9, making its economy the 131st freest in the 2015 *Index*. Its overall score has decreased by 0.2 point since last year, with improvements in labor freedom, freedom from corruption, and monetary freedom outweighed by notable declines in investment freedom and business freedom. Bangladesh is ranked 27th out of 42 countries in the Asia–Pacific region.

Over the past five years, Bangladesh's economic freedom has fluctuated at the lower end of the "mostly unfree" category. Modest score improvements have occurred in just four of the 10 economic freedoms (financial freedom, labor freedom, freedom from corruption, and trade freedom), and overall policy reform appears to have stalled.

A general disregard for the rule of law, rampant corruption, and a judicial system that suffers from political interference provide a weak foundation for economic modernization. Lack of a national consensus on the direction of future policy changes has diminished the momentum for economic reforms, and deteriorating prospects for near-term improvements in economic freedom make it unlikely that the relatively high growth rates of recent years can be maintained.

BACKGROUND: Prime Minister Sheikh Hasina was reelected in January 2014. The opposition boycotted the election and blocked roads and highways. The government's use of force to open thoroughfares led to violent clashes, and Bangladeshis suffered economically. In 2014, the war crimes tribunal set up to investigate human rights violations committed during the 1971 war for independence handed down several death sentences that led to rioting by Islamists. Despite a decade of overall economic and social gains for much of the population, Bangladesh remains one of the world's poorest nations. Garment manufacturing accounts for over 90 percent of export earnings, and the collapse of the Rana Plaza garment factory in April 2013, which killed over 1,000 people, has focused international attention on working conditions and labor and safety standards.

Freedom Trend

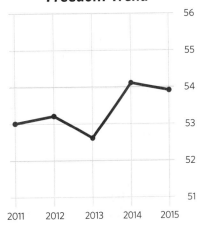

56
55
54
53
52
51

2011   2012   2013   2014   2015

Country Comparisons

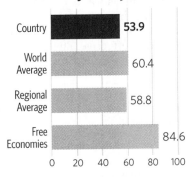

Country — **53.9**
World Average — 60.4
Regional Average — 58.8
Free Economies — 84.6

0   20   40   60   80   100

Quick Facts

Population: 156.3 million
GDP (PPP): $325.1 billion
5.8% growth in 2013
5-year compound annual growth 6.1%
$2,080 per capita
Unemployment: 4.3%
Inflation (CPI): 7.5%
FDI Inflow: $1.6 billion
Public Debt: 39.7% of GDP

2013 data unless otherwise noted.
Data compiled as of September 2014.

THE TEN ECONOMIC FREEDOMS

		Score	Country	World Average	Rank	1-Year Change

RULE OF LAW

Property Rights 20.0 — 138th — 0
Freedom from Corruption 27.0 — 141st — +3.7

Institutional accountability is not well established, and the judiciary is not clearly separated from the executive. Government effectiveness is undermined by pervasive graft. Contract enforcement and dispute settlement procedures are inefficient. Antiquated real property laws and poor record-keeping systems complicate land and property transactions. Poor governance is one of the main barriers to foreign direct investment.

GOVERNMENT SIZE

Fiscal Freedom 72.7 — 128th — +0.2
Government Spending 92.0 — 8th — −0.3

Bangladesh's top individual income tax rate is 25 percent, and its top corporate tax rate is 45 percent. Other taxes include a value-added tax. Despite relatively high rates, tax revenue remains low at around 10 percent of gross domestic product. Public expenditures account for about 16.3 percent of the domestic economy, and public debt has grown to a level equal to about 40 percent of GDP.

REGULATORY EFFICIENCY

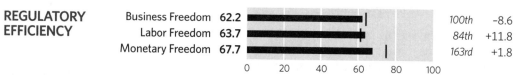

Business Freedom 62.2 — 100th — −8.6
Labor Freedom 63.7 — 84th — +11.8
Monetary Freedom 67.7 — 163rd — +1.8

Reform measures in recent years have streamlined the procedures for establishing a business, but other institutional deficiencies such as pervasive corruption and poor access to credit discourage start-ups. The labor market remains underdeveloped, and the enforcement of labor rules is ineffective. The government maintains an extensive system of price controls and subsidies for basic food staples, fuels, fertilizers, and electricity.

OPEN MARKETS

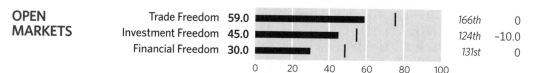

Trade Freedom 59.0 — 166th — 0
Investment Freedom 45.0 — 124th — −10.0
Financial Freedom 30.0 — 131st — 0

Bangladesh has a relatively high 13.0 percent average tariff rate, and tariffs are a significant source of government revenue. Efforts are underway to improve customs processes. Foreign investors face bureaucratic hurdles. The financial sector remains underdeveloped despite modernization efforts. State-owned commercial banks account for over 30 percent of total banking system assets. Stock market capitalization is low.

Long-Term Score Change (since 1995)

RULE OF LAW		GOVERNMENT SIZE		REGULATORY EFFICIENCY		OPEN MARKETS	
Property Rights	−10.0	Fiscal Freedom	+28.7	Business Freedom	+22.2	Trade Freedom	+59.0
Freedom from Corruption	+17.0	Government Spending	+0.5	Labor Freedom	−0.4	Investment Freedom	−5.0
				Monetary Freedom	−5.2	Financial Freedom	0

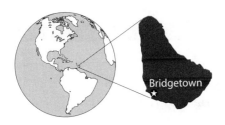

BARBADOS

Economic Freedom Score

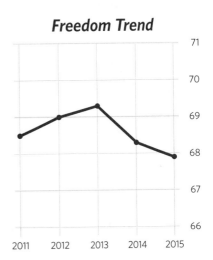

67.9

Least free 0   25   50   75   100 Most free

World Rank: 46   **Regional Rank: 7**

Barbados's economic freedom score is 67.9, making its economy the 46th freest in the 2015 *Index*. Its score is 0.4 point worse than last year due to declines in half of the 10 economic freedoms including the control of public spending, labor freedom, and freedom from corruption. Barbados is ranked 7th out of 29 countries in the South and Central America/Caribbean region, and its overall score remains well above the global and regional averages.

Barbados is one of the Caribbean region's most prosperous economies, and offshore finance and tourism have been important sources of economic growth. With relatively strong foundations of economic freedom supported by a high degree of transparency and an efficient judiciary, the economy has focused on attracting international companies and long-term investment.

Over the past five years, Barbados's economic freedom has declined by about 0.5 point. Improvements in such areas as investment freedom, trade freedom, and fiscal freedom have been offset by notable deteriorations in business freedom, labor freedom, and the management of government spending. Large fiscal deficits have driven an increase in government debt, which is now almost equal to the size of the economy.

BACKGROUND: Barbados is a politically stable parliamentary democracy. Prime Minister Freundel Stuart and his Democratic Labour Party won a five-year term in office in 2013. Barbados has transformed itself from a low-income, agricultural economy producing mainly sugar and rum into a middle-income economy built on tourism and offshore banking that generates one of the highest per capita incomes in the Caribbean. However, tourism revenues have declined, and financial services and construction have never fully recovered from the Great Recession that began in 2008. The government is trying to diversify away from tourism, which has been the main source of external vulnerability. In 2014, in an effort to reduce its large fiscal deficit, the government imposed an asset tax on banks and laid off 3,000 public-sector workers.

Freedom Trend

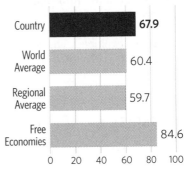

	2011	2012	2013	2014	2015

Country Comparisons

Country	67.9
World Average	60.4
Regional Average	59.7
Free Economies	84.6

0   20   40   60   80   100

Quick Facts

Population: 0.3 million
GDP (PPP): $7.0 billion
–0.7% growth in 2013
5-year compound annual growth –0.8%
$25,181 per capita
Unemployment: 12.2%
Inflation (CPI): 2.3%
FDI Inflow: $376.4 million
Public Debt: 92.0% of GDP

2013 data unless otherwise noted.
Data compiled as of September 2014.

How Do We Measure Economic Freedom?
See page 475 for an explanation of the methodology or visit the *Index* Web site at *heritage.org/index*.

119

THE TEN ECONOMIC FREEDOMS

	Score		Rank	1-Year Change
RULE OF LAW	Property Rights 80.0		20th	0
	Freedom from Corruption 75.0		15th	−2.9

Corruption is not a major problem in Barbados. There are criminal penalties for official corruption, and the government's enforcement of anti-corruption measures is generally effective. The court system is based on British common law and is generally unbiased and efficient. The protection of property rights is strong, and the rule of law is respected.

	Score		Rank	1-Year Change
GOVERNMENT SIZE	Fiscal Freedom 73.8		120th	−0.2
	Government Spending 42.1		148th	−7.7

The top individual income tax rate is 35 percent, and the top corporate tax rate is 25 percent. Other taxes include a value-added tax and a property tax. The overall tax burden equals 27.8 percent of domestic income, and government spending is equivalent to around 43.9 percent of the total domestic economy. At 92 percent of GDP, public debt is high for a small island nation.

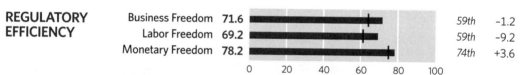

	Score		Rank	1-Year Change
REGULATORY EFFICIENCY	Business Freedom 71.6		59th	−1.2
	Labor Freedom 69.2		59th	−9.2
	Monetary Freedom 78.2		74th	+3.6

There is no minimum capital requirement, but starting a business requires eight procedures and takes more than two weeks. On average, obtaining permits for construction takes over 400 days. Despite relatively flexible employment regulations, a well-functioning labor market has not fully developed. The government maintains price controls on basic food commodities but removed its fuel subsidy for public service vehicles in 2014.

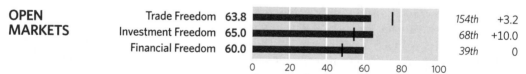

	Score		Rank	1-Year Change
OPEN MARKETS	Trade Freedom 63.8		154th	+3.2
	Investment Freedom 65.0		68th	+10.0
	Financial Freedom 60.0		39th	0

Barbados has a relatively high 13.1 percent average tariff due to its reliance on tariff revenue to finance the government. Foreign and domestic investors are generally treated equally, but investment in some sectors is regulated. The banking sector has grown, offering a wider range of services for domestic and foreign investors. The securities market lacks depth and remains relatively illiquid.

Long-Term Score Change (since 1996)

RULE OF LAW		GOVERNMENT SIZE		REGULATORY EFFICIENCY		OPEN MARKETS	
Property Rights	+30.0	Fiscal Freedom	+13.0	Business Freedom	+1.6	Trade Freedom	+14.8
Freedom from Corruption	+45.0	Government Spending	−29.4	Labor Freedom	−10.8	Investment Freedom	−5.0
				Monetary Freedom	−10.8	Financial Freedom	−10.0

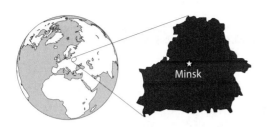

BELARUS

Economic Freedom Score

49.8

Belarus's economic freedom score is 49.8, making its economy the 153rd freest in the 2015 *Index*. Its overall score is 0.3 point lower than last year, reflecting declines in half of the 10 economic freedoms including investment freedom, the control of government spending, and fiscal freedom. Belarus is ranked 42nd among the 43 countries in the Europe region.

Despite this year's decline, Belarus's economic freedom score has improved by nearly 2 points over the past five years. Marked improvements in overall fiscal management and a decline in perceived corruption have bolstered overall economic freedom. However, the score decline in the 2015 *Index* has pushed the country back into the "repressed" category.

Belarus remains one of the world's most controlled economies. The state directs or interferes in many areas of the economy. Proposed labor laws include a so-called serfdom decree that threatens to limit the free movement of agricultural workers. These policies, along with centralized state control and harsh redistribution, have stifled Belarus's prosperity and economic freedom compared to the rest of Europe.

BACKGROUND: President Alexander Lukashenko, in power since 1994, rules all branches of government. The U.N. Human Rights Council has appointed a human rights investigator for Belarus. The European Union imposed targeted economic sanctions following beatings and arrests of opposition figures after Lukashenko falsified the December 2010 election results. Parliamentary elections in 2012 were rigged, and the two main opposition parties boycotted the elections. Belarus's industries and state-controlled agriculture are not competitive. Corruption and inflation plague the economy. Russia maintains huge political influence in the government and economy, and a significant portion of Russian oil and gas exports passes through the country. In May 2014, Belarus signed an agreement with Russia to create a Eurasian Economic Union.

Freedom Trend

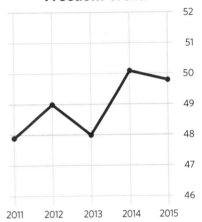

Country Comparisons

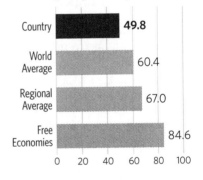

Country	49.8
World Average	60.4
Regional Average	67.0
Free Economies	84.6

Quick Facts

Population: 9.5 million
GDP (PPP): $149.1 billion
0.9% growth in 2013
5-year compound annual growth 3.2%
$15,753 per capita
Unemployment: 5.9%
Inflation (CPI): 18.3%
FDI Inflow: $2.2 billion
Public Debt: 36.7% of GDP

2013 data unless otherwise noted.
Data compiled as of September 2014.

THE TEN ECONOMIC FREEDOMS

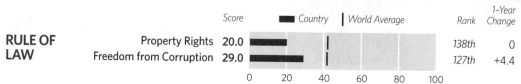

	Score		Rank	1-Year Change

RULE OF LAW
Property Rights — 20.0 — 138th — 0
Freedom from Corruption — 29.0 — 127th — +4.4

President Alexander Lukashenko presides over an authoritarian system that has destroyed checks and balances and dominates all branches of government. The state controls 70 percent of the economy, feeding widespread corruption. Graft is also enabled by the lack of transparency and accountability in government. Soviet-era state ownership of land and government-controlled collective farms continues.

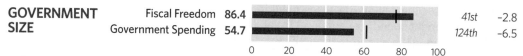

GOVERNMENT SIZE
Fiscal Freedom — 86.4 — 41st — -2.8
Government Spending — 54.7 — 124th — -6.5

Belarus's flat individual income tax rate is 12 percent, and its corporate tax rate is 18 percent. Income earned in technology parks is taxed at a lesser rate. Other taxes include a value-added tax and excise taxes. The overall tax burden equals 29.8 percent of gross domestic income. Government spending has reached 38.9 percent of domestic income, and public debt equals 37 percent of GDP.

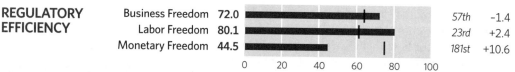

REGULATORY EFFICIENCY
Business Freedom — 72.0 — 57th — -1.4
Labor Freedom — 80.1 — 23rd — +2.4
Monetary Freedom — 44.5 — 181st — +10.6

Simplified registration formalities facilitate business formation, but obtaining necessary permits remains time-consuming and burdensome. A well-functioning labor market has not developed, and the public sector is the main source of employment. The state subsidizes prices for energy and many household goods and fixes artificially low prices for products made by state-owned enterprises.

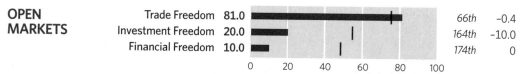

OPEN MARKETS
Trade Freedom — 81.0 — 66th — -0.4
Investment Freedom — 20.0 — 164th — -10.0
Financial Freedom — 10.0 — 174th — 0

Belarus has a relatively low 2.0 percent average tariff rate. It is a member of the Eurasian Customs Union and has not joined the World Trade Organization. The government reviews foreign investment. The financial sector, dominated by banking, remains heavily government-influenced, with commercial banks' lending practices subject to state pressure. The stock market is small and largely dormant.

Long-Term Score Change (since 1995)

RULE OF LAW		GOVERNMENT SIZE		REGULATORY EFFICIENCY		OPEN MARKETS	
Property Rights	-30.0	Fiscal Freedom	+44.4	Business Freedom	+2.0	Trade Freedom	+21.0
Freedom from Corruption	+19.0	Government Spending	+23.2	Labor Freedom	+8.1	Investment Freedom	-30.0
				Monetary Freedom	+44.5	Financial Freedom	-40.0

BELGIUM

Economic Freedom Score

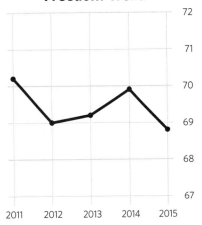

25   50   75

Least free   0   100   Most free

68.8

World Rank: 40   **Regional Rank: 18**

Belgium's economic freedom score is 68.8, making its economy the 40th freest in the 2015 *Index*. Its overall score has decreased by 1.1 points from last year, with declines in labor freedom, the management of public spending, and fiscal freedom outweighing improvements in monetary freedom, business freedom, and freedom from corruption. Belgium is ranked 18th among the 43 countries in the Europe region, and its overall score is above the regional and global averages.

Over the past five years, Belgium's economic freedom score has slipped by 1.4 points, moving the country further away from the rank of "mostly free" that it last achieved in 2011. Long-term declines in four of the 10 economic freedoms, including the management of public spending, business freedom, labor freedom, and monetary freedom, have caused this deterioration. In particular, Belgium's government spending score has declined by nearly 15 points.

Policy responses during and after the eurozone financial crisis have exacerbated long-term structural weaknesses. A rigid labor market and high taxation have undermined any broad-based recovery, and government spending has increased substantially, pushing public debt close to the size of the economy. Labor market reforms and fiscal prudence must be at the top of the policy agenda in order to secure broad-based economic freedom and growth.

BACKGROUND: Belgium is a federal state with three culturally different regions: Flanders, Wallonia, and the capital city of Brussels. Brussels also serves as the headquarters of NATO and the European Union. In October 2011, an electoral reform package was adopted with the aim of avoiding a situation similar to the one that occurred when the country went 541 days without forming a government after the 2010 elections. The first federal elections under these reforms were in May 2014. Bart De Wever's center-right New Flemish Alliance won a plurality but not a majority. Services account for 75 percent of economic activity. Leading exports are electrical equipment, vehicles, diamonds, and chemicals.

Freedom Trend

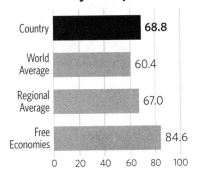

72

71

70

69

68

67

2011   2012   2013   2014   2015

Country Comparisons

Country	68.8
World Average	60.4
Regional Average	67.0
Free Economies	84.6

0   20   40   60   80   100

Quick Facts

Population: 11.2 million
GDP (PPP): $422.8 billion
0.2% growth in 2013
5-year compound annual growth 0.3%
$37,881 per capita
Unemployment: 8.6%
Inflation (CPI): 1.2%
FDI Inflow: –$2.4 billion
Public Debt: 99.8% of GDP

2013 data unless otherwise noted.
Data compiled as of September 2014.

How Do We Measure Economic Freedom?
See page 475 for an explanation of the methodology
or visit the *Index* Web site at *heritage.org/index*.

THE TEN ECONOMIC FREEDOMS

		Score		Rank	1-Year Change
RULE OF LAW	Property Rights	80.0		20th	0
	Freedom from Corruption	75.0		15th	+0.8

Notwithstanding ongoing political difficulties between the two linguistic communities, corruption remains minimal in Belgium. The government prohibits and punishes all forms of bribery. Property rights are well protected by law. Laws are well-codified, and the judicial system is generally respected, but the courts can be slow. Enforcement actions to protect intellectual property rights can be protracted.

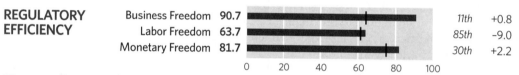

		Score		Rank	1-Year Change
GOVERNMENT SIZE	Fiscal Freedom	43.6		178th	-1.2
	Government Spending	10.2		172nd	-4.6

Belgium's top individual income tax rate is 50 percent, and its top corporate income tax rate is 33 percent. Other taxes include a value-added tax and an estate tax. The overall tax burden equals 45.3 percent of gross domestic product. Government spending is equivalent to 54.7 percent of the domestic economy, and public debt is approaching nearly 100 percent of GDP.

		Score		Rank	1-Year Change
REGULATORY EFFICIENCY	Business Freedom	90.7		11th	+0.8
	Labor Freedom	63.7		85th	-9.0
	Monetary Freedom	81.7		30th	+2.2

The overall regulatory environment is efficient and transparent. The cost of establishing a company has been reduced, and starting a business takes only three days and four procedures. Although employment regulations have become less burdensome, the non-salary cost of hiring a worker remains high. The state controls the prices of a wide range of fuels and other items and spends almost 1 percent of GDP on coal subsidies.

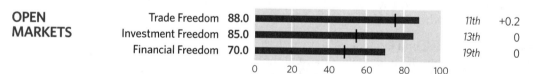

		Score		Rank	1-Year Change
OPEN MARKETS	Trade Freedom	88.0		11th	+0.2
	Investment Freedom	85.0		13th	0
	Financial Freedom	70.0		19th	0

EU members have a 1.0 percent average tariff rate. Although some non-tariff barriers exist, the EU is relatively open to external trade. Foreign and domestic investors are generally treated equally in Belgium. The financial sector remains vibrant and generally free from government involvement. Some institutions received bailouts during the economic slowdown, and the recently passed Financial Crisis Law grants the state stronger powers during crises.

Long-Term Score Change (since 1996)

RULE OF LAW		GOVERNMENT SIZE		REGULATORY EFFICIENCY		OPEN MARKETS	
Property Rights	-10.0	Fiscal Freedom	+9.7	Business Freedom	+20.7	Trade Freedom	+10.2
Freedom from Corruption	-15.0	Government Spending	+2.9	Labor Freedom	-4.3	Investment Freedom	+15.0
				Monetary Freedom	-3.3	Financial Freedom	0

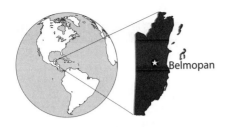
★ Belmopan

BELIZE

Economic Freedom Score

Least free 0   Most free 100

56.8

Belize's economic freedom score is 56.8, making its economy the 117th freest in the 2015 *Index*. Its overall score is about the same as last year, with improvements in investment freedom and the control of government spending counterbalanced by declines in business and labor freedoms. Belize is ranked 20th out of 29 countries in the South and Central America/Caribbean region.

Over the past five years, Belize's economic freedom has declined by 7 points. Deterioration has occurred in half of the 10 economic freedoms since 2011, with double-digit declines in freedom from corruption, business freedom, and labor freedom. Given the patchy efforts to advance economic reforms, economic dynamism in Belize remains constrained by structural weaknesses that undermine prospects for broad-based economic development.

Corruption has become prevalent, with Belize's score on freedom from corruption declining by more than 20 points over the past half-decade. A weak and politically vulnerable judiciary has been ineffective in upholding the rule of law, and the country has become a haven for money laundering and drug transit. Despite a comparatively high level of trade freedom, dynamic gains from trade have been undercut by the lack of progress in reforming the investment climate and the financial sector.

BACKGROUND: Belize is a parliamentary democracy. Prime Minister Dean Barrow of the United Democratic Party won reelection for a five-year term in March 2012, more than a year earlier than constitutionally mandated. Since taking office in 2008, Barrow's government has undermined investment by expropriating the leading private telecommunications and electricity companies and the water company. However, Belize has reached an agreement with bondholders to restructure its $544 million external debt, also referred to as the "superbond." The economy is based primarily on tourism followed by exports of marine products, citrus, sugar, and bananas. Oil reserves are declining. Belize has high crime rates, a prevalence of HIV/AIDS, and significant unemployment.

Freedom Trend

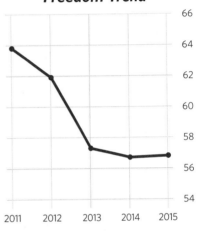

Country Comparisons

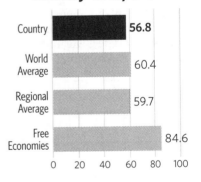

Country	56.8
World Average	60.4
Regional Average	59.7
Free Economies	84.6

Quick Facts

Population: 0.3 million
GDP (PPP): $3.0 billion
1.6% growth in 2013
5-year compound annual growth 2.2%
$8,716 per capita
Unemployment: 8.2%
Inflation (CPI): 0.5%
FDI Inflow: $89.3 million
Public Debt: 75.5% of GDP

2013 data unless otherwise noted.
Data compiled as of September 2014.

THE TEN ECONOMIC FREEDOMS

		Score			Rank	1-Year Change
RULE OF LAW	Property Rights	30.0			94th	0
	Freedom from Corruption	6.7			185th	0

A government commission to monitor, prevent, and combat corruption has not met for several years. Business owners complain that government officials, police, and others often solicit bribes or show favoritism. The judiciary, although independent, is influenced by the executive. As of May 2014, the government had not compensated the owners of expropriated foreign-owned electricity and telecommunications companies.

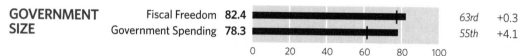

		Score			Rank	1-Year Change
GOVERNMENT SIZE	Fiscal Freedom	82.4			63rd	+0.3
	Government Spending	78.3			55th	+4.1

The top individual income and corporate tax rates are 25 percent. Other taxes include a goods and services tax and a stamp duty. The overall tax burden is equal to 22.5 percent of the domestic economy. Government expenditures are equivalent to 26.9 percent of gross domestic product, and public debt amounts to 76 percent of the size of the domestic economy.

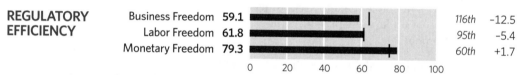

		Score			Rank	1-Year Change
REGULATORY EFFICIENCY	Business Freedom	59.1			116th	-12.5
	Labor Freedom	61.8			95th	-5.4
	Monetary Freedom	79.3			60th	+1.7

The process for setting up a business and completing regulatory requirements has been streamlined, but entrepreneurial activity often faces such challenges as poor enforcement of the commercial code and lack of regulatory transparency. A formal labor market has not been fully developed. The government maintains price controls on various products such as rice, sugar, and flour and subsidizes the cost of electricity.

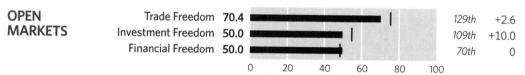

		Score			Rank	1-Year Change
OPEN MARKETS	Trade Freedom	70.4			129th	+2.6
	Investment Freedom	50.0			109th	+10.0
	Financial Freedom	50.0			70th	0

Belize has a 9.8 percent average tariff rate. The government relies heavily on tariff revenue, and import licensing affects some agricultural imports. Both foreign and domestic investors may find it difficult to title land. Despite efforts to improve efficiency, the government-controlled financial sector does not meet private-sector credit needs sufficiently. The banking sector remains burdened with nonperforming loans.

Long-Term Score Change (since 1995)

RULE OF LAW		GOVERNMENT SIZE		REGULATORY EFFICIENCY		OPEN MARKETS	
Property Rights	-40.0	Fiscal Freedom	+19.2	Business Freedom	-10.9	Trade Freedom	+28.4
Freedom from Corruption	-43.3	Government Spending	+13.6	Labor Freedom	-21.5	Investment Freedom	-20.0
				Monetary Freedom	-7.2	Financial Freedom	0

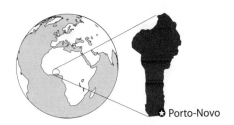

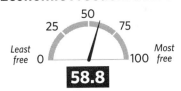

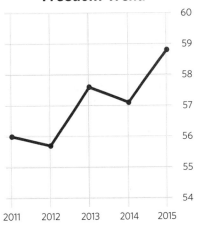

BENIN

Economic Freedom Score

25   50   75

Least free 0   100 Most free

58.8

World Rank: 99   **Regional Rank: 11**

Benin's economic freedom score is 58.8, making its economy the 99th freest in the 2015 *Index*. Its overall score is 1.7 points better than last year, with notable improvements in freedom from corruption and in the area of regulatory efficiency consisting of business freedom, labor freedom, and monetary freedom. Benin is ranked 11th out of 46 countries in the Sub-Saharan Africa region, and its overall score is higher than the regional average.

Over the past five years, economic freedom in Benin has advanced by 2.8 points. Six of the 10 economic freedoms, notably investment freedom, business freedom, and freedom from corruption, have improved by close to 10 points or more.

Nonetheless, as a "mostly unfree" economy in which the foundations of economic freedom remain fragile and uneven across the country, Benin continues to lack the broad-based economic dynamism that is necessary to ensure long-term economic development. Though some previously government-owned enterprises have been privatized, lingering government interference and inefficiency continue to crowd out private-sector development. Further reforms in the rule of law and financial freedom are urgently needed to improve productivity and raise incomes.

BACKGROUND: President Thomas Boni Yayi was elected in 2006 and re-elected for another five-year term in 2011. Police foiled a coup against Yayi in March 2013. His former associate, Patrice Talon, was linked to the alleged assassination plot. Talon was arrested in Paris; however, a Paris court blocked his extradition on the grounds that he would be denied a fair trial in Benin. Although it is one of Africa's largest cotton producers, Benin remains underdeveloped and dependent on subsistence agriculture and regional trade.

Freedom Trend

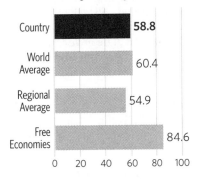

Country Comparisons

Country	58.8
World Average	60.4
Regional Average	54.9
Free Economies	84.6

0   20   40   60   80   100

Quick Facts

Population: 10.3 million
GDP (PPP): $16.7 billion
5.6% growth in 2013
5-year compound annual growth 3.9%
$1,623 per capita
Unemployment: 1.0%
Inflation (CPI): 1.0%
FDI Inflow: $320.1 million
Public Debt: 29.8% of GDP

2013 data unless otherwise noted.
Data compiled as of September 2014.

How Do We Measure Economic Freedom?
See page 475 for an explanation of the methodology
or visit the *Index* Web site at *heritage.org/index.*

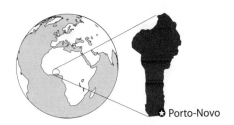

127

THE TEN ECONOMIC FREEDOMS

		Score		Rank	1-Year Change
RULE OF LAW	Property Rights	30.0		94th	0
	Freedom from Corruption	36.0		95th	+6.5

The business environment is undermined by the government's failure to meet contractual obligations, ensure an independent judiciary, and accept adverse court decisions. Corruption persists in customs administration, government procurement, and the judicial system. There are no separate commercial courts, and backlogs of civil cases cause long delays. There is extensive smuggling of food and fuel across the border with Nigeria.

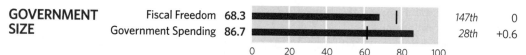

		Score		Rank	1-Year Change
GOVERNMENT SIZE	Fiscal Freedom	68.3		147th	0
	Government Spending	86.7		28th	+0.6

The top individual income tax rate is 45 percent, and the top corporate tax rate is 30 percent. Companies engaged in hydrocarbon exploration, extraction, and sales pay between 35 percent and 45 percent. Other taxes include a value-added tax. The overall tax burden equals 15.5 percent of gross domestic income. Government spending accounts for 21 percent of the domestic economy, and government debt equals 30 percent of GDP.

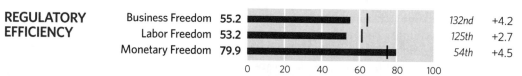

		Score		Rank	1-Year Change
REGULATORY EFFICIENCY	Business Freedom	55.2		132nd	+4.2
	Labor Freedom	53.2		125th	+2.7
	Monetary Freedom	79.9		54th	+4.5

The entrepreneurial environment remains burdensome. Bureaucratic procedures are not streamlined and lack transparency. Despite some progress, obtaining business licenses is time-consuming and costly. Outmoded employment regulations hinder job creation and productivity growth. The government subsidizes the production of cotton, and the country relies on subsidized gasoline and diesel fuel smuggled from Nigeria.

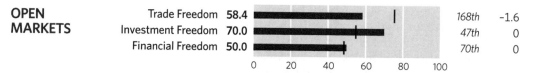

		Score		Rank	1-Year Change
OPEN MARKETS	Trade Freedom	58.4		168th	-1.6
	Investment Freedom	70.0		47th	0
	Financial Freedom	50.0		70th	0

Benin has a 15.8 percent average tariff rate. It has implemented a one-stop shop for customs documents to facilitate trade. The slow-moving court system can impede international trade and investment. The banking sector is predominantly private, and foreign ownership is allowed, but despite the noticeable development of microfinance institutions, overall access to credit remains low.

Long-Term Score Change (since 1996)

RULE OF LAW		GOVERNMENT SIZE		REGULATORY EFFICIENCY		OPEN MARKETS	
Property Rights	-20.0	Fiscal Freedom	-3.8	Business Freedom	-14.8	Trade Freedom	+58.4
Freedom from Corruption	-14.0	Government Spending	-3.8	Labor Freedom	+0.6	Investment Freedom	+20.0
				Monetary Freedom	+22.0	Financial Freedom	0

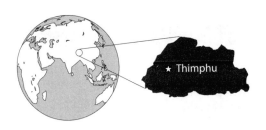

★ Thimphu

BHUTAN

Economic Freedom Score

50

25   75

Least   Most
free 0   100 free

57.4

World Rank: **115**   Regional Rank: **24**

Bhutan's economic freedom score is 57.4, making its economy the 115th freest in the 2015 *Index*. Its score has increased 0.7 point from last year, with improvements in freedom from corruption, the management of government spending, and business freedom partially offset by declines in labor freedom and fiscal freedom. Bhutan is ranked 24th out of 42 countries in the Asia–Pacific region, and its overall score is below the global and regional averages.

Over the past five years, Bhutan has charted a V-shaped trend in economic freedom. Bolstered by improvements in freedom from corruption and business freedom, it has bounced back from its lowest economic freedom score ever in 2013. Nonetheless, Bhutan continues to be in the ranks of the "mostly unfree," with scores on many of the 10 economic freedoms remaining below the world averages.

Efforts to diversify the economy have been at the top of the policymaking agenda in the past few years. Hydropower production and development, led by the government, has been a large driver of growth, but the poverty rate remains persistently high. Landlocked and mountainous, Bhutan remains relatively isolated from the world economy and has yet to open itself fully to international trade and global financial flows.

BACKGROUND: Bhutan is a small Himalayan constitutional monarchy that made the transition from absolute monarchy to parliamentary democracy in March 2008. In July 2013, it completed its second democratic handover of power after the People's Democratic Party won the majority of seats in the National Assembly. Bhutan has one of the world's smallest and least-developed economies. Until a few decades ago, it was largely agrarian, with few roads, little electricity, and no modern hospitals. Recent interregional economic cooperation, particularly involving trade with Bangladesh and India, is helping to encourage economic growth. Connections to global markets are limited and dominated significantly by India.

Freedom Trend

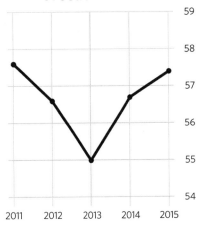

59

58

57

56

55

54

2011   2012   2013   2014   2015

Country Comparisons

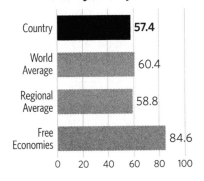

Country   **57.4**

World
Average   60.4

Regional
Average   58.8

Free
Economies   84.6

0   20   40   60   80   100

Quick Facts

Population: 0.7 million
GDP (PPP): $4.7 billion
5.0% growth in 2013
5-year compound annual growth 7.3%
$6,370 per capita
Unemployment: 2.1%
Inflation (CPI): 8.7%
FDI Inflow: $21.3 million
Public Debt: 110.7% of GDP

2013 data unless otherwise noted.
Data compiled as of September 2014.

How Do We Measure Economic Freedom?
See page 475 for an explanation of the methodology
or visit the *Index* Web site at *heritage.org/index*.

BHUTAN (continued)

THE TEN ECONOMIC FREEDOMS

	Score			Rank	1-Year Change
■ Country			❘ World Average		

RULE OF LAW
	Score		Rank	1-Year Change
Property Rights	60.0		41st	0
Freedom from Corruption	63.0		31st	+4.2

The government operates with limited transparency and accountability, but a new performance management system was implemented in 2014 to improve efficiency. Misuses of resources, bribery, collusion, and nepotism are major problems. Bhutan's civil and criminal codes include many modern provisions based on English common law. Property rights are generally better protected than in other South Asian countries.

GOVERNMENT SIZE

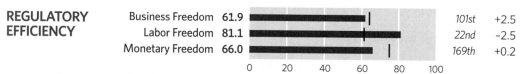

	Score		Rank	1-Year Change
Fiscal Freedom	82.6		62nd	−0.3
Government Spending	60.1		113th	+2.9

Bhutan's top individual income tax rate is 25 percent, and its top corporate tax rate is 30 percent. Other taxes include a property tax and an excise tax. The overall tax burden amounts to 14.8 percent of domestic income. Government expenditures are equivalent to 36.5 percent of gross domestic product, and public debt equals 110 percent of domestic output.

REGULATORY EFFICIENCY

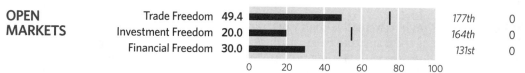

	Score		Rank	1-Year Change
Business Freedom	61.9		101st	+2.5
Labor Freedom	81.1		22nd	−2.5
Monetary Freedom	66.0		169th	+0.2

A modern regulatory framework has not been fully developed. Despite recent efforts, the business climate is still hampered by inconsistent enforcement of regulations. On average, it takes 36 days to start a company. The imbalance between labor supply and demand persists, and unemployment has risen in recent years. In July 2014, India renewed its LPG and kerosene subsidy program for Bhutan.

OPEN MARKETS

	Score		Rank	1-Year Change
Trade Freedom	49.4		177th	0
Investment Freedom	20.0		164th	0
Financial Freedom	30.0		131st	0

As of 2007, Bhutan had a 17.8 percent tariff rate. The cost and time required to import goods are relatively high. The government may screen new foreign investment. The financial sector is small, and an underdeveloped regulatory framework limits access to capital for local entrepreneurs. Competition has improved with the gradual opening of the sector to more foreign partnerships, but banking remains state-controlled.

Long-Term Score Change (since 2009)

RULE OF LAW		GOVERNMENT SIZE		REGULATORY EFFICIENCY		OPEN MARKETS	
Property Rights	0	Fiscal Freedom	−1.0	Business Freedom	+0.2	Trade Freedom	+7.4
Freedom from Corruption	+13.0	Government Spending	+1.8	Labor Freedom	−4.7	Investment Freedom	−10.0
				Monetary Freedom	−9.9	Financial Freedom	0

★ La Paz

BOLIVIA

Economic Freedom Score

50
25   75
Least free 0   100 Most free

46.8

World Rank: 163   **Regional Rank: 26**

Bolivia's economic freedom score is 46.8, making its economy the 163rd freest in the 2015 *Index*. Its overall score is 1.6 points worse than last year, with notable deteriorations in six of the 10 economic freedoms including financial freedom, investment freedom, and labor freedom. Bolivia is ranked 26th out of 29 countries in the South and Central America/Caribbean region, and its overall score is far below the world and regional averages.

Over the past five years, Bolivia's economic freedom has declined by 3.2 points, registering its lowest score ever in the 2015 *Index*. Modest improvements in freedom from corruption and fiscal and monetary freedoms are more than offset by declines in half of the 10 factors, including double-digit declines in labor, investment, and financial freedoms.

Weak investment protections, rigid labor rules, and an increased cost of business add to a perception of rising economic subjugation under President Evo Morales, whose government has expropriated over 20 private companies since 2006. Growth has been driven largely by windfall gains from high commodity prices that are unlikely to be distributed broadly. Reforms across all sectors are needed to guarantee long-term economic growth.

BACKGROUND: President Evo Morales, in power since 2006, imposed a new constitution in 2009 to expand his executive powers and nationalize the economy. He has pledged to move Bolivia toward "communitarian socialism." Constitutionally limited to two terms, Morales was elected to a third term in October 2014. Bolivia has strong alliances with Cuba, Venezuela, and Iran. Although its economic growth rate since 2010 is one of the highest in Latin America and its macroeconomic environment seems stable thanks to revenues from gas exports, the rate of private investment is among the region's lowest, and foreign direct investment is concentrated in natural resources. Half of all Bolivians live in poverty, and nearly 60 percent of working arrangements are informal. Bolivia is one of the world's three main cocaine-producing countries and a significant transit zone for Peruvian cocaine.

Freedom Trend

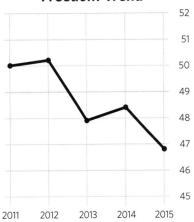

2011 2012 2013 2014 2015

Country Comparisons

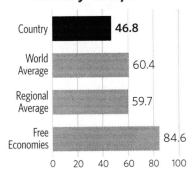

Country	46.8
World Average	60.4
Regional Average	59.7
Free Economies	84.6

0 20 40 60 80 100

Quick Facts

Population: 11.0 million
GDP (PPP): $59.2 billion
6.8% growth in 2013
5-year compound annual growth 4.9%
$5,364 per capita
Unemployment: 3.2%
Inflation (CPI): 5.7%
FDI Inflow: $1.7 billion
Public Debt: 33.1% of GDP

2013 data unless otherwise noted.
Data compiled as of September 2014.

How Do We Measure Economic Freedom?
See page 475 for an explanation of the methodology or visit the *Index* Web site at *heritage.org/index*.

131

THE TEN ECONOMIC FREEDOMS

		Score	Rank	1-Year Change
RULE OF LAW	Property Rights	10.0	165th	0
	Freedom from Corruption	34.0	107th	+5.9

Corruption continues to be a serious problem in Bolivia. The constitution specifically allows expropriation in cases of public necessity or where property is not serving a public function. In recent years, there has been a series of mob invasions of rural and mining properties, which authorities seem unable or unwilling to deter.

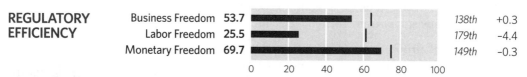

		Score	Rank	1-Year Change
GOVERNMENT SIZE	Fiscal Freedom	86.8	40th	−0.3
	Government Spending	60.9	111th	−1.6

Bolivia's top individual income tax rate is 13 percent, and the top corporate tax rate is 25 percent. Other taxes include a value-added tax and a transactions tax. In the most recent year, tax revenue equaled 22.9 percent of domestic output. Supported by hydrocarbon savings, government expenditures have been steady at 36.1 percent of gross domestic product. Public debt is equivalent to 33 percent of the domestic economy.

		Score	Rank	1-Year Change
REGULATORY EFFICIENCY	Business Freedom	53.7	138th	+0.3
	Labor Freedom	25.5	179th	−4.4
	Monetary Freedom	69.7	149th	−0.3

The regulatory environment is burdened with red tape and inconsistent enforcement of commercial regulations. With 15 procedures required, on average, it takes more than a month to start a business. The labor market is not fully developed, and employment regulations are not conducive to productivity growth. Fuel prices, subsidized and controlled by the government, are frozen for years at a time. Electricity is also subsidized.

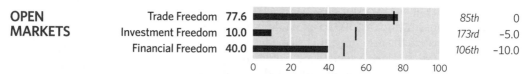

		Score	Rank	1-Year Change
OPEN MARKETS	Trade Freedom	77.6	85th	0
	Investment Freedom	10.0	173rd	−5.0
	Financial Freedom	40.0	106th	−10.0

Bolivia has a 3.7 percent average tariff rate. Government procurement processes may favor domestic firms. New foreign investment may be subject to government screening. New legislation on financial services enacted in August 2013 increases the state's interference in the financial sector, introduces more controls, and directs banks to increase the availability of credit to certain sectors.

Long-Term Score Change (since 1995)

RULE OF LAW		GOVERNMENT SIZE		REGULATORY EFFICIENCY		OPEN MARKETS	
Property Rights	−40.0	Fiscal Freedom	−4.2	Business Freedom	−1.3	Trade Freedom	+12.2
Freedom from Corruption	+24.0	Government Spending	+0.2	Labor Freedom	−22.2	Investment Freedom	−60.0
				Monetary Freedom	−9.8	Financial Freedom	+10.0

BOSNIA AND HERZEGOVINA

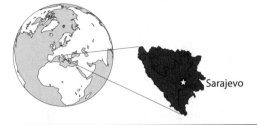

Sarajevo

World Rank: 97   **Regional Rank: 38**

Economic Freedom Score

25 50 75

Least free 0   Most free 100

59.0

Bosnia and Herzegovina's economic freedom score is 59.0, making its economy the 97th freest in the 2015 *Index*. Its overall score has increased by 0.6 point, with improvements in freedom from corruption, monetary freedom, and labor freedom partially offset by declines in investment freedom and business freedom. Bosnia and Herzegovina is ranked 38th out of 43 countries in the Europe region, and its score is below the global and regional averages.

Over the past five years, Bosnia and Herzegovina's economic freedom has advanced by 1.5 points, registering its highest score ever in the 2015 *Index*. Reforms have led to improvements in half of the 10 factors, including government spending and labor, monetary, and trade freedoms, with an especially notable 12-point gain in freedom from corruption.

Despite a decade of concerted effort to improve economic prospects through broad, gradual institutional improvements, however, Bosnia and Herzegovina's economy remains in the "mostly unfree" category, and deeper structural and institutional reforms are needed. In particular, fully eradicating corruption, guaranteeing the independence of the judiciary, and consistently enforcing property rights are vital to propelling the country to higher levels of economic freedom and prosperity.

BACKGROUND: The 1995 Dayton Agreement ended three years of war in the former Yugoslavia and finalized Bosnia and Herzegovina's independence. Two separate entities exist under a loose central government: the Republika Srpska (Serbian) and Federation of Bosnia and Herzegovina (Muslim/Croat). The European Union signed a Stabilization and Association Agreement with Bosnia and Herzegovina in 2008. Bosnia also received a NATO Membership Action Plan in 2010 and is one of four official candidates for NATO membership. The country is one of Europe's poorest. There has been some privatization, but agriculture and industry require modernization. Corruption is widespread, and a weak central government makes implementation of economic reforms difficult. Violent unrest and protests in February 2014 were fueled in part by rampant youth unemployment.

How Do We Measure Economic Freedom?
See page 475 for an explanation of the methodology or visit the *Index* Web site at *heritage.org/index*.

Freedom Trend

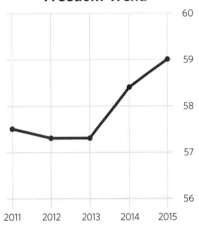

Country Comparisons

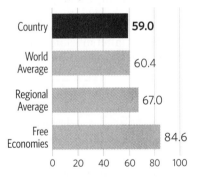

Country	59.0
World Average	60.4
Regional Average	67.0
Free Economies	84.6

0 20 40 60 80 100

Quick Facts

Population: 3.9 million
GDP (PPP): $32.1 billion
1.2% growth in 2013
5-year compound annual growth -0.2%
$8,280 per capita
Unemployment: 28.6%
Inflation (CPI): -0.1%
FDI Inflow: $331.7 million
Public Debt: 42.7% of GDP

2013 data unless otherwise noted.
Data compiled as of September 2014.

THE TEN ECONOMIC FREEDOMS

		Score	Country	World Average	Rank	1-Year Change
RULE OF LAW	Property Rights	20.0			138th	0
	Freedom from Corruption	42.0			72nd	+8.1

Public procurement is a principal source of corruption and fraud in Bosnia and Herzegovina. According to a 2014 estimate, around 60 percent of institutions ignore the procurement law, and about 25 percent of contracts are processed through public tenders. The complex system of government lends itself to deadlock and prevents reform. Property registries are largely unreliable, leaving transfers open to dispute.

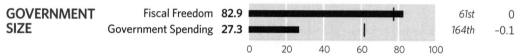

		Score			Rank	Change
GOVERNMENT SIZE	Fiscal Freedom	82.9			61st	0
	Government Spending	27.3			164th	−0.1

Tax policies in Bosnia and Herzegovina vary depending on the governing entity. The top individual and corporate income tax rates are 10 percent. Other taxes include a value-added tax and a property tax. The overall tax burden reached 38.8 percent of GDP in the most recent year. Public expenditures amount to 49.2 percent of domestic output, and public debt is equal to 43 percent of the domestic economy.

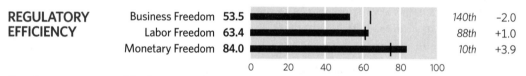

		Score			Rank	Change
REGULATORY EFFICIENCY	Business Freedom	53.5			140th	−2.0
	Labor Freedom	63.4			88th	+1.0
	Monetary Freedom	84.0			10th	+3.9

Starting a company still takes more than a month, and licensing requirements remain burdensome. Labor regulations' complex administrative structure has inspired a dual labor market. The unemployment rate, particularly among the young, is one of the highest in the region. Energy-related subsidies amount to nearly 10 percent of GDP. The government also subsidizes agricultural production and controls some prices.

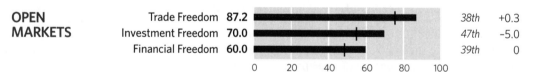

		Score			Rank	Change
OPEN MARKETS	Trade Freedom	87.2			38th	+0.3
	Investment Freedom	70.0			47th	−5.0
	Financial Freedom	60.0			39th	0

Bosnia and Herzegovina's 1.4 percent average tariff is relatively low. Non-tariff barriers have been reduced, and customs procedures have improved. Foreign investors face bureaucratic hurdles. About 80 percent of banking capital is privately owned, and around 90 percent of banks are foreign-owned. Difficulties in contract enforcement and an insecure regulatory environment limit the availability of credit for start-up businesses.

Long-Term Score Change (since 1998)

RULE OF LAW		GOVERNMENT SIZE		REGULATORY EFFICIENCY		OPEN MARKETS	
Property Rights	+10.0	Fiscal Freedom	+4.1	Business Freedom	+13.5	Trade Freedom	+17.8
Freedom from Corruption	+32.0	Government Spending	+10.6	Labor Freedom	+8.6	Investment Freedom	+40.0
				Monetary Freedom	+84.0	Financial Freedom	+50.0

Gaborone

BOTSWANA

Economic Freedom Score

50

25   75

Least
free   0   100   Most
free

69.8

World Rank: **36**	Regional Rank: **2**

Botswana's economic freedom score is 69.8, making its economy the 36th freest in the 2015 *Index*. Its overall score is 2.2 points worse than last year, reflecting considerable declines in half of the 10 economic freedoms, including trade freedom, the management of government spending, and investment freedom. Although Botswana has registered the fourth-largest score drop in the 2015 *Index*, it remains the second-freest economy in the Sub-Saharan Africa region, and its overall score is well above the regional and world averages.

A significant increase in the trade-weighted tariff rate has resulted in a decline in Botswana's trade freedom score. This increase, along with deterioration in the management of public spending, has moved Botswana out of the "mostly free" category.

Nonetheless, Botswana's scores on many of the 10 economic freedoms are consistently among the region's highest. The level of corruption is the lowest in Africa. An independent judiciary enforces contracts effectively and protects property rights, buttressing competitiveness.

BACKGROUND: The Botswana Democratic Party has governed this multi-party democracy since independence from Britain in 1966. Ian Khama assumed the presidency in 2008 upon his predecessor's resignation, won a five-year term in 2009, and won a second term in October 2014. Gomolemo Motswaledi, head of the opposition Botswana Movement for Democracy and vice president of the opposition Umbrella for Democratic Change coalition, died in a car crash in July 2014, increasing tensions in the run-up to the fall elections. With abundant natural resources and a market-oriented economy, Botswana has Africa's highest sovereign credit rating. Diamonds account for one-third of GDP (about US$3.3 billion), and the diamond industry has transformed Botswana into a middle-income country. In an attempt to diversify the economy through tourism, Botswana has focused on conservation and developing extensive nature preserves. Botswana has one of the world's highest HIV/AIDS infection rates but is also among Africa's leaders in combating the disease.

Freedom Trend

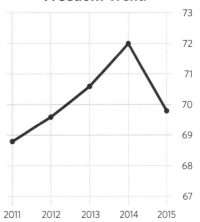

73

72

71

70

69

68

67

2011   2012   2013   2014   2015

Country Comparisons

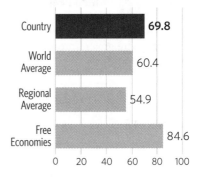

Country	69.8
World Average	60.4
Regional Average	54.9
Free Economies	84.6

0   20   40   60   80   100

Quick Facts

Population: 2.1 million
GDP (PPP): $34.1 billion
3.9% growth in 2013
5-year compound annual growth 2.8%
$16,377 per capita
Unemployment: 18.4%
Inflation (CPI): 5.8%
FDI Inflow: $188.2 million
Public Debt: 15.9% of GDP

2013 data unless otherwise noted.
Data compiled as of September 2014.

How Do We Measure Economic Freedom?
See page 475 for an explanation of the methodology
or visit the *Index* Web site at *heritage.org/index*.

THE TEN ECONOMIC FREEDOMS

	Score		Rank	1-Year Change

RULE OF LAW

	Score		Rank	1-Year Change
Property Rights	70.0		30th	0
Freedom from Corruption	64.0		30th	+2.8

Although Botswana continues to be rated Africa's least corrupt country, there are almost no restrictions on the private business activities of public servants (the president is a large stakeholder in the tourism sector), and political ties often play a role in awarding government jobs and tenders. The legal system is sufficient to enforce secure commercial dealings, but the process is lengthy and time-consuming.

GOVERNMENT SIZE

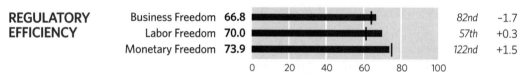

	Score		Rank	1-Year Change
Fiscal Freedom	79.5		89th	-1.5
Government Spending	61.9		104th	-7.9

The top individual income tax rate is 25 percent, and the top corporate tax rate is 22 percent. Other taxes include a sales tax, a value-added tax, and a property tax. The overall tax burden equals 30.7 percent of GDP. Public expenditures amount to 35.7 percent of domestic income, and public debt equals 16 percent of the domestic economy. A sovereign wealth fund helps to ease fiscal cycles.

REGULATORY EFFICIENCY

	Score		Rank	1-Year Change
Business Freedom	66.8		82nd	-1.7
Labor Freedom	70.0		57th	+0.3
Monetary Freedom	73.9		122nd	+1.5

A more streamlined licensing process has eased business start-up procedures, but the overall pace of reform has slowed. Employment regulations are moderately flexible, and the non-salary cost of hiring a worker is relatively low. The inefficient agricultural sector is highly subsidized by the government, which also influences prices through state-owned enterprises and service providers.

OPEN MARKETS

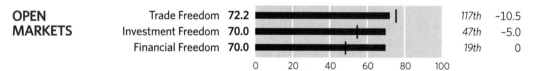

	Score		Rank	1-Year Change
Trade Freedom	72.2		117th	-10.5
Investment Freedom	70.0		47th	-5.0
Financial Freedom	70.0		19th	0

Botswana's average tariff rate is 6.4 percent. Importing goods can be costly. There are some limits on land sales to foreign investors. Botswana's competitive banking sector is one of Africa's most advanced. Credit is allocated on market terms, although the government provides some subsidized loans. The government has abolished exchange controls, and the Botswana Stock Exchange is growing.

Long-Term Score Change (since 1995)

RULE OF LAW		GOVERNMENT SIZE		REGULATORY EFFICIENCY		OPEN MARKETS	
Property Rights	0	Fiscal Freedom	+25.8	Business Freedom	-3.2	Trade Freedom	+26.0
Freedom from Corruption	+14.0	Government Spending	+6.8	Labor Freedom	+3.4	Investment Freedom	+20.0
				Monetary Freedom	+8.0	Financial Freedom	+20.0

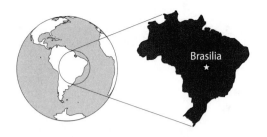

BRAZIL

Economic Freedom Score

56.6

B razil's economic freedom score is 56.6, making its economy the 118th freest in the 2015 *Index*. Its score is 0.3 point worse than last year, reflecting declines in half of the 10 economic freedoms including investment freedom, the management of government spending, and monetary freedom. Brazil is ranked 21st out of 29 countries in the South and Central America/Caribbean region, and its overall score is below the world average.

Over the past five years, Brazil's economic freedom has advanced by less than 0.5 point. Improvements in financial freedom and freedom from corruption have been largely offset by deteriorations in the area of regulatory efficiency, including business freedom and labor freedom.

The negative economic impact of stagnant economic freedom has largely been masked by strong growth driven by high commodity prices over the past decade, but a deteriorating international environment and diminished growth expectations have brought these structural issues to the forefront. More broad-based and consistent reforms will be needed to guarantee long-term economic development.

BACKGROUND: Preparations for the 2014 World Cup and 2016 Rio Olympic games have tested President Dilma Rousseff's government. Public discontent was reflected in the unexpectedly strong showing by Socialist Party candidate Marina Silva, but Rousseff was re-elected to a second term in October 2014. Brazil is spending heavily to host marquee sporting events, but Brazilians resent the fact that they are left to contend with poor public services, antiquated and insufficient infrastructure, high taxes, inflation, corruption, and sluggish economic growth. Brazil's "Bolsa Família," a conditional cash transfer program for the poor, has helped the government to win support in some sectors. Brazil is the world's seventh-largest economy, and its population of almost 200 million is heavily concentrated on the Atlantic coast. The middle class is growing, and millions have been lifted out of poverty, but government intervention in the economy continues to cause the misallocation of capital and limit mobility, fueling a sense of injustice.

Freedom Trend

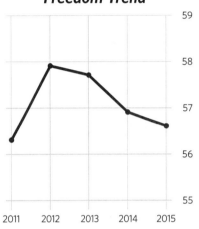

Country Comparisons

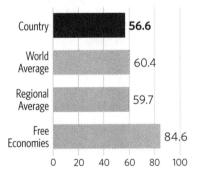

Country	**56.6**
World Average	60.4
Regional Average	59.7
Free Economies	84.6

Quick Facts

Population: 198.3 million
GDP (PPP): $2.4 trillion
2.3% growth in 2013
5-year compound annual growth 2.6%
$12,221 per capita
Unemployment: 6.6%
Inflation (CPI): 6.2%
FDI Inflow: $64.0 billion
Public Debt: 66.3% of GDP

2013 data unless otherwise noted.
Data compiled as of September 2014.

THE TEN ECONOMIC FREEDOMS

		Score		Rank	1-Year Change
RULE OF LAW	Property Rights	50.0		56th	0
	Freedom from Corruption	42.0		72nd	+4.1

Public discontent about new state-funded World Cup stadiums while public services remain deficient is reflected in a 2014 survey, which indicates that 85 percent of Brazilians disapprove of President Rousseff's policies on corruption and crime. The judiciary is inefficient and subject to political and economic influence. The court system is generally overburdened, and contract disputes can be lengthy and complex.

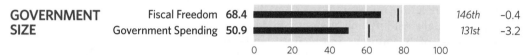

		Score		Rank	1-Year Change
GOVERNMENT SIZE	Fiscal Freedom	68.4		146th	-0.4
	Government Spending	50.9		131st	-3.2

The top individual income tax rate is 27.5 percent. The top corporate tax rate of 34 percent includes a 15 percent corporate tax, a corporate surtax, and a 9 percent social contributions tax on net profits. There are other federal, state, and municipal taxes. The tax burden is equivalent to 35.3 percent of domestic income. Public spending equals 40.4 percent of GDP, and public debt amounts to 66 percent of the economy.

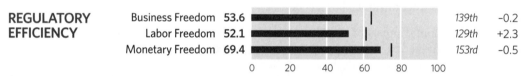

		Score		Rank	1-Year Change
REGULATORY EFFICIENCY	Business Freedom	53.6		139th	-0.2
	Labor Freedom	52.1		129th	+2.3
	Monetary Freedom	69.4		153rd	-0.5

Progress in reforming the regulatory framework has been uneven. Bureaucratic hurdles include lengthy processes for launching a business and obtaining permits. The non-salary cost of employing a worker adds to the cost of doing business, and labor regulations remain stringent. Inflation has increased steadily since 2011, and the government has imposed economically distortionary price controls and subsidies.

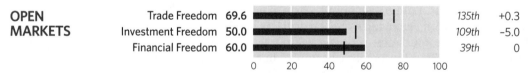

		Score		Rank	1-Year Change
OPEN MARKETS	Trade Freedom	69.6		135th	+0.3
	Investment Freedom	50.0		109th	-5.0
	Financial Freedom	60.0		39th	0

Brazil's average tariff rate is 7.7 percent. The government has worked to improve customs procedures, but non-tariff barriers deter imports of goods and services. Foreign investment in aviation, insurance, and other sectors is limited. The financial sector is diversified and competitive, but the state's role remains significant. State-owned banks control over a quarter of assets and direct loans to certain preferred sectors.

Long-Term Score Change (since 1995)

RULE OF LAW		GOVERNMENT SIZE		REGULATORY EFFICIENCY		OPEN MARKETS	
Property Rights	0	Fiscal Freedom	-8.3	Business Freedom	-1.4	Trade Freedom	+13.2
Freedom from Corruption	-8.0	Government Spending	-23.5	Labor Freedom	-12.5	Investment Freedom	0
				Monetary Freedom	+69.4	Financial Freedom	+10.0

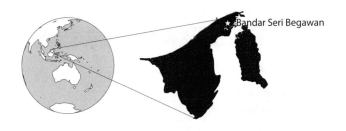
★ Bandar Seri Begawan

BRUNEI

Economic Freedom Score

Least free 0   Most free 100

68.9

Brunei's economic freedom score is 68.9, making its economy the 39th freest in the 2015 *Index*. Its overall score is essentially the same as last year's, with improvements in freedom from corruption, monetary freedom, and labor freedom counterbalanced by declines in property rights, fiscal freedom, and the management of public spending. Brunei is ranked 10th out of 42 countries in the Asia–Pacific region, and its overall score is higher than the regional and world averages.

Brunei was graded in the *Index* for the first time in 2014 and continues to perform competitively in most aspects of economic freedom. Relatively high market openness facilitates integration into the global economy, particularly in the oil and natural gas sectors. Macroeconomic stability has been a staple of development, which has been supported by a well-developed legal system, secure property rights, and a commitment to investment.

Improving access to private-sector financing remains critical if the government wishes to diversify away from the oil and gas industry. The small financial sector, largely insulated from the global financial crisis, has seen a boom in Islamic finance in recent years. Streamlined investment rules and regulations would improve openness and encourage economic growth.

BACKGROUND: The Sultan of Brunei is prime minister, minister of defense, and minister of finance. He is advised by several councils, including a Legislative Council and Privy Council, which he appoints. Imposition of a new Sharia Penal Code, which includes harsh penalties (including death) for a variety of offenses, in 2014 generated widespread international criticism. The oil and gas industry, which accounts for over half of GDP and 90 percent of government revenues, funds a sizable welfare state, and most of the population works directly for the government. Brunei has extremely low manufacturing capacity and imports most of its manufactured goods and food. The government is seeking integration into the global economy as a member of the Trans-Pacific Partnership negotiations.

Freedom Trend

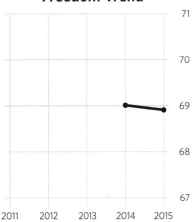

Country Comparisons

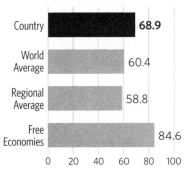

Country	68.9
World Average	60.4
Regional Average	58.8
Free Economies	84.6

Quick Facts

Population: 0.4 million
GDP (PPP): $21.7 billion
–1.2% growth in 2013
5-year compound annual growth 0.8%
$53,431 per capita
Unemployment: 3.7%
Inflation (CPI): 0.4%
FDI Inflow: $895.0 million
Public Debt: 2.5% of GDP

2013 data unless otherwise noted.
Data compiled as of September 2014.

How Do We Measure Economic Freedom?
See page 475 for an explanation of the methodology
or visit the *Index* Web site at *heritage.org/index*.

THE TEN ECONOMIC FREEDOMS

		Score		Rank	1-Year Change
RULE OF LAW	Property Rights	35.0		87th	–5.0
	Freedom from Corruption	60.0		37th	+6.7

Human rights concerns arose in 2014 as the government began to implement Shari'ah (Islamic) law in Brunei. Protection of private property is weak. Only citizens of Brunei may purchase land; foreign firms must have a local partner. The constitution does not provide for an independent judiciary, and the sultan wields broad powers. No direct legislative elections have been held since 1962.

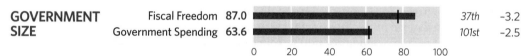

		Score		Rank	1-Year Change
GOVERNMENT SIZE	Fiscal Freedom	87.0		37th	–3.2
	Government Spending	63.6		101st	–2.5

Brunei has no income tax, and the top corporate tax rate is 20 percent for most companies. The corporate tax rate for oil and gas companies is 55 percent. Other taxes include a social security tax. The overall tax burden is equivalent to 30 percent of gross domestic output. Government spending equals around 35 percent of the domestic economy, and public debt is below 3 percent of GDP.

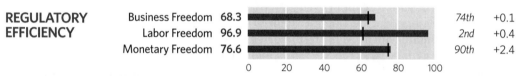

		Score		Rank	1-Year Change
REGULATORY EFFICIENCY	Business Freedom	68.3		74th	+0.1
	Labor Freedom	96.9		2nd	+0.4
	Monetary Freedom	76.6		90th	+2.4

Incorporating new businesses takes more than three months, but there is no minimum capital requirement. Licensing requirements consume 17 procedures and 88 days on average. A supply-and-demand imbalance persists in the labor market. The public sector remains the main source of employment. The government provides large price-distorting subsidies for nearly everything the average citizen needs.

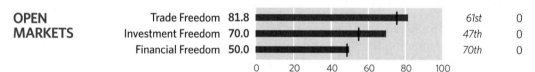

		Score		Rank	1-Year Change
OPEN MARKETS	Trade Freedom	81.8		61st	0
	Investment Freedom	70.0		47th	0
	Financial Freedom	50.0		70th	0

Brunei's average tariff rate is 4.1 percent. Non-tariff barriers are low, but numerous state-owned enterprises affect trade and investment. There is no foreign ownership of land. The government restricts foreign investment in certain sectors of the economy. The small but growing financial sector is dominated by commercial banks, which remain well-capitalized. Despite some progress, the banking sector lacks competition.

Long-Term Score Change (since 2014)

RULE OF LAW		GOVERNMENT SIZE		REGULATORY EFFICIENCY		OPEN MARKETS	
Property Rights	–5.0	Fiscal Freedom	–3.2	Business Freedom	+0.1	Trade Freedom	0
Freedom from Corruption	+6.7	Government Spending	–2.5	Labor Freedom	+0.4	Investment Freedom	0
				Monetary Freedom	+2.4	Financial Freedom	0

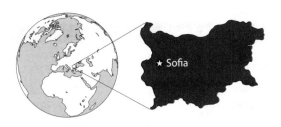

BULGARIA

Economic Freedom Score

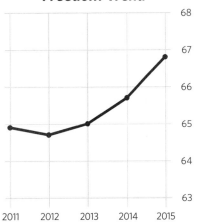

66.8

World Rank: 55   **Regional Rank: 26**

Bulgaria's economic freedom score is 66.8, making its economy the 55th freest in the 2015 *Index*. Its overall score is 1.1 points better than last year due to improvements in investment freedom, freedom from corruption, and monetary freedom that outweigh declines in business freedom and labor freedom. Bulgaria is ranked 26th out of 43 countries in the Europe region, and its overall score is above the world average but below the regional average.

Over the past five years, economic freedom in Bulgaria has advanced by nearly 2.0 points, led by a more open investment environment, improvements in the fiscal outlook, diminished perceptions of corruption, and low inflation. Gains were recorded in six of the 10 factors, led by investment and monetary freedom, which advanced 10 points and 7.7 points, respectively.

Bulgaria has taken steps to control budget deficits and public debt more effectively, but further reform is necessary to achieve broad-based economic freedom and growth. In particular, institutional reforms must promote judicial independence and tackle corruption in order to solidify the foundations of economic freedom and ensure progress toward greater prosperity.

BACKGROUND: Bulgaria joined the European Union in January 2007. Former Finance Minister Plamen Oresharski became prime minister in May 2013 at the head of a Socialist Party–led coalition. In June 2014, amid protests against low standards of living, high energy costs, and corruption, President Rosen Plevneliev announced that he was dissolving Parliament because of banking instability. Tourism, information technology and telecommunications, agriculture, pharmaceuticals, and textiles are leading industries. Despite EU protests, Bulgaria has refused to stop work on its section of Russia's South Stream pipeline and the Azerbaijan/Turkey-backed Trans-Anatolian Natural Gas pipeline. Sluggishness in the economy has been exacerbated by the EU crisis and internal instability. Bulgaria remains one of the EU's poorest countries. Prospects for adoption of the euro have declined.

Freedom Trend

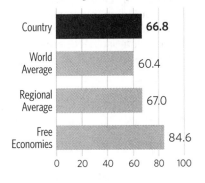

Country Comparisons

Country	66.8
World Average	60.4
Regional Average	67.0
Free Economies	84.6

Quick Facts

Population: 7.2 million
GDP (PPP): $105.0 billion
0.9% growth in 2013
5-year compound annual growth -0.4%
$14,499 per capita
Unemployment: 13.1%
Inflation (CPI): 0.4%
FDI Inflow: $1.5 billion
Public Debt: 17.6% of GDP

2013 data unless otherwise noted.
Data compiled as of September 2014.

How Do We Measure Economic Freedom?
See page 475 for an explanation of the methodology
or visit the *Index* Web site at *heritage.org/index.*

THE TEN ECONOMIC FREEDOMS

RULE OF LAW

	Score		Rank	1-Year Change
Property Rights	30.0		94th	0
Freedom from Corruption	41.0		77th	+5.8

Corrupt and inconsistent public administration, a weak judiciary, and organized crime continue to hamper Bulgaria's economic prospects. Human trafficking, narcotics, and contraband smuggling contribute to corruption. In May 2014, the parliament approved a five-year residency requirement for foreign purchase of agricultural land. The judicial system does not enforce property rights effectively.

GOVERNMENT SIZE

	Score		Rank	1-Year Change
Fiscal Freedom	91.0		27th	-0.2
Government Spending	64.5		100th	0

Bulgaria's top individual and corporate income tax rates are 10 percent. Other taxes include a value-added tax and an estate tax. Total tax revenue equaled 26.5 percent of gross domestic product in the most recent year. Public expenditures account for 34.4 percent of GDP, and public debt remains under 18 percent of the size of the economy.

REGULATORY EFFICIENCY

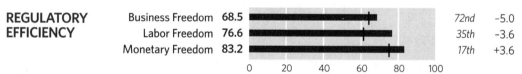

	Score		Rank	1-Year Change
Business Freedom	68.5		72nd	-5.0
Labor Freedom	76.6		35th	-3.6
Monetary Freedom	83.2		17th	+3.6

The overall regulatory framework supports entrepreneurial activity. Launching a business is less time-consuming, and the minimum capital requirement has been eliminated. However, obtaining licenses still takes more than three months. The labor market needs further reform. Although most prices are determined by market forces, rising and unevenly distributed agricultural subsidies from the European Union have distorted land values.

OPEN MARKETS

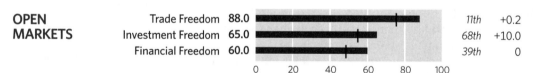

	Score		Rank	1-Year Change
Trade Freedom	88.0		11th	+0.2
Investment Freedom	65.0		68th	+10.0
Financial Freedom	60.0		39th	0

EU members have a 1.0 percent average tariff rate. Although some non-tariff barriers exist, the EU is relatively open to external trade. Bulgaria's regulatory and court systems can be a hurdle for foreign investors. The financial sector, dominated by banks, has benefited from increased competition. A June 2014 run on deposits at Corpbank prompted the central bank to seize control of the bank and freeze its operations.

Long-Term Score Change (since 1995)

RULE OF LAW		GOVERNMENT SIZE		REGULATORY EFFICIENCY		OPEN MARKETS	
Property Rights	-20.0	Fiscal Freedom	+45.0	Business Freedom	+13.5	Trade Freedom	+15.6
Freedom from Corruption	+11.0	Government Spending	+14.0	Labor Freedom	-3.7	Investment Freedom	-5.0
				Monetary Freedom	+56.9	Financial Freedom	+10.0

BURKINA FASO

Ouagadougou

Economic Freedom Score

50
25   75
Least free 0   100 Most free

58.6

Burkina Faso's economic freedom score is 58.6, making its economy the 102nd freest in the 2015 *Index*. Its overall score has decreased by 0.3 point since last year, with improvements in half of the 10 economic freedom, including freedom from corruption and investment freedom, offset by declines in business freedom and property rights. Burkina Faso is ranked 13th out of 46 countries in the Sub-Saharan Africa region, and its overall score is above the regional average.

Over the past five years, Burkina Faso's economic freedom has been declining. Since 2011, when it registered its highest economic freedom score ever, Burkina Faso has fallen back to the "mostly unfree" category. Improvements in investment freedom, labor freedom, and monetary freedom have been counterbalanced by significant declines in business freedom, financial freedom, and trade freedom.

Deeper structural and institutional reforms are critically needed to maintain stability and ensure long-term economic development. Systemic weaknesses in the protection of property rights, exacerbated by an inefficient judicial system that remains vulnerable to political influence, hinder the development of a more vibrant entrepreneurial environment.

BACKGROUND: President Blaise Compaoré had ruled the former French colony since seizing power in 1987, but was ousted in a coup in late 2014. The country now faces a year of political transition. In 2013, Burkina Faso sent 500 troops to Mali to help secure the northern half of the country from Tuareg separatists and groups linked to al-Qaeda. As many as 33,000 Malian refugees remain in Burkina Faso, despite efforts to repatriate the refugees back to Mali. Burkina Faso is the world's third-poorest country, with an estimated poverty rate of 46 percent, and relies heavily on cotton and gold exports. Approximately 90 percent of the population depends on subsistence agriculture. Ongoing problems include inflation and endemic corruption.

Freedom Trend

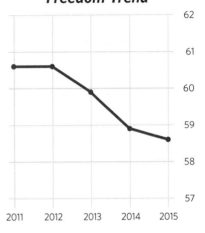

2011   2012   2013   2014   2015

Country Comparisons

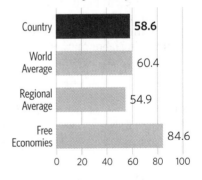

Country	58.6
World Average	60.4
Regional Average	54.9
Free Economies	84.6

0 20 40 60 80 100

Quick Facts

Population: 16.8 million
GDP (PPP): $26.6 billion
6.8% growth in 2013
5-year compound annual growth 6.4%
$1,585 per capita
Unemployment: 3.1%
Inflation (CPI): 2.0%
FDI Inflow: $374.3 million
Public Debt: 33.3% of GDP

2013 data unless otherwise noted.
Data compiled as of September 2014.

How Do We Measure Economic Freedom?
See page 475 for an explanation of the methodology or visit the *Index* Web site at *heritage.org/index*.

THE TEN ECONOMIC FREEDOMS

		Score	■ Country	│ World Average	Rank	1-Year Change

RULE OF LAW

	Score		Rank	1-Year Change
Property Rights	25.0		124th	–5.0
Freedom from Corruption	38.0		83rd	+6.7

Burkina Faso, one of the world's poorest and least developed countries, has never experienced a peaceful transition of power. President Compaoré, who seized power in 1987, was ousted in a coup in 2014. Corruption is widespread, especially in public procurement, and the judiciary is weak. Members of the presidential family and the ruling party have controlled key economic activities.

GOVERNMENT SIZE

	Score		Rank	1-Year Change
Fiscal Freedom	82.4		65th	–0.6
Government Spending	79.8		46th	–2.5

The top individual income and corporate tax rates are 27.5 percent. Other taxes include a value-added tax. The overall tax burden is equivalent to 15.8 percent of gross domestic product. Government expenditures make up 25.9 percent of the domestic economy, and public debt amounts to 33 percent of total domestic output.

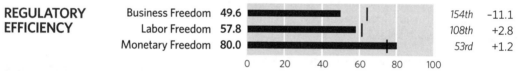

REGULATORY EFFICIENCY

	Score		Rank	1-Year Change
Business Freedom	49.6		154th	–11.1
Labor Freedom	57.8		108th	+2.8
Monetary Freedom	80.0		53rd	+1.2

The inefficient business environment continues to impede broader economic development. The minimum capital required to start a business exceeds three times the level of average annual income. Getting necessary permits takes more than 100 days. In the absence of a well-functioning labor market, informal labor activity persists in many sectors. The state subsidizes fuels and electricity and maintains price supports for cotton.

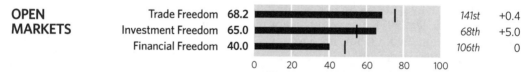

OPEN MARKETS

	Score		Rank	1-Year Change
Trade Freedom	68.2		141st	+0.4
Investment Freedom	65.0		68th	+5.0
Financial Freedom	40.0		106th	0

Burkina Faso has an average tariff rate of 8.4 percent. Importing goods is time-consuming and expensive. The government must compensate investors in the event of expropriation of property. The financial system remains underdeveloped. Banks have continued to increase their domestic assets, and there are several microfinance institutions, but overall access to credit remains limited.

Long-Term Score Change (since 1996)

RULE OF LAW		GOVERNMENT SIZE		REGULATORY EFFICIENCY		OPEN MARKETS	
Property Rights	–5.0	Fiscal Freedom	+15.7	Business Freedom	+9.6	Trade Freedom	+13.2
Freedom from Corruption	+28.0	Government Spending	–4.5	Labor Freedom	+14.0	Investment Freedom	–5.0
				Monetary Freedom	+20.9	Financial Freedom	+10.0

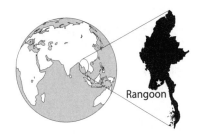

BURMA

Economic Freedom Score

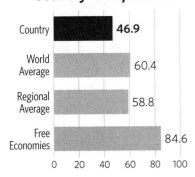

46.9

Burma's economic freedom score is 46.9, making its economy the 161st freest in the 2015 *Index*. Its score is 0.4 point better than last year due to improvements in five of the 10 economic freedoms, including freedom from corruption, labor freedom, and monetary freedom, that outweigh a substantial decline in the control of government spending. Burma is ranked 38th out of 42 countries in the Asia–Pacific region, and its overall score is much lower than the regional average.

Over the past five years, economic freedom in Burma has advanced by about 9.0 points, the second-best improvement among graded countries. From a low base, Burma has made considerable strides in liberalizing its economy and opening itself to the outside world. Gains in eight of the 10 economic freedoms include greater price stability and double-digit improvements in labor freedom and investment freedom.

Nevertheless, Burma remains a "repressed" economy due to years of state intervention, poor institutional structures, and autarkic investment and financial regimes. To solidify and build on the past half-decade's gains, the government must continue its reform agenda with particular emphasis on stamping out corruption, enforcing property rights, creating an independent judiciary, and further opening up the economy to the international marketplace.

BACKGROUND: Burma has been a military dictatorship since 1962 but since 2010 has pursued limited political and economic reform, including releases of political prisoners, relaxation of media censorship, and exchange rate reform. Sectarian violence and continued persecution of Muslim and Christian minorities remain problems. National League for Democracy leader and Nobel laureate Aung San Suu Kyi was released from jail in November 2010 and won a seat in parliament in 2012. The United States and the European Union eased some sanctions in response to Burma's limited changes, but state-sponsored repression has led many to urge caution before lifting all sanctions. Heavy government intervention in the economy has made Burma one of the world's poorest countries.

Freedom Trend

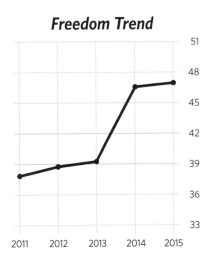

Country Comparisons

Country	46.9
World Average	60.4
Regional Average	58.8
Free Economies	84.6

Quick Facts

Population: 64.9 million
GDP (PPP): $113.0 billion
7.5% growth in 2013
5-year compound annual growth 6.2%
$1,740 per capita
Unemployment: 3.5%
Inflation (CPI): 5.8%
FDI Inflow: $2.6 billion
Public Debt: 42.7% of GDP

2013 data unless otherwise noted.
Data compiled as of September 2014.

How Do We Measure Economic Freedom?
See page 475 for an explanation of the methodology
or visit the *Index* Web site at *heritage.org/index*.

THE TEN ECONOMIC FREEDOMS

		Score				Rank	1-Year Change
RULE OF LAW	Property Rights	10.0				165th	0
	Freedom from Corruption	21.0				165th	+9.4

Burma's emerging but deeply flawed democratic reform process will likely lose momentum in the run-up to the 2015 elections. Corruption is endemic. Due to a complex and capricious regulatory/legal environment and extremely low government salaries, rent-seeking is ubiquitous. Rule of law and protection of property rights are weak. Judicial decisions are often influenced by government interference, personal relationships, or bribes.

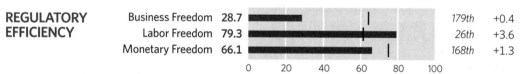

		Score		Rank	1-Year Change
GOVERNMENT SIZE	Fiscal Freedom	86.9		39th	0
	Government Spending	77.9		59th	-11.3

Burma's top individual income tax rate is 20 percent, and its top corporate tax rate is 30 percent. Commercial and capital gains taxes add to government revenue, but the overall tax burden remains less than 5 percent of gross domestic product. Public expenditures amount to 27.2 percent of the domestic economy, and public debt is equal to around 43 percent of total domestic output.

		Score		Rank	1-Year Change
REGULATORY EFFICIENCY	Business Freedom	28.7		179th	+0.4
	Labor Freedom	79.3		26th	+3.6
	Monetary Freedom	66.1		168th	+1.3

Significant bureaucratic impediments to entrepreneurial activity and economic development persist. The labor market remains underdeveloped, and enforcement of the labor codes is ineffective. The informal sector continues to be an important source of employment. Inflation is expected to remain elevated, led by higher prices for rice and other staple foods and electricity.

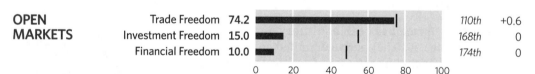

		Score		Rank	1-Year Change
OPEN MARKETS	Trade Freedom	74.2		110th	+0.6
	Investment Freedom	15.0		168th	0
	Financial Freedom	10.0		174th	0

Burma's average tariff rate is 3.2 percent, and some imports face additional restrictions. The government reviews new foreign investment, and state-owned enterprises dominate some sectors of the economy. The financial system remains underdeveloped, and the banking sector is dominated by state-owned banks. Most loans are directed to government-led projects, and access to credit remains very poor.

Long-Term Score Change (since 1996)

RULE OF LAW		GOVERNMENT SIZE		REGULATORY EFFICIENCY		OPEN MARKETS	
Property Rights	-20.0	Fiscal Freedom	+5.1	Business Freedom	-11.3	Trade Freedom	+24.2
Freedom from Corruption	+11.0	Government Spending	-3.4	Labor Freedom	+59.3	Investment Freedom	-15.0
				Monetary Freedom	+12.8	Financial Freedom	-20.0

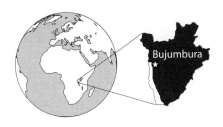

Bujumbura

BURUNDI

Economic Freedom Score

50
25   75
Least   Most
free 0   100 free

53.7

World Rank: 132   **Regional Rank: 27**

Burundi's economic freedom score is 53.7, making its economy the 132nd freest in the 2015 *Index*. Its overall score is 2.3 points better than last year, reflecting improvements in six of the 10 economic freedoms including the management of government spending, labor freedom, and freedom from corruption. Burundi is ranked 27th out of 46 countries in the Sub-Saharan Africa region, and its score is worse than the world average.

Over the past five years, economic freedom in Burundi has advanced by 4.1 points. Business freedom, control of government spending, and investment freedom have improved by 5.0 points or more. This year, Burundi has achieved its highest economic freedom score ever, registering the seventh-biggest improvement in the 2015 *Index*.

Despite these improvements, Burundi remains in the ranks of the "mostly unfree." The lack of capable public institutions and the weak rule of law continue to undermine the implementation of other critical reforms. Tariff and non-tariff barriers, coupled with burdensome investment regulations, still hamper development of a more dynamic private sector and interfere with diversification of the economic base.

BACKGROUND: The 1993 assassination of Hutu President Melchior Ndadaye sparked a civil war between Hutus and Tutsis that also significantly influenced the Hutu-led 1994 Rwandan genocide. Negotiations mediated by South Africa led to a power-sharing government in 2001. Pierre Nkurunziza, elected president by the National Assembly under a new constitution in 2005, was re-elected in 2010 in a disputed vote. His regime's repressive policies and attacks on the opposition and media have led to fears of renewed violence. Burundi is active in the African Union's AMISOM peacekeeping mission in Somalia and deployed troops to the Central African Republic as part of an international effort to prevent civil war in 2014. The economy is dominated by subsistence agriculture, and half of the population lives below the poverty line. Corruption is endemic.

Freedom Trend

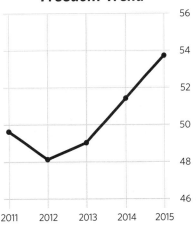

56
54
52
50
48
46

2011 2012 2013 2014 2015

Country Comparisons

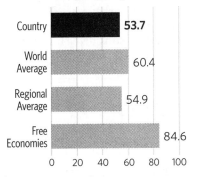

Country — **53.7**
World Average — 60.4
Regional Average — 54.9
Free Economies — 84.6

0 20 40 60 80 100

Quick Facts

Population: 9.0 million
GDP (PPP): $5.8 billion
4.5% growth in 2013
5-year compound annual growth 4.3%
$642 per capita
Unemployment: 8.5%
Inflation (CPI): 8.8%
FDI Inflow: $6.8 million
Public Debt: 31.7% of GDP

2013 data unless otherwise noted.
Data compiled as of September 2014.

How Do We Measure Economic Freedom?
See page 475 for an explanation of the methodology
or visit the *Index* Web site at *heritage.org/index.*

THE TEN ECONOMIC FREEDOMS

		Score	Country	World Average	Rank	1-Year Change

RULE OF LAW
Property Rights 20.0 — 138th — 0
Freedom from Corruption 21.0 — 165th — +5.1

Land-locked Burundi is one of the world's poorest nations and one of the most corrupt countries in sub-Saharan Africa. Government procurement is conducted nontransparently amid allegations of cronyism, and customs officials reportedly extort bribes. The judiciary is nominally independent, but judges are subject to undue political pressure. Private property is vulnerable to government expropriation and armed banditry.

GOVERNMENT SIZE

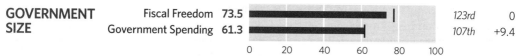

Fiscal Freedom 73.5 — 123rd — 0
Government Spending 61.3 — 107th — +9.4

Burundi's top individual and corporate income tax rates are 35 percent. Other taxes, including a value-added tax, add to government revenue that equates to 14.1 percent of domestic output. Foreign assistance also helps to support government expenditures that equal about 35.9 percent of gross domestic product. Public debt equals 32 percent of the domestic economy.

REGULATORY EFFICIENCY

Business Freedom 61.4 — 104th — +1.6
Labor Freedom 68.1 — 65th — +5.0
Monetary Freedom 69.8 — 148th — +1.6

Reform measures in recent years have streamlined the procedures for incorporating a business, but start-ups are discouraged by time-consuming licensing requirements. With the labor market relatively underdeveloped, the public sector accounts for most formal employment. The state subsidizes fuel, rations subsidized electricity, and influences other prices through state-owned enterprises and agriculture-support programs.

OPEN MARKETS

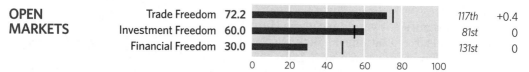

Trade Freedom 72.2 — 117th — +0.4
Investment Freedom 60.0 — 81st — 0
Financial Freedom 30.0 — 131st — 0

Burundi's average tariff rate is 6.4 percent. Importers may face customs delays, and importing goods is expensive. Although the country is relatively open to foreign investment, corruption may be a problem. The underdeveloped financial sector remains dominated by banks that are plagued by nonperforming loans and inadequate capitalization. Much of the population relies on informal lending.

Long-Term Score Change (since 1997)

RULE OF LAW		GOVERNMENT SIZE		REGULATORY EFFICIENCY		OPEN MARKETS	
Property Rights	−10.0	Fiscal Freedom	+29.9	Business Freedom	+6.4	Trade Freedom	+2.0
Freedom from Corruption	+11.0	Government Spending	−20.2	Labor Freedom	+14.4	Investment Freedom	+30.0
				Monetary Freedom	+11.2	Financial Freedom	0

CABO VERDE

Economic Freedom Score

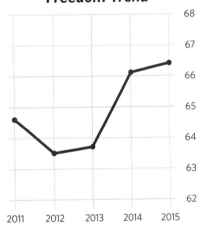

50
25   75

Least
free 0   100 Most
free

66.4

World Rank: **60**   Regional Rank: **3**

Cabo Verde's economic freedom score is 66.4, making its economy the 60th freest in the 2015 *Index*. Its overall score is 0.3 point better than last year due to advancements in monetary stability and the rule of law as measured by property rights and freedom from corruption. Cabo Verde is ranked 3rd out of 46 countries in the Sub-Saharan Africa region, and its overall score continues to be much higher than the global and regional averages.

Over the past five years, economic freedom in Cabo Verde has advanced by close to 2.0 points, reflecting broad-based improvements in six of the 10 economic freedoms, including investment freedom, fiscal freedom, and the protection of property rights. In the 2015 *Index*, Cabo Verde has recorded its highest economic freedom score ever, progressing further into the ranks of the "moderately free."

With macroeconomic stability well maintained and good governance firmly in place, Cabo Verde has made notable progress in economic growth and development. Its impressive transition to a more open and flexible economic system has been facilitated by policies that promote open markets and regulatory efficiency, buttressed by a transparent legal framework that upholds the rule of law.

BACKGROUND: Cabo Verde is a stable, multi-party parliamentary democracy. Prime Minister Jose Maria Neves of the Independence for Cabo Verde Party took office in 2001 and was re-elected in 2006 and 2011. Opposition leader Jose Carlos Fonseca of the Movement for Democracy won presidential elections in 2011. The Cabo Verde islands have few natural resources. Severe droughts in the 20th century caused the deaths of 200,000 people and prompted heavy emigration. As a result, Cabo Verde's expatriate population is larger than its domestic population. Services dominate the economy, and about 82 percent of the country's food is imported. Economic reforms aim to boost foreign investment and diversify the economy.

Freedom Trend

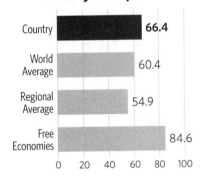

68
67
66
65
64
63
62

2011   2012   2013   2014   2015

Country Comparisons

Country — 66.4
World Average — 60.4
Regional Average — 54.9
Free Economies — 84.6

0   20   40   60   80   100

Quick Facts

Population: 0.5 million
GDP (PPP): $2.2 billion
0.5% growth in 2013
5-year compound annual growth 1.1%
$4,338 per capita
Unemployment: 8.6%
Inflation (CPI): 1.5%
FDI Inflow: $18.7 million
Public Debt: 95.0% of GDP

2013 data unless otherwise noted.
Data compiled as of September 2014.

How Do We Measure Economic Freedom?
See page 475 for an explanation of the methodology or visit the *Index* Web site at *heritage.org/index*.

THE TEN ECONOMIC FREEDOMS

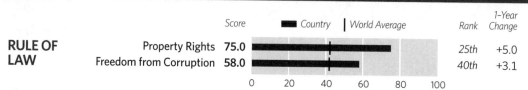

RULE OF LAW

	Score		Rank	1-Year Change
Property Rights	75.0		25th	+5.0
Freedom from Corruption	58.0		40th	+3.1

Although Cabo Verde is among Sub-Saharan Africa's least corrupt countries, the government launched a new program in 2014 to combat "serious ethical problems and strong indication of corruption" in the civil service. Private property is reasonably well protected. The constitutional provision for an independent judiciary is generally respected, but the judicial system is inefficient, and the case backlog causes significant delays.

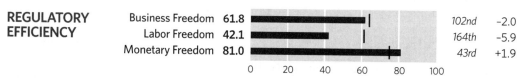

GOVERNMENT SIZE

	Score		Rank	1-Year Change
Fiscal Freedom	78.3		102nd	+0.9
Government Spending	67.9		92nd	-0.7

The top individual income tax rate is 35 percent, and the top corporate tax rate is 25 percent. Other taxes include a value-added tax. The overall tax burden is equal to 18 percent of the domestic economy. Public expenditures equal 32.7 percent of gross domestic product, and public debt is nearly equivalent to the total size of the economy.

REGULATORY EFFICIENCY

	Score		Rank	1-Year Change
Business Freedom	61.8		102nd	-2.0
Labor Freedom	42.1		164th	-5.9
Monetary Freedom	81.0		43rd	+1.9

Steps to introduce greater regulatory efficiency have been implemented in recent years. It takes seven procedures and 10 days on average to incorporate a business, and no minimum capital is required. Despite reform efforts, labor market rigidity persists. The market determines most prices, but the government subsidizes electricity and water as well as a state-owned, loss-making airline.

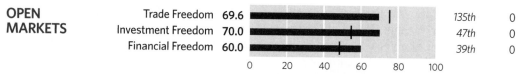

OPEN MARKETS

	Score		Rank	1-Year Change
Trade Freedom	69.6		135th	0
Investment Freedom	70.0		47th	0
Financial Freedom	60.0		39th	0

Cabo Verde's average tariff rate is 10.2 percent, and non-tariff barriers are relatively low for the region. Domestic and foreign investors are generally treated equally under the law. Banks dominate the small financial sector. They remain well-capitalized, and the number of nonperforming loans is decreasing. Small and medium-sized companies have access to credit that is allocated on market terms, but capital markets are not fully developed.

Long-Term Score Change (since 1996)

RULE OF LAW		GOVERNMENT SIZE		REGULATORY EFFICIENCY		OPEN MARKETS	
Property Rights	+5.0	Fiscal Freedom	+14.0	Business Freedom	+6.8	Trade Freedom	+24.6
Freedom from Corruption	+28.0	Government Spending	+37.0	Labor Freedom	-14.8	Investment Freedom	0
				Monetary Freedom	+8.7	Financial Freedom	+50.0

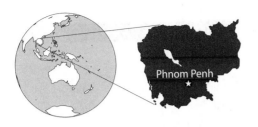
★ Phnom Penh

CAMBODIA

World Rank: 110   **Regional Rank: 23**

Cambodia's economic freedom score is 57.5, making its economy the 110th freest in the 2015 *Index*. Its overall score is essentially unchanged from last year, with improvements in labor freedom and freedom from corruption largely offset by declines in business freedom and property rights. Cambodia is ranked 23rd out of 42 countries in the Asia–Pacific region, and its overall score is lower than the regional average.

Over the past five years, economic freedom in Cambodia has stagnated, with potential gains from a liberalized labor market and a small opening to international markets undermined by a weakening business environment, looser fiscal policy, and a decline in property rights.

Little progress has been made in tackling corruption, which is by far the most serious threat to advancing economic freedom in Cambodia. The government must do more to strengthen the institutional environment underpinning the rule of law, including improving the judiciary and reinforcing property rights. These issues, along with a poor business environment and government interference in the economy, continue to undermine the dynamic investment flows enjoyed by regional neighbors.

BACKGROUND: Between 1975 and 1979, Pol Pot's Khmer Rouge regime killed an estimated 3 million Cambodians. The Khmer Rouge Tribunal, established under an agreement with the United Nations to prosecute senior officials involved in the atrocities, has been slow to deliver justice. Though it is nominally a democracy, Cambodia has been ruled by former Khmer Rouge member and Vietnamese puppet Prime Minister Hun Sen since 1993. The 2013 election nearly unseated Hun Sen and remains hotly contested by the opposition party. In 2012, Cambodia took its turn chairing the Association of Southeast Asian Nations, drawing increased international attention to and criticism of its undemocratic policies and close ties to China. Cambodia's economy depends heavily on tourism and apparel assembly.

Freedom Trend

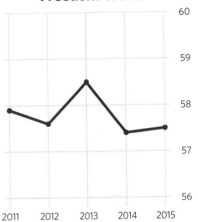

60

59

58

57

56

2011   2012   2013   2014   2015

Country Comparisons

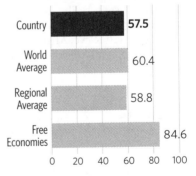

Country	57.5
World Average	60.4
Regional Average	58.8
Free Economies	84.6

0   20   40   60   80   100

Quick Facts

Population: 15.4 million
GDP (PPP): $39.7 billion
7.0% growth in 2013
5-year compound annual growth 5.5%
$2,576 per capita
Unemployment: 0.3%
Inflation (CPI): 3.0%
FDI Inflow: $1.4 billion
Public Debt: 28.1% of GDP

2013 data unless otherwise noted.
Data compiled as of September 2014.

THE TEN ECONOMIC FREEDOMS

	Score	Country	World Average	Rank	1-Year Change

RULE OF LAW

	Score			Rank	1-Year Change
Property Rights	25.0			124th	−5.0
Freedom from Corruption	20.0			168th	+1.3

The perverse effects of decades of international intervention and foreign aid have contributed to rampant corruption in Cambodia. Three new judicial "reform" laws approved in 2014 will further entrench the ruling party. Weak and inconsistent courts do not protect private property effectively. Investments in many economic sectors frequently are accompanied by land grabs by powerful politicians, bureaucrats, and military officers.

GOVERNMENT SIZE

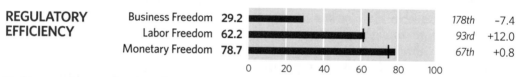

	Score			Rank	1-Year Change
Fiscal Freedom	90.5			29th	−0.3
Government Spending	87.5			23rd	−0.9

The top individual and corporate income tax rates are 20 percent. Businesses in the petroleum and gas sectors are assessed at a 30 percent rate. Other taxes include a value-added tax and an excise tax. Total tax revenue equals 12.2 percent of GDP. Government expenditures amount to around 20 percent of the domestic economy, and public debt is equivalent to 28 percent of total domestic output.

REGULATORY EFFICIENCY

	Score			Rank	1-Year Change
Business Freedom	29.2			178th	−7.4
Labor Freedom	62.2			93rd	+12.0
Monetary Freedom	78.7			67th	+0.8

Red tape and inconsistent enforcement of the laws hinder the development of a critically needed private sector. The formal labor market remains distorted by state intervention that sets public-sector wages and influences wage-setting in the market. Enforcement of the labor code remains ineffective. Although most prices are determined by the market, the government has been increasing subsidies for fuel.

OPEN MARKETS

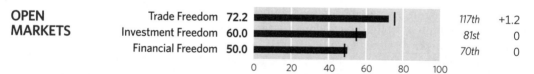

	Score			Rank	1-Year Change
Trade Freedom	72.2			117th	+1.2
Investment Freedom	60.0			81st	0
Financial Freedom	50.0			70th	0

Cambodia has an average tariff rate of 8.9 percent. Non-tariff barriers at the border further restrict trade. The slow-moving bureaucracy and court system present challenges for foreign investors. Development of the financial sector has progressed gradually, although large state banks have recorded notable growth and continue to dominate the banking system.

Long-Term Score Change (since 1997)

RULE OF LAW		GOVERNMENT SIZE		REGULATORY EFFICIENCY		OPEN MARKETS	
Property Rights	−5.0	Fiscal Freedom	−1.2	Business Freedom	−25.8	Trade Freedom	+57.2
Freedom from Corruption	−10.0	Government Spending	−4.3	Labor Freedom	+18.3	Investment Freedom	+10.0
				Monetary Freedom	+16.6	Financial Freedom	0

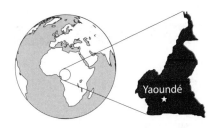

CAMEROON

51.9

| World Rank: **146** | Regional Rank: **35** |

Cameroon's economic freedom score is 51.9, making its economy the 146th freest in the 2015 *Index*. Its overall score is 0.7 point worse than last year, with declines in labor freedom, business freedom, property rights, and trade freedom outweighing improvements in monetary freedom and freedom from corruption. Cameroon is ranked 35th out of 46 countries in the Sub-Saharan Africa region, and its overall score is lower than the regional average.

Over the past half-decade, economic freedom in Cameroon has stagnated. The country made progress in a four of the 10 economic freedoms—freedom from corruption, fiscal freedom, labor freedom, and monetary freedom—but registered no improvements in opening markets to integrate more fully into the global economy.

Although Cameroon has risen from the ranks of the "repressed" where it was over a decade ago, it has made little headway in capitalizing on reform momentum, and growth from an oil and commodity boom has lessened pressure for needed changes. Institutional reforms to tackle nepotism and cronyism and to promote an independent judiciary remain vital for laying the foundations of economic freedom and spurring the broad-based growth that is needed to deal with high rates of poverty.

BACKGROUND: President Paul Biya has held office since 1982 and was re-elected in October 2011 for another seven-year term in an election that was marred by irregularities. Cameroon is rife with corruption and often accused of failing to ensure equality under the law. The economy is dependent on commodity exports and subject to burdensome regulation. Economic growth was seriously affected by the global economic slowdown. Cameroonian security forces are at war with Nigerian Islamist terrorist group Boko Haram, which has attacked and infiltrated villages along the 1,800-km Cameroon–Nigerian border. Cameroon currently hosts approximately 35,000 refugees from the Central African Republic.

Freedom Trend

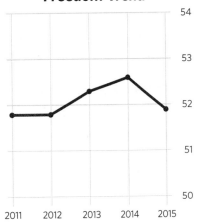

Country Comparisons

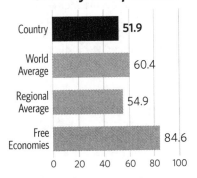

Quick Facts

Population: 22.0 million
GDP (PPP): $53.3 billion
4.6% growth in 2013
5-year compound annual growth 3.7%
$2,423 per capita
Unemployment: 4.0%
Inflation (CPI): 2.1%
FDI Inflow: $572.0 million
Public Debt: 18.6% of GDP

2013 data unless otherwise noted.
Data compiled as of September 2014.

THE TEN ECONOMIC FREEDOMS

		Score		Rank	1-Year Change
RULE OF LAW	Property Rights	25.0		124th	−5.0
	Freedom from Corruption	25.0		149th	+3.1

In power since 1982, President Paul Biya's unwieldy government includes over 50 ministers and secretaries of state, mostly from his Beti ethnic group. Cronyism and corruption are endemic. Revenues from oil, gas, and mining are not openly reported. Protection of real property rights is weak, and the judicial system is slow, inefficient, and vulnerable to political interference. Intellectual property rights are routinely violated.

		Score		Rank	1-Year Change
GOVERNMENT SIZE	Fiscal Freedom	71.7		133rd	0
	Government Spending	87.8		21st	+1.8

The top individual income tax rate is 35 percent, and the top corporate tax rate is 38.5 percent (a 35 percent tax rate and 10 percent surcharge). Other taxes include a value-added tax and inheritance taxes. The overall tax burden amounts to 11.0 percent of gross domestic output. Public expenditures equal 20.2 percent of GDP, and public debt is equal in size to 19 percent of the domestic economy.

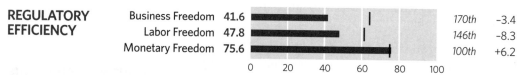

		Score		Rank	1-Year Change
REGULATORY EFFICIENCY	Business Freedom	41.6		170th	−3.4
	Labor Freedom	47.8		146th	−8.3
	Monetary Freedom	75.6		100th	+6.2

Bureaucracy and a lack of transparency make business formation costly and burdensome. Business start-up has been streamlined, but obtaining necessary licenses remains time-consuming. Labor regulations are rigid, and restrictions on work hours are stringent. In 2014, the government reduced subsidies for most energy products to stem the growth of budget deficits that had undermined public infrastructure investment.

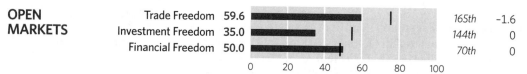

		Score		Rank	1-Year Change
OPEN MARKETS	Trade Freedom	59.6		165th	−1.6
	Investment Freedom	35.0		144th	0
	Financial Freedom	50.0		70th	0

Cameroon's average tariff rate is 12.7 percent. As with other members of the Central African Economic and Monetary Community, importing goods may be costly. Foreign investors may face bureaucratic hurdles. The financial sector remains relatively resilient and continues to expand. Despite increased market competition, however, state-owned financial institutions dominate the sector and influence lending.

Long-Term Score Change (since 1995)

RULE OF LAW		GOVERNMENT SIZE		REGULATORY EFFICIENCY		OPEN MARKETS	
Property Rights	−25.0	Fiscal Freedom	+20.6	Business Freedom	−13.4	Trade Freedom	+34.6
Freedom from Corruption	+15.0	Government Spending	−2.0	Labor Freedom	−4.2	Investment Freedom	−15.0
				Monetary Freedom	−5.3	Financial Freedom	0

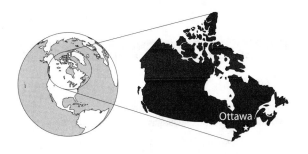

CANADA

Economic Freedom Score

Least free 0

Most free 100

79.1

Canada's economic freedom score is 79.1, making its economy the 6th freest in the 2015 *Index*. Its overall score is 1.1 points lower than last year, with modest improvements in monetary freedom and the control of government spending outweighed by declines in labor freedom and freedom from corruption. Canada continues to be the freest economy in the North America region.

Over the past five years, Canada's economic freedom score has declined by 1.7 points, highlighting a trend that has pushed the country into the "mostly free" category for the first time since 2007. Score declines have been spread over five of the 10 economic freedoms, with an increase in the level of perceived corruption contributing the most to the moderate slide in Canada's score.

Nonetheless, Canada remains one of the world's most stable business climates and an attractive investment destination. With the world's second-best property rights regime buttressing openness to global commerce, Canada has a solid foundation of economic freedom. The financial sector is competitive, and its efficiency is supported by prudent lending practices and sound oversight.

BACKGROUND: Prime Minister Stephen Harper and his Conservative Party have governed since 2011 with a strong parliamentary majority of 166 out of 308 seats. With 103 seats, the social democratic New Democratic Party has become the leading opposition party for the first time. The next election must be held no later than October 19, 2015, when 30 new seats will be added to the House of Commons to increase representation of provinces with growing populations. Canada's diversity and geographic size are reflected in a democratic system that provides substantial autonomy to its 13 provinces and territories. The 20 percent of Canadians for whom French is the native language are heavily concentrated in Quebec. Canada is a major exporter of oil, minerals, automobiles, manufactured goods, and forest products, and its economy is closely linked to the U.S. economy.

Freedom Trend

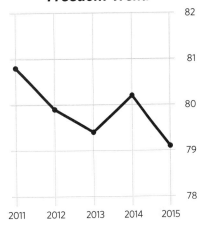

Country Comparisons

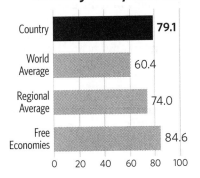

Quick Facts

Population: 35.1 million
GDP (PPP): $1.5 trillion
2.0% growth in 2013
5-year compound annual growth 1.4%
$43,472 per capita
Unemployment: 7.1%
Inflation (CPI): 1.0%
FDI Inflow: $62.3 billion
Public Debt: 89.1% of GDP

2013 data unless otherwise noted.
Data compiled as of September 2014.

THE TEN ECONOMIC FREEDOMS

		Score	Rank	1-Year Change
RULE OF LAW	Property Rights	90.0	3rd	0
	Freedom from Corruption	81.0	9th	-6.7

Canada's robust economic freedom rests on a judicial system with an impeccable record of independence and transparency. The government prosecutes corruption vigorously. Private property is well protected. In 2014, the Supreme Court for the first time confirmed an indigenous land title. Enforcement of contracts is very secure, and expropriation is highly unusual. Protection of intellectual property rights is consistent with world standards.

		Score	Rank	1-Year Change
GOVERNMENT SIZE	Fiscal Freedom	79.9	86th	+0.2
	Government Spending	48.3	135th	+1.0

Canada's top federal individual income tax rate is 29 percent, and its top corporate tax rate is 15 percent. Other taxes include a property tax and a value-added tax. The overall tax burden is equivalent to 30.7 percent of gross domestic product. Government expenditures amount to 41.5 percent of domestic output, and public debt is equal to 89 percent of the domestic economy.

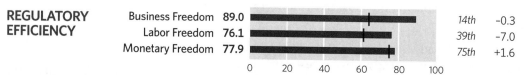

		Score	Rank	1-Year Change
REGULATORY EFFICIENCY	Business Freedom	89.0	14th	-0.3
	Labor Freedom	76.1	39th	-7.0
	Monetary Freedom	77.9	75th	+1.6

With no minimum capital requirement, establishing a business takes only one procedure and five days, but completing licensing requirements takes over 200 days on average. The labor market remains relatively flexible, and labor costs are moderate. The government provides extensive energy and agricultural subsidies and controls virtually all prices for health care through a mandatory "single-payer" nationalized program.

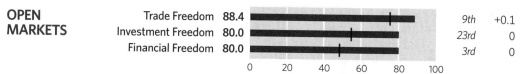

		Score	Rank	1-Year Change
OPEN MARKETS	Trade Freedom	88.4	9th	+0.1
	Investment Freedom	80.0	23rd	0
	Financial Freedom	80.0	3rd	0

Canada's average tariff rate is a low 0.8 percent. Canada continues to negotiate free trade agreements but restricts dairy imports. Foreign investment in some sectors of the economy, including airlines and telecommunications, is regulated. Financial institutions offer a wide range of services, and credit is readily available on market terms. The banking sector remains stable, and securities markets are well developed.

Long-Term Score Change (since 1995)

RULE OF LAW		GOVERNMENT SIZE		REGULATORY EFFICIENCY		OPEN MARKETS	
Property Rights	0	Fiscal Freedom	+15.7	Business Freedom	+4.0	Trade Freedom	+13.2
Freedom from Corruption	-9.0	Government Spending	+33.5	Labor Freedom	-6.1	Investment Freedom	+30.0
				Monetary Freedom	-8.0	Financial Freedom	+10.0

CENTRAL AFRICAN REPUBLIC

★ Bangui

Economic Freedom Score

25   **50**   75

Least free   0   100   Most free

45.9

World Rank: 166   **Regional Rank: 41**

The Central African Republic's economic freedom score is 45.9, making its economy the 166th freest in the 2015 *Index*. Its overall score is 0.8 point lower than last year, with modest gains in the rule of law undermined by declines in six other areas. The CAR is ranked 41st out of 46 countries in the Sub-Saharan Africa region, and its overall score is lower than the regional average.

Over the past five years, economic freedom in the CAR has declined by 3.4 points, with score decreases in the past two years wiping out steady improvements earlier in the decade. Score declines in eight of the 10 economic freedoms indicate deteriorations across such key policy areas as market openness and regulatory efficiency. In the 2015 *Index*, the CAR has registered its lowest economic freedom score ever.

The Central African Republic's overall entrepreneurial environment remains severely constrained, burdened by over-regulation that pushes many entrepreneurs into the informal sector. Poor access to credit and high financing costs further suppress the development of a vibrant private sector. Since 2013, state institutions have collapsed, and the economy has contracted sharply.

BACKGROUND: In 2013, Seleka rebels ousted President François Bozizé and seized power under the leadership of Michel Djotodia. Widespread atrocities carried out by the Seleka militia spurred the emergence of the "anti-balaka" militia, comprised of Christians opposed to Seleka rule. France sent forces to the former French colony in December 2013, and a U.N. peacekeeping force was deployed in September 2014. Djotodia stepped down early in 2014 after failing to stop sectarian violence and was replaced by interim President Catherine Samba-Panza. General elections are scheduled for early 2015. The CAR is one of the world's least-developed countries. More than half of the population lives in rural areas and depends on subsistence agriculture. The CAR has abundant timber, diamonds gold, uranium, and prospects for oil exploration.

Freedom Trend

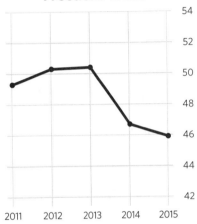

2011   2012   2013   2014   2015

54
52
50
48
46
44
42

Country Comparisons

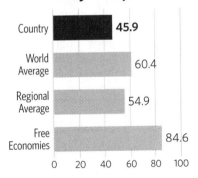

Country   **45.9**
World Average   60.4
Regional Average   54.9
Free Economies   84.6

0   20   40   60   80   100

Quick Facts

Population: 4.6 million
GDP (PPP): $2.5 billion
–36.0% growth in 2013
5-year compound annual growth –6.3%
$542 per capita
Unemployment: 8.8%
Inflation (CPI): 6.6%
FDI Inflow: $0.8 million
Public Debt: 50.8% of GDP

2013 data unless otherwise noted.
Data compiled as of September 2014.

How Do We Measure Economic Freedom?
See page 475 for an explanation of the methodology
or visit the *Index* Web site at *heritage.org/index*.

THE TEN ECONOMIC FREEDOMS

		Score	■ Country	❘ World Average		Rank	1-Year Change

RULE OF LAW

Property Rights 15.0 — 157th +5.0
Freedom from Corruption 25.0 — 149th +4.4

A 2013 coup d'état disrupted the economy and amplified a state of lawlessness, and despite growing financial and military support, the interim government is struggling to restore stability. Corruption remains pervasive. Armed groups are involved in the illicit trade and exploitation of natural resources, especially gold and diamonds, which account for more than half of export earnings. Protection of property rights is weak.

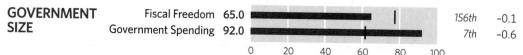

GOVERNMENT SIZE

Fiscal Freedom 65.0 — 156th −0.1
Government Spending 92.0 — 7th −0.6

The Central African Republic's top individual income tax rate is 50 percent, and its top corporate tax rate is 30 percent. Other taxes include a value-added tax. The overall tax burden equals 9.8 percent of gross domestic product. Government expenditures equal 16.3 percent of the domestic economy, and public debt is about half the size of the domestic economy.

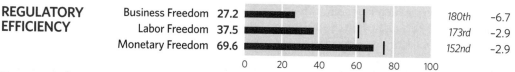

REGULATORY EFFICIENCY

Business Freedom 27.2 — 180th −6.7
Labor Freedom 37.5 — 173rd −2.9
Monetary Freedom 69.6 — 152nd −2.9

Progress in improving the business framework has been slow and uneven. Labor regulations are not generally enforced, and the labor market remains poorly developed. Most of the population is employed outside of the formal sector, primarily in agriculture. Government distortions of the economy through subsidies and wage/price controls are aggravated by political instability that undermines the basic functioning of state institutions.

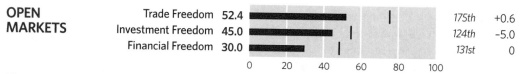

OPEN MARKETS

Trade Freedom 52.4 — 175th +0.6
Investment Freedom 45.0 — 124th −5.0
Financial Freedom 30.0 — 131st 0

The Central African Republic's average tariff rate is 16.3 percent. Imports of products like sugar face additional restrictions, and exports may be subject to taxation. Political instability continues to be a serious deterrent to foreign investment. Poor access to credit significantly hinders private-sector growth. The banking system remains highly dependent on the government and state-owned companies.

Long-Term Score Change (since 2002)

RULE OF LAW		GOVERNMENT SIZE		REGULATORY EFFICIENCY		OPEN MARKETS	
Property Rights	−35.0	Fiscal Freedom	−0.3	Business Freedom	−27.8	Trade Freedom	+4.2
Freedom from Corruption	−5.0	Government Spending	+4.0	Labor Freedom	−12.2	Investment Freedom	−25.0
				Monetary Freedom	−12.4	Financial Freedom	−20.0

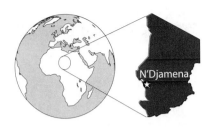

CHAD

World Rank: 165　　　　　**Regional Rank: 40**

Economic Freedom Score

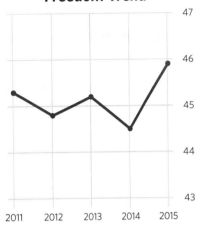

Least free 0　　　　　Most free 100

45.9

Chad's economic freedom score is 45.9, making its economy the 165th freest in the 2015 *Index*. Its overall score is 1.4 points better than last year, reflecting improvements in five of the 10 economic freedoms, particularly in policy areas related to regulatory efficiency such as monetary freedom, labor freedom, and business freedom. Chad is ranked 40th out of 46 countries in the Sub-Saharan Africa region, and its overall score is lower than the regional average.

Over the past five years, Chad's economic freedom has advanced by 0.6 points, but with a trend that has seen it bounce between yearly score gains and losses. Score improvements have been modest and evenly spread among four of the 10 economic freedoms: freedom from corruption, business freedom, labor freedom, and monetary freedom. Price stability has improved the most.

Despite these modest improvements, the state continues to interfere heavily but ineffectively in the economy, and the quality of governance is low. Price controls continue to distort the markets for essential goods, and poor maintenance of the rule of law causes uncertainty, corruption, and lax enforcement of property rights. These factors gravely undermine the prospects for long-term economic development that could combat rampant poverty.

BACKGROUND: President Idriss Déby, who seized power in 1990, won a fourth term in 2011 in a highly dubious election. President Déby continues to face armed revolt by the opposition as well as charges of corruption. Security forces foiled coup plots in 2006, 2008, and 2013. Chad has sent troops to assist peacekeeping forces in Darfur, the Central African Republic, and the Democratic Republic of Congo to reduce cross-border violence and instability. Conflict in eastern Chad and unrest in Sudan's Darfur region have created hundreds of thousands of refugees. In January 2014, Chad began a two-year rotation on the U.N. Security Council.

Freedom Trend

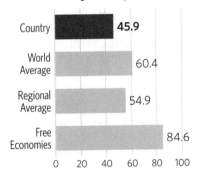

Country Comparisons

Country 45.9
World Average 60.4
Regional Average 54.9
Free Economies 84.6

Quick Facts

Population: 11.0 million
GDP (PPP): $28.0 billion
3.6% growth in 2013
5-year compound annual growth 6.0%
$2,539 per capita
Unemployment: 8.6%
Inflation (CPI): 0.2%
FDI Inflow: $538.4 million
Public Debt: 30.2% of GDP

2013 data unless otherwise noted.
Data compiled as of September 2014.

How Do We Measure Economic Freedom?
See page 475 for an explanation of the methodology
or visit the *Index* Web site at *heritage.org/index*.

THE TEN ECONOMIC FREEDOMS

		Score	■ Country		World Average		Rank	1-Year Change

RULE OF LAW

Property Rights 20.0 — 138th — 0
Freedom from Corruption 19.0 — 171st — +3.1

Although several high-profile officials were arrested on corruption charges in 2013, Chad remains one of the world's most corrupt countries. The president's inner circle continues to siphon off the nation's oil wealth. The rule of law is weak, and most key officials in the constitutionally independent judiciary are named by the president. Protection of private property is inadequate, and fraud is common in property transactions.

GOVERNMENT SIZE

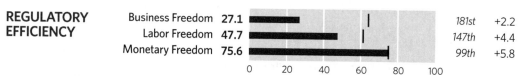

Fiscal Freedom 46.2 — 177th — 0
Government Spending 83.6 — 35th — +3.6

Chad's top individual income tax rate is the world's highest: 60 percent. Its top corporate tax rate is 45 percent. Other taxes include a value-added tax and a property tax. Lax enforcement results in an overall tax burden of just 5.1 percent of domestic income. Government expenditures equal 23.4 percent of gross domestic product, and public debt equals 30 percent of the domestic economy.

REGULATORY EFFICIENCY

Business Freedom 27.1 — 181st — +2.2
Labor Freedom 47.7 — 147th — +4.4
Monetary Freedom 75.6 — 99th — +5.8

Burdensome regulations continue to hinder private-sector development. The regulatory system lacks transparency and clarity, and regulations are enforced inconsistently. The formal labor market is underdeveloped. Inflation has fallen, but the state continues to subsidize state-owned enterprises such as an oil refinery, a tractor assembly plant, and electricity, water, and cotton companies.

OPEN MARKETS

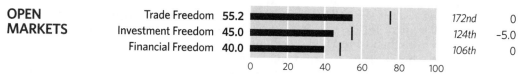

Trade Freedom 55.2 — 172nd — 0
Investment Freedom 45.0 — 124th — −5.0
Financial Freedom 40.0 — 106th — 0

Chad's average tariff rate is 14.9 percent. Chad is a member of the Central African Economic and Monetary Community. Exports may be subject to taxation, and state-owned enterprises operate in several sectors of the economy. The high cost of credit and scarce access to financing hold back private-sector development. A large part of the population remains outside of the formal banking sector.

Long-Term Score Change (since 1997)

RULE OF LAW		GOVERNMENT SIZE		REGULATORY EFFICIENCY		OPEN MARKETS	
Property Rights	−10.0	Fiscal Freedom	0	Business Freedom	−27.9	Trade Freedom	+1.8
Freedom from Corruption	+9.0	Government Spending	−5.5	Labor Freedom	+4.4	Investment Freedom	+15.0
				Monetary Freedom	+13.2	Financial Freedom	+10.0

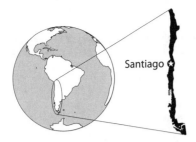

Santiago ☆

CHILE

Economic Freedom Score

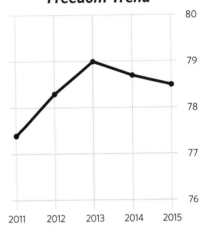

Least free 0 ... 100 Most free

78.5

Chile's economic freedom score is 78.5, making its economy the 7th freest in the 2015 *Index*. Its overall score is 0.2 point lower than last year, with an improvement in monetary freedom outweighed by declines in labor freedom, freedom from corruption, and the control of government spending. Still one of the 10 freest economies in the *Index*, Chile enjoys the highest degree of economic freedom in the South and Central America/Caribbean region.

Over the past five years, Chile's economic freedom has advanced by 1.1 points, securing Chile's place as the first South and Central American country to reach the top 10 in the rankings. Improvements in five of the 10 economic freedoms have been led by sizeable gains in property rights, price stability, and the investment climate.

Despite recent declines, Chile remains a global leader in economic freedom and an example for other Latin American countries. Aided by prudent public financial management and successful countercyclical fiscal policy, it has kept public debt low and budget deficits under control. Chile is second in the world in protecting property rights and has been renewing its commitment to open trade and investment by participating in the Trans-Pacific Partnership talks.

BACKGROUND: Socialist President Michelle Bachelet began her second (non-consecutive) four-year term in 2014, succeeding Sebastian Piñera, and immediately proposed tax increases to fund higher government spending on education and other services while discounting concerns that this would dampen future growth. Even if Bachelet largely maintains market-based institutions and economic policies, her campaign promises to reform Chile's constitution could have significant undesirable effects, and Chile's commitment to the Pacific Alliance could weaken. Nonetheless, Chile retains the region's best reputation among foreign investors. It was the first South American country to join the Organisation for Economic Co-operation and Development and is the world's leading producer of copper. The economy is very open to imports but is also an export powerhouse in minerals, wood, fruit, seafood, and wine.

Freedom Trend

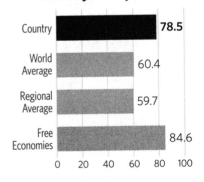

Country Comparisons

Country	78.5
World Average	60.4
Regional Average	59.7
Free Economies	84.6

Quick Facts

Population: 17.6 million
GDP (PPP): $334.8 billion
4.2% growth in 2013
5-year compound annual growth 4.0%
$19,067 per capita
Unemployment: 5.9%
Inflation (CPI): 1.8%
FDI Inflow: $20.3 billion
Public Debt: 12.2% of GDP

2013 data unless otherwise noted.
Data compiled as of September 2014.

How Do We Measure Economic Freedom?
See page 475 for an explanation of the methodology
or visit the *Index* Web site at *heritage.org/index*.

THE TEN ECONOMIC FREEDOMS

RULE OF LAW

	Score		Rank	1-Year Change
Property Rights	90.0		3rd	0
Freedom from Corruption	71.0		22nd	−1.3

Chile is among South America's least corrupt countries. Courts are generally free from political interference. Although President Bachelet campaigned in 2013 on a promise to reform the constitution, adopted in 1980 during the return to democratic self-government, Chile most likely will retain its independent and competent judiciary. Property rights and contracts are strongly respected, and expropriation is rare.

GOVERNMENT SIZE

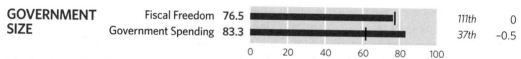

	Score		Rank	1-Year Change
Fiscal Freedom	76.5		111th	0
Government Spending	83.3		37th	−0.5

The top individual income tax rate remains 40 percent, and the top corporate tax rate is 20 percent. Other taxes include a value-added tax and a property tax. The total tax burden is equivalent to 18.8 percent of domestic income. Government expenditures equal 23.6 percent of total domestic output, and public debt amounts to less than 15 percent of gross domestic product.

REGULATORY EFFICIENCY

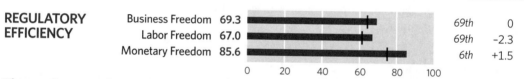

	Score		Rank	1-Year Change
Business Freedom	69.3		69th	0
Labor Freedom	67.0		69th	−2.3
Monetary Freedom	85.6		6th	+1.5

The regulatory regime sustains business formation and operation. Starting a business takes seven procedures and six days on average and costs less than 1 percent of the level of average annual income. Labor regulations are rigid, with broad wage settlements and high unionization. Government price supports for agriculture are less than 5 percent of total farm receipts, one of the lowest rates among OECD countries.

OPEN MARKETS

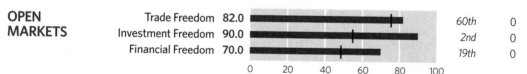

	Score		Rank	1-Year Change
Trade Freedom	82.0		60th	0
Investment Freedom	90.0		2nd	0
Financial Freedom	70.0		19th	0

Chile has a 4.0 percent average tariff rate. Most imports enter duty-free, and tariffs have been reduced through the Pacific Alliance. Chile is very open to foreign investment. A well-capitalized and dynamic banking sector provides a wide range of services, and the financial system remains one of the region's most advanced. Credit is issued on market terms, and domestic and foreign financial firms receive equal treatment.

Long-Term Score Change (since 1995)

RULE OF LAW		GOVERNMENT SIZE		REGULATORY EFFICIENCY		OPEN MARKETS	
Property Rights	0	Fiscal Freedom	−2.9	Business Freedom	−15.7	Trade Freedom	+19.0
Freedom from Corruption	+21.0	Government Spending	−3.7	Labor Freedom	−10.3	Investment Freedom	+20.0
				Monetary Freedom	+19.4	Financial Freedom	+20.0

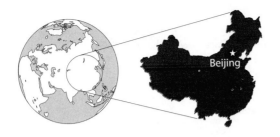

CHINA

Economic Freedom Score

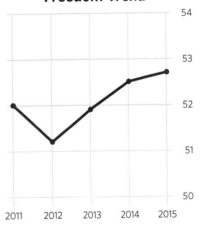

25   **50**   75

Least free 0   100 Most free

52.7

China's economic freedom score is 52.7, making its economy the 139th freest in the 2015 *Index*. Its overall score is 0.2 point higher than last year, with modest improvements in freedom from corruption, business freedom, and labor freedom largely offset by declines in investment freedom and the control of government spending. China is ranked 30th out of 42 countries in the Asia–Pacific region, and its overall score is lower than the global and regional averages.

Over the past five years, economic freedom in China has improved by less than 1.0 point, continuing its patchy and uneven progress since 1995. The one bright spot has been an 8.1-point improvement in labor freedom since 2011. A restrictive residency permitting system remains in place, and gains in labor freedom have been largely offset by losses in other factors, including a 5.5-point decline in the control of government spending.

A more comprehensive set of economic reforms is desperately needed, especially a loosening of the government's stranglehold on investment flows. The Communist Party's control of all levels of government continues to undermine confidence in the rule of law and interfere with the development of an independent judiciary. Institutionalized cronyism is prevalent.

BACKGROUND: Under the government of Communist Party General Secretary Xi Jinping, China has talked about the need for economic "rebalancing" (the shifting of power and wealth from state-owned enterprises and local governments to the household sector), but real changes in power relationships have been hard to detect. Reforms to improve labor mobility have gained no traction. Tensions in the South and East China Seas have increased with Beijing's unilateral declaration of an Air Defense Identification Zone and its deployment of an oil rig in Vietnamese waters. China has achieved impressive GDP growth based on economic reforms and greater integration into the world trading and financial systems since the late 1970s. The size of its industrial and manufacturing sector now rivals that of the United States.

Freedom Trend

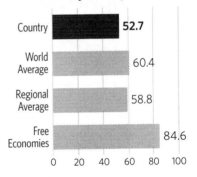

	2011	2012	2013	2014	2015

Chart range: 50 to 54

Country Comparisons

Country **52.7**
World Average 60.4
Regional Average 58.8
Free Economies 84.6

0   20   40   60   80   100

Quick Facts

Population: 1.36 billion
GDP (PPP): $13.4 trillion
7.7% growth in 2013
5-year compound annual growth 8.9%
$9,844 per capita
Unemployment: 4.6%
Inflation (CPI): 2.6%
FDI Inflow: $123.9 billion
Public Debt: 22.4% of GDP

2013 data unless otherwise noted.
Data compiled as of September 2014.

THE TEN ECONOMIC FREEDOMS

		Score			Rank	1-Year Change
RULE OF LAW	Property Rights	20.0			138th	0
	Freedom from Corruption	40.0			80th	+5.0

Xi Jinping began his first year in power with an anti-corruption campaign that netted several high-ranking officials, but corruption remains endemic. With Chinese cyber espionage visibly on the rise in 2014, protection of property rights has clearly deteriorated. China's weak judicial system is highly vulnerable to political influence. The giant urban migrant workforce has little legal protection despite promises of reform.

		Score			Rank	1-Year Change
GOVERNMENT SIZE	Fiscal Freedom	69.7			139th	-0.2
	Government Spending	81.5			43rd	-1.4

China's top individual income tax rate is 45 percent, and its top corporate tax rate is 25 percent. Other taxes include a value-added tax and a real estate tax. The total tax burden equaled 19.4 percent of gross domestic product in the most recent year. Total government expenditures account for 24.8 percent of domestic output, and public debt equals 22 percent of GDP.

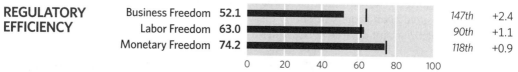

		Score			Rank	1-Year Change
REGULATORY EFFICIENCY	Business Freedom	52.1			147th	+2.4
	Labor Freedom	63.0			90th	+1.1
	Monetary Freedom	74.2			118th	+0.9

Regulatory reform has progressed gradually and unevenly. Incorporating a business takes 11 procedures and about a month. Bureaucratic hurdles still add to the cost of completing licensing requirements. Labor regulations are relatively flexible, but enforcement of labor laws is not consistent. The government provides large fossil fuel and electricity subsidies and also funds significant agricultural subsidies.

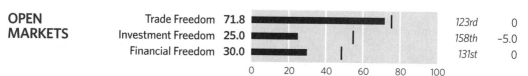

		Score			Rank	1-Year Change
OPEN MARKETS	Trade Freedom	71.8			123rd	0
	Investment Freedom	25.0			158th	-5.0
	Financial Freedom	30.0			131st	0

China's average tariff rate is 4.1 percent. Export taxes, subsidies to state-owned enterprises, anti-dumping barriers, and other measures restrict trade. The government screens foreign investment and still tightly controls the financial system. State-owned enterprises benefit from greater access to capital and lower financing costs, but small and medium-sized companies continue to suffer from the lack of access to credit.

Long-Term Score Change (since 1995)

RULE OF LAW		GOVERNMENT SIZE		REGULATORY EFFICIENCY		OPEN MARKETS	
Property Rights	-10.0	Fiscal Freedom	-0.9	Business Freedom	-2.9	Trade Freedom	+51.8
Freedom from Corruption	+10.0	Government Spending	-12.2	Labor Freedom	-2.0	Investment Freedom	-25.0
				Monetary Freedom	+5.8	Financial Freedom	-20.0

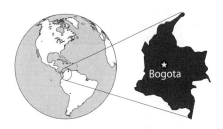

COLOMBIA

Economic Freedom Score

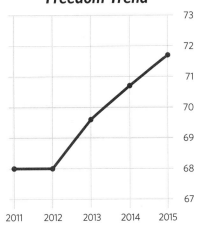

Least free 0   25   50   75   Most free 100

71.7

World Rank: 28   **Regional Rank: 2**

Colombia's economic freedom score is 71.7, making its economy the 28th freest in the 2015 *Index*. Its overall score is 1.0 point higher than last year, with improvements in six of the 10 economic freedoms, including investment freedom, freedom from corruption, and trade freedom. Recording its highest score ever in the 2015 *Index*, Colombia has solidified its ranking as the 2nd freest out of 29 countries in the South and Central America/Caribbean region.

Over the past five years, economic freedom in Colombia has risen by 3.7 points as reform has gained momentum. Impressive gains in market openness include double-digit improvements in both investment and financial freedom and an 8.0-point improvement in trade freedom.

Colombia's relatively open economy has benefited from a petrochemical boom and diminished threat of risk as the government engages in talks with the militant group FARC. This has allowed greater fiscal flexibility while the government implements a reform program to open the country further to trade, investment, and financial flows. Corruption is perceived as widespread.

BACKGROUND: President Juan Manuel Santos, elected in 2010 and re-elected in 2014, has tried to distance himself from former President Alvaro Uribe. Uribe's "democratic security" agenda significantly reduced crime and violence and reestablished the state's presence in rural areas. Uribe also boosted business confidence. Santos has made peace talks with FARC and ELN guerrillas the centerpiece of his government. He has promised that guerrillas will be given no immunity, but the FARC leadership has stated that it will not spend a single day in jail. Santos faces the challenge of delivering peace while ensuring justice for victims of the FARC and ELN. Colombia's economy depends heavily on exports of petroleum, coffee, and cut flowers. It has replaced Argentina as Latin America's third-largest economy, surpassed only by Brazil and Mexico. Colombia is a founding member of the Pacific Alliance. Inflation is low, and the poverty rate is decreasing.

Freedom Trend

Country Comparisons

Country	71.7
World Average	60.4
Regional Average	59.7
Free Economies	84.6

0   20   40   60   80   100

Quick Facts

Population: 47.2 million
GDP (PPP): $527.6 billion
4.3% growth in 2013
5-year compound annual growth 4.1%
$11,189 per capita
Unemployment: 10.5%
Inflation (CPI): 2.0%
FDI Inflow: $16.8 billion
Public Debt: 31.8% of GDP

2013 data unless otherwise noted.
Data compiled as of September 2014.

How Do We Measure Economic Freedom?
See page 475 for an explanation of the methodology
or visit the *Index* Web site at *heritage.org/index*.

THE TEN ECONOMIC FREEDOMS

		Score	Country	World Average	Rank	1-Year Change
RULE OF LAW	Property Rights	50.0			56th	0
	Freedom from Corruption	36.0			95th	+2.8

Settlement of the 50-year internal conflict could strengthen governance in large areas of Colombia, but drug trafficking and the violence and corruption that it engenders will continue to erode institutions. Corruption occurs at multiple levels of public administration. The courts have demonstrated a degree of independence from the executive, but the justice system remains compromised by corruption and extortion.

		Score			Rank	1-Year Change
GOVERNMENT SIZE	Fiscal Freedom	80.3			79th	-0.3
	Government Spending	76.0			65th	+1.1

Colombia's top individual income tax rate is 33 percent, and its top corporate income tax rate is 25 percent. Other taxes include a value-added tax and a financial transactions tax. The overall tax burden is equivalent to 16.1 percent of domestic income. Total government expenditures account for 28.3 percent of the domestic economy, and public debt equals 32 percent of gross domestic product.

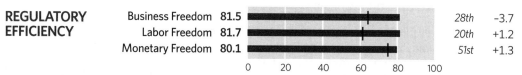

		Score			Rank	1-Year Change
REGULATORY EFFICIENCY	Business Freedom	81.5			28th	-3.7
	Labor Freedom	81.7			20th	+1.2
	Monetary Freedom	80.1			51st	+1.3

Incorporating a business takes fewer than 10 procedures, with no paid-in minimum capital required, but completing licensing requirements remains time-consuming. The non-salary cost of hiring a worker is moderate, and regulation of work hours is relatively flexible. In 2014, the government reduced subsidies to coffee farmers in light of higher market prices. Other state subsidies remain below regional averages.

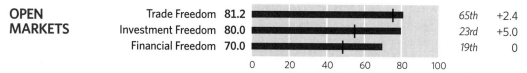

		Score			Rank	1-Year Change
OPEN MARKETS	Trade Freedom	81.2			65th	+2.4
	Investment Freedom	80.0			23rd	+5.0
	Financial Freedom	70.0			19th	0

The average tariff rate is 4.4 percent. Colombia is a member of the Pacific Alliance with Chile, Costa Rica, Mexico, and Peru. Foreign and domestic investors are generally treated equally under the law. Following a decade of significant consolidation, private institutions dominate the growing financial sector. Credit is allocated on market terms, and foreign firms receive equal treatment. Access to long-term financing can be difficult.

Long-Term Score Change (since 1995)

RULE OF LAW		GOVERNMENT SIZE		REGULATORY EFFICIENCY		OPEN MARKETS	
Property Rights	0	Fiscal Freedom	-0.2	Business Freedom	-3.5	Trade Freedom	+16.2
Freedom from Corruption	+26.0	Government Spending	-10.0	Labor Freedom	+18.9	Investment Freedom	+10.0
				Monetary Freedom	+16.4	Financial Freedom	0

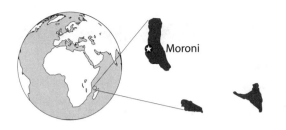

Moroni

COMOROS

Economic Freedom Score

Least free 0   Most free 100

52.1

Comoros's economic freedom score is 52.1, making its economy the 142nd freest in the 2015 *Index*. Its overall score is 0.7 point higher than last year, reflecting improvements in half of the 10 economic freedoms, including freedom from corruption, investment freedom, monetary freedom, and labor freedom. Comoros is ranked 32nd out of 46 countries in the Sub-Saharan Africa region, and its overall score is lower than the regional average.

Over the past five years, economic freedom in Comoros has advanced by 8.3 points, the second-best improvement by any country. Comoros has recorded impressive score improvements in five straight years, led by double-digit gains in labor freedom, trade freedom, investment freedom, and financial freedom. Investment freedom has improved by 30 points since 2011.

Comoros has been graded only since 2009. It moved out of the ranks of the "repressed" last year and registered its highest score ever in the 2015 *Index*. Institutionalizing and improving on gains made in the past half-decade will be essential. Comoros continues to lag far behind on rule of law, and corruption remains pervasive. Despite opening to foreign investment, the repressive domestic regulatory environment hinders entrepreneurial dynamism. The government must also do more to promote competition, as financial and investment regimes remain among the world's least free.

BACKGROUND: The three-island Union of the Comoros has endured more than 20 coups since independence in 1975. Under a 2001 constitution granting each island increased autonomy, the presidency rotates among the three islands every four years. The transfer of power to President Ikililou Dhoinine in 2011 was peaceful. Although Comoros is a leading producer of ylang-ylang, cloves, and vanilla, its narrow export base leaves it vulnerable to external shocks. It also has poor transportation links. Comoros remains heavily dependent on foreign aid and remittances. In 2012, the International Monetary Fund and the World Bank provided $176 million in debt relief to Comoros.

Freedom Trend

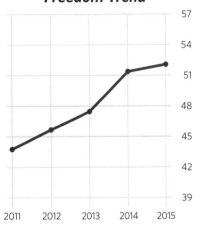

Country Comparisons

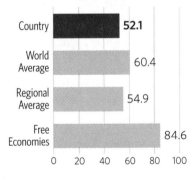

Country	52.1
World Average	60.4
Regional Average	54.9
Free Economies	84.6

Quick Facts

Population: 0.7 million
GDP (PPP): $0.9 billion
3.5% growth in 2013
5-year compound annual growth 2.5%
$1,287 per capita
Unemployment: 7.9%
Inflation (CPI): 2.3%
FDI Inflow: $13.9 million
Public Debt: 19.0% of GDP

2013 data unless otherwise noted.
Data compiled as of September 2014.

How Do We Measure Economic Freedom?
See page 475 for an explanation of the methodology
or visit the *Index* Web site at *heritage.org/index.*

THE TEN ECONOMIC FREEDOMS

	Score	Rank	1-Year Change
RULE OF LAW Property Rights	30.0	94th	0
Freedom from Corruption	28.0	132nd	+5.9

Although President Dhoinine is pursuing governance reforms, corruption remains a serious problem at all levels of the government, judiciary, and civil service, as well as among the police and security forces. The judicial system, based on both Sharia (Islamic) law and the French legal code, is relatively weak and subject to influence by the executive branch and other elites. The top individual income tax rate is 30 percent, and the top corporate tax rate is 50 percent.

	Score	Rank	1-Year Change
GOVERNMENT SIZE Fiscal Freedom	64.5	158th	0
Government Spending	78.8	51st	-6.5

Other taxes include a value-added tax and an insurance tax. The overall tax burden is 12.3 percent of GDP. Government expenditures equal 26.6 percent of the domestic economy. Public debt has fallen to 19 percent of the domestic economy as debt forgiveness continues under the Highly Indebted Poor Country initiative.

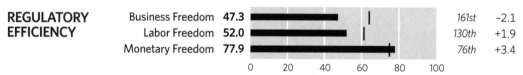

	Score	Rank	1-Year Change
REGULATORY EFFICIENCY Business Freedom	47.3	161st	-2.1
Labor Freedom	52.0	130th	+1.9
Monetary Freedom	77.9	76th	+3.4

Simplifying the business start-up process has progressed unevenly, and private enterprises still face costly and time-consuming regulatory hurdles. Launching a company costs more than the level of average annual income, and completing licensing requirements takes over 100 days. The formal labor market is not fully developed. The government subsidizes state-owned utilities (water, electricity, and oil) and controls other prices.

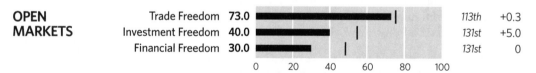

	Score	Rank	1-Year Change
OPEN MARKETS Trade Freedom	73.0	113th	+0.3
Investment Freedom	40.0	131st	+5.0
Financial Freedom	30.0	131st	0

Comoros has an average tariff rate of 6.0 percent. It is a member of the Common Market for Eastern and Southern Africa. Lack of a strong court system to enforce contracts can deter foreign investors. The financial sector remains limited in scope and depth, and much of the population has very limited access to financial services. The majority of bank loans are for short terms only.

Long-Term Score Change (since 2009)

RULE OF LAW		GOVERNMENT SIZE		REGULATORY EFFICIENCY		OPEN MARKETS	
Property Rights	0	Fiscal Freedom	-0.1	Business Freedom	+0.8	Trade Freedom	+45.8
Freedom from Corruption	+2.0	Government Spending	-9.3	Labor Freedom	+20.2	Investment Freedom	+20.0
				Monetary Freedom	-1.0	Financial Freedom	+10.0

DEMOCRATIC REPUBLIC OF **CONGO**

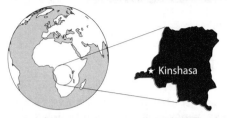

★ Kinshasa

World Rank: 168　　　　**Regional Rank: 42**

Economic Freedom Score

25　**50**　75

Least free　0　　　　100　Most free

45.0

The Democratic Republic of Congo's economic freedom score is 45.0, making it the 168th freest economy in the 2015 *Index*. Its overall score is 4.4 points better than last year, with double-digit gains in business freedom, monetary freedom, and the control of government spending. Nonetheless, the DRC is ranked 42nd out of 46 countries in the Sub-Saharan Africa region, and its score is far below the regional average.

Over the past five years, the DRC's economic freedom has advanced by 4.3 points, with especially strong gains in the past two years. Monetary freedom has improved by over 28 points, but advancement has been broad-based, with gains in six of the 10 factors. The DRC has registered its highest economic freedom score ever in the 2015 *Index*.

Despite this welcome progress, the DRC's level of economic freedom remains among the lowest in the world, still well within the "repressed" category. Inadequate institutions make the formation of a vibrant private sector difficult.

BACKGROUND: The Democratic Republic of Congo remains plagued by wide-ranging conflict between government forces that historically have been backed by Angola, Namibia, and Zimbabwe and rebels supported by Uganda and Rwanda. Much of the eastern part of the country remains embroiled in conflict. In 2006, Joseph Kabila won the first multi-party election in 40 years. He was re-elected in December 2011 in a flawed and violent election. Rebel groups including the Lord's Resistance Army, M23, and the Democratic Forces for the Liberation of Rwanda remain active in the eastern regions. Renewed violence has led to massive population displacement and atrocities against civilians. The DRC continues to host the U.N.'s largest peacekeeping mission. Political instability, lack of transparency, and systematic corruption undermine economic growth. The DRC's immense natural resources, including copper, cobalt, and diamonds, have fueled conflict, forcing foreign businesses to limit their operations. The DRC suffered from an Ebola outbreak in the summer of 2014.

Freedom Trend

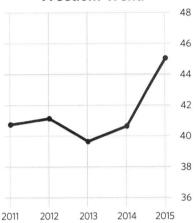

48
46
44
42
40
38
36

2011　2012　2013　2014　2015

Country Comparisons

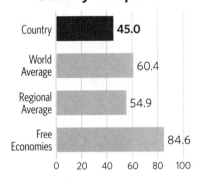

Country　**45.0**

World Average　60.4

Regional Average　54.9

Free Economies　84.6

0　20　40　60　80　100

Quick Facts

Population: 77.0 million
GDP (PPP): $49.9 billion
8.5% growth in 2013
5-year compound annual growth 6.5%
$648 per capita
Unemployment: 7.9%
Inflation (CPI): 0.8%
FDI Inflow: $2.1 billion
Public Debt: 21.6% of GDP

How Do We Measure Economic Freedom?
See page 475 for an explanation of the methodology
or visit the *Index* Web site at *heritage.org/index*.

2013 data unless otherwise noted.
Data compiled as of September 2014.

169

DEMOCRATIC REPUBLIC OF CONGO (continued)

THE TEN ECONOMIC FREEDOMS

		Score		Rank	1-Year Change
RULE OF LAW	Property Rights	10.0		165th	0
	Freedom from Corruption	22.0		161st	+4.4

An uncertain legal framework, conflicts with armed militias for control of eastern Congo's rich mineral deposits, endemic corruption, and a lack of transparency in government policy are long-term problems for the mining sector and the economy as a whole. Protection of property rights remains weak and dependent on a dysfunctional public administration and judicial system. Human rights abuses and banditry deter economic activity.

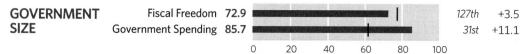

		Score		Rank	1-Year Change
GOVERNMENT SIZE	Fiscal Freedom	72.9		127th	+3.5
	Government Spending	85.7		31st	+11.1

The top individual income tax rate is 30 percent, and the top corporate income tax rate is 40 percent. Other taxes include a tax on vehicles and a tax on rentals. The overall tax burden equals 14.5 percent of the domestic economy. Government spending is equal to 21.8 percent of domestic production, and public debt amounts to 22 percent of gross domestic product.

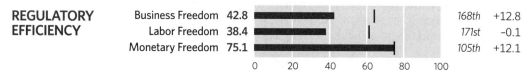

		Score		Rank	1-Year Change
REGULATORY EFFICIENCY	Business Freedom	42.8		168th	+12.8
	Labor Freedom	38.4		171st	-0.1
	Monetary Freedom	75.1		105th	+12.1

Despite some progress, the regulatory environment still remains significantly burdensome. Minimum capital requirements to launch a company are about five times the level of average annual income. With development of a modern labor market lagging, the informal sector is the source of most employment. Prices are controlled and regulated by the government, which also subsidizes electricity.

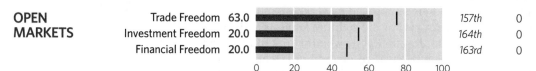

		Score		Rank	1-Year Change
OPEN MARKETS	Trade Freedom	63.0		157th	0
	Investment Freedom	20.0		164th	0
	Financial Freedom	20.0		163rd	0

The Democratic Republic of Congo's average tariff rate is 11.0 percent. Bureaucratic and regulatory barriers impede the free flow of trade and discourage foreign direct investment. Over the past five years, the banking sector has recorded considerable growth. The level of financial inclusion has also increased, but the financial system, dominated by banks, remains one of the region's least developed.

Long-Term Score Change (since 1995)

RULE OF LAW		GOVERNMENT SIZE		REGULATORY EFFICIENCY		OPEN MARKETS	
Property Rights	-40.0	Fiscal Freedom	+22.0	Business Freedom	-12.2	Trade Freedom	+14.0
Freedom from Corruption	+12.0	Government Spending	-11.5	Labor Freedom	+3.9	Investment Freedom	-10.0
				Monetary Freedom	+75.1	Financial Freedom	-10.0

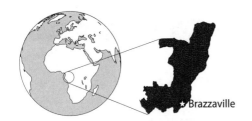

*Brazzaville

REPUBLIC OF **CONGO**

Economic Freedom Score

50
25   75
Least
free   0   100   Most
free

42.7

The Republic of Congo's economic freedom score is 42.7, making its economy the 170th freest in the 2015 *Index*. Its overall score is 1.0 point worse than last year, with improvements in investment freedom, trade freedom, business freedom, and freedom from corruption counterbalanced by declines in the control of government spending and labor freedom. Congo is ranked 43rd out of 46 countries in the Sub-Saharan Africa region, and its overall score is much lower than the global and regional averages.

Large sections of the population remain trapped in poverty. Government remains involved in leading economic sectors, and institutional constraints force many small entrepreneurs to operate informally. Lack of an effective independent judiciary, corruption, and an oppressive regulatory environment hamper the development of a dynamic private sector.

These institutional difficulties are reflected in Congo's declining score over the past five years. Economic freedom has fallen significantly in three of the 10 factors. A 19-point decline in government spending highlights the government's continued interference in the domestic economy, and the regulatory environment has become particularly burdensome for entrepreneurs and workers.

BACKGROUND: Congo became independent in 1960. After seizing power in 1979, Denis Sassou-Nguesso governed the country as a Marxist–Leninist state before moderating economic policy and allowing multi-party elections in 1992. He lost to Pascal Lissouba but seized power again following a 1997 civil war, won a flawed election in 2002, and won a seven-year term in 2009 in a similarly dubious election. Civil war militias remain active in the southern Pool region. Congo is sub-Saharan Africa's fourth-largest oil producer, but lack of infrastructure has prevented the exploitation of its sizable natural gas reserves and significant hydropower potential. Seventy percent of the population lives in poverty. As of mid-2013, Congo hosted more than 60,000 refugees from Angola, the Central African Republic, Chad, the Democratic Republic of Congo, and Rwanda.

Freedom Trend

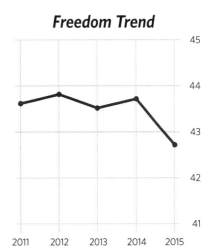

45

44

43

42

41

2011   2012   2013   2014   2015

Country Comparisons

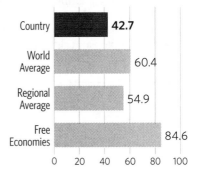

Country	**42.7**
World Average	60.4
Regional Average	54.9
Free Economies	84.6

0   20   40   60   80   100

Quick Facts

Population: 4.2 million
GDP (PPP): $20.0 billion
4.5% growth in 2013
5-year compound annual growth 5.6%
$4,791 per capita
Unemployment: 7.8%
Inflation (CPI): 4.6%
FDI Inflow: $2.0 billion
Public Debt: 30.8% of GDP

2013 data unless otherwise noted.
Data compiled as of September 2014.

THE TEN ECONOMIC FREEDOMS

		Score	■ Country ┃ World Average	Rank	1-Year Change
RULE OF LAW	Property Rights	10.0		165th	0
	Freedom from Corruption	22.0		161st	+1.4

Corruption is almost invariably linked to doing business in Congo. There is an absence of substantiated figures on government revenues and spending. Contract terms are not transparent, and "informal" tax collectors regularly solicit bribes. The judiciary is underfunded and crippled by institutional weakness and a lack of technical capability. The state oil company is directly controlled by the president's family and advisers.

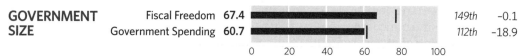

		Score		Rank	Change
GOVERNMENT SIZE	Fiscal Freedom	67.4		149th	−0.1
	Government Spending	60.7		112th	−18.9

The top individual income tax rate is 45 percent, and the top corporate tax rate is 34 percent. Other taxes include a value-added tax, a tax on rental values, and an apprenticeship tax. The overall tax burden equals 8.7 percent of gross domestic output. Government spending is equivalent to 36.2 percent of GDP, and public debt equals about 25 percent of the domestic economy. Rebels continue to undermine tax collection.

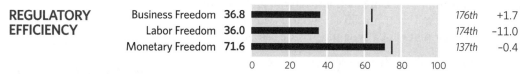

		Score		Rank	Change
REGULATORY EFFICIENCY	Business Freedom	36.8		176th	+1.7
	Labor Freedom	36.0		174th	−11.0
	Monetary Freedom	71.6		137th	−0.4

The process for establishing a company is now more streamlined, but paid-in minimum capital required to launch a business almost equals the level of average annual income. The formal labor market is not fully developed, and cumbersome labor codes hinder job growth. Government ownership and subsidization of the large public sector affect the prices of a range of goods and services.

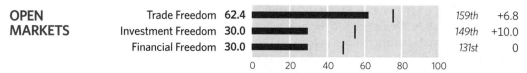

		Score		Rank	Change
OPEN MARKETS	Trade Freedom	62.4		159th	+6.8
	Investment Freedom	30.0		149th	+10.0
	Financial Freedom	30.0		131st	0

The average tariff rate is 14.7 percent. Congo is a member of the Central African Economic and Monetary Community. Exports may be taxed, and imports of sugar are restricted. Foreign investors face bureaucratic hurdles. The financial sector remains limited in depth and scope. The number of banks has increased to 10, but the sector remains underdeveloped, and total assets equal only about 20 percent of GDP.

Long-Term Score Change (since 1996)

RULE OF LAW		GOVERNMENT SIZE		REGULATORY EFFICIENCY		OPEN MARKETS	
Property Rights	−20.0	Fiscal Freedom	+17.8	Business Freedom	−18.2	Trade Freedom	+10.0
Freedom from Corruption	+12.0	Government Spending	+5.9	Labor Freedom	−7.9	Investment Freedom	0
				Monetary Freedom	+20.7	Financial Freedom	0

COSTA RICA

Economic Freedom Score

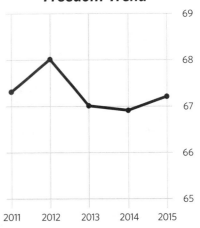

Least free 0 ... 25 ... 50 ... 75 ... 100 Most free

67.2

Costa Rica's economic freedom score is 67.2, making its economy the 51st freest in the 2015 *Index*. Its overall score has increased by 0.3 point from last year, reflecting improvements in labor freedom and freedom from corruption that outweigh a combined decline in monetary freedom, business freedom, and the control of government spending. Costa Rica is ranked 10th out of 29 countries in the South and Central America/Caribbean region, and its overall score is higher than the global and regional averages.

Economic development has focused on orienting the economy to the global marketplace. Costa Rica has one of the highest levels of foreign direct investment in Latin America, and the government's limited economic presence has facilitated a business environment based on tourism, agriculture, and technology.

The small increase in Costa Rica's overall score this year has reversed a multi-year decline. Over the past five years, Costa Rica's economic freedom has declined in four of the 10 factors, including property rights, fiscal freedom, labor freedom, and trade freedom. Changes in the corporate income tax regime to help pay for security services have undermined fiscal freedom.

BACKGROUND: Luis Guillermo Solís of the Partido Acción Ciudadana was elected president in 2014, ousting the incumbent Partido Liberación Nacional amid concerns over corruption. The peaceful transfer of power highlighted the long history of democratic stability that has contributed to one of Latin America's highest levels of foreign direct investment per capita. Nevertheless, many people live in poverty and work in the underground economy. Fiscal and structural reforms to liberalize the economy are long overdue. While Costa Rica remains safer than many of its neighbors, crime rates are rising. There is an ongoing border dispute with Nicaragua. Costa Rica has benefited from foreign investments in electronics and health care, and the Central America–Dominican Republic–United States Free Trade Agreement (CAFTA–DR) has opened insurance and telecommunications to private investors.

Freedom Trend

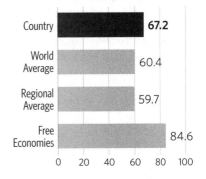

Country Comparisons

Country	67.2
World Average	60.4
Regional Average	59.7
Free Economies	84.6

0   20   40   60   80   100

Quick Facts

Population: 4.8 million
GDP (PPP): $61.6 billion
3.5% growth in 2013
5-year compound annual growth 3.4%
$12,942 per capita
Unemployment: 7.7%
Inflation (CPI): 5.2%
FDI Inflow: $2.7 billion
Public Debt: 37.0% of GDP

2013 data unless otherwise noted.
Data compiled as of September 2014.

THE TEN ECONOMIC FREEDOMS

		Score			Rank	1-Year Change
			■ Country	| World Average		

RULE OF LAW

	Score		Rank	1-Year Change
Property Rights	50.0		56th	0
Freedom from Corruption	53.0		48th	+2.1

Corruption is lower than elsewhere in the region, and Costa Rica has avoided the infiltration of its state institutions by organized crime, but drug-related activity has increased in the past two years as Mexican cartels move into Central America. The judicial branch is independent, but there are often substantial delays in the judicial process. Property rights are secure, and contracts are generally upheld.

GOVERNMENT SIZE

	Score		Rank	1-Year Change
Fiscal Freedom	80.0		84th	0
Government Spending	89.9		11th	−0.1

The top individual income tax rate is 25 percent, and the top corporate tax rate is 30 percent. Other taxes include a general sales tax and a real property tax. The overall tax burden equals 21.9 percent of the domestic economy. Government spending amounts to 18.3 percent of gross domestic product, and public debt is equivalent to around 37 percent of yearly domestic income.

REGULATORY EFFICIENCY

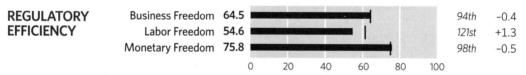

	Score		Rank	1-Year Change
Business Freedom	64.5		94th	−0.4
Labor Freedom	54.6		121st	+1.3
Monetary Freedom	75.8		98th	−0.5

The environment for business formation is now more streamlined, but regulatory compliance remains time-consuming. Obtaining necessary permits still takes more than 100 days. The labor market remains relatively flexible, although a modest increase in the minimum wage went into force in July 2013. The government maintains price controls and in 2014 announced a one-year extension of price supports for rice.

OPEN MARKETS

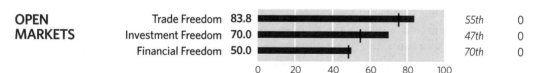

	Score		Rank	1-Year Change
Trade Freedom	83.8		55th	0
Investment Freedom	70.0		47th	0
Financial Freedom	50.0		70th	0

Costa Rica's average tariff rate is 3.1 percent, and the government has upgraded its customs procedures. Domestic and foreign investors are treated similarly, but investment in some sectors of the economy is restricted. The growing financial sector has gradually become more open to competition, but state-owned banks continue to dominate the sector. Capital markets are not fully developed.

Long-Term Score Change (since 1995)

RULE OF LAW		GOVERNMENT SIZE		REGULATORY EFFICIENCY		OPEN MARKETS	
Property Rights	0	Fiscal Freedom	−2.6	Business Freedom	−5.5	Trade Freedom	+5.8
Freedom from Corruption	+3.0	Government Spending	−0.9	Labor Freedom	−6.5	Investment Freedom	0
				Monetary Freedom	+4.9	Financial Freedom	0

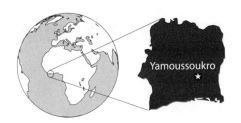

CÔTE D'IVOIRE

Economic Freedom Score

25   50   75

Least free   0   100   Most free

58.5

World Rank: 103   **Regional Rank: 14**

Côte d'Ivoire's economic freedom score is 58.5, making its economy the 103rd freest in the 2015 *Index*. Its score is 0.8 point higher than last year, reflecting improvements in half of the 10 economic freedoms, including business freedom, property rights, investment freedom, and freedom from corruption. Registering its highest score ever in the 2015 *Index*, Côte d'Ivoire has advanced to 14th out of 46 countries in the Sub-Saharan Africa region, and its overall score is now slightly above the regional average.

Over the past five years, economic freedom in Côte d'Ivoire has expanded by 3.1 points, led by 20-point gains in business and investment freedoms. The largely market-based economy has benefited in recent years from the international trade in coffee and palm oil.

However, the weak rule of law, affected by corruption and unclear property rights, still undermines the institutional environment necessary for sustained economic growth. Regulatory inefficiencies and insufficient investor protections have retarded the development of a more dynamic entrepreneurial environment.

BACKGROUND: In 2002, civil war split Côte d'Ivoire between a rebel-controlled North and a government-controlled South. Renewed violence flared in 2004 and 2010. In 2010, when Alassane Ouattara was internationally recognized as winner of the presidential election, incumbent Laurent Gbagbo refused to hand over power and was removed by U.N. and French forces. Gbagbo is currently awaiting trial in The Hague for crimes against humanity that he allegedly committed during the post-election period. Political tensions have cooled under Ouattara's leadership, but because of his poor health and the country's upcoming elections in 2015, instability could return. The African Development Bank, after leaving the country 11 years ago for Tunisia due to unrest, has reopened its headquarters in Abidjan. Côte d'Ivoire is West Africa's second-largest economy and a leading producer of cocoa and cashews.

Freedom Trend

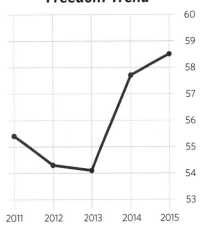

2011   2012   2013   2014   2015

Country Comparisons

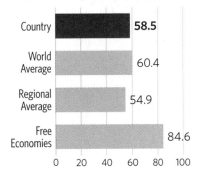

Country	58.5
World Average	60.4
Regional Average	54.9
Free Economies	84.6

0   20   40   60   80   100

Quick Facts

Population: 24.1 million
GDP (PPP): $43.8 billion
8.1% growth in 2013
5-year compound annual growth 3.7%
$1,818 per capita
Unemployment: 3.9%
Inflation (CPI): 2.6%
FDI Inflow: $371.0 million
Public Debt: 43.2% of GDP

2013 data unless otherwise noted.
Data compiled as of September 2014.

How Do We Measure Economic Freedom?
See page 475 for an explanation of the methodology
or visit the *Index* Web site at *heritage.org/index*.

THE TEN ECONOMIC FREEDOMS

		Score			Rank	1-Year Change
RULE OF LAW	Property Rights	35.0			87th	+5.0
	Freedom from Corruption	27.0			141st	+4.9

Although the government has improved the investment climate, private and public corruption persists, especially with respect to judicial proceedings, contract awards, customs, and tax issues. Obtaining an official stamp, a copy of a birth or death certificate, or an automobile title often requires payment of a supplemental "commission." Protection of property rights is fragile, and land titles are rare outside of urban areas.

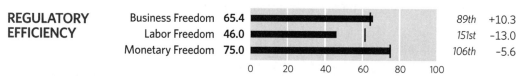

		Score			Rank	1-Year Change
GOVERNMENT SIZE	Fiscal Freedom	77.7			104th	−1.4
	Government Spending	82.4			40th	+2.6

Côte d'Ivoire's top individual income tax rate is 36 percent, and its top corporate tax rate is 25 percent. Other taxes include a value-added tax and a tax on interest. Total tax revenue amounts to 17.6 percent of domestic output, and public expenditures are equal to about 24.2 percent of domestic production. Public debt amounts to 43 percent of gross domestic product.

		Score			Rank	1-Year Change
REGULATORY EFFICIENCY	Business Freedom	65.4			89th	+10.3
	Labor Freedom	46.0			151st	−13.0
	Monetary Freedom	75.0			106th	−5.6

Considerable improvements have been made in streamlining the entrepreneurial framework. The time and number of procedures required to incorporate a business have been reduced. In the absence of well-functioning efficient labor markets, informal labor activity persists in many sectors. In 2013, the government abandoned a decade of sector liberalization to guarantee a minimum price for cocoa farmers, and it still regulates many other prices.

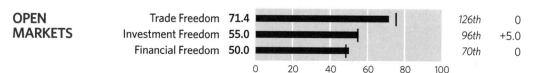

		Score			Rank	1-Year Change
OPEN MARKETS	Trade Freedom	71.4			126th	0
	Investment Freedom	55.0			96th	+5.0
	Financial Freedom	50.0			70th	0

The average tariff rate is 6.8 percent. Côte d'Ivoire is a member of the West Africa Economic and Monetary Union. The government has announced plans to privatize many state-owned enterprises. Efforts to modernize and restructure the financial sector have been made. The banking penetration rate remains under 15 percent, but telephone banking has been growing. Access to loans, particularly short-term working capital, remains a challenge.

Long-Term Score Change (since 1995)

RULE OF LAW		GOVERNMENT SIZE		REGULATORY EFFICIENCY		OPEN MARKETS	
Property Rights	−15.0	Fiscal Freedom	+25.5	Business Freedom	−4.6	Trade Freedom	+58.8
Freedom from Corruption	−3.0	Government Spending	−3.7	Labor Freedom	−13.9	Investment Freedom	+5.0
				Monetary Freedom	−4.7	Financial Freedom	0

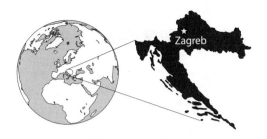
Zagreb

CROATIA

Economic Freedom Score

50
25   75
Least   Most
free   0   100   free

61.5

C roatia's economic freedom score is 61.5, making its econo-my the 81st freest in the 2015 *Index*. Its overall score is 1.1 points better than last year, reflecting improvements in five of the 10 economic freedoms including freedom from corruption, fiscal freedom, and labor freedom. Croatia has registered its highest score ever in the 2015 *Index*, but it continues to lag behind many other emerging economies in the region, and its overall score remains below the regional average.

Despite its accession to the European Union in 2013, Croatia still suffers some of the difficulties facing other transitional economies. An independent judiciary has not been fully established, and there are delays and backlogs in adjudicating cases. High levels of corruption persist in business, education, and basic government services. Land registry offices need further reform to guarantee clearly defined property rights.

An uncertain civic environment and fiscal pressures will continue to challenge efforts to build on Croatia's modest improvements in economic freedom over the past five years. Reforms to open up the investment regime should help the country to integrate more fully into the European market.

BACKGROUND: Croatia declared its independence in 1991, contributing to the breakup of Yugoslavia along ethnic and religious lines. Years of Croat/Serb conflict ended formally in 1995 with the Dayton Peace Accords. Croatia joined NATO in April 2009 and the European Union in July 2013. In December 2011, former Prime Minister Jadranka Kosor, credited with making the final push toward EU accession, was defeated by center-left Prime Minister Zoran Milanovic. Turnout for Croatia's first-ever elections for the EU Parliament, held in April 2013, was only 20.8 percent. Growth has been hurt by the global financial crisis and overreliance on tourism, and domestic demand is weak. The slow pace of privatization of state-owned businesses has been a drag on the economy, which has been shrinking since 2008 despite membership in the EU.

Freedom Trend

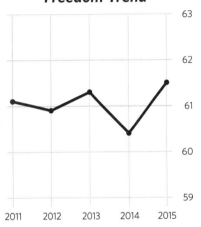

63

62

61

60

59

2011   2012   2013   2014   2015

Country Comparisons

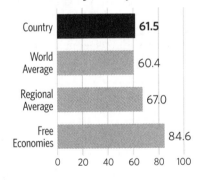

Country — **61.5**
World Average — 60.4
Regional Average — 67.0
Free Economies — 84.6

0   20   40   60   80   100

Quick Facts

Population: 4.3 million
GDP (PPP): $77.9 billion
–1.0% growth in 2013
5-year compound annual growth –2.5%
$18,191 per capita
Unemployment: 17.2%
Inflation (CPI): 2.2%
FDI Inflow: $580.1 million
Public Debt: 59.8% of GDP

2013 data unless otherwise noted.
Data compiled as of September 2014.

How Do We Measure Economic Freedom?
See page 475 for an explanation of the methodology
or visit the *Index* Web site at *heritage.org/index*.

THE TEN ECONOMIC FREEDOMS

		Score		Rank	1-Year Change
RULE OF LAW	Property Rights	40.0		70th	0
	Freedom from Corruption	48.0		57th	+6.9

Corruption is perceived as prevalent in major public companies, the health sector, universities, public procurement systems, the construction sector, and land registry offices. In 2014, a former prime minister was found guilty of masterminding a scheme to siphon off $2.7 million from state companies. Although some reforms are being implemented, the court system is cumbersome, inefficient, and time-consuming.

		Score		Rank	1-Year Change
GOVERNMENT SIZE	Fiscal Freedom	74.9		118th	+5.5
	Government Spending	46.5		140th	+0.7

Croatia's top individual income tax rate is 40 percent, and its top corporate tax rate is 20 percent. Other taxes include a value-added tax and an excise tax. The overall tax burden amounts to 22.6 percent of gross domestic product. Government spending is equal to 42.2 percent of the domestic economy, and public debt is equivalent to 60 percent of domestic income.

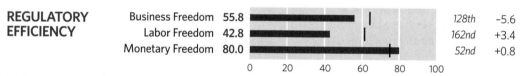

		Score		Rank	1-Year Change
REGULATORY EFFICIENCY	Business Freedom	55.8		128th	−5.6
	Labor Freedom	42.8		162nd	+3.4
	Monetary Freedom	80.0		52nd	+0.8

Reform measures have streamlined the procedures for establishing a business, but the overall regulatory environment remains burdensome and inefficient. Despite some progress, the labor market remains rigid. In 2014, the government pledged to cut subsidies and raise excise taxes on petrol and telecom operators to meet EU budget requirements. The state still attempts to influence price levels through various mechanisms.

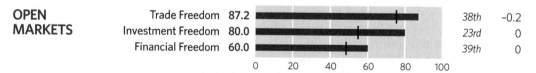

		Score		Rank	1-Year Change
OPEN MARKETS	Trade Freedom	87.2		38th	−0.2
	Investment Freedom	80.0		23rd	0
	Financial Freedom	60.0		39th	0

EU members have a 1.0 percent average tariff rate. Although some non-tariff barriers exist, the EU is relatively open to external trade. In Croatia, foreign and domestic firms are generally treated equally under the law. The financial system has become more competitive. The consolidated banking sector is relatively efficient, with over 30 commercial banks. Croatia's capital market is not fully developed and lags behind other key markets in the EU.

Long-Term Score Change (since 1996)

RULE OF LAW		GOVERNMENT SIZE		REGULATORY EFFICIENCY		OPEN MARKETS	
Property Rights	−10.0	Fiscal Freedom	−2.5	Business Freedom	+0.8	Trade Freedom	+18.2
Freedom from Corruption	+18.0	Government Spending	−4.0	Labor Freedom	−1.5	Investment Freedom	+30.0
				Monetary Freedom	+80.0	Financial Freedom	+10.0

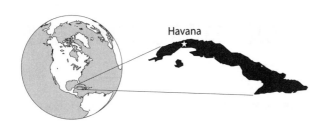

Havana

CUBA

Economic Freedom Score

25 50 75

Least free 0

Most free 100

29.6

Cuba's economic freedom score is 29.6, making its economy one of the world's least free. Its overall score is 0.9 point higher than last year, with a slight deterioration in monetary freedom outweighed by improvements in three of the 10 economic freedoms, including trade freedom, fiscal freedom, and freedom from corruption. Cuba is ranked least free of 29 countries in the South and Central America/Caribbean region, and its overall score is significantly lower than the regional average.

In recent years, the government has made measured concessions to encourage more entrepreneurship and private-sector growth. Communist Party–endorsed reforms to cut government payrolls and expand approved professions have not been broad enough to ensure any meaningful advancement in overall economic freedom. The state continues to interfere in most economic activity. Price controls are pervasive, and the two-tiered exchange rate regime continues to distort prices.

Despite membership in the World Trade Organization, the economy remains relatively cut off from the international marketplace. Only state enterprises are allowed to engage in international trade and investment. The state uses an oppressive regulatory environment to suppress entrepreneurial activity and controls most means of production. Shallow credit markets impede access to credit for business activities.

BACKGROUND: A one-party Communist state, Cuba depends on external assistance (chiefly oil subsidies provided by Venezuela and remittances from Cuban émigrés) and a captive labor force to survive. Property rights are severely restricted. Fidel Castro's 83-year-old brother Raúl continues to lead both the government and the Cuban Communist Party. Workers' wages are not enough to live on, the agriculture sector is starved for investment, and tourism revenue is volatile. Under Raúl Castro, violent repression of civil society and of dissidents has increased dramatically. Much-touted "free-market reforms" have proven to be cosmetic changes in what remains a socialist state. Restrictions on foreign travel have been eased, but certain Cubans are still barred from leaving.

Freedom Trend

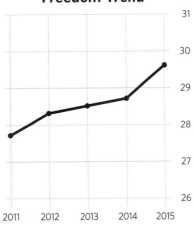

2011 2012 2013 2014 2015

Country Comparisons

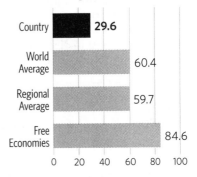

Country	29.6
World Average	60.4
Regional Average	59.7
Free Economies	84.6

0 20 40 60 80 100

Quick Facts

Population: 11.2 million
GDP (PPP): $130.0 billion
2.8% growth in 2013
5-year compound annual growth 2.3%
$11,610 per capita
Unemployment: n/a
Inflation (CPI): 6.0%
FDI Inflow: n/a
Public Debt: 37.5% of GDP

2013 data unless otherwise noted.
Data compiled as of September 2014.

THE TEN ECONOMIC FREEDOMS

RULE OF LAW

	Score	Rank	1-Year Change
Property Rights	10.0	165th	0
Freedom from Corruption	46.0	63rd	+4.8

Although the perceived level of corruption has traditionally been far lower in Cuba than in other Latin American countries, it remains a considerable systemic problem. Low salaries for public officials and the dual exchange rate provide incentives for illicit enrichment. Only state enterprises may enter into economic agreements with foreigners as minority partners. Most means of production are owned by the state.

GOVERNMENT SIZE

	Score	Rank	1-Year Change
Fiscal Freedom	61.8	165th	+1.8
Government Spending	0.0	176th	0

Cuba's top individual income tax rate is 50 percent, and its top corporate tax rate is 30 percent. Other taxes include a property transfer tax and a sales tax. The overall tax burden equals 20.5 percent of domestic production. Public expenditures account for 60.2 percent of the domestic economy, and public debt is equal to about 38 percent of gross domestic product.

REGULATORY EFFICIENCY

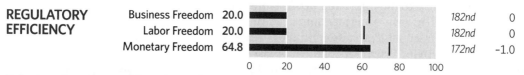

	Score	Rank	1-Year Change
Business Freedom	20.0	182nd	0
Labor Freedom	20.0	182nd	0
Monetary Freedom	64.8	172nd	–1.0

Private entrepreneurship exists only on a very small scale. The inconsistent and non-transparent application of regulations impedes the creation of new businesses. The rigid, state-controlled labor market has helped to create a large informal economy. The government tries to contain inflation directly by using price controls and regulating the limited areas of free-market activity and indirectly by controlling monetary growth.

OPEN MARKETS

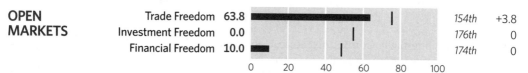

	Score	Rank	1-Year Change
Trade Freedom	63.8	154th	+3.8
Investment Freedom	0.0	176th	0
Financial Freedom	10.0	174th	0

Cuba's average tariff rate is 8.1 percent. The country's centrally planned economy is a barrier to the free flow of international trade and investment. The financial sector is tightly controlled by the state. Over a dozen foreign banks have opened representative offices, but they are not allowed to operate freely. Credit is not allocated on market terms, and capital markets remain underdeveloped.

Long-Term Score Change (since 1995)

RULE OF LAW		GOVERNMENT SIZE		REGULATORY EFFICIENCY		OPEN MARKETS	
Property Rights	0	Fiscal Freedom	+14.2	Business Freedom	–20.0	Trade Freedom	+3.8
Freedom from Corruption	+36.0	Government Spending	0	Labor Freedom	0	Investment Freedom	–10.0
				Monetary Freedom	+1.9	Financial Freedom	0

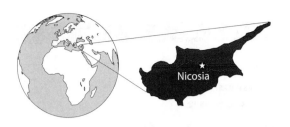

CYPRUS

Economic Freedom Score

25 — 50 — 75

Least free 0

Most free 100

67.9

World Rank: 45　　　　**Regional Rank: 20**

Cyprus's economic freedom score is 67.9, making its economy the 45th freest in the 2015 *Index*. Its overall score is up by 0.3 point from last year due to improvements in trade freedom, investment freedom, and monetary freedom that outweigh declines in labor freedom and freedom from corruption. Cyprus is ranked 20th out of 43 countries in the Europe region.

Over the past five years, spurred by government responses to the financial crisis and the difficult external environment, economic freedom in Cyprus has declined by 5.4 points, the second-largest decline in the European region. With scores dropping in nine of the 10 economic freedoms, Cyprus has been rated "moderately free" since 2013.

The eurozone crisis has severely strained Cyprus's economy. Multiple bailouts to prop up government finances and the financial sector have increased the country's relative debt load to one of the highest in Europe. To reverse this trend, the government will have to demonstrate that it is willing to reopen its market to free trade and capital flows. A renewed commitment to easing the regulatory environment will be needed to promote entrepreneurial activity and reorient the economy away from offshore financial services.

BACKGROUND: A U.N. buffer zone has separated the Greek Cypriot Republic of Cyprus from the Turkish Republic of Northern Cyprus since 1974. The Republic of Cyprus joined the European Union in 2004 and acts as the island's internationally recognized administration. Despite deep mutual hostility, Greek and Turkish leaders continue to negotiate on possible reunification through U.N.-brokered talks. Center-right Cyprus President Nicos Anastasiades took office in February 2013. After the collapse of the banking sector in 2013, Cyprus received a €10 billion bailout plan from the EU. However, draconian measures that include taxing bank deposits were imposed as part of the bailout. The economy remains very weak, and the unemployment rate is one of Europe's highest.

Freedom Trend

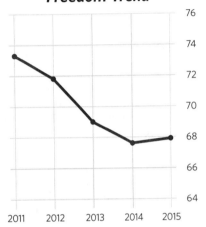

Country Comparisons

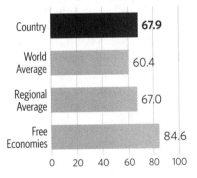

Country	67.9
World Average	60.4
Regional Average	67.0
Free Economies	84.6

0　20　40　60　80　100

Quick Facts

Population: 0.9 million
GDP (PPP): $22.3 billion
–6.0% growth in 2013
5-year compound annual growth –1.7%
$25,265 per capita
Unemployment: 15.7%
Inflation (CPI): 0.4%
FDI Inflow: $533.3 million
Public Debt: 112.0% of GDP

2013 data unless otherwise noted.
Data compiled as of September 2014.

How Do We Measure Economic Freedom?
See page 475 for an explanation of the methodology
or visit the *Index* Web site at *heritage.org/index.*

THE TEN ECONOMIC FREEDOMS

		Score	■ Country		World Average	Rank	1-Year Change

RULE OF LAW

	Score	Rank	1-Year Change
Property Rights	70.0	30th	0
Freedom from Corruption	63.0	31st	–1.0

Despite renewed efforts by the two governments in 2014 to reach a political settlement concerning the Turkish-controlled region, the division of the island continues. Corruption, patronage, and a lack of transparency will continue to flourish in that area and pose inherent risks for foreign investors. The independent judiciary in the Republic of Cyprus operates according to the British tradition, upholding due process rights.

GOVERNMENT SIZE

	Score	Rank	1-Year Change
Fiscal Freedom	79.5	90th	–0.2
Government Spending	36.7	157th	+0.5

The top individual income tax rate is 35 percent, and the top corporate tax rate is 12.5 percent. Other taxes include a value-added tax and a real estate tax. The overall tax burden amounts to 25.9 percent of gross domestic product. Government expenditures are equal to 45.9 percent of domestic income, and public debt is equivalent to 112 percent of annual domestic production.

REGULATORY EFFICIENCY

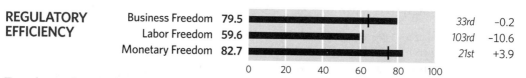

	Score	Rank	1-Year Change
Business Freedom	79.5	33rd	–0.2
Labor Freedom	59.6	103rd	–10.6
Monetary Freedom	82.7	21st	+3.9

Forming and operating a business is relatively straightforward within the regulatory framework. With no minimum capital required, it takes less than a week to launch a company. Relatively flexible labor regulations facilitate employment and productivity growth, although union power remains strong. EU subsidies to Cyprus increased after the 2013 banking crisis, and the government mandated price controls on food staples.

OPEN MARKETS

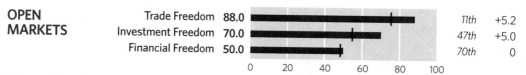

	Score	Rank	1-Year Change
Trade Freedom	88.0	11th	+5.2
Investment Freedom	70.0	47th	+5.0
Financial Freedom	50.0	70th	0

EU members have a 1.0 percent average tariff rate. Although some non-tariff barriers exist, the EU is relatively open to external trade. In most sectors of the Cypriot economy, foreign and domestic investors are treated similarly. Capital controls imposed during the 2013 banking crisis have been lifted. Despite reorganizations following the bailout, the banking sector remains unstable, with a high level of nonperforming loans.

Long-Term Score Change (since 1996)

RULE OF LAW		GOVERNMENT SIZE		REGULATORY EFFICIENCY		OPEN MARKETS	
Property Rights	+20.0	Fiscal Freedom	+7.6	Business Freedom	–5.5	Trade Freedom	+19.6
Freedom from Corruption	+13.0	Government Spending	–31.2	Labor Freedom	–10.4	Investment Freedom	0
				Monetary Freedom	+6.7	Financial Freedom	–20.0

CZECH REPUBLIC

★ Prague

World Rank: 24　　　　　　　　**Regional Rank: 13**

Economic Freedom Score

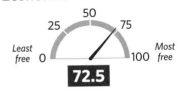

72.5

The Czech Republic's economic freedom score is 72.5, making its economy the 24th freest in the 2015 *Index*. Its overall score is 0.3 point better than last year, with declines in the management of public spending, business freedom, and labor freedom outweighed by improvements in the area of the rule of law as measured by property rights and freedom from corruption. The Czech Republic is ranked 13th out of 43 countries in the Europe region, and its overall score is higher than the regional and global averages.

Over the past five years, the Czech Republic's transition to a market economy has been facilitated by a strong commitment to economic freedom. Since 2011, its economic freedom score has improved by 2.1 points, reinforcing the country's position in the "mostly free" category. Score improvements in six of the 10 economic freedoms have been led by double-digit improvements in investment freedom and property rights.

With a vibrant automotive production base, the Czech Republic has established itself as an open and dynamic market economy, a sharp reversal after decades of Communism. However, further efforts to institutionalize the independence of the judiciary and stamp out corruption remain critical.

BACKGROUND: The end of Czechoslovakia's Communist dictatorship in 1989 led to the election of dissident playwright Vaclav Havel as president. The Czech Republic separated from Slovakia in 1993 and joined NATO in 1999 and the European Union in 2004. Prospects for adoption of the euro are uncertain because of the EU economic crisis, but the government appears to be moving toward closer alignment with the eurozone. The first directly elected president, Miloš Zeman, appointed a caretaker government in August 2013, and legislative elections followed in October. In January 2014, Zeman asked Social Democrat leader Bohuslav Sobotka to form a government. The Czech Republic is an export economy, but foreign trade decreased in 2013.

Freedom Trend

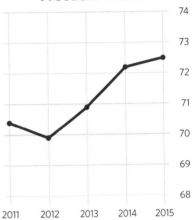

Country Comparisons

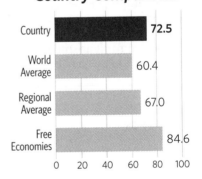

Quick Facts

Population: 10.5 million
GDP (PPP): $286.0 billion
–0.9% growth in 2013
5-year compound annual growth –0.5%
$27,200 per capita
Unemployment: 7.0%
Inflation (CPI): 1.4%
FDI Inflow: $5.0 billion
Public Debt: 47.9% of GDP

2013 data unless otherwise noted.
Data compiled as of September 2014.

How Do We Measure Economic Freedom?
See page 475 for an explanation of the methodology
or visit the *Index* Web site at *heritage.org/index*.

THE TEN ECONOMIC FREEDOMS

RULE OF LAW

	Score		Rank	1-Year Change
Property Rights	75.0		25th	+5.0
Freedom from Corruption	48.0		57th	+2.7

An abuse-of-power scandal toppled the government in 2013 and propelled the rise of the "ANO 2011" anti-corruption party. The new government's anti-graft program applies to all governmental departments and offices. The judiciary's independence is largely respected, though its complexity and multilayered composition lead to the slow delivery of judgments. Property rights are relatively well protected, and contracts are generally secure.

GOVERNMENT SIZE

	Score		Rank	1-Year Change
Fiscal Freedom	81.5		68th	-0.2
Government Spending	40.6		151st	-3.2

The top individual income tax rate is 15 percent, and the top corporate tax rate is 19 percent. Other taxes include a value-added tax and an inheritance tax. The overall tax burden is equal to 35.5 percent of the domestic economy. Government spending equals 44.5 percent of domestic income, and public debt is equivalent to 48 percent of gross domestic product.

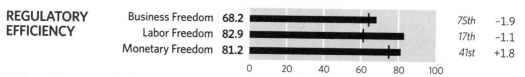

REGULATORY EFFICIENCY

	Score		Rank	1-Year Change
Business Freedom	68.2		75th	-1.9
Labor Freedom	82.9		17th	-1.1
Monetary Freedom	81.2		41st	+1.8

With minimum capital required, starting a company involves nine bureaucratic procedures. Obtaining necessary permits still takes over 100 days. Hiring and dismissal regulations are not onerous, but the non-salary cost of employing a worker can be burdensome. Although a number of price controls are maintained, the government has taken steps to reduce subsidies for state pensions and green energy.

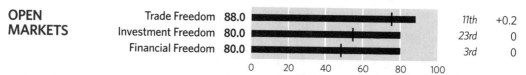

OPEN MARKETS

	Score		Rank	1-Year Change
Trade Freedom	88.0		11th	+0.2
Investment Freedom	80.0		23rd	0
Financial Freedom	80.0		3rd	0

EU members have a 1.0 percent average tariff rate. Although some non-tariff barriers exist, the EU is relatively open to external trade. The Czech financial system is relatively well developed and open to competition. Foreign banks dominate the banking sector, and direct government involvement is minimal. Capital markets are not fully developed.

Long-Term Score Change (since 1995)

RULE OF LAW		GOVERNMENT SIZE		REGULATORY EFFICIENCY		OPEN MARKETS	
Property Rights	+5.0	Fiscal Freedom	+34.8	Business Freedom	-31.8	Trade Freedom	+12.0
Freedom from Corruption	-2.0	Government Spending	+2.4	Labor Freedom	+25.2	Investment Freedom	+10.0
				Monetary Freedom	+12.0	Financial Freedom	-10.0

Copenhagen

DENMARK

Economic Freedom Score

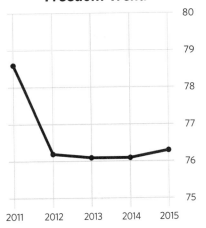

25   50   75

Least free 0   100 Most free

76.3

World Rank: 11   **Regional Rank: 4**

Denmark's economic freedom score is 76.3, making its economy the 11th freest in the 2015 *Index*. Its overall score is up by 0.2 point from last year, with improvements in six of the 10 economic freedoms, including monetary freedom and property rights, partially offset by declines in financial freedom and freedom from corruption. Denmark is ranked 4th out of 43 countries in the Europe region.

Although economic freedom in Denmark has generally flourished in the past, the recent eurozone crisis has taken a toll. Over the past half-decade, Denmark's economic freedom score has declined by 2.3 points. Contributing to this decrease have been declines in half of the 10 economic freedom factors, including freedom from corruption, fiscal freedom, government spending, business freedom, and financial freedom.

Negative growth rates in recent years have put intense pressure on government finances, with Denmark's government spending score declining by nearly 18 points since 2011. Nevertheless, economic freedom continues to flourish in one of Europe's most stable economies. The rule of law and property rights are well entrenched, and the economy is open to global trade and investment.

BACKGROUND: Social Democrat Prime Minister Helle Thorning-Schmidt heads a center-left coalition that defeated Prime Minister Lars Løkke Rasmussen in the September 2011 parliamentary elections. She is Denmark's first female prime minister. Denmark has been a member of the European Union since 1973. Its economy depends heavily on foreign trade, and the private sector includes many small and medium-size companies. Increased immigration spurred by the 2011 uprisings in North Africa has led the government to consider more restrictive immigration laws. Although not party to the euro, Denmark has felt the impact of the European economic crisis. Economic growth has been sluggish, though unemployment remains relatively low. There are no significant natural resources, and the economy relies almost totally on services.

Freedom Trend

	80
	79
	78
	77
	76
	75

2011   2012   2013   2014   2015

Country Comparisons

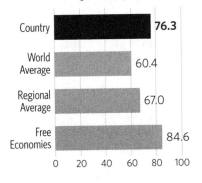

Country   **76.3**
World Average 60.4
Regional Average 67.0
Free Economies 84.6

0   20   40   60   80   100

Quick Facts

Population: 5.6 million
GDP (PPP): $211.9 billion
0.4% growth in 2013
5-year compound annual growth –0.7%
$37,900 per capita
Unemployment: 7.1%
Inflation (CPI): 0.8%
FDI Inflow: $2.1 billion
Public Debt: 45.2% of GDP

2013 data unless otherwise noted.
Data compiled as of September 2014.

How Do We Measure Economic Freedom?
See page 475 for an explanation of the methodology
or visit the *Index* Web site at *heritage.org/index*.

THE TEN ECONOMIC FREEDOMS

		Score	■ Country	| World Average	Rank	1-Year Change

RULE OF LAW

	Score	Rank	1-Year Change
Property Rights	95.0	1st	+5.0
Freedom from Corruption	91.0	1st	-2.7

Levels of corruption are generally very low in Denmark, which was tied with New Zealand for first place out of 177 countries surveyed in Transparency International's 2013 Corruption Perceptions Index. Protections for property rights are strongly enforced, and an independent and fair judicial system is institutionalized throughout the economy. Intellectual property rights are respected, and enforcement is consistent with world standards.

GOVERNMENT SIZE

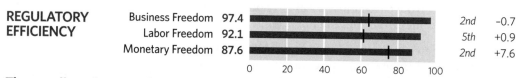

	Score	Rank	1-Year Change
Fiscal Freedom	39.6	180th	+0.3
Government Spending	1.8	175th	+1.3

Denmark's top individual income tax rate is 56.0 percent, and its top corporate tax rate is down slightly at 24.5 percent. Other taxes include a value-added tax and an inheritance tax. The overall tax burden equals 48.0 percent of the domestic economy. Government spending amounts to 57.2 percent of gross domestic product, and public debt is equivalent to 45 percent of GDP.

REGULATORY EFFICIENCY

	Score	Rank	1-Year Change
Business Freedom	97.4	2nd	-0.7
Labor Freedom	92.1	5th	+0.9
Monetary Freedom	87.6	2nd	+7.6

The overall regulatory environment remains one of the world's most transparent and efficient. Minimum capital requirements for limited liability companies have been reduced, and launching a business involves only four procedures. Flexible and modern employment regulations sustain the labor market. Monetary stability is well established, but rents are controlled and medications are heavily subsidized. Green energy subsidies were cut in 2013.

OPEN MARKETS

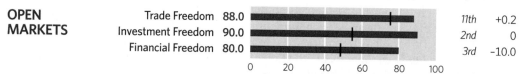

	Score	Rank	1-Year Change
Trade Freedom	88.0	11th	+0.2
Investment Freedom	90.0	2nd	0
Financial Freedom	80.0	3rd	-10.0

EU members have a 1.0 percent average tariff rate. Some non-tariff barriers exist, but the EU is relatively open to external trade. Denmark is very open to foreign investment and generally treats foreign and domestic investors equally under the law. The modern and diversified financial sector has undergone some instability, with several banks performing poorly. The three largest banks account for over half of total banking assets.

Long-Term Score Change (since 1996)

RULE OF LAW		GOVERNMENT SIZE		REGULATORY EFFICIENCY		OPEN MARKETS	
Property Rights	+5.0	Fiscal Freedom	+8.1	Business Freedom	+12.4	Trade Freedom	+10.2
Freedom from Corruption	+1.0	Government Spending	+1.8	Labor Freedom	-7.8	Investment Freedom	+20.0
				Monetary Freedom	-3.8	Financial Freedom	+10.0

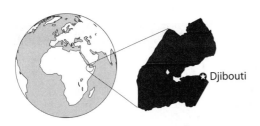
⭐ Djibouti

DJIBOUTI

Economic Freedom Score

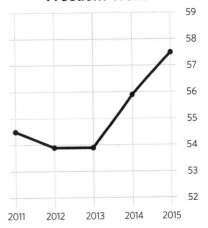

25　50　75
Least free　0　Most free　100

57.5

World Rank: 112　　　　**Regional Rank: 18**

Djibouti's economic freedom score is 57.5, making its economy the 112th freest in the 2015 *Index*. Its overall score is 1.6 points better than last year, reflecting improvements in six of the 10 economic freedoms, including business freedom, freedom from corruption, and investment freedom. Djibouti is ranked 18th out of 46 countries in the Sub-Saharan Africa region.

Djibouti has achieved gradual improvements in economic freedom over the past five years. Since 2011, its economic freedom score has risen by 3.0 points, led by gains in freedom from corruption, government spending, monetary freedom, and investment freedom. Strategically located at the mouth of the Red Sea, Djibouti has developed as a vital port and transshipment terminal for international trade.

Nevertheless, Djibouti has remained "mostly unfree" throughout its history in the *Index*. Its integration with the world economy as a transshipment point contrasts sharply with a trade freedom score that sits well below the world average. Tariff and non-tariff barriers exacerbate well-known food security issues. Strategic attempts to reorient the economy toward financial services and communication are undermined by an increasingly onerous regulatory regime.

BACKGROUND: President Ismael Omar Guelleh, whose multi-party, multi-ethnic coalition controls all levels of government, was re-elected to a third term in 2011. One of Djibouti's comparative advantages is its geostrategic location at the mouth of the Red Sea. Port facilities and the railway are key assets. Djibouti is also home to French, Japanese, and American military facilities. The main port serves as a key staging point for international antipiracy operations. Djibouti is active in the African Union's AMISOM peacekeeping mission in Somalia. Djibouti has few natural resources and imports most of its food. The government relies on foreign assistance to pay its bills and finance development projects. In 2013, Guelleh announced that Djibouti would focus on improving and expanding its financial and communications sectors.

Freedom Trend

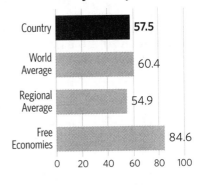

59
58
57
56
55
54
53
52

2011　2012　2013　2014　2015

Country Comparisons

Country　**57.5**
World Average　60.4
Regional Average　54.9
Free Economies　84.6

0　20　40　60　80　100

Quick Facts

Population: 0.9 million
GDP (PPP): $2.5 billion
5.0% growth in 2013
5-year compound annual growth 4.6%
$2,746 per capita
Unemployment: n/a
Inflation (CPI): 2.5%
FDI Inflow: $286.0 million
Public Debt: 34.8% of GDP

2013 data unless otherwise noted.
Data compiled as of September 2014.

How Do We Measure Economic Freedom?
See page 475 for an explanation of the methodology or visit the *Index* Web site at *heritage.org/index*.

THE TEN ECONOMIC FREEDOMS

		Score	■ Country	| World Average	Rank	1-Year Change
RULE OF LAW	Property Rights	25.0			124th	−5.0
	Freedom from Corruption	36.0			95th	+5.1

Despite tepid efforts to curb corruption, power remains concentrated in the hands of the president, and political repression increased in 2014. Public officials do not have to disclose their assets. Trials and judicial proceedings are time-consuming, prone to corruption, and politically manipulated. Protection of private property is weak. The judicial system is based on the French civil code, but Sharia law prevails in family matters.

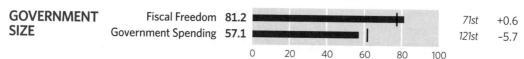

		Score			Rank	1-Year Change
GOVERNMENT SIZE	Fiscal Freedom	81.2			71st	+0.6
	Government Spending	57.1			121st	−5.7

The top individual income tax rate is 30 percent, and the top corporate tax rate is 25 percent. Other taxes include a property tax and an excise tax. Overall tax revenue is equivalent to 18.9 percent of gross domestic product. Government expenditures equal 37.8 percent of domestic income, and public debt amounts to 35 percent of the gross domestic economy.

		Score			Rank	1-Year Change
REGULATORY EFFICIENCY	Business Freedom	55.4			130th	+12.7
	Labor Freedom	66.6			72nd	+1.5
	Monetary Freedom	78.9			64th	+1.7

The regulatory system lacks clarity and efficiency. Launching a business remains burdensome, and the minimum capital required amounts to about twice the level of average annual income. A modern labor market has not fully developed. Several goods and services are subject to price controls. In 2013, the IMF urged the government to replace costly subsidies on food and fuel with targeted assistance.

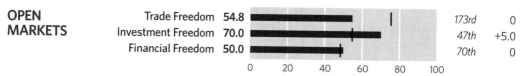

		Score			Rank	1-Year Change
OPEN MARKETS	Trade Freedom	54.8			173rd	0
	Investment Freedom	70.0			47th	+5.0
	Financial Freedom	50.0			70th	0

Djibouti's average tariff rate is 17.6 percent. Non-tariff barriers are relatively low for the region. Domestic and foreign investors generally receive equal treatment under the law, but investment in some sectors of the economy is restricted. The banking sector has expanded as more banks, particularly foreign banks, have entered the market and increased competition in recent years.

Long-Term Score Change (since 1997)

RULE OF LAW		GOVERNMENT SIZE		REGULATORY EFFICIENCY		OPEN MARKETS	
Property Rights	−25.0	Fiscal Freedom	−2.9	Business Freedom	+0.4	Trade Freedom	+3.8
Freedom from Corruption	+6.0	Government Spending	+12.6	Labor Freedom	+6.9	Investment Freedom	+20.0
				Monetary Freedom	+3.4	Financial Freedom	0

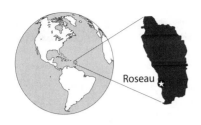

Roseau

DOMINICA

Economic Freedom Score

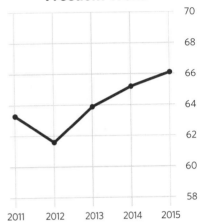

50
25   75
Least free   0   100   Most free

66.1

Dominica's economic freedom score is 66.1, making its economy the 61st freest in the 2015 *Index*. Its overall score is 0.9 point higher than last year, due primarily to improvements in investment freedom, freedom from corruption, and monetary freedom. Dominica is ranked 11th out of 29 countries in the South and Central America/Caribbean region. It has recorded its highest economic freedom score ever in the 2015 *Index*, and its overall score is above the world average.

Over the past five years, economic freedom in Dominica has improved by 2.8 points, advancing in half of the 10 factors. Efforts to develop an offshore medical and financial industry have been assisted by improvements in labor freedom and an easing of the investment regime.

However, Dominica still falls short of the world average in the four economic freedoms in the areas of finance, trade, fiscal policy, and the management of government spending. Diversifying the economy from agriculture to services and eco-tourism requires more serious restructuring, particularly in opening the economy to the global marketplace.

BACKGROUND: Dominica has a unicameral parliamentary government with a president and prime minister. Prime Minister Roosevelt Skerrit took office in 2004; his Dominica Labour Party was re-elected in 2009 and will face the voters again in 2015. In 2008, Dominica was among the first Caribbean nations to join the Bolivarian Alliance for the Americas (ALBA), a restrictive trade organization led by socialist Venezuela. ALBA's continuing interference in the Caribbean Community (CARICOM) threatens to undermine progress in free-market democratic institutions and regional integration. In 2010, Dominica entered into an economic union with other members of the Organization of Eastern Caribbean States. In an effort to diversify the economy, the government encourages investments in non-traditional agricultural exports such as coffee, patchouli, aloe vera, exotic fruits, and cut flowers. It also plans to sign agreements with private-sector investors to develop geothermal energy resources.

Freedom Trend

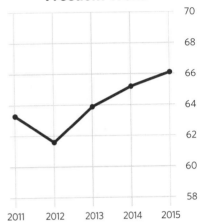

70
68
66
64
62
60
58

2011   2012   2013   2014   2015

Country Comparisons

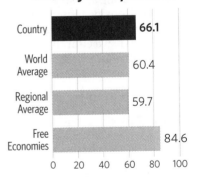

Country	66.1
World Average	60.4
Regional Average	59.7
Free Economies	84.6

0   20   40   60   80   100

Quick Facts

Population: 0.1 million
GDP (PPP): $1.0 billion
0.8% growth in 2013
5-year compound annual growth 0.0%
$14,283 per capita
Unemployment: n/a
Inflation (CPI): –0.4%
FDI Inflow: $17.9 million
Public Debt: 75.0% of GDP

2013 data unless otherwise noted.
Data compiled as of September 2014.

How Do We Measure Economic Freedom?
See page 475 for an explanation of the methodology or visit the *Index* Web site at *heritage.org/index*.

THE TEN ECONOMIC FREEDOMS

RULE OF LAW

	Score	Rank	1-Year Change
Property Rights	60.0	41st	0
Freedom from Corruption	58.0	40th	+4.5

Dominica does not have a major corruption problem, although anti-corruption statutes are sometimes not implemented effectively. It has an independent judiciary based on English common law, and private property rights are generally respected. Public trials are considered fair. Pirated copyrighted material is sold openly. Non-bank financial institutions are monitored to combat money laundering and the financing of terrorism.

GOVERNMENT SIZE

	Score	Rank	1-Year Change
Fiscal Freedom	73.6	121st	+0.7
Government Spending	61.5	106th	-0.2

Dominica's top individual income tax rate is 35 percent, and its top corporate tax rate is 30 percent. Other taxes include a value-added tax and an environment tax. Overall tax revenue equals 22.6 percent of the domestic economy. Government expenditures are equivalent to 35.8 percent of domestic income, and public debt amounts to 75 percent of gross domestic product.

REGULATORY EFFICIENCY

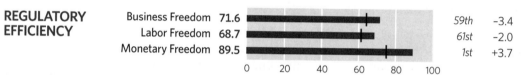

	Score	Rank	1-Year Change
Business Freedom	71.6	59th	-3.4
Labor Freedom	68.7	61st	-2.0
Monetary Freedom	89.5	1st	+3.7

Incorporating a business takes about two weeks, and no minimum capital is required. Completing licensing requirements still takes over three months on average. The non-salary cost of employing a worker is moderate, but restrictions on work hours are rigid. An ongoing and comprehensive effort by government to restructure the economy includes the elimination of price controls.

OPEN MARKETS

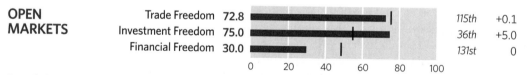

	Score	Rank	1-Year Change
Trade Freedom	72.8	115th	+0.1
Investment Freedom	75.0	36th	+5.0
Financial Freedom	30.0	131st	0

Dominica's average tariff rate is 8.6 percent. Government procurement rules can favor domestic firms. Foreign and domestic investors are generally treated equally under the law, but there are some restrictions on foreign ownership of land. The financial sector remains underdeveloped. Shallow capital markets and a lack of available financial instruments restrict overall access to credit.

Long-Term Score Change (since 2009)

RULE OF LAW		GOVERNMENT SIZE		REGULATORY EFFICIENCY		OPEN MARKETS	
Property Rights	0	Fiscal Freedom	+6.2	Business Freedom	-4.8	Trade Freedom	-1.4
Freedom from Corruption	+2.0	Government Spending	+9.3	Labor Freedom	-1.3	Investment Freedom	+15.0
				Monetary Freedom	+9.7	Financial Freedom	0

DOMINICAN REPUBLIC

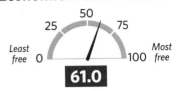

Santo Domingo ★

World Rank: 86   **Regional Rank: 16**

Economic Freedom Score

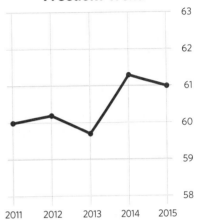

Least free 0   Most free 100

61.0

The Dominican Republic's economic freedom score is 61.0, making its economy the 86th freest in the 2015 *Index*. Its overall score is 0.3 point lower than last year due to considerable declines in the control of government spending and business freedom that outweigh gains in labor freedom and freedom from corruption. The Dominican Republic is ranked 16th out of 29 countries in the South and Central America/Caribbean region, and its score is just above the regional average.

A free trade agreement with the United States and a strategic location in the Caribbean have facilitated economic growth in the Dominican Republic. Over the past half-decade, however, the Dominican Republic has recorded positive changes in only two of the 10 economic freedoms. Labor freedom improved only marginally, but investment freedom advanced by 20 points.

Once an agricultural economy, the Dominican Republic now boasts a robust tourism and services sector. Liberalization of the investment regime has facilitated growth surrounding free trade zones along the coast. However, entrepreneurship and private-sector development remain constrained by inefficient government services and weak rule of law. Corruption is still pervasive in the economy, exacerbated by drug trafficking in recent years. Institutionalizing free-market principles will be vital for securing long-term growth.

BACKGROUND: Danilo Medina of the center-left Dominican Liberation Party (PLD) won the presidency in August 2012, succeeding three-term President Leonel Fernández, also of the PLD. Haitian immigration is a hot political issue. A 2013 Supreme Court ruling that limited the rights of Haitians who are unlawfully present in the country and their Dominican-born children was partially undone by a Medina-sponsored law in 2014. The Dominican Republic is the second-largest economy in the Caribbean. The traditional agricultural economy has shifted in recent years toward greater reliance on tourism and manufacturing. Remittances from the United States account for about 10 percent of GDP. Drug and human trafficking undermine the rule of law.

Freedom Trend

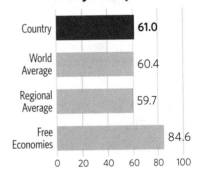

Country Comparisons

Country	61.0
World Average	60.4
Regional Average	59.7
Free Economies	84.6

0   20   40   60   80   100

Quick Facts

Population: 10.4 million
GDP (PPP): $103.2 billion
4.1% growth in 2013
5-year compound annual growth 4.7%
$9,911 per capita
Unemployment: 15.0%
Inflation (CPI): 4.8%
FDI Inflow: $2.0 billion
Public Debt: 33.8% of GDP

2013 data unless otherwise noted.
Data compiled as of September 2014.

How Do We Measure Economic Freedom?
See page 475 for an explanation of the methodology
or visit the *Index* Web site at *heritage.org/index.*

THE TEN ECONOMIC FREEDOMS

	Score	Country	World Average	Rank	1-Year Change

RULE OF LAW

	Score		Rank	1-Year Change
Property Rights	30.0		94th	0
Freedom from Corruption	29.0		127th	+1.7

Late in 2013, the government launched an effort to improve public-sector transparency, but it seems unlikely to make the institutional reforms needed to reduce widespread graft, and bureaucratic processes will probably remain vulnerable to corruption. The judiciary is politicized and riddled with corruption, and the legal system offers little recourse to those who lack money or influence. Enforcement of intellectual property rights is poor.

GOVERNMENT SIZE

	Score		Rank	1-Year Change
Fiscal Freedom	84.1		57th	+0.4
Government Spending	87.1		25th	-5.2

The top individual income tax rate is 25 percent, and the top corporate tax rate has been reduced from 29 percent to 28 percent. Other taxes include a value-added tax and a tax on net wealth. Overall tax revenue is 13.5 percent of gross domestic product. Government expenditures equal 20.7 percent of the domestic economy, and public debt equals 34 percent of annual domestic income.

REGULATORY EFFICIENCY

	Score		Rank	1-Year Change
Business Freedom	53.5		140th	-2.6
Labor Freedom	57.5		109th	+2.3
Monetary Freedom	76.0		97th	+0.3

Launching a business takes seven procedures, and the minimum capital required equals about half the level of average annual income. Obtaining necessary permits takes over 150 days on average. The non-salary cost of employing a worker is moderate, but the labor market lacks flexibility in other areas. The government's SIUBEN system includes targeted conditional cash transfers, electricity and cooking gas subsidies, and subsidized health insurance.

OPEN MARKETS

	Score		Rank	1-Year Change
Trade Freedom	77.8		84th	0
Investment Freedom	75.0		36th	0
Financial Freedom	40.0		106th	0

The Dominican Republic's average tariff rate is 6.1 percent. Imports of used cars are restricted, and government procurement rules can benefit domestic companies. Foreign investors sometimes find it challenging to deal with the bureaucracy. The small financial sector has been modernized and consolidated, but confidence in banking has been shaky. Capital markets are underdeveloped, and long-term financing is hard to obtain.

Long-Term Score Change (since 1995)

RULE OF LAW		GOVERNMENT SIZE		REGULATORY EFFICIENCY		OPEN MARKETS	
Property Rights	0	Fiscal Freedom	-0.2	Business Freedom	-1.5	Trade Freedom	+46.8
Freedom from Corruption	-1.0	Government Spending	-8.2	Labor Freedom	+0.6	Investment Freedom	+25.0
				Monetary Freedom	-0.2	Financial Freedom	-10.0

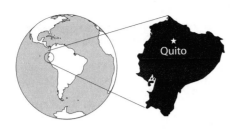

Quito

ECUADOR

Economic Freedom Score

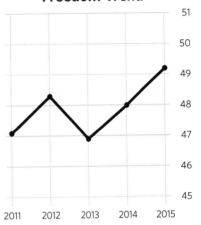

50
25   75
Least   Most
free 0 ──────── 100 free

49.2

World Rank: **156**   Regional Rank: **25**

Ecuador's economic freedom score is 49.2, making its economy the 156th freest in the 2015 *Index*. Its overall score is 1.2 points higher than last year due to significant improvements in freedom from corruption, the control of government spending, and monetary freedom. Scores in five other economic freedoms declined. Ecuador is ranked 25th out of 29 countries in the South and Central America/Caribbean region, and its overall score is far below world and regional averages.

Ecuador's improvement of 2.1 points over the past five years masks long-term deterioration in economic freedom since scoring began in 1995. Once considered "moderately free," Ecuador has fallen into the ranks of the "repressed" economies since 2010.

Ecuador continues to lag significantly in promoting the rule of law and has yet to establish a judicial system that is free from political interference. Deep petroleum reserves have enhanced financial growth, and Ecuador returned to the bond market in 2014. However, a history of fiscal incompetence, along with a restrictive investment climate, continues to suppress overall economic freedom.

BACKGROUND: President Rafael Correa was re-elected in 2013 for the third time, having amended the constitution in 2008 to ease presidential term limits. The ruling Alianza PAIZ has proposed legislation to abolish the limits altogether, which would allow Correa to run again in 2017. Other constitutional amendments passed in 2011 increased Correa's control of media and reduced the judicial system's independence. The Inter-American Human Rights Commission has criticized Ecuador for restricting freedom of the press. Ecuador is part of the Bolivarian Alliance for the Americas (ALBA), led by socialist Venezuela, and has strengthened its relations with Iran and China. By 2013, Ecuador was sending most of its oil exports to China. Ecuador returned to international credit markets in June 2014 for the first time since its $3.2 billion default in 2008. Approximately one-third of the population lives below the poverty line.

Freedom Trend

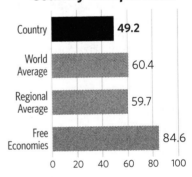

51
50
49
48
47
46
45

2011   2012   2013   2014   2015

Country Comparisons

Country   **49.2**
World Average   60.4
Regional Average   59.7
Free Economies   84.6

0   20   40   60   80   100

Quick Facts

Population: 15.8 million
GDP (PPP): $159.0 billion
4.2% growth in 2013
5-year compound annual growth 4.2%
$10,080 per capita
Unemployment: 4.5%
Inflation (CPI): 2.7%
FDI Inflow: $702.8 million
Public Debt: 24.3% of GDP

2013 data unless otherwise noted.
Data compiled as of September 2014.

How Do We Measure Economic Freedom?
See page 475 for an explanation of the methodology
or visit the *Index* Web site at *heritage.org/index*.

THE TEN ECONOMIC FREEDOMS

		Score	Rank	1-Year Change
RULE OF LAW	Property Rights	15.0	157th	–5.0
	Freedom from Corruption	35.0	103rd	+9.0

The government's anti-corruption agency reported in 2013 that cronyism, impunity, excessive discretion, fragmented anticorruption policies, lack of correspondence between offenses and sanctions, and collusion were among the factors that have favored the persistence of corruption in Ecuador. Judicial processes are slow and subject to political influence. The government decriminalized intellectual property rights violations in 2014.

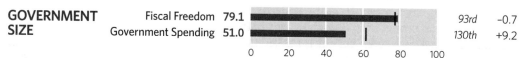

		Score	Rank	1-Year Change
GOVERNMENT SIZE	Fiscal Freedom	79.1	93rd	–0.7
	Government Spending	51.0	130th	+9.2

The top individual income tax rate is 35 percent, and the top corporate tax rate is 22 percent. A lower rate of 12 percent applies to profits that are reinvested. Other taxes include a value-added tax and an inheritance tax. Overall revenue equals 19.4 percent of domestic income. Public expenditures are equivalent to 40.4 percent of the overall domestic economy, and public debt equals 24 percent of GDP.

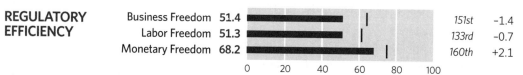

		Score	Rank	1-Year Change
REGULATORY EFFICIENCY	Business Freedom	51.4	151st	–1.4
	Labor Freedom	51.3	133rd	–0.7
	Monetary Freedom	68.2	160th	+2.1

Commercial laws are applied inconsistently, and launching a business takes about two months and 13 procedures. Completing licensing requirements takes over 100 days. Job-tenure regulations create a disincentive for new hiring, and employers resort to short-term contracts. Although dollarization produces a modicum of monetary stability, the state makes extensive use of subsidies and price controls.

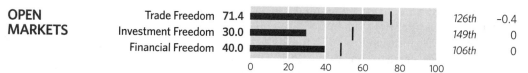

		Score	Rank	1-Year Change
OPEN MARKETS	Trade Freedom	71.4	126th	–0.4
	Investment Freedom	30.0	149th	0
	Financial Freedom	40.0	106th	0

Ecuador's average tariff rate is 4.3 percent. Additional barriers to trade include export taxes and government promotion of "import substitution." Foreign investment in several sectors of the economy is restricted. The financial system lacks efficiency and depth, and capital markets are underdeveloped. Lack of financing options hampers private-sector growth, and the number of nonperforming loans has increased.

Long-Term Score Change (since 1995)

RULE OF LAW		GOVERNMENT SIZE		REGULATORY EFFICIENCY		OPEN MARKETS	
Property Rights	–35.0	Fiscal Freedom	–2.7	Business Freedom	–3.6	Trade Freedom	+10.4
Freedom from Corruption	+25.0	Government Spending	–43.9	Labor Freedom	+11.5	Investment Freedom	–40.0
				Monetary Freedom	+21.9	Financial Freedom	–10.0

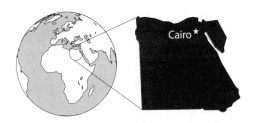

EGYPT

World Rank: 124   **Regional Rank: 12**

Egypt's economic freedom score is 55.2, making its economy the 124th freest in the 2015 *Index*. Its overall score is 2.3 points higher than last year due to improvements in six of the 10 economic freedoms, including labor freedom, monetary freedom, and investment freedom, that outweigh declines in trade freedom and the control of government spending. Egypt is ranked 12th out of 15 countries in the Middle East/North Africa region, and its overall score is below the world average.

Over the past five years, Egypt's economic freedom score has declined by nearly 4.0 points, pushed down by double-digit losses in property rights, investment freedom, and financial freedom. However, this decline has come to a halt in the 2015 *Index*.

Further action to restore and improve economic freedom is essential to counter economic stagnation and poverty. Long-established weaknesses in the institutional framework that include price controls and government subsidies of gasoline have greatly burdened the budget and forced the government to seek a bailout from both the IMF and other Arab states. The rule of law is ineffective and arbitrary, and judicial procedures are long and costly.

BACKGROUND: The army ousted President Hosni Mubarak in February 2011, and the Supreme Council of the Armed Forces assumed power pending election of a new civilian government. The parliament was dissolved in June 2012 after one-third of its members were found to have won their seats illegitimately. Mohamed Morsi of the Muslim Brotherhood's Freedom and Justice Party was elected president in June 2012 and granted himself sweeping new powers in November. His increasingly authoritarian rule triggered huge demonstrations and a July 2013 army coup. Field Marshal Abdel Fattah el-Sisi was elected president in May 2014. Three years of political instability have hurt tourism and foreign investment, both of which are important sources of foreign exchange. There have been limited market reforms, but food, energy, and other key commodities remain heavily subsidized.

Freedom Trend

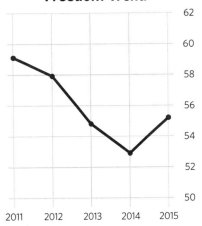

62
60
58
56
54
52
50

2011   2012   2013   2014   2015

Country Comparisons

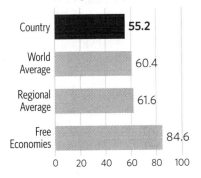

Country	**55.2**
World Average	60.4
Regional Average	61.6
Free Economies	84.6

0   20   40   60   80   100

Quick Facts

Population: 84.2 million
GDP (PPP): $553.6 billion
2.1% growth in 2013
5-year compound annual growth 3.2%
$6,579 per capita
Unemployment: 12.7%
Inflation (CPI): 6.9%
FDI Inflow: $5.6 billion
Public Debt: 89.2% of GDP

2013 data unless otherwise noted.
Data compiled as of September 2014.

How Do We Measure Economic Freedom?
See page 475 for an explanation of the methodology
or visit the *Index* Web site at *heritage.org/index.*

THE TEN ECONOMIC FREEDOMS

	Score		Rank	1-Year Change

RULE OF LAW

Property Rights	20.0	138th	0
Freedom from Corruption	32.0	116th	+3.4

Long before the 2013–2014 political upheaval, corruption was pervasive at all levels of government. The rule of law has been highly unstable across the country, and the judicial system's independence is poorly institutionalized. Judicial procedures tend to be protracted, costly, and subject to political pressure. Property rights are not protected effectively, and titles to real property may be difficult to establish.

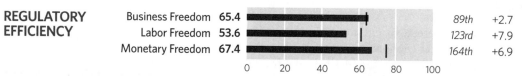

GOVERNMENT SIZE

Fiscal Freedom	85.8	45th	+0.2
Government Spending	68.0	91st	−1.6

Egypt's top individual and corporate income tax rates are 25 percent. Other taxes include a property tax and a general sales tax. Total tax revenue is equal to 12.9 percent of domestic income. Government spending equals 32.7 percent of the domestic economy, and public debt has risen to 89 percent of GDP. Measures to reduce the budget deficit by lowering energy subsidies are underway.

REGULATORY EFFICIENCY

Business Freedom	65.4	89th	+2.7
Labor Freedom	53.6	123rd	+7.9
Monetary Freedom	67.4	164th	+6.9

Previous regulatory reforms have made starting a business less time-consuming. However, without restructuring in other policy areas, those reforms have failed to create real momentum for dynamic entrepreneurial growth. Informal labor activity persists in many sectors. The government introduced significant electricity and fuel price increases in 2014 in a move to cut state subsidies.

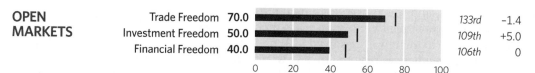

OPEN MARKETS

Trade Freedom	70.0	133rd	−1.4
Investment Freedom	50.0	109th	+5.0
Financial Freedom	40.0	106th	0

Egypt's average tariff rate is 8.1 percent. The government increased tariffs on luxury goods in 2013. Foreign ownership of land in some regions is restricted. Despite the uncertainty generated by political turmoil that has included the overthrow of two governments, the banking sector remains integrated into international markets and has shown a high level of resilience. Banks continue to be relatively well capitalized.

Long-Term Score Change (since 1995)

RULE OF LAW		GOVERNMENT SIZE		REGULATORY EFFICIENCY		OPEN MARKETS	
Property Rights	−10.0	Fiscal Freedom	+39.8	Business Freedom	+10.4	Trade Freedom	+45.0
Freedom from Corruption	+2.0	Government Spending	+14.3	Labor Freedom	−6.1	Investment Freedom	0
				Monetary Freedom	−4.6	Financial Freedom	−10.0

EL SALVADOR

Economic Freedom Score

Least free 0

25

50

75

100 Most free

65.7

World Rank: 62   **Regional Rank: 12**

El Salvador's economic freedom score is 65.7, making its economy the 62nd freest in the 2015 *Index*. Its overall score is 0.5 point lower than last year, with declines in labor freedom, business freedom, and property rights outweighing improvements in trade freedom, investment freedom, and freedom from corruption. El Salvador is ranked 12th out of 29 countries in the South and Central America/Caribbean region, and its overall score remains above the world average.

Over the past five years, economic freedom in El Salvador has declined by over 3.0 points, and the country has recorded its lowest score ever in the 2015 *Index*. Declines in half of the 10 economic freedoms include especially serious deteriorations in fiscal freedom and regulatory efficiency.

El Salvador's deteriorating economic freedom undermines an already weak institutional environment. Rampant violent crime further incapacitates a legal environment that is already subject to lingering corruption and obstructionism. However, relatively open trading and investment environments have fueled growth and offset other weaknesses.

BACKGROUND: After the end of El Salvador's 12-year civil war in 1992, three successive presidents from the National Republican Alliance (ARENA) sought to liberalize the economy in order to spur growth. A fourth, Antonio Saca (2004–2009), broke with that line of thinking. Corruption and deteriorating property rights during the Saca administration alienated foreign investors and drove the electorate to look for another option. Mauricio Funes of the Farabundo Martí Liberation Front (FMLN), elected in 2009, stepped into the vacuum, but his policies further undermined the rule of law. FMLN member and former guerrilla commander Salvador Sánchez Cerén succeeded Funes in March 2014. The disintegration of a gang truce has led to an increase in homicides, and El Salvador currently has the world's fourth-highest murder rate. Two days after Sánchez Cerén's inauguration, El Salvador became a member of Petrocaribe, an alliance formed by former Venezuelan President Hugo Chávez.

Freedom Trend

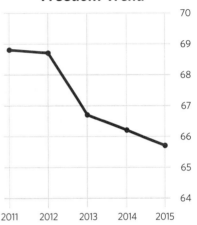

2011 2012 2013 2014 2015

Country Comparisons

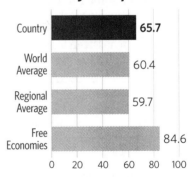

Country	65.7
World Average	60.4
Regional Average	59.7
Free Economies	84.6

0   20   40   60   80   100

Quick Facts

Population: 6.3 million
GDP (PPP): $47.5 billion
1.6% growth in 2013
5-year compound annual growth 0.8%
$7,515 per capita
Unemployment: 6.3%
Inflation (CPI): 0.8%
FDI Inflow: $140.1 million
Public Debt: 54.9% of GDP

2013 data unless otherwise noted.
Data compiled as of September 2014.

How Do We Measure Economic Freedom?
See page 475 for an explanation of the methodology
or visit the *Index* Web site at *heritage.org/index*.

THE TEN ECONOMIC FREEDOMS

		Score		Rank	1-Year Change
RULE OF LAW	Property Rights	35.0		87th	−5.0
	Freedom from Corruption	38.0		83rd	+3.7

In 2014, an arrest warrant was issued for a former president on corruption charges including embezzlement and illicit gains, but few high-level public officials have ever been convicted. The judicial system is somewhat independent but still subject to corruption and obstructionism. Property rights are not strongly respected, and law enforcement is inefficient and uneven. Violent crime, much of it gang-related, remains a problem.

		Score		Rank	1-Year Change
GOVERNMENT SIZE	Fiscal Freedom	79.4		91st	−0.2
	Government Spending	85.5		32nd	−0.3

El Salvador's top individual and corporate income tax rates are 30 percent. Other taxes include a value-added tax and excise taxes. Total tax revenue equals 16 percent of gross domestic product. Government spending has reached 22 percent of the total domestic economy in the most recent year, and public debt is equivalent to 55 percent of domestic income.

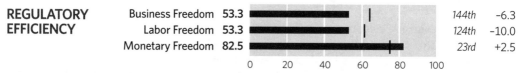

		Score		Rank	1-Year Change
REGULATORY EFFICIENCY	Business Freedom	53.3		144th	−6.3
	Labor Freedom	53.3		124th	−10.0
	Monetary Freedom	82.5		23rd	+2.5

Despite ongoing reform efforts, the overall regulatory environment remains burdensome. Starting a business takes over two weeks on average, and obtaining necessary permits involves 25 procedures. Lack of flexibility in the labor market hinders job growth. Although electricity generation has been largely privatized, the government partially subsidizes fuels and imposes price controls on several goods and services.

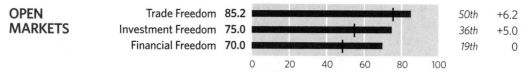

		Score		Rank	1-Year Change
OPEN MARKETS	Trade Freedom	85.2		50th	+6.2
	Investment Freedom	75.0		36th	+5.0
	Financial Freedom	70.0		19th	0

El Salvador's average tariff rate is 2.4 percent. Imports of agricultural products can face additional barriers. Foreign and domestic investors are generally subject to the same rules. Banks, largely foreign-owned and private, dominate the evolving financial system. The two state-owned banks account for less than 5 percent of all loans. A weak legal framework constrains local capital market development.

Long-Term Score Change (since 1995)

RULE OF LAW		GOVERNMENT SIZE		REGULATORY EFFICIENCY		OPEN MARKETS	
Property Rights	−15.0	Fiscal Freedom	−4.4	Business Freedom	−16.7	Trade Freedom	+20.2
Freedom from Corruption	−12.0	Government Spending	−8.1	Labor Freedom	−14.8	Investment Freedom	+5.0
				Monetary Freedom	+13.1	Financial Freedom	0

EQUATORIAL GUINEA

Economic Freedom Score

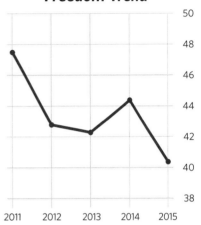

50

25   75

Least
free   0   100   Most
free

40.4

World Rank: 173   **Regional Rank: 44**

E quatorial Guinea's economic freedom score is 40.4, making its economy the 173rd freest in the 2015 *Index*. Its overall score has dropped by 4.0 points, the biggest decline in this year's *Index*. Equatorial Guinea is ranked 44th out of 46 countries in the Sub-Saharan Africa region, and its score is far below the regional and world averages.

Economic freedom in Equatorial Guinea has declined by over 7 points over the past half-decade, and the country has registered its lowest score ever in the 2015 *Index*. Led by a 49-point deterioration in its score for government spending, it has dropped even further into the "repressed" category. Scores for financial freedom and property rights have plummeted by over 10 points.

Abundant oil reserves have generated high economic growth, but most Equatorial Guineans remain trapped in poverty. A corrupt government and the small group of presidential cronies and other elites have captured billions of dollars in petroleum rents. The government continues to influence foreign investment decisions, subsidize key industries, control the flow of capital, and generally maintain its pervasive presence in the economy. The judiciary is one of the weakest in the world and is directly influenced by the president's office.

BACKGROUND: President Teodoro Obiang Nguema Mbasogo seized power in 1979 and continues to control the military and the government. Human rights organizations criticize Obiang for using an oil boom to enrich himself at the expense of his people. In 2011, U.S. authorities filed suit to seize $71 million worth of assets allegedly obtained illegally by the president's family. Equatorial Guinea is one of Africa's fastest-growing economies and Africa's third-largest oil producer. The oil boom has led to a dramatic increase in government revenue in recent years, but the standard of living has been slow to increase due to endemic corruption, mismanagement of oil revenues, and an absence of the rule of law.

Freedom Trend

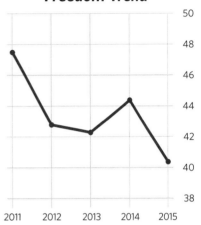

				50
				48
				46
				44
				42
				40
				38

2011   2012   2013   2014   2015

Country Comparisons

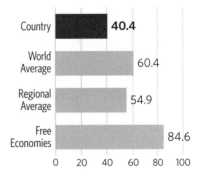

Country   **40.4**

World
Average   60.4

Regional
Average   54.9

Free
Economies   84.6

0   20   40   60   80   100

Quick Facts

Population: 0.8 million
GDP (PPP): $17.7 billion
–4.9% growth in 2013
5-year compound annual growth –1.3%
$23,370 per capita
Unemployment: 9.1%
Inflation (CPI): 3.2%
FDI Inflow: $1.9 billion
Public Debt: 8.8% of GDP

How Do We Measure Economic Freedom?
See page 475 for an explanation of the methodology
or visit the *Index* Web site at *heritage.org/index*.

2013 data unless otherwise noted.
Data compiled as of September 2014.

THE TEN ECONOMIC FREEDOMS

		Score	Country	World Average	Rank	1-Year Change
RULE OF LAW	Property Rights	10.0			165th	0
	Freedom from Corruption	19.0			171st	+2.4

President Obiang and his inner circle dominate the economic landscape with absolute power. Graft is rampant. In 2014, the French government announced a formal investigation into money laundering by Obiang's son, Teodorìn, Equatorial Guinea's second vice president. U.S. authorities are also investigating. The judiciary is not independent as the president is the chief magistrate. Protection of property rights is poor.

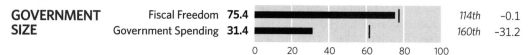

		Score			Rank	1-Year Change
GOVERNMENT SIZE	Fiscal Freedom	75.4			114th	-0.1
	Government Spending	31.4			160th	-31.2

Equatorial Guinea's top individual and corporate income tax rates are 35 percent. Other taxes include a value-added tax and a tax on inheritance. The overall tax burden equals 2.4 percent of gross domestic product. Government spending, which stands at 47.8 percent of the domestic economy, is mostly funded by hydrocarbon revenue. Public debt equals 9 percent of domestic income.

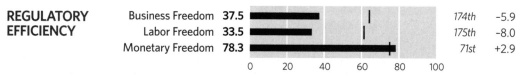

		Score			Rank	1-Year Change
REGULATORY EFFICIENCY	Business Freedom	37.5			174th	-5.9
	Labor Freedom	33.5			175th	-8.0
	Monetary Freedom	78.3			71st	+2.9

Starting a business costs about the level of average annual income, and completing licensing requirements takes over 140 days. The inefficient labor market lacks flexibility, and imbalances persist in the demand for and supply of skilled workers. The government has misused its substantial oil revenues to subsidize strategic sectors such as fisheries, agriculture, and ecotourism.

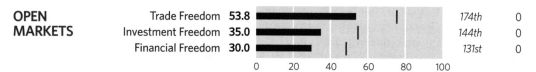

		Score			Rank	1-Year Change
OPEN MARKETS	Trade Freedom	53.8			174th	0
	Investment Freedom	35.0			144th	0
	Financial Freedom	30.0			131st	0

Equatorial Guinea's average tariff rate was 15.6 percent as of 2007. It may take weeks to import goods. The government screens foreign investment and imposes additional sectoral restrictions. The small financial sector remains underdeveloped, with only four commercial banks in operation. The high costs of finance and limited access to credit instruments hinder entrepreneurial activities. There is no stock exchange.

Long-Term Score Change (since 1999)

RULE OF LAW		GOVERNMENT SIZE		REGULATORY EFFICIENCY		OPEN MARKETS	
Property Rights	0	Fiscal Freedom	-13.9	Business Freedom	-17.5	Trade Freedom	-0.6
Freedom from Corruption	+9.0	Government Spending	-50.0	Labor Freedom	-13.9	Investment Freedom	+5.0
				Monetary Freedom	+12.3	Financial Freedom	+20.0

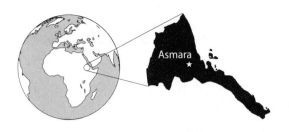

ERITREA

Economic Freedom Score

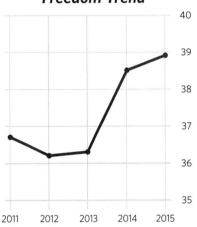

Least free 0   Most free 100

38.9

Eritrea's economic freedom score is 38.9, making its economy one of the most "repressed" in the 2015 *Index*. Its overall score is 0.4 point better than last year, with improvements in labor freedom and the control of government spending offset by declines in freedom from corruption and business freedom. Although Eritrea has recorded its highest economic freedom score ever in the 2015 *Index*, it is ranked 45th out of the 46 countries in the Sub-Saharan Africa region and remains the world's fifth least free economy.

Located on the Red Sea and with a burgeoning mining sector, Eritrea has experienced a half-decade of strong GDP growth that, along with more prudent spending and a slightly more stable monetary outlook, has led to a modest increase in economic freedom. However, improvements have occurred in only three of the 10 factors.

Over the past five years, scores have declined in the areas of corruption, taxation, and labor policy, further burdening an already weak institutional framework. An oppressive central government controls investment and the financial sector and distorts prices. Corruption is endemic. The judiciary is highly politicized and fails to check government expropriations of private property.

BACKGROUND: Isaias Afwerki has ruled this one-party state since 1993. According to a U.N. report in 2014, 4,000 Eritreans flee every month because of government repression. Eritrea is subject to U.N. military and economic sanctions for supporting armed opposition groups in Horn of Africa countries. Border conflicts persist between Ethiopia and Eritrea. Although Eritrea is one of Africa's faster-growing countries in percentage terms, growth in absolute terms is relatively meager. Copper and gold are important exports, but military spending drains resources from development of public infrastructure. An estimated 70 percent of Eritreans cannot meet basic food needs, and the government declines international food aid. Roughly three-quarters of Eritreans depend on small-scale agriculture and fishing, and up to two-thirds reportedly rely on government assistance.

Freedom Trend

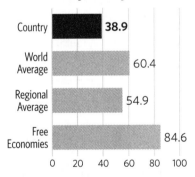

Country Comparisons

Country **38.9**
World Average 60.4
Regional Average 54.9
Free Economies 84.6

0   20   40   60   80   100

Quick Facts

Population: 6.3 million
GDP (PPP): $4.5 billion
1.3% growth in 2013
5-year compound annual growth 4.6%
$707 per capita
Unemployment: 8.9%
Inflation (CPI): 12.3%
FDI Inflow: $43.9 million
Public Debt: 126.0% of GDP

2013 data unless otherwise noted.
Data compiled as of September 2014.

THE TEN ECONOMIC FREEDOMS

		Score	Rank	1-Year Change
RULE OF LAW	Property Rights	10.0	165th	0
	Freedom from Corruption	20.0	168th	-2.9

The autocratic regime of the president and his small circle of senior advisers and military commanders is widely considered to be one of the world's most repressive. Corruption is a major problem. The politicized judiciary, understaffed and unprofessional, has never ruled against the government. Protection of property rights is poor. The state has often expropriated private property without notice, explanation, or compensation.

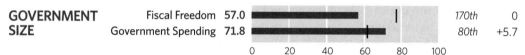

		Score	Rank	1-Year Change
GOVERNMENT SIZE	Fiscal Freedom	57.0	170th	0
	Government Spending	71.8	80th	+5.7

The top individual and corporate income tax rates are 30 percent. Other taxes include a controversial 2 percent levy on the Eritrean diaspora. The overall tax burden equals 50 percent of the domestic economy. Government expenditures equal 30.7 percent of domestic income, and public debt is larger than the size of the economy at over 125 percent of gross domestic product.

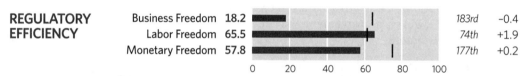

		Score	Rank	1-Year Change
REGULATORY EFFICIENCY	Business Freedom	18.2	183rd	-0.4
	Labor Freedom	65.5	74th	+1.9
	Monetary Freedom	57.8	177th	+0.2

Cumbersome procedures and high compliance costs continue to be impediments to business formation. In the absence of private-sector employment opportunities, an organized labor market has not emerged. Existing labor regulations are outmoded and create challenging barriers to hiring. Monetary stability remains weak overall. Subsidies and price controls have been a core feature of the country's command economy.

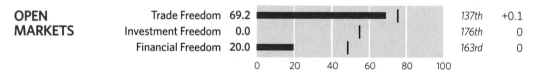

		Score	Rank	1-Year Change
OPEN MARKETS	Trade Freedom	69.2	137th	+0.1
	Investment Freedom	0.0	176th	0
	Financial Freedom	20.0	163rd	0

Eritrea's average tariff rate was 5.4 percent as of 2006. Importing goods can be a time-consuming process. Eritrea's economy is dominated by the state and provides a difficult environment for foreign investors. The financial system remains very underdeveloped. All banks are majority-owned by the state, and private-sector involvement in the system remains limited.

Long-Term Score Change (since 2009)

RULE OF LAW		GOVERNMENT SIZE		REGULATORY EFFICIENCY		OPEN MARKETS	
Property Rights	0	Fiscal Freedom	-29.4	Business Freedom	-0.1	Trade Freedom	0
Freedom from Corruption	-8.0	Government Spending	+61.9	Labor Freedom	-8.4	Investment Freedom	-10.0
				Monetary Freedom	-1.2	Financial Freedom	0

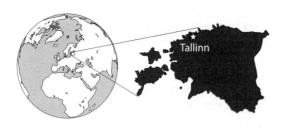

Tallinn

ESTONIA

Economic Freedom Score

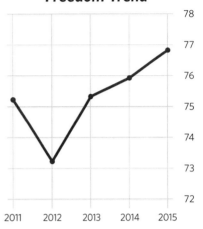

World Rank: 8   **Regional Rank: 2**

Estonia's economic freedom score is 76.8, making its economy the 8th freest in the 2015 *Index*. Its overall score is 0.9 point higher than last year, reflecting improvements in six of the 10 economic freedoms, including business freedom, freedom from corruption, and labor freedom. Estonia is ranked 2nd out of 43 countries in the Europe region, and its overall score is well above the regional and world averages.

Despite the eurozone crisis and a half-decade of weak regional growth, Estonia's domestic economy has proven resilient, and economic freedom has advanced. Since 2011, economic freedom has increased in a majority of the 10 factors, with strong improvements in the property rights regime and the entrepreneurial environment.

An increase in its overall score for the past three years has helped to confirm Estonia as a regional leader in economic freedom, reestablished as one of the world's 10 freest economies for the first time since 2007. Minimal state interference has been accompanied by a prudent fiscal policy, a commitment to open markets, and overall regulatory efficiency. In addition, the government has reinforced the rule of law and promoted an independent judiciary since independence from the Soviet Union in 1991.

BACKGROUND: Estonia regained its independence from the Soviet Union in 1991 and is a stable multi-party democracy. It joined NATO and the European Union in 2004 and the Organisation for Economic Co-operation and Development in 2010. In 2011, it became the first former Soviet state to adopt the euro. With a liberal investment climate, foreign investments have risen substantially. In March 2014, Prime Minister Taavi Röivas of the center-right Reform Party replaced Andrus Ansip, also of the Reform Party, who had served for nine years. Estonia is one of the world's most dynamic and modern economies. It profits from strong electronics and telecommunication sectors and has strong trade relations with Russia, Germany, Sweden, and Finland.

Freedom Trend

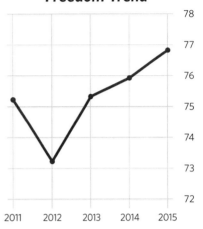

Country Comparisons

Quick Facts

Population: 1.3 million
GDP (PPP): $29.8 billion
0.8% growth in 2013
5-year compound annual growth 0.2%
$23,144 per capita
Unemployment: 8.5%
Inflation (CPI): 3.5%
FDI Inflow: $949.8 million
Public Debt: 11.3% of GDP

2013 data unless otherwise noted.
Data compiled as of September 2014.

How Do We Measure Economic Freedom?
See page 475 for an explanation of the methodology or visit the *Index* Web site at *heritage.org/index*.

THE TEN ECONOMIC FREEDOMS

	Score		Rank	1-Year Change
RULE OF LAW				
Property Rights	90.0		3rd	0
Freedom from Corruption	68.0		28th	+3.8

There are occasional problems with government corruption. In 2013, senior members of the governing Reform Party were implicated in a business corruption scandal involving a now-defunct company owned by the environment minister's father. Estonia's judiciary is effectively insulated from government influence. Property rights and contracts are well enforced and secure. Commercial codes are applied consistently.

	Score		Rank	1-Year Change
GOVERNMENT SIZE				
Fiscal Freedom	80.6		76th	+0.2
Government Spending	53.2		126th	-2.8

The top individual income tax rate is 21 percent, and the corporate tax is 21 percent of the net amount of profit distribution. Other taxes include a value-added tax and excise taxes. Total government revenue equals 32.5 percent of the domestic economy, and government spending equals 39.5 percent of domestic income. Public debt is a relatively low 11 percent of gross domestic product.

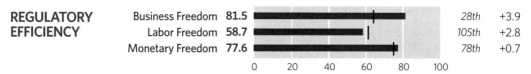

	Score		Rank	1-Year Change
REGULATORY EFFICIENCY				
Business Freedom	81.5		28th	+3.9
Labor Freedom	58.7		105th	+2.8
Monetary Freedom	77.6		78th	+0.7

Recent reforms have facilitated insolvent firms' restructuring, making bankruptcy procedures less costly and improving regulatory efficiency. Enhancing labor productivity has been a key goal, and the recently enacted labor law aims to reduce the costs of dismissing employees. In 2014, the government reduced the "renewable energy fee" on monthly electricity bills to cushion the effect of higher prices from liberalization.

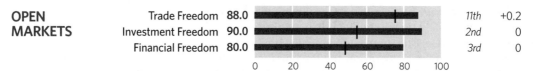

	Score		Rank	1-Year Change
OPEN MARKETS				
Trade Freedom	88.0		11th	+0.2
Investment Freedom	90.0		2nd	0
Financial Freedom	80.0		3rd	0

EU members have a 1.0 percent average tariff rate. Although some non-tariff barriers exist, the EU is relatively open to external trade. Foreign and domestic investors are generally treated equally under Estonian law. The relatively well regulated financial market continues to grow steadily. The banking sector remains competitively open and resilient, offering a wider range of financial products.

Long-Term Score Change (since 1995)

RULE OF LAW		GOVERNMENT SIZE		REGULATORY EFFICIENCY		OPEN MARKETS	
Property Rights	+20.0	Fiscal Freedom	-1.4	Business Freedom	-3.5	Trade Freedom	+11.0
Freedom from Corruption	+18.0	Government Spending	-10.1	Labor Freedom	+11.3	Investment Freedom	0
				Monetary Freedom	+77.6	Financial Freedom	+10.0

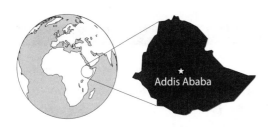

ETHIOPIA

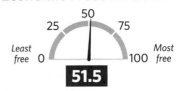

Economic Freedom Score

50
25   75
Least free 0   Most free 100

51.5

Ethiopia's economic freedom score is 51.5, making its economy the 149th freest in the 2015 *Index*. Its overall score is 1.5 points higher than last year, reflecting considerable improvements in monetary freedom, freedom from corruption, and labor freedom. Ethiopia is ranked 37th out of 46 countries in the Sub-Saharan Africa region, and its overall score continues to be below the regional average.

With a large domestic market and promising economic prospects, Ethiopia has the potential to become a regional economic powerhouse, but persistent state intervention in the relatively closed economy has suppressed the growth of economic freedom over the past five years. Since 2011, Ethiopia's economic freedom has expanded by a modest 1.0 point.

Overall, the institutional basis of economic freedom in Ethiopia is still weak. A nominally independent judiciary continues to follow government policy advice, and corruption remains endemic. The government has made significant investments in major development projects, including the Grand Renaissance Dam, but restricts foreign investment in major industries and keeps important sectors of the economy closed to global trade and investment.

BACKGROUND: Prime Minister Hailemariam Desalegn's Ethiopian People's Revolutionary Democratic Front and allied parties hold all but two seats in parliament. Elections are scheduled for 2015. Desalegn served a one-year term as the elected chairman of the African Union. In May 2014, Ethiopia, Kenya, Burundi, and Rwanda agreed to send troops to South Sudan to prevent renewed fighting between government troops and rebel forces. After years of unilateral intervention to secure border buffer zones in Somalia, Ethiopia joined the African Union's peacekeeping mission there in 2014. Border tensions continue between Ethiopia and Eritrea. Ethiopia has had 10 years of steady economic growth, but not enough to reduce poverty. Its per capita income remains among the world's lowest. Ethiopia is a leading coffee producer. Its economy is largely based on agriculture and is vulnerable to droughts and external shocks.

Freedom Trend

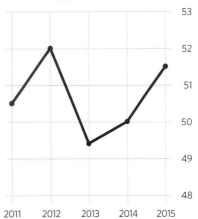

2011 2012 2013 2014 2015

Country Comparisons

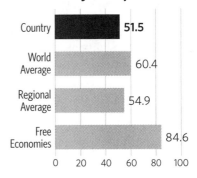

Country	51.5
World Average	60.4
Regional Average	54.9
Free Economies	84.6

0 20 40 60 80 100

Quick Facts

Population: 88.9 million
GDP (PPP): $121.4 billion
9.7% growth in 2013
5-year compound annual growth 10.1%
$1,366 per capita
Unemployment: 5.7%
Inflation (CPI): 8.0%
FDI Inflow: $953.0 million
Public Debt: 22.2% of GDP

2013 data unless otherwise noted.
Data compiled as of September 2014.

How Do We Measure Economic Freedom?
See page 475 for an explanation of the methodology or visit the *Index* Web site at *heritage.org/index.*

THE TEN ECONOMIC FREEDOMS

		Score		Rank	1-Year Change
RULE OF LAW	Property Rights	30.0		94th	0
	Freedom from Corruption	33.0		113th	+6.0

Corruption is a significant problem in Ethiopia. State institutions are dominated by ruling EPRDF officials who reportedly receive preferential access to credit, land leases, and jobs. Under the government's "villagization" program, hundreds of thousands of indigenous people have been forcibly relocated to new villages with inadequate infrastructure so that the state can lease their lands to commercial agricultural foreign investors.

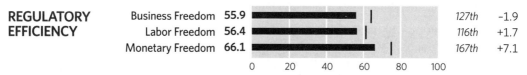

		Score		Rank	1-Year Change
GOVERNMENT SIZE	Fiscal Freedom	77.4		108th	-0.1
	Government Spending	91.4		10th	+1.5

Ethiopia's top individual income tax rate is 35 percent, and its top corporate tax rate remains at 30 percent. Other taxes include a value-added tax and a tax on capital gains. The overall tax burden equals 11.6 percent of the domestic economy, and government spending accounts for 16.9 percent of gross domestic product. Public debt equals 22 percent of annual production.

		Score		Rank	1-Year Change
REGULATORY EFFICIENCY	Business Freedom	55.9		127th	-1.9
	Labor Freedom	56.4		116th	+1.7
	Monetary Freedom	66.1		167th	+7.1

Inconsistent enforcement of regulations often impedes business activity and undermines economic development. The minimum capital requirement for launching a business is higher than the level of average annual income. Much of the labor force is employed in the informal sector. Monetary stability has been weak, and subsidies for the government's state-led development model are hindering private-sector growth.

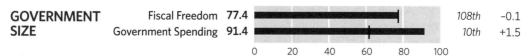

		Score		Rank	1-Year Change
OPEN MARKETS	Trade Freedom	64.4		152nd	+0.2
	Investment Freedom	20.0		164th	0
	Financial Freedom	20.0		163rd	0

Ethiopia has a 10.3 percent average tariff rate. It is not a member of the WTO, and government procurement processes can favor domestic companies. Foreign investment is heavily regulated. There is no constitutional right to own land. The small financial sector continues to evolve and is largely dominated by banks. The capital market remains underdeveloped, and there is no stock exchange.

Long-Term Score Change (since 1995)

RULE OF LAW		GOVERNMENT SIZE		REGULATORY EFFICIENCY		OPEN MARKETS	
Property Rights	0	Fiscal Freedom	+36.4	Business Freedom	+0.9	Trade Freedom	+37.4
Freedom from Corruption	+3.0	Government Spending	+2.9	Labor Freedom	-5.2	Investment Freedom	+10.0
				Monetary Freedom	-5.9	Financial Freedom	-10.0

FIJI

Economic Freedom Score

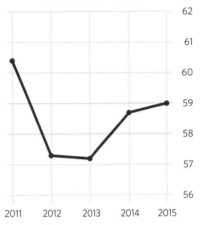

59.0

Least free 0 · 25 · 50 · 75 · 100 Most free

World Rank: 98   **Regional Rank: 20**

Fiji's economic freedom score is 59.0, making its economy the 98th freest in the 2015 *Index*. Its overall score is 0.3 point higher than last year, with improvements in monetary freedom, freedom from corruption, and labor freedom partially offset by a combined decline in business freedom, the control of government spending, and fiscal freedom. Fiji is ranked 20th out of 42 countries in the Asia–Pacific region, and its overall score is about average, both for the world and the region.

Over the past five years, Fiji's economic freedom has declined by 1.4 points, a trend that has pushed the economy into the "mostly unfree" category. Led by score declines in freedom from corruption, financial freedom, and government spending, economic freedom in Fiji has fallen in half of the 10 categories measured.

Reflecting the lack of progress in structural and institutional reforms, Fiji continues to underperform in many policy areas critical to economic freedom. The autocratic and centralized government undercuts the effective development of an independent judiciary. Government spending has been growing, with subsidies and price controls undermining overall monetary stability and fiscal soundness.

BACKGROUND: The Pacific island nation of Fiji is ruled by military strongman Commodore Frank Bainimarama, who has dominated island politics for a decade. There is a long history of ethnic tension between the indigenous, mostly Christian population and a large minority of Hindu and Muslim Indo–Fijians. Sanctions imposed in 2006 by Fiji's main trading partners, including the European Union and Australia, in reaction to the coup that installed Bainimarama hurt the vital agriculture, apparel, and fishing industries. In September 2009, Fiji was suspended from the Commonwealth of Nations. In July 2012, Australia and New Zealand restored diplomatic ties in response to Fiji's preparations for democratic elections in 2014. A reform of the industrial sector has done little to boost growth.

Freedom Trend

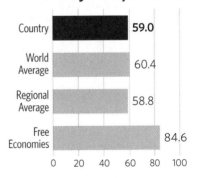

Country Comparisons

Country	59.0
World Average	60.4
Regional Average	58.8
Free Economies	84.6

0   20   40   60   80   100

Quick Facts

Population: 0.9 million
GDP (PPP): $4.5 billion
3.0% growth in 2013
5-year compound annual growth 1.8%
$5,085 per capita
Unemployment: 8.0%
Inflation (CPI): 2.9%
FDI Inflow: $272.1 million
Public Debt: 52.9% of GDP

2013 data unless otherwise noted.
Data compiled as of September 2014.

How Do We Measure Economic Freedom?
See page 475 for an explanation of the methodology or visit the *Index* Web site at *heritage.org/index*.

THE TEN ECONOMIC FREEDOMS

		Score		Rank	1-Year Change
RULE OF LAW	Property Rights	25.0		124th	0
	Freedom from Corruption	22.3		160th	+2.3

Since seizing power in 2006, the military government has suspended the constitution, neutralized political opponents, and crippled democratic institutions. Official corruption is widespread, and government decision-making is not transparent. Eight percent of the land is freehold; the rest (indigenous and government land) can only be leased. Protection of property is highly uncertain, and obtaining land titles is difficult.

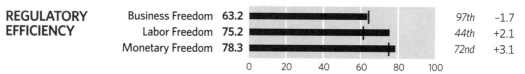

		Score		Rank	1-Year Change
GOVERNMENT SIZE	Fiscal Freedom	81.3		70th	-1.0
	Government Spending	74.6		67th	-1.6

Fiji's top individual income tax rate is 29 percent, and its top corporate tax rate is 20 percent. Other taxes include a value-added tax and a land sales tax. The overall tax burden is 25 percent of domestic income. Government spending equals 29.1 percent of domestic output, and public debt equals 52 percent of gross domestic product.

		Score		Rank	1-Year Change
REGULATORY EFFICIENCY	Business Freedom	63.2		97th	-1.7
	Labor Freedom	75.2		44th	+2.1
	Monetary Freedom	78.3		72nd	+3.1

Incorporating a business has become less time-consuming, but other regulatory requirements increase the overall cost of conducting business. The minimum capital requirement for starting a business has been eliminated. The underdeveloped labor market traps much of the labor force in informal economic activity. The government maintains price controls on various goods and continues to subsidize electricity for residential customers.

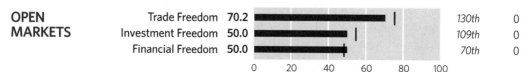

		Score		Rank	1-Year Change
OPEN MARKETS	Trade Freedom	70.2		130th	0
	Investment Freedom	50.0		109th	0
	Financial Freedom	50.0		70th	0

Fiji has a 9.9 percent average tariff rate. There are few formal non-tariff barriers. Most land is owned by the government. The financial sector, dominated by commercial banks, is relatively well developed and stable. The central bank has relaxed several foreign exchange controls in recent years. The capital market remains underdeveloped, with 18 companies listed in the stock exchange as of 2014.

Long-Term Score Change (since 1995)

RULE OF LAW		GOVERNMENT SIZE		REGULATORY EFFICIENCY		OPEN MARKETS	
Property Rights	-25.0	Fiscal Freedom	+24.2	Business Freedom	+8.2	Trade Freedom	+17.6
Freedom from Corruption	-7.7	Government Spending	+2.1	Labor Freedom	-8.4	Investment Freedom	0
				Monetary Freedom	+2.8	Financial Freedom	0

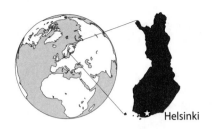

Helsinki

FINLAND

Economic Freedom Score

50

25   75

Least free 0   100 Most free

73.4

Finland's economic freedom score is 73.4, making its economy the 19th freest in the 2015 *Index*. Its score is unchanged from last year, with improvements in labor freedom, fiscal freedom, monetary freedom, and trade freedom counterbalanced by declines in the management of government spending, freedom from corruption, and business freedom. Finland is ranked 9th out of 43 countries in the Europe region, and its overall score is well above the world average.

Finland, a top performer in economic freedom in both Europe and the world, remains a dynamic and flexible economy. However, over the past five years, its strong growth in economic freedom has ended, with declines in business freedom, monetary freedom, and control of government spending offsetting significant improvements in labor freedom. Economic growth has also stagnated.

A European leader in information and communications technology, Finland has developed a strong domestic market with openness, efficiency, and flexibility at its core. The rule of law is buttressed by strong property rights, and the perceived level of corruption is one of the world's lowest. As with other Nordic countries, government spending is high relative to the domestic economy, but the government remains committed to meeting deficit targets.

BACKGROUND: With about one-fourth of its land mass above the Arctic Circle, Finland is sparsely populated. Prime Minister Jyrki Katainen of the center-right National Coalition Party stepped down in 2014. His successor, Alexander Stubb, formed a five-party government coalition in June. Finland joined the European Union in 1995 and adopted the euro as its currency in 1999. It also became a member of NATO's Partnership for Peace in 1994 and sits on the Euro–Atlantic Council. Public debate on pursuing full NATO membership has renewed in response to recent Russian aggression against Ukraine. Although growth remains sluggish, Finland's economy is modern and competitive, with a focus on international trade and vibrant information and communications-technology sectors.

Freedom Trend

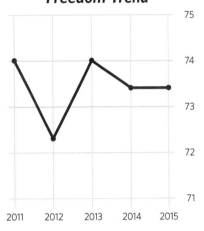

75

74

73

72

71

2011   2012   2013   2014   2015

Country Comparisons

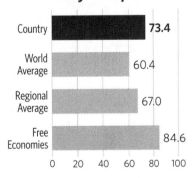

Country   73.4

World Average   60.4

Regional Average   67.0

Free Economies   84.6

0   20   40   60   80   100

Quick Facts

Population: 5.5 million
GDP (PPP): $194.2 billion
–1.4% growth in 2013
5-year compound annual growth –1.0%
$35,617 per capita
Unemployment: 8.1%
Inflation (CPI): 2.2%
FDI Inflow: –$1.1 billion
Public Debt: 57.0% of GDP

2013 data unless otherwise noted.
Data compiled as of September 2014.

THE TEN ECONOMIC FREEDOMS

		Score		Rank	1-Year Change
RULE OF LAW	Property Rights	90.0		3rd	0
	Freedom from Corruption	89.0		3rd	−4.4

Corruption is not a significant problem in Finland, which was ranked second out of 177 countries surveyed in Transparency International's 2013 Corruption Perceptions Index. Secured interests in movable and real property are recognized and enforced. Contractual agreements are strictly honored. The quality of the judiciary is generally high. Finland adheres to many international agreements that aim to protect intellectual property.

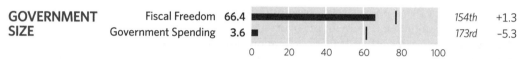

				Rank	1-Year Change
GOVERNMENT SIZE	Fiscal Freedom	66.4		154th	+1.3
	Government Spending	3.6		173rd	−5.3

Finland's top individual income tax rate is 31.8 percent, and its top corporate tax rate has been reduced from 24.5 percent to 20 percent. Other taxes include a 28 percent flat tax on capital income and a value-added tax. The total tax burden equals 44.1 percent of domestic income, and government spending is equivalent to 56.7 percent of domestic output. Public debt equals 57 percent of GDP.

				Rank	1-Year Change
REGULATORY EFFICIENCY	Business Freedom	92.6		7th	−1.0
	Labor Freedom	54.8		120th	+8.3
	Monetary Freedom	79.9		55th	+1.0

The overall regulatory framework is transparent and competitive. Launching a business is subject to minimum capital requirements but takes only three procedures. Bankruptcy procedures are modern and efficient. Labor regulations are relatively rigid, and the non-salary cost of employing a worker is high. Monetary stability has been well maintained, but the government subsidizes numerous biogas, wind, and solar energy projects.

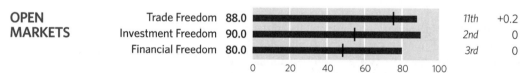

				Rank	1-Year Change
OPEN MARKETS	Trade Freedom	88.0		11th	+0.2
	Investment Freedom	90.0		2nd	0
	Financial Freedom	80.0		3rd	0

EU members have a 1.0 percent average tariff rate. Although some non-tariff barriers exist, the EU is relatively open to external trade. The Finnish government generally treats foreign and domestic investors equally. The financial sector, market-driven and competitive, offers a wide range of financing options. Supervision of banking is prudent, and regulations are largely consistent with international norms. Credit is allocated on market terms.

Long-Term Score Change (since 1996)

RULE OF LAW		GOVERNMENT SIZE		REGULATORY EFFICIENCY		OPEN MARKETS	
Property Rights	0	Fiscal Freedom	+8.0	Business Freedom	+37.6	Trade Freedom	+10.2
Freedom from Corruption	−1.0	Government Spending	+3.6	Labor Freedom	+4.9	Investment Freedom	+20.0
				Monetary Freedom	−2.4	Financial Freedom	+30.0

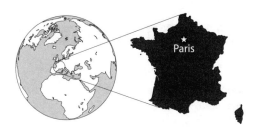

FRANCE

Economic Freedom Score

62.5

France's economic freedom score is 62.5, making its economy the 73rd freest in the 2015 *Index*. Its overall score has decreased by 1.0 point, with particularly large declines in labor freedom and the management of government spending. France is ranked 33rd out of 43 countries in the Europe region, and its overall score is higher than the world average but below the regional average.

Over the past five years, France's economic freedom has waned as the size and reach of government have expanded. A stagnating domestic economic environment has led to persistently high unemployment, particularly among young people, and structural deficiencies have suppressed dynamic private-sector expansion. Since 2011, economic freedom in France has declined by over 2.0 points, falling in five of the 10 economic freedoms including the control of government spending, fiscal freedom, and labor freedom.

However, with such institutional strengths as strong protection of property rights and a relatively efficient legal framework, the French economy is diversified and modern. The entrepreneurial environment is generally facilitated by a sophisticated and relatively resilient financial sector. The government has pursued reform measures to increase the economy's competitiveness and flexibility, but progress has been slow and patchy.

BACKGROUND: François Hollande was elected president in May 2012, and his Socialist Party has majority control of the National Assembly. Hollande's poor handling of the economy has led to low approval ratings. French voters punished the mainstream parties in the 2014 European Parliament elections, which resulted in the far-right National Front taking the most seats. Formally reintegrated into NATO's military command structures, France was a leading participant in NATO's March 2011 military engagement in Libya and recently sent troops to Mali and the Central African Republic to counter advancing Islamic militants. The economy is diversified but also is the top recipient of market-distorting agricultural subsidies under the European Union's Common Agricultural Policy.

Freedom Trend

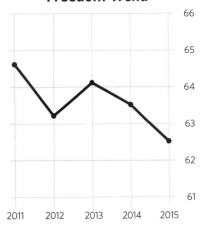

Country Comparisons

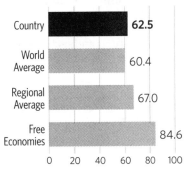

Quick Facts

Population: 63.7 million
GDP (PPP): $2.3 trillion
0.3% growth in 2013
5-year compound annual growth 0.2%
$35,784 per capita
Unemployment: 10.5%
Inflation (CPI): 1.0%
FDI Inflow: $4.9 billion
Public Debt: 93.9% of GDP

2013 data unless otherwise noted.
Data compiled as of September 2014.

How Do We Measure Economic Freedom?
See page 475 for an explanation of the methodology
or visit the *Index* Web site at *heritage.org/index*.

THE TEN ECONOMIC FREEDOMS

		Score	■ Country	│ World Average	Rank	1-Year Change

RULE OF LAW

Property Rights 80.0 — 20th — 0
Freedom from Corruption 71.0 — 22nd — +1.1

France has an independent judiciary, and the rule of law is firmly established. In 2014, however, former President Nicolas Sarkozy was detained for questioning about long-running accusations of corruption. Property rights and contract enforcement are secure, but complex and inefficient regulations help to make property in France among the most expensive in the world, despite weak demand and slowing construction activity.

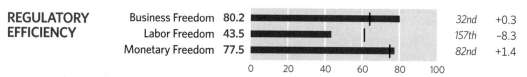

GOVERNMENT SIZE

Fiscal Freedom 47.5 — 176th — –0.9
Government Spending 2.5 — 174th — –3.1

France's top individual income tax rate is 45 percent, and its top corporate tax rate is 34.3 percent. Other taxes include a value-added tax and a tax on inheritance. Overall tax revenue equals about 45.3 percent of domestic income, and government spending equals 57.0 percent of gross domestic product. Public debt is close to 94 percent of annual domestic output.

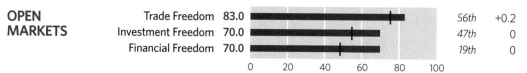

REGULATORY EFFICIENCY

Business Freedom 80.2 — 32nd — +0.3
Labor Freedom 43.5 — 157th — –8.3
Monetary Freedom 77.5 — 82nd — +1.4

With no minimum capital requirement for launching a firm, business start-up is straightforward. Completing licensing requirements takes over three months on average. The rigid labor market lacks the capacity to generate more vibrant employment growth. Price controls affect many products and services, and state subsidies to increase renewable energy capacity threaten the competitiveness of the French power industry.

OPEN MARKETS

Trade Freedom 83.0 — 56th — +0.2
Investment Freedom 70.0 — 47th — 0
Financial Freedom 70.0 — 19th — 0

EU members have a 1.0 percent average tariff rate. France protects its film industry from competition and imposes quotas on the broadcast of foreign television shows and music. The government screens foreign investment in some sectors. The competitive financial sector, dominated by banks, stable, and open to competition, offers a wide range of services. Foreign financial firms have gained considerable market share.

Long-Term Score Change (since 1995)

RULE OF LAW		GOVERNMENT SIZE		REGULATORY EFFICIENCY		OPEN MARKETS	
Property Rights	+10.0	Fiscal Freedom	–13.3	Business Freedom	–4.8	Trade Freedom	+5.2
Freedom from Corruption	–19.0	Government Spending	–13.2	Labor Freedom	–10.8	Investment Freedom	+20.0
				Monetary Freedom	–3.0	Financial Freedom	+20.0

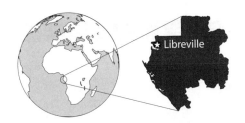

★ Libreville

GABON

Economic Freedom Score

25   **50**   75

Least free   0   100   Most free

58.3

Gabon's economic freedom score is 58.3, making its economy the 104th freest in the 2015 *Index*. Its overall score has increased by 0.5 point, reflecting improvements in freedom from corruption, monetary freedom, and fiscal freedom that outweigh declines in the management of government spending and business freedom. Gabon is ranked 15th out of 46 countries in the Sub-Saharan Africa region, and its overall score is lower than the world average.

Over the past five years, Gabon's economic freedom score has advanced by 1.6 points. Led by relatively broad-based gains in six of the 10 economic freedoms, Gabon has registered a score decline since 2011 only in the management of public spending.

While economic freedom has increased, Gabon has failed to fully use the wealth generated by its vast oil to produce greater prosperity for its people by restructuring and modernizing its economy. In particular, the rule of law remains weak and not fully institutionalized. Natural resource revenues encourage rent-seeking and graft, and the judicial system continues to be arbitrary and used for political ends. An IMF bailout in 2007 has not prevented the deterioration of public finances in recent years. A closed domestic marketplace exacerbates sensitivity to price fluctuations in key industries.

BACKGROUND: President Omar Bongo ruled Gabon from 1967 until his death in 2009 when his son, Ali Ben Bongo, replaced him. Opposition leaders accused the Bongo family of electoral fraud to ensure dynastic succession. In 2011, President Bongo's Gabonese Democratic Party (PDG) took 95 percent of the seats in flawed parliamentary elections. The Bongo family is the subject of a long-running corruption investigation in France. Gabon is the fifth-largest oil producer in sub-Saharan Africa, but oil production has been declining steadily in recent years. The government is working to reduce dependence on oil and to diversify the economy by spending more on education and infrastructure.

Freedom Trend

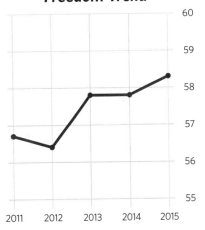

Country Comparisons

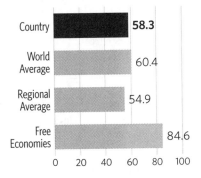

Country	58.3
World Average	60.4
Regional Average	54.9
Free Economies	84.6

0   20   40   60   80   100

Quick Facts

Population: 1.6 million
GDP (PPP): $30.4 billion
5.9% growth in 2013
5-year compound annual growth 4.4%
$19,478 per capita
Unemployment: 19.2%
Inflation (CPI): 0.5%
FDI Inflow: $856.0 million
Public Debt: 22.9% of GDP

2013 data unless otherwise noted.
Data compiled as of September 2014.

THE TEN ECONOMIC FREEDOMS

		Score		Rank	1-Year Change
RULE OF LAW	Property Rights	40.0		70th	0
	Freedom from Corruption	34.0		107th	+4.9

Corruption is rampant, although Gabon ranked as less corrupt than most of its Central African neighbors in 2013. Payoffs are common in the commercial and business arenas, especially in the energy sector. The judiciary is inefficient and not independent. Some prosecutions of former government officials appear to target opposition members. Protections for property rights and contracts are not strongly enforced.

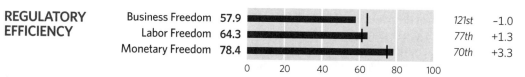

		Score		Rank	1-Year Change
GOVERNMENT SIZE	Fiscal Freedom	77.5		107th	+3.0
	Government Spending	74.6		68th	-7.1

The top individual income tax rate is 35 percent. The top corporate tax rate was cut from 35 percent to 30 percent in 2013 (extractive industries and other companies can qualify for lower rates). Other taxes include a value-added tax. The overall tax burden equals 11.2 percent of economic activity. Government spending amounts to 29.1 percent of domestic output, and public debt equals 23 percent of GDP.

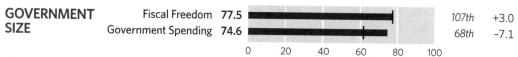

		Score		Rank	1-Year Change
REGULATORY EFFICIENCY	Business Freedom	57.9		121st	-1.0
	Labor Freedom	64.3		77th	+1.3
	Monetary Freedom	78.4		70th	+3.3

Despite recent reform efforts, administrative procedures for incorporating businesses remain time-consuming. On average, it takes about 200 days to complete licensing requirements. Labor regulations are outmoded, and the labor market does not function well. The state influences prices through subsidies to state-owned enterprises and direct control of the prices of other products.

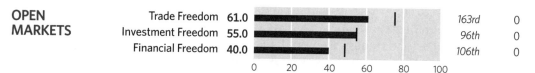

		Score		Rank	1-Year Change
OPEN MARKETS	Trade Freedom	61.0		163rd	0
	Investment Freedom	55.0		96th	0
	Financial Freedom	40.0		106th	0

Gabon's average tariff rate is 14.5 percent. Imports of sugar, eggs, and used cars are restricted. Gabon's Investment Charter guarantees the right of foreign investors to repatriate profits. The financial sector remains state-controlled. Credit costs are high, and access to financing is scarce, with fewer than 10 commercial banks in operation. The government controls long-term lending through the state-owned development bank.

Long-Term Score Change (since 1995)

RULE OF LAW		GOVERNMENT SIZE		REGULATORY EFFICIENCY		OPEN MARKETS	
Property Rights	-10.0	Fiscal Freedom	+28.1	Business Freedom	-12.1	Trade Freedom	+37.4
Freedom from Corruption	-16.0	Government Spending	-1.4	Labor Freedom	+4.1	Investment Freedom	-15.0
				Monetary Freedom	-0.5	Financial Freedom	-10.0

Banjul

THE **GAMBIA**

Economic Freedom Score

25   50   75

Least
free   0 100   Most
                            free

57.5

The Gambia's economic freedom score is 57.5, making its economy the 113th freest in the 2015 *Index*. Its overall score is 2.0 points worse than last year, with especially notable declines in the management of government spending, property rights, freedom from corruption, and fiscal freedom. The Gambia is ranked 19th out of 46 countries in the Sub-Saharan Africa region, and its overall score is below the world average.

With few natural resources and high rates of poverty, The Gambia has been behind many developing countries in implementing policies that advance economic freedom. Over the past five years, improvements to open the economy to greater trade and investment have been offset by declines in six of the 10 economic freedoms including the control of government spending and property rights. The Gambia's overall score decline is the fifth-largest in the 2015 *Index*.

Investments in the institutions vital to growth and prosperity are stagnant. Despite small improvements, high tariffs and relatively closed domestic markets limit investment in promising sectors like agriculture and tourism. Rampant government corruption and patronage are exacerbated by the judiciary's lack of independence. Despite recent reform efforts, inefficiency in business and labor regulations continues to inhibit entrepreneurial growth.

BACKGROUND: Yahya Jammeh, who came to power in a bloodless coup in 1994, won his fourth term in 2011 in flawed elections. Jammeh's Alliance for Patriotic Reorientation and Construction won a major victory in the 2012 legislative elections, which were boycotted by opposition parties. The government restrains civil liberties and harasses political opponents. In 2013, President Jammeh withdrew The Gambia from the Commonwealth. The Gambia has few natural resources. Government revenue depends heavily on peanut exports, leaving the state vulnerable to price fluctuations and market shocks. Due to its unique location along the Gambia River, the country is also a natural hub for tourism and trade.

Freedom Trend

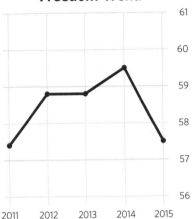

| 2011 | 2012 | 2013 | 2014 | 2015 |

Country Comparisons

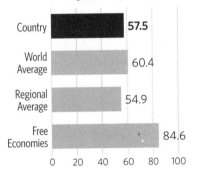

Country	**57.5**
World Average	60.4
Regional Average	54.9
Free Economies	84.6

0   20   40   60   80   100

Quick Facts

Population: 1.9 million
GDP (PPP): $3.7 billion
6.3% growth in 2013
5-year compound annual growth 4.0%
$1,962 per capita
Unemployment: 8.6%
Inflation (CPI): 5.2%
FDI Inflow: $25.3 million
Public Debt: 82.1% of GDP

2013 data unless otherwise noted.
Data compiled as of September 2014.

THE TEN ECONOMIC FREEDOMS

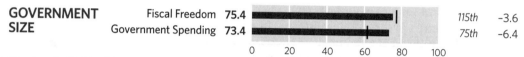

	Score		Rank	1-Year Change
RULE OF LAW	Property Rights 25.0		124th	–5.0
	Freedom from Corruption 28.0		132nd	–3.7

President Jammeh retains an increasingly erratic but firm grip on power with a combination of patronage and repression. Although the judiciary is constitutionally independent, the president fired the chief justice and his own justice minister early in 2014. The judicial system recognizes customary law and Sharia (Islamic) law in family matters. Impunity for members of the security forces remains a serious problem.

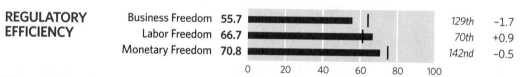

	Score		Rank	1-Year Change
GOVERNMENT SIZE	Fiscal Freedom 75.4		115th	–3.6
	Government Spending 73.4		75th	–6.4

The top individual income tax rate is 35 percent, and the top corporate tax rate is 32 percent. Other taxes include a capital gains tax and a sales tax. The overall tax burden equals 14.4 percent of the domestic economy. Government spending is equivalent to 29.8 percent of total domestic output, and government debt equals about 82 percent of GDP.

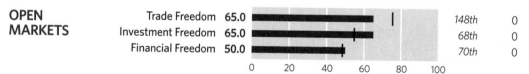

	Score		Rank	1-Year Change
REGULATORY EFFICIENCY	Business Freedom 55.7		129th	–1.7
	Labor Freedom 66.7		70th	+0.9
	Monetary Freedom 70.8		142nd	–0.5

The overall regulatory framework remains hampered by red tape and a lack of transparency. Inconsistent application of commercial regulations remains a considerable impediment to business. The stagnant labor market perpetuates high unemployment and underemployment. The government heavily subsidizes the parastatal water and electricity companies, which are among the least efficient operators on the African continent.

	Score		Rank	1-Year Change
OPEN MARKETS	Trade Freedom 65.0		148th	0
	Investment Freedom 65.0		68th	0
	Financial Freedom 50.0		70th	0

The Gambia's average tariff rate is 12.5 percent. Foreign and domestic investors are generally treated equally under the law. The banking sector has gradually expanded and benefits from increased competition. Almost all of the 13 commercial banks are majority-owned by foreign banks. Credit to the private sector has been increasing, and nonperforming loans are less than 10 percent of total loans. There is no stock exchange.

Long-Term Score Change (since 1997)

RULE OF LAW		GOVERNMENT SIZE		REGULATORY EFFICIENCY		OPEN MARKETS	
Property Rights	–45.0	Fiscal Freedom	+2.9	Business Freedom	+0.7	Trade Freedom	+7.0
Freedom from Corruption	+18.0	Government Spending	–7.4	Labor Freedom	–8.4	Investment Freedom	+35.0
				Monetary Freedom	+0.9	Financial Freedom	+20.0

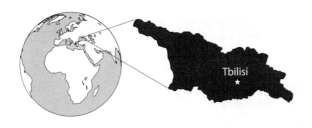

GEORGIA

Economic Freedom Score

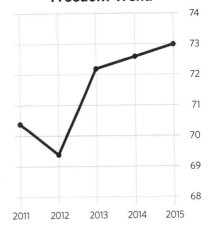

73.0

Least free 0 ... Most free 100

25 50 75

World Rank: 22   **Regional Rank: 11**

Georgia's economic freedom score is 73.0, making its economy the 22nd freest in the 2015 *Index*. Its overall score has increased by 0.4 point since last year, primarily reflecting improvements in freedom from corruption, monetary freedom, and the management of government spending that outweigh a notable decline in labor freedom. Georgia is ranked 11th out of 43 countries in the Europe region, and its score is well above the regional average.

With a 2.6-point score increase over the past five years, Georgia has registered improvements in five of the economic freedoms, including freedom from corruption, the control of government spending, business freedom, monetary freedom, and investment freedom. Achieving its highest score ever in the 2015 *Index*, Georgia has advanced further into the category of "mostly free."

A decade of solid increases in economic freedom has contributed to the dynamic expansion of Georgia's economy. Sound public finances and policies that support open markets have boosted prosperity and reinforced Georgia's commitment to economic freedom. However, not all of the pillars of economic freedom are fully entrenched. Rule of law remains weak, and the perceived level of corruption, though improving, is higher than average for a European country.

BACKGROUND: A leading economic reformer among the former Soviet satellites, Georgia has been particularly effective in reducing regulations, taxes, and corruption. Russia invaded Georgia in 2008 and continues to occupy the territories of South Ossetia and Abkhazia. In 2012, billionaire Bidzina Ivanishvili and his Georgian Dream coalition defeated President Mikheil Saakashvili's United National Movement. After serving briefly as prime minister, Ivanishvili voluntarily resigned in November 2013 and named Irakli Garibashvili as his successor. The Georgian Dream coalition's political dominance was reinforced with a victory in the 2013 presidential elections. Although economic growth remains solid, foreign direct investment has decreased. Georgia has been committed to Euro-Atlantic integration. It hopes to join NATO and in June 2014 signed Association Agreements with the EU.

Freedom Trend

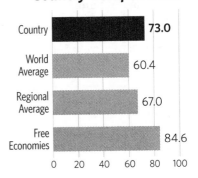

Country Comparisons

Country — 73.0
World Average — 60.4
Regional Average — 67.0
Free Economies — 84.6

0 20 40 60 80 100

Quick Facts

Population: 4.5 million
GDP (PPP): $27.6 billion
3.2% growth in 2013
5-year compound annual growth 3.7%
$6,145 per capita
Unemployment: 14.3%
Inflation (CPI): –0.5%
FDI Inflow: $1.0 billion
Public Debt: 31.8% of GDP

2013 data unless otherwise noted.
Data compiled as of September 2014.

How Do We Measure Economic Freedom?
See page 475 for an explanation of the methodology
or visit the *Index* Web site at *heritage.org/index*.

THE TEN ECONOMIC FREEDOMS

		Score		Rank	1-Year Change
RULE OF LAW	Property Rights	40.0		70th	0
	Freedom from Corruption	49.0		55th	+6.2

In 2014, a former prime minister and senior figure in the main opposition party was found guilty of corruption and misuse of public funds. Several members of the current government were also removed from office for alleged graft. Georgia continues to struggle with the lingering effects of Soviet-era corruption. There are ongoing efforts to improve the security of property rights.

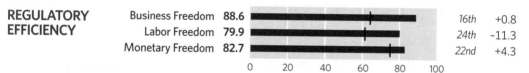

GOVERNMENT SIZE	Fiscal Freedom	87.2		34th	−0.1
	Government Spending	73.8		74th	+4.1

Georgia's top individual income tax rate is 20 percent, and its top corporate tax rate is 15 percent. Other taxes include a value-added tax and a tax on dividends. The overall tax burden equals 25.5 percent of domestic output. Government spending amounts to 29.6 percent of the domestic economy, and public debt is equivalent to 32 percent of gross domestic product.

REGULATORY EFFICIENCY	Business Freedom	88.6		16th	+0.8
	Labor Freedom	79.9		24th	−11.3
	Monetary Freedom	82.7		22nd	+4.3

The competitive and efficient regulatory framework facilitates entrepreneurial activity. With no minimum capital required, it takes two days and two procedures to start a business. Completing licensing requirements can be difficult, taking about two months on average. The labor market is relatively flexible and still evolving. Prices are generally set in the market, but the state maintains price-control measures and subsidizes fuel.

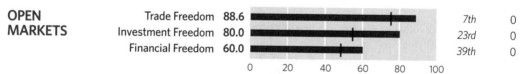

OPEN MARKETS	Trade Freedom	88.6		7th	0
	Investment Freedom	80.0		23rd	0
	Financial Freedom	60.0		39th	0

Georgia's average tariff rate is 0.7 percent. After gaining independence, it pursued a policy of unilateral tariff cuts and free trade. Foreign and domestic investors are generally treated equally under the law. The financial sector, dominated by banks, remains stable. With the state's role limited primarily to regulatory enforcement, banking has become more competitive. The capital market remains underdeveloped with a small stock exchange.

Long-Term Score Change (since 1996)

RULE OF LAW		GOVERNMENT SIZE		REGULATORY EFFICIENCY		OPEN MARKETS	
Property Rights	+10.0	Fiscal Freedom	−4.8	Business Freedom	+33.6	Trade Freedom	+19.6
Freedom from Corruption	+39.0	Government Spending	+12.5	Labor Freedom	+13.1	Investment Freedom	+30.0
				Monetary Freedom	+82.7	Financial Freedom	+30.0

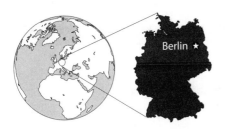

Berlin ★

GERMANY

Economic Freedom Score

50
25   75

Least
free 0   100   Most
free

73.8

Germany's economic freedom score is 73.8, making its economy the 16th freest in the 2015 *Index*. Its overall score is up by 0.4 point from last year, with improvements in the management of public spending and labor freedom outweighing declines in freedom from corruption and business freedom. Germany is ranked 7th out of 43 countries in the Europe region, and its score exceeds the world and regional averages.

Germany has achieved its highest score ever in the 2015 *Index*. Since 2011, a 2.0-point increase in economic freedom has been led by marked improvements in labor freedom and in policy areas related to market openness. Overall, economic freedom has increased in five of the 10 measured categories.

Germany's judicial system, independent and free of corruption, enforces contracts reliably. Openness to global trade and investment has enabled Germany to become one of the world's most competitive and flexible economies. The government has held firm to policies emphasizing sound public finance, keeping spending under control through deficit-cutting measures. In response to changing economic conditions, employers and workers have worked to adjust wages and work hours.

BACKGROUND: Chancellor Angela Merkel's Christian Democratic Union won the biggest share of the national vote in the September 2013 election, but its coalition partner, the economically liberal Free Democratic Party, is no longer in the Bundestag. In December 2013, Merkel's party reached an agreement with the Social Democratic Party to form a coalition government. Economic reforms remain stalled, with most policy attention focused on rescuing the euro. Germany has funded the lion's share of large rescue packages for fellow eurozone members. Its industrialized economy, the largest in Europe, is well integrated into the global marketplace and generates average per capita incomes that are among the world's highest. Germany has one of Europe's lowest unemployment rates, and shortages of skilled labor may be developing. Germany remains, both politically and economically, the most influential nation in the EU.

Freedom Trend

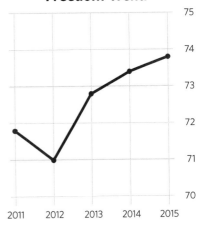

75

74

73

72

71

70

2011   2012   2013   2014   2015

Country Comparisons

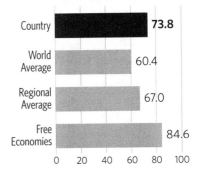

Country	**73.8**
World Average	60.4
Regional Average	67.0
Free Economies	84.6

0   20   40   60   80   100

Quick Facts

Population: 80.8 million
GDP (PPP): $3.2 trillion
0.5% growth in 2013
5-year compound annual growth 0.7%
$40,007 per capita
Unemployment: 5.3%
Inflation (CPI): 1.6%
FDI Inflow: $26.7 billion
Public Debt: 78.1% of GDP

2013 data unless otherwise noted.
Data compiled as of September 2014.

How Do We Measure Economic Freedom?
See page 475 for an explanation of the methodology
or visit the *Index* Web site at *heritage.org/index*.

THE TEN ECONOMIC FREEDOMS

RULE OF LAW

	Score		Rank	1-Year Change
Property Rights	90.0		3rd	0
Freedom from Corruption	78.0		12th	-2.1

Although government transparency is high and anti-corruption measures are enforced effectively, the auto industry, construction, and public contracting, in conjunction with questionable political party influence and party donations, are areas of continuing concern. Property owned by foreigners is fully protected under German law, and secured interests in both chattel and real property are recognized and enforced.

GOVERNMENT SIZE

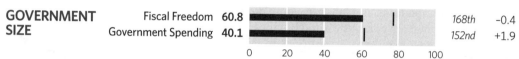

	Score		Rank	1-Year Change
Fiscal Freedom	60.8		168th	-0.4
Government Spending	40.1		152nd	+1.9

Germany's top individual income tax rate is 47.5 percent, and its top corporate tax rate is 15.8 percent. Other taxes include a value-added tax and a capital gains tax. The overall tax burden equals 37.6 percent of domestic output. Government expenditures are equivalent to 44.7 percent of gross domestic product, and public debt is equal to 75 percent of domestic output.

REGULATORY EFFICIENCY

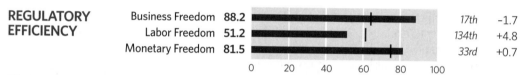

	Score		Rank	1-Year Change
Business Freedom	88.2		17th	-1.7
Labor Freedom	51.2		134th	+4.8
Monetary Freedom	81.5		33rd	+0.7

The regulatory regime supports innovative business formation and operation. Starting a business takes nine procedures and costs about 9 percent of the level of average annual income. Labor regulations are rigid, with broad wage settlements and high unionization. Monetary stability is well maintained, although the government uses a surcharge on monthly electricity bills to subsidize the cost of renewable power generation.

OPEN MARKETS

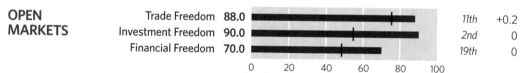

	Score		Rank	1-Year Change
Trade Freedom	88.0		11th	+0.2
Investment Freedom	90.0		2nd	0
Financial Freedom	70.0		19th	0

EU members have a 1.0 percent average tariff rate. Although some non-tariff barriers exist, the EU is relatively open to external trade. Germany generally applies the same rules to foreign and domestic investment. The competitive financial sector remains dynamic and well developed, offering a full range of financing options. Despite consolidation, the traditional three-tiered system of private, public, and cooperative banks is intact.

Long-Term Score Change (since 1995)

RULE OF LAW		GOVERNMENT SIZE		REGULATORY EFFICIENCY		OPEN MARKETS	
Property Rights	0	Fiscal Freedom	+27.6	Business Freedom	+3.2	Trade Freedom	+10.2
Freedom from Corruption	-12.0	Government Spending	+9.5	Labor Freedom	+2.5	Investment Freedom	+20.0
				Monetary Freedom	-0.1	Financial Freedom	0

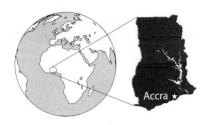

GHANA

Economic Freedom Score

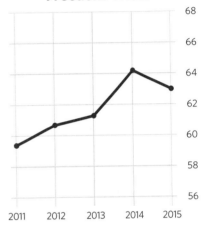

25 50 75

Least free 0   100 Most free

63.0

Ghana's economic freedom score is 63.0, making its economy the 71st freest in the 2015 *Index*. Its overall score is 1.2 points lower than last year, with improvements in freedom from corruption and monetary freedom outweighed by declines in the management of government spending, investment freedom, and labor freedom. Ghana is ranked 5th out of 46 countries in the Sub-Saharan Africa region, and its overall score remains above the world average.

Over the past five years, economic freedom in Ghana has increased by 3.6 points. Along with an improvement of more than 20 points in its score for control of government spending, the country's scores have advanced in half of the 10 economic freedoms including freedom from corruption and monetary freedom. These improvements have propelled Ghana into the ranks of the "moderately free."

These steady advances, however, have masked deeper structural and institutional problems. Ghana remains well short of solidifying the foundations of macroeconomic fundamentals necessary for sustained growth and prosperity. Fiscal improvements have been overshadowed by the malinvestment of future oil revenues, forcing the government to seek IMF assistance in 2014. The judiciary is poorly funded and subject to bribery. Land titles are hard to obtain, and the process is lengthy, compromising the ability of individuals and firms to invest in their property.

BACKGROUND: Ghana has been a stable democracy since 1992. Following the death of President John Atta Mills in July 2012, Vice President John Dramani Mahama became interim head of state. Mahama was elected president in December 2012. Ghana is rich in natural resources, including gold, diamonds, manganese ore, and bauxite, as well as oil. It is Africa's second-biggest gold producer after South Africa. In 2013, Ghana deported thousands of Chinese nationals for illegally mining gold. Economic challenges include managing new oil revenue while maintaining fiscal discipline.

Freedom Trend

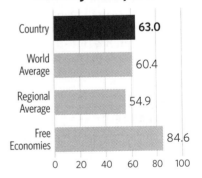

68
66
64
62
60
58
56

2011 2012 2013 2014 2015

Country Comparisons

Country	63.0
World Average	60.4
Regional Average	54.9
Free Economies	84.6

0 20 40 60 80 100

Quick Facts

Population: 25.6 million
GDP (PPP): $88.5 billion
5.5% growth in 2013
5-year compound annual growth 8.0%
$3,461 per capita
Unemployment: 4.5%
Inflation (CPI): 11.7%
FDI Inflow: $3.2 billion
Public Debt: 60.1% of GDP

2013 data unless otherwise noted.
Data compiled as of September 2014.

How Do We Measure Economic Freedom?
See page 475 for an explanation of the methodology
or visit the *Index* Web site at *heritage.org/index*.

THE TEN ECONOMIC FREEDOMS

		Score	Rank	1-Year Change
RULE OF LAW	Property Rights	50.0	56th	0
	Freedom from Corruption	46.0	63rd	+5.6

Successive governments have deployed robust legal and institutional frameworks to combat corruption in Ghana, which is comparatively less corrupt than neighboring countries, but few Ghanaians feel that the situation has improved. Scarce resources compromise and delay the judicial process, and poorly paid judges can be tempted by bribes. The process for obtaining clear title to land is often difficult, complicated, and lengthy.

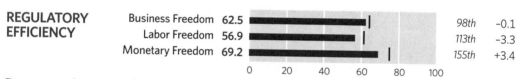

		Score	Rank	1-Year Change
GOVERNMENT SIZE	Fiscal Freedom	84.6	51st	-0.8
	Government Spending	70.8	81st	-12.5

Ghana's top individual and corporate income tax rates are 25 percent. Other taxes include a national insurance levy, a value-added tax, and a capital gains tax. The total tax burden equaled 17.1 percent of GDP in the most recent year. Public expenditures equal 31.2 percent of gross domestic product, and public debt equals 60 percent of domestic output.

		Score	Rank	1-Year Change
REGULATORY EFFICIENCY	Business Freedom	62.5	98th	-0.1
	Labor Freedom	56.9	113th	-3.3
	Monetary Freedom	69.2	155th	+3.4

Recent regulatory reform measures have yielded reductions in bureaucracy, but progress in enhancing overall regulatory efficiency has lagged compared to other economies. Labor regulations have been under modernization, but informal labor activity remains significant. The government has reinstated a fuel-price adjustment mechanism to eliminate subsidies and has sharply increased electricity and water tariffs to reduce the fiscal deficit.

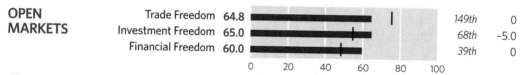

		Score	Rank	1-Year Change
OPEN MARKETS	Trade Freedom	64.8	149th	0
	Investment Freedom	65.0	68th	-5.0
	Financial Freedom	60.0	39th	0

Ghana has an 8.6 percent average tariff rate. Government procurement procedures can favor domestic firms. Freely repatriating profits, foreign investors are typically treated equally with domestic investors under the law. The financial sector has undergone restructuring, and there are over 20 commercial banks. However, high interest rates on bank loans limit financing opportunities for new firms.

Long-Term Score Change (since 1995)

RULE OF LAW		GOVERNMENT SIZE		REGULATORY EFFICIENCY		OPEN MARKETS	
Property Rights	0	Fiscal Freedom	+18.3	Business Freedom	+7.5	Trade Freedom	+33.6
Freedom from Corruption	-24.0	Government Spending	-11.0	Labor Freedom	+6.7	Investment Freedom	+35.0
				Monetary Freedom	+3.0	Financial Freedom	+10.0

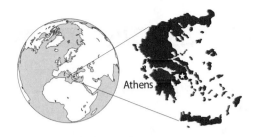

GREECE

Economic Freedom Score

Least free 0   100 Most free

54.0

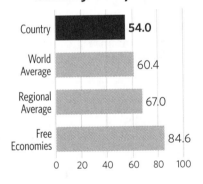

World Rank: **130**   Regional Rank: **40**

Greece's economic freedom score is 54.0, making its economy the 130th freest in the 2015 *Index*. Its score has declined by 1.7 points since last year due to a substantial deterioration in the control of government spending and smaller declines in business freedom, labor freedom, and fiscal freedom. Greece is ranked 40th out of 43 countries in the Europe region, and its overall score is below the world and regional averages.

Since 2011, Greece's economic freedom has declined by 6.3 points, with scores falling in seven of the 10 measured categories. Once ranked in the "moderately free" category, Greece is now considered "mostly unfree." With the 10th largest score decline in the 2015 *Index*, Greece has recorded its lowest economic freedom score ever this year.

Large continued declines in the management of government spending bode ill for a government still reeling from a sovereign debt crisis and multiple international bailouts. The rule of law remains problematic, with property rights weakly enforced, tax evasion on the rise, and corruption pervasive. Despite efforts to create a more business-friendly regulatory environment, the labor market remains rigid and slow to adjust to market realities.

BACKGROUND: Greece joined NATO in 1952 and the European Union in 1981. It adopted the euro in 2002. In response to a Greek sovereign debt crisis in 2010, the European Central Bank and the International Monetary Fund provided emergency loans in exchange for austerity measures. Elections in June 2012 led to formation of a "pro-Euro" coalition led by Antonis Samaras and his center-right New Democracy party. In June 2013, the Democratic Left Party left the coalition, forcing a reshuffle that gave the center-left Pan-Hellenic Socialist Movement an expanded role in the government. Greece's economy, which depends heavily on shipping, tourism, and services, has been in recession for six years. International creditors expected it to expand slightly in 2014. Greek unemployment is among the highest in the eurozone.

Freedom Trend

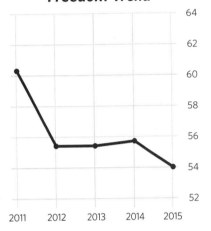

Country Comparisons

Country	54.0
World Average	60.4
Regional Average	67.0
Free Economies	84.6

0   20   40   60   80   100

Quick Facts

Population: 11.1 million
GDP (PPP): $265.6 billion
–3.9% growth in 2013
5-year compound annual growth –5.2%
$24,012 per capita
Unemployment: 27.6%
Inflation (CPI): –0.9%
FDI Inflow: $2.6 billion
Public Debt: 173.8% of GDP

2013 data unless otherwise noted.
Data compiled as of September 2014.

THE TEN ECONOMIC FREEDOMS

		Score		Rank	1-Year Change
RULE OF LAW	Property Rights	40.0		70th	0
	Freedom from Corruption	40.0		80th	+6.8

Successive governments have made election promises to root out deeply entrenched corruption in Greece, but progress has been very slow. Ninety percent of households surveyed in 2013 consider Greece's political parties to be corrupt or extremely corrupt. Nevertheless, the judiciary is independent, and the constitution provides for public trials. Protection of property rights is not strongly enforced.

		Score		Rank	1-Year Change
GOVERNMENT SIZE	Fiscal Freedom	64.2		159th	-1.7
	Government Spending	0.0		176th	-19.2

Greece's top individual income tax rate is 42 percent, and its top corporate tax rate is 26 percent. Other taxes include a value-added tax and a real estate tax. Overall tax revenue amounts to 33.8 percent of gross domestic product, and public expenditures equal 58.5 percent of domestic output. Public debt is equivalent to over 170 percent of gross domestic product.

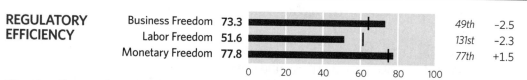

		Score		Rank	1-Year Change
REGULATORY EFFICIENCY	Business Freedom	73.3		49th	-2.5
	Labor Freedom	51.6		131st	-2.3
	Monetary Freedom	77.8		77th	+1.5

The overall pace of regulatory reform lags behind other countries. With no minimum capital required, launching a business takes five procedures and 13 days. However, completing licensing requirements still takes about four months on average. Despite reform efforts, the labor market remains rigid and stagnant. Monetary stability is weak, and Greece is receiving substantial subsidies from the European Union.

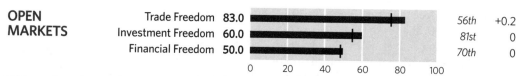

		Score		Rank	1-Year Change
OPEN MARKETS	Trade Freedom	83.0		56th	+0.2
	Investment Freedom	60.0		81st	0
	Financial Freedom	50.0		70th	0

EU members have a 1.0 percent average tariff rate. Although some non-tariff barriers exist, the EU is relatively open to external trade. Greece maintains additional barriers to the provision of some professional services. Foreign investment in some sectors is capped. The financial system remains under strain. In the banking sector, nonperforming loans account for over 30 percent of total loans.

Long-Term Score Change (since 1995)

RULE OF LAW		GOVERNMENT SIZE		REGULATORY EFFICIENCY		OPEN MARKETS	
Property Rights	-30.0	Fiscal Freedom	+1.7	Business Freedom	+3.3	Trade Freedom	+5.2
Freedom from Corruption	-10.0	Government Spending	-55.3	Labor Freedom	-4.5	Investment Freedom	-10.0
				Monetary Freedom	+12.5	Financial Freedom	+20.0

GUATEMALA

Economic Freedom Score

60.4

World Rank: **87**   Regional Rank: **17**

Guatemala's economic freedom score is 60.4, making its economy the 87th freest in the 2015 *Index*. Its score is down by 0.8 point, reflecting declines in property rights, business freedom, and trade freedom that are partially offset by improvements in labor freedom, the management of government spending, and freedom from corruption. Guatemala is ranked 17th out of 29 countries in the South and Central America/Caribbean region, and its overall score is equal to the world average.

Over the past five years, Guatemala's economic freedom has declined by 1.5 points. Longer-term declines have been concentrated largely in four of the 10 economic freedoms: property rights, freedom from corruption, government spending, and labor freedom. Property rights scores have dropped sharply.

The rule of law is weakly established, and crime, violence, and corruption are endemic. Poverty is high, and inefficient business regulations continue to inhibit entrepreneurship and employment. Despite a relatively high degree of trade freedom and low tariff rates, the dynamic economic gains from trade are undercut by the absence of progress in reforming other policies that are critical to sustaining open markets in the financial and investment areas.

BACKGROUND: Center-right President Otto Pérez Molina succeeded social democrat Alvaro Colom in 2012. Guatemala withdrew from the Venezuela-led Petrocaribe oil alliance in 2013 after failing to negotiate favorable rates. As the administrative hub for the Central American Integration System, Guatemala is tasked with improving regional economic cooperation. Agriculture accounts for 11 percent of GDP. The economy was seriously damaged during the global recession but has rebounded since 2012. More than half of the population lives below the poverty line. Guatemala works closely with the U.S. on security issues, but Mexican drug cartels continue to expand their influence in the country. Former President Alfonso Portillo was extradited to the U.S. in 2013 and pleaded guilty to charges of money laundering in 2014.

Freedom Trend

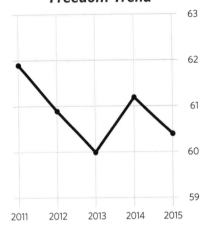

Country Comparisons

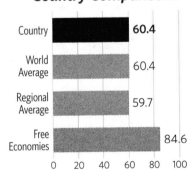

Quick Facts

Population: 15.5 million
GDP (PPP): $81.8 billion
3.5% growth in 2013
5-year compound annual growth 2.8%
$5,282 per capita
Unemployment: 2.8%
Inflation (CPI): 4.3%
FDI Inflow: $1.3 billion
Public Debt: 24.4% of GDP

2013 data unless otherwise noted.
Data compiled as of September 2014.

How Do We Measure Economic Freedom?
See page 475 for an explanation of the methodology
or visit the *Index* Web site at *heritage.org/index*.

THE TEN ECONOMIC FREEDOMS

		Score	Country	World Average	Rank	1-Year Change
RULE OF LAW	Property Rights	20.0			138th	−5.0
	Freedom from Corruption	29.0			127th	+0.3

In 2014, former President Alfonso Portillo pleaded guilty to taking $2.5 million in Taiwanese government bribes and attempting to launder the money through U.S. banks. A government study reports that corruption in customs offices costs $1.5 billion annually. Organized crime has infiltrated key state institutions. The judiciary is characterized by corruption, inefficiency, capacity shortages, and intimidation of judges, prosecutors, and witnesses.

		Score			Rank	1-Year Change
GOVERNMENT SIZE	Fiscal Freedom	79.6			88th	0
	Government Spending	94.1			3rd	+0.5

Guatemala's top individual and corporate income tax rates are 31 percent. Other taxes include a value-added tax and a tax on real estate. The overall tax burden is 10.9 percent of the domestic economy. Government expenditures are equivalent to 14.1 percent of domestic output, and public debt is equal to about 24 percent of gross domestic output.

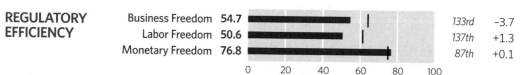

		Score			Rank	1-Year Change
REGULATORY EFFICIENCY	Business Freedom	54.7			133rd	−3.7
	Labor Freedom	50.6			137th	+1.3
	Monetary Freedom	76.8			87th	+0.1

Progress in improving the regulatory framework has been uneven. Bureaucratic hurdles, including lengthy processes for obtaining necessary permits, remain common. Completing licensing requirements takes over five months on average. Labor regulations are rigid, and a large portion of the workforce is employed in the informal sector. The state maintains few price controls but subsidizes numerous key economic activities and products.

		Score			Rank	1-Year Change
OPEN MARKETS	Trade Freedom	84.6			53rd	−0.8
	Investment Freedom	65.0			68th	0
	Financial Freedom	50.0			70th	0

Guatemala's average tariff rate is 2.7 percent. Foreign investors can repatriate profits. There are some limits on foreign ownership of land. The financial system is dominated by bank-centered financial conglomerates. The banking sector remains stable and open to competition, but fewer than 20 banks are now in operation. Foreign insurance companies may open branches under a recently enacted insurance law.

Long-Term Score Change (since 1995)

RULE OF LAW		GOVERNMENT SIZE		REGULATORY EFFICIENCY		OPEN MARKETS	
Property Rights	−30.0	Fiscal Freedom	−7.2	Business Freedom	−0.3	Trade Freedom	+32.2
Freedom from Corruption	−21.0	Government Spending	−2.5	Labor Freedom	−10.0	Investment Freedom	+15.0
				Monetary Freedom	+9.9	Financial Freedom	0

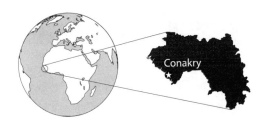

Conakry

GUINEA

Economic Freedom Score

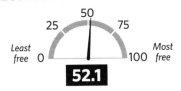

25 50 75

Least free 0   100 Most free

52.1

World Rank: 144   **Regional Rank: 33**

Guinea's economic freedom score is 52.1, making its economy the 144th freest in the 2015 *Index*. Its overall score has decreased by 1.4 points, reflecting declines in half of the 10 economic freedoms, including investment freedom, property rights, the management of public spending, and fiscal freedom. Guinea is ranked 33rd out of 46 countries in the Sub-Saharan Africa region, and its overall score is below the world and regional averages.

Wracked by political instability and violence after a military coup in 2008, Guinea has yet to return to the levels of economic freedom witnessed in the mid-2000s. With significant bauxite reserves, a main source of aluminum, Guinea's relatively closed economy relies on export earnings to fund the importation of food. The financial sector is underdeveloped and poorly integrated, and many Guineans do not hold formal bank accounts. The government's myriad rules and regulations deter investors.

Entrepreneurial activity faces many hurdles. The business licensing process is lengthy and expensive, and the formal labor market remains underdeveloped and resistant to economic changes. The public sector dominates formal employment. Ineffective rule of law and rampant corruption undermine private-sector economic activity that could lift many Guineans out of poverty.

BACKGROUND: In 2010, Alpha Conde won Guinea's first presidential election since independence from France in 1958. The election was marred by irregularities and political violence. In 2013, Conde's Rally of the Guinean People party won a majority of seats in flawed parliamentary elections. According to the U.N., roughly 10,000 refugees from Côte d'Ivoire, Liberia, and Sierra Leone resided in Guinea in 2014. This has strained government services, generated ethnic tensions, and soured relations with bordering nations. Guinea has two-thirds of the world's bauxite reserves and large deposits of iron ore, gold, and diamonds, but the population remains impoverished due to the lack of property rights, rampant corruption, poor government administration, limited infrastructure, and political instability.

Freedom Trend

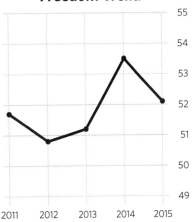

55
54
53
52
51
50
49

2011 2012 2013 2014 2015

Country Comparisons

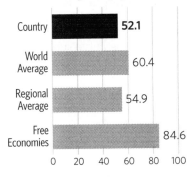

Country	52.1
World Average	60.4
Regional Average	54.9
Free Economies	84.6

0 20 40 60 80 100

Quick Facts

Population: 11.1 million
GDP (PPP): $12.5 billion
2.5% growth in 2013
5-year compound annual growth 2.4%
$1,125 per capita
Unemployment: 3.1%
Inflation (CPI): 12.0%
FDI Inflow: $24.8 million
Public Debt: 37.8% of GDP

2013 data unless otherwise noted.
Data compiled as of September 2014.

How Do We Measure Economic Freedom?
See page 475 for an explanation of the methodology
or visit the *Index* Web site at *heritage.org/index*.

THE TEN ECONOMIC FREEDOMS

		Score	■ Country	| World Average	Rank	1-Year Change

RULE OF LAW

	Score		Rank	1-Year Change
Property Rights	15.0		157th	−5.0
Freedom from Corruption	24.0		156th	+4.8

0 20 40 60 80 100

Despite rich natural resources, most Guineans live in poverty, partly because of rampant corruption. A 2014 FBI investigation found that a British front company (BGSR) bribed government officials to win a mining concession for $165 million; BGSR later sold 51 percent of the mine to Brazilian firm Vale for $2.5 billion. The courts are subject to political interference, and protection of property rights is weak.

GOVERNMENT SIZE

	Score		Rank	1-Year Change
Fiscal Freedom	68.1		148th	−1.2
Government Spending	79.5		47th	−6.7

0 20 40 60 80 100

The top individual income tax rate is 40 percent, and the top corporate tax rate is 35 percent. Other taxes include a value-added tax and an inheritance tax. Overall tax revenue equals 19 percent of gross domestic product, and government spending is equivalent to 26.1 percent of the domestic economy. Public debt equals 38 percent of GDP after debt forgiveness by the IMF in 2012.

REGULATORY EFFICIENCY

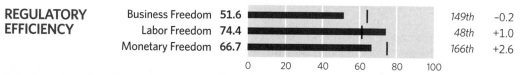

	Score		Rank	1-Year Change
Business Freedom	51.6		149th	−0.2
Labor Freedom	74.4		48th	+1.0
Monetary Freedom	66.7		166th	+2.6

0 20 40 60 80 100

Private enterprises face numerous hurdles. The minimum capital requirement for launching a company exceeds four times the level of average annual income, and completing licensing requirements takes more than three months. The formal labor market is underdeveloped. Despite substantial subsidies provided to the state electrical utility, there are widespread and frequent power shortages. The government cut fuel subsidies in 2014.

OPEN MARKETS

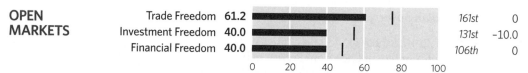

	Score		Rank	1-Year Change
Trade Freedom	61.2		161st	0
Investment Freedom	40.0		131st	−10.0
Financial Freedom	40.0		106th	0

0 20 40 60 80 100

Guinea's average tariff rate is 11.9 percent. Non-tariff barriers including restrictions on imports like rice, flour, and sugar further impede trade. The government has expressed a desire to attract foreign investment, but the uncertain political climate is a deterrent. The financial sector remains underdeveloped. Most economic activity remains outside of the formal banking sector as there are fewer than 10 commercial banks.

Long-Term Score Change (since 1995)

RULE OF LAW		GOVERNMENT SIZE		REGULATORY EFFICIENCY		OPEN MARKETS	
Property Rights	−35.0	Fiscal Freedom	−3.2	Business Freedom	−18.4	Trade Freedom	+10.2
Freedom from Corruption	+14.0	Government Spending	−6.9	Labor Freedom	+3.9	Investment Freedom	−10.0
				Monetary Freedom	−9.2	Financial Freedom	−30.0

GUINEA-BISSAU

Economic Freedom Score

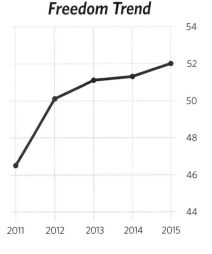

25   50   75

Least free 0   100   Most free

52.0

World Rank: **145**　　　　Regional Rank: **34**

Guinea–Bissau's economic freedom score is 52.0, making its economy the 145th freest in the 2015 *Index*. Its score has increased by 0.7 point, reflecting improvements in trade freedom, monetary freedom, and the control of government spending that outweigh declines in freedom from corruption and business freedom. Guinea-Bissau is ranked 34th out of 46 countries in the Sub-Saharan Africa region, and its overall score remains well below the world and regional averages.

Despite continued instability resulting from the 2012 military coup, Guinea–Bissau has made steady progress in improving economic freedom for its citizens over the past half-decade. Since 2011, the economy has advanced in the *Index* by 5.5 points, the third-biggest gain in the Sub-Saharan Africa region. Led by double-digit score improvements in both the control of government spending and business freedom, Guinea–Bissau has risen out of the "repressed" category.

Improvements so far have put in place a foundation of basic economic market structures, but much more must be done to solidify an institutional environment that will foster sustained growth. The economy remains closed to outside investment and trade, and the financial sector operates largely informally. Rigid business regulations condemn much of the population to informal work arrangements, stifling dynamism and perpetuating subsistence agriculture as the dominant economic activity.

BACKGROUND: Guinea–Bissau had a civil war in the late 1990s, and there have been multiple military coups, most recently in April 2012. In May 2014, Jose Mario Vaz was elected president of the former Portuguese colony. Guinea–Bissau is one of the world's poorest countries. It also is a major transit point for illegal South American drugs bound for Europe, and several senior military officials are allegedly involved in the drug trade. Guinea–Bissau remains highly dependent on subsistence agriculture, the export of cashew nuts (the country's most important commercial crop), and foreign assistance.

Freedom Trend

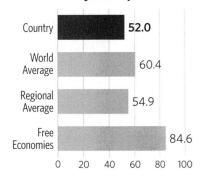

54
52
50
48
46
44

2011　2012　2013　2014　2015

Country Comparisons

Country	52.0
World Average	60.4
Regional Average	54.9
Free Economies	84.6

0　20　40　60　80　100

Quick Facts

Population: 1.6 million
GDP (PPP): $1.9 billion
0.3% growth in 2013
5-year compound annual growth 2.1%
$1,206 per capita
Unemployment: 8.5%
Inflation (CPI): 0.6%
FDI Inflow: $14.5 million
Public Debt: 61.0% of GDP

2013 data unless otherwise noted.
Data compiled as of September 2014.

How Do We Measure Economic Freedom?
See page 475 for an explanation of the methodology
or visit the *Index* Web site at *heritage.org/index*.

229

THE TEN ECONOMIC FREEDOMS

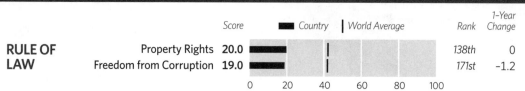

	Score		Rank	1-Year Change
RULE OF LAW				
Property Rights	20.0		138th	0
Freedom from Corruption	19.0		171st	-1.2

Corruption is pervasive and has been aggravated by Guinea-Bissau's prominent role in international narco-trafficking and political instability before the re-establishment of constitutional rule in the spring of 2014. Scant budgets and endemic corruption severely challenge judicial independence. Judges and magistrates are poorly trained, irregularly paid, and highly susceptible to graft and political pressure.

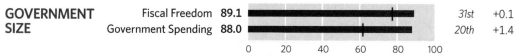

	Score		Rank	1-Year Change
GOVERNMENT SIZE				
Fiscal Freedom	89.1		31st	+0.1
Government Spending	88.0		20th	+1.4

Guinea-Bissau's top individual income tax rate is 20 percent, and its top corporate tax rate is 25 percent. Other taxes include a sales tax. The overall tax burden is equivalent to 8.3 percent of gross domestic product, and government expenditures equal 20.0 percent of the domestic economy. Public debt is equivalent to 61 percent of domestic output.

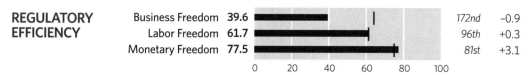

	Score		Rank	1-Year Change
REGULATORY EFFICIENCY				
Business Freedom	39.6		172nd	-0.9
Labor Freedom	61.7		96th	+0.3
Monetary Freedom	77.5		81st	+3.1

The cost of incorporating a business has been reduced considerably, and the time has been cut from over 200 days to nine, but completing licensing requirements still takes over 100 days. Much of the labor force is employed in the public sector or the informal economy. The government uses reference prices for fuel and basic foods to control prices of key products.

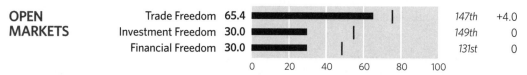

	Score		Rank	1-Year Change
OPEN MARKETS				
Trade Freedom	65.4		147th	+4.0
Investment Freedom	30.0		149th	0
Financial Freedom	30.0		131st	0

Guinea-Bissau has an average tariff rate of 9.8 percent. It is a member of the Economic Community of West African States and the West African Economic and Monetary Union. The uncertain political and economic climate deters foreign investment. Much of the population is still outside of the formal banking sector. High credit costs and scarce access to financing severely impede entrepreneurial activity.

Long-Term Score Change (since 1999)

RULE OF LAW		GOVERNMENT SIZE		REGULATORY EFFICIENCY		OPEN MARKETS	
Property Rights	+10.0	Fiscal Freedom	+23.6	Business Freedom	-0.4	Trade Freedom	+36.0
Freedom from Corruption	+9.0	Government Spending	+22.1	Labor Freedom	+10.1	Investment Freedom	0
				Monetary Freedom	+36.9	Financial Freedom	+20.0

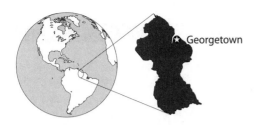

Georgetown

GUYANA

Economic Freedom Score

50
25 　 75

Least
free　0

Most
free　100

55.5

Guyana's economic freedom score is 55.5, making its economy the 123rd freest in the 2015 *Index*. Its overall score is 0.2 point worse than last year, with improvements in freedom from corruption and labor freedom counterbalanced by declines in property rights and the management of government spending. Guyana is ranked 22nd out of 29 countries in the South and Central America/Caribbean region, and its overall score is well below the world and regional averages.

Over the past five years, Guyana has recorded the largest score improvement of any South and Central American country. Since 2011, its economic freedom has advanced by 6.1 points, with impressive score increases in government spending and investment freedom. As a result, Guyana's economy has moved from "repressed" to "mostly unfree."

Nevertheless, the underlying institutional environment is still weak. Large improvements in investment freedom have come from a relatively low base. Political unrest and poor access to financing continue to undermine foreign direct investment. Poorly institutionalized rule of law deters investors and entrepreneurs. The cocaine trade has generated corruption and violence.

BACKGROUND: President Donald Ramotar, an economist and head of the left-wing People's Progressive Party (PPP), was elected to a five-year term in 2011. The PPP has been in power since 1992. Local municipal government elections have not been held for almost two decades. Political reform has been attempted only under framework agreements with international organizations. Although the risk of political violence is low, relations between the ruling Indo-Guyanese PPC/Civic parties and the Afro-Guyanese People's National Congress/Reform parties remain hostile. Exports of sugar, gold, bauxite, shrimp, timber, and rice represent nearly 60 percent of formal GDP and are susceptible to weather conditions and fluctuations in commodity prices. Violent crime and drug trafficking are endemic, and the informal economy is driven primarily by drug proceeds.

Freedom Trend

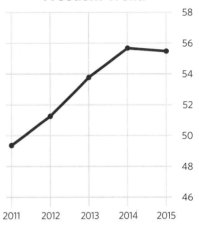

2011	2012 2013 2014 2015

58
56
54
52
50
48
46

Country Comparisons

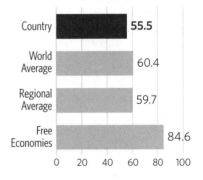

Country	55.5
World Average	60.4
Regional Average	59.7
Free Economies	84.6

0　20　40　60　80　100

Quick Facts

Population: 0.8 million
GDP (PPP): $6.6 billion
4.8% growth in 2013
5-year compound annual growth 4.5%
$8,250 per capita
Unemployment: 11.2%
Inflation (CPI): 3.5%
FDI Inflow: $240.3 million
Public Debt: 63.9% of GDP

How Do We Measure Economic Freedom?
See page 475 for an explanation of the methodology
or visit the *Index* Web site at *heritage.org/index*.

2013 data unless otherwise noted.
Data compiled as of September 2014.

THE TEN ECONOMIC FREEDOMS

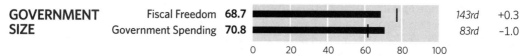

		Score	Country	World Average	Rank	1-Year Change
RULE OF LAW	Property Rights	25.0			124th	–5.0
	Freedom from Corruption	27.0			141st	+2.6

In November 2013, Guyana was blacklisted by the Caribbean Financial Action Task Force after the government failed to strengthen anti–money laundering legislation. Organized criminal activity and narco-trafficking have increased, and violent crime is a major problem. The judicial system is generally perceived as slow and ineffective in enforcing contracts or resolving disputes. Protection of property rights is poor.

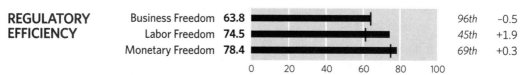

		Score			Rank	1-Year Change
GOVERNMENT SIZE	Fiscal Freedom	68.7			143rd	+0.3
	Government Spending	70.8			83rd	–1.0

Guyana's top individual income tax rate is 33.3 percent, and its top corporate tax rate is 40 percent. Other taxes include a value-added tax and a property tax. The overall tax burden equals 20.5 percent of domestic income. Public expenditures are equal to 31.2 percent of the domestic economy, and public debt is equivalent to 63 percent of gross domestic product.

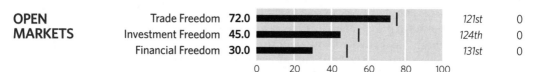

		Score			Rank	1-Year Change
REGULATORY EFFICIENCY	Business Freedom	63.8			96th	–0.5
	Labor Freedom	74.5			45th	+1.9
	Monetary Freedom	78.4			69th	+0.3

Reform measures have streamlined the procedures for establishing a business, and the cost of licenses has been reduced, but the overall pace of regulatory reform has lagged behind other countries. A well-functioning private labor market has not yet emerged. The government influences prices through state-owned utilities and enterprises and provides significant subsidies for electricity, transportation, and the sugar industry.

		Score			Rank	1-Year Change
OPEN MARKETS	Trade Freedom	72.0			121st	0
	Investment Freedom	45.0			124th	0
	Financial Freedom	30.0			131st	0

Guyana has an average tariff rate of 6.5 percent. It is a member of the Caribbean Community and Common Market. Political unrest is a concern. The banking sector remains relatively well capitalized, and nonperforming loans are around 5 percent of total loans, but high credit costs and scarce access to financing remain barriers to private-sector development. The capital market is not fully developed.

Long-Term Score Change (since 1995)

RULE OF LAW		GOVERNMENT SIZE		REGULATORY EFFICIENCY		OPEN MARKETS	
Property Rights	–25.0	Fiscal Freedom	+12.9	Business Freedom	+8.8	Trade Freedom	+6.0
Freedom from Corruption	+17.0	Government Spending	+40.5	Labor Freedom	+12.0	Investment Freedom	–5.0
				Monetary Freedom	+14.4	Financial Freedom	0

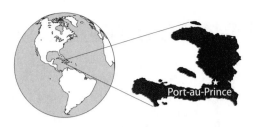

HAITI

Economic Freedom Score

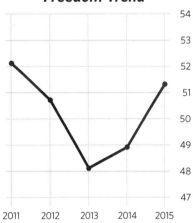

Least free 0   25   50   75   100 Most free

51.3

H aiti's economic freedom score is 51.3, making its economy the 151st freest in the 2015 *Index*. Its overall score is 2.4 points better than last year, reflecting notable improvements in the control of government spending, business freedom, trade freedom, and freedom from corruption. Haiti is ranked 24th out of 29 countries in the South and Central America/ Caribbean region, and its overall score is below the regional average.

Haiti has recorded the fourth largest score improvement in the 2015 *Index*, but its economy is still reeling from the destruction of the 2010 earthquake. Despite some progress, institutional and economic foundations remain fragile, with economic freedom declining by close to 1.0 point over the past five years.

Of particular concern is the poor regard for rule of law. Corruption is rampant, and the judicial system is ineffective and inefficient. Smuggling remains a huge problem and is exacerbated by poor trade freedom. Entrepreneurs find Haiti one of the world's most difficult places to do business, as the regulatory environment for both business and labor is outdated and inefficient.

BACKGROUND: President Michel Martelly took office in 2011 promising a fresh start for Haiti, but his policies have had little effect on the daily economic struggle that most Haitians face. Inflation and corruption remain popular grievances, weakening his political capital. Relations with the Dominican Republic have been strained since Santo Domingo revoked the citizenship of thousands of Dominican-born people of Haitian descent. The United Nations Stabilization Mission in Haiti, established in 2004 to ensure security, extended its mandate until October 2014 but reduced the number of U.N. peacekeeping troops in the country. Haiti is still recovering from a 2010 earthquake, and reconstruction is far from complete. More than 90 percent of the government's budget comes from an agreement with Petrocaribe, a Venezuela-led oil alliance. Extreme poverty, weak government institutions, and violent crime are still major problems.

Freedom Trend

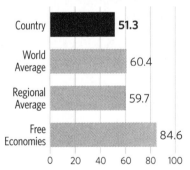

Country Comparisons

Country	51.3
World Average	60.4
Regional Average	59.7
Free Economies	84.6

Quick Facts

Population: 10.3 million
GDP (PPP): $13.6 billion
4.3% growth in 2013
5-year compound annual growth 2.0%
$1,315 per capita
Unemployment: 7.1%
Inflation (CPI): 6.8%
FDI Inflow: $190.0 million
Public Debt: 21.3% of GDP

2013 data unless otherwise noted.
Data compiled as of September 2014.

How Do We Measure Economic Freedom?
See page 475 for an explanation of the methodology
or visit the *Index* Web site at *heritage.org/index*.

THE TEN ECONOMIC FREEDOMS

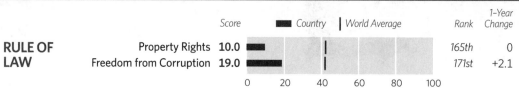

		Score		Rank	1-Year Change
RULE OF LAW	Property Rights	10.0		165th	0
	Freedom from Corruption	19.0		171st	+2.1

In 2013, Transparency International's Corruption Perceptions Index ranked Haiti as the most corrupt country in the Western Hemisphere. Haiti is a major narco-trafficking transshipment point. The dysfunctional judicial system is underfunded, inefficient, corrupt, and burdened by a large backlog of cases, outdated legal codes, and poor facilities. There is no comprehensive civil registry. Clear property titles are virtually nonexistent.

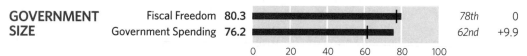

		Score		Rank	1-Year Change
GOVERNMENT SIZE	Fiscal Freedom	80.3		78th	0
	Government Spending	76.2		62nd	+9.9

The top individual and corporate income tax rates are 30 percent. Other taxes include a value-added tax and a capital gains tax. The overall tax burden is equal to 12.9 percent of domestic output, and government expenditures amount to 28.2 percent of domestic income. Public debt has been growing and exceeds a level equal to 21 percent of gross domestic product.

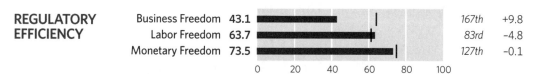

		Score		Rank	1-Year Change
REGULATORY EFFICIENCY	Business Freedom	43.1		167th	+9.8
	Labor Freedom	63.7		83rd	-4.8
	Monetary Freedom	73.5		127th	-0.1

Launching a business has become more streamlined and takes only 12 procedures, but the cost of obtaining necessary licenses remains about twice the level of average annual income. The labor market is inefficient, and much of the labor force is employed in the informal sector. The state-owned electrical utility receives an annual government subsidy of $170 million but serves only 25 percent of the population.

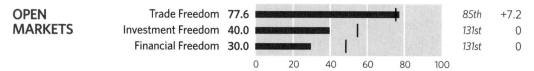

		Score		Rank	1-Year Change
OPEN MARKETS	Trade Freedom	77.6		85th	+7.2
	Investment Freedom	40.0		131st	0
	Financial Freedom	30.0		131st	0

Haiti's average tariff rate is 3.7 percent. Importing goods can take several weeks. Foreign and domestic investors are treated equally under the law, but navigating the legal system is difficult, as are titling and selling land. Scarce access to financing impedes private-sector development. The financial sector is dominated by banking, but much of the population remains outside of the formal banking sector.

Long-Term Score Change (since 1995)

RULE OF LAW		GOVERNMENT SIZE		REGULATORY EFFICIENCY		OPEN MARKETS	
Property Rights	0	Fiscal Freedom	+1.7	Business Freedom	+3.1	Trade Freedom	-2.4
Freedom from Corruption	+9.0	Government Spending	-19.3	Labor Freedom	+1.8	Investment Freedom	+30.0
				Monetary Freedom	+20.7	Financial Freedom	+20.0

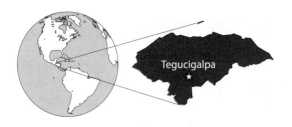

HONDURAS

Economic Freedom Score

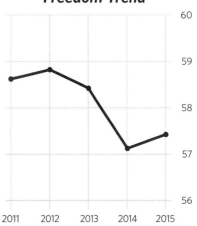

25   50   75

Least free   0   100   Most free

57.4

World Rank: 116   **Regional Rank: 19**

H onduras's economic freedom score is 57.4, making its economy the 116th freest in the 2015 *Index*. Its overall score has increased by 0.3 point since last year, with improvements in freedom from corruption, trade freedom, and labor freedom offsetting declines in business freedom and the control of government spending. Honduras is ranked 19th out of 29 countries in the South and Central America/Caribbean region, and its overall score is lower than the world and regional averages.

Over the past decade, Honduras has been developing "charter cities" with more reasonable business and trade regulations to attract trade and investment. Overall economic freedom, however, has fallen by 1.2 points over the past five years. Score deteriorations in three of the 10 economic freedoms have included drops of close to 10 points in the management of government spending and labor freedom.

The decline in economic freedom has undermined an economic environment that already lacks strong institutional foundations. As in many other Latin American countries, political and social instability related to the drug trade destabilizes the rule of law and encourages corruption. The labor market remains one of the world's most rigid, and procedural and licensing requirements make it prohibitive for entrepreneurs to enter the formal sector.

BACKGROUND: Juan Orlando Hernández of the conservative National Party of Honduras took office in January 2014, defeating Xiomara Castro, leftist candidate and wife of ousted President Manuel Zelaya. Hernández has created the National Investment Board to facilitate dialogue between the private and public sectors and to promote foreign investment and growth. Honduras plans to launch a "Zone for Employment and Economic Development," and Hernández has encouraged El Salvador and Nicaragua to join him in making Central America more competitive. Honduras remains one of Latin America's poorest countries, with more than two-thirds of the population living in poverty. Hernández faces the challenge of reducing a rising deficit and endemic corruption. Honduras still has the world's highest homicide rate.

Freedom Trend

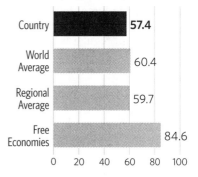

	60
	59
	58
	57
	56

2011   2012   2013   2014   2015

Country Comparisons

Country	57.4
World Average	60.4
Regional Average	59.7
Free Economies	84.6

0   20   40   60   80   100

Quick Facts

Population: 8.1 million
GDP (PPP): $39.2 billion
2.6% growth in 2013
5-year compound annual growth 2.3%
$4,839 per capita
Unemployment: 4.2%
Inflation (CPI): 5.2%
FDI Inflow: $1.1 billion
Public Debt: 40.2% of GDP

2013 data unless otherwise noted.
Data compiled as of September 2014.

THE TEN ECONOMIC FREEDOMS

		Score	Rank	1-Year Change
RULE OF LAW	Property Rights	30.0	94th	0
	Freedom from Corruption	26.0	145th	+2.3

Rampant corruption and weak state institutions make it almost impossible to combat threats posed by transnational gangs and organized criminal groups. Honduras has the world's highest murder rate. The court system is weak and inefficient, and resolution of disputed cases can take years. Laws and practices regarding real estate differ substantially from those in more developed countries, and fraudulent deeds and titles are common.

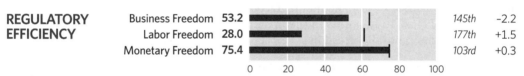

		Score	Rank	1-Year Change
GOVERNMENT SIZE	Fiscal Freedom	84.9	50th	0
	Government Spending	78.7	53rd	-1.1

The top individual and corporate income tax rates are 25 percent. Other taxes include a 5 percent social contribution tax for corporations, a capital gains tax, and a sales tax. The overall tax burden is equivalent to 16.1 percent of domestic income, and government expenditures amount to 26.6 percent of domestic output. Public debt is equal to 40 percent of gross domestic product.

		Score	Rank	1-Year Change
REGULATORY EFFICIENCY	Business Freedom	53.2	145th	-2.2
	Labor Freedom	28.0	177th	+1.5
	Monetary Freedom	75.4	103rd	+0.3

Application of regulations has been inconsistent and non-transparent. Starting a new business is fairly easy, but obtaining operating licenses still takes close to three months on average. In the absence of a well-functioning labor market, informal labor activity persists. Although the government regulates the prices of key products (e.g., fuel) and services, it took steps in 2014 to reduce electricity and other subsidies.

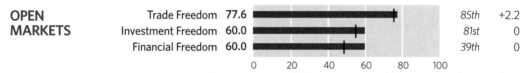

		Score	Rank	1-Year Change
OPEN MARKETS	Trade Freedom	77.6	85th	+2.2
	Investment Freedom	60.0	81st	0
	Financial Freedom	60.0	39th	0

The average tariff rate for Honduras is 6.5 percent. Additional barriers impede imports of agricultural goods. The government is attempting to create special economic development zones to attract foreign investment. The small financial sector remains relatively stable. The reasonably sound regulatory framework and financial system infrastructure have helped to enhance the public's access to formal banking institutions and credits.

Long-Term Score Change (since 1995)

RULE OF LAW		GOVERNMENT SIZE		REGULATORY EFFICIENCY		OPEN MARKETS	
Property Rights	-20.0	Fiscal Freedom	+19.4	Business Freedom	-1.8	Trade Freedom	+16.6
Freedom from Corruption	-4.0	Government Spending	-4.7	Labor Freedom	-16.7	Investment Freedom	+10.0
				Monetary Freedom	+7.6	Financial Freedom	+10.0

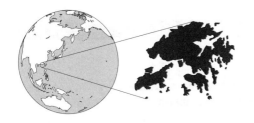

HONG KONG

World Rank: 1   **Regional Rank: 1**

Hong Kong's economic freedom score is 89.6. Its overall score has declined by 0.5 point since last year, reflecting a higher level of perceived corruption that outweighs small improvements in business freedom, labor freedom, and fiscal freedom. Hong Kong continues to be the top-rated economy in the *Index*.

Hong Kong, a global free port and financial hub, continues to thrive on the free flow of goods, services, and capital. As the economic and financial gateway to China, and with an efficient regulatory framework, low and simple taxation, and sophisticated capital markets, the territory continues to offer the most convenient platform for international companies doing business on the mainland. An impressive level of resilience has enabled it to navigate global economic swings and domestic shocks.

However, the economy's institutional uniqueness, enshrined in its exceptional commitment to economic freedom and a high degree of autonomy pledged by the mainland, has faded a bit. Although Hong Kong maintains the features of an economically free society, economic decision-making has become somewhat more bureaucratic and politicized, and the government's administrative scope and reach have expanded. Recent political events appear to have undermined public trust and confidence in the administration.

BACKGROUND: Hong Kong became part of the People's Republic of China in 1997, but under the "one country, two systems" agreement, China promised not to impose its socialist policies on Hong Kong and to allow Hong Kong a high degree of autonomy in all matters except foreign and defense policy for 50 years. The critical issue today is the shape and form that "universal suffrage," promised for 2017 by Chinese authorities, will take. Although the government controls all land in Hong Kong, the economy has benefited from its commitment to small government, low taxes, and light regulation. Major industries include financial services and shipping; manufacturing has largely migrated to the mainland. Hong Kong's economy has become increasingly integrated with China through trade, tourism, and financial links.

Freedom Trend

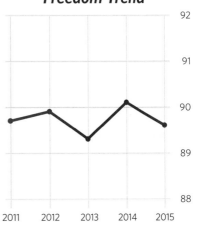

Country Comparisons

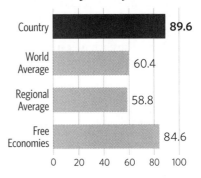

Country	89.6
World Average	60.4
Regional Average	58.8
Free Economies	84.6

Quick Facts

Population: 7.2 million
GDP (PPP): $381.9 billion
2.9% growth in 2013
5-year compound annual growth 2.7%
$52,722 per capita
Unemployment: 3.3%
Inflation (CPI): 4.3%
FDI Inflow: $76.6 billion
Public Debt: 0.5% of GDP

2013 data unless otherwise noted.
Data compiled as of September 2014.

How Do We Measure Economic Freedom?
See page 475 for an explanation of the methodology
or visit the *Index* Web site at *heritage.org/index*.

THE TEN ECONOMIC FREEDOMS

		Score		Rank	1-Year Change
RULE OF LAW	Property Rights	90.0		3rd	0
	Freedom from Corruption	75.0		15th	-7.3

Hong Kong continues to enjoy relatively low rates of corruption, although business interests exercise a strong influence in the unicameral legislature and executive branch. Beijing's heavy-handed efforts in 2014 to assert greater control from the mainland have galvanized pro-democracy sentiments. The rule of law is respected, and the efficient and capable judiciary remains independent. Property rights are well protected.

		Score		Rank	1-Year Change
GOVERNMENT SIZE	Fiscal Freedom	93.2		17th	+0.2
	Government Spending	89.7		12th	0

The standard income tax rate is 15 percent, and the top corporate tax rate is 16.5 percent. The overall tax burden equals 13.7 percent of domestic income. Government expenditures amount to 18.5 percent of gross domestic product. Public debt is low, and a budget surplus has been maintained, but population aging and greater spending on social programs have increased fiscal pressures.

		Score		Rank	1-Year Change
REGULATORY EFFICIENCY	Business Freedom	100.		1st	+1.1
	Labor Freedom	0		4th	+0.4
	Monetary Freedom	95.9		28th	-0.2

The competitive and transparent regulatory framework supports dynamic business formation and operation. The labor market is vibrant, with flexible and well-enforced labor codes. Working hours and wages are largely determined by the market. Monetary stability is maintained through the exchange-rate peg to the U.S. dollar. The government provides some low-cost housing and green energy subsidies.

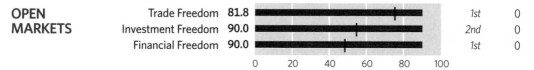

		Score		Rank	1-Year Change
OPEN MARKETS	Trade Freedom	81.8		1st	0
	Investment Freedom	90.0		2nd	0
	Financial Freedom	90.0		1st	0

Hong Kong has a 0 percent average tariff rate and remains one of the world's most open economies for international trade and investment. The highly developed and prudently regulated financial system offers a wide range of innovative financing options. The banking sector is dynamic and resilient. The large and growing financial exposure to the mainland continues to deepen.

Long-Term Score Change (since 1995)

RULE OF LAW		GOVERNMENT SIZE		REGULATORY EFFICIENCY		OPEN MARKETS	
Property Rights	0	Fiscal Freedom	+0.2	Business Freedom	0	Trade Freedom	0
Freedom from Corruption	-15.0	Government Spending	-3.8	Labor Freedom	+9.4	Investment Freedom	0
				Monetary Freedom	+1.0	Financial Freedom	+20.0

HUNGARY

Economic Freedom Score

25   50   75

Least free 0   Most free 100

66.8

Hungary's economic freedom score is 66.8, making its economy the 54th freest in the 2015 *Index*. Its score is down by 0.2 point from last year, with declines in property rights, business freedom, fiscal freedom, and the control of public spending outweighing improvements in monetary freedom, labor freedom, and freedom from corruption. Hungary is ranked 25th out of 43 countries in the Europe region, and its overall score is above the world average but below the regional average.

Hungary's economic freedom peaked in 2013, and declines in the past two years, particularly in property rights and business freedom, have raised questions about the momentum for further reform.

Hungary's longer-term economic transition to an open market economy has been highlighted by improvements in the trade and investment regimes. The business environment is relatively encouraging to entrepreneurship and risk-taking, and capital markets are developed and open to foreign investment. Concerns about the rule of law have been increasing over the past few years, and the government has been struggling with a burgeoning budget and foreign currency debt.

BACKGROUND: Hungary has been a member of NATO since 1999 and a member of the European Union since 2004. The April 2014 parliamentary election was held in accordance with a new constitution, which went into force in January 2012. The center-right Fidesz–Hungarian Civic Alliance won the majority of seats, and Prime Minister Viktor Orbán, who has been in office since May 2010, formed a new government. Despite achieving broad electoral support, Orbán so far has achieved only limited economic success. Hungary exited from recession in early 2013, but with only a modest recovery. The low-skilled labor supply greatly exceeds demand, generating high unemployment. Hard currency indebtedness remains a key vulnerability.

Freedom Trend

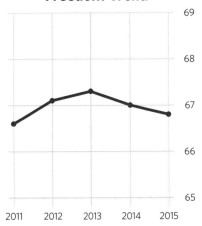

69

68

67

66

65

2011   2012   2013   2014   2015

Country Comparisons

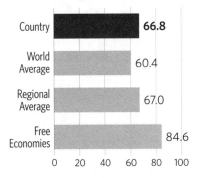

Country   **66.8**

World Average   60.4

Regional Average   67.0

Free Economies   84.6

0   20   40   60   80   100

Quick Facts

Population: 9.9 million
GDP (PPP): $198.2 billion
1.1% growth in 2013
5-year compound annual growth –1.0%
$20,065 per capita
Unemployment: 10.5%
Inflation (CPI): 1.7%
FDI Inflow: $3.1 billion
Public Debt: 79.2% of GDP

2013 data unless otherwise noted.
Data compiled as of September 2014.

How Do We Measure Economic Freedom?
See page 475 for an explanation of the methodology
or visit the *Index* Web site at *heritage.org/index*.

THE TEN ECONOMIC FREEDOMS

		Score	■ Country	World Average	Rank	1-Year Change

RULE OF LAW

Property Rights 55.0 — 50th — −5.0
Freedom from Corruption 54.0 — 46th — +5.4

Hungary ranked low among EU members in Transparency International's 2013 Corruption Perceptions Index, partly because government watchdog institutions are weak and headed by party loyalists. Corruption has long been rampant in public procurement and state aid; in 2014, it was estimated that firms routinely pay bribes of up to 20 percent of a project's value. Recent reforms have undermined the independence of the judiciary.

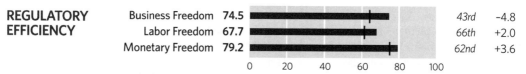

GOVERNMENT SIZE

Fiscal Freedom 78.7 — 98th — −2.4
Government Spending 25.9 — 166th — −0.9

Hungary's individual income tax rate is a flat 16 percent, and its top corporate tax rate is 19 percent. Other taxes include a value-added tax and a property tax. Total tax revenues equal 38.9 percent of domestic output. Government expenditures are equivalent to 49.7 percent of domestic income, and public debt equals 79 percent of gross domestic product.

REGULATORY EFFICIENCY

Business Freedom 74.5 — 43rd — −4.8
Labor Freedom 67.7 — 66th — +2.0
Monetary Freedom 79.2 — 62nd — +3.6

The entrepreneurial framework is relatively transparent and efficient. Starting a business takes four procedures and five days on average, but licensing can be time-consuming. The labor market lacks flexibility, but the non-salary cost of employment is not high in comparison to other countries in the region. Hungary will receive nearly €2 billion in agricultural subsidies from the EU between 2014 and 2020.

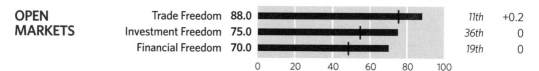

OPEN MARKETS

Trade Freedom 88.0 — 11th — +0.2
Investment Freedom 75.0 — 36th — 0
Financial Freedom 70.0 — 19th — 0

EU members have a 1.0 percent average tariff rate. Although some non-tariff barriers exist, the EU is relatively open to external trade. Foreign and domestic investors are generally treated equally under Hungarian law. The financial sector is dominated by banks, many of which are foreign-owned. The banking sector remains plagued by low profitability and uncertainty. Since 2010, commercial banks have suffered from higher taxes.

Long-Term Score Change (since 1995)

RULE OF LAW		GOVERNMENT SIZE		REGULATORY EFFICIENCY		OPEN MARKETS	
Property Rights	−15.0	Fiscal Freedom	+31.9	Business Freedom	−10.5	Trade Freedom	+27.0
Freedom from Corruption	+4.0	Government Spending	+25.9	Labor Freedom	−0.5	Investment Freedom	+5.0
				Monetary Freedom	+15.0	Financial Freedom	+20.0

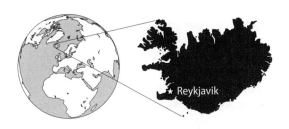

ICELAND

Economic Freedom Score

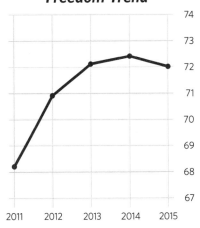

50
25   75
Least free   0   100   Most free

72.0

World Rank: 26   **Regional Rank: 14**

Iceland's economic freedom score is 72.0, making its economy the 26th freest in the 2015 *Index*. Its overall score has decreased by 0.4 point since last year, with combined declines in freedom from corruption, fiscal freedom, business freedom, and the management of public spending outweighing improvements in labor freedom and monetary freedom. Iceland is ranked 14th out of 43 countries in the Europe region, and its overall score remains well above the world and regional averages.

Iceland's score change in the 2015 *Index* is negative for the first time in five years. Nonetheless, economic freedom has still advanced by 3.8 points in the past half-decade, led by gains in fiscal freedom, government spending, labor freedom, monetary freedom, and investment freedom.

Despite recent setbacks, Iceland has consistently remained among the "mostly free," falling below this threshold only once in its history in the *Index*. Supported by one of the strongest property rights regimes in the world, Iceland has built a society based on the rule of law and open markets. Fiscal policy has ranked poorly in recent years due to a collapsing revenue base and bank bailouts.

BACKGROUND: The pro–European Union Social Democrats lost the April 2013 parliamentary elections. Sigmundur Davíð Gunnlaugsson of the Progressive Party was elected prime minister in a coalition government of the Progressive Party and Independence Party. The new government indefinitely suspended accession talks with the EU in May 2013 and then, in May 2014, postponed plans to withdraw its application for EU membership. To join the EU, the government must win a public referendum, and public opinion remains divided. Iceland already enjoys EU-related benefits that include free trade and movement of capital, labor, goods, and services within the region. It also has membership in the Schengen Zone, which allows visa-free travel in 26 European countries. The economy, dependent on tourism and fishing, is expected to grow slowly in 2014 and 2015.

Freedom Trend

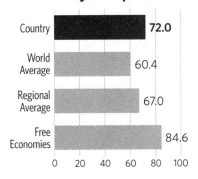

74
73
72
71
70
69
68
67

2011   2012   2013   2014   2015

Country Comparisons

Country	**72.0**
World Average	60.4
Regional Average	67.0
Free Economies	84.6

0   20   40   60   80   100

Quick Facts

Population: 0.3 million
GDP (PPP): $13.2 billion
2.9% growth in 2013
5-year compound annual growth –0.8%
$41,000 per capita
Unemployment: 5.6%
Inflation (CPI): 3.9%
FDI Inflow: $347.1 million
Public Debt: 90.2% of GDP

2013 data unless otherwise noted.
Data compiled as of September 2014.

How Do We Measure Economic Freedom?
See page 475 for an explanation of the methodology
or visit the *Index* Web site at *heritage.org/index*.

THE TEN ECONOMIC FREEDOMS

		Score		Rank	1-Year Change
RULE OF LAW	Property Rights	90.0		3rd	0
	Freedom from Corruption	78.0		12th	−6.2

The institutionalization of accountability and transparency results from 1,000 years of parliamentary government. Isolated cases of corruption occur but are not an obstacle to foreign investment. Private property is well protected. Iceland has a solid legislative and institutional framework to enforce intellectual property protection laws. The constitution provides for an independent judiciary, and trials are generally public and fair.

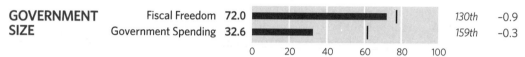

		Score		Rank	1-Year Change
GOVERNMENT SIZE	Fiscal Freedom	72.0		130th	−0.9
	Government Spending	32.6		159th	−0.3

The top individual income tax rate is 31.8 percent, and the top corporate tax rate is 20 percent. Other taxes include a value-added tax and an estate tax. The total tax burden is equal to 37.2 percent of total domestic income. Public expenditures equal 47.4 percent of gross domestic product. Public debt has fallen steadily but is still equivalent to 90 percent of GDP.

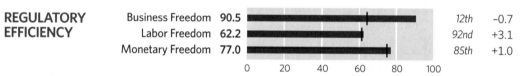

		Score		Rank	1-Year Change
REGULATORY EFFICIENCY	Business Freedom	90.5		12th	−0.7
	Labor Freedom	62.2		92nd	+3.1
	Monetary Freedom	77.0		85th	+1.0

The overall regulatory framework is transparent and competitive. Launching a business is subject to minimum capital requirements but takes only five procedures. Bankruptcy procedures are modern and efficient. Labor regulations are relatively rigid, and the non-salary cost of employing a worker is high. Despite the challenging economic situation, inflation was controlled in 2014, and monetary stability has been maintained.

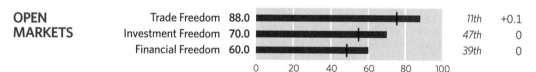

		Score		Rank	1-Year Change
OPEN MARKETS	Trade Freedom	88.0		11th	+0.1
	Investment Freedom	70.0		47th	0
	Financial Freedom	60.0		39th	0

Iceland's average tariff rate is 1.0 percent. Imports of agricultural goods, including meat and dairy products, are restricted. Capital controls put in place in 2008 have not been fully removed, and investment in some economic sectors is capped. Extensive reforms of financial market regulations have been implemented, and reform is ongoing. The financial system has regained stability, with the banking sector recapitalized.

Long-Term Score Change (since 1997)

RULE OF LAW		GOVERNMENT SIZE		REGULATORY EFFICIENCY		OPEN MARKETS	
Property Rights	0	Fiscal Freedom	+10.4	Business Freedom	+20.5	Trade Freedom	+7.2
Freedom from Corruption	−12.0	Government Spending	−8.0	Labor Freedom	−2.4	Investment Freedom	0
				Monetary Freedom	−4.3	Financial Freedom	+10.0

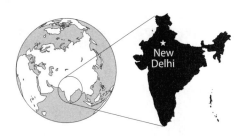

INDIA

World Rank: 128   **Regional Rank: 26**

Economic Freedom Score

I ndia's economic freedom score is 54.6, making its economy the 128th freest in the 2015 *Index*. Its score is down by 1.1 points from last year, with modest improvements in business freedom, property rights, and freedom from corruption offset by declines in labor freedom and trade freedom. India is ranked 26th out of 41 countries in the Asia–Pacific region, and its overall score continues to be below the regional and world averages.

India's level of economic freedom is unchanged over five years. The state's presence in the economy remains extensive through state-owned enterprises and wasteful subsidy programs that cause chronically high budget deficits. In the absence of a well-functioning legal and regulatory framework, a weak rule of law exacerbated by corruption in many areas of economic activity undermines the emergence of a more vibrant private sector. India remains a "mostly unfree" economy.

The reform-minded Modi administration has undertaken some necessary structural adjustments with a focus on reforming the inefficient and bloated government sector, better managing public finance, and improving the business and investment environments. The first budget presented in July 2014, however, was short on detail about plans to restructure wasteful subsidy programs and reignite economic growth.

BACKGROUND: India is a relatively stable democracy. It is 80 percent Hindu but is still home to one of the world's largest Muslim populations. The Bharatiya Janata Party, led by Narendra Modi, won a sweeping victory in the 2014 national elections, held over a five-week period. The previous Congress Party–led government was unseated amid corruption scandals and a faltering economy. After decade-low GDP growth in 2013, Prime Minister Modi has promised to implement economic reform in order to attract private-sector investment. Corruption, poor infrastructure, and fiscal deficits are major obstacles to economic growth. India is a significant force in world trade, but its economy continues to operate far below its potential.

Freedom Trend

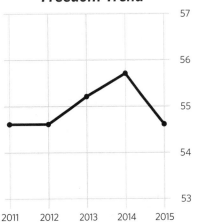

Country Comparisons

Country	54.6
World Average	60.4
Regional Average	58.8
Free Economies	84.6

Quick Facts

Population: 1.24 billion
GDP (PPP): $5.1 trillion
4.4% growth in 2013
5-year compound annual growth 6.9%
$4,077 per capita
Unemployment: 3.7%
Inflation (CPI): 9.5%
FDI Inflow: $28.2 billion
Public Debt: 66.7% of GDP

2013 data unless otherwise noted.
Data compiled as of September 2014.

How Do We Measure Economic Freedom?
See page 475 for an explanation of the methodology
or visit the *Index* Web site at *heritage.org/index*.

THE TEN ECONOMIC FREEDOMS

		Score		Rank	1-Year Change
RULE OF LAW	Property Rights	55.0		50th	+5.0
	Freedom from Corruption	36.0		95th	+4.5

In a poll, 96 percent of Indians said chronic corruption was holding back their country. Corruption has had a negative effect on government efficiency and economic performance. The judiciary is independent, but Indian courts are understaffed and lack the technology necessary to clear an enormous backlog, estimated by the U.N. to total 30 million–40 million pending cases.

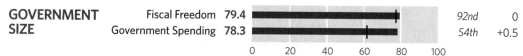

GOVERNMENT SIZE	Fiscal Freedom	79.4		92nd	0
	Government Spending	78.3		54th	+0.5

The top individual income tax rate is 30.9 percent (including an education tax). The top corporate tax rate is 32.4 percent. The overall tax burden equals 7.3 percent of domestic income, and government expenditures amount to 26.9 percent of the domestic economy. Public debt equals approximately 67 percent of GDP. The fiscal deficit has declined but remains above 4 percent of GDP.

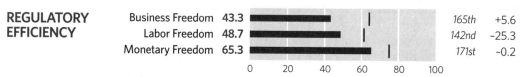

REGULATORY EFFICIENCY	Business Freedom	43.3		165th	+5.6
	Labor Freedom	48.7		142nd	-25.3
	Monetary Freedom	65.3		171st	-0.2

Business registration fees have been considerably reduced, but completing licensing requirements remains time-consuming. Although minimum wages are low, the labor market remains plagued by low labor productivity and the relatively high non-salary cost of hiring a worker. The government had announced its intention to cut badly targeted fuel subsidies but has yet to set out a clear plan.

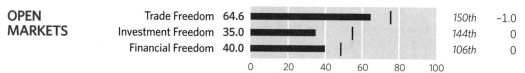

OPEN MARKETS	Trade Freedom	64.6		150th	-1.0
	Investment Freedom	35.0		144th	0
	Financial Freedom	40.0		106th	0

India's average tariff rate is 7.7 percent. Non-tariff barriers further interfere with the flow of goods and services. Government procurement policies can favor domestic firms. The government screens new foreign investment. The evolving financial sector remains vulnerable to state interference. The government retains considerable ownership in the banking sector, and the level of nonperforming loans is relatively high.

Long-Term Score Change (since 1995)

RULE OF LAW		GOVERNMENT SIZE		REGULATORY EFFICIENCY		OPEN MARKETS	
Property Rights	+5.0	Fiscal Freedom	+32.6	Business Freedom	-11.7	Trade Freedom	+64.6
Freedom from Corruption	+26.0	Government Spending	-14.1	Labor Freedom	-13.0	Investment Freedom	-15.0
				Monetary Freedom	-6.4	Financial Freedom	+10.0

Jakarta

INDONESIA

Economic Freedom Score

50
25   75
Least   Most
free 0   100 free

58.1

Indonesia's economic freedom score is 58.1, making its economy the 105th freest in the 2015 *Index*. Its score has deteriorated by 0.4 point since last year, reflecting declines in business freedom, the control of government spending, and monetary freedom that counterbalance improvements in freedom from corruption and labor freedom. Indonesia is ranked 22nd out of 41 countries in the Asia–Pacific region, and its overall score is below the world and regional averages.

Steady growth in economic freedom over the past five years has tapered off more recently. However, since 2011, economic freedom in Indonesia has advanced by over 2.0 points, reflecting a more sustained commitment to opening up the financial sectors and improving the investment regime. Other changes have led to score advances in six of the 10 economic freedoms, reflecting relatively broad-based policy improvements.

Nonetheless, economic freedom remains weakly entrenched in Indonesia. The judiciary has demonstrated some independence, but corruption is present. Overregulation of the business and labor markets leads to inefficiencies in labor supply and business formation. Despite its presence in a dynamic East Asian trading network, Indonesia remains relatively closed off from the global marketplace.

BACKGROUND: Indonesia is the world's most populous Muslim-majority democracy. Since 1998, when long-standing authoritarian ruler General Suharto stepped down, Indonesia's 250 million people have enjoyed a widening range of political freedoms, and participation in the political process is high. Joko Widodo, former businessman and governor of Jakarta, won a tight race for the presidency in 2014, pledging to end corruption and promote economic reform. Weak rule of law remains a major impediment to attracting capital. As a member of the G-20 and a driving force within the Association of Southeast Asian Nations, Indonesia plays a growing role at the multilateral level. Its increasingly modern and diversified economy has recovered from the 2009 global recession.

Freedom Trend

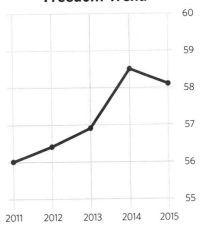

60

59

58

57

56

55

2011   2012   2013   2014   2015

Country Comparisons

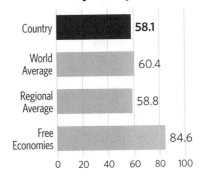

Country   **58.1**
World Average   60.4
Regional Average   58.8
Free Economies   84.6

0   20   40   60   80   100

Quick Facts

Population: 248.0 million
GDP (PPP): $1.3 trillion
5.8% growth in 2013
5-year compound annual growth 5.9%
$5,214 per capita
Unemployment: 6.0%
Inflation (CPI): 6.4%
FDI Inflow: $18.4 billion
Public Debt: 26.1% of GDP

2013 data unless otherwise noted.
Data compiled as of September 2014.

THE TEN ECONOMIC FREEDOMS

		Score	■ Country | World Average	Rank	1-Year Change
RULE OF LAW	Property Rights	30.0		94th	0
	Freedom from Corruption	32.0		116th	+4.0

Corruption remains endemic, including in the parliament and other key institutions like the police. The judicial process is slow and inefficient. In June 2014, the former Constitutional Court chief justice was sentenced to life imprisonment for accepting more than $4.8 million in exchange for favorable rulings in regional election disputes. Property rights are generally respected, but enforcement is inefficient and uneven.

		Score		Rank	1-Year Change
GOVERNMENT SIZE	Fiscal Freedom	83.3		59th	-0.1
	Government Spending	88.3		19th	-1.5

The top individual income tax rate is 30 percent, and the top corporate tax rate is 25 percent. Other taxes include a value-added tax and a property tax. Overall tax revenue equals 11.9 percent of domestic income. Public expenditures are equivalent to 19.7 percent of the domestic economy, and public debt corresponds to 26 percent of gross domestic product.

		Score		Rank	1-Year Change
REGULATORY EFFICIENCY	Business Freedom	49.3		155th	-5.5
	Labor Freedom	48.7		143rd	+0.9
	Monetary Freedom	74.9		110th	-1.5

Progress in improving the entrepreneurial environment has been modest. Launching a business takes 10 procedures on average, and meeting licensing requirements takes 200 days. The labor market lacks flexibility, and complex regulations hinder job growth. Fuel subsidies consumed 13 percent of GDP in 2014, although President Widodo announced that he will phase out fuel subsidies entirely within the next four years.

		Score		Rank	1-Year Change
OPEN MARKETS	Trade Freedom	74.8		106th	0
	Investment Freedom	40.0		131st	0
	Financial Freedom	60.0		39th	0

Indonesia's average tariff rate is 2.6 percent, and non-tariff barriers are numerous. State-owned enterprises play a large role in the economy. Foreign investment in several sectors is capped. The government still retains ownership in the banking sector, which is stable and evolving. Supervision of the sector has recently been transferred from the central bank to the Financial Services Authority.

Long-Term Score Change (since 1995)

RULE OF LAW		GOVERNMENT SIZE		REGULATORY EFFICIENCY		OPEN MARKETS	
Property Rights	-20.0	Fiscal Freedom	+10.2	Business Freedom	-5.7	Trade Freedom	+29.8
Freedom from Corruption	+22.0	Government Spending	-1.4	Labor Freedom	-0.4	Investment Freedom	-10.0
				Monetary Freedom	+4.0	Financial Freedom	+10.0

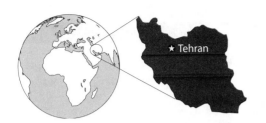
★ Tehran

IRAN

Economic Freedom Score

41.8

25   50   75

Least free 0   100 Most free

Iran's economic freedom score is 41.8, making its economy the 171st freest in the 2015 *Index*. Its score has increased by 1.5 points since last year, with improvements in five of the 10 economic freedoms, including labor freedom, the control of government spending, and monetary freedom, outweighing a decline in business freedom. Iran is ranked last out of 15 countries in the Middle East/North Africa region, and its overall score is well below the world and regional averages.

International isolation and a faltering domestic economy have undermined economic freedom in Iran. Over the past five years, its score has declined by 0.3 point, with losses concentrated in three of the 10 economic freedoms. In particular, rising business regulations have made it harder for entrepreneurs to do business. Capital flight and increased inflation due to currency devaluation also have affected the petroleum-dependent economy.

Weak rule of law and autarkic trade and investment policies have long undermined the foundations of economic freedom in Iran. Political and religious interference in judicial matters is common. All investment must be approved by the government and is limited to certain sectors. Small-business entrepreneurs struggle to register businesses or acquire capital.

BACKGROUND: Iran had one of the Middle East's most advanced economies before the 1979 Islamic revolution. Today, the economy is in shambles thanks to an agenda characterized by large subsidies to favored sectors, a bloated public sector, and high inflation. Corruption is another serious problem. Economic sanctions imposed by the U.S. and European Union in response to Iran's illicit nuclear weapons program have had devastating effects. Petroleum exports, which provide about 85 percent of government revenues, declined to about 1.5 million barrels per day in 2012 from about 2.5 million per day in 2011. President Hassan Rowhani, elected in June 2013, will find it difficult to revive the economy unless he can secure the removal of Western sanctions by negotiating a deal to curb Iran's nuclear program.

Freedom Trend

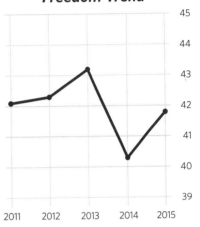

Country Comparisons

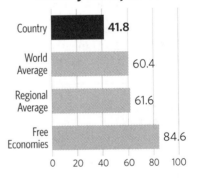

Country	41.8
World Average	60.4
Regional Average	61.6
Free Economies	84.6

0   20   40   60   80   100

Quick Facts

Population: 77.1 million
GDP (PPP): $945.5 billion
–1.7% growth in 2013
5-year compound annual growth 1.0%
$12,264 per capita
Unemployment: 13.2%
Inflation (CPI): 35.2%
FDI Inflow: $3.0 billion
Public Debt: 10.6% of GDP

2013 data unless otherwise noted.
Data compiled as of September 2014.

How Do We Measure Economic Freedom?
See page 475 for an explanation of the methodology or visit the *Index* Web site at *heritage.org/index.*

THE TEN ECONOMIC FREEDOMS

		Score	■ Country | World Average	Rank	1-Year Change
RULE OF LAW	Property Rights	10.0		165th	0
	Freedom from Corruption	25.0		149th	+1.6

Corruption is pervasive. The hard-line clerical establishment has gained great wealth through control of tax-exempt foundations that dominate many economic sectors. The government long ago abolished independent financial watchdogs. The judicial system is not independent; the supreme leader appoints the head of the judiciary, who in turn appoints senior judges. The government has confiscated property belonging to religious minorities.

		Score		Rank	1-Year Change
GOVERNMENT SIZE	Fiscal Freedom	81.2		72nd	+0.6
	Government Spending	93.0		6th	+7.1

Iran's top individual income tax rate is 35 percent, and its top corporate tax rate is 25 percent. Other taxes include a value-added tax and a property tax. The overall tax burden is equal to 5.9 percent of domestic output. Total government expenditures equal 15.3 percent of gross domestic product, and public debt is equivalent to 11 percent of GDP.

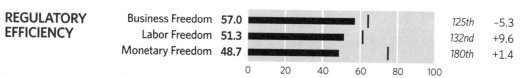

		Score		Rank	1-Year Change
REGULATORY EFFICIENCY	Business Freedom	57.0		125th	−5.3
	Labor Freedom	51.3		132nd	+9.6
	Monetary Freedom	48.7		180th	+1.4

Bureaucracy and a lack of transparency often make business formation and operation costly and burdensome. Business start-up is now more streamlined, but obtaining necessary licenses remains time-consuming. Labor regulations are rigid, and informal labor activity is substantial. In April 2014, Iran cut gasoline subsidies as part of a fiscal consolidation program; gas prices increased by 75 percent.

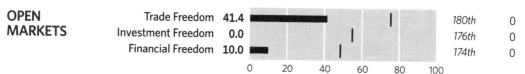

		Score		Rank	1-Year Change
OPEN MARKETS	Trade Freedom	41.4		180th	0
	Investment Freedom	0.0		176th	0
	Financial Freedom	10.0		174th	0

Iran's average tariff rate is 21.8 percent. Importing goods is time-consuming. The government reviews proposed foreign investment and maintains several sectoral restrictions. Iran's financial sector remains heavily affected by state interference. A small number of private banks operate under strict restrictions directed by the government. State-owned commercial banks and specialized financial institutions direct credit allocation.

Long-Term Score Change (since 1996)

RULE OF LAW		GOVERNMENT SIZE		REGULATORY EFFICIENCY		OPEN MARKETS	
Property Rights	0	Fiscal Freedom	+39.7	Business Freedom	+2.0	Trade Freedom	−3.6
Freedom from Corruption	+15.0	Government Spending	+0.9	Labor Freedom	−25.1	Investment Freedom	−10.0
				Monetary Freedom	−2.6	Financial Freedom	0

Baghdad

IRAQ

Economic Freedom Score

50
25   75

Least free 0
Most free 100

This economy is not graded

World Rank: Not Ranked   Regional Rank: Not Ranked

Iraq remains unranked in the 2015 *Index* because of the lack of sufficiently reliable data on economic freedom within the country. The Iraqi economy has slowly recovered from the hostilities that began in 2003, but much of this progress has been patchy or even reversed. The country faces worsening political and security challenges. Iraq was last graded in the 2002 *Index*, when it received an overall score of 15.6.

A higher degree of political instability and violence has plagued Iraq over the past year and undermined its reconstruction. Endowed with abundant oil wealth, the government has failed to address problems in economic freedom that hold back private-sector development and improvements in productivity.

Inefficient business regulations undermine the entrepreneurial environment, preventing the diversification of the economy away from oil production. Monetary and fiscal policies are poorly enforced, and the government has trouble maintaining proper bookkeeping or budgetary functions. Corruption is endemic and undermines the development of a dynamic private sector. Sectarian favoritism in government bureaucracies leads to arbitrary economic policies that favor particular groups.

BACKGROUND: Iraq grew increasingly unstable in 2013 due to the bloody comeback of radical Islamists in the form of the Islamic State in Iraq and Syria (ISIS), the successor to al-Qaeda in Iraq, which spearheaded a Sunni Arab revolt against Prime Minister Nuri al-Maliki's Shia-dominated coalition government. Maliki, whose party won the largest number of seats in the April 2014 parliamentary elections, alienated Iraq's Sunni Arabs and Kurds with a heavy-handed sectarian agenda. He stepped down in August in favor of Haider al-Abadi. The oil industry provides more than 90 percent of government revenue. Inadequate infrastructure, weak property rights, bureaucratic red tape, high unemployment, and widespread corruption continue to impede development.

Freedom Trend

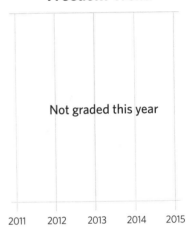

Not graded this year

2011   2012   2013   2014   2015

Country Comparisons

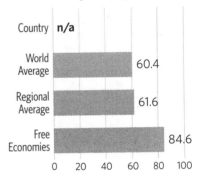

Country	n/a
World Average	60.4
Regional Average	61.6
Free Economies	84.6

0   20   40   60   80   100

Quick Facts

Population: 34.8 million
GDP (PPP): $257.0 billion
4.2% growth in 2013
5-year compound annual growth 7.2%
$7,391 per capita
Unemployment: 16.1%
Inflation (CPI): 1.9%
FDI Inflow: $2.9 billion
Public Debt: 31.3% of GDP

2013 data unless otherwise noted.
Data compiled as of September 2014.

How Do We Measure Economic Freedom?
See page 475 for an explanation of the methodology
or visit the *Index* Web site at *heritage.org/index.*

THE TEN ECONOMIC FREEDOMS

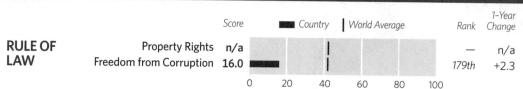

	Score		Rank	1-Year Change

RULE OF LAW

Property Rights — n/a — — — — n/a
Freedom from Corruption — 16.0 — 179th — +2.3

Until the Islamic State incursion in 2014, the Iraqi state, with its history of authoritarian and intrusive regimes, could be quite efficient at enforcing contracts, albeit through subjective legal processes. Post-ISIS, however, central government control has been weakened, and vested interests and corruption have increased. In such a political environment, property rights are not well protected.

GOVERNMENT SIZE

Fiscal Freedom — n/a — — — — n/a
Government Spending — 43.8 — 144th — +3.5

Iraq's individual and corporate income tax rates are 15 percent. Oil and gas companies pay a corporate tax of 35 percent. There are few other taxes. Taxation remains erratic and poorly enforced. Most government revenue comes from hydrocarbon rents. Government expenditures equal 43.3 percent of domestic output, and public debt is equivalent to 31 percent of gross domestic product.

REGULATORY EFFICIENCY

Business Freedom — 57.7 — 123rd — +0.8
Labor Freedom — 74.4 — 48th — +1.0
Monetary Freedom — 73.6 — 125th — +3.6

Before the ongoing security turmoil, the business environment, lacking transparency and efficiency, had improved only marginally. The labor market, which had already suffered from state interference and control, has been severely affected by the devastating conflicts. The government uses oil revenues to subsidize basic goods and services and maintains tight price controls on food and medicine.

OPEN MARKETS

Trade Freedom — n/a — — — — n/a
Investment Freedom — n/a — — — — n/a
Financial Freedom — n/a — — — — n/a

Iraq's legal and regulatory regime discourages the free flow of foreign trade and investment. The uncertain security environment also impedes international commerce. Inadequate supervision, political uncertainty, and a lack of security have severely undermined the financial system. Banks suffer from a lack of liquidity. The state has used banks to finance deficit spending and has required loans to state-owned enterprises.

Long-Term Score Change: n/a

RULE OF LAW		GOVERNMENT SIZE		REGULATORY EFFICIENCY		OPEN MARKETS	
Property Rights	**n/a**	Fiscal Freedom	**n/a**	Business Freedom	**n/a**	Trade Freedom	**n/a**
Freedom from Corruption		Government Spending	**n/a**	Labor Freedom	**n/a**	Investment Freedom	**n/a**
				Monetary Freedom	**n/a**	Financial Freedom	**n/a**

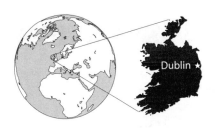

IRELAND

Economic Freedom Score

Least free 0 · 25 · 50 · 75 · 100 Most free

76.6

| World Rank: **9** | Regional Rank: **3** |

Ireland's economic freedom score is 76.6, making its economy the 9th freest in the 2015 *Index*. Its score is up by 0.4 point from last year, with a notable combined improvement in the management of government spending and monetary freedom outweighing declines in half of the 10 economic freedoms including property rights, labor freedom, and freedom from corruption. The Irish economy is ranked third out of 43 countries in the Europe region, and its score is far above the world and regional averages.

Two years of gains in economic freedom have not totally reversed losses earlier in the past half-decade. During that period, Ireland's economic freedom has declined by over 2.0 points, with ratings for freedom from corruption and business freedom recording the largest declines.

This erosion of economic freedom has undermined competitiveness and hindered economic recovery in a difficult external environment. Nonetheless, by adhering to its commitment to policies that sustain open markets and reducing the costs of a bloated public sector to restore fiscal soundness, Ireland has been able to reemerge as one of the world's 10 freest economies.

BACKGROUND: Prime Minister Enda Kenny's Fine Gael government was elected in February 2011. Ireland's modern, highly industrialized economy performed extraordinarily well throughout the 1990s and most of the next decade, encouraged by free-market policies that attracted investment capital. However, a speculative housing bubble burst in 2008 and generated a financial crisis. A 2010 National Recovery Plan was implemented after the government nationalized several banks, and Ireland accepted a $90 billion European Union–International Monetary Fund rescue package. The policy agenda aims to get the economy back on a solid footing by 2015. In February 2013, Ireland reached agreement with the European Central Bank to restructure loans and ease the debt burden incurred when the Anglo Irish Bank was nationalized in 2009. Ireland's economy was expected to grow in 2014, but the ratio of public debt to GDP remains very high.

Freedom Trend

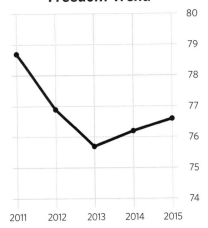

Country Comparisons

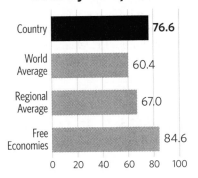

Country	76.6
World Average	60.4
Regional Average	67.0
Free Economies	84.6

Quick Facts

Population: 4.8 million
GDP (PPP): $188.9 billion
–0.3% growth in 2013
5-year compound annual growth –1.1%
$39,547 per capita
Unemployment: 13.6%
Inflation (CPI): 0.5%
FDI Inflow: $35.5 billion
Public Debt: 122.8% of GDP

2013 data unless otherwise noted.
Data compiled as of September 2014.

How Do We Measure Economic Freedom?
See page 475 for an explanation of the methodology
or visit the *Index* Web site at *heritage.org/index.*

251

THE TEN ECONOMIC FREEDOMS

		Score			Rank	1-Year Change
RULE OF LAW	Property Rights	85.0			19th	–5.0
	Freedom from Corruption	72.0			21st	–2.8

More than four-fifths of the Irish think that corruption is a major problem, according to a 2014 EU report. Corruption, including cronyism, political patronage, and illegal donations, is in fact a recurring issue. Nevertheless, contracts are secure, and expropriation is rare. Ireland's legal system is based on common law, and the judiciary is independent. Property rights are well protected.

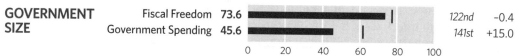

		Score			Rank	1-Year Change
GOVERNMENT SIZE	Fiscal Freedom	73.6			122nd	–0.4
	Government Spending	45.6			141st	+15.0

Ireland's top individual income tax rate is 41 percent, and its top corporate tax rate is 12.5 percent. Other taxes include a value-added tax and a capital gains tax. Total tax revenue is equivalent to 28.3 percent of domestic output. Government expenditures equal 42.6 percent of gross domestic product, and public debt corresponds to 123 percent of the size of the domestic economy.

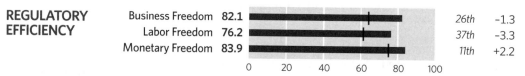

		Score			Rank	1-Year Change
REGULATORY EFFICIENCY	Business Freedom	82.1			26th	–1.3
	Labor Freedom	76.2			37th	–3.3
	Monetary Freedom	83.9			11th	+2.2

Launching a business takes four procedures and six days, and no minimum capital is required, but obtaining necessary permits takes 150 days on average. Relatively flexible hiring and dismissal regulations sustain an efficient labor market. Monetary stability has been relatively well maintained. Prices are generally set by market forces, but the government subsidizes some industries (e.g., wind energy).

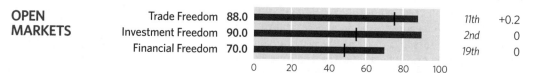

		Score			Rank	1-Year Change
OPEN MARKETS	Trade Freedom	88.0			11th	+0.2
	Investment Freedom	90.0			2nd	0
	Financial Freedom	70.0			19th	0

EU members have a 1.0 percent average tariff rate. Although some non-tariff barriers exist, the EU is relatively open to external trade. Ireland has few barriers to international trade and investment. Foreign and domestic investors are generally treated equally under the law. Massive recapitalization and restructuring since 2009 have changed the banking sector substantially. Major domestic banks have become almost fully nationalized.

Long-Term Score Change (since 1995)

RULE OF LAW		GOVERNMENT SIZE		REGULATORY EFFICIENCY		OPEN MARKETS	
Property Rights	–5.0	Fiscal Freedom	+24.5	Business Freedom	–2.9	Trade Freedom	+10.2
Freedom from Corruption	+22.0	Government Spending	+6.9	Labor Freedom	–2.0	Investment Freedom	+20.0
				Monetary Freedom	–2.2	Financial Freedom	0

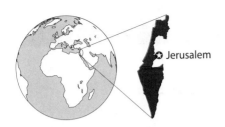
⊕ Jerusalem

ISRAEL

Economic Freedom Score

25   50   75

Least
free 0 .... 100 Most
free

70.5

I srael's economic freedom score is 70.5, making its econo-my the 33rd freest in the 2015 *Index*. Its overall score is 2.1 points better than last year, with improvements in six of the 10 economic freedoms, including the management of government spending, trade freedom, labor freedom, and fiscal freedom. Registering the 10th largest score increase in the 2015 *Index*, Israel has achieved its highest score ever. Israel is ranked 4th out of 15 countries in the Middle East/North Africa region, and its overall score is above the world and regional averages.

Broad, sustained improvements in property rights and the regulatory sectors over the past five years have propelled Israel into the ranks of the "mostly free" for the first time. Since 2011, economic freedom has advanced by 2.0 points, with scores advancing broadly in six of the 10 categories measured. Improvements in property rights and the regulatory environment have been the backbone of this advance.

A democratic and free-market bastion in the Middle East, Israel has entrenched the principles of economic freedom during its development. A small, open economy, Israel relies on its competitive regulatory environment and well-established rule of law to attract international investment. While government spending is sizeable, the government has not interfered heavily with industrial activity.

BACKGROUND: Israel gained independence in 1948, and its vibrant democracy remains unique in the region. Prime Minister Benjamin Netanyahu, re-elected in January 2013, leads a right-of-center coalition government. Israel has developed a modern market economy with a thriving high-technology sector that attracts considerable foreign investment because of reliable property rights. The recent discovery of large offshore natural gas deposits has improved Israel's energy security and balance-of-payments prospects. Despite the 2006 war against Hezbollah in Lebanon and the 2008–2009, 2012, and 2014 wars against Hamas in Gaza, and despite the constant threat of terrorism, Israel's economy remains fundamentally sound, growing by over 3 percent in 2013.

Freedom Trend

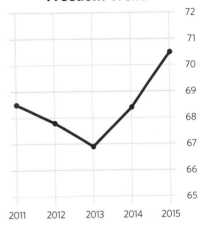

2011   2012   2013   2014   2015

Country Comparisons

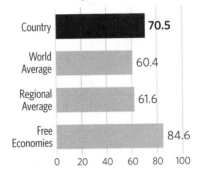

Country — 70.5
World Average — 60.4
Regional Average — 61.6
Free Economies — 84.6

0   20   40   60   80   100

Quick Facts

Population: 7.9 million
GDP (PPP): $273.7 billion
3.3% growth in 2013
5-year compound annual growth 3.6%
$34,770 per capita
Unemployment: 6.7%
Inflation (CPI): 1.5%
FDI Inflow: $11.8 billion
Public Debt: 66.7% of GDP

2013 data unless otherwise noted.
Data compiled as of September 2014.

How Do We Measure Economic Freedom?
See page 475 for an explanation of the methodology
or visit the *Index* Web site at *heritage.org/index*.

THE TEN ECONOMIC FREEDOMS

		Score		Rank	1-Year Change
RULE OF LAW	Property Rights	75.0		25th	0
	Freedom from Corruption	61.0		35th	+1.7

Fairly frequent high-level corruption investigations (e.g., leading to the 2014 bribery conviction of a former prime minister), coupled with a strong societal intolerance for graft, have led to a governance environment with relatively low levels of corruption. Israel has a modern and independent legal system that provides effective means for enforcing property and contractual rights.

		Score		Rank	1-Year Change
GOVERNMENT SIZE	Fiscal Freedom	61.9		164th	+1.8
	Government Spending	47.8		136th	+7.5

The top individual income tax rate is 48 percent, and the top corporate tax rate is now 26.5 percent. Other taxes include a value-added tax and a capital gains tax. The overall tax burden is equivalent to 28.3 percent of domestic production. Government expenditures equal 41.7 percent of domestic output, and public debt equals 67 percent of gross domestic product.

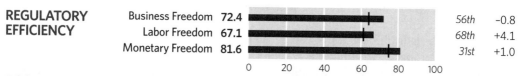

		Score		Rank	1-Year Change
REGULATORY EFFICIENCY	Business Freedom	72.4		56th	−0.8
	Labor Freedom	67.1		68th	+4.1
	Monetary Freedom	81.6		31st	+1.0

With no minimum capital requirement, incorporating a business takes five procedures, but completing licensing requirements takes over 200 days on average. The labor market remains relatively flexible, and labor costs are moderate. Prices are generally set by market forces, but the government controls food prices and subsidizes some political priorities (e.g., West Bank settlement housing and green energy initiatives).

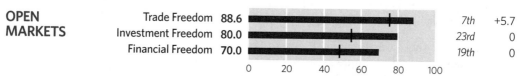

		Score		Rank	1-Year Change
OPEN MARKETS	Trade Freedom	88.6		7th	+5.7
	Investment Freedom	80.0		23rd	0
	Financial Freedom	70.0		19th	0

Israel's average tariff rate is 0.7 percent. The government has worked to facilitate trade. It maintains some sectoral restrictions on foreign investment but generally welcomes investment. The evolving financial system, dominated by banks, functions without undue government influence. Credit is allocated on market terms, and relatively sound regulation and supervision assure free flows of financial resources.

Long-Term Score Change (since 1995)

RULE OF LAW		GOVERNMENT SIZE		REGULATORY EFFICIENCY		OPEN MARKETS	
Property Rights	+5.0	Fiscal Freedom	+17.1	Business Freedom	−12.6	Trade Freedom	+8.2
Freedom from Corruption	+31.0	Government Spending	+17.8	Labor Freedom	+2.9	Investment Freedom	−10.0
				Monetary Freedom	+8.4	Financial Freedom	+20.0

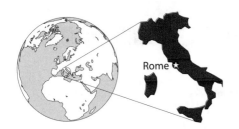

Rome ★

ITALY

Economic Freedom Score

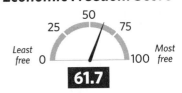

25 **50** 75

Least free 0   100 Most free

61.7

Italy's economic freedom score is 61.7, making its economy the 80th freest in the 2015 *Index*. Its overall score has increased by 0.8 point since last year, with improvements in five of the 10 economic freedoms, including property rights, freedom from corruption, labor freedom, and monetary freedom, outweighing declines in business freedom, management of government spending, and fiscal freedom. Italy is ranked 34th out of 43 countries in the Europe region, and its score is above the world average but below the regional average.

Despite the eurozone's challenging economic environment, economic freedom in Italy has advanced by 1.4 points since 2011, maintaining the country's "moderately free" rating. Medium-term gains have occurred in only three of the 10 economic freedoms but have been enough to advance Italy's overall score. Improvements in labor and investment freedom have led sectoral gains.

However, more substantial reforms are needed. A rigid labor market delays hiring and firing, causing supply and demand mismatches. Government spending that consumes about 50 percent of the domestic economy crowds out productive investment. Growth is hindered by a property rights regime and rule of law that are weakly established by European standards.

BACKGROUND: After a February 2013 general election that produced no clear winner, center-left Democratic Party leader Enrico Letta was chosen to form a government and serve as prime minister. A year later, former Florence mayor Matteo Renzi won 80 percent of the vote to become Italy's youngest prime minister ever. He leads a coalition government consisting of the center-left Democratic Party, the center-right People of Freedom Party led by former Prime Minister Silvio Berlusconi, and the centrist Civic Choice Party. Renzi has pledged to reform entitlements, taxes, and labor laws, and he remains broadly popular. Italy has an immense public debt, entrenched organized crime, a large informal sector, and high unemployment, particularly among the young. The North is industrialized and prosperous, while the South is less developed.

Freedom Trend

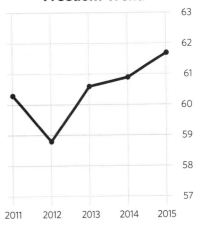

2011   2012   2013   2014   2015

Country Comparisons

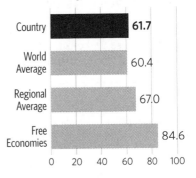

Country	61.7
World Average	60.4
Regional Average	67.0
Free Economies	84.6

0   20   40   60   80   100

Quick Facts

Population: 59.7 million
GDP (PPP): $1.8 trillion
–1.9% growth in 2013
5-year compound annual growth –1.5%
$30,289 per capita
Unemployment: 12.2%
Inflation (CPI): 1.3%
FDI Inflow: $16.5 billion
Public Debt: 132.5% of GDP

2013 data unless otherwise noted.
Data compiled as of September 2014.

How Do We Measure Economic Freedom?
See page 475 for an explanation of the methodology or visit the *Index* Web site at *heritage.org/index*.

THE TEN ECONOMIC FREEDOMS

		Score		Rank	1-Year Change
■■ Country	| World Average				

RULE OF LAW
Property Rights 55.0 — 50th +5.0
Freedom from Corruption 43.0 — 69th +4.5

Former Prime Minister Berlusconi's expulsion from parliament late in 2013 following his conviction for tax fraud led to the election in 2014 of a new government pledged to fight corruption. The legal system, however, remains vulnerable to political interference. Property rights and contracts are secure, but court procedures are extremely slow. Protection of intellectual property is below EU norms.

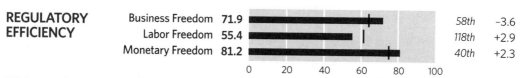

GOVERNMENT SIZE
Fiscal Freedom 54.2 — 171st −1.3
Government Spending 23.2 — 169th −2.4

The top individual income tax rate is 43 percent, and the top corporate tax rate is 27.5 percent. Other taxes include a value-added tax and an inheritance tax. The total tax burden equals 44.4 percent of domestic production, and government expenditures account for 50.6 percent of domestic output. Public debt remains high at 133 percent of GDP, but sovereign financing concerns have abated.

REGULATORY EFFICIENCY
Business Freedom 71.9 — 58th −3.6
Labor Freedom 55.4 — 118th +2.9
Monetary Freedom 81.2 — 40th +2.3

With no minimum capital required, business formation takes only five procedures, but burdensome licensing requirements require over three months on average, discouraging dynamic entrepreneurial growth. The labor market remains stagnant. The rigid labor code hurts competitiveness and employment prospects. Monetary stability has been relatively well maintained, and the government has reduced subsidies for renewable energy.

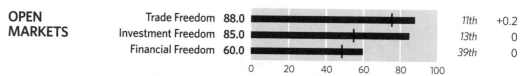

OPEN MARKETS
Trade Freedom 88.0 — 11th +0.2
Investment Freedom 85.0 — 13th 0
Financial Freedom 60.0 — 39th 0

EU members have a 1.0 percent average tariff rate. Although some non-tariff barriers exist, the EU is relatively open to external trade. Foreign and domestic investments are generally treated equally under Italian law. The financial system, dominated by banks, remains vulnerable to state interference. There are about 700 banks. Nonperforming loans have increased considerably since 2007.

Long-Term Score Change (since 1995)

RULE OF LAW		GOVERNMENT SIZE		REGULATORY EFFICIENCY		OPEN MARKETS	
Property Rights	−15.0	Fiscal Freedom	+10.6	Business Freedom	−13.1	Trade Freedom	+10.2
Freedom from Corruption	−27.0	Government Spending	+19.6	Labor Freedom	−19.1	Investment Freedom	+15.0
				Monetary Freedom	+0.1	Financial Freedom	+10.0

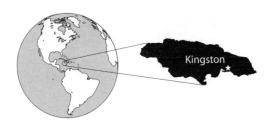

JAMAICA

Economic Freedom Score

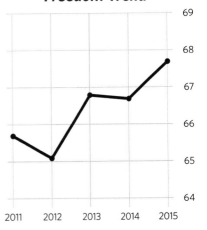

Least free 0

Most free 100

67.7

| World Rank: **48** | Regional Rank: **9** |

J amaica's economic freedom score is 67.7, making its economy the 48th freest in the 2015 *Index*. Its score has increased by 1.0 point since last year, reflecting gains in five of the 10 economic freedoms, including freedom from corruption, fiscal freedom, and the management of government spending, that outweigh a decline in monetary freedom. Jamaica ranks 9th out of 29 countries in the South and Central America/ Caribbean region.

Action to correct terms of trade issues and poor fiscal policy has helped Jamaica to improve its overall economic freedom score over the past five years. Since 2011, economic freedom on the island has improved by 2.0 points, led by advances in five of the 10 economic freedoms including freedom from corruption, the management of government spending, and fiscal freedom. In the 2015 *Index*, Jamaica has achieved its highest economic freedom score ever.

However, the foundations of economic freedom in Jamaica are still weak. Corruption is common, and the rule of law is weakly enforced. Violence related to the drug trade has been prevalent. Jamaica scores only about average on trade and financial freedom, a serious problem for an island nation dependent on imports for basic goods and fuel.

BACKGROUND: Prime Minister Portia Simpson-Miller's People's National Party was re-elected in December 2011 with a large parliamentary majority. Simpson-Miller has maintained market-friendly policies, but high interest rates and government debt burden the economy. A $1.27 billion standby agreement with the International Monetary Fund signed in 2010 required a commitment to major fiscal reforms that have been slow to materialize. An extended IMF agreement was approved in 2013. Most foreign exchange comes from remittances, tourism, and bauxite production, all of which declined sharply during the 2009 recession and have not recovered. Unemployment remains high, particularly in the formal sector. Services account for more than 60 percent of GDP. Jamaica is a member of the Venezuela-led Petrocaribe oil alliance.

Freedom Trend

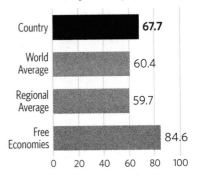

Country Comparisons

Country	67.7
World Average	60.4
Regional Average	59.7
Free Economies	84.6

Quick Facts

Population: 2.8 million
GDP (PPP): $25.2 billion
0.5% growth in 2013
5-year compound annual growth –0.7%
$9,048 per capita
Unemployment: 15.0%
Inflation (CPI): 9.4%
FDI Inflow: $567.1 million
Public Debt: 138.9% of GDP

2013 data unless otherwise noted.
Data compiled as of September 2014.

How Do We Measure Economic Freedom?
See page 475 for an explanation of the methodology
or visit the *Index* Web site at *heritage.org/index*.

THE TEN ECONOMIC FREEDOMS

	Score		Rank	1-Year Change
RULE OF LAW	Property Rights	40.0	70th	0
	Freedom from Corruption	38.0	83rd	+5.0

Jamaicans see corruption as a root cause of their high crime rate. The government has yet to send a strong signal against corruption. In May 2014, a license to a Hong Kong–based company for a major power project was revoked amid allegations of improper handling of the tender process. The inefficient legal system weakens property rights and the rule of law.

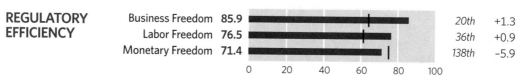

GOVERNMENT SIZE	Fiscal Freedom	81.5	67th	+4.3
	Government Spending	73.2	76th	+3.8

Jamaica's top individual income tax rate is 25 percent, and its corporate tax rate is down to 25 percent from 33.3 percent. Other taxes include a property transfer tax and a general consumption tax. Overall tax revenue equals 24.4 percent of domestic income. Government expenditures equal 29.9 percent of domestic production, and public debt is equivalent to 139 percent of gross domestic product.

REGULATORY EFFICIENCY	Business Freedom	85.9	20th	+1.3
	Labor Freedom	76.5	36th	+0.9
	Monetary Freedom	71.4	138th	-5.9

With no minimum capital required, the business start-up process takes only two procedures. However, completing licensing requirements continues to be time-consuming, taking over four months on average. Inefficiencies in the labor market continue to cause chronically high unemployment and underemployment. Most prices are set by the market, but the government regulates the prices of several goods and services.

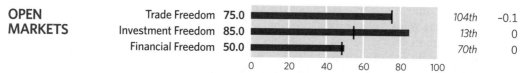

OPEN MARKETS	Trade Freedom	75.0	104th	-0.1
	Investment Freedom	85.0	13th	0
	Financial Freedom	50.0	70th	0

Jamaica's average tariff rate is 7.5 percent. Tariffs are an important source of government revenue. Some imports require a license. The government does not automatically screen foreign investment. The banking sector is diversified, providing a wide range of financial services. Incorporating new provisions related to the evolving financial system, the Banking Services Act was approved in June 2014.

Long-Term Score Change (since 1995)

RULE OF LAW		GOVERNMENT SIZE		REGULATORY EFFICIENCY		OPEN MARKETS	
Property Rights	-10.0	Fiscal Freedom	+4.0	Business Freedom	+15.9	Trade Freedom	+10.0
Freedom from Corruption	-12.0	Government Spending	-3.3	Labor Freedom	+8.1	Investment Freedom	+15.0
				Monetary Freedom	+20.5	Financial Freedom	-20.0

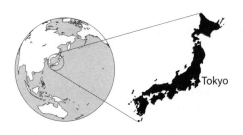

JAPAN

Economic Freedom Score

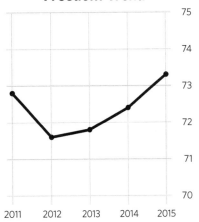

73.3

World Rank: 20　　　　　　**Regional Rank: 6**

Japan's economic freedom score is 73.3, making its economy the 20th freest in the 2015 *Index*. Its score has increased by 0.9 point since last year, with improvements in labor freedom, business freedom, and trade freedom outweighing modest declines in freedom from corruption, monetary freedom, and fiscal freedom. Japan is ranked 6th out of 41 countries in the Asia–Pacific region, and its overall score is above the world and regional averages.

Over the past five years, Japan's economic freedom has experienced a turnaround, with early losses overcome by recent gains. In particular, improvements in labor and trade freedom have contributed to overall score gains.

While the government's three arrows of reform have generated substantial enthusiasm, key structural issues continue to hold back economic freedom and growth. Government spending has been high, and deficit spending most recently has been funded by a multi-year increase in the sales tax. The financial sector is difficult for foreign investors and subject to political influence. Propelling Japan out of its decades-long malaise will require targeted reforms to improve economic freedom and remove institutional constraints.

BACKGROUND: Prime Minister Shinzo Abe's Liberal Democratic Party has held power since 2012. Abe has reversed a 13-year trend of steadily decreasing defense spending, pushed forward on collective self-defense, and stood up to Chinese assertiveness near the Japanese-controlled Senkaku Islands. But his revisionist comments on Japan's wartime actions, a visit to the controversial Yasukuni Shrine, and his unwillingness to discipline politicians for making provocative and egregious comments have hindered his ability to achieve international support for defense reform that would allow Japan a larger regional role. Abe has taken preliminary steps toward structural economic reform as part of his "Abenomics" plan to pull Japan from a two-decade economic slump, but he faces resistance from entrenched special interests. Japan is a significant force in world trade, but its economy continues to operate far below its potential.

Freedom Trend

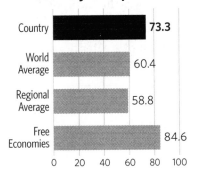

Country Comparisons

Country	73.3
World Average	60.4
Regional Average	58.8
Free Economies	84.6

Quick Facts

Population: 127.3 million
GDP (PPP): $4.7 trillion
1.5% growth in 2013
5-year compound annual growth 0.3%
$36,899 per capita
Unemployment: 4.1%
Inflation (CPI): 0.4%
FDI Inflow: $2.3 billion
Public Debt: 243.2% of GDP

2013 data unless otherwise noted.
Data compiled as of September 2014.

How Do We Measure Economic Freedom?
See page 475 for an explanation of the methodology
or visit the *Index* Web site at *heritage.org/index*.

THE TEN ECONOMIC FREEDOMS

		Score	Rank	1-Year Change
RULE OF LAW	Property Rights	80.0	20th	0
	Freedom from Corruption	74.0	18th	-3.8

While the direct exchange of cash for favors from government officials is extremely rare in Japan, a web of close relationships among companies, politicians, government agencies, and other groups fosters an inwardly cooperative business climate conducive to corruption, most often the rigging of bids on government public works projects. The judiciary is independent and provides secure protection of real and intellectual property.

		Score	Rank	1-Year Change
GOVERNMENT SIZE	Fiscal Freedom	68.7	144th	-0.5
	Government Spending	47.1	137th	0

The top individual income tax rate is 40.8 percent, and the top corporate tax rate is 25.5 percent (28.05 percent with a fiscal surtax). The government plans to increase the sales tax to 10 percent by 2015. The overall tax burden amounts to 28.6 percent of domestic output, and public spending is equivalent to about 42 percent of domestic production. Public debt exceeds twice the size of the economy.

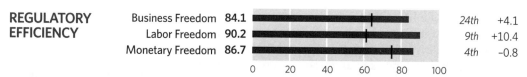

		Score	Rank	1-Year Change
REGULATORY EFFICIENCY	Business Freedom	84.1	24th	+4.1
	Labor Freedom	90.2	9th	+10.4
	Monetary Freedom	86.7	4th	-0.8

The process for incorporating a business is relatively streamlined, but entrepreneurial growth is discouraged by unaddressed structural problems. The labor market is well functioning, but a propensity for lifetime employment guarantees and seniority-based wages impedes the development of greater flexibility. Prices are generally set by market forces, but the government subsidizes numerous industries and sectors.

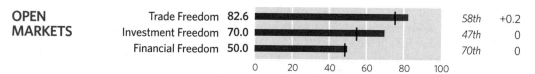

		Score	Rank	1-Year Change
OPEN MARKETS	Trade Freedom	82.6	58th	+0.2
	Investment Freedom	70.0	47th	0
	Financial Freedom	50.0	70th	0

Japan has a 1.2 percent average tariff rate. Imports and foreign direct investment are low relative to GDP, and agricultural imports face significant barriers. Investment in some economic sectors may be screened. The financial sector is competitive but vulnerable to political influence. The government retains considerable shares in the banking sector, which includes 100 percent ownership in Japan Post Holding as of 2014.

Long-Term Score Change (since 1995)

RULE OF LAW		GOVERNMENT SIZE		REGULATORY EFFICIENCY		OPEN MARKETS	
Property Rights	-10.0	Fiscal Freedom	+15.1	Business Freedom	-0.9	Trade Freedom	+0.6
Freedom from Corruption	-16.0	Government Spending	-20.6	Labor Freedom	+6.9	Investment Freedom	+20.0
				Monetary Freedom	-0.3	Financial Freedom	-20.0

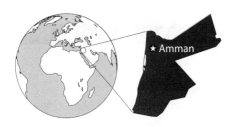 ★ Amman

JORDAN

Economic Freedom Score

Least free 0   100 Most free

69.3

Jordan's economic freedom score is 69.3, making its economy the 38th freest in the 2015 *Index*. Its score is essentially unchanged from last year, with a change of 0.1 point reflecting improvements in the management of government spending and labor freedom that are largely counterbalanced by declines in business freedom, monetary freedom, and freedom from corruption. Jordan is ranked 5th out of 15 countries in the Middle East/North Africa region, and its overall score continues to be well above the world and regional averages.

Steady improvement in economic freedom in the early half of the past decade has tapered off in recent years. Over the past five years, Jordan's economic freedom has advanced by just 0.4 point, primarily due to a deteriorating regulatory environment and an increased level of perceived corruption that offset gains in the control of government spending and property rights.

Despite challenges, economic freedom in Jordan continues its gradual advance, and the economy has moved closer to the "mostly free" category. Jordan is relatively open to global investment and trade. Property rights are generally respected, but improvements are needed to combat corruption and reinforce the judiciary's independence.

BACKGROUND: Jordan is a constitutional monarchy with relatively few natural resources. Foreign loans, international aid, and remittances from expatriate workers support the economy. In 2011, King Abdullah responded to "Arab Spring" demonstrations by dismissing his cabinet and ceding greater authority to the judiciary and parliament. The government also implemented two economic relief packages and a supplementary budget to subsidize the middle class and the poor. In 2000, Jordan joined the World Trade Organization and signed a free trade agreement with the United States; in 2001, it signed an association agreement with the European Union. Jordan negotiated a $2.1 billion standby arrangement with the International Monetary Fund in 2012 to finance its budgetary and balance-of-payments deficits. The presence of more than 600,000 Syrian refugees causes serious administrative and resource problems.

Freedom Trend

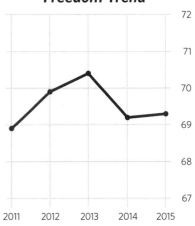

Country Comparisons

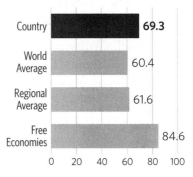

Country	69.3
World Average	60.4
Regional Average	61.6
Free Economies	84.6

Quick Facts

Population: 6.5 million
GDP (PPP): $40.0 billion
3.3% growth in 2013
5-year compound annual growth 3.2%
$6,115 per capita
Unemployment: 12.6%
Inflation (CPI): 5.5%
FDI Inflow: $1.8 billion
Public Debt: 87.7% of GDP

2013 data unless otherwise noted.
Data compiled as of September 2014.

How Do We Measure Economic Freedom?
See page 475 for an explanation of the methodology
or visit the *Index* Web site at *heritage.org/index*.

THE TEN ECONOMIC FREEDOMS

		Score	■ Country	| World Average	Rank	1-Year Change
RULE OF LAW	Property Rights	60.0			41st	0
	Freedom from Corruption	45.0			66th	−0.6

As in most Middle-Eastern states, *wasta* (the use of family, business, and other personal connections to advance one's interests) is endemic in Jordan. Officials are sometimes influenced in government procurement processes and in dispute settlement. Anti-corruption efforts have yielded mixed results. Property rights are respected for the most part. The judiciary is generally independent, but the king is the ultimate authority.

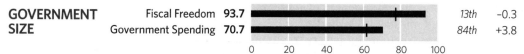

		Score		Rank	1-Year Change
GOVERNMENT SIZE	Fiscal Freedom	93.7		13th	−0.3
	Government Spending	70.7		84th	+3.8

The top individual and corporate income tax rates are 14 percent. Other taxes include a value-added tax and a property tax. The overall tax burden is equal to 15.3 percent of domestic production. Public expenditures are equivalent to 31.2 percent of gross domestic product, and public debt corresponds to about 88 percent of domestic output.

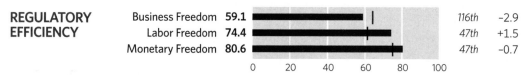

		Score		Rank	1-Year Change
REGULATORY EFFICIENCY	Business Freedom	59.1		116th	−2.9
	Labor Freedom	74.4		47th	+1.5
	Monetary Freedom	80.6		47th	−0.7

Incorporating a business takes seven procedures, and no minimum capital is required, but completing licensing requirements takes about two months. The labor market remains rigid, and the public sector employs much of the labor force. The government, facing budget deficits, plans to eliminate electricity subsidies by 2017 and has increased prices for fuel, but it has increased agricultural subsidies.

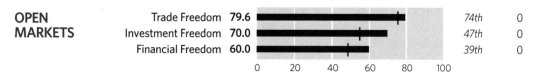

		Score		Rank	1-Year Change
OPEN MARKETS	Trade Freedom	79.6		74th	0
	Investment Freedom	70.0		47th	0
	Financial Freedom	60.0		39th	0

Jordan has a 5.2 percent average tariff rate. Imports of agricultural products may be subject to licensing requirements. The Jordan Investment Board reviews new investments. Despite a challenging economic environment and ongoing uncertainty stemming from regional security turmoil, banking remains resilient and well capitalized. There are 26 banks in operation, and the capital market continues to develop.

Long-Term Score Change (since 1995)

RULE OF LAW		GOVERNMENT SIZE		REGULATORY EFFICIENCY		OPEN MARKETS	
Property Rights	−10.0	Fiscal Freedom	+47.1	Business Freedom	−10.9	Trade Freedom	+20.4
Freedom from Corruption	+15.0	Government Spending	+0.1	Labor Freedom	+0.5	Investment Freedom	0
				Monetary Freedom	+3.1	Financial Freedom	−10.0

KAZAKHSTAN

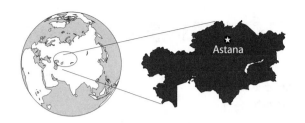

Astana

World Rank: 69 **Regional Rank: 11**

Economic Freedom Score

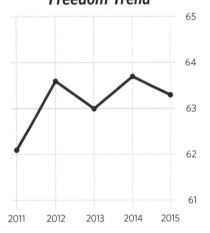

25   50   75

Least free 0   100 Most free

63.3

Kazakhstan's economic freedom score is 63.3, making its economy the 69th freest in the 2015 *Index*. Its score has decreased by 0.4 point since last year, with declines in property rights and business freedom outweighing a modest combined improvement in half of the 10 economic freedoms, including trade freedom, labor freedom, and freedom from corruption. Kazakhstan ranks 11th out of 42 countries in the Asia–Pacific region, and its overall score is above the world and regional averages.

With strong fiscal restraint, low taxes, and stabilizing monetary policy, Kazakhstan has made steady gains in economic freedom. Over the past five years, its *Index* score has advanced by 1.2 points with improvements in fiscal freedom, government spending, monetary freedom, and investment freedom.

Kazakhstan's transition to a market-led economy has been steady, but further reforms are necessary to solidify past gains. Its overall investment and trade regime remains relatively closed to foreign investors compared to regional and global peers. The judiciary lacks statutory independence and is subservient to the executive branch. Corruption is prevalent and reaches into all branches of government.

BACKGROUND: In May 2014, Kazakhstan signed a treaty with Russia and Belarus to bring the Eurasian Economic Union into being on January 1, 2015. The EEU will have a GDP of $2.7 trillion and a population of 170 million. President Nursultan Nazarbayev, whose rule began in 1989 when Kazakhstan was still a Soviet republic, won a fifth five-year term in 2011 and is likely to stay in power until at least the end of his term in 2016. The opposition is marginalized, and the lack of a succession plan creates longer-term political uncertainty. Production in the giant Kashagan oil field off the northern shore of the Caspian Sea is expected to begin by 2016 and could help Kazakhstan extract 3 million barrels per day by 2030. Kazakhstan is also the world's largest producer of uranium.

Freedom Trend

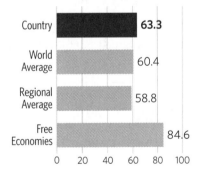

65

64

63

62

61

2011   2012   2013   2014   2015

Country Comparisons

Country	63.3
World Average	60.4
Regional Average	58.8
Free Economies	84.6

0   20   40   60   80   100

Quick Facts

Population: 17.2 million
GDP (PPP): $246.9 billion
6.0% growth in 2013
5-year compound annual growth 5.4%
$14,391 per capita
Unemployment: 5.2%
Inflation (CPI): 5.8%
FDI Inflow: $9.7 billion
Public Debt: 13.5% of GDP

2013 data unless otherwise noted.
Data compiled as of September 2014.

How Do We Measure Economic Freedom?
See page 475 for an explanation of the methodology or visit the *Index* Web site at *heritage.org/index*.

THE TEN ECONOMIC FREEDOMS

		Score		Rank	1-Year Change

RULE OF LAW

	Score	Rank	1-Year Change
Property Rights	25.0	124th	–5.0
Freedom from Corruption	26.0	145th	+0.3

Corruption pervades public services, the judiciary, the security forces, and the economy generally. It also contributes to capital flight. Kazakhstan fell by seven places in the 2013 Corruption Perceptions Index, ranking just 140th out of 177 countries. New procedures were introduced in 2014 to expedite property transfers and registration, but courts lack the capacity to protect property rights effectively.

GOVERNMENT SIZE

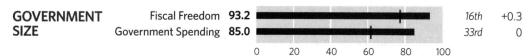

	Score	Rank	1-Year Change
Fiscal Freedom	93.2	16th	+0.3
Government Spending	85.0	33rd	0

The top individual income tax rate is 10 percent, and the top corporate tax rate is 20 percent. Other taxes include a value-added tax and excise taxes. Overall tax revenues equal 13.5 percent of domestic production. Oil revenues contribute to public expenditures that total 22.4 percent of domestic output. Public debt equals approximately 14 percent of gross domestic product.

REGULATORY EFFICIENCY

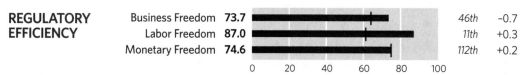

	Score	Rank	1-Year Change
Business Freedom	73.7	46th	–0.7
Labor Freedom	87.0	11th	+0.3
Monetary Freedom	74.6	112th	+0.2

No minimum capital is required to start a company, which takes six procedures and 10 days, but obtaining necessary operating permits requires over five months on average. The labor market needs more flexibility to accommodate rapid economic transformation. Monetary stability is well maintained, but the government subsidizes agriculture and imposes price controls on fuel.

OPEN MARKETS

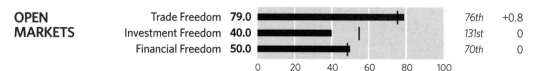

	Score	Rank	1-Year Change
Trade Freedom	79.0	76th	+0.8
Investment Freedom	40.0	131st	0
Financial Freedom	50.0	70th	0

Kazakhstan's average tariff rate is 3.0 percent. Kazakhstan is working to join the WTO, but nontariff barriers impede imports of agricultural products. Government procurement processes can favor domestic firms. Foreign investors may not purchase agricultural land. The financial sector is dominated by banks in which the government holds considerable ownership. Nonperforming loans account for over 30 percent of total assets.

Long-Term Score Change (since 1998)

RULE OF LAW		GOVERNMENT SIZE		REGULATORY EFFICIENCY		OPEN MARKETS	
Property Rights	–5.0	Fiscal Freedom	+19.9	Business Freedom	+18.7	Trade Freedom	+18.0
Freedom from Corruption	+16.0	Government Spending	–0.7	Labor Freedom	+4.4	Investment Freedom	+10.0
				Monetary Freedom	+74.6	Financial Freedom	+20.0

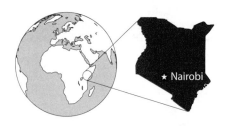

KENYA

Economic Freedom Score

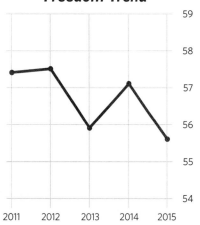

55.6

Least free 0

Most free 100

World Rank: 122   **Regional Rank: 23**

Kenya's economic freedom score is 55.6, making its economy the 122nd freest in the 2015 *Index*. Its score is down by 1.5 points from last year, with an improvement in freedom from corruption outweighed by declines in five of the 10 economic freedoms, including trade freedom, business freedom, and the control of government spending. Kenya is ranked 23rd out of 46 countries in the Sub-Saharan Africa region, and its overall score is just above the regional average.

Over the past half-decade, Kenya's economic freedom score has declined by 1.8 points, pushing the economy further down into the ranks of the "mostly unfree." Declines in four of the 10 economic freedoms include alarming deteriorations in business and trade freedom that could threaten local entrepreneurs and Kenya's integration into global trading networks.

Kenya ranks higher than the global average in just three of the 10 economic freedoms. Property rights are poorly protected, much of the population lacks land titles, and corruption throughout all levels of government undermines basic procurement of government services.

BACKGROUND: In March 2013, Uhuru Kenyatta won the first presidential election under the 2010 constitution. Both he and running mate William Ruto have faced International Criminal Court charges of crimes against humanity related to post-election violence in 2007. In November 2011, Kenya launched a military incursion into Somalia in response to terrorist activity and kidnappings by Somalia's al-Shabaab. Kenya joined the African Union peacekeeping mission in Somalia in 2012. In September 2013, al-Shabaab terrorists attacked a Nairobi mall, killing 67 people. In April 2014, Kenya and several other East African states agreed to send troops to South Sudan. There has been a moderate economic recovery since the 2007–2008 ethnic clashes, but poor infrastructure, systemic corruption, high unemployment, and a lack of public security undermine economic development. A $25.5 billion trade corridor in the port of Lamu is scheduled for completion by 2017.

Freedom Trend

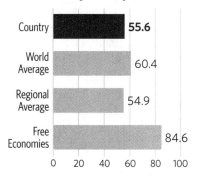

Country Comparisons

Country	55.6
World Average	60.4
Regional Average	54.9
Free Economies	84.6

Quick Facts

Population: 44.4 million
GDP (PPP): $80.4 billion
5.6% growth in 2013
5-year compound annual growth 4.6%
$1,812 per capita
Unemployment: 9.2%
Inflation (CPI): 5.7%
FDI Inflow: $514.4 million
Public Debt: 50.5% of GDP

2013 data unless otherwise noted.
Data compiled as of September 2014.

How Do We Measure Economic Freedom?
See page 475 for an explanation of the methodology or visit the *Index* Web site at *heritage.org/index*.

THE TEN ECONOMIC FREEDOMS

		Score	Country	World Average	Rank	1-Year Change
RULE OF LAW	Property Rights	30.0			94th	0
	Freedom from Corruption	27.0			141st	+6.0

Corruption is a serious problem. The 2010 constitution increased transparency and the independence of the judiciary, but no top officials have been prosecuted successfully. In 2013, the head of the state anti-corruption agency was charged with corruption, and an IMF request to publicize agreements between the government and mining corporations was rejected. The lower courts remain understaffed, underfinanced, and slow.

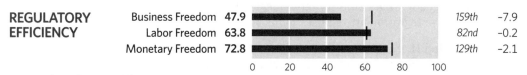

		Score			Rank	1-Year Change
GOVERNMENT SIZE	Fiscal Freedom	78.0			103rd	0
	Government Spending	72.1			78th	-2.5

The top individual and corporate income tax rates are 30 percent. Other taxes include a value-added tax and a tax on interest. Total tax revenues are equivalent to 20.1 percent of gross domestic product. Government expenditures equal 30.5 percent of Kenya's GDP, and government debt is equal to 50 percent of annual output.

		Score			Rank	1-Year Change
REGULATORY EFFICIENCY	Business Freedom	47.9			159th	-7.9
	Labor Freedom	63.8			82nd	-0.2
	Monetary Freedom	72.8			129th	-2.1

Implementation of reforms to enhance regulatory efficiency has been uneven. Launching a firm still takes 10 procedures and 30 days, and completing licensing requirements takes a month. The public sector is the main source of employment, and the informal economy employs much of the labor force. The government still regulates prices through subsidies, agricultural marketing boards, and state-owned enterprises.

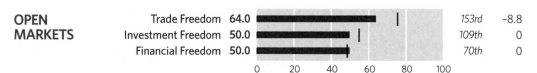

		Score			Rank	1-Year Change
OPEN MARKETS	Trade Freedom	64.0			153rd	-8.8
	Investment Freedom	50.0			109th	0
	Financial Freedom	50.0			70th	0

Kenya's average tariff rate is 10.5 percent. Efforts to facilitate trade through customs improvements are underway with other members of the East African Community. Foreign investors face regulatory hurdles. The state still owns or holds shares in several domestic financial institutions and continues to influence the allocation of credit. Financial inclusion has increased through mobile banking.

Long-Term Score Change (since 1995)

RULE OF LAW		GOVERNMENT SIZE		REGULATORY EFFICIENCY		OPEN MARKETS	
Property Rights	-20.0	Fiscal Freedom	+10.0	Business Freedom	-7.1	Trade Freedom	+10.4
Freedom from Corruption	-23.0	Government Spending	+9.1	Labor Freedom	+4.4	Investment Freedom	0
				Monetary Freedom	+22.4	Financial Freedom	0

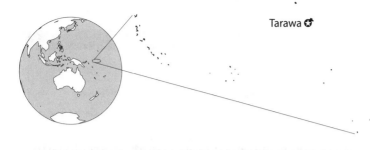

Tarawa ✪

KIRIBATI

Economic Freedom Score

25   50   75

Least free   0   100   Most free

46.4

World Rank: 164   **Regional Rank: 39**

Kiribati's economic freedom score is 46.4, making its economy the 164th freest in the 2015 *Index*. Its score is essentially the same as last year's, with a change of 0.1 point reflecting improvements in fiscal freedom and labor freedom that are offset by declines in business freedom and monetary freedom. Kiribati is ranked 39th out of 42 countries in the Asia–Pacific region, and its overall score is below the world and regional averages.

Kiribati's economy has institutionalized few of the basic principles of economic freedom. Over the past five years, the country's low overall score, near the bottom ranks of the *Index*, has improved by 1.6 points. This modest advancement has occurred in just three of the 10 economic freedoms: fiscal freedom, monetary freedom, and freedom from corruption.

Kiribati is one of the countries least open to trade. Tariffs remain a significant source of revenue, removing the incentive to liberalize to a more open trading environment. Government spending supports over half of the domestic economy, and government payrolls make up a significant portion of employment. Much of the population is engaged in subsistence agriculture. The rule of law is weakly enforced, and respect for business contracts is uneven.

BACKGROUND: The Pacific archipelago of Kiribati gained its independence from Britain in 1979 and has a democratic form of government. Third-term President Anote Tong is barred from re-election. Kiribati was once rich in phosphates and highly dependent on mining, but deposits were exhausted in 1979. Today, it depends on a $500 million Revenue Equalization Reserve Fund created using phosphates earnings, as well as foreign assistance, remittances from overseas, and revenue from fishing licenses, exports of fish and coconuts, and tourism. Crippling algae in the corals surrounding Kiribati seriously threaten the fishing industry, and preservation of the coral ecosystem, the South Pacific's largest marine reserve, continues to be a priority.

Freedom Trend

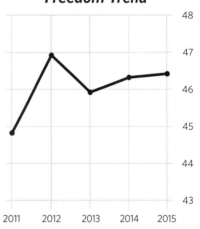

48

47

46

45

44

43

2011   2012   2013   2014   2015

Country Comparisons

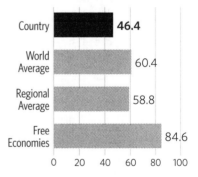

Country	46.4
World Average	60.4
Regional Average	58.8
Free Economies	84.6

0   20   40   60   80   100

Quick Facts

Population: 0.1 million
GDP (PPP): $0.7 billion
2.9% growth in 2013
5-year compound annual growth 1.5%
$6,391 per capita
Unemployment: n/a
Inflation (CPI): 2.0%
FDI Inflow: $9.0 billion
Public Debt: 4.6% of GDP

2013 data unless otherwise noted.
Data compiled as of September 2014.

How Do We Measure Economic Freedom?
See page 475 for an explanation of the methodology
or visit the *Index* Web site at *heritage.org/index*.

267

THE TEN ECONOMIC FREEDOMS

		Score			Rank	1-Year Change
RULE OF LAW	Property Rights	30.0			94th	0
	Freedom from Corruption	29.2			126th	0

Official corruption and abuse are serious problems, and international donors continue to demand improved governance and transparency. The judicial system is modeled on English common law and provides adequate due process rights, but the rule of law remains uneven across the country. Traditional customs permit corporal punishment. Contracts are weakly enforced, and courts are relatively inexperienced in commercial litigation.

GOVERNMENT SIZE	Fiscal Freedom	73.0			126th	+1.6
	Government Spending	0.0			176th	0

The top individual and corporate income tax rates are 35 percent. Tax administration is erratic, and government expenditures have been more reliant on fishing license revenue. The total tax burden equals 15.7 percent of the domestic economy, but government expenditures, including transfer payments, exceed 109 percent of domestic production. Public debt is low.

REGULATORY EFFICIENCY	Business Freedom	56.8			126th	−0.2
	Labor Freedom	83.9			14th	+0.3
	Monetary Freedom	80.6			48th	−0.7

Commercial regulations are not enforced consistently and lack the capacity to spur dynamic entrepreneurial growth. Only a small share of the labor force participates in the formal economy. The government is the major source of employment. Although monetary instability is mitigated by use of the Australian dollar as the official currency, the state funds price-distorting subsidies for some agricultural products.

OPEN MARKETS	Trade Freedom	55.4			171st	0
	Investment Freedom	25.0			158th	0
	Financial Freedom	30.0			131st	0

Kiribati's average tariff rate was 17.3 percent as of 2006. Tariffs are an important source of revenue. The government may screen new foreign investment, and there are restrictions on foreign ownership of land. High credit costs and constrained access to financing severely impede private-sector development. A large proportion of the population remains outside the formal banking system.

Long-Term Score Change (since 2009)

RULE OF LAW		GOVERNMENT SIZE		REGULATORY EFFICIENCY		OPEN MARKETS	
Property Rights	0	Fiscal Freedom	+30.8	Business Freedom	−5.7	Trade Freedom	+0.4
Freedom from Corruption	−3.8	Government Spending	0	Labor Freedom	−1.7	Investment Freedom	−5.0
				Monetary Freedom	−8.1	Financial Freedom	0

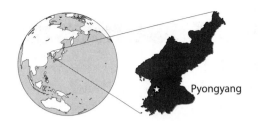

Pyongyang

NORTH KOREA

Economic Freedom Score

Least free 0 · 25 · 50 · 75 · 100 Most free

1.3

World Rank: **178**	Regional Rank: **42**

North Korea remains a closed society. Timely collection of data is extremely difficult, and reported economic statistics must be considered highly speculative. Nevertheless, it is possible to determine that North Korea scores some minimal points only in property rights and freedom from corruption, and its overall score is only 1.3 points, hardly measurable on the *Index* scale. North Korea continues to be the world's least free economy.

North Korea is an unreformed dictatorial state. Little is known about the economic policy intentions of Kim Jong-un, the hermit kingdom's third-generation "supreme leader," but his time in power has been marked by inconsistencies.

Calling for North Korea to become an "economic giant," Kim has attempted to attract more foreign direct investment with such measures as designating new economic development zones. There have been few takers. Additionally, a new Ministry of External Economic Affairs was formed in June 2014. The regime firmly upholds the development of its military and nuclear strength as key priorities, severely undercutting any chance of economic reform and development.

BACKGROUND: Western-educated North Korean dictator Kim Jong-un rules a totalitarian state unchanged since his father died in 2011. Kim rejects any alterations in the status quo, warning of the dangers of outside contagion to the stability of the country. He has maintained Pyongyang's aggressive rhetoric and provocative behavior toward its neighbors and the international community. North Korea continues to conduct nuclear and missile tests in violation of U.N. Security Council resolutions. It has threatened nuclear attacks on the United States and its allies, and it continues to augment and refine its nuclear and missile-delivery capabilities. Typically, Pyongyang escalates and then lowers tensions in attempts to win diplomatic and economic benefits. The Obama Administration, South Korea, and Japan have refused to resume negotiations on denuclearizing the Korean Peninsula without tangible signs of change in North Korean policy.

Freedom Trend

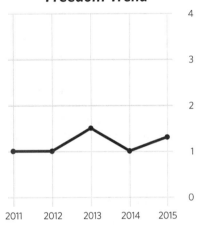

Country Comparisons

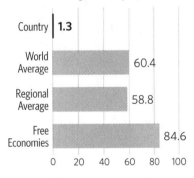

Quick Facts

Population: 24.7 million
GDP (PPP): $40.0 billion (2011)
0.8% growth in 2011
5-year compound annual growth n/a
$1,800 per capita (2011)
Unemployment: n/a
Inflation (CPI): n/a
FDI Inflow: n/a
Public Debt: n/a

2013 data unless otherwise noted.
Data compiled as of September 2014.

How Do We Measure Economic Freedom?
See page 475 for an explanation of the methodology
or visit the *Index* Web site at *heritage.org/index*.

269

THE TEN ECONOMIC FREEDOMS

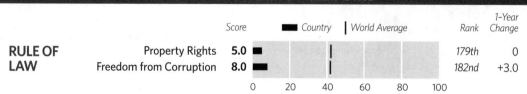

		Score		Rank	1-Year Change
RULE OF LAW	Property Rights	5.0		179th	0
	Freedom from Corruption	8.0		182nd	+3.0

Bribery is pervasive, and corruption is endemic at every level of the state and economy. A modern, independent judiciary does not exist. The Workers' Party, the Korean People's Army, and cabinet officials run companies that compete to earn foreign exchange. Almost all property belongs to the state. Government control extends to all imports and exports as well as domestically produced goods.

		Score		Rank	1-Year Change
GOVERNMENT SIZE	Fiscal Freedom	0.0		181st	0
	Government Spending	0.0		176th	0

No effective tax system is in place. The state commands almost every part of the economy and directs all significant economic activity. The government sets production levels for most products, and state-owned industries account for nearly all GDP. Large military spending further drains scarce resources. Despite attempts to crack down on them, black markets have grown.

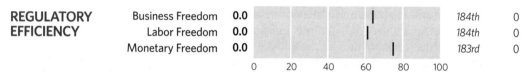

		Score		Rank	1-Year Change
REGULATORY EFFICIENCY	Business Freedom	0.0		184th	0
	Labor Freedom	0.0		184th	0
	Monetary Freedom	0.0		183rd	0

The state regulates the economy through central planning and control. The private sector is virtually nonexistent. Since the 2002 economic reforms, factory managers have had limited autonomy to offer incentives, but the government controls the labor market. The botched currency reform in late 2009 has exacerbated monetary instability. "Yuanization" of the economy, especially in areas abutting China, is increasing.

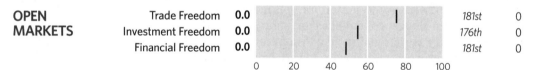

		Score		Rank	1-Year Change
OPEN MARKETS	Trade Freedom	0.0		181st	0
	Investment Freedom	0.0		176th	0
	Financial Freedom	0.0		181st	0

North Korea is isolated from the global economy. International trade and investment are tightly controlled by the government. Limited foreign participation is allowed in the economy through special economic zones, investment in which is approved on a case-by-case basis. The limited financial sector is tightly controlled by the state.

Long-Term Score Change (since 1995)

RULE OF LAW		GOVERNMENT SIZE		REGULATORY EFFICIENCY		OPEN MARKETS	
Property Rights	−5.0	Fiscal Freedom	0	Business Freedom	−40.0	Trade Freedom	0
Freedom from Corruption	−2.0	Government Spending	0	Labor Freedom	0	Investment Freedom	−10.0
				Monetary Freedom	0	Financial Freedom	−10.0

SOUTH KOREA

Economic Freedom Score

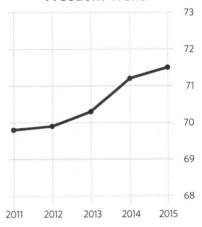

71.5

World Rank: 29   **Regional Rank: 7**

South Korea's economic freedom score is 71.5, making its economy the 29th freest in the 2015 *Index*. Its score is 0.3 point higher than last year, with improvements in property rights, labor freedom, and monetary freedom exceeding declines in the management of government spending and business freedom. South Korea is ranked 7th out of 42 countries in the Asia–Pacific region, and its overall score is above the world and regional averages.

Over the past five years, South Korea's economic freedom has improved by 1.7 points, further advancing the country into the "mostly free" category. The export-oriented, dynamic economy scores above the world average in seven of the 10 economic freedoms. Openness to global trade and investment has been institutionalized through free trade agreements, and the regulatory environment has become more efficient and competitive.

Nonetheless, South Korea's overall economic freedom is limited by corruption and a low level of labor freedom. Despite a sound legal framework, corruption continues to erode equity and trust in government; despite reform efforts, the rigid labor market undermines competitiveness and results in a high level of underemployment.

BACKGROUND: Conservative President Park Geun-hye assumed office in February 2013 vowing a new policy toward North Korea. Her "trustpolitik" strategy balances enhancing South Korea's ability to deter North Korean attacks with a willingness to engage Pyongyang in conditional, reciprocal diplomacy. North Korea has demanded that it first be granted unconditional aid and developmental subsidies from Seoul. Pyongyang rejected Park's "Dresden Declaration," a vision for Korean reconciliation articulated during a visit to Germany, as an attempt at "unification through absorption." At home, Park has yet to deliver on pledges of a mixture of business-friendly economic policies to jump-start the economy and increased government "social welfarism" to redress economic disparities. Scandals involving senior administration officials have reduced her popularity and political capital. The country remains a world leader in electronics, telecommunications, automobile production, and shipbuilding.

Freedom Trend

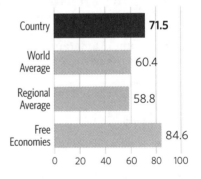

Country Comparisons

Country		**71.5**
World Average		60.4
Regional Average		58.8
Free Economies		84.6

Quick Facts

Population: 50.2 million
GDP (PPP): $1.7 trillion
2.8% growth in 2013
5-year compound annual growth 3.0%
$33,189 per capita
Unemployment: 3.2%
Inflation (CPI): 1.3%
FDI Inflow: $12.2 billion
Public Debt: 36.7% of GDP

2013 data unless otherwise noted.
Data compiled as of September 2014.

How Do We Measure Economic Freedom?
See page 475 for an explanation of the methodology or visit the *Index* Web site at *heritage.org/index*.

THE TEN ECONOMIC FREEDOMS

		Score		Rank	1-Year Change
RULE OF LAW	Property Rights	75.0		25th	+5.0
	Freedom from Corruption	55.0		45th	+1.0

Despite the political system's overall health, bribery, influence peddling, and extortion continue in politics, business, and everyday life. Since 2013, there have been several investigations into allegations of corruption among high-ranking officials. A well-functioning modern legal framework ensures strong protection of private property rights. The rule of law is effective, and the judicial system is independent and efficient.

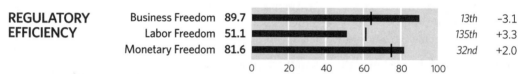

		Score		Rank	1-Year Change
GOVERNMENT SIZE	Fiscal Freedom	72.5		129th	−0.1
	Government Spending	67.9		92nd	−4.7

The top individual income tax rate is 35 percent, and the top corporate tax rate is 22 percent (with a 10 percent surtax on individual and corporate rates). Other taxes include a value-added tax. The overall tax burden is equivalent to 26.8 percent of domestic income. Government spending equals 32.7 percent of total domestic output, and public debt amounts to approximately 37 percent of GDP.

		Score		Rank	1-Year Change
REGULATORY EFFICIENCY	Business Freedom	89.7		13th	−3.1
	Labor Freedom	51.1		135th	+3.3
	Monetary Freedom	81.6		32nd	+2.0

The competitive regulatory framework facilitates business formation and innovation. With no minimum capital required, incorporating a business takes three procedures and four days on average. The labor market is dynamic, but costs of hiring and dismissing a worker remain burdensome. Monetary stability has been well maintained, but the government subsidizes numerous renewable energy projects, child care, and medical care.

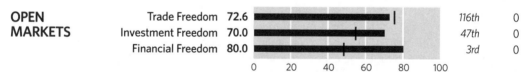

		Score		Rank	1-Year Change
OPEN MARKETS	Trade Freedom	72.6		116th	0
	Investment Freedom	70.0		47th	0
	Financial Freedom	80.0		3rd	0

The average tariff rate is 8.7 percent. South Korea continues to pursue its "World's Best Customs" strategy. Foreign investment in some sectors is regulated or capped. The financial system has become more sophisticated and competitive, offering a wide range of options, but business start-ups and small and medium-sized companies struggle to obtain timely financing. The banking sector remains largely stable.

Long-Term Score Change (since 1995)

RULE OF LAW		GOVERNMENT SIZE		REGULATORY EFFICIENCY		OPEN MARKETS	
Property Rights	−15.0	Fiscal Freedom	+9.2	Business Freedom	+19.7	Trade Freedom	+3.4
Freedom from Corruption	−15.0	Government Spending	−17.7	Labor Freedom	−5.5	Investment Freedom	+20.0
				Monetary Freedom	+1.5	Financial Freedom	+10.0

Pristina

KOSOVO

Economic Freedom Score

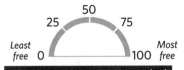

Least free 0

Most free 100

This economy is not graded

Kosovo's economy is not graded in the 2015 *Index* due to insufficient data. Facets of economic freedom for which data are available have been scored individually. Kosovo will receive an overall economic freedom score and ranking in future editions as more reliable information becomes available.

Kosovo's continued transition to a market-based economy has yielded dividends over the past five years. Its move from a centrally planned to a market-based economy has proceeded steadily, and the government has engaged in a series of high-profile privatizations. Limited by political and geographic constraints, the young nation has opened its borders to trade and investment and now relies heavily on remittances and foreign direct investment.

Continued progress is hindered by weak institutional capacity, and the government has yet to show a sustained commitment to economic freedom. Corruption is still prevalent and undermines the already restricted business environment. Political interference in the judiciary is troubling. Remnants of the centrally planned economy still linger in a government bureaucracy that makes business formation costly and onerous.

BACKGROUND: Transitioning from a centrally planned economy to a more market-based economy, Kosovo has been privatizing many of its state-owned assets. The nation has opened its borders to trade and investment, with services and manufacturing accounting for a large majority of economic activity. Parliamentary elections in May 2014 produced political deadlock, further hampering progress on economic reform. Half of Kosovo's population is under 25, unemployment remains high at 35 percent, and informal networks and transactions remain a large portion of the economy. Despite progress since independence, institutional capacity remains weak, and remittances account for around 15 percent of GDP. A truly independent judiciary is not yet a reality. Intrusive bureaucracy and costly registration procedures reflect a history of central planning. Greater political commitment is needed to implement the significant reforms necessary to jump-start the economy and stamp out corruption.

Freedom Trend

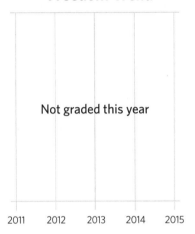

Not graded this year

2011   2012   2013   2014   2015

Country Comparisons

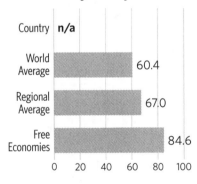

Country   **n/a**

World Average   60.4

Regional Average   67.0

Free Economies   84.6

0   20   40   60   80   100

Quick Facts

Population: 1.85 million
GDP (PPP): $14.0 billion
2.5% growth in 2013
5-year compound annual growth 3.2%
$7,600 per capita
Unemployment: 30.9%
Inflation (CPI): 1.9%
FDI Inflow: n/a
Public Debt: 9.1% of GDP

2013 data unless otherwise noted.
Data compiled as of September 2014.

How Do We Measure Economic Freedom?
See page 475 for an explanation of the methodology
or visit the *Index* Web site at *heritage.org/index*.

273

THE TEN ECONOMIC FREEDOMS

		Score		Rank	1-Year Change
RULE OF LAW	Property Rights	30.0		94th	0
	Freedom from Corruption	33.0		113th	+4.4

Political corruption is one of Kosovo's greatest challenges. Several reforms were implemented in 2013 to improve the transparency of campaign financing, but high-level senior officials involved in corruption are not routinely punished. In general, the current institutional framework is not designed to resolve claims and challenges to property rights in an efficient and effective manner.

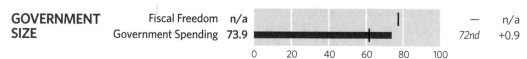

		Score		Rank	1-Year Change
GOVERNMENT SIZE	Fiscal Freedom	n/a		—	n/a
	Government Spending	73.9		72nd	+0.9

Kosovo's top individual and corporate income tax rates are 10 percent. Other taxes include a value-added tax and a property tax. Government revenue is largely dependent on the VAT, excise and trade taxes, and transfers from abroad. Taxation is poorly enforced. Public expenditures equal 29.5 percent of domestic output, and public debt equals approximately 9 percent of GDP.

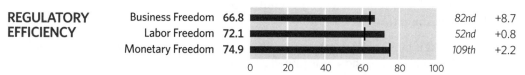

		Score		Rank	1-Year Change
REGULATORY EFFICIENCY	Business Freedom	66.8		82nd	+8.7
	Labor Freedom	72.1		52nd	+0.8
	Monetary Freedom	74.9		109th	+2.2

With no minimum capital required, it takes five procedures and less than a week to start a company, but completing licensing requirements takes about five months on average. The labor market is underdeveloped, and informal labor activity is substantial. Agricultural and energy-related subsidies from the government and international donors amount to more than one-third of GDP.

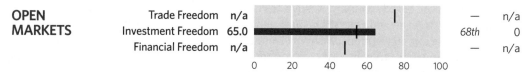

		Score		Rank	1-Year Change
OPEN MARKETS	Trade Freedom	n/a		—	n/a
	Investment Freedom	65.0		68th	0
	Financial Freedom	n/a		—	n/a

Kosovo is a member of the Central European Free Trade Agreement (CEFTA) region. Most sectors of the economy are open to foreign investment. Kosovo has several state-owned enterprises. The financial system, dominated by a small number of banks, remains limited in scope and depth. A lack of readily available financing hinders the development of a dynamic private sector.

Long-Term Score Change: n/a

RULE OF LAW		GOVERNMENT SIZE		REGULATORY EFFICIENCY		OPEN MARKETS	
Property Rights	n/a	Fiscal Freedom	n/a	Business Freedom	n/a	Trade Freedom	n/a
Freedom from Corruption	n/a	Government Spending	n/a	Labor Freedom	n/a	Investment Freedom	n/a
				Monetary Freedom	n/a	Financial Freedom	n/a

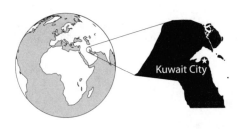

Kuwait City

KUWAIT

Economic Freedom Score

Least free 0   Most free 100

62.5

Kuwait's economic freedom score is 62.5, making its economy the 74th freest in the 2015 *Index*. Its score is 0.2 point better than last year, reflecting improvements in the management of government spending, business freedom, monetary freedom, and labor freedom that offset declines in property rights, freedom from corruption, and trade freedom. Kuwait is ranked 7th out of 15 countries in the Middle East/North Africa region, and its overall score is slightly above the regional and world averages.

Over the past five years, economic freedom in Kuwait has declined by 2.4 points. Score declines have occurred in six of the 10 economic freedoms, led by deteriorations in the control of government spending, business freedom, and trade freedom.

High oil revenues have excused policymakers from making tough choices to liberalize the economy, including privatizing some state-owned enterprises. Structural reforms remain critically necessary to spur dynamic growth and ensure long-term economic development. While Kuwait continues to benefit from an open trading regime that attracts investment flows, rising protectionism must be controlled in order to maintain international trade linkages.

BACKGROUND: Kuwait, one of the richest Arab nations, is a constitutional monarchy ruled by the al-Sabah dynasty. During the Arab Spring of 2011, young activists called for political reforms, and residents unlawfully in the country demanded citizenship and jobs. After Islamists scored major gains in parliamentary elections in February 2012, Amir Sabah al-Ahmad al-Jabr al-Sabah annulled the results and changed the election laws. This sparked protests and triggered a boycott of the new election in December. The results of that election were annulled by the Constitutional Court, and in new balloting held in July 2013, pro-government Sunni candidates achieved a significant majority. Kuwait controls roughly 6 percent of the world's oil reserves. The oil and gas sector accounts for nearly 50 percent of GDP and 95 percent of export revenues.

Freedom Trend

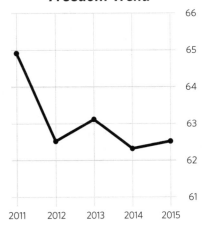

Country Comparisons

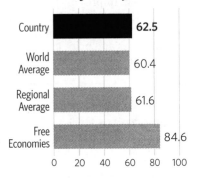

Country	62.5
World Average	60.4
Regional Average	61.6
Free Economies	84.6

Quick Facts

Population: 3.9 million
GDP (PPP): $154.5 billion
0.8% growth in 2013
5-year compound annual growth 0.6%
$39,706 per capita
Unemployment: 3.1%
Inflation (CPI): 2.7%
FDI Inflow: $2.3 billion
Public Debt: 5.3% of GDP

2013 data unless otherwise noted.
Data compiled as of September 2014.

How Do We Measure Economic Freedom?
See page 475 for an explanation of the methodology
or visit the *Index* Web site at *heritage.org/index*.

THE TEN ECONOMIC FREEDOMS

		Score	■ Country │ World Average	Rank	1-Year Change
RULE OF LAW	Property Rights	45.0		66th	–5.0
	Freedom from Corruption	43.0		69th	–0.7

Five opposition members of parliament resigned in May 2014 after they were denied a request to question the prime minister about corruption. There are occasional accusations of attempted bribery in the government's lengthy procurement process. The legal framework is not well developed, and the rule of law remains weak. Foreigners face difficulties enforcing contract provisions in the local courts.

		Score		Rank	1-Year Change
GOVERNMENT SIZE	Fiscal Freedom	97.7		7th	0
	Government Spending	61.1		109th	+5.5

Kuwait has no individual income tax. Foreign-owned companies are subject to a 15 percent tax. Taxes make up a small portion of government revenue, with most financing coming from oil and gas windfalls. Overall tax revenue is less than 1 percent of domestic output. Public expenditures equal 36 percent of domestic production, and government debt amounts to 5 percent of gross domestic product.

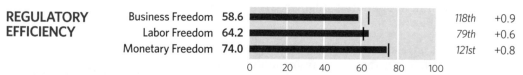

		Score		Rank	1-Year Change
REGULATORY EFFICIENCY	Business Freedom	58.6		118th	+0.9
	Labor Freedom	64.2		79th	+0.6
	Monetary Freedom	74.0		121st	+0.8

Progress in improving Kuwait's regulatory framework has been uneven. Incorporating a business still takes more than 30 days, and bureaucratic hurdles continue to add to the cost of business. Overall labor regulations lack flexibility. The government has an extensive system of subsidies and price controls through state-owned utilities and enterprises, although diesel fuel subsidies were cut in 2014.

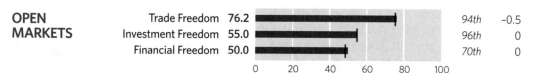

		Score		Rank	1-Year Change
OPEN MARKETS	Trade Freedom	76.2		94th	–0.5
	Investment Freedom	55.0		96th	0
	Financial Freedom	50.0		70th	0

Kuwait's average tariff rate is 4.4 percent. Government procurement may favor domestic firms, and imports of books and media deemed detrimental to public morals are not allowed. The relatively well-developed financial system offers a wide range of services. Restrictions on foreign banks include a ban on competing in the retail sector. Foreign banks are limited to providing investment banking services.

Long-Term Score Change (since 1996)

RULE OF LAW		GOVERNMENT SIZE		REGULATORY EFFICIENCY		OPEN MARKETS	
Property Rights	–45.0	Fiscal Freedom	–2.2	Business Freedom	–26.4	Trade Freedom	–0.8
Freedom from Corruption	–27.0	Government Spending	+50.2	Labor Freedom	–16.0	Investment Freedom	+25.0
				Monetary Freedom	–7.7	Financial Freedom	0

KYRGYZ REPUBLIC

Bishkek

Economic Freedom Score

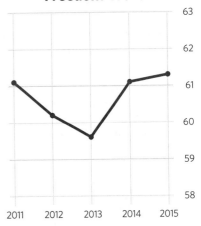

25 **50** 75

Least free 0   100 Most free

61.3

World Rank: 82   **Regional Rank: 15**

The Kyrgyz Republic's economic freedom score is 61.3, making its economy the 82nd freest in the 2015 *Index*. Its score has increased by 0.2 point since last year, with improvements in trade freedom, freedom from corruption, and labor freedom outweighing declines in the control of government spending, fiscal freedom, and business freedom. The Kyrgyz Republic is ranked 15th out of 42 countries in the Asia–Pacific region, and its overall score is above the regional and world averages.

Over the past two years, the Kyrgyz Republic has re-established the positive growth in economic freedom it had achieved prior to 2010. Solid gains have been made in opening the economy to trade and investment, but the control of government spending continues to deteriorate.

Compared to transitioning economies in Eastern Europe, the Kyrgyz Republic lags behind in key indicators of economic freedom. Trade freedom has only recently surpassed the global average, and the rule of law remains weak. Corruption, particularly surrounding the president's family and office, has been well documented. Courts remain largely unreformed, and property rights are weak.

BACKGROUND: The Kyrgyz Republic is one of Central Asia's poorest and least stable countries and is sharply divided along ethnic lines. Former Prime Minister Almazbek Atambayev, elected president in 2011 with Moscow's support, has used questionable legal maneuvers to persecute opponents. Weak governance has encouraged extremist threats, organized crime, and corruption. The government has accumulated high levels of external debt and is heavily dependent on foreign aid. The economy depends heavily on gold exports and remittances from Kyrgyzstani migrant workers, primarily in Russia. Cotton, tobacco, wool, and meat are the main agricultural products, but only tobacco and cotton are exported in any quantity. There has been strong foreign investment, particularly from Russia. In May 2014, Atambayev signed a road map for membership in the Russia-dominated Eurasian Economic Union, saying that his country has little choice but to join.

Freedom Trend

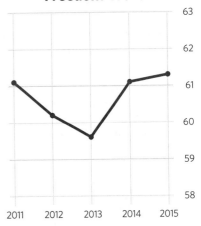

63
62
61
60
59
58

2011   2012   2013   2014   2015

Country Comparisons

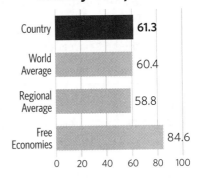

Country   **61.3**

World Average   60.4

Regional Average   58.8

Free Economies   84.6

0   20   40   60   80   100

Quick Facts

Population: 5.6 million
GDP (PPP): $14.7 billion
10.5% growth in 2013
5-year compound annual growth 3.5%
$2,611 per capita
Unemployment: 7.9%
Inflation (CPI): 6.6%
FDI Inflow: $757.6 million
Public Debt: 47.7% of GDP

2013 data unless otherwise noted.
Data compiled as of September 2014.

THE TEN ECONOMIC FREEDOMS

		Score			Rank	1-Year Change
RULE OF LAW	Property Rights	20.0			138th	0
	Freedom from Corruption	24.0			156th	+4.8

Corruption is pervasive, and despite many rounds of constitutional and statutory changes, the Kyrgyz Republic has been trapped in a cycle in which political elites rotate from opposition to power and use government resources to reward clients. Government anti-corruption efforts mostly target the opposition. The courts are largely unreformed, judges are often corrupt, and the legal framework is weak.

		Score			Rank	1-Year Change
GOVERNMENT SIZE	Fiscal Freedom	93.6			14th	-1.0
	Government Spending	53.2			125th	-7.0

The Kyrgyz Republic's individual and corporate income tax rates are a flat 10 percent. Other taxes include a value-added tax and excise taxes. The overall tax burden corresponds to 21 percent of domestic production. Non-tax revenue from gold deposits is sizeable. Government expenditures equal 39.5 percent of domestic output, and public debt is equivalent to 48 percent of gross domestic product.

		Score			Rank	1-Year Change
REGULATORY EFFICIENCY	Business Freedom	73.7			46th	-0.5
	Labor Freedom	85.0			12th	+1.2
	Monetary Freedom	73.8			124th	+0.1

Requirements for starting a business have been simplified, but regulatory inefficiency and lack of transparency persist. Completing licensing requirements still takes over 140 days. The labor market remains inefficient, and informal labor activity is high. The 12-month inflation rate reached 6.3 percent in March 2014, but core inflation has been in the single digits since May 2013.

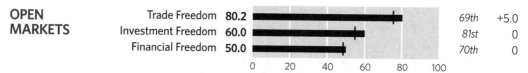

		Score			Rank	1-Year Change
OPEN MARKETS	Trade Freedom	80.2			69th	+5.0
	Investment Freedom	60.0			81st	0
	Financial Freedom	50.0			70th	0

The Kyrgyz Republic's average tariff rate is 2.4 percent. Tariffs on imported clothing are relatively high. The legal and regulatory environment is challenging for foreign investors. Financial intermediation has increased, but high credit costs severely undermine private-sector development. Credits provided by a banking sector that remains vulnerable to state interference equal less than 15 percent of GDP.

Long-Term Score Change (since 1998)

RULE OF LAW		GOVERNMENT SIZE		REGULATORY EFFICIENCY		OPEN MARKETS	
Property Rights	-10.0	Fiscal Freedom	+21.3	Business Freedom	+18.7	Trade Freedom	+15.2
Freedom from Corruption	-6.0	Government Spending	-19.4	Labor Freedom	+20.2	Investment Freedom	+10.0
				Monetary Freedom	+32.7	Financial Freedom	0

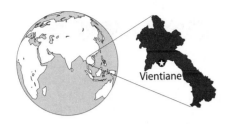

LAOS

Economic Freedom Score

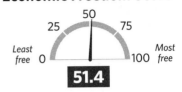

51.4

L aos's economic freedom score is 51.4, making its economy the 150th freest in the 2015 *Index*. Its overall score is 0.2 point higher than last year, reflecting improvements in freedom from corruption and labor freedom that outweigh declines in investment freedom, business freedom, and monetary freedom. Laos is ranked 33rd out of 42 countries in the Asia–Pacific region, and its overall score is below the world and regional averages.

Economic freedom in Laos has scarcely budged over the past five years, highlighting the apparent lack of commitment to economic reform in the East Asian economy. While the country did register its highest score ever in the 2015 *Index*, progress has been inconsequential. Five-year improvements in half of the 10 economic freedoms, including the control of government spending and labor freedom, have been counterbalanced by deteriorations in property rights, government spending, monetary freedom, and trade freedom.

Laos remains largely absent from the East Asian trading network, and its trade freedom remains well below the global average. Government corruption is widespread, and the judiciary is largely ineffective. Businesses, especially entrepreneurs, find that business formation and capital accumulation are difficult because of regulatory costs and underdeveloped financial markets.

BACKGROUND: The Communist government of Laos, in power since 1975, wrecked the economy in the early years of its rule. Slow liberalization, begun in 1986, has yielded limited success. Corruption is endemic, laws are applied erratically, and the country remains highly dependent on international aid. Basic civil liberties are heavily restricted. Seventy-five percent of the workforce is employed in subsistence farming. In 2013, following a 15-year negotiation process, Laos became a member of the World Trade Organization.

Freedom Trend

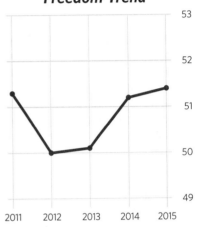

Country Comparisons

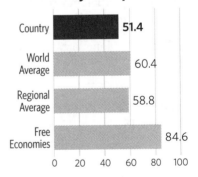

Quick Facts

Population: 6.8 million
GDP (PPP): $20.8 billion
8.2% growth in 2013
5-year compound annual growth 7.9%
$3,068 per capita
Unemployment: 1.4%
Inflation (CPI): 6.4%
FDI Inflow: $296.0 million
Public Debt: 62.0% of GDP

2013 data unless otherwise noted.
Data compiled as of September 2014.

How Do We Measure Economic Freedom?
See page 475 for an explanation of the methodology
or visit the *Index* Web site at *heritage.org/index.*

THE TEN ECONOMIC FREEDOMS

	Score	Rank	1-Year Change
RULE OF LAW Property Rights	15.0	157th	0
Freedom from Corruption	26.0	145th	+7.4

Widespread corruption among government officials fuels public discontent and causes problems in tax collection and degraded public services. In late 2013, more than 50 officials in a provincial government were investigated for fraud. Senior civilian and military officials are often involved in logging, mining, and other extractive enterprises. The judicial system is inefficient, and protections for property rights are weak.

	Score	Rank	1-Year Change
GOVERNMENT SIZE Fiscal Freedom	86.2	43rd	-0.4
Government Spending	86.8	27th	+0.1

Laos's top individual and corporate income tax rates are 24 percent. Other taxes include a vehicle tax and excise taxes. The overall tax burden equals 24 percent of domestic production. Government expenditures are equal to 21 percent of domestic output, and public debt is equivalent to 62 percent of gross domestic product.

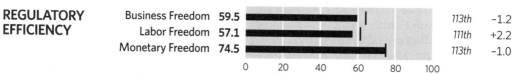

	Score	Rank	1-Year Change
REGULATORY EFFICIENCY Business Freedom	59.5	113th	-1.2
Labor Freedom	57.1	111th	+2.2
Monetary Freedom	74.5	113th	-1.0

Regulatory efficiency remains poor, and the application of regulations is inconsistent and non-transparent. On average, it requires over 90 days to incorporate a company, and obtaining necessary permits takes over two months. The labor market lacks flexibility and hinders job growth. Monetary stability has strengthened somewhat. The government influences many prices through subsidies and state-owned enterprises and utilities.

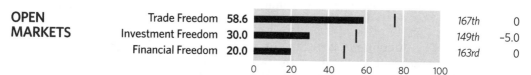

	Score	Rank	1-Year Change
OPEN MARKETS Trade Freedom	58.6	167th	0
Investment Freedom	30.0	149th	-5.0
Financial Freedom	20.0	163rd	0

Laos has an average tariff rate of 13.2 percent. Some goods are subject to import licensing, and foreign-based service providers may face barriers. Foreign investors typically must overcome multiple regulatory hurdles. The financial system is underdeveloped and subject to political interference. Three state-owned banks dominate the banking sector, and the government controls credit allocation.

Long-Term Score Change (since 1996)

RULE OF LAW		GOVERNMENT SIZE		REGULATORY EFFICIENCY		OPEN MARKETS	
Property Rights	+5.0	Fiscal Freedom	+53.9	Business Freedom	+19.5	Trade Freedom	-22.4
Freedom from Corruption	+16.0	Government Spending	-3.4	Labor Freedom	-4.2	Investment Freedom	+20.0
				Monetary Freedom	+11.7	Financial Freedom	+10.0

★ Riga

LATVIA

Economic Freedom Score

50

25　75

Least free　0　　100　Most free

69.7

L atvia's economic freedom score is 69.7, making its economy the 37th freest in the 2015 *Index*. Its score has increased by 1.0 point since last year, with improvements in freedom from corruption, the management of government spending, and monetary freedom outweighing declines in labor freedom, business freedom, and fiscal freedom. Latvia is ranked 17th out of 43 countries in the Europe region, and its overall score is above the regional and world averages.

Commitment to pursuing greater economic freedom has pushed Latvia higher in the "moderately free" category over the past five years. Since 2011, economic freedom in Latvia has increased by 3.9 points, the second highest overall score increase in Europe during that period. Most impressive, Latvia recorded no score declines, sustaining improvements in all 10 economic freedoms except property rights and financial freedom, scores for which were unchanged. In the 2015 *Index*, Latvia has recorded its highest economic freedom score ever.

Latvia's ongoing transition to a free-market economy has been facilitated by openness to global commerce and efficient regulation. Prudent fiscal policies and low taxes have limited the government's presence in the economy and fostered a dynamic private sector. Although Latvia remains poised to continue to reap the benefits of advancing economic freedom, more institutional reforms must be implemented to shore up a weak judiciary and the property rights regime and to tackle pervasive corruption effectively.

BACKGROUND: Latvia regained its independence from the Soviet Union in 1991 and joined the European Union and NATO in 2004. Prime Minister Laimdota Straujuma of the conservative Union Party heads a four-party coalition that also includes the National Alliance, the Reform Party, and the Union of Greens and Farmers. Latvia's economic standing and credit rating have improved following pro-market reforms. Low productivity remains a problem, and there is a large underground economy. Latvia joined the eurozone in 2014.

Freedom Trend

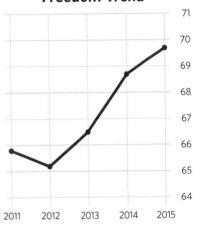

71

70

69

68

67

66

65

64

2011　2012　2013　2014　2015

Country Comparisons

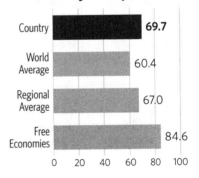

Country　**69.7**

World Average　60.4

Regional Average　67.0

Free Economies　84.6

0　20　40　60　80　100

Quick Facts

Population: 2.0 million
GDP (PPP): $38.9 billion
4.1% growth in 2013
5-year compound annual growth –1.3%
$19,120 per capita
Unemployment: 10.9%
Inflation (CPI): 0.0%
FDI Inflow: $808.3 million
Public Debt: 32.1% of GDP

2013 data unless otherwise noted.
Data compiled as of September 2014.

THE TEN ECONOMIC FREEDOMS

		Score		Rank	1-Year Change
RULE OF LAW	Property Rights	50.0		56th	0
	Freedom from Corruption	53.0		48th	+9.4

In a 2013 Transparency International poll, 25 percent of Latvians reported paying bribes to government officials. In late 2013, the long-time prime minister resigned after suspicions that a supermarket collapse in Riga that killed over 50 people was due in part to corruption in the construction safety permit process. The judicial system is independent, but improvements are needed.

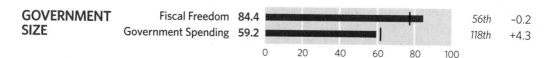

		Score		Rank	1-Year Change
GOVERNMENT SIZE	Fiscal Freedom	84.4		56th	-0.2
	Government Spending	59.2		118th	+4.3

Latvia's top individual income tax rate is 24 percent, and its top corporate tax rate is 15 percent. Other taxes include a value-added tax and a tax on capital gains. The overall tax burden equals 27.6 percent of gross domestic product. Public expenditures correspond to 36.9 percent of total domestic production, and public debt equals 32 percent of gross domestic output.

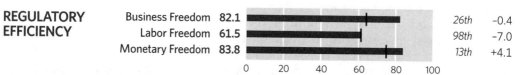

		Score		Rank	1-Year Change
REGULATORY EFFICIENCY	Business Freedom	82.1		26th	-0.4
	Labor Freedom	61.5		98th	-7.0
	Monetary Freedom	83.8		13th	+4.1

Incorporating a business takes four procedures on average, and no paid-in minimum capital is required, but completing licensing requirements remains time-consuming. Despite reform efforts, the relatively rigid labor market hinders dynamic job growth. The government created a social support mechanism for poor households to limit potential increases in rates following full opening of the electricity market in 2014.

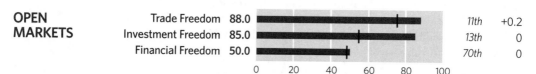

		Score		Rank	1-Year Change
OPEN MARKETS	Trade Freedom	88.0		11th	+0.2
	Investment Freedom	85.0		13th	0
	Financial Freedom	50.0		70th	0

EU members have a 1.0 percent average tariff rate. Although some non-tariff barriers exist, the EU is relatively open to external trade. Latvia generally welcomes foreign investment, but foreign ownership of agricultural land is restricted. The banking sector, largely recapitalized since the recent global financial crisis, has recovered its financial stability. The number of non-performing loans has declined.

Long-Term Score Change (since 1996)

RULE OF LAW		GOVERNMENT SIZE		REGULATORY EFFICIENCY		OPEN MARKETS	
Property Rights	0	Fiscal Freedom	+6.4	Business Freedom	+12.1	Trade Freedom	+33.0
Freedom from Corruption	+3.0	Government Spending	+8.4	Labor Freedom	-2.0	Investment Freedom	+35.0
				Monetary Freedom	+42.7	Financial Freedom	0

LEBANON

Economic Freedom Score

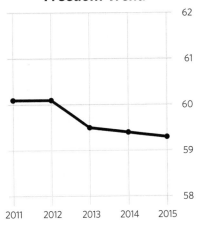

25 · 50 · 75

Least free 0 · Most free 100

59.3

L ebanon's economic freedom score is 59.3, making its economy the 94th freest in the 2015 *Index*. Its score is essentially unchanged from last year, with a loss of 0.1 point reflecting declines in the control of government spending, monetary freedom, and business freedom that offset improvements in freedom from corruption, labor freedom, and fiscal freedom. Lebanon is ranked 10th out of 15 countries in the Middle East/North Africa region, and its overall score is below the world average.

Political instability and diminishing confidence in the domestic economy reflect the slow degradation of Lebanon's economic freedom over the past five years. A decline of 0.8 point since 2011 reflects deteriorations in four of the 10 economic freedoms, including property rights, monetary freedom, and trade freedom.

These declines have weakened the already fragile structural and institutional environment. Restrictive business and labor regulations inhibit business formation and the development of a dynamic private sector. Prevalent corruption has undermined the basic political institutions of society. The banking sector is relatively well developed, but the economy remains more closed to trade and investment than many of its regional peers.

BACKGROUND: Since 1975, Lebanon's economy has been disrupted by civil war, Syrian occupation, Hezbollah clashes with Israel, political uncertainty, and sectarian tensions. Syria was forced to withdraw its army in 2005 after its government was implicated in the assassination of former Lebanese Prime Minister Rafiq Hariri. In 2006, Lebanon-based Hezbollah forces instigated a conflict with Israel. Hariri's son, Saad Hariri, was elected prime minister in June 2009, but his government collapsed in January 2011 when Hezbollah engineered the elevation of Najib Mikati as prime minister. Mikati resigned in March 2013, and Tammam Salam was asked to form a caretaker government until new elections slated for November 2014. Economic growth has fallen dramatically due to the civil war in neighboring Syria and growing instability triggered by rising Sunni–Shia sectarian tensions.

Freedom Trend

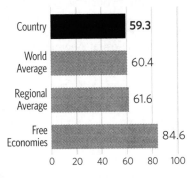

62
61
60
59
58

2011 2012 2013 2014 2015

Country Comparisons

Country	59.3
World Average	60.4
Regional Average	61.6
Free Economies	84.6

0   20   40   60   80   100

Quick Facts

Population: 4.5 million
GDP (PPP): $66.3 billion
1.0% growth in 2013
5-year compound annual growth 4.5%
$14,845 per capita
Unemployment: 6.6%
Inflation (CPI): 3.2%
FDI Inflow: $2.8 billion
Public Debt: 139.7% of GDP

2013 data unless otherwise noted.
Data compiled as of September 2014.

THE TEN ECONOMIC FREEDOMS

		Score		Rank	1-Year Change
RULE OF LAW	Property Rights	20.0		138th	0
	Freedom from Corruption	28.0		132nd	+3.5

Corruption pervades the public sector, and Lebanon's proximity to the Syrian crisis heightens political instability. The sectarian political system and the powerful role of foreign patrons limit elected officials' accountability to the public. Lebanon's judicial system is in need of root-and-branch reform to change both its procedures and many of its junior, middle-ranking, and senior personnel.

		Score		Rank	1-Year Change
GOVERNMENT SIZE	Fiscal Freedom	91.3		25th	+0.4
	Government Spending	70.6		85th	-3.1

Lebanon's top individual income tax rate is 20 percent, and its top corporate tax rate is 15 percent. Other taxes include an inheritance tax and a value-added tax. The overall tax burden equals 15.7 percent of domestic production. Public expenditures are equal to 31.3 percent of domestic output, and public debt is equivalent to 139 percent of gross domestic product.

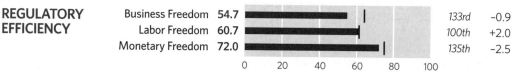

		Score		Rank	1-Year Change
REGULATORY EFFICIENCY	Business Freedom	54.7		133rd	-0.9
	Labor Freedom	60.7		100th	+2.0
	Monetary Freedom	72.0		135th	-2.5

Launching a business takes slightly more than a week, and minimum capital requirements cost about one-third of the level of average annual income. Obtaining necessary licenses takes over eight months on average. Outmoded labor laws undermine the development of a dynamic labor market. The state-owned and heavily subsidized electricity sector's annual deficit consumes about a third of government revenue.

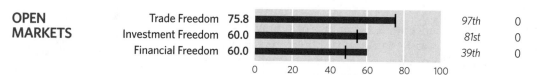

		Score		Rank	1-Year Change
OPEN MARKETS	Trade Freedom	75.8		97th	0
	Investment Freedom	60.0		81st	0
	Financial Freedom	60.0		39th	0

Lebanon's average tariff rate is 4.8 percent. Imports of used cars and goods from Israel are restricted, as is foreign investment in several sectors of the economy. The financial sector is not well diversified and is dominated by banks. Competition among private banks has contributed to greater efficiency. With a high degree of resilience, banking remains the cornerstone of the economy.

Long-Term Score Change (since 1996)

RULE OF LAW		GOVERNMENT SIZE		REGULATORY EFFICIENCY		OPEN MARKETS	
Property Rights	-30.0	Fiscal Freedom	-6.7	Business Freedom	-15.3	Trade Freedom	+0.8
Freedom from Corruption	+18.0	Government Spending	-9.3	Labor Freedom	+1.5	Investment Freedom	+10.0
				Monetary Freedom	+5.6	Financial Freedom	-10.0

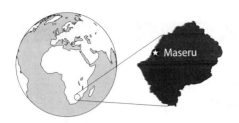

★ Maseru

LESOTHO

Economic Freedom Score

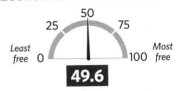

25   **50**   75

Least   0   100   Most
free   free

49.6

Lesotho's economic freedom score is 49.6, making its economy the 155th freest in the 2015 *Index*. Its score is essentially the same as last year's, with a change of 0.1 point reflecting improvements in freedom from corruption, labor freedom, and fiscal freedom that outweigh declines in property rights, investment freedom, and trade freedom. Lesotho is ranked 38th out of 46 countries in the Sub-Saharan Africa region, and its overall score is below the world average.

Over the past five years, economic freedom in Lesotho has advanced by 2.1 points, reflecting marked improvements in six of the 10 economic freedoms, but a gain of over 20 points in fiscal freedom has been more than offset by a decline of over 20 points in the management of government spending.

Corruption remains a serious problem and pervades all levels of government. High tariffs on agricultural and other products exacerbate food security issues and increase costs. Outmoded labor laws undermine the development of a formal labor market, and inefficient business regulations inhibit business formation.

BACKGROUND: Following independence from the United Kingdom in 1966, Lesotho was subject to frequent coups and foreign military interventions for nearly three decades. Lesotho is a parliamentary constitutional monarchy. King Letsie III is ceremonial head of state. Thomas Thabane, elected prime minister in May 2012, was forced to flee in August 2014 following an attempted coup by a renegade general. He was reinstated following a peace deal brokered by the South African government. Geographically surrounded by and economically integrated with South Africa, Lesotho relies on customs duties from the Southern Africa Customs Union for government revenue and remittances from laborers employed in South Africa for much of its national income. Principal exports include diamonds and water. In 2012, one of the worst food crises in human history hit Lesotho after its crops failed due to extraordinary weather circumstances. Lesotho has the world's third-highest HIV rate.

Freedom Trend

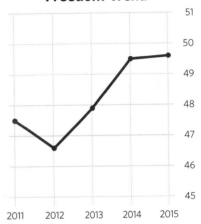

51
50
49
48
47
46
45

2011   2012   2013   2014   2015

Country Comparisons

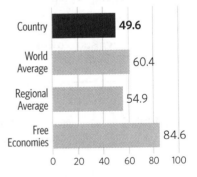

Country	**49.6**
World Average	60.4
Regional Average	54.9
Free Economies	84.6

0   20   40   60   80   100

Quick Facts

Population: 1.9 million
GDP (PPP): $4.3 billion
5.8% growth in 2013
5-year compound annual growth 5.2%
$2,255 per capita
Unemployment: 27.0%
Inflation (CPI): 5.3%
FDI Inflow: $44.1 million
Public Debt: 39.6% of GDP

2013 data unless otherwise noted.
Data compiled as of September 2014.

THE TEN ECONOMIC FREEDOMS

		Score		Rank	1-Year Change
RULE OF LAW	Property Rights	35.0		87th	–5.0
	Freedom from Corruption	49.0		55th	+11.9

In 2013, the water minister became the first cabinet member ever to be dismissed because of corruption. Corruption pervades all sectors of public service, and cronyism is prevalent in state bidding procedures. The judiciary is relatively independent but politicized and chronically underfunded. Protection of private property rights is ineffective, but expropriation is unlikely.

		Score		Rank	1-Year Change
GOVERNMENT SIZE	Fiscal Freedom	68.5		145th	+1.1
	Government Spending	0.0		176th	0

Lesotho's top individual income tax rate is 35 percent, and its top corporate tax rate is 25 percent. Other taxes include a value-added tax and a tax on dividends. Tax revenue equals about 36.1 percent of domestic output, and public expenditures have reached 61.1 percent of domestic production. Public debt is equivalent to about 40 percent of gross domestic product.

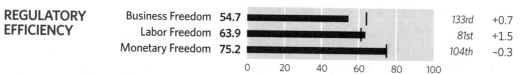

		Score		Rank	1-Year Change
REGULATORY EFFICIENCY	Business Freedom	54.7		133rd	+0.7
	Labor Freedom	63.9		81st	+1.5
	Monetary Freedom	75.2		104th	–0.3

Starting a business takes seven procedures, and no minimum capital is required, but completing licensing requirements still takes over 150 days on average. The labor market remains stagnant. A large portion of the workforce is in the informal sector. The government influences prices through state-owned enterprises. Monetary stability is affected by inflationary pressures in South Africa.

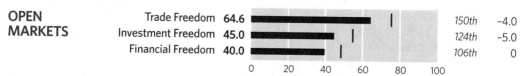

		Score		Rank	1-Year Change
OPEN MARKETS	Trade Freedom	64.6		150th	–4.0
	Investment Freedom	45.0		124th	–5.0
	Financial Freedom	40.0		106th	0

Lesotho's average tariff rate is 12.7 percent. Imports of agricultural products or used clothing and cars may require a license. Foreign and domestic investments are treated equally under the law. The financial system is closely linked to South Africa's and dominated by South African-owned banks. Much of the population lacks adequate access to banking services. There is no stock exchange.

Long-Term Score Change (since 1996)

RULE OF LAW		GOVERNMENT SIZE		REGULATORY EFFICIENCY		OPEN MARKETS	
Property Rights	–15.0	Fiscal Freedom	+9.4	Business Freedom	–0.3	Trade Freedom	+19.6
Freedom from Corruption	+19.0	Government Spending	–38.7	Labor Freedom	–8.0	Investment Freedom	–5.0
				Monetary Freedom	+9.9	Financial Freedom	+10.0

LIBERIA

Economic Freedom Score

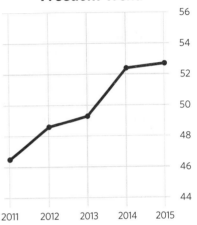

25   50   75

Least free 0   100 Most free

52.7

Liberia's economic freedom score is 52.7, making its economy the 141st freest in the 2015 *Index*. Its score is 0.3 point higher than last year, reflecting improvements in freedom from corruption and trade freedom that offset declines in six of the 10 economic freedoms, including property rights, labor freedom, and business freedom. Liberia is ranked 31st out of 46 countries in the Sub-Saharan Africa region, and its overall rating remains below the world and regional averages.

Liberia's high economic growth rates have corresponded with five years of strong advances in economic freedom. With Sub-Saharan Africa's third largest increase in economic freedom over the past half-decade, Liberia's score has advanced by 6.2 points. Progress in reducing corruption, improving fiscal accounts, and opening the economy to trade and investment have further cemented Liberia's progression out of the "repressed" category.

Nevertheless, the judicial system and the property rights regime remain weak. Efforts to reform land titling are progressing but not fully implemented. Business and labor regulations are becoming more efficient, but more progress is needed to promote sustained entrepreneurial and job growth.

BACKGROUND: In the 1990s, civil war killed a quarter of a million Liberians. A peace agreement was reached in 1995, and Charles Taylor was elected president. He was forced to step down and was subsequently found guilty of war crimes in April 2012. Ellen Johnson Sirleaf, elected president in 2005 and re-elected in 2011, was awarded the Nobel Peace Prize in 2011. The country remains fragile. In 2013, the United Nations Refugee Agency repatriated 155,000 Liberians who had fled during the civil war. Rampant corruption, high unemployment, and widespread illiteracy hinder development. Political instability and international sanctions have destroyed most large businesses and driven out many foreign investors. Liberia is rich in natural resources including rubber, mineral resources, and iron ore. It has suffered significantly from the 2014 Ebola virus outbreak in West Africa.

Freedom Trend

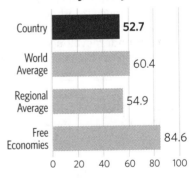

Country Comparisons

Country	52.7
World Average	60.4
Regional Average	54.9
Free Economies	84.6

0   20   40   60   80   100

Quick Facts

Population: 4.1 million
GDP (PPP): $2.9 billion
8.0% growth in 2013
5-year compound annual growth 7.0%
$703 per capita
Unemployment: 3.8%
Inflation (CPI): 7.6%
FDI Inflow: $1.1 billion
Public Debt: 29.5% of GDP

2013 data unless otherwise noted.
Data compiled as of September 2014.

How Do We Measure Economic Freedom?
See page 475 for an explanation of the methodology
or visit the *Index* Web site at *heritage.org/index.*

THE TEN ECONOMIC FREEDOMS

		Score			Rank	1-Year Change
RULE OF LAW	Property Rights	25.0			124th	–5.0
	Freedom from Corruption	38.0			83rd	+4.2

The Senate candidacy of the president's son in the October 2014 elections focused public attention on claims of nepotism and graft. Despite government efforts to fight it, corruption is endemic. Property rights are not strongly protected, and the rule of law remains uneven across the country. The judiciary lacks adequate facilities. Legislation to reconcile statutory and customary land tenure systems is pending.

		Score			Rank	1-Year Change
GOVERNMENT SIZE	Fiscal Freedom	83.0			60th	–0.6
	Government Spending	69.9			86th	–0.6

Liberia's top individual and corporate income tax rates are 25 percent. Other taxes include a property tax and a goods and services tax. The overall tax burden equals 21.1 percent of gross domestic product. Government expenditures are equivalent to 31.7 percent of the domestic economy, and public debt is equal to around 30 percent of domestic output.

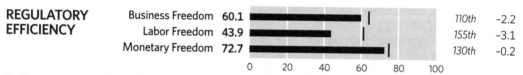

		Score			Rank	1-Year Change
REGULATORY EFFICIENCY	Business Freedom	60.1			110th	–2.2
	Labor Freedom	43.9			155th	–3.1
	Monetary Freedom	72.7			130th	–0.2

Reform measures have streamlined the procedures for establishing a business, but start-ups are discouraged by other institutional deficiencies such as pervasive corruption and very limited access to credit. Obtaining necessary licenses remains time-consuming. The labor market remains underdeveloped. The effectiveness of Liberian monetary policy is limited in the near term, given the high dollarization of the economy.

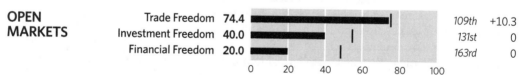

		Score			Rank	1-Year Change
OPEN MARKETS	Trade Freedom	74.4			109th	+10.3
	Investment Freedom	40.0			131st	0
	Financial Freedom	20.0			163rd	0

Liberia's average tariff rate is 5.3 percent. Imports may face customs delays, and state-owned enterprises may distort the economy. Foreign investment in several sectors is restricted. The rate of nonperforming loans is high. The high cost of credit and scarce access to financing hold back private-sector development. A large part of the population remains outside of the formal banking sector.

Long-Term Score Change (since 2009)

RULE OF LAW		GOVERNMENT SIZE		REGULATORY EFFICIENCY		OPEN MARKETS	
Property Rights	0	Fiscal Freedom	+9.2	Business Freedom	+19.9	Trade Freedom	+20.6
Freedom from Corruption	+17.0	Government Spending	–27.3	Labor Freedom	–5.9	Investment Freedom	+10.0
				Monetary Freedom	+2.6	Financial Freedom	0

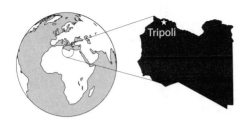
Tripoli

LIBYA

Economic Freedom Score

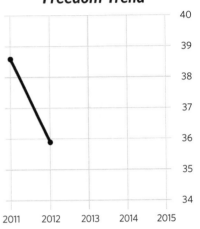

25   50   75

Least free 0   Most free 100

This economy is not graded

Numerical grading of Libya's overall economic freedom remains suspended for the third year in a row in the 2015 *Index* because ongoing political turmoil has resulted in deterioration in the quality of publicly available economic statistics. Facets of economic freedom for which data are still available have been individually scored. As a "repressed" economy with a score of 35.9, Libya was ranked last in the Middle East/North Africa region when it was last graded in the 2012 *Index*.

Political unrest, violence, and militia rule have continued to plague Libya ever since Muammar Qadhafi's ouster in 2011. Years of dictatorial rule left the economy largely dependent on oil resources. Structural and institutional mechanisms to guarantee sustained growth have been absent. Limited efforts to diversify the economy away from oil have been unsuccessful.

Libya faces serious long-term and short-term challenges. In the short term, a political transition must be achieved that limits violence and political instability. Establishing the rule of law and effective governance will be critical if the weak central government is to repair the crumbling economic infrastructure destroyed during the civil war.

BACKGROUND: Dictator Muammar Qadhafi was overthrown in 2011, and elections were held in July 2012. The new government under President Mohammed Magarief and Prime Minister Ali Zeidan struggled to rein in militias fighting for control of territory and resources. Zeidan stepped down in March 2014 and was replaced by Ahmed Maiteg in May. As fighting between militias and Islamist terrorist groups continued, Libya held legislative elections in June. Oil and natural gas provide about 80 percent of GDP, 95 percent of export revenues, and 99 percent of government revenues. Economic recovery began in 2012, and the energy sector is producing at pre-war levels. The government faces major challenges in disarming and demobilizing militias, improving the rule of law, and reforming the state-dominated socialist economy.

Freedom Trend

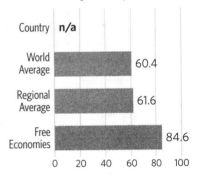

Country Comparisons

Country	n/a
World Average	60.4
Regional Average	61.6
Free Economies	84.6

0   20   40   60   80   100

Quick Facts

Population: 6.1 million
GDP (PPP): $70.4 billion
–9.4% growth in 2013
5-year compound annual growth –6.0%
$11,498 per capita
Unemployment: 9.0%
Inflation (CPI): 2.6%
FDI Inflow: $702.0 million
Public Debt: n/a

2013 data unless otherwise noted.
Data compiled as of September 2014.

How Do We Measure Economic Freedom?
See page 475 for an explanation of the methodology
or visit the *Index* Web site at *heritage.org/index*.

THE TEN ECONOMIC FREEDOMS

		Score		Rank	1-Year Change
RULE OF LAW	Property Rights	10.0		165th	0
	Freedom from Corruption	15.0		180th	-3.3

Institutional effectiveness continues to be undermined by security problems. Many experienced technocrats who served under the Qadhafi regime are blocked from assuming leadership roles in which they might be able to execute effective policy. In 2014, numerous investigations of foreign companies allegedly complicit in improper business practices in Libya under the Gaddafi regime continued.

		Score		Rank	Change
GOVERNMENT SIZE	Fiscal Freedom	95.0		11th	0
	Government Spending	37.5		155th	+37.5

Libya's top individual income tax rate is 10 percent, and its corporate tax rate is 20 percent (plus a 4 percent surcharge for a Jihad Fund). Oil revenue makes up 96 percent of all government revenue, and security concerns make tax administration erratic. Overall tax revenue amounts to less than one percent of gross domestic product, and expenditures equal 45.7 percent of GDP.

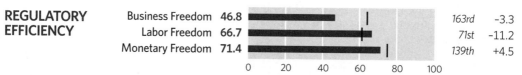

		Score		Rank	Change
REGULATORY EFFICIENCY	Business Freedom	46.8		163rd	-3.3
	Labor Freedom	66.7		71st	-11.2
	Monetary Freedom	71.4		139th	+4.5

The business environment, lacking transparency and efficiency, remains very poor and fragile. The labor market, which already suffered from state interference and control, has been severely affected by political instability and uncertainty. In the 2014 budget, the government committed to subsidy reform by January 2015, starting with the conversion of goods and fuel subsidies into cash subsidies.

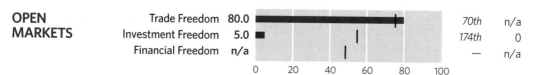

		Score		Rank	Change
OPEN MARKETS	Trade Freedom	80.0		70th	n/a
	Investment Freedom	5.0		174th	0
	Financial Freedom	n/a		—	n/a

Libya has a 0 percent average tariff rate. The country's regulatory regime interferes with trade. State-owned enterprises distort the economy, and political unrest discourages international trade and investment. The financial sector has many shortcomings in its diversification and scope. The central bank owns four of the major banks that dominate the banking sector.

Long-Term Score Change: n/a

RULE OF LAW		GOVERNMENT SIZE		REGULATORY EFFICIENCY		OPEN MARKETS	
Property Rights	n/a	Fiscal Freedom	n/a	Business Freedom	n/a	Trade Freedom	n/a
Freedom from Corruption	n/a	Government Spending	n/a	Labor Freedom	n/a	Investment Freedom	n/a
				Monetary Freedom	n/a	Financial Freedom	n/a

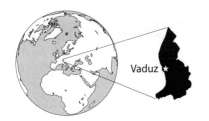

Vaduz ★

LIECHTENSTEIN

Economic Freedom Score

Least free 0

Most free

This economy is not graded

World Rank: Not Ranked   Regional Rank: Not Ranked

Liechtenstein's economic freedom score remains unrated in the 2015 *Index* because of a lack of sufficient comparable data. Those aspects of economic freedom for which data are available have been individually scored. The country will receive an overall economic freedom score and ranking in future editions as more information becomes available.

Liechtenstein is a modern and diversified economy that has made dynamic engagement with global commerce the cornerstone of its economic policy. An efficient regulatory environment that is open to trade and investment has contributed to the development of a robust banking sector. Tax rates are competitive, and labor laws allow employers and employees to respond efficiently to changing market dynamics.

Enhanced levels of political and social stability have facilitated the development of a high-value service industry that has capitalized on a well-entrenched rule of law. Property rights are respected, and the judicial system is transparent. The absence of corruption minimizes potential drags on the economy and encourages entrepreneurialism.

BACKGROUND: Prince of Liechtenstein Hans-Adam II is head of state, but his son Prince Alois wields considerable power as regent. The center-right Progressive Citizens' Party won the March 2013 parliamentary elections, and Prime Minister Adrian Hasler now heads the government. Liechtenstein has a vibrant free-enterprise economy. Low taxes and traditions of strict bank secrecy (though less secret than before) have helped financial institutions to attract funds. Still, the worldwide financial crisis led to a sharp contraction in the banking sector. In 2009, the Organisation for Economic Cooperation and Development removed Liechtenstein from its list of uncooperative tax havens. The principality's economy is closely linked to Switzerland, whose currency it shares, and the European Union. Liechtenstein is a member of the European Free Trade Association and the European Economic Area but not the EU.

Freedom Trend

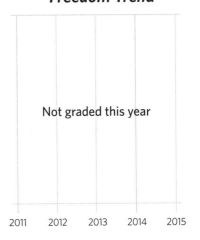

Not graded this year

2011   2012   2013   2014   2015

Country Comparisons

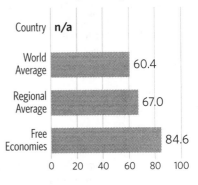

Country   n/a
World Average   60.4
Regional Average   67.0
Free Economies   84.6

0   20   40   60   80   100

Quick Facts

Population: 37,313
GDP (nominal): $5.8 billion (2012)
1.8% growth in 2012
5-year compound annual growth n/a
$158,976 per capita (nominal, 2012)
Unemployment: 2.3% (2012)
Inflation (CPI): -0.7% (2012)
FDI Inflow: n/a
Public Debt: n/a

2013 data unless otherwise noted.
Data compiled as of September 2014.

How Do We Measure Economic Freedom?
See page 475 for an explanation of the methodology
or visit the *Index* Web site at *heritage.org/index*.

291

THE TEN ECONOMIC FREEDOMS

		Score	■ Country │ World Average	Rank	1-Year Change

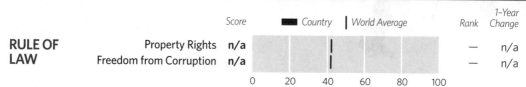

RULE OF LAW

	Score	Rank	1-Year Change
Property Rights	n/a	—	n/a
Freedom from Corruption	n/a	—	n/a

Liechtenstein is largely free of corruption, although as an offshore banking center, it must continue to work to prevent money laundering in its banking system. The judiciary is independent and impartial despite the appointment of judges by the hereditary monarch. Property rights and contracts are secure. Intellectual property laws are based on Switzerland's IPR protection regimes.

GOVERNMENT SIZE

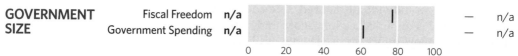

	Score	Rank	1-Year Change
Fiscal Freedom	n/a	—	n/a
Government Spending	n/a	—	n/a

Tax reform that went into effect in 2011 lowered rates, modernized administration, and improved transparency. The top individual income tax rate is 7 percent, and the top corporate tax rate is 12.5 percent. A value-added tax is administered by Switzerland. Although the fiscal system lacks some transparency, government fiscal management has been relatively sound.

REGULATORY EFFICIENCY

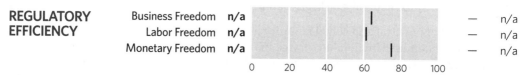

	Score	Rank	1-Year Change
Business Freedom	n/a	—	n/a
Labor Freedom	n/a	—	n/a
Monetary Freedom	n/a	—	n/a

The efficient regulatory framework facilitates entrepreneurial activity. Government generally takes a hand-off approach in sectors dominated by small businesses. Unemployment has been low, and labor market policies have focused on minimizing youth unemployment. Liechtenstein has a de facto monetary union with Switzerland but no vote in the Swiss National Bank's monetary policy.

OPEN MARKETS

	Score	Rank	1-Year Change
Trade Freedom	90.0	1st	0
Investment Freedom	85.0	13th	0
Financial Freedom	80.0	3rd	0

Liechtenstein has a 0 percent average tariff rate. The government maintains an open trade and investment regime and generally does not discriminate against foreign investors. There are no restrictions on repatriation of profits or currency transfers. Liechtenstein is a major financial center, particularly in private banking. The banking sector remains stable under a prudent regulatory regime.

Long-Term Score Change: n/a

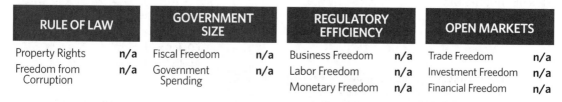

RULE OF LAW		GOVERNMENT SIZE		REGULATORY EFFICIENCY		OPEN MARKETS	
Property Rights	n/a	Fiscal Freedom	n/a	Business Freedom	n/a	Trade Freedom	n/a
Freedom from Corruption	n/a	Government Spending	n/a	Labor Freedom	n/a	Investment Freedom	n/a
				Monetary Freedom	n/a	Financial Freedom	n/a

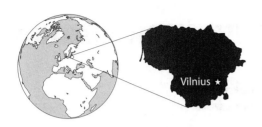

LITHUANIA

Economic Freedom Score

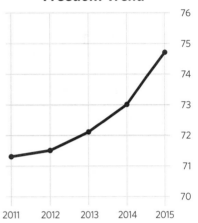

74.7

World Rank: 15   **Regional Rank: 6**

Lithuania's economic freedom score is 74.7, making its economy the 15th freest in the 2015 *Index*. Its overall score is up by 1.7 points from last year, reflecting improvements in half of the 10 economic freedoms including freedom from corruption, the management of public spending, labor freedom, and monetary freedom. Lithuania is ranked 6th out of 43 countries in the Europe region, and its overall score is well above the world and regional averages.

Recording its fifth straight year of advancing economic freedom, Lithuania achieved its highest score ever in the 2015 *Index*. Since 2011, its economic freedom has advanced by 3.4 points, with gains in seven of the 10 economic freedoms driven by prudent fiscal and monetary policies and declining levels of perceived corruption. Remarkably, Lithuania has experienced no score declines in any factor over this period.

Lithuania's transition to a dynamic economy open to global commerce is facilitated by low tariff barriers and open financial markets. Investors are attracted by an efficient regulatory environment with low barriers to entry. The economy scores above average on rule of law, but institutional issues in the judiciary and property rights regime persist.

BACKGROUND: Lithuania, largest of the three Baltic States, regained its independence from the Soviet Union in 1991. It joined the European Union and NATO in 2004. Lithuania is a parliamentary republic with some attributes of a semi-presidential system. Under President Dalia Grybauskaite, re-elected in May 2014, the country has worked to improve transparency in parliamentary elections, on judicial reforms, and on energy and financial security. Prime Minister Algirdas Butkevicius of the Social Democratic Party presides over a center-left coalition. Lithuania is heavily dependent on Russia for natural gas and is building the region's largest offshore liquefied natural gas terminal to access other sources of energy. The construction, financial services, and retail sectors have grown.

Freedom Trend

Country Comparisons

Quick Facts

Population: 3.0 million
GDP (PPP): $67.6 billion
3.3% growth in 2013
5-year compound annual growth -0.4%
$22,747 per capita
Unemployment: 12.1%
Inflation (CPI): 1.2%
FDI Inflow: $531.1 million
Public Debt: 39.3% of GDP

2013 data unless otherwise noted.
Data compiled as of September 2014.

How Do We Measure Economic Freedom?
See page 475 for an explanation of the methodology
or visit the *Index* Web site at *heritage.org/index*.

THE TEN ECONOMIC FREEDOMS

		Score		Rank	1-Year Change

RULE OF LAW

	Score	Rank	1-Year Change
Property Rights	60.0	41st	0
Freedom from Corruption	57.0	42nd	+7.1

Corruption is present at all levels of state governance and public administration. State procurement is also a problem; it is often claimed that tender requirements, for example, are tailored to fit specific bidders. In 2013, a court found four Labor Party officials guilty of a fraud scheme to benefit the party. EU membership has strengthened judicial independence, but many improvements are still needed.

GOVERNMENT SIZE

	Score	Rank	1-Year Change
Fiscal Freedom	92.9	18th	0
Government Spending	61.3	107th	+5.4

The top individual and corporate income tax rates are 15 percent. Some small businesses qualify for a reduced rate of 5 percent. Other taxes include an inheritance tax and a value-added tax. Total revenue is equal to 16 percent of domestic production. Public expenditures amounts to 35.9 percent of domestic output, and public debt equals 39 percent of gross domestic product.

REGULATORY EFFICIENCY

	Score	Rank	1-Year Change
Business Freedom	84.9	22nd	–0.8
Labor Freedom	62.0	94th	+3.0
Monetary Freedom	81.2	39th	+2.6

Incorporating a firm involves three procedures, and no minimum capital is required. Labor market dynamics have improved, and a ceiling on unemployment benefits has been introduced. The government used its EU presidency in 2013 to push for reductions in EU Common Agricultural Policy subsidies, but it must further reduce its own state subsidies when it joins the eurozone in 2015.

OPEN MARKETS

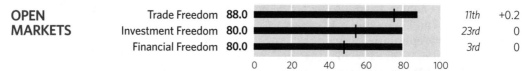

	Score	Rank	1-Year Change
Trade Freedom	88.0	11th	+0.2
Investment Freedom	80.0	23rd	0
Financial Freedom	80.0	3rd	0

EU members have a 1.0 percent average tariff rate. Although some non-tariff barriers exist, the EU is relatively open to external trade. Lithuania's policies welcome investment, but foreign purchases of agricultural land are restricted. The financial sector remains stable. Although a mid-sized domestic bank failed in 2013, financial stability has not been impaired.

Long-Term Score Change (since 1996)

RULE OF LAW		GOVERNMENT SIZE		REGULATORY EFFICIENCY		OPEN MARKETS	
Property Rights	+10.0	Fiscal Freedom	+16.3	Business Freedom	+14.9	Trade Freedom	+23.0
Freedom from Corruption	+27.0	Government Spending	–1.1	Labor Freedom	+6.2	Investment Freedom	+30.0
				Monetary Freedom	+68.3	Financial Freedom	+50.0

LUXEMBOURG

World Rank: 21   **Regional Rank: 10**

Economic Freedom Score

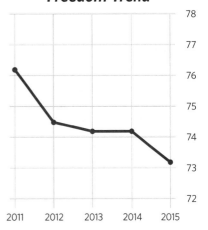

25   **50**   75

Least free 0   100 Most free

73.2

L uxembourg's economic freedom score is 73.2, making its economy the 21st freest in the 2015 *Index*. Its overall score has decreased by 1.0 point since last year, with declines in the management of government spending, freedom from corruption, and business freedom outweighing improvements in monetary freedom and trade freedom. Luxembourg is ranked 10th out of 43 countries in the Europe region, and its overall score continues to be above the world and regional averages.

Luxembourg's economic freedom score has fallen steadily for five years. A decline of 3.0 points has been led by double-digit drops in the management of public finance and in policy areas related to regulatory efficiency. Once a "free" economy, Luxembourg has dropped to well within the ranks of the "mostly free."

Small and landlocked, Luxembourg has made engagement with the global economy the cornerstone of its economic policy. Investment freedom, the world's most highly ranked, has led to the development of a robust banking sector. Regulations are relatively efficient, but labor markets are somewhat inelastic. Fiscal accounts must be managed more prudently for the economy to promote growth and return to the top ranks of the *Index*.

BACKGROUND: A founding member of the European Union in 1957 and the euro in 1999, the Grand Duchy of Luxembourg continues to promote European integration. Prime Minister Xavier Bettel of the Democratic Party was elected in December 2013, defeating the Christian Social People's Party that had been in power since 1979. Luxembourgers have one of the world's highest income levels, although the global economic crisis provoked the first recession in 60 years in 2009. During the 20th century, Luxembourg evolved into a mixed manufacturing and services economy with incredibly strong financial services. The government is trying to diversify the economy by promoting Luxembourg as an information technology and e-commerce hub. The country has a skilled workforce and well-developed infrastructure.

Freedom Trend

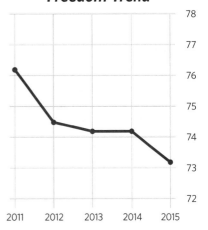

	78
	77
	76
	75
	74
	73
	72

2011   2012   2013   2014   2015

Country Comparisons

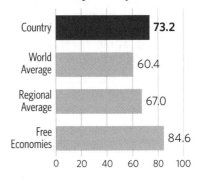

Country	**73.2**
World Average	60.4
Regional Average	67.0
Free Economies	84.6

0   20   40   60   80   100

Quick Facts

Population: 0.5 million
GDP (PPP): $42.6 billion
2.0% growth in 2013
5-year compound annual growth 0.2%
$78,670 per capita
Unemployment: 5.7%
Inflation (CPI): 1.7%
FDI Inflow: $30.1 billion
Public Debt: 22.9% of GDP

2013 data unless otherwise noted.
Data compiled as of September 2014.

THE TEN ECONOMIC FREEDOMS

	Score	Rank	1-Year Change
RULE OF LAW			
Property Rights	90.0	3rd	0
Freedom from Corruption	80.0	11th	-4.1

The government is largely free from corruption, but the prime minister resigned in July 2013 amid disclosures of abuses by the State Intelligence Service, including secret recordings of politicians taking payments in return for access to local officials. The judiciary is independent, and the legal framework strongly supports the rule of law. Private property rights are protected, and contracts are secure.

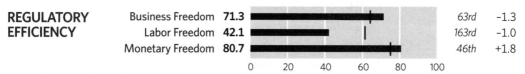

	Score	Rank	1-Year Change
GOVERNMENT SIZE			
Fiscal Freedom	62.3	163rd	-0.5
Government Spending	42.2	147th	-5.4

The top individual income tax rate is 43.6 percent, and the top corporate tax rate is 21 percent. Other taxes include a surtax for the unemployment fund, a value-added tax, and an inheritance tax. Overall tax revenues amount to 37.8 percent of domestic output, and public expenditures are equivalent to 43.9 percent of domestic production. Public debt equals about 23 percent of gross domestic product.

	Score	Rank	1-Year Change
REGULATORY EFFICIENCY			
Business Freedom	71.3	63rd	-1.3
Labor Freedom	42.1	163rd	-1.0
Monetary Freedom	80.7	46th	+1.8

The regulatory framework generally facilitates entrepreneurial activity. Launching a business takes six procedures, but obtaining necessary permits remains time-consuming. Hiring and dismissal regulations are burdensome, with generous fringe benefits among the world's costliest. Monetary stability has been well maintained. The agricultural sector is highly subsidized by the government and through the EU's Common Agricultural Policy.

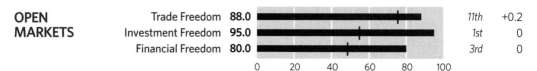

	Score	Rank	1-Year Change
OPEN MARKETS			
Trade Freedom	88.0	11th	+0.2
Investment Freedom	95.0	1st	0
Financial Freedom	80.0	3rd	0

EU members have a 1.0 percent average tariff rate. Although some non-tariff barriers exist, the EU is relatively open to external trade. Luxembourg treats foreign and domestic investors equally under the law. The competitive financial sector provides a wide range of financing options. As a global financial hub, the sophisticated banking sector remains well capitalized. The capital market is vibrant.

Long-Term Score Change (since 1996)

RULE OF LAW		GOVERNMENT SIZE		REGULATORY EFFICIENCY		OPEN MARKETS	
Property Rights	0	Fiscal Freedom	+15.7	Business Freedom	-13.7	Trade Freedom	+9.0
Freedom from Corruption	-10.0	Government Spending	+5.1	Labor Freedom	-9.3	Investment Freedom	+25.0
				Monetary Freedom	-4.0	Financial Freedom	+10.0

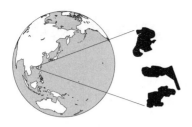

MACAU

Economic Freedom Score

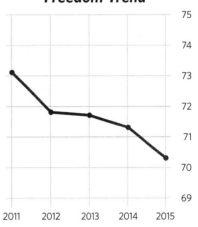

Least free 0   25   50   75   100   Most free

70.3

World Rank: 34   **Regional Rank: 9**

Macau's economic freedom score is 70.3, making its economy the 34th freest in the 2015 *Index*. Its overall score is 1.0 point lower than last year, reflecting declines in labor freedom and monetary freedom that outweigh small improvements in the management of government spending and fiscal freedom. Macau is ranked 9th out of 42 countries in the Asia–Pacific region, and its overall score is well above the world and regional averages.

Macau has one of the world's highest economic growth rates, driven largely by gambling and tourism. However, over the past five years, its economic freedom has declined by nearly 3.0 points, led by large declines in labor and monetary freedoms. Its economy is now well down in the ranks of the "mostly free," and prospects for more diversified development are unclear.

Despite this disappointing trend, Macau's long-standing history as a free port city and its openness to international trade and investment provide strong foundations for economic freedom. The judiciary largely respects property rights, and the government has stepped up enforcement of anti–money laundering efforts. Taxes are low, and government spending is prudent.

BACKGROUND: Macau was colonized by the Portuguese in the 16th century and became the first European settlement in the Far East. It became a Special Administrative Region of China in 1999, and its chief executive is appointed by Beijing. Under China's "one country, two systems" policy, Macau enjoys a high degree of autonomy except in matters of national defense and foreign policy. Macau is one of the world's largest gaming centers, and gaming-related taxes accounted for 85 percent of government revenue in 2013. Much of the island's economic activity is driven by Chinese tourists. Manufacturing of textiles and apparel, once the mainstay of the economy, has largely migrated to the mainland. Macau's currency is fully convertible into the Hong Kong dollar, which in turn is pegged to the U.S. dollar.

Freedom Trend

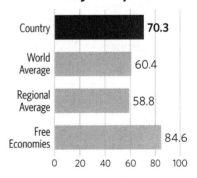

75
74
73
72
71
70
69

2011   2012   2013   2014   2015

Country Comparisons

Country	**70.3**
World Average	60.4
Regional Average	58.8
Free Economies	84.6

0   20   40   60   80   100

Quick Facts

Population: 0.6 million
GDP (PPP): $51.7 billion
11.9% growth in 2013
5-year compound annual growth n/a
$88,700 per capita
Unemployment: 2.0%
Inflation (CPI): 5.5%
FDI Inflow: $2.3 billion
Public Debt: 0.0% of GDP

2013 data unless otherwise noted.
Data compiled as of September 2014.

How Do We Measure Economic Freedom?
See page 475 for an explanation of the methodology or visit the *Index* Web site at *heritage.org/index*.

THE TEN ECONOMIC FREEDOMS

	Score		Rank	1-Year Change
RULE OF LAW				
Property Rights	60.0		41st	0
Freedom from Corruption	49.7		54th	0

Beijing's crackdown on corruption and tax evasion caused casino revenues to decline in 2014. A proposed law that would grant outgoing chief executives immunity from criminal charges sparked public demonstrations and was dropped in May 2014. Macau has its own judicial system with a high court; the legal framework is based largely on Portuguese law. Property rights and commercial contracts are secure.

	Score		Rank	1-Year Change
GOVERNMENT SIZE				
Fiscal Freedom	71.8		132nd	+0.4
Government Spending	91.8		9th	+0.1

Macau's top individual income tax rate is 12 percent, and its top corporate tax rate is 39 percent. Gaming and gambling account for a large portion of both tax and overall revenue, which is equal to 34 percent of domestic production. Public expenditures are 16.5 percent of gross domestic product, and there is no public debt.

	Score		Rank	1-Year Change
REGULATORY EFFICIENCY				
Business Freedom	60.0		111th	0
Labor Freedom	50.0		140th	-5.0
Monetary Freedom	74.9		108th	-4.9

Macau's overall regulatory framework is relatively efficient, but reform efforts are largely absent. On average, it takes three to four weeks to incorporate a business. Licensing requirements vary by type of economic activity. The labor market lacks dynamic growth and remains highly segmented. Monetary stability has been relatively well maintained, but government subsidies to households quadrupled between 2008 and 2014.

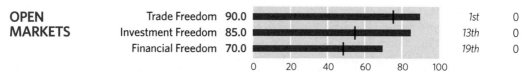

	Score		Rank	1-Year Change
OPEN MARKETS				
Trade Freedom	90.0		1st	0
Investment Freedom	85.0		13th	0
Financial Freedom	70.0		19th	0

Macau has a 0 percent average tariff rate. Non-tariff barriers are low. Foreign investors receive national treatment. A relatively small financial sector, dominated by banks, provides a range of financial services. The banking system, dominated by banks owned by China and Hong Kong, remains stable and well capitalized, with a very low rate of nonperforming loans.

Long-Term Score Change (since 2009)

RULE OF LAW		GOVERNMENT SIZE		REGULATORY EFFICIENCY		OPEN MARKETS	
Property Rights	0	Fiscal Freedom	-7.5	Business Freedom	0	Trade Freedom	0
Freedom from Corruption	-7.3	Government Spending	-1.5	Labor Freedom	-10.0	Investment Freedom	+15.0
				Monetary Freedom	-5.4	Financial Freedom	0

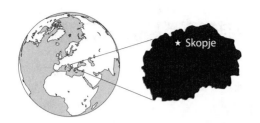

★ Skopje

MACEDONIA

Economic Freedom Score

50
25   75

Least free 0   100 Most free

67.1

World Rank: 53   **Regional Rank: 24**

Macedonia's economic freedom score is 67.1, making its economy the 53rd freest in the 2015 *Index*. Its overall score has decreased by 1.5 points since last year, with improvements in freedom from corruption and trade freedom outweighed by declines in labor freedom, business freedom, the management of government spending, and monetary freedom. Macedonia is ranked 24th out of 43 countries in the Europe region, and its overall score is above the world and regional averages.

Macedonia's transition to a more market-based economy has been facilitated by relatively high social and political stability that has enabled the economy to adapt to comprehensive reform measures. Over the past five years, Macedonia's economic freedom has advanced by 1.1 points with notable score improvements in half of the 10 economic freedoms, including business freedom, freedom from corruption, and trade freedom.

Macedonia has made considerable progress in income growth and overall poverty reduction. Competitive flat tax rates and a permissive trade regime, buttressed by a relatively efficient regulatory framework, have encouraged the emergence of a dynamic private sector. Implementation of deeper institutional reforms will be critical to ensuring more dynamic long-term development.

BACKGROUND: The Republic of Macedonia gained its independence from the former Yugoslavia in 1991 and has achieved considerable political and economic stability. Prime Minister Nikola Gruevski of the conservative party VMRO-DPMNE prevailed in the April 2014 presidential and parliamentary elections in a coalition with the Democratic Union for Integration. Macedonia completed NATO's Membership Action Plan in 2008, but Greece continues to block its accession to the alliance because it objects to Macedonia's name. This dispute is delaying Macedonia's accession to the European Union as well. Macedonia is a developing country with a substantial fiscal deficit, but its economy is growing. Improvements in the legal framework are creating a stable environment for foreign and domestic investment.

Freedom Trend

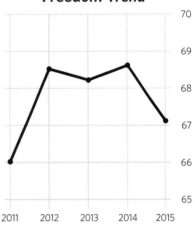

70

69

68

67

66

65

2011   2012   2013   2014   2015

Country Comparisons

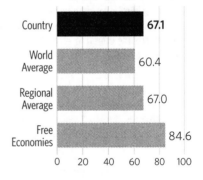

Country **67.1**

World Average 60.4

Regional Average 67.0

Free Economies 84.6

0   20   40   60   80   100

Quick Facts

Population: 2.1 million
GDP (PPP): $22.6 billion
3.1% growth in 2013
5-year compound annual growth 1.5%
$10,904 per capita
Unemployment: 29.7%
Inflation (CPI): 2.8%
FDI Inflow: $333.9 million
Public Debt: 35.8% of GDP

2013 data unless otherwise noted.
Data compiled as of September 2014.

How Do We Measure Economic Freedom?
See page 475 for an explanation of the methodology or visit the *Index* Web site at *heritage.org/index*.

THE TEN ECONOMIC FREEDOMS

	Score		Rank	1-Year Change
RULE OF LAW				
Property Rights	35.0		87th	0
Freedom from Corruption	44.0		67th	+4.4

Corruption and cronyism are prevalent in public administration and procurement procedures, increasing costs for businesses and chilling foreign investment. Macedonia remains an important transit and destination point for human trafficking to Western Europe, as well as for the smuggling of arms, drugs, and stolen cars. Registering real property and obtaining land titles continue to be difficult.

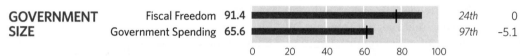

	Score		Rank	1-Year Change
GOVERNMENT SIZE				
Fiscal Freedom	91.4		24th	0
Government Spending	65.6		97th	-5.1

Individual and corporate income tax rates are a flat 10 percent. Other taxes include a value-added tax and a property transfer tax. Tax revenue constitutes 25.6 percent of domestic income, and government spending accounts for 33.8 percent of the domestic economy. Public debt is equal to about 36 percent of gross domestic product.

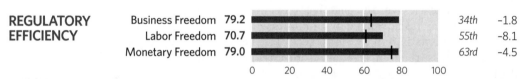

	Score		Rank	1-Year Change
REGULATORY EFFICIENCY				
Business Freedom	79.2		34th	-1.8
Labor Freedom	70.7		55th	-8.1
Monetary Freedom	79.0		63rd	-4.5

Forming a business takes two procedures and two days, with no minimum capital required, but completing licensing requirements remains relatively time-consuming. The labor market lacks flexibility, hindering more dynamic job growth. The state has tried to maintain fiscal discipline to bolster its case for eventual membership in the eurozone, but spending on agricultural subsidies increased again in 2014.

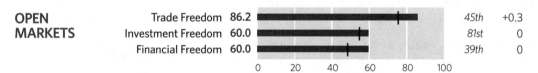

	Score		Rank	1-Year Change
OPEN MARKETS				
Trade Freedom	86.2		45th	+0.3
Investment Freedom	60.0		81st	0
Financial Freedom	60.0		39th	0

Macedonia's average tariff rate is 1.9 percent. The country has worked to reduce trade barriers since joining the WTO. Non-tariff barriers are relatively low, and foreign and domestic investors are generally treated equally. The financial sector has been restructured. The banking sector is more open to foreign banks and has withstood the global financial turmoil relatively well. The capital market is evolving.

Long-Term Score Change (since 2002)

RULE OF LAW		GOVERNMENT SIZE		REGULATORY EFFICIENCY		OPEN MARKETS	
Property Rights	+5.0	Fiscal Freedom	+10.4	Business Freedom	+24.2	Trade Freedom	+23.2
Freedom from Corruption	+11.0	Government Spending	+2.3	Labor Freedom	+14.5	Investment Freedom	+10.0
				Monetary Freedom	+1.8	Financial Freedom	-10.0

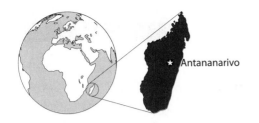

MADAGASCAR

★ Antananarivo

Economic Freedom Score

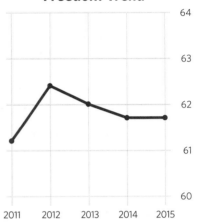

61.7

Least free 0 — Most free 100

| World Rank: **79** | Regional Rank: **7** |

Madagascar's economic freedom score is 61.7, making its economy the 79th freest in the 2015 *Index*. Its score is unchanged from last year, with improvements in six of the 10 economic freedoms, including property rights, the control of government spending, and monetary freedom, offset by significant deteriorations in trade freedom and investment freedom. Madagascar is ranked 7th out of 46 countries in the Sub-Saharan Africa region, and its overall score is above the world and regional averages.

Over the past five years, Madagascar's economic freedom has advanced by 0.6 point. Although the country remains in the ranks of the "moderately free," the absence of committed reforms has undermined overall competitiveness, turned away investors, and eroded the rule of law.

Corruption is pervasive and has contributed to political unrest and a general distrust of the ruling elite. Economic losses from corruption inhibit the development of a strong entrepreneurial environment, a situation that is compounded by inefficient business and labor regulations. Because financial services have not proliferated, the expansion of small businesses and entrepreneurs is stunted.

BACKGROUND: The former French colony of Madagascar has endured decades of military coups, political violence, and corruption but has stabilized in recent years. Following four years of political stalemate and a mediation process led by the Southern African Development Community, Hery Rajaonarimampianina was elected president in January 2014. In April, Roger Kolo was appointed prime minister, and a new government was established. Following a coup in 2009, international organizations and foreign donors severed ties with Madagascar, but in light of the last election, many have expressed their willingness to normalize economic relations. Madagascar's economy is largely agricultural. Sitting just off the east coast of Africa, it is highly vulnerable to natural disasters and weather shocks. The World Bank estimates that 92 percent of Malagasy live on less than $2 a day.

Freedom Trend

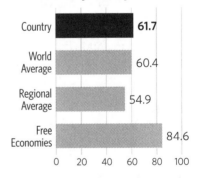

Country Comparisons

Country	61.7
World Average	60.4
Regional Average	54.9
Free Economies	84.6

Quick Facts

Population: 23.0 million
GDP (PPP): $22.3 billion
2.4% growth in 2013
5-year compound annual growth 0.6%
$970 per capita
Unemployment: 3.8%
Inflation (CPI): 5.8%
FDI Inflow: $837.5 million
Public Debt: 38.4% of GDP

2013 data unless otherwise noted.
Data compiled as of September 2014.

How Do We Measure Economic Freedom?
See page 475 for an explanation of the methodology
or visit the *Index* Web site at *heritage.org/index*.

THE TEN ECONOMIC FREEDOMS

		Score		Rank	1-Year Change
RULE OF LAW	Property Rights	45.0		66th	+5.0
	Freedom from Corruption	28.0		132nd	+0.7

After a democratically elected government took office in 2014, the prime minister announced that 40 percent of his country's budget is lost to graft and pledged to fight it. In June 2014, the Extractive Industries Transparency Initiative reinstated Madagascar's membership, which had been suspended in the wake of a coup in 2009. The judiciary remains susceptible to corruption and executive influence.

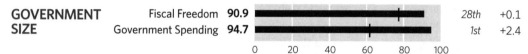

		Score		Rank	1-Year Change
GOVERNMENT SIZE	Fiscal Freedom	90.9		28th	+0.1
	Government Spending	94.7		1st	+2.4

Madagascar's individual and corporate income tax rates are 20 percent. Other taxes include a value-added tax and a capital gains tax. The overall tax burden is 10.3 percent of domestic output. Government expenditures are equivalent to 13.3 percent of domestic production. Public debt is equal to about 39 percent of gross domestic product.

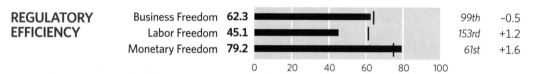

		Score		Rank	1-Year Change
REGULATORY EFFICIENCY	Business Freedom	62.3		99th	-0.5
	Labor Freedom	45.1		153rd	+1.2
	Monetary Freedom	79.2		61st	+1.6

Previous reforms have reduced the number of days and procedures required to launch a new business, but completing licensing requirements still takes over four months on average. Much of the workforce is employed in the informal sector. In a 2014 IMF agreement, the government pledged to maintain fiscal and monetary discipline and reduce costly fuel price subsidies with better-targeted anti-poverty programs.

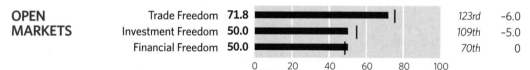

		Score		Rank	1-Year Change
OPEN MARKETS	Trade Freedom	71.8		123rd	-6.0
	Investment Freedom	50.0		109th	-5.0
	Financial Freedom	50.0		70th	0

Madagascar's average tariff rate is 9.1 percent. The government relies on tariffs for revenue but maintains few non-tariff barriers. Investors face an unsettled political environment. The financial system includes over 40 credit institutions and 11 banks. There is no stock exchange, and financing for new businesses is not readily available. State-issued treasury bills are used to bridge budget deficits.

Long-Term Score Change (since 1995)

RULE OF LAW		GOVERNMENT SIZE		REGULATORY EFFICIENCY		OPEN MARKETS	
Property Rights	+15.0	Fiscal Freedom	+16.2	Business Freedom	-7.7	Trade Freedom	+34.2
Freedom from Corruption	+18.0	Government Spending	+6.8	Labor Freedom	-3.8	Investment Freedom	0
				Monetary Freedom	+5.2	Financial Freedom	+20.0

Lilongwe ★

MALAWI

Economic Freedom Score

50

25   75

Least free 0   100 Most free

54.8

| World Rank: **126** | Regional Rank: **25** |

Malawi's economic freedom score is 54.8, making its economy the 126th freest in the 2015 *Index*. Its score is 0.6 point lower than last year, reflecting declines in property rights, the control of government spending, monetary freedom, and trade freedom that outweigh gains in business freedom, investment freedom, and freedom from corruption. Malawi is ranked 25th out of 46 countries in the Sub-Saharan Africa region, and its overall score is below the world average.

Malawi has yet to develop the basic institutional framework to improve economic freedom and address poverty. Government efforts to reverse some anti-market policies in an attempt to attract donors have largely been offset by high levels of government spending and soaring inflation.

A weak institutional foundation and structural shortcomings keep Malawi "mostly unfree." The independence of the judiciary is recognized in the constitution but not always observed in practice. Business regulations are among the world's most inefficient, and the labor market is rigid. The financial sector is underdeveloped and does not effectively allocate capital to productive means. Trade freedom is below the world average.

BACKGROUND: Malawi achieved independence from the British in 1964 and was ruled as a one-party state by Dr. Hastings Kamuzu Banda for 30 years. President Bingu wa Mutharika, elected in 2004 and re-elected in 2009, died in April 2012 and was replaced by Vice President Joyce Banda. In May 2014, Peter Mutharika, brother of the late president, was elected president in elections regarded as flawed. Malawi is one of Africa's most densely populated countries. More than half of the population lives below the poverty line, and over 85 percent depend on subsistence agriculture. Tobacco, tea, and sugar are the most important exports. In late 2013, international donors suspended aid to protest a scandal that involved the public looting of roughly 1 percent of Malawi's annual GDP over six months.

Freedom Trend

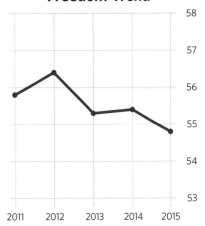

58

57

56

55

54

53

2011   2012   2013   2014   2015

Country Comparisons

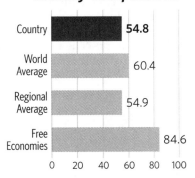

Country		54.8
World Average		60.4
Regional Average		54.9
Free Economies		84.6

0   20   40   60   80   100

Quick Facts

Population: 17.1 million
GDP (PPP): $15.0 billion
5.0% growth in 2013
5-year compound annual growth 5.3%
$879 per capita
Unemployment: 7.6%
Inflation (CPI): 27.7%
FDI Inflow: $118.4 million
Public Debt: 68.9% of GDP

2013 data unless otherwise noted.
Data compiled as of September 2014.

How Do We Measure Economic Freedom?
See page 475 for an explanation of the methodology
or visit the *Index* Web site at *heritage.org/index*.

303

THE TEN ECONOMIC FREEDOMS

		Score		Rank	1-Year Change
RULE OF LAW	Property Rights	40.0		70th	-5.0
	Freedom from Corruption	37.0		92nd	+5.1

Treason charges against President Mutharika citing efforts to block the democratic accession of his predecessor, Joyce Banda, to the presidency were quickly dropped following his May 2014 election victory, raising concerns about the judiciary's independence. Corruption remains endemic, with an estimated 30 percent of Malawi's budget lost to fraud (e.g., through "Cashgate" transactions using the government's automated payments system).

		Score		Rank	1-Year Change
GOVERNMENT SIZE	Fiscal Freedom	78.5		100th	+0.5
	Government Spending	49.0		134th	-14.0

Malawi's individual and corporate income tax rates are 30 percent. Other taxes include a value-added tax and a capital gains tax. The overall tax burden has reached 18.8 percent of gross domestic product. Public expenditures are equal to 41.2 percent of total domestic economic activity, and public debt is equivalent to about 69 percent of GDP.

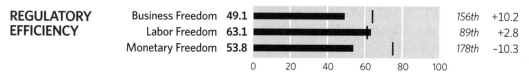

		Score		Rank	1-Year Change
REGULATORY EFFICIENCY	Business Freedom	49.1		156th	+10.2
	Labor Freedom	63.1		89th	+2.8
	Monetary Freedom	53.8		178th	-10.3

The inefficient business environment continues to impede broader economic development. Incorporating a business takes over a month on average, although there is no minimum capital requirement. In the absence of a well-functioning labor market, informal labor activity persists in many sectors. The new government has embraced higher subsidies, and the inflation rate is over 25 percent.

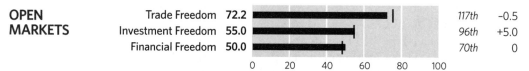

		Score		Rank	1-Year Change
OPEN MARKETS	Trade Freedom	72.2		117th	-0.5
	Investment Freedom	55.0		96th	+5.0
	Financial Freedom	50.0		70th	0

Malawi's average tariff rate is 6.4 percent. Importing goods can take weeks. Foreign and domestic investments are generally treated equally under the law, but investors face bureaucratic hurdles. The financial sector is underdeveloped, and less than 20 percent of the population has access to banking services. The high cost of credit suppresses business formation. The state owns the two largest banks.

Long-Term Score Change (since 1995)

RULE OF LAW		GOVERNMENT SIZE		REGULATORY EFFICIENCY		OPEN MARKETS	
Property Rights	-10.0	Fiscal Freedom	+9.2	Business Freedom	-5.9	Trade Freedom	+8.2
Freedom from Corruption	+7.0	Government Spending	-15.1	Labor Freedom	+5.2	Investment Freedom	+5.0
				Monetary Freedom	-6.4	Financial Freedom	0

Kuala Lumpur

MALAYSIA

Economic Freedom Score

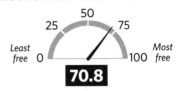

50

25   75

Least   Most
free 0   100 free

70.8

| World Rank: **31** | Regional Rank: **8** |

Malaysia's economic freedom score is 70.8, making its economy the 31st freest in the 2015 *Index*. Its score has increased by 1.2 points since last year, with improvements in freedom from corruption, business freedom, and trade freedom outweighing declines in labor freedom and the management of government spending. Malaysia is ranked 8th out of 42 countries in the Asia–Pacific region, and its overall score is above the world and regional averages.

Malaysia has risen to the "mostly free" category. Since 2011, its economic freedom has advanced by 4.5 points, the third largest point increase in the Asia–Pacific region. Gains in six of the 10 economic freedoms have been led by double-digit increases in investment, financial, and business freedoms.

A relatively open economy, Malaysia is a vital part of the East Asian manufacturing network. The business environment encourages the development of a vibrant private sector. Malaysia scores well in the area of open markets measured by trade freedom, investment freedom, and financial freedom compared to the global averages. The financial sector is robust, and foreign investment is being permitted to a greater degree. While the rule of law remains weak, the government has taken steps to tackle corruption more effectively.

BACKGROUND: The United Malays National Organization (UMNO) has ruled the ethnically and religiously diverse constitutional monarchy of Malaysia since independence in 1957. Dissatisfaction with pro-Malay affirmative-action programs and corruption generated important opposition gains in the March 2008 elections. In the 2013 elections, the UMNO-led coalition retained power but failed for the first time to win more than 50 percent of the popular vote. The government maintains investments in such key sectors as banking, media, automobiles, and airlines. In 2014, a Malaysia Airlines plane was lost in the Indian Ocean, and another was shot down in Ukraine. Malaysia is a leading exporter of electronics and information technology products; other industries include agricultural products and automobiles.

Freedom Trend

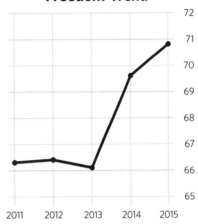

Country Comparisons

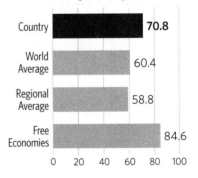

Quick Facts

Population: 29.6 million
GDP (PPP): $525.7 billion
4.7% growth in 2013
5-year compound annual growth 4.2%
$17,748 per capita
Unemployment: 3.2%
Inflation (CPI): 2.1%
FDI Inflow: $12.3 billion
Public Debt: 58.2% of GDP

2013 data unless otherwise noted.
Data compiled as of September 2014.

How Do We Measure Economic Freedom?
See page 475 for an explanation of the methodology
or visit the *Index* Web site at *heritage.org/index*.

THE TEN ECONOMIC FREEDOMS

		Score		Rank	1-Year Change
RULE OF LAW	Property Rights	55.0		50th	0
	Freedom from Corruption	50.0		52nd	+5.7

The continuous 50-year hold on power by the United Malays National Organization and the other parties in the ruling coalition, government favoritism, blurred distinctions between public and private enterprises, and the imperfections of the bureaucratic system have encouraged the perpetuation of corruption in political and economic life. Judicial independence is compromised by extensive executive influence.

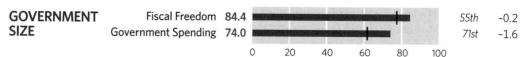

		Score		Rank	1-Year Change
GOVERNMENT SIZE	Fiscal Freedom	84.4		55th	−0.2
	Government Spending	74.0		71st	−1.6

Malaysia's top individual income tax rate is 26 percent, and its top corporate tax rate is 25 percent. Other taxes include a sales tax and a capital gains tax. Overall tax revenue amounts to 16.1 percent of domestic income. Government spending amounts to 29.5 percent of the domestic economy, and public debt is equal to 58 percent of gross domestic product.

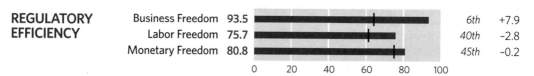

		Score		Rank	1-Year Change
REGULATORY EFFICIENCY	Business Freedom	93.5		6th	+7.9
	Labor Freedom	75.7		40th	−2.8
	Monetary Freedom	80.8		45th	−0.2

The regulatory framework generally facilitates entrepreneurial activity. With no minimum capital required, incorporating a business takes three procedures. Relatively flexible labor regulations support the development of an efficient labor market. In 2013, the government cut fuel subsidies and later hiked electricity tariffs to reduce budget deficits. Other economically distortionary subsidies and price controls remain in place.

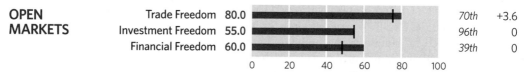

		Score		Rank	1-Year Change
OPEN MARKETS	Trade Freedom	80.0		70th	+3.6
	Investment Freedom	55.0		96th	0
	Financial Freedom	60.0		39th	0

Malaysia's average tariff rate is 4.0 percent. Malaysia has benefited from unilateral tariff cuts and trade agreements that have reduced trade barriers. Foreign investment in many economic sectors is capped. Measures to open the financial sector to greater competition have been implemented, but state-owned enterprises retain sizable shares in the banking sector, including the two largest banks.

Long-Term Score Change (since 1995)

RULE OF LAW		GOVERNMENT SIZE		REGULATORY EFFICIENCY		OPEN MARKETS	
Property Rights	−15.0	Fiscal Freedom	+10.3	Business Freedom	+8.5	Trade Freedom	+13.0
Freedom from Corruption	−20.0	Government Spending	−4.3	Labor Freedom	+3.7	Investment Freedom	−15.0
				Monetary Freedom	−1.7	Financial Freedom	+10.0

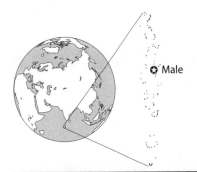

Male

MALDIVES

Economic Freedom Score

50
25   75
Least
free 0   100 Most
free

53.4

The Maldives' economic freedom score is 53.4, making its economy the 134th freest in the 2015 *Index*. Its score has increased by 2.4 points, reflecting improvements in six of the 10 economic freedoms, including the control of government spending, investment freedom, property rights, and monetary freedom. The country has recorded its highest economic freedom score ever in this year's *Index*. Ranked 28th out of 42 countries in the Asia–Pacific region, its overall score remains below the world and regional averages.

The Maldives is heavily dependent on fishing and tourism and has yet to achieve the benefits of diversification that follow from higher levels of economic freedom. A 5.0-point advance in its economic freedom score over the past five years has enabled the country to move out of the "repressed" category, but this advance has been led in large measure by a nearly 50-point improvement in government spending, meaning that improvements have been concentrated and not broad-based.

Weaknesses in the rule of law and protectionist measures that keep the domestic economy relatively closed continue to hold back economic development in the Maldives. Tariffs are over 20 percent. Political unrest and a strict investment regime deter potential foreign investors. The island economy's political situation undermines the judiciary and has led to increased perceptions of corruption. A more broad-based commitment to institutional and structural reforms is necessary to allow the progress made in advancing economic freedom in recent years to bear fruit.

BACKGROUND: The military forced President Mohammed Nasheed to step down in February 2012 after several weeks of anti-government street protests instigated by former dictator Maumoon Abdul Gayoom. In November 2013, Gayoom's half-brother Abdulla Yameen was elected, putting an end to nearly two years of political turmoil. Tourism is the centerpiece of the economy, contributing 28 percent of GDP and over 90 percent of government tax revenue.

Freedom Trend

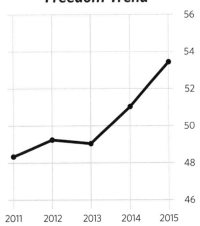

56

54

52

50

48

46

2011 2012 2013 2014 2015

Country Comparisons

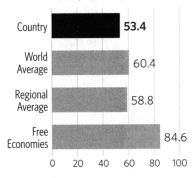

Country   **53.4**

World
Average   60.4

Regional
Average   58.8

Free
Economies   84.6

0   20   40   60   80   100

Quick Facts

Population: 0.3 million
GDP (PPP): $3.1 billion
3.7% growth in 2013
5-year compound annual growth 2.8%
$9,173 per capita
Unemployment: 11.7%
Inflation (CPI): 4.0%
FDI Inflow: $325.3 million
Public Debt: 80.7% of GDP

2013 data unless otherwise noted.
Data compiled as of September 2014.

How Do We Measure Economic Freedom?
See page 475 for an explanation of the methodology
or visit the *Index* Web site at *heritage.org/index*.

THE TEN ECONOMIC FREEDOMS

		Score			Rank	1-Year Change
RULE OF LAW	Property Rights	25.0			124th	+5.0
	Freedom from Corruption	21.9			164th	0

The government has been functioning more normally, allowing the democratic election in late 2013 of a president from the political opposition. In recent years, a new, independent auditor general has provided greater transparency and shed light on pervasive corruption. Nevertheless, the rule of law remains uneven across the country, and the inefficient judicial system is subject to political influence.

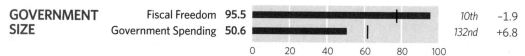

GOVERNMENT SIZE	Fiscal Freedom	95.5			10th	–1.9
	Government Spending	50.6			132nd	+6.8

The Maldives has no individual or corporate income taxes. Commercial banks are subject to a tax rate of 25 percent. Other taxes include taxes on foreign-source income and tourism goods and services. The overall tax burden equals 21.2 percent of domestic income. Government expenditures equal 40.6 percent of domestic output, and public debt equals about 81 percent of GDP.

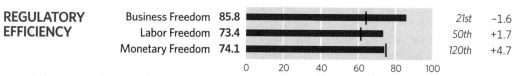

REGULATORY EFFICIENCY	Business Freedom	85.8			21st	–1.6
	Labor Freedom	73.4			50th	+1.7
	Monetary Freedom	74.1			120th	+4.7

Incorporating a business takes five procedures and nine days on average, but completing licensing requirements takes over 100 days. The labor market is underdeveloped. Much of the labor force is employed in the large public sector. Although high public spending has moderated, increases in state-funded pensions and health benefits added to fiscal pressures in 2014.

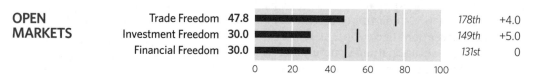

OPEN MARKETS	Trade Freedom	47.8			178th	+4.0
	Investment Freedom	30.0			149th	+5.0
	Financial Freedom	30.0			131st	0

The Maldives' average tariff rate is 20.6 percent. The government relies on tariffs for revenue. Quotas restrict some agricultural imports. The government reviews proposed new foreign investment. The financial sector remains rudimentary, and much of the population operates outside of the formal banking sector. High credit costs and scarce access to financing continue to constrain the small private sector.

Long-Term Score Change (since 2009)

RULE OF LAW		GOVERNMENT SIZE		REGULATORY EFFICIENCY		OPEN MARKETS	
Property Rights	–5.0	Fiscal Freedom	–0.3	Business Freedom	+2.6	Trade Freedom	+3.8
Freedom from Corruption	–11.1	Government Spending	+50.6	Labor Freedom	–16.7	Investment Freedom	0
				Monetary Freedom	–2.4	Financial Freedom	0

MALI

Economic Freedom Score

50

25   75

Least free 0   100 Most free

56.4

Mali's economic freedom score is 56.4, making its economy the 119th freest in the 2015 *Index*. Its score has increased by 0.9 point since last year, with improvements in property rights, monetary freedom, investment freedom, and the control of government spending outweighing a notable loss in labor freedom. Mali is ranked 21st out of 46 countries in the Sub-Saharan Africa region, and its score is below the world average but higher than the regional average.

Over the past five years, improvements in investment freedom and fiscal freedom have been offset by declines in labor freedom and property rights. Mali's weak institutional framework traps many of its citizens in subsistence agriculture and poverty. Political instability and the struggle against Islamist rebels in the North have distracted policymakers from making much-needed reforms to spur growth and reduce poverty.

Mali has yet to open its domestic economy to global markets. Tariff rates remain high, and political unrest and security concerns deter foreign investment. These issues are exacerbated by a weak rule of law. Corruption is present in all levels of government and has spilled over into the judiciary, which remains notoriously inefficient.

BACKGROUND: After President Amadou Toumani Touré was ousted in a March 2012 military coup, Tuareg separatists and militants linked to al-Qaeda took control of Northern Mali and declared independence. French armed forces restored government control in the major cities in January 2013, and Tuareg rebels signed a peace accord in June. In August 2013, former Prime Minister Ibrahim Boubacar Keita won the presidential election in a second-round ballot. In May 2014, peace talks with Tuareg separatists in the North broke down, and rebels seized control of several northern cities. Approximately 1,500 French troops remain in the country along with a U.N. peacekeeping operation. The economy depends on agricultural exports such as cotton for revenue, and price fluctuations and drought have contributed to poverty and political instability.

Freedom Trend

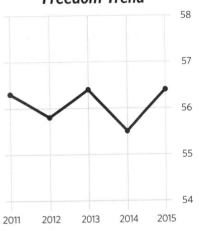

58

57

56

55

54

2011   2012   2013   2014   2015

Country Comparisons

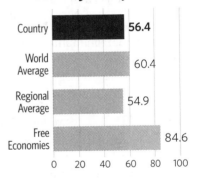

Country	56.4
World Average	60.4
Regional Average	54.9
Free Economies	84.6

0   20   40   60   80   100

Quick Facts

Population: 16.9 million
GDP (PPP): $18.6 billion
1.7% growth in 2013
5-year compound annual growth 2.9%
$1,103 per capita
Unemployment: 8.5%
Inflation (CPI): –0.6%
FDI Inflow: $410.3 million
Public Debt: 31.5% of GDP

2013 data unless otherwise noted.
Data compiled as of September 2014.

How Do We Measure Economic Freedom?
See page 475 for an explanation of the methodology or visit the *Index* Web site at *heritage.org/index*.

THE TEN ECONOMIC FREEDOMS

		Score			Rank	1-Year Change
RULE OF LAW	Property Rights	25.0			124th	+5.0
	Freedom from Corruption	28.0			132nd	+0.3

Mali held presidential and parliamentary elections in 2013 after a coup in 2012. The new president has pledged to restore his predecessor's anti-corruption initiatives, including creation of a general auditor's office. Nevertheless, corruption remains a problem in government, public procurement, and both public and private contracting. The judicial system is inefficient and prone to corruption.

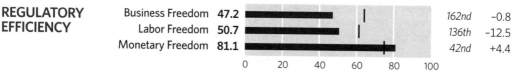

GOVERNMENT SIZE	Fiscal Freedom	69.6			140th	−0.2
	Government Spending	89.2			14th	+7.5

Mali's top individual income tax rate is 40 percent, and its top corporate tax rate is 35 percent. Other taxes include a value-added tax. The overall tax burden equals 14.5 percent of gross domestic product. Government expenditures are equal to 19 percent of domestic production, and government debt is equivalent to about 32 percent of domestic output.

REGULATORY EFFICIENCY	Business Freedom	47.2			162nd	−0.8
	Labor Freedom	50.7			136th	−12.5
	Monetary Freedom	81.1			42nd	+4.4

The non-transparent and costly regulatory framework continues to discourage entrepreneurial dynamism. Labor regulations are not enforced effectively, and the informal sector employs a large share of the workforce. As Mali seeks to return to political stability with the help of the international community, the government is trying to strengthen public financial management to help accelerate economic growth.

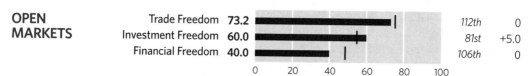

OPEN MARKETS	Trade Freedom	73.2			112th	0
	Investment Freedom	60.0			81st	+5.0
	Financial Freedom	40.0			106th	0

Mali's average tariff rate is 8.4 percent, and importing goods can be expensive. Foreign and domestic investors are generally treated equally under the law. The environment for foreign investment has improved. The financial sector is concentrated in urban areas and remains underdeveloped. The small banking sector provides a limited range of financial services. The cost of long-term financing is high.

Long-Term Score Change (since 1995)

RULE OF LAW		GOVERNMENT SIZE		REGULATORY EFFICIENCY		OPEN MARKETS	
Property Rights	−5.0	Fiscal Freedom	+20.7	Business Freedom	−7.8	Trade Freedom	+8.2
Freedom from Corruption	+18.0	Government Spending	+8.6	Labor Freedom	−12.6	Investment Freedom	−10.0
				Monetary Freedom	−1.0	Financial Freedom	+10.0

★ Valletta

MALTA

Economic Freedom Score

50

25   75

Least   Most
free 0   100 free

66.5

Malta's economic freedom score is 66.5, making its economy the 58th freest in the 2015 *Index*. Its overall score is up by 0.1 point from last year, with improvements in freedom from corruption, labor freedom, monetary freedom, and trade freedom offsetting declines in the control of government spending, business freedom, and fiscal freedom. Malta is ranked 28th out of 43 countries in the Europe region, and its overall score is below the regional average but above the world average.

Unlike some other eurozone countries, Malta has advanced its economic freedom over the past five years. A 0.8-point improvement since 2011 has been led by gains in seven of the 10 factors, with losses only in business freedom and labor freedom. Dependent on imports for most foodstuffs, Malta has created a relatively open economy with low tariffs and efficient investment rules.

Budget shocks have alerted authorities to serious structural problems that stem largely from an inefficient bureaucracy, a weak public pension system, and persistent fiscal imbalances. Taxes remain high, and government spending makes up over two-fifths of the domestic economy.

BACKGROUND: Malta joined the European Union in 2004 and the eurozone in 2008. Labour Party leader Joseph Muscat won the March 2013 elections and became prime minister. With few natural resources, Malta imports most of its food and fresh water and 100 percent of its energy. The economy depends on tourism, trade, and manufacturing. Well-trained workers, low labor costs, and membership in the EU attract foreign investment, but the government maintains a sprawling socialist bureaucracy, with the majority of spending allocated to housing, education, and health care. Unemployment is relatively low. Early in 2013, excessive public borrowing led to an EU warning to reduce the budget deficit, which exceeded EU guidelines. Since then, the government has taken steps to reduce the deficit. Substantial immigration from North Africa remains a concern.

Freedom Trend

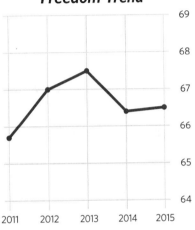

69

68

67

66

65

64

2011   2012   2013   2014   2015

Country Comparisons

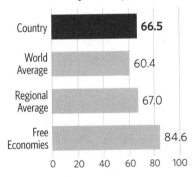

Country   **66.5**

World
Average   60.4

Regional
Average   67.0

Free
Economies   84.6

0   20   40   60   80   100

Quick Facts

Population: 0.4 million
GDP (PPP): $11.6 billion
2.4% growth in 2013
5-year compound annual growth 1.1%
$27,840 per capita
Unemployment: 6.5%
Inflation (CPI): 1.0%
FDI Inflow: –$2.1 billion
Public Debt: 71.7% of GDP

How Do We Measure Economic Freedom?
See page 475 for an explanation of the methodology
or visit the *Index* Web site at *heritage.org/index*.

2013 data unless otherwise noted.
Data compiled as of September 2014.

THE TEN ECONOMIC FREEDOMS

		Score		Rank	1-Year Change
RULE OF LAW	Property Rights	75.0		25th	0
	Freedom from Corruption	56.0		44th	+0.2

A 2013 Eurobarometer survey revealed that 83 percent of Maltese saw corruption as a major problem in politics and business. Malta still lacks appropriate institutions to implement and monitor anti-corruption activities. The judiciary is independent both constitutionally and in practice. Property rights are protected, and expropriation is unlikely. Foreigners do not have full rights to buy property.

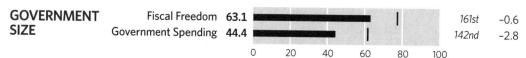

		Score		Rank	1-Year Change
GOVERNMENT SIZE	Fiscal Freedom	63.1		161st	−0.6
	Government Spending	44.4		142nd	−2.8

Malta's individual and corporate income tax rates are 35 percent. Other taxes include a value-added tax and a capital gains tax. Tax revenue is equal to 35.2 percent of domestic income, and government expenditures are equivalent to 43.1 percent of gross domestic product. Public debt equals 72 percent of total domestic output.

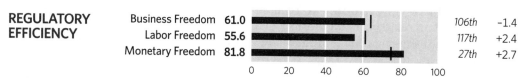

		Score		Rank	1-Year Change
REGULATORY EFFICIENCY	Business Freedom	61.0		106th	−1.4
	Labor Freedom	55.6		117th	+2.4
	Monetary Freedom	81.8		27th	+2.7

Malta has adopted transparent and effective regulations to foster competition, but the pace of reform has slowed. Business regulations are relatively straightforward and applied uniformly most of the time. The labor market remains relatively rigid. Although it maintained macroeconomic stability during the eurozone crisis, Malta faces deteriorating public finances and needs to reform pension and health care subsidies.

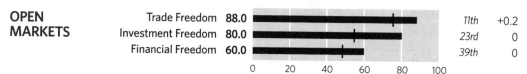

		Score		Rank	1-Year Change
OPEN MARKETS	Trade Freedom	88.0		11th	+0.2
	Investment Freedom	80.0		23rd	0
	Financial Freedom	60.0		39th	0

EU members have a 1.0 percent average tariff rate. Although some non-tariff barriers exist, the EU is relatively open to external trade. Malta generally welcomes foreign investment, but some state-owned enterprises have yet to be privatized. The financial sector is dominated by banks. The large banking sector, which consists of subsidiaries of foreign banks, has shown notable resilience.

Long-Term Score Change (since 1995)

RULE OF LAW		GOVERNMENT SIZE		REGULATORY EFFICIENCY		OPEN MARKETS	
Property Rights	+25.0	Fiscal Freedom	−5.1	Business Freedom	−9.0	Trade Freedom	+24.4
Freedom from Corruption	+46.0	Government Spending	−7.4	Labor Freedom	−4.4	Investment Freedom	+10.0
				Monetary Freedom	+8.4	Financial Freedom	+10.0

MAURITANIA

★ Nouakchott

Economic Freedom Score

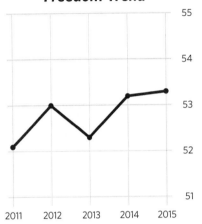

25   50   75

Least free 0   100 Most free

53.3

World Rank: 135   **Regional Rank: 28**

Mauritania's economic freedom score is 53.3, making its economy the 135th freest in the 2015 *Index*. Its score is essentially unchanged from last year, with improvements in business freedom, freedom from corruption, and monetary freedom offset by declines in fiscal freedom and labor freedom and a collapse in the control of government spending. Mauritania is ranked 28th out of 46 countries in the Sub-Saharan Africa region, and its overall score is below the world and regional averages.

Mauritania's trend in economic freedom has been characterized by alternating years of advances and losses, but the overall change has been positive over the past five years. Since 2011, economic freedom has improved by over 1.0 point. A double-digit improvement in investment freedom has led advances concentrated in four of the 10 economic freedoms.

The modest gain in overall economic freedom has occurred despite a weak institutional framework that has yet to experience measureable reform. Corruption remains endemic, and political instability has undermined society's basic institutions. The judicial system's lack of independence makes it vulnerable to political influence. Mauritania scores below the global average in all policy areas of open markets measured by trade freedom, investment freedom, and financial freedom.

BACKGROUND: A military junta ruled the former French colony of Mauritania from 1978 until 1992, when the first multiparty elections were held. In 2008, General Mohamed Ould Abdel Aziz overthrew President Sidi Ould Cheikh Abdallahi. Aziz won elections in July 2009 and again in June 2014, but opposition groups boycotted the elections. There are recurring ethnic tensions within the mixed population of Moors and black Africans. Mauritania faces the growing threat of al-Qaeda terrorists in the Islamic Maghreb who have kidnapped and killed several foreigners. Mining and fishing dominate the economy. Mauritania is one of Africa's newest oil producers, and offshore gas production is expected to begin in 2015.

Freedom Trend

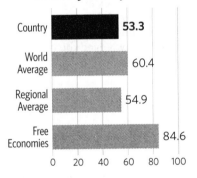

Country Comparisons

Country   53.3
World Average   60.4
Regional Average 54.9
Free Economies 84.6

0   20   40   60   80   100

Quick Facts

Population: 3.7 million
GDP (PPP): $8.2 billion
6.7% growth in 2013
5-year compound annual growth 4.1%
$2,218 per capita
Unemployment: 30.9%
Inflation (CPI): 4.1%
FDI Inflow: $1.2 billion
Public Debt: 87.7% of GDP

2013 data unless otherwise noted.
Data compiled as of September 2014.

How Do We Measure Economic Freedom?
See page 475 for an explanation of the methodology
or visit the *Index* Web site at *heritage.org/index*.

THE TEN ECONOMIC FREEDOMS

		Score			Rank	1–Year Change

RULE OF LAW

		Score	Rank	1–Year Change
Property Rights	25.0		124th	0
Freedom from Corruption	30.0		121st	+6.1

Corruption is a serious problem. In recent years, for the first time, several senior officials have been charged with corruption, but either these cases have been dismissed or officials have been ordered to reimburse the government for the amount they supposedly embezzled with no further legal consequences. The judicial system is chaotic, corrupt, and heavily influenced by the government.

GOVERNMENT SIZE

		Score	Rank	1–Year Change
Fiscal Freedom	80.2		80th	–1.5
Government Spending	59.8		115th	–16.0

Mauritania's top individual income tax rate is 30 percent, and its top corporate tax rate is 25 percent. Other taxes include a value-added tax. Taxes consume about 21.3 percent of gross domestic product, and government expenditures amount to about 36.6 percent of domestic output. Government debt equals approximately 88 percent of the size of the domestic economy.

REGULATORY EFFICIENCY

		Score	Rank	1–Year Change
Business Freedom	50.5		153rd	+12.5
Labor Freedom	52.1		128th	–1.0
Monetary Freedom	76.6		88th	+1.1

The regulatory environment remains burdensome. The minimum capital required to launch a business is about three times the level of average annual income, and completing licensing requirements takes over 100 days. The labor market remains underdeveloped. The government has acknowledged the need to shrink the public sector and reduce food and fuel subsidies but has yet to act.

OPEN MARKETS

		Score	Rank	1–Year Change
Trade Freedom	69.0		138th	0
Investment Freedom	50.0		109th	0
Financial Freedom	40.0		106th	0

Mauritania's average tariff rate is 10.1 percent. Customs procedures have been improved, but importing goods can still be time-consuming. The slow-moving court system may deter foreign investment. Commercial banks, regulated by the central bank, dominate the small financial sector, and diversification remains limited. Less than 5 percent of the population has access to banking services.

Long-Term Score Change (since 1996)

RULE OF LAW		GOVERNMENT SIZE		REGULATORY EFFICIENCY		OPEN MARKETS	
Property Rights	–5.0	Fiscal Freedom	+30.4	Business Freedom	–4.5	Trade Freedom	+14.0
Freedom from Corruption	0	Government Spending	–20.5	Labor Freedom	+5.1	Investment Freedom	+20.0
				Monetary Freedom	+7.0	Financial Freedom	+30.0

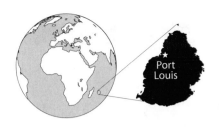

MAURITIUS

Economic Freedom Score

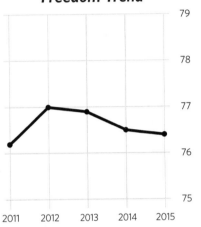

76.4

Least free 0

Most free 100

25 50 75

World Rank: 10　　　　**Regional Rank: 1**

Mauritius's economic freedom score is 76.4, making its economy the 10th freest in the 2015 *Index*. Its overall score is essentially unchanged from last year, with a negative score change of 0.1 point reflecting a significant decline in labor freedom that overshadows gains in the control of government spending, business freedom, and monetary freedom. Mauritius is ranked 1st out of 46 countries in the Sub-Saharan African region, and it scores well above the regional and global averages.

Adherence to stable fiscal policy and openness to global trade and investment have established Mauritius as one of the world's 10 freest economies. Since 2007, Mauritius has led the Sub-Saharan Africa region in economic freedom.

Economic development in Mauritius has been facilitated by a stable macroeconomic environment, prudent policy decisions, and openness to competition. Adoption of open-market policies has been accompanied by the development of growing financial and tourism sectors that have helped to supplant traditional subsistence agriculture. The rule of law has been enforced effectively within a framework of transparency and accountability, although corruption remains a concern.

BACKGROUND: Independent since 1968, Mauritius is the only African country ranked as a "full democracy" in the Economist Intelligence Unit's Democracy Index. Navin Ramgoolam of the Mauritius Labour Party has been prime minister since 2005, and Rajkeswur Purryag has been president since 2012. The government is trying to encourage modernization of the sugar and textile industries while promoting diversification into such areas as information and communications technology, financial and business services, seafood processing, and exports. Services and tourism remain the main economic drivers. Mauritius has made maritime security a priority and in 2012 signed a deal with Britain's Royal Navy for the transfer of suspected pirates captured by Britain to Mauritius for prosecution. Both Mauritius and Seychelles claim control of the Chagos Islands, administered by Britain and home to a U.S. military base.

Freedom Trend

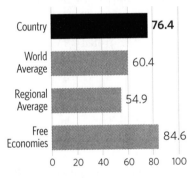

79

78

77

76

75

2011　2012　2013　2014　2015

Country Comparisons

Country **76.4**

World Average 60.4

Regional Average 54.9

Free Economies 84.6

0　20　40　60　80　100

Quick Facts

Population: 1.3 million
GDP (PPP): $20.9 billion
3.1% growth in 2013
5-year compound annual growth 3.5%
$16,056 per capita
Unemployment: 8.1%
Inflation (CPI): 3.5%
FDI Inflow: $258.6 million
Public Debt: 53.8% of GDP

2013 data unless otherwise noted.
Data compiled as of September 2014.

How Do We Measure Economic Freedom?
See page 475 for an explanation of the methodology
or visit the *Index* Web site at *heritage.org/index*.

THE TEN ECONOMIC FREEDOMS

		Score		Rank	1-Year Change

RULE OF LAW

| Property Rights | 65.0 | 40th | 0 |
| Freedom from Corruption | 52.0 | 51st | –1.4 |

A generally positive reputation for transparency and accountability has been hurt by several high-profile scandals. Critics allege, for example, that in its August 2013 investigation of the minister of higher education, the government's anti-corruption commission was used as a political tool. The judiciary continues to be independent, however, and the legal system is generally non-discriminatory and transparent.

GOVERNMENT SIZE

| Fiscal Freedom | 91.9 | 21st | –0.3 |
| Government Spending | 87.4 | 24th | +5.6 |

The top individual and corporate income tax rates in Mauritius are 15 percent. Other taxes include a value-added tax. The overall tax burden amounts to about 18.9 percent of the size of the domestic economy. Government expenditures equal about 20.5 percent of domestic output, and public debt is equivalent to about 54 percent of gross domestic product.

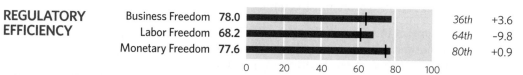

REGULATORY EFFICIENCY

Business Freedom	78.0	36th	+3.6
Labor Freedom	68.2	64th	–9.8
Monetary Freedom	77.6	80th	+0.9

No minimum capital is required to start a business, and the start-up process has been simplified. The labor market remains relatively flexible, but the mismatch between demand for and supply of labor persists. Inflation is well controlled, and the government is trying to promote private sector–led economic growth, but it needs to make more progress in reducing subsidies.

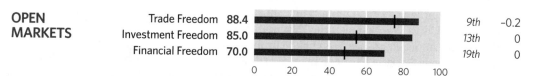

OPEN MARKETS

Trade Freedom	88.4	9th	–0.2
Investment Freedom	85.0	13th	0
Financial Freedom	70.0	19th	0

Mauritius has an average tariff rate of 0.8 percent and has cut tariffs unilaterally. The government generally welcomes foreign investment, although new investment is subject to review. The competitive financial system provides a range of financing tools. Banking is resilient and open to competition. The Stock Exchange of Mauritius is considered one of the most innovative in the region.

Long-Term Score Change (since 1999)

RULE OF LAW		GOVERNMENT SIZE		REGULATORY EFFICIENCY		OPEN MARKETS	
Property Rights	–5.0	Fiscal Freedom	+15.9	Business Freedom	–7.0	Trade Freedom	+31.4
Freedom from Corruption	+2.0	Government Spending	+2.3	Labor Freedom	–8.2	Investment Freedom	+35.0
				Monetary Freedom	+4.0	Financial Freedom	0

MEXICO

Economic Freedom Score

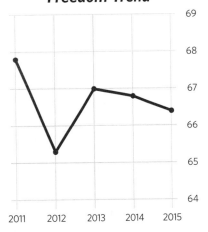

66.4

Least free 0   Most free 100

Mexico's economic freedom score is 66.4, making its economy the 59th freest in the 2015 *Index*. Its score has declined by 0.4 point since last year, with improvements in three of the 10 economic freedoms, including freedom from corruption and labor freedom, offset by declines in the management of government spending, fiscal freedom, and business freedom. Mexico is ranked 3rd out of three countries in the North America region, but its score is well above the world average.

Over the past five years, economic freedom in Mexico has declined by 1.4 points. Deteriorations in the fiscal and regulatory environments have occurred in an environment of slow economic growth despite a reform-minded leadership bent on increasing competition and opening the economy to trade and investment.

Mexico's economic growth has been driven largely by integration with Canada and the U.S. in NAFTA, but economic performance remains far below potential. Despite a more open economic environment, business regulations continue to undermine economic efficiency. Ensuring more dynamic growth will require broader-based reforms to improve the investment climate and enhance the rule of law.

BACKGROUND: President Enrique Peña Nieto took office in December 2012 and has made solid progress in reforming the constitution in the areas of education, energy, and telecommunications, but whether new legislation will boost competition is unclear. The government has moved to centralize power further with a fiscal reform that raised taxes and promised a return to deficit spending. A new anti-trust law has increased investor uncertainty. Efforts to reform the criminal justice system and combat endemic corruption that began in 2008 have lagged and are not expected to meet 2016 targets. The recent migration crisis on the border with the United States and the rise of citizen militias in Michoacán highlight weaknesses in Mexico's security forces. The Peña Nieto administration contends that the homicide rate has declined, but conflicting government findings indicate otherwise. Organized crime is endemic.

Freedom Trend

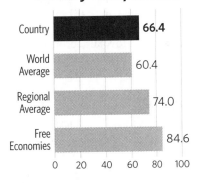

Country Comparisons

Country	66.4
World Average	60.4
Regional Average	74.0
Free Economies	84.6

0   20   40   60   80   100

Quick Facts

Population: 118.4 million
GDP (PPP): $1.8 trillion
1.1% growth in 2013
5-year compound annual growth 1.8%
$15,563 per capita
Unemployment: 5.0%
Inflation (CPI): 3.8%
FDI Inflow: $38.3 billion
Public Debt: 46.5% of GDP

2013 data unless otherwise noted.
Data compiled as of September 2014.

How Do We Measure Economic Freedom?
See page 475 for an explanation of the methodology
or visit the *Index* Web site at *heritage.org/index.*

THE TEN ECONOMIC FREEDOMS

		Score		Rank	1-Year Change
RULE OF LAW	Property Rights	50.0		56th	0
	Freedom from Corruption	34.0		107th	+4.3

Corruption is deeply embedded culturally and remains pervasive at all levels of society, fed by and entrenching the power of monopolists, party bosses, and other mafias. Billions of narco-dollars that enter Mexico each year from the U.S. affect politics, particularly at the state and local levels. Contracts are generally upheld, but courts are inefficient and vulnerable to political interference.

		Score		Rank	
GOVERNMENT SIZE	Fiscal Freedom	77.8		73rd	−3.1
	Government Spending	78.0		58th	−0.9

The top individual income tax rate has been raised to 35 percent, and the corporate tax rate is a flat 30 percent. Other taxes include a value-added tax. Tax revenues are equivalent to 10 percent of domestic income, and public expenditures equal 27.1 percent of domestic production. Public debt is equal to 46 percent of gross domestic product.

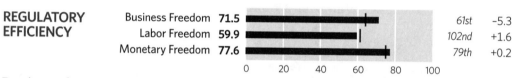

		Score		Rank	
REGULATORY EFFICIENCY	Business Freedom	71.5		61st	−5.3
	Labor Freedom	59.9		102nd	+1.6
	Monetary Freedom	77.6		79th	+0.2

Previous reforms have enhanced the regulatory framework, but the pace of reform has slowed in comparison to other emerging economies. Completing licensing requirements still takes about three months. Rigid and outdated labor codes create incentives for firms to operate outside of the formal sector. The government has implemented extensive energy and fiscal reforms but must further reduce subsidies and inflation.

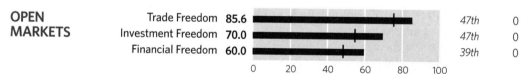

		Score		Rank	
OPEN MARKETS	Trade Freedom	85.6		47th	0
	Investment Freedom	70.0		47th	0
	Financial Freedom	60.0		39th	0

Mexico has a 2.2 percent average tariff rate. It has reduced tariff and non-tariff barriers unilaterally and through trade agreements like the Pacific Alliance. A law passed in December 2013 will partially open the energy sector to foreign investment. The financial sector is relatively small and lacks dynamism. Mexico needs to build a deeper and more accessible banking system.

Long-Term Score Change (since 1995)

RULE OF LAW		GOVERNMENT SIZE		REGULATORY EFFICIENCY		OPEN MARKETS	
Property Rights	−20.0	Fiscal Freedom	+5.4	Business Freedom	+16.5	Trade Freedom	+19.4
Freedom from Corruption	−16.0	Government Spending	−8.8	Labor Freedom	−1.5	Investment Freedom	0
				Monetary Freedom	+9.8	Financial Freedom	+30.0

MICRONESIA

⊗ Palikir

World Rank: 154   **Regional Rank: 35**

Economic Freedom Score

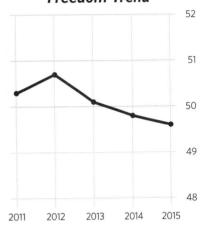

49.6

Micronesia's economic freedom score is 49.6, making its economy the 154th freest in the 2015 *Index*. Its score has decreased by 0.2 points since last year, reflecting declines in business freedom and fiscal freedom that outweigh improvements in labor freedom and monetary freedom. Micronesia is ranked 35th out of 42 countries in the Asia–Pacific region, and its overall score is lower than the world and regional averages.

Over the past five years, economic freedom has declined in the archipelago, pushing the Micronesian economy further into the "repressed" category. Higher taxes, inflation, and the lack of progress in reforming the entrepreneurial environment have gradually undermined Micronesia's economic freedom.

A weak institutional foundation is holding back advancements in economic freedom. Enforcing the rule of law evenly on over 600 islands remains a challenge, exacerbated by the prevalence of corruption that undermines effective governance. The underdeveloped financial system hampers the emergence of a vibrant private sector, leading to high financing costs and denying many Micronesians access to formal banking services. The restrictive investment regime makes capital accumulation from outside sources unlikely.

BACKGROUND: Politically organized as a confederation of four states—the island groups of Pohnpei, Chuuk, Yap, and Kosrae—the 607-island South Pacific archipelago of Micronesia has a central government with limited powers. The president is elected by the small unicameral legislature from among its at-large members. Formerly administered by the United States as a U.N. Trust Territory, Micronesia became independent in 1986 and signed a Compact of Free Association with the United States. Under an amended compact, it receives about $130 million annually in direct assistance from the U.S. The government sector employs more than half of the workforce, and economic development is hampered by poor infrastructure in electricity and water.

Freedom Trend

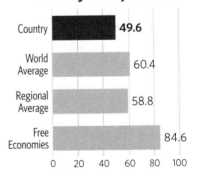

Country Comparisons

Country	49.6
World Average	60.4
Regional Average	58.8
Free Economies	84.6

Quick Facts

Population: 0.1 million
GDP (PPP): $0.8 billion
0.6% growth in 2013
5-year compound annual growth 1.3%
$7,288 per capita
Unemployment: n/a
Inflation (CPI): 4.0%
FDI Inflow: $0.8 million
Public Debt: 26.3% of GDP

2013 data unless otherwise noted.
Data compiled as of September 2014.

How Do We Measure Economic Freedom?
See page 475 for an explanation of the methodology
or visit the *Index* Web site at *heritage.org/index*.

THE TEN ECONOMIC FREEDOMS

	Score		Rank	1-Year Change
RULE OF LAW				
Property Rights	30.0		94th	0
Freedom from Corruption	30.0		121st	0

Official corruption remains a major source of public discontent. The government awarded a contract to a Chinese consortium to build a 10,000-room casino and tourism complex on the island of Yap, but the head of the company disappeared unexpectedly in 2014 during an anti-corruption investigation. Corruption and political influence are serious problems in the chronically underfunded judicial system.

	Score		Rank	1-Year Change
GOVERNMENT SIZE				
Fiscal Freedom	93.2		15th	–4.3
Government Spending	0.0		176th	0

Micronesia administers a 10 percent tax on individual income and a 21 percent tax on corporate income. Other taxes include regional sales taxes and import taxes. The overall tax burden equals 11.6 percent of the domestic economy. Government expenditures amount to 65.2 percent of domestic production, and public debt is equal to 26 percent of gross domestic product.

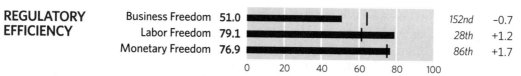

	Score		Rank	1-Year Change
REGULATORY EFFICIENCY				
Business Freedom	51.0		152nd	–0.7
Labor Freedom	79.1		28th	+1.2
Monetary Freedom	76.9		86th	+1.7

Procedures for establishing a business are opaque. Regulations are not applied consistently, and the non-transparent regulatory framework continues to discourage private-sector development. Labor regulations are not enforced effectively, and the labor market is rudimentary. Pressure for public-sector reforms has been reduced as a result of continued large flows of U.S. foreign aid.

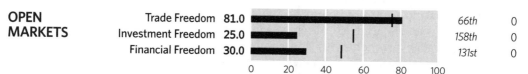

	Score		Rank	1-Year Change
OPEN MARKETS				
Trade Freedom	81.0		66th	0
Investment Freedom	25.0		158th	0
Financial Freedom	30.0		131st	0

Micronesia's average tariff rate was 4.5 percent as of 2006, and imports can face delays. Foreign investors may not own land, and the government caps most foreign investments. The financial sector remains underdeveloped, leaving much of the population without formal access to banking services. Constrained access to financing severely impedes entrepreneurial activity and private-sector development.

Long-Term Score Change (since 2009)

RULE OF LAW		GOVERNMENT SIZE		REGULATORY EFFICIENCY		OPEN MARKETS	
Property Rights	0	Fiscal Freedom	–4.2	Business Freedom	–8.8	Trade Freedom	0
Freedom from Corruption	0	Government Spending	0	Labor Freedom	–3.2	Investment Freedom	–5.0
				Monetary Freedom	+0.2	Financial Freedom	0

Chişinău

MOLDOVA

Economic Freedom Score

50
25   75
Least   Most
free 0   100 free

57.5

Moldova's economic freedom score is 57.5, making its economy the 111th freest in the 2015 *Index*. Its score has increased by 0.2 point since last year, with gains in freedom from corruption, labor freedom, and monetary freedom outweighing declines in business freedom and the control of government spending. Moldova is ranked 39th among 43 countries in the Europe region, and its overall score is below the regional and world averages.

Reversing a previous sharp drop in economic freedom, Moldova has experienced three straight years of gains. Since 2011, Moldova has advanced its economic freedom by 1.8 points. Modest score improvements highlight a continued effort to transform the formerly Communist economy into a free-market system.

Nonetheless, the weak rule of law and a lack of progress in implementing open-market policies continue to prevent broader and more dynamic economic development. Economic performance is far below potential. Lingering state interference in the private sector increases economic risk in a volatile political environment. Political instability has left fiscal policy fragmented, and there is significant corruption in most areas of the bureaucracy.

BACKGROUND: Moldova gained independence after the collapse of the Soviet Union in 1991 but faces a secessionist pro-Russian movement in its Transnistria region. The country is poor, and excessive dependence on Russia threatens its sovereignty. In April 2013, the center-right Liberal Democrat Party (LDP) government of Prime Minister Vlad Filat lost a no-confidence vote. He was replaced by Iurie Leancă, also of the LDP, who put together a slightly different coaltion. Leancă supports European integration and favors EU candidate status for Moldova in 2015. Association Agreements signed with the EU in June 2014 include Deep and Comprehensive Free Trade Area (DCFTA) accords, and exports to the EU are increasing. Foodstuffs, wine, and agricultural products are the main exports, although the technology sector is developing slowly. Corruption undermines public trust in government.

Freedom Trend

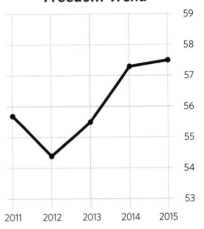

59
58
57
56
55
54
53

2011   2012   2013   2014   2015

Country Comparisons

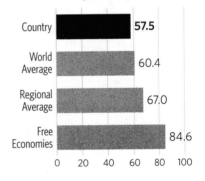

Country	57.5
World Average	60.4
Regional Average	67.0
Free Economies	84.6

0   20   40   60   80   100

Quick Facts

Population: 3.6 million
GDP (PPP): $13.3 billion
8.9% growth in 2013
5-year compound annual growth 3.0%
$3,736 per capita
Unemployment: 5.9%
Inflation (CPI): 4.6%
FDI Inflow: $231.3 million
Public Debt: 24.4% of GDP

2013 data unless otherwise noted.
Data compiled as of September 2014.

THE TEN ECONOMIC FREEDOMS

		Score		Rank	1-Year Change

RULE OF LAW

	Score	Rank	1-Year Change
Property Rights	40.0	70th	0
Freedom from Corruption	35.0	103rd	+5.5

Most Moldovans see corruption as one of the country's major challenges. Corruption is systemic and deeply embedded in Moldova's public institutions, especially in law enforcement, the judicial system, public service, political parties, the educational system, and the legislature. The constitution provides for an independent judiciary, but the legal framework is ineffective, and lack of funds undermines reform efforts.

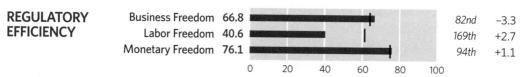

GOVERNMENT SIZE

	Score	Rank	1-Year Change
Fiscal Freedom	85.1	48th	-0.7
Government Spending	51.8	128th	-2.6

The top individual income tax rate is 18 percent, and the top corporate tax rate is 12 percent. Other taxes include a value-added tax. The overall tax burden amounts to 32 percent of domestic income. Government expenditures are equivalent to 40.1 percent of domestic output, and public debt equals approximately 24 percent of gross domestic product.

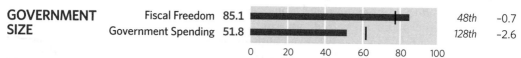

REGULATORY EFFICIENCY

	Score	Rank	1-Year Change
Business Freedom	66.8	82nd	-3.3
Labor Freedom	40.6	169th	+2.7
Monetary Freedom	76.1	94th	+1.1

Bureaucracy and lack of transparency can make the formation and operation of private enterprises burdensome. The non-salary cost of employing a worker is relatively high, and restrictions on work hours are stringent. The government has increased agricultural subsidies in support of eventual EU membership. The rapid depreciation of the leu in 2014 and looser fiscal policy threaten the inflation target.

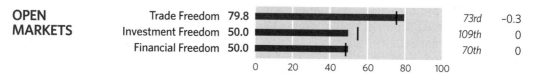

OPEN MARKETS

	Score	Rank	1-Year Change
Trade Freedom	79.8	73rd	-0.3
Investment Freedom	50.0	109th	0
Financial Freedom	50.0	70th	0

Moldova has a 2.6 percent average tariff rate. Some products are subject to import quotas. Foreign and domestic investments are generally treated equally under the law. The financial system still faces major challenges stemming from a poor regulatory environment and weak governance. The banking sector remains underdeveloped and does not offer a range of readily available financing options.

Long-Term Score Change (since 1995)

RULE OF LAW		GOVERNMENT SIZE		REGULATORY EFFICIENCY		OPEN MARKETS	
Property Rights	-10.0	Fiscal Freedom	+47.8	Business Freedom	-3.2	Trade Freedom	+62.2
Freedom from Corruption	+25.0	Government Spending	-20.3	Labor Freedom	-24.2	Investment Freedom	+20.0
				Monetary Freedom	+76.1	Financial Freedom	+40.0

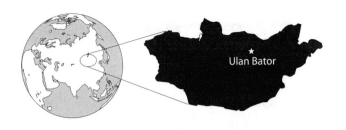

MONGOLIA

Economic Freedom Score

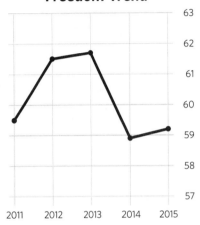

59.2

Mongolia's economic freedom score is 59.2, making its economy the 96th freest in the 2015 *Index*. Its overall score has increased by 0.3 point since last year, with improvements in four of the 10 economic freedoms, led by freedom from corruption and fiscal freedom, outweighing declines in business freedom, the management of public spending, and monetary freedom. Mongolia is ranked 19th out of 42 countries in the Asia–Pacific region, and its overall score is above the regional average but below the world average.

A massive investment boom has reshaped Mongolia's economy into a leading coal exporter. However, gains in economic freedom made after 2011 have been undermined by a subsequent decline that revealed underlying structural weaknesses and has pushed Mongolia into the "mostly unfree" category.

At the root of this negative development are increasing fiscal indiscipline and weak rule of law. The government's direct interest in the coal project has exposed it to cyclical revenue changes. The budgetary outlook discounts benefits from future mining windfalls by expanding spending in the short term. The judicial framework remains vulnerable to political influence, and the perceived level of corruption is still high.

BACKGROUND: Mongolia emerged from the shadow of the former Soviet Union in 1990 with a new constitution and a multi-party system. Its transition to democracy has been accompanied by the gradual introduction of free-market reforms. Despite political tensions exacerbated by the 2009 economic crisis, Mongolia has enjoyed relative political stability in recent years. President Tsakhiagiin Elbegdorj, whose Democratic Party coalition controls parliament, is serving his second term and cannot run for re-election. Agriculture and mining are the most important sectors of the economy, although uncertainty over investment rules has caused investment in the mineral sector to ebb and flow. While improving overall relations with the U.S., Japan, and South Korea, Mongolia has maintained strong ties with Russia and China.

Freedom Trend

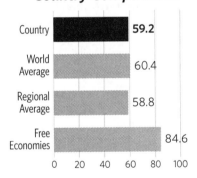

Country Comparisons

Country	59.2
World Average	60.4
Regional Average	58.8
Free Economies	84.6

Quick Facts

Population: 2.9 million
GDP (PPP): $17.1 billion
11.7% growth in 2013
5-year compound annual growth 9.2%
$5,885 per capita
Unemployment: 4.9%
Inflation (CPI): 9.6%
FDI Inflow: $2.0 billion
Public Debt: 63% of GDP

2013 data unless otherwise noted.
Data compiled as of September 2014.

How Do We Measure Economic Freedom?
See page 475 for an explanation of the methodology
or visit the *Index* Web site at *heritage.org/index.*

THE TEN ECONOMIC FREEDOMS

		Score	Country	World Average	Rank	1-Year Change

RULE OF LAW
Property Rights 30.0 — 94th — 0
Freedom from Corruption 38.0 — 83rd — +9.8

Corruption is viewed as pervasive. Graft is endemic, and weak institutions do not enforce anti-corruption measures effectively. The judiciary is independent but inefficient and vulnerable to political interference. Corruption persists among judges. Property and contractual rights are recognized, but enforcement is weak. The government lacks the capacity to enforce intellectual property rights laws.

GOVERNMENT SIZE
Fiscal Freedom 83.9 — 58th — +2.1
Government Spending 35.6 — 158th — –3.5

Mongolia's top individual income tax rate is 10 percent, and its top corporate tax rate is 25 percent. Other taxes include a value-added tax and an excise tax. The total tax burden equals 29.8 percent of domestic income, and public spending equals 46.3 percent of domestic production. Public debt has increased to over half the size of the economy.

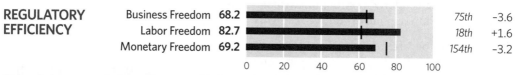

REGULATORY EFFICIENCY
Business Freedom 68.2 — 75th — –3.6
Labor Freedom 82.7 — 18th — +1.6
Monetary Freedom 69.2 — 154th — –3.2

The minimum capital requirement for incorporating has been removed, and starting a business takes only five procedures, but completing licensing requirements still takes over 130 days. Despite some progress, the labor market still lacks dynamism and remains segmented. The central bank's large mortgage subsidy program and liquidity injection in 2013 distorted markets and ratcheted up inflation.

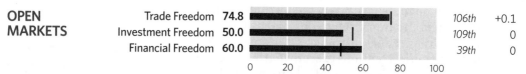

OPEN MARKETS
Trade Freedom 74.8 — 106th — +0.1
Investment Freedom 50.0 — 109th — 0
Financial Freedom 60.0 — 39th — 0

Mongolia has a 5.1 percent average tariff rate. Importing goods is time-consuming. The 2012 Strategic Entities Foreign Investment Law limits investment in some sectors of the economy. The financial system, dominated by banks, has undergone restructuring and modernization. In recent years, the banking sector has had vulnerabilities arising from highly concentrated loan portfolios and high loan-to-deposit ratios.

Long-Term Score Change (since 1995)

RULE OF LAW		GOVERNMENT SIZE		REGULATORY EFFICIENCY		OPEN MARKETS	
Property Rights	–40.0	Fiscal Freedom	+36.3	Business Freedom	–1.8	Trade Freedom	+19.8
Freedom from Corruption	–12.0	Government Spending	+18.3	Labor Freedom	+12.3	Investment Freedom	–20.0
				Monetary Freedom	+69.2	Financial Freedom	+10.0

MONTENEGRO

Economic Freedom Score

25   50   75

Least free 0   100 Most free

64.7

Montenegro's economic freedom score is 64.7, making its economy the 66th freest in the 2015 *Index*. Its score is 1.1 points higher than last year, with gains in half of the 10 economic freedoms, including labor freedom, freedom from corruption, and trade freedom, slightly offset by declines in the management of government spending and business freedom. Montenegro is ranked 31st out of 43 countries in the Europe region, and its overall score is above the world average but below the regional average.

Economic freedom in Montenegro has expanded by 2.2 points during the past five years and has reached its highest level ever in the 2015 *Index*. Improvements in seven of the 10 economic freedoms include strong gains in investment freedom and the control of government spending that help to offset a double-digit decline in labor freedom.

Fallout from the global financial and eurozone crisis has hurt growth, but economic reforms have proceeded and have become more broad-based. Open-market policies continue to facilitate privatization of state-owned enterprises. The pace of judicial reform has been sluggish, and the perceived level of corruption remains high.

BACKGROUND: The Republic of Montenegro declared its independence from Serbia in 2006. Upon gaining independence, it introduced significant privatization and adopted the euro as its currency despite not being a member of the eurozone. Milo Đukanovic, leader of the Coalition for European Montenegro, an alliance between the Democratic Party of Socialists of Montenegro and two other center-left parties that won the October 2012 parliamentary elections, became prime minister in December 2012. Montenegro was invited to launch a NATO Membership Action Plan in 2009, became a candidate for membership in the European Union in 2010, and joined the World Trade Organization in 2011. Its economy relies heavily on tourism and exports of refined metals, but real estate is gaining importance. Unprofitable state companies burden public finances, and unemployment is high.

Freedom Trend

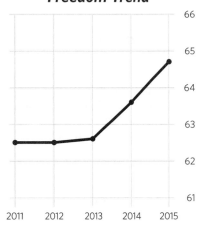

Country Comparisons

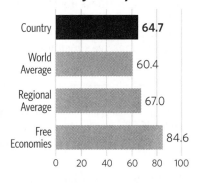

Country	64.7
World Average	60.4
Regional Average	67.0
Free Economies	84.6

0   20   40   60   80   100

Quick Facts

Population: 0.6 million
GDP (PPP): $7.4 billion
3.4% growth in 2013
5-year compound annual growth 0.1%
$11,913 per capita
Unemployment: 19.7%
Inflation (CPI): 2.2%
FDI Inflow: $447.4 million
Public Debt: 56.8% of GDP

2013 data unless otherwise noted.
Data compiled as of September 2014.

How Do We Measure Economic Freedom?
See page 475 for an explanation of the methodology
or visit the *Index* Web site at *heritage.org/index*.

THE TEN ECONOMIC FREEDOMS

		Score			Rank	1-Year Change

RULE OF LAW
	Score	Rank	1-Year Change
Property Rights	40.0	70th	0
Freedom from Corruption	44.0	67th	+6.2

Corruption remains pervasive. According to a 2013 European Commission report, graft and misconduct are widespread in such key areas as health care and public procurement, convictions in high-profile cases are low, and oversight of conflicts of interest is relatively weak. Organized crime significantly influences both the public and private sectors. Politicization of the judiciary is a long-standing problem.

GOVERNMENT SIZE
	Score	Rank	1-Year Change
Fiscal Freedom	92.6	19th	+0.1
Government Spending	36.7	156th	-5.9

Montenegro's individual and corporate income tax rates are a flat 9 percent. Other taxes include a value-added tax and an inheritance tax. Tax revenue equals 24 percent of domestic production, and public expenditures are equal to 45.9 percent of the size of the domestic economy. Public debt is equivalent to about 57 percent of gross domestic product.

REGULATORY EFFICIENCY
	Score	Rank	1-Year Change
Business Freedom	77.1	39th	-0.5
Labor Freedom	77.5	32nd	+8.9
Monetary Freedom	79.7	58th	+1.1

Starting a business now takes six procedures and slightly less than a week, with no minimum capital required. However, licensing requirements continue to be costly and time-consuming. The labor market continues to evolve, but unemployment and underemployment remain high. Ongoing massive subsidies for a bankrupt, state-supported Communist-era aluminum factory have distorted the economy.

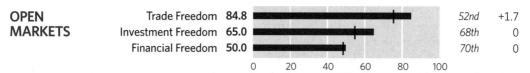

OPEN MARKETS
	Score	Rank	1-Year Change
Trade Freedom	84.8	52nd	+1.7
Investment Freedom	65.0	68th	0
Financial Freedom	50.0	70th	0

Montenegro's average tariff rate is 2.6 percent. Foreign and domestic investors are treated equally under the law, but the court system moves slowly. The financial system has gradually become more open and diversified. However, the system, particularly the banking sector, remains plagued by low profitability, and nonperforming loans have increased to about 20 percent of total loans.

Long-Term Score Change (since 2009)

RULE OF LAW		GOVERNMENT SIZE		REGULATORY EFFICIENCY		OPEN MARKETS	
Property Rights	0	Fiscal Freedom	+3.5	Business Freedom	+8.4	Trade Freedom	+4.6
Freedom from Corruption	+11.0	Government Spending	-8.6	Labor Freedom	+20.3	Investment Freedom	+25.0
				Monetary Freedom	+0.8	Financial Freedom	0

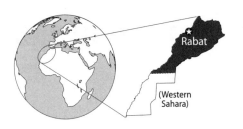

MOROCCO

Economic Freedom Score

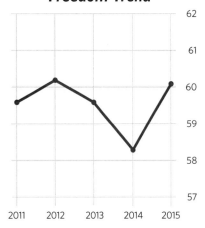

Least free 0   Most free 100

60.1

M orocco's economic freedom score is 60.1, making its economy the 89th freest in the 2015 *Index*. Its score is 1.8 points better than last year, with a very large improvement in trade freedom and smaller gains in freedom from corruption, labor freedom, and monetary freedom outweighing declines in business freedom and the management of government spending. Morocco is ranked 9th out of 15 countries in the Middle East/North Africa region, and its overall score is just below the world average.

Committed to economic reform, Morocco remained largely immune from significant Arab Spring protests. Over the past five years, gains in five of the 10 economic freedoms, including labor freedom, monetary freedom, and investment freedom, have offset declines in the management of public spending and business freedom. Morocco has regained "moderately free" status in the 2015 *Index*.

Proximity to Europe and a free trade agreement with the United States have helped to establish a foundation for dynamic economic growth. Openness to global trade and investment has facilitated the development of a modern and competitive financial sector. Relatively prudent fiscal policy has encouraged macroeconomic stability and greater structural reform.

BACKGROUND: Morocco, a constitutional monarchy with an elected parliament, has been a key ally in the struggle against Islamist extremism. Constitutional amendments proposed by a commission authorized by King Mohammed VI and approved by referendum in 2011 are designed to increase the power and independence of the prime minister and provide greater civil liberties. In November 2011, the Justice and Development Party became the first Islamist party to lead the government, but the king retains significant power as chief executive. Reforms were adopted in 2014 to reduce government subsidies. In addition to a large tourism industry and a growing manufacturing sector, a nascent aeronautics industry is attracting new foreign direct investment. Agriculture accounts for about 15 percent of GDP and employs almost 45 percent of the labor force.

Freedom Trend

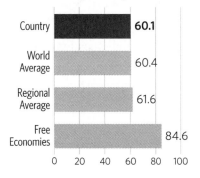

Country Comparisons

Country — 60.1
World Average — 60.4
Regional Average — 61.6
Free Economies — 84.6

Quick Facts

Population: 32.9 million
GDP (PPP): $179.2 billion
4.5% growth in 2013
5-year compound annual growth 4.1%
$5,456 per capita
Unemployment: 9.2%
Inflation (CPI): 1.9%
FDI Inflow: $3.4 billion
Public Debt: 61.9% of GDP

2013 data unless otherwise noted.
Data compiled as of September 2014.

How Do We Measure Economic Freedom?
See page 475 for an explanation of the methodology
or visit the *Index* Web site at *heritage.org/index*.

THE TEN ECONOMIC FREEDOMS

		Score	■ Country	| World Average	Rank	1-Year Change

RULE OF LAW

	Score	Rank	1-Year Change
Property Rights	40.0	70th	0
Freedom from Corruption	37.0	92nd	+3.7

Widespread corruption undermines investor sentiment and raises the cost of operating a business. Recent cases have involved the embezzlement of millions by public servants. In addition to his public role, the king is the majority stakeholder in a vast array of private and public-sector firms. The courts are inadequate and cannot be relied upon to rule quickly or fairly.

GOVERNMENT SIZE

	Score	Rank	1-Year Change
Fiscal Freedom	70.9	135th	-0.4
Government Spending	61.0	110th	-3.1

Morocco's top individual income tax rate is 38 percent, and its corporate tax rate is a flat 30 percent. Other taxes include a value-added tax and a gift tax. Overall tax revenue equals 23.7 percent of gross domestic product. Public expenditures equal 36.1 percent of domestic production, and public debt corresponds to 62 percent of the size of the domestic economy.

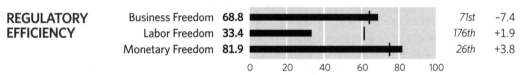

REGULATORY EFFICIENCY

	Score	Rank	1-Year Change
Business Freedom	68.8	71st	-7.4
Labor Freedom	33.4	176th	+1.9
Monetary Freedom	81.9	26th	+3.8

Incorporating a business takes five procedures and less than a week, with no minimum capital required, but completing licensing requirements still takes about three months on average. Labor market rigidity continues to discourage dynamic job growth. In January 2014, the government ended costly gasoline and fuel oil subsidies, but it maintained some food subsidies.

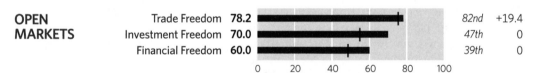

OPEN MARKETS

	Score	Rank	1-Year Change
Trade Freedom	78.2	82nd	+19.4
Investment Freedom	70.0	47th	0
Financial Freedom	60.0	39th	0

The average tariff rate is 3.4 percent. Tariffs have fallen, but regulatory issues may delay trade. Foreign investors cannot buy agricultural land, and investment in some economic sectors is regulated. The financial system has undergone modernization and expansion. Morocco's banking sector is one of the most liberalized in North Africa. The stock market does not restrict foreign participation.

Long-Term Score Change (since 1995)

RULE OF LAW		GOVERNMENT SIZE		REGULATORY EFFICIENCY		OPEN MARKETS	
Property Rights	-30.0	Fiscal Freedom	+13.4	Business Freedom	-1.2	Trade Freedom	+28.4
Freedom from Corruption	-13.0	Government Spending	-11.8	Labor Freedom	-8.7	Investment Freedom	0
				Monetary Freedom	+6.9	Financial Freedom	+10.0

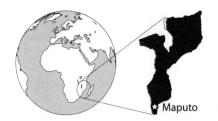

Maputo

MOZAMBIQUE

Economic Freedom Score

Least free 0   Most free 100

54.8

Mozambique's economic freedom score is 54.8, making its economy the 125th freest in the 2015 *Index*. Its overall score has declined by 0.2 point since last year, with improvements in freedom from corruption, government spending, labor freedom, and monetary freedom outweighed by sizeable declines in business freedom and investment freedom. Mozambique is ranked 24th out of 46 countries in the Sub-Saharan Africa region, and its overall score is just below the regional average.

Relative peace after years of civil war and the discovery of promising natural gas reserves have propelled Mozambique's economic growth in recent years, but improvements in economic freedom have not followed. Over the past five years, economic freedom in Mozambique has declined by 2.0 points, with losses in a majority of the 10 factors. Particularly worrying is a large score decline in the management of government spending. Continued fiscal intransigence could undermine the productive use of commodity windfalls.

This downward trend undermines an already weak economic foundation. The judiciary remains ineffective and vulnerable to political influence, and corruption remains pervasive in the public sector. Much of the population is stuck in subsistence agriculture due to burdensome business regulations that inhibit entrepreneurship, and the rigid labor market exacerbates unemployment and underemployment.

BACKGROUND: The Frelimo party, currently headed by President Armando Guebuza, has been in power since independence from Portugal in 1975. Following independence, there was a 16-year civil war between Frelimo and the rebel movement Renamo that ended with the Rome Peace Accords in 1992. In October 2013, after several clashes with Frelimo, Renamo announced that it was pulling out of the peace accord. Both parties reached a peace deal in September 2014 ahead of the country's national elections in October. Despite political instability, Mozambique has emerged as one of the world's fastest-growing economies and is expected to become one of the world's largest exporters of coal and gas.

Freedom Trend

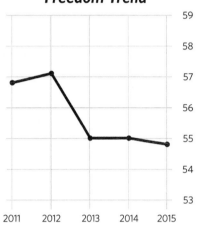

Country Comparisons

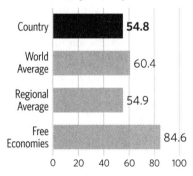

Quick Facts

Population: 25.9 million
GDP (PPP): $28.2 billion
7.1% growth in 2013
5-year compound annual growth 7.0%
$1,090 per capita
Unemployment: 8.5%
Inflation (CPI): 4.2%
FDI Inflow: $5.9 billion
Public Debt: 43.3% of GDP

2013 data unless otherwise noted.
Data compiled as of September 2014.

How Do We Measure Economic Freedom?
See page 475 for an explanation of the methodology
or visit the *Index* Web site at *heritage.org/index*.

329

THE TEN ECONOMIC FREEDOMS

		Score		Rank	1-Year Change
RULE OF LAW	Property Rights	30.0		94th	0
	Freedom from Corruption	30.0		121st	+3.8

Corruption remains pervasive in government and business despite the passing of a new anti-corruption law and the delegation of new powers to the Central Office for Combating Corruption in 2012. The police and judicial bodies in charge of enforcing anti-corruption measures are themselves often corrupt. Property rights are not strongly respected, and law enforcement is inefficient and uneven.

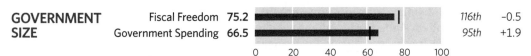

		Score		Rank	1-Year Change
GOVERNMENT SIZE	Fiscal Freedom	75.2		116th	−0.5
	Government Spending	66.5		95th	+1.9

The top individual and corporate income tax rates are 32 percent. Other taxes include a value-added tax and an inheritance tax. The overall tax burden equals 20.8 percent of the domestic economy. Government expenditures are equal to 33.4 percent of gross domestic product, and public debt is equivalent to 43 percent of annual domestic output.

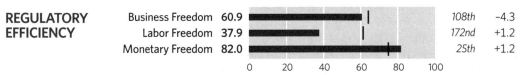

		Score		Rank	1-Year Change
REGULATORY EFFICIENCY	Business Freedom	60.9		108th	−4.3
	Labor Freedom	37.9		172nd	+1.2
	Monetary Freedom	82.0		25th	+1.2

With no minimum capital required, forming a business takes nine procedures and 13 days on average, but completing licensing requirements still takes over 140 days on average. The public and energy sectors employ much of the formal labor force. The labor market lacks flexibility. The government maintains administered prices for fuels and subsidizes state-owned enterprises such as the electricity company.

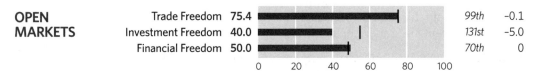

		Score		Rank	1-Year Change
OPEN MARKETS	Trade Freedom	75.4		99th	−0.1
	Investment Freedom	40.0		131st	−5.0
	Financial Freedom	50.0		70th	0

Mozambique's average tariff rate is 4.8 percent. Customs delays may interfere with trade. Land is state-owned, and the government screens new foreign investment. The financial system remains underdeveloped. About 10 percent of Mozambicans have access to formal financial services, and less than 5 percent have access to credit. The three largest banks, all foreign-owned, dominate the system.

Long-Term Score Change (since 1995)

RULE OF LAW		GOVERNMENT SIZE		REGULATORY EFFICIENCY		OPEN MARKETS	
Property Rights	0	Fiscal Freedom	+14.8	Business Freedom	+5.9	Trade Freedom	+0.4
Freedom from Corruption	+20.0	Government Spending	−8.3	Labor Freedom	+2.7	Investment Freedom	+10.0
				Monetary Freedom	+38.1	Financial Freedom	+20.0

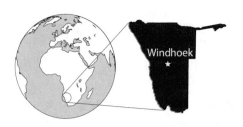

Windhoek ★

NAMIBIA

Economic Freedom Score

25   50   75

Least free 0   100 Most free

59.6

Namibia's economic freedom score is 59.6, making its economy the 93rd freest in the 2015 *Index*. Its score is up by 0.2 point from last year, reflecting improvements in labor freedom, investment freedom, and freedom from corruption that outweigh declines in half of the 10 economic freedoms led by a significant deterioration in trade freedom. Namibia is ranked 10th out of 46 countries in the Sub-Saharan Africa region, and its overall score is below the world average but above the regional average.

Over the past five years, Namibia's economic freedom has been on a downward trend, declining by 3.1 points, the third biggest score drop in the Sub-Saharan Africa region. Deteriorations have largely been concentrated in the management of government spending and trade freedom, which have declined by 15 points and 18 points, respectively.

Overall, Namibia's progress toward greater economic freedom has been patchy. Open-market policies have been advanced only marginally, with layers of tariff and non-tariff barriers as well as lingering regulatory restrictions continuing to undercut productivity growth and impede diversification of the economy. The absence of an independent and fair judiciary weakens the rule of law and undermines prospects for long-term economic development. Corruption is pervasive, and the effectiveness of government services is poor.

BACKGROUND: Namibia has enjoyed political stability since independence from South Africa in 1990. President Hifikepunye Pohamba won a second five-year term in 2009. The next elections are scheduled for 2014. Namibia benefits from good governance and a market-led economy. The economy is centered on agriculture, which is vulnerable to external shocks. It is also closely linked to South Africa's economy, with the Namibian dollar pegged to the South African rand since 1993. There has been official pressure on white and foreign landowners to sell their property to the government so that "historically disadvantaged" and landless Namibians can be resettled.

Freedom Trend

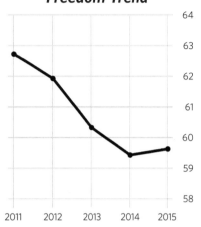

2011   2012   2013   2014   2015

Country Comparisons

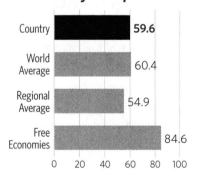

Country	59.6
World Average	60.4
Regional Average	54.9
Free Economies	84.6

0   20   40   60   80   100

Quick Facts

Population: 2.2 million
GDP (PPP): $17.8 billion
4.3% growth in 2013
5-year compound annual growth 4.0%
$8,191 per capita
Unemployment: 17.7%
Inflation (CPI): 6.2%
FDI Inflow: $699.1 million
Public Debt: 26.6% of GDP

2013 data unless otherwise noted.
Data compiled as of September 2014.

THE TEN ECONOMIC FREEDOMS

		Score		Rank	1-Year Change
RULE OF LAW	Property Rights	30.0		94th	0
	Freedom from Corruption	48.0		57th	+3.8

According to an April 2014 Ernest & Young survey, nearly 80 percent of Namibian businesses view fraud and corruption as a significant risk to their operations. The rule of law remains weak, and access to justice is obstructed by economic and geographic barriers, a shortage of public defenders, and delays. Property rights are not protected effectively.

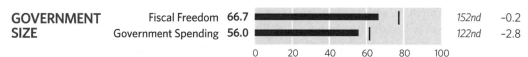

		Score		Rank	1-Year Change
GOVERNMENT SIZE	Fiscal Freedom	66.7		152nd	-0.2
	Government Spending	56.0		122nd	-2.8

Namibia's top individual income tax rate is 37 percent, and its top corporate tax rate is 34 percent. Other taxes include a value-added tax. Overall tax revenue is equal to 28.4 percent of the domestic economy, and public expenditures are equivalent to 38.3 percent of domestic output. Public debt equals approximately 27 percent of gross domestic product.

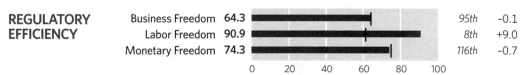

		Score		Rank	1-Year Change
REGULATORY EFFICIENCY	Business Freedom	64.3		95th	-0.1
	Labor Freedom	90.9		8th	+9.0
	Monetary Freedom	74.3		116th	-0.7

The regulatory environment is not conducive to business formation and operation. Launching a business takes 10 procedures and 66 days on average, and licensing takes over four months. The labor market is underdeveloped. Much of the labor force is employed in the public sector. Inflation remained high in 2013, spurred by a 13 percent increase in the tariff for bulk electricity.

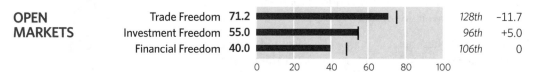

		Score		Rank	1-Year Change
OPEN MARKETS	Trade Freedom	71.2		128th	-11.7
	Investment Freedom	55.0		96th	+5.0
	Financial Freedom	40.0		106th	0

Namibia, a member of the Southern African Customs Union, has a 6.9 percent average tariff rate. Government procurement policies can be challenging for foreign firms. Foreign and domestic investments are generally treated equally under the law. Limited access to credit and the high costs of financing impede entrepreneurial activity. Progress in modernizing the financial sector has been sluggish and limited.

Long-Term Score Change (since 1997)

RULE OF LAW		GOVERNMENT SIZE		REGULATORY EFFICIENCY		OPEN MARKETS	
Property Rights	-40.0	Fiscal Freedom	-1.0	Business Freedom	+9.3	Trade Freedom	+35.0
Freedom from Corruption	-2.0	Government Spending	-4.5	Labor Freedom	+4.3	Investment Freedom	-15.0
				Monetary Freedom	-0.6	Financial Freedom	-30.0

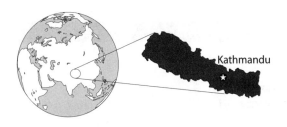

NEPAL

Economic Freedom Score

25 50 75

Least free 0   100 Most free

51.3

World Rank: 152   **Regional Rank: 34**

N epal's economic freedom score is 51.3, making its economy the 152nd freest in the 2015 *Index*. Its score has increased by 1.2 points since last year, driven mainly by improvements in freedom from corruption and business freedom that outweigh a decline in monetary freedom. Nepal is ranked 34th out of 42 countries in the Asia–Pacific region, and its score remains below the world and regional averages.

Much of Nepal's population has been trapped in poverty for years. A failure to implement consistent economic reforms has perpetuated this condition and left the Nepalese economy barely above the "repressed" category in terms of economic freedom.

Although economic freedom has advanced by 1.2 points over the past five years, seven of the 10 categories measured still score below the global averages. Improvements have occurred only in freedom from corruption and business freedom. The rule of law is not evenly enforced, and this has deterred investors from investing in Nepal's promising hydroelectric industry. Even small entrepreneurs and laborers are inhibited from entering the formal marketplace due to inefficient and excessive regulation.

BACKGROUND: Eight years after the end of a Maoist insurgency and abolition of the monarchy, Nepal still has only an interim constitution. In May 2012, the first Constituent Assembly was dissolved after failing to produce a new constitution. Elections were postponed for nearly 18 months. In November 2013, the Nepali Congress party won enough seats to form a coalition government headed by Prime Minister Sushi Koirala, who pledged to complete a new constitution within a year with a goal of making the transition from a constitutional monarchy to a federal republic. The reintegration of former Maoist fighters into the national army remains controversial. A poor, landlocked country bordering the Himalayan Mountains, Nepal attracts little foreign direct investment. Agriculture accounts for one-third of GDP.

Freedom Trend

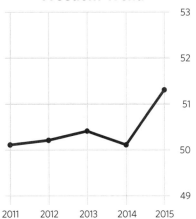

2011 2012 2013 2014 2015

Country Comparisons

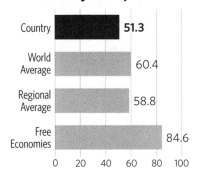

Country 51.3
World Average 60.4
Regional Average 58.8
Free Economies 84.6

0 20 40 60 80 100

Quick Facts

Population: 27.9 million
GDP (PPP): $42.1 billion
3.6% growth in 2013
5-year compound annual growth 4.3%
$1,508 per capita
Unemployment: 2.7%
Inflation (CPI): 9.9%
FDI Inflow: $73.6 million
Public Debt: 31.0% of GDP

2013 data unless otherwise noted.
Data compiled as of September 2014.

How Do We Measure Economic Freedom?
See page 475 for an explanation of the methodology
or visit the *Index* Web site at *heritage.org/index*.

333

THE TEN ECONOMIC FREEDOMS

RULE OF LAW

	Score	Rank	1-Year Change
Property Rights	30.0	94th	0
Freedom from Corruption	31.0	118th	+9.7

Corruption is endemic in politics and government. Many legislators have been accused or convicted of corruption, but high-level officials are rarely prosecuted. Graft is particularly prevalent in the judiciary, with payoffs to judges for favorable rulings, and in the police force, which has been accused of extensive involvement in organized crime. Protections for property rights are not enforced effectively.

GOVERNMENT SIZE

	Score	Rank	1-Year Change
Fiscal Freedom	85.6	46th	-0.3
Government Spending	88.9	16th	-0.7

Nepal's top individual and corporate income tax rates are 25 percent. Other taxes include a value-added tax and a property tax. The overall tax burden is equivalent to 13.9 percent of domestic income. Government expenditures equal 19.2 percent of gross domestic product, and public debt stands at 31 percent of the size of the domestic economy.

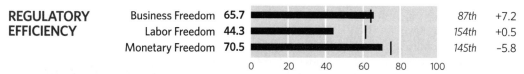

REGULATORY EFFICIENCY

	Score	Rank	1-Year Change
Business Freedom	65.7	87th	+7.2
Labor Freedom	44.3	154th	+0.5
Monetary Freedom	70.5	145th	-5.8

Commercial regulations are not implemented or enforced effectively. Economic diversification has lagged, and much private-sector activity takes place outside of the formal economy. Labor regulations, although not fully enforced, are relatively rigid and outmoded. Inflation increased in late 2013 due to higher import bills caused by depreciation of the Nepali rupee against the Chinese yuan and the U.S. dollar.

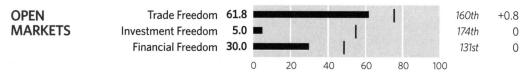

OPEN MARKETS

	Score	Rank	1-Year Change
Trade Freedom	61.8	160th	+0.8
Investment Freedom	5.0	174th	0
Financial Freedom	30.0	131st	0

Nepal's average tariff rate is 11.6 percent. Some goods may be subject to export taxes, and beef imports are restricted. New foreign investment is screened by the government. The financial sector, dominated by banking, remains underdeveloped, and a full range of modern financing tools is not readily available. Capital transactions and foreign exchange accounts are also limited.

Long-Term Score Change (since 1996)

RULE OF LAW		GOVERNMENT SIZE		REGULATORY EFFICIENCY		OPEN MARKETS	
Property Rights	0	Fiscal Freedom	-0.8	Business Freedom	+10.7	Trade Freedom	+8.6
Freedom from Corruption	+21.0	Government Spending	-2.4	Labor Freedom	-3.2	Investment Freedom	-25.0
				Monetary Freedom	+3.5	Financial Freedom	0

NETHERLANDS

Amsterdam

Economic Freedom Score

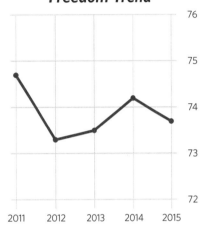

Least free 0

Most free 100

73.7

The Netherlands' economic freedom score is 73.7, making its economy the 17th freest in the 2015 *Index*. Its score has decreased by 0.5 point since last year, reflecting declines in four of the 10 economic freedoms, including business freedom and freedom from corruption, that outweigh a significant gain in labor freedom. The Netherlands is ranked 8th out of 43 countries in the Europe region.

The Netherlands has a long history of openness to global commerce and economic freedom. Its ports of Rotterdam and Antwerp are among the busiest in the world and serve as primary entry points for goods to Europe. However, over the past five years, the country's traditional commitment to the free market has been under stress. Since 2011, economic freedom has declined by 1.0 point, largely as a result of excessive government spending and increased perceptions of corruption.

Despite some negative trends, The Netherlands' economy still rests on strong foundations of economic freedom. The property rights and investment regimes are the second freest in the world. Business regulations are more efficient than those of regional peers, providing a comparative advantage. However, fiscal policy does remain a concern. Taxes are high, but government spending is even higher, pushing up levels of public debt.

BACKGROUND: The center-right coalition led by Prime Minister Mark Rutte collapsed in April 2012 when the Freedom Party's Geert Wilders refused to back Rutte's austerity package. Rutte's party and its principal coalition partner, the center-left Labor Party, won increased support to maintain power during elections in September 2012. The Netherlands is a founding member of the European Union and under Rutte's leadership has been one of the most outspoken supporters of turning power back to EU member states. The Netherlands is a center of international commerce.

Freedom Trend

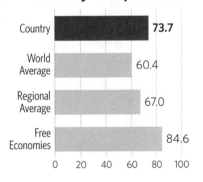

Country Comparisons

Country	73.7
World Average	60.4
Regional Average	67.0
Free Economies	84.6

Quick Facts

Population: 16.8 million
GDP (PPP): $700.5 billion
–0.8% growth in 2013
5-year compound annual growth –0.7%
$41,711 per capita
Unemployment: 6.7%
Inflation (CPI): 2.6%
FDI Inflow: $24.4 billion
Public Debt: 74.9% of GDP

2013 data unless otherwise noted.
Data compiled as of September 2014.

THE TEN ECONOMIC FREEDOMS

		Score		Rank	1-Year Change
RULE OF LAW	Property Rights	90.0		3rd	0
	Freedom from Corruption	83.0		8th	-5.0

The Netherlands has few problems with corruption. Effective anti-corruption measures ensure government integrity, and public tolerance for graft is low. A new campaign financing law took effect in May 2013. The legal framework ensures strong protection of private property rights and enforcement of contracts. Independent of political interference, the judiciary is respected and provides fair adjudication of disputes.

		Score		Rank	1-Year Change
GOVERNMENT SIZE	Fiscal Freedom	51.8		174th	+0.1
	Government Spending	23.8		168th	-1.8

The Netherlands' top individual income tax rate is 52 percent, and its top corporate tax rate is 25 percent. Other taxes include a value-added tax, environmental taxes, and inheritance taxes. Overall tax revenue equals 38.6 percent of domestic income, and government expenditures equal 50.4 percent of domestic output. Public debt is equivalent to 75 percent of gross domestic product.

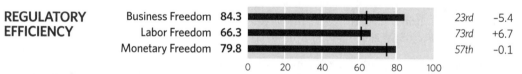

		Score		Rank	1-Year Change
REGULATORY EFFICIENCY	Business Freedom	84.3		23rd	-5.4
	Labor Freedom	66.3		73rd	+6.7
	Monetary Freedom	79.8		57th	-0.1

It takes four procedures and four days to start a business on average, with no minimum capital required, but completing licensing requirements remains time-consuming. The non-salary cost of employing a worker is high, although severance payments are not overly burdensome. Monetary stability has been well maintained, and the government has cut subsidies to offshore wind power projects.

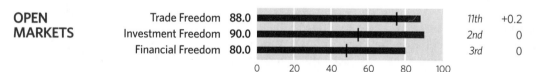

		Score		Rank	1-Year Change
OPEN MARKETS	Trade Freedom	88.0		11th	+0.2
	Investment Freedom	90.0		2nd	0
	Financial Freedom	80.0		3rd	0

EU members have a 1.0 percent average tariff rate. Although some non-tariff barriers exist, the EU is relatively open to external trade. The Netherlands generally treats foreign and domestic investors equally. The competitive financial sector offers a wide range of financing instruments. The government has nationalized several banks in recent years but is planning to sell some of its holdings.

Long-Term Score Change (since 1996)

RULE OF LAW		GOVERNMENT SIZE		REGULATORY EFFICIENCY		OPEN MARKETS	
Property Rights	0	Fiscal Freedom	+18.0	Business Freedom	-0.7	Trade Freedom	+10.2
Freedom from Corruption	-7.0	Government Spending	+17.2	Labor Freedom	+4.8	Investment Freedom	+20.0
				Monetary Freedom	-4.6	Financial Freedom	-10.0

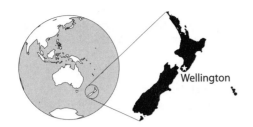

NEW ZEALAND

Economic Freedom Score

Least free 0

25

50

75

100 Most free

82.1

World Rank: **3**   Regional Rank: **3**

N ew Zealand's economic freedom score is 82.1, making its economy the 3rd freest in the 2015 *Index*. Its score is up by 0.9 point, with improvements in the management of government spending, monetary freedom, and labor freedom outweighing declines in freedom from corruption, fiscal freedom, and business freedom. New Zealand is ranked 3rd out of 42 countries in the Asia–Pacific region and 3rd in the world.

New Zealand's economic development over the past few decades has been built on principles of market openness and free trade. Reforms in the 1980s opened the economy to imports, reduced the size of government, and lowered the tax burden. These changes, enhanced in recent decades, have solidified the economy's ranking among the world's freest, with a high standard of living and low rates of poverty.

New Zealand's prosperity rests on its well-established rule of law. The economy is the least corrupt in the world, and property rights, including intellectual property, are strongly protected. Entrepreneurs generally find regulations efficient, and the labor market is efficient in allocating labor. Despite having one of the world's most open financial sectors, New Zealand banks avoided the worst effects of the global financial crisis.

BACKGROUND: New Zealand is a parliamentary democracy and one of the Asia–Pacific region's most prosperous countries. After 10 years of Labor Party–dominated governments, the center-right National Party, led by Prime Minister John Key, returned to power in November 2008 and was re-elected in November 2011. Far-reaching deregulation and privatization in the 1980s and 1990s largely liberated the economy, which is powered mainly by agriculture but also benefits from a flourishing manufacturing sector, thriving tourism, and a strong renewable geothermal energy resource base. Following a sizable contraction during the global economic recession, the economy has been expanding since 2010.

Freedom Trend

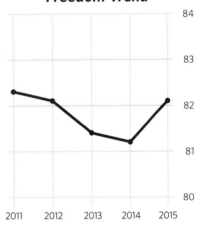

Country Comparisons

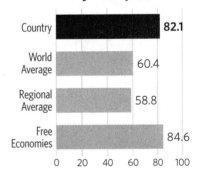

Quick Facts

Population: 4.5 million
GDP (PPP): $136.6 billion
2.4% growth in 2013
5-year compound annual growth 1.5%
$30,493 per capita
Unemployment: 6.4%
Inflation (CPI): 1.1%
FDI Inflow: $986.5 million
Public Debt: 35.9% of GDP

2013 data unless otherwise noted.
Data compiled as of September 2014.

How Do We Measure Economic Freedom?
See page 475 for an explanation of the methodology or visit the *Index* Web site at *heritage.org/index*.

THE TEN ECONOMIC FREEDOMS

		Score	Country	World Average	Rank	1-Year Change
RULE OF LAW	Property Rights	95.0			1st	0
	Freedom from Corruption	91.0			1st	-3.0

New Zealand is tied with Denmark for first place out of 177 countries in Transparency International's 2013 Corruption Perceptions Index. It is renowned for its efforts to penalize bribery and ensure a transparent, competitive, and corruption-free government procurement system. The judicial system is independent and functions well. Private property rights are strongly protected, and contracts are notably secure.

		Score			Rank	Change
GOVERNMENT SIZE	Fiscal Freedom	70.4			136th	-0.8
	Government Spending	43.0			146th	+10.7

The top individual income tax rate is 33 percent, and the top corporate tax rate is 28 percent. Other taxes include a goods and services tax and environmental taxes. Overall tax revenue equals 32.9 percent of gross domestic product. Public expenditures equal 43.6 percent of GDP, and public debt is equivalent to approximately 35 percent of annual economic activity.

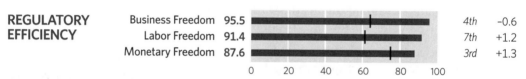

		Score			Rank	Change
REGULATORY EFFICIENCY	Business Freedom	95.5			4th	-0.6
	Labor Freedom	91.4			7th	+1.2
	Monetary Freedom	87.6			3rd	+1.3

The entrepreneurial framework is transparent and efficient. Starting a business takes one procedure and one day on average. The labor market is flexible, with moderate non-salary costs and flexible work-hours regulations. New Zealand has the lowest subsidies of any OECD country. It removed all farm subsidies two decades ago and spurred the development of a diversified agriculture sector.

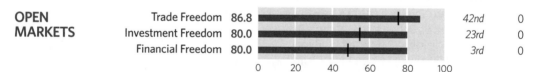

		Score			Rank	Change
OPEN MARKETS	Trade Freedom	86.8			42nd	0
	Investment Freedom	80.0			23rd	0
	Financial Freedom	80.0			3rd	0

New Zealand's average tariff rate is 1.6 percent. Non-tariff barriers are low as a result of unilateral trade liberalization and participation in trade agreements. Foreign investment is welcomed, but the government may screen some large investments. The open financial sector is highly competitive and well developed. Prudent regulations allowed firms to withstand the global financial turmoil with little disruption.

Long-Term Score Change (since 1996)

RULE OF LAW		GOVERNMENT SIZE		REGULATORY EFFICIENCY		OPEN MARKETS	
Property Rights	+5.0	Fiscal Freedom	+5.3	Business Freedom	+10.5	Trade Freedom	+8.2
Freedom from Corruption	+1.0	Government Spending	-5.6	Labor Freedom	+0.3	Investment Freedom	+10.0
				Monetary Freedom	+1.6	Financial Freedom	-10.0

NICARAGUA

Economic Freedom Score

57.6

Nicaragua's economic freedom score is 57.6, making its economy the 108th freest in the 2015 *Index*. Its score is 0.8 point lower than last year due to declines in half of the 10 economic freedoms, including property rights, monetary freedom, labor freedom, and the management of government spending, that outweigh modest improvements in business freedom and freedom from corruption. Nicaragua is ranked 18th out of 29 countries in the South and Central America/Caribbean region.

On a net basis, economic freedom in Nicaragua has dropped by 1.2 points over the past half-decade. Declines in half of the 10 economic freedoms include large drops in property rights, labor freedom, and investment freedom.

Nicaragua's shaky institutional infrastructure makes any score declines potentially damaging. Protections for contracts and property rights are uneven, reflecting the incompetence of the judiciary. Corruption remains pervasive, and attempts to target corrupt officials have turned into political battles. Entrepreneurs find it hard to do business, and the labor market is rigid. This forces many small businesses into the informal sector. The inefficiency of the financial sector inhibits capital formation.

BACKGROUND: Despite a constitutional prohibition, Sandinista President Daniel Ortega was re-elected in November 2011, and constitutional changes approved by the National Assembly early in 2014 will allow him to stay in power indefinitely. Ortega has weathered domestic opposition thanks to economic assistance from Venezuela, divisions among his opponents, and a policy agenda that maintains relative economic openness. The Central America–Dominican Republic–United States Free Trade Agreement (CAFTA–DR) has helped to diversify the economy. Agricultural goods and textile production account for 50 percent of exports. Nicaragua is the second poorest nation in the Americas. Much of the workforce is underemployed in the formal sector. The government has granted a Chinese company a concession to construct a transatlantic canal, but the feasibility of the project has been questioned.

Freedom Trend

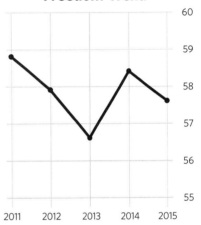

Country Comparisons

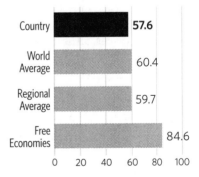

Quick Facts

Population: 6.1 million
GDP (PPP): $27.9 billion
4.2% growth in 2013
5-year compound annual growth 3.2%
$4,554 per capita
Unemployment: 7.2%
Inflation (CPI): 7.4%
FDI Inflow: $848.7 million
Public Debt: 42.4% of GDP

2013 data unless otherwise noted.
Data compiled as of September 2014.

How Do We Measure Economic Freedom?
See page 475 for an explanation of the methodology or visit the *Index* Web site at *heritage.org/index.*

THE TEN ECONOMIC FREEDOMS

		Score			Rank	1-Year Change
RULE OF LAW	Property Rights	10.0			165th	–5.0
	Freedom from Corruption	28.0			132nd	+3.9

Democracy was further weakened in 2014 by Daniel Ortega's authoritarian tendencies and efforts to subvert the constitution for political benefit. Ortega's significant influence over all state organs, including the Supreme Court and the Supreme Electoral Council, has undermined checks on the executive. Protection of private property rights is not enforced effectively, and contracts are not always secure.

		Score			Rank	1-Year Change
GOVERNMENT SIZE	Fiscal Freedom	78.4			101st	–0.2
	Government Spending	76.6			61st	–3.4

Nicaragua's top individual and corporate income tax rates are 30 percent. Other taxes include a value-added tax and a capital gains tax. With adjustments in the income tax thresholds, revenue generation has reached 18.9 percent of domestic income. Public expenditures equal 28 percent of gross domestic product, and public debt equals approximately 42 percent of the domestic economy.

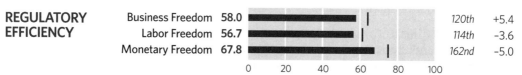

		Score			Rank	1-Year Change
REGULATORY EFFICIENCY	Business Freedom	58.0			120th	+5.4
	Labor Freedom	56.7			114th	–3.6
	Monetary Freedom	67.8			162nd	–5.0

Requirements for launching a business are not time-consuming, but the licensing process still takes more than 200 days to complete. Labor regulations are not efficient enough to support a vibrant labor market. Substantial energy and cash subsidies from Venezuela have distorted domestic prices, although the level of that aid could fall because of Venezuela's growing economic problems.

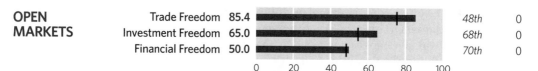

		Score			Rank	1-Year Change
OPEN MARKETS	Trade Freedom	85.4			48th	0
	Investment Freedom	65.0			68th	0
	Financial Freedom	50.0			70th	0

Nicaragua's average tariff rate is 2.3 percent. Imports of used cars and genetically modified food are restricted. The legal and regulatory environment may be difficult for foreign investors. The small financial sector has been evolving, particularly in the urban areas. A limited number of commercial credit instruments are available to the private sector, and capital markets are rudimentary.

Long-Term Score Change (since 1995)

RULE OF LAW		GOVERNMENT SIZE		REGULATORY EFFICIENCY		OPEN MARKETS	
Property Rights	–20.0	Fiscal Freedom	+0.1	Business Freedom	+3.0	Trade Freedom	+31.0
Freedom from Corruption	+18.0	Government Spending	+1.5	Labor Freedom	–16.2	Investment Freedom	+15.0
				Monetary Freedom	+67.8	Financial Freedom	+20.0

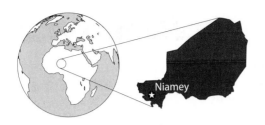

NIGER

Economic Freedom Score

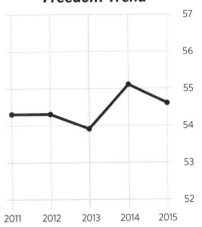

54.6

Least free 0

Most free 100

World Rank: 127   **Regional Rank: 26**

N iger's economic freedom score is 54.6, making its economy the 127th freest in the 2015 *Index*. Its score has decreased by 0.5 point since last year, reflecting declines in monetary freedom, the management of government spending, and labor freedom that outweigh gains in freedom from corruption and business freedom. Niger is ranked 26th out of 46 countries in the Sub-Saharan Africa region, and its overall score is slightly above the regional average.

Niger has experienced fast growth in recent years thanks to an expansion of its mining and uranium sectors, but economic freedom has not followed this trend. Over the past five years, broad gains have been largely offset by a sharp decline in trade freedom.

Nearly half of the government's budget comes from foreign donors, political unrest has undermined the rule of law, and the post-coup civilian government is working to combat widespread corruption and judicial incompetence. A high level of monetary freedom provides some economic stability, but a poor entrepreneurial environment, ineffective capital allocation, and closed domestic markets keep the majority of citizens in poverty.

BACKGROUND: President Mamadou Tandja was overthrown in a military coup in February 2010. A year later, in March 2011, opposition leader Mahamadou Issoufou won presidential elections that were deemed free and fair by the international community, and his Social Democratic Party coalition won a majority in the National Assembly. A Tuareg rebellion in northern Niger, spillover violence from conflicts in Libya and Mali, and the growing presence of groups linked to al-Qaeda are serious threats. Niger has one of the world's fastest population growth rates. Poor infrastructure and frequent weather disasters contribute to economic hardship. With the exception of uranium and (as of 2011) oil, substantial mineral resources, including gold, have yet to be exploited. According to a 2014 United Nations report, Niger currently hosts upwards of 50,000 refugees from Mali and Nigeria.

Freedom Trend

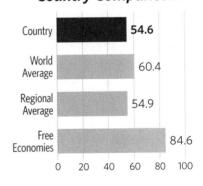

Country Comparisons

Country	54.6
World Average	60.4
Regional Average	54.9
Free Economies	84.6

Quick Facts

Population: 16.6 million
GDP (PPP): $13.8 billion
3.6% growth in 2013
5-year compound annual growth 4.8%
$829 per capita
Unemployment: 5.0%
Inflation (CPI): 2.3%
FDI Inflow: $631.4 million
Public Debt: 33.8% of GDP

2013 data unless otherwise noted.
Data compiled as of September 2014.

How Do We Measure Economic Freedom?
See page 475 for an explanation of the methodology
or visit the *Index* Web site at *heritage.org/index.*

THE TEN ECONOMIC FREEDOMS

		Score		Rank	1-Year Change
RULE OF LAW	Property Rights	30.0		94th	0
	Freedom from Corruption	34.0		107th	+8.0

Corruption remains a serious problem in Niger. In 2014, a court in Niamey lifted the immunity of former President Tandja, opening the way for a possible investigation into the disappearance of nearly $800 million of public money. The rule of law is hampered by an ineffective judicial framework, and a weak court system remains vulnerable to political interference.

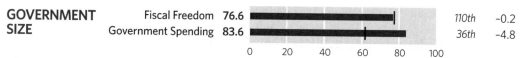

		Score		Rank	1-Year Change
GOVERNMENT SIZE	Fiscal Freedom	76.6		110th	−0.2
	Government Spending	83.6		36th	−4.8

Niger's top individual income tax rate is 35 percent, and its top corporate tax rate is 30 percent. Other taxes include a value-added tax and a tax on interest and capital gains. The overall tax burden equals 14.5 percent of domestic income, and government expenditures equal 23.4 percent of domestic output. Public debt amounts to 34 percent of gross domestic product.

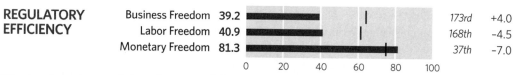

		Score		Rank	1-Year Change
REGULATORY EFFICIENCY	Business Freedom	39.2		173rd	+4.0
	Labor Freedom	40.9		168th	−4.5
	Monetary Freedom	81.3		37th	−7.0

The inadequate regulatory framework hampers private-sector development. Onerous and inconsistent regulations impose substantial costs on business. The minimum capital required to incorporate a business is still nearly five times the level of annual average income. The labor market is poorly developed, and much of the labor force works in the informal sector. The state influences prices through state-owned utilities.

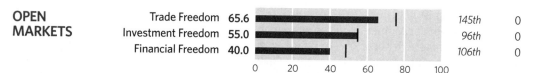

		Score		Rank	1-Year Change
OPEN MARKETS	Trade Freedom	65.6		145th	0
	Investment Freedom	55.0		96th	0
	Financial Freedom	40.0		106th	0

Niger's average tariff rate is 9.7 percent. Importing goods may be time-consuming and costly. In most cases, domestic and foreign investors are treated equally under the law. Despite some progress toward modernizing the financial sector, financing options for starting and expanding private businesses are limited. Overall bank credit to the private sector remains low.

Long-Term Score Change (since 1996)

RULE OF LAW		GOVERNMENT SIZE		REGULATORY EFFICIENCY		OPEN MARKETS	
Property Rights	0	Fiscal Freedom	+30.5	Business Freedom	−15.8	Trade Freedom	+0.6
Freedom from Corruption	+24.0	Government Spending	−8.4	Labor Freedom	−3.3	Investment Freedom	+25.0
				Monetary Freedom	+26.8	Financial Freedom	+10.0

NIGERIA

Economic Freedom Score

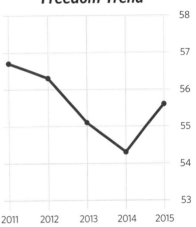

Least free 0

Most free 100

55.6

World Rank: 120   **Regional Rank: 22**

Nigeria's economic freedom score is 55.6, making its economy the 120th freest in the 2015 *Index*. Its score has increased by 1.3 points since last year, with improvements in five of the 10 economic freedoms, including labor freedom, freedom from corruption, and the management of government spending, outweighing a decline in monetary freedom. Nigeria is ranked 22nd out of 46 countries in the Sub-Saharan Africa region, and its overall score is below the world average.

Attempts to diversify Nigeria's economy away from oil and gas have fallen flat. Over the past five years, economic freedom in Nigeria has declined by 1.1 points, with losses concentrated largely in the regulatory area.

Nigeria's rule of law remains weak, and the corruption that accompanies high levels of government spending and pervades the oil sector inhibits private-sector growth. Strong linkage to global markets through the trade in crude oil is the only bright spot in trade and investment regimes that are protectionist and adverse to competition.

BACKGROUND: Nigeria achieved independence from Britain in 1960. Goodluck Jonathan became president after the sudden death of President Umaru Yar'Adua in 2010. Jonathan's re-election in 2011 was heavily criticized among northern Muslims for not following the traditional Muslim–Christian rotating power agreement. In 2013, the government declared a state of emergency in three northern states and deployed security forces to combat the terrorist group Boko Haram. In April 2014, the al-Qaeda–linked Boko Haram kidnapped nearly 300 schoolgirls. Nigeria is Africa's most populous nation and leading oil producer and has sub-Saharan Africa's largest natural gas reserves. Security issues in the Niger Delta, political instability, corruption, and mismanagement hinder energy production. In 2014, Nigeria surpassed South Africa as the continent's largest economy, but an estimated 61 percent of Nigerians live on less than $1 a day. Nigeria suffered from the 2014 Ebola virus outbreak in West Africa.

Freedom Trend

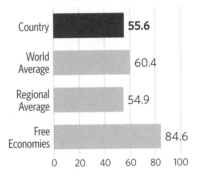

Country Comparisons

Country	55.6
World Average	60.4
Regional Average	54.9
Free Economies	84.6

Quick Facts

Population: 169.3 million
GDP (PPP): $479.3 billion
6.3% growth in 2013
5-year compound annual growth 7.0%
$2,831 per capita
Unemployment: 7.5%
Inflation (CPI): 8.5%
FDI Inflow: $5.6 billion
Public Debt: 19.4% of GDP

2013 data unless otherwise noted.
Data compiled as of September 2014.

How Do We Measure Economic Freedom?
See page 475 for an explanation of the methodology
or visit the *Index* Web site at *heritage.org/index.*

THE TEN ECONOMIC FREEDOMS

		Score		Rank	1-Year Change
RULE OF LAW	Property Rights	30.0		94th	0
	Freedom from Corruption	25.0		149th	+2.3

Moderately strengthened institutional capacity has checked some of the more blatant forms of corruption, but rent-seeking officials and politicians have found more subtle ways to defraud the Treasury with continued corrosive effects on politics and economic management. The public sector remains overstaffed, highly bureaucratic, and largely ineffective. One of the world's least efficient property registration systems weakens property rights.

		Score		Rank	1-Year Change
GOVERNMENT SIZE	Fiscal Freedom	85.2		47th	+0.2
	Government Spending	76.1		63rd	+1.6

The top individual income tax rate is 24 percent, and the top corporate tax rate is 30 percent. Other taxes include a value-added tax and a capital gains tax. Overall tax revenue accounts for 3 percent of domestic income. Government expenditures equal 28.2 percent of domestic output, and public debt is equivalent to 19 percent of gross domestic product.

		Score		Rank	1-Year Change
REGULATORY EFFICIENCY	Business Freedom	48.3		158th	+0.3
	Labor Freedom	77.7		31st	+11.3
	Monetary Freedom	70.4		146th	-2.7

Although the business environment has improved, regulatory procedures remain time-consuming and costly. The minimum capital requirement for starting a business has been eliminated, but completing licensing requirements still takes over 100 days. Much of the formal labor force is employed in the public or energy sectors. The state subsidizes and administers the prices of imported fuel and electricity.

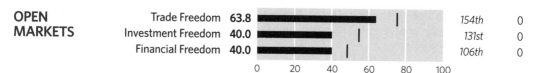

		Score		Rank	1-Year Change
OPEN MARKETS	Trade Freedom	63.8		154th	0
	Investment Freedom	40.0		131st	0
	Financial Freedom	40.0		106th	0

Nigeria's average tariff rate is 10.6 percent. Additional barriers restrict some agricultural imports, and imports may face customs delays. The legal and regulatory bureaucracies may be challenging for foreign investors. With 24 commercial banks, the financial sector continues to grow. The Nigerian Stock Exchange, with about 200 companies listed, has become a desirable financing option.

Long-Term Score Change (since 1995)

RULE OF LAW		GOVERNMENT SIZE		REGULATORY EFFICIENCY		OPEN MARKETS	
Property Rights	-20.0	Fiscal Freedom	+9.8	Business Freedom	-6.7	Trade Freedom	+18.8
Freedom from Corruption	-25.0	Government Spending	+76.1	Labor Freedom	+4.5	Investment Freedom	-10.0
				Monetary Freedom	+20.2	Financial Freedom	-10.0

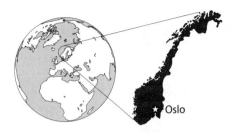

Oslo

NORWAY

Economic Freedom Score

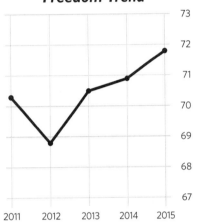

50

25   75

Least
free   0   100   Most
free

71.8

N orway's economic freedom score is 71.8, making its economy the 27th freest in the 2015 *Index*. Its score has increased by 0.9 point since last year, with solid improvements in six of the 10 economic freedoms, including labor freedom, monetary freedom, and the management of public spending, outweighing a decline in freedom from corruption. Norway is ranked 15th out of 43 countries in the Europe region, and its overall score is well above the world and regional averages.

Improvements in the regulatory environment and trade freedom have caused Norway's economic freedom score to expand by 1.1 points over the past five years. The only decline was in government spending as the government responded to low economic growth with additional spending.

Steady improvements in the 10 economic freedoms have underlined Norway's development of strong institutions. A small, open economy, Norway has low barriers to entry for foreign businesses and an investment regime that encourages international participation. The business environment is welcoming to new entrepreneurs, although the labor code remains rigid. High taxes and government spending are supplemented by the world's largest sovereign wealth fund. The property rights regime is the world's second best.

BACKGROUND: Norway has been a member of NATO since 1949. Voters have twice rejected membership in the European Union, but Norway is a party to a European Free Trade Association agreement. Prime Minister Erna Solberg of the Conservative Party was elected in September 2013 to lead a new center-right coalition minority government. Solberg's government has promised to lower taxes, decrease reliance on oil production, increase investment in infrastructure, and curtail immigration. Norway is one of the world's most prosperous countries. Fisheries, metal, and oil are the most important commodities. Norway saves a large portion of its petroleum-sector revenues, including dividends from the partially state-owned Statoil and taxes from oil and gas companies operating in Norway, in its Government Pension Fund–Global.

Freedom Trend

73

72

71

70

69

68

67

2011   2012   2013   2014   2015

Country Comparisons

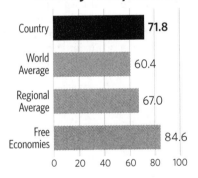

Country   71.8

World
Average   60.4

Regional
Average   67.0

Free
Economies   84.6

0   20   40   60   80   100

Quick Facts

Population: 5.1 million
GDP (PPP): $280.0 billion
0.8% growth in 2013
5-year compound annual growth 0.8%
$54,947 per capita
Unemployment: 3.5%
Inflation (CPI): 2.1%
FDI Inflow: $9.3 billion
Public Debt: 29.5% of GDP

2013 data unless otherwise noted.
Data compiled as of September 2014.

How Do We Measure Economic Freedom?
See page 475 for an explanation of the methodology
or visit the *Index* Web site at *heritage.org/index.*

THE TEN ECONOMIC FREEDOMS

		Score		Rank	1-Year Change

RULE OF LAW
Property Rights 90.0 — 3rd — 0
Freedom from Corruption 86.0 — 5th — −2.1

Norway is ranked 5th out of 177 countries in Transparency International's 2013 Corruption Perceptions Index. Well-established anti-corruption measures reinforce a cultural emphasis on government integrity. The judiciary is independent, and the court system operates fairly at the local and national levels. Private property rights are securely protected, and commercial contracts are reliably enforced.

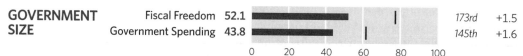

GOVERNMENT SIZE
Fiscal Freedom 52.1 — 173rd — +1.5
Government Spending 43.8 — 145th — +1.6

Norway's top individual income tax rate is 47.8 percent, and its top corporate tax rate is 27 percent. Other taxes include a value-added tax, a tax on net wealth, and environmental taxes. The overall tax burden equals 42.2 percent of the domestic economy. Public expenditures amount to 43.3 percent of domestic production, and public debt is equal to 30 percent of GDP.

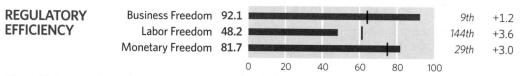

REGULATORY EFFICIENCY
Business Freedom 92.1 — 9th — +1.2
Labor Freedom 48.2 — 144th — +3.6
Monetary Freedom 81.7 — 29th — +3.0

The efficient and transparent business framework supports private-sector development. Incorporating a business costs about 1 percent of the level of average annual income and takes four procedures. The non-salary cost of employing a worker is high, but severance payments are not overly burdensome. Monetary stability has been well maintained, although the government subsidizes numerous renewable energy projects.

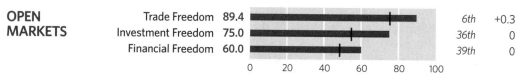

OPEN MARKETS
Trade Freedom 89.4 — 6th — +0.3
Investment Freedom 75.0 — 36th — 0
Financial Freedom 60.0 — 39th — 0

Norway has a 0.3 percent average tariff rate, but the agricultural sector is subsidized and protected from competition. There are few government barriers to international trade and investment, and foreign investors generally receive national treatment. The well-developed financial system provides a wide range of services. Banking remains generally well capitalized. The state retains ownership of the largest financial institutions.

Long-Term Score Change (since 1996)

RULE OF LAW		GOVERNMENT SIZE		REGULATORY EFFICIENCY		OPEN MARKETS	
Property Rights	0	Fiscal Freedom	−6.8	Business Freedom	+22.1	Trade Freedom	+20.4
Freedom from Corruption	−4.0	Government Spending	+34.9	Labor Freedom	−1.1	Investment Freedom	+5.0
				Monetary Freedom	0	Financial Freedom	+10.0

OMAN

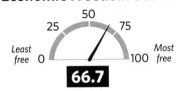

Economic Freedom Score

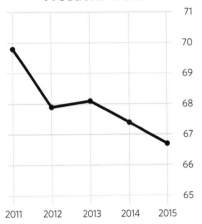

Least free 0

Most free 100

66.7

Oman's economic freedom score is 66.7, making its economy the 56th freest in the 2015 *Index*. Its score is 0.7 point lower than last year due to declines in the management of government spending, trade freedom, and freedom from corruption that outweigh improvements in four of the 10 economic freedoms, including property rights and monetary freedom. Oman is ranked 6th out of 15 countries in the Middle East/North Africa region, and its overall score is above the world and regional averages.

Oman's efforts to diversify beyond a declining oil and gas sector have been undermined by what seems to have become an aversion to economic freedom. Over the past five years, economic freedom in Oman has declined by 3.1 points. Double-digit declines in labor freedom and management of government spending have headlined reductions in half of the economic freedoms.

Serious reforms to improve the rule of law and market access for goods and capital are needed to return Oman to higher levels of economic freedom. The judiciary lacks independence and is subordinate to the sultan. Property rights differ for foreign and domestic property holders, as foreigners are not allowed to own land.

BACKGROUND: In early 2011, in response to turmoil throughout the region, Sultan Qabus bin Said changed cabinet ministers and promised political and economic reforms and more government jobs. A Consultative Council elected in October 2011 has been given expanded regulatory and legislative powers. Municipal councils were elected in December 2012 to advise the executive branch on local needs. Oman is a relatively small oil exporter. The government is trying to expand exports of liquefied natural gas, develop gas-based industries, and encourage foreign investment in petrochemicals, electric power, and telecommunications. It also stresses "Omanization" (replacing foreign workers with local staff to reduce chronically high unemployment). Oman joined the World Trade Organization in 2000 and signed a free trade agreement with the United States in 2006.

Freedom Trend

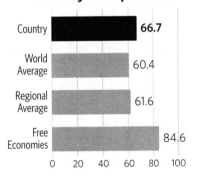

Country Comparisons

Country	66.7
World Average	60.4
Regional Average	61.6
Free Economies	84.6

Quick Facts

Population: 3.2 million
GDP (PPP): $95.0 billion
5.1% growth in 2013
5-year compound annual growth 4.7%
$29,813 per capita
Unemployment: 8.0%
Inflation (CPI): 1.3%
FDI Inflow: $1.6 billion
Public Debt: 7.0% of GDP

2013 data unless otherwise noted.
Data compiled as of September 2014.

How Do We Measure Economic Freedom?
See page 475 for an explanation of the methodology
or visit the *Index* Web site at *heritage.org/index.*

THE TEN ECONOMIC FREEDOMS

		Score		Rank	1-Year Change
RULE OF LAW	Property Rights	55.0		50th	+5.0
	Freedom from Corruption	47.0		61st	-1.2

A crackdown on corruption that began in 2012 has led to prosecutions of company executives and government officials. In May 2014, a former commerce minister was sentenced to three years in prison for corruption and fined $2 million. The judiciary is not independent and remains subordinate to the sultan and the Ministry of Justice. Property rights are well protected.

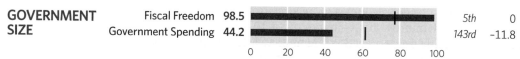

		Score		Rank	1-Year Change
GOVERNMENT SIZE	Fiscal Freedom	98.5		5th	0
	Government Spending	44.2		143rd	-11.8

Oman has no individual income tax. The corporate tax rate is 12 percent, but income from petroleum sales is subject to a 55 percent rate. There is no value-added tax or consumption tax. Formal tax revenue equals 2.5 percent of domestic income. Public spending is equal to 43.1 percent of domestic production, and government debt equals 7 percent of GDP.

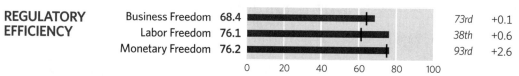

		Score		Rank	1-Year Change
REGULATORY EFFICIENCY	Business Freedom	68.4		73rd	+0.1
	Labor Freedom	76.1		38th	+0.6
	Monetary Freedom	76.2		93rd	+2.6

Starting a business takes an average of five procedures and one week, but licensing requirements remain burdensome. The labor laws enforce the "Omanization" policy requiring firms to meet quotas for hiring native Omani workers. The state influences prices through an extensive subsidy system, which grew by 8 percent in 2013, driven mainly by subsidies for petroleum products and electricity.

		Score		Rank	1-Year Change
OPEN MARKETS	Trade Freedom	76.8		89th	-1.9
	Investment Freedom	65.0		68th	0
	Financial Freedom	60.0		39th	0

Oman's average tariff rate is 4.1 percent. "Morally objectionable" imports may be restricted. Foreign investors may not buy land. The state dominates a significant portion of the banking sector. Most credit is offered at market rates, but subsidized loans are used to promote investment. The capital market is not fully developed, but the stock exchange is open to foreign investors.

Long-Term Score Change (since 1995)

RULE OF LAW		GOVERNMENT SIZE		REGULATORY EFFICIENCY		OPEN MARKETS	
Property Rights	-15.0	Fiscal Freedom	+23.5	Business Freedom	-16.6	Trade Freedom	+3.8
Freedom from Corruption	-23.0	Government Spending	-8.5	Labor Freedom	+2.3	Investment Freedom	+15.0
				Monetary Freedom	-9.5	Financial Freedom	-10.0

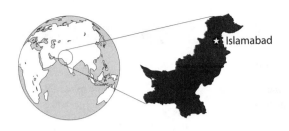

★ Islamabad

PAKISTAN

Economic Freedom Score

25   50   75

Least free 0 .... 100 Most free

55.6

Pakistan's economic freedom score is 55.6, making its economy the 121st freest in the 2015 *Index*. Its score has increased by 0.4 point since last year, reflecting improvements in investment freedom and freedom from corruption that are largely counterbalanced by deteriorations in labor freedom and business freedom. Pakistan is ranked 25th out of 42 countries in the Asia–Pacific region, and its overall score is below the world and regional averages.

Pakistan's economic freedom has advanced modestly in recent years. Since 2011, economic freedom in Pakistan has increased by 0.5 point, led by advances in investment freedom, monetary freedom, and freedom from corruption. However, gains have been outnumbered by losses among the 10 economic freedoms.

Large sections of the population live in poverty and survive through subsistence agriculture. Inefficient regulatory agencies inhibit business formation. Access to bank credit also undermines entrepreneurship, and the financial sector's seclusion from the outside world has slowed innovation and growth.

BACKGROUND: Prime Minister Nawaz Sharif took office in June 2013 and has had to contend with terrorism, sectarian violence, and a well-organized insurgency along the border with Afghanistan. The army stepped up its military operations in North Waziristan in June 2014 following a major attack on the Karachi airport that killed nearly 36 people. Sustained street demonstrations in August and September 2014 led by Tehreek-e-Insaf party chief Imran Khan and religious leader Tahir ul-Qadri have weakened Sharif and increased civil–military tensions. Pakistan has privatized some state-run industries, but the economy is still heavily regulated, and poor security discourages foreign investment.

Freedom Trend

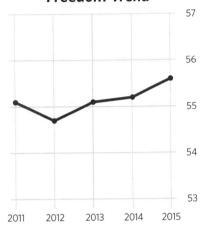

57

56

55

54

53

2011   2012   2013   2014   2015

Country Comparisons

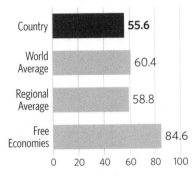

Country	55.6
World Average	60.4
Regional Average	58.8
Free Economies	84.6

0   20   40   60   80   100

Quick Facts

Population: 182.6 million
GDP (PPP): $575.0 billion
3.6% growth in 2013
5-year compound annual growth 2.9%
$3,149 per capita
Unemployment: 5.2%
Inflation (CPI): 7.4%
FDI Inflow: $1.3 billion
Public Debt: 63.1% of GDP

How Do We Measure Economic Freedom?
See page 475 for an explanation of the methodology
or visit the *Index* Web site at *heritage.org/index*.

2013 data unless otherwise noted.
Data compiled as of September 2014.

THE TEN ECONOMIC FREEDOMS

		Score			Rank	1-Year Change
RULE OF LAW	Property Rights	30.0			94th	0
	Freedom from Corruption	28.0			132nd	+5.3

Corruption, lack of accountability, and lack of transparency continue to pervade all levels of government, politics, and the military despite some improvements in democratic processes. Oversight mechanisms remain weak. Property rights are not protected effectively. The functioning of the higher judiciary has improved, but delays, corruption, intimidation, and political interference are endemic in the broader justice system.

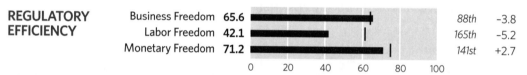

GOVERNMENT SIZE	Fiscal Freedom	77.7			106th	-2.9
	Government Spending	86.1			29th	-2.2

Pakistan's top individual income tax rate is 35 percent. The rate for salaried employment is lower. The top corporate tax rate is 35 percent. Other taxes include a value-added tax and a tax on interest. Overall tax revenue equals 10.4 percent of domestic income. Public expenditures amount to 21.5 percent of domestic output, and public debt equals 63 percent of GDP.

REGULATORY EFFICIENCY	Business Freedom	65.6			88th	-3.8
	Labor Freedom	42.1			165th	-5.2
	Monetary Freedom	71.2			141st	+2.7

Starting a business takes an average of 19 days and 10 procedures. Completing licensing requirements still takes about 250 days. The rigid labor market keeps a large portion of the workforce in the informal sector. The government controls fuel prices but in 2014 reduced electric power subsidies to narrow the budget deficit and meet the terms of IMF conditionality.

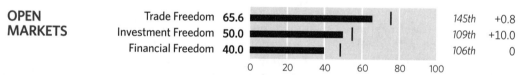

OPEN MARKETS	Trade Freedom	65.6			145th	+0.8
	Investment Freedom	50.0			109th	+10.0
	Financial Freedom	40.0			106th	0

Pakistan's average tariff rate is 9.5 percent. Imports may face additional bureaucratic barriers. Pakistan's "Investment Policy 2013" was designed to facilitate foreign direct investment, but the security environment is a deterrent. The financial system remains subject to government interference, and the state retains considerable ownership in the banking sector. The government often directs banks' lending to priority sectors.

Long-Term Score Change (since 1995)

RULE OF LAW		GOVERNMENT SIZE		REGULATORY EFFICIENCY		OPEN MARKETS	
Property Rights	-40.0	Fiscal Freedom	+18.6	Business Freedom	+10.6	Trade Freedom	+33.2
Freedom from Corruption	+18.0	Government Spending	+4.0	Labor Freedom	-17.5	Investment Freedom	-20.0
				Monetary Freedom	+1.3	Financial Freedom	-30.0

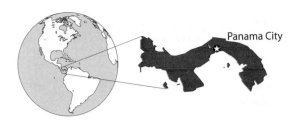
Panama City

PANAMA

Economic Freedom Score

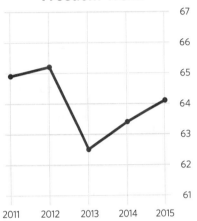

25 — 50 — 75

Least free 0 — 100 Most free

64.1

| World Rank: **68** | Regional Rank: **14** |

Panama's economic freedom score is 64.1, making its economy the 68th freest in the 2015 *Index*. Its score has increased by 0.7 point since last year, with improvements in six of the 10 economic freedoms, led by trade freedom and labor freedom, outweighing a decline in business freedom. Panama is ranked 14th out of 29 countries in the South and Central America/Caribbean region, and its overall score is above the world average.

Panama's economic freedom has stagnated over the past five years. Large declines in property rights and the management of government spending have undercut a substantial increase in investment freedom, and Panama has dropped from 59th to 68th place in the rankings.

Development of a vibrant logistics, financial, and international business sector has been facilitated by openness to international trade and investment. The financial sector remains open to investment and has been shielded from the global financial crisis by prudent regulations. However, a rigid labor market and corruption undermine the entrepreneurial environment. Business regulations and the rule of law need to be improved to enable the non-urban population to escape from poverty.

BACKGROUND: Panama's incumbent Vice President Juan Carlos Varela won the May 2014 presidential election and took office in July. Varela's win was unexpected, and the ruling Panameñista Party has only 11 of the 71 seats in Congress. A week after inauguration, the center-right Varela announced price controls on 22 items in the basic food basket, generating concerns about his economic policy plans. Since the opening of the Panama Canal in 1914, Panama has been a strategic hub for commerce and security in the Americas, with transportation, services, and banking serving as the main engines of economic growth. Following a series of setbacks, the Panama Canal Authority hopes to complete its expansion by late 2015. A third set of locks will enable the canal to handle post-Panamax ships, essentially doubling its capacity.

Freedom Trend

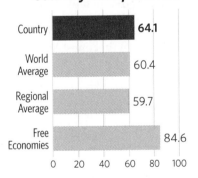

2011	
2012	
2013	
2014	
2015	

(67, 66, 65, 64, 63, 62, 61)

Country Comparisons

Country	64.1
World Average	60.4
Regional Average	59.7
Free Economies	84.6

0 20 40 60 80 100

Quick Facts

Population: 3.7 million
GDP (PPP): $62.0 billion
8.0% growth in 2013
5-year compound annual growth 8.2%
$16,658 per capita
Unemployment: 4.0%
Inflation (CPI): 4.0%
FDI Inflow: $4.7 billion
Public Debt: 41.3% of GDP

2013 data unless otherwise noted.
Data compiled as of September 2014.

How Do We Measure Economic Freedom?
See page 475 for an explanation of the methodology or visit the *Index* Web site at *heritage.org/index*.

THE TEN ECONOMIC FREEDOMS

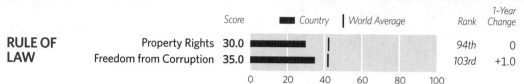

		Score	■ Country	| World Average	Rank	1-Year Change
RULE OF LAW	Property Rights	30.0			94th	0
	Freedom from Corruption	35.0			103rd	+1.0

President Juan Carlos Varela took office in July 2014, promising to fight corruption and return strength and credibility to Panama's democracy and institutions. The judicial system remains overburdened, inefficient, politicized, and prone to corruption. Its capacity to resolve contractual and property disputes is weak. Most land in Panama (and almost all land outside of Panama City) is not titled.

		Score			Rank	1-Year Change
GOVERNMENT SIZE	Fiscal Freedom	84.5			53rd	+0.2
	Government Spending	78.8			52nd	+0.1

Panama's top individual and corporate income tax rates are 25 percent. Other taxes include a value-added tax and a capital gains tax. Overall tax revenue equals 17.4 percent of domestic income. Public expenditures are equivalent to 26.6 percent of domestic production, and public debt equals 41 percent of gross domestic product. A canal-funded sovereign wealth fund helps to support public spending.

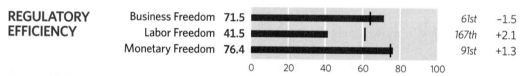

		Score			Rank	1-Year Change
REGULATORY EFFICIENCY	Business Freedom	71.5			61st	-1.5
	Labor Freedom	41.5			167th	+2.1
	Monetary Freedom	76.4			91st	+1.3

The overall regulatory environment is efficient, but the pace of reform has slowed in recent years. With no minimum capital requirements, starting a business takes six days and five procedures. Despite some improvement, the labor market lacks flexibility. The new president announced that one of his first orders would be to regulate prices for staple food products.

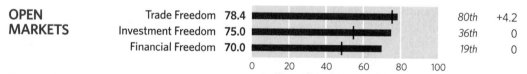

		Score			Rank	1-Year Change
OPEN MARKETS	Trade Freedom	78.4			80th	+4.2
	Investment Freedom	75.0			36th	0
	Financial Freedom	70.0			19th	0

Panama's average tariff rate is 7.6 percent, and the country is relatively open to international trade. The government generally welcomes foreign investment, but investment levels in several sectors are capped. The financial sector, vibrant and generally well-regulated as a regional financial hub, provides a wide range of financing options. Capital markets are relatively sophisticated and continue to expand.

Long-Term Score Change (since 1995)

RULE OF LAW		GOVERNMENT SIZE		REGULATORY EFFICIENCY		OPEN MARKETS	
Property Rights	-20.0	Fiscal Freedom	+7.0	Business Freedom	+1.5	Trade Freedom	+14.0
Freedom from Corruption	-15.0	Government Spending	-5.2	Labor Freedom	-3.7	Investment Freedom	+5.0
				Monetary Freedom	-12.3	Financial Freedom	-20.0

PAPUA NEW GUINEA

Port Moresby

World Rank: 137　　　**Regional Rank: 29**

Economic Freedom Score

25　50　75

Least free 0　　　100　Most free

53.1

Papua New Guinea's economic freedom score is 53.1, making its economy the 137th freest in the 2015 *Index*. Its score is 0.8 point lower than last year, with declines in the management of government spending, business freedom, and monetary freedom outweighing improvements in freedom from corruption and labor freedom. Papua New Guinea is ranked 29th out of 42 countries in the Asia–Pacific region, and its overall score is lower than the world and regional averages.

Papua New Guinea's commodity-based economy has recorded only modest improvements in economic freedom over the past five years. Failure to pursue a more vigorous reform agenda has contributed to the persistence of poverty, subsistence economic activity, and a large informal sector. Rapid expansion of the mining and petroleum sector has increased the risk of rent-seeking and cronyism among the elite and politically connected.

The judiciary lacks independence and a well-defined institutional framework. Corruption is prevalent, and nepotism undermines effective governance. An externally oriented commodity sector has taken advantage of low tariffs and the lack of non-tariff barriers. However, new investments require government approval, and an underdeveloped financial sector limits domestically funded capital formation.

BACKGROUND: Papua New Guinea is a parliamentary democracy with nearly 7 million people and over 840 different languages. A year-long constitutional crisis subsided in August 2012 with the re-election of Prime Minister Peter O'Neill, whose People's National Congress Party won the most seats in parliament. Sir Michael Somare, O'Neill's chief rival, announced that they would form a joint government. O'Neill is currently embroiled in a legal battle over alleged misuse of government funds. Gold and copper mining, oil, and natural gas dominate the formal economy, but the vast majority of Papua New Guineans depend on subsistence hunting or agriculture and the informal economy. Australia provides around US$480 million a year in assistance. Corruption, weak governance, crime, and poverty are endemic.

Freedom Trend

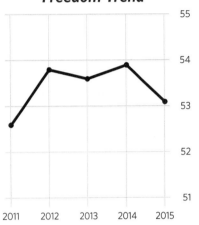

Country Comparisons

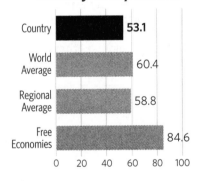

Country	**53.1**
World Average	60.4
Regional Average	58.8
Free Economies	84.6

Quick Facts

Population: 7.0 million
GDP (PPP): $19.8 billion
4.6% growth in 2013
5-year compound annual growth 7.4%
$2,834 per capita
Unemployment: 2.4%
Inflation (CPI): 3.8%
FDI Inflow: $18.2 million
Public Debt: 32.6% of GDP

2013 data unless otherwise noted.
Data compiled as of September 2014.

How Do We Measure Economic Freedom?
See page 475 for an explanation of the methodology or visit the *Index* Web site at *heritage.org/index*.

THE TEN ECONOMIC FREEDOMS

		Score		Rank	1-Year Change
RULE OF LAW	Property Rights	20.0		138th	0
	Freedom from Corruption	25.0		149th	+4.8

Prime Minister O'Neill pledged to fight widespread official abuse and corruption fueled by large foreign investment windfalls in mining and petroleum, but the government's "Taskforce Sweep" anti-corruption unit alleged in 2014 that O'Neill himself authorized $30 million in illegal payments to a law firm. A modern, well-functioning judicial framework is not firmly in place. Land is often held communally.

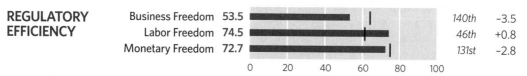

GOVERNMENT SIZE	Fiscal Freedom	66.9		150th	+0.2
	Government Spending	68.7		88th	-6.7

The top individual income tax rate is 42 percent, and the top corporate tax rate is 30 percent. Other taxes include a value-added tax and an excise tax. The overall tax burden amounts to 25.4 percent of domestic income. Public expenditures equal 32.3 percent of domestic production, and public debt equals 33 percent of gross domestic product.

REGULATORY EFFICIENCY	Business Freedom	53.5		140th	-3.5
	Labor Freedom	74.5		46th	+0.8
	Monetary Freedom	72.7		131st	-2.8

Incorporating a business and completing licensing requirements continue to be onerous and time-consuming. A small share of the labor force participates in the formal economy, and the public sector is the major source of employment. The government heavily subsidizes state-owned enterprises that provide substandard service in such areas as power, water, banking, telecommunications, air travel, and seaports.

OPEN MARKETS	Trade Freedom	85.0		51st	-0.1
	Investment Freedom	35.0		144th	0
	Financial Freedom	30.0		131st	0

Papua New Guinea's average tariff rate is 2.5 percent. Government procurement policies can favor domestic firms. The government screens new foreign investment. The financial sector remains underdeveloped, leaving much of the population without formal access to banking services. Constrained access to financing severely impedes entrepreneurial activity and the sustained development of a vibrant private sector.

Long-Term Score Change (since 1996)

RULE OF LAW		GOVERNMENT SIZE		REGULATORY EFFICIENCY		OPEN MARKETS	
Property Rights	-30.0	Fiscal Freedom	-14.6	Business Freedom	-16.5	Trade Freedom	+39.2
Freedom from Corruption	-25.0	Government Spending	-0.6	Labor Freedom	-6.6	Investment Freedom	-15.0
				Monetary Freedom	-8.5	Financial Freedom	0

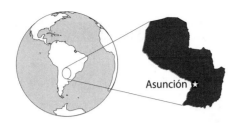

PARAGUAY

Economic Freedom Score

Least free 0   100 Most free

61.1

Paraguay's economic freedom score is 61.1, making its economy the 83rd freest in the 2015 *Index*. Its score has decreased by 0.9 point since last year, with improvements in freedom from corruption, business freedom, and trade freedom counterbalanced by declines in the management of government spending, monetary freedom, and labor freedom. Paraguay is ranked 15th out of 29 countries in the South and Central America/Caribbean region. As a "moderately free" economy, its overall score is above the world average.

Over the past five years, Paraguay's economic freedom has fallen by 1.2 points with declines in five of the 10 economic freedoms, including the control of public finance and business freedom. The government has pursued a series of structural reforms to enhance the entrepreneurial environment, but inefficient business and labor regulations force much of the population into the informal sector.

Economic freedom in Paraguay remains particularly challenged by the weak rule of law. Political instability has undermined efforts to combat corruption and improve governance. The previous president's promises to address corruption have been undermined by his constitutional removal from power. Soya remains a vital export, facilitated by a commitment to open trade and investment policies.

BACKGROUND: President Horacio Cartes of the traditionally dominant Colorado Party was elected in 2013, succeeding Federico Franco, who served temporarily following the impeachment of left-leaning Fernando Lugo in 2012. Paraguay was suspended from the MERCOSUR regional trade bloc after Lugo's impeachment. In 2013, Cartes made a deal in which Paraguay voted to approve Venezuela as a new member in exchange for readmission. Paraguay had also been suspended from summits of the South American Union but was welcomed back that same year. After a recession in 2012, the economy rebounded strongly in 2013. Corruption is pervasive, and government attempts to reduce smuggling and scrutinize suspected terrorist groups in the tri-border area with Brazil and Argentina have met with little success.

Freedom Trend

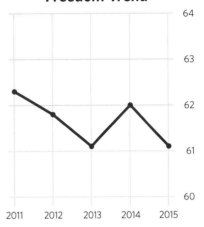

Country Comparisons

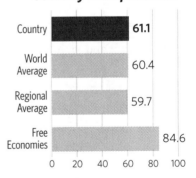

Quick Facts

Population: 6.8 million
GDP (PPP): $46.4 billion
13.0% growth in 2013
5-year compound annual growth 4.8%
$6,823 per capita
Unemployment: 5.2%
Inflation (CPI): 2.7%
FDI Inflow: $382.4 million
Public Debt: 15.2% of GDP

*2013 data unless otherwise noted.
Data compiled as of September 2014.*

How Do We Measure Economic Freedom?
See page 475 for an explanation of the methodology or visit the *Index* Web site at *heritage.org/index.*

THE TEN ECONOMIC FREEDOMS

		Score		Rank	1-Year Change
RULE OF LAW	Property Rights	30.0		94th	0
	Freedom from Corruption	24.0		156th	+3.5

President Cartes took office in August 2013 pledging to end the corruption and cronyism that pervades the government, the judiciary, and the police. Yet the president himself is suspected of money laundering and involvement in Paraguay's growing drug trafficking network. A lack of consistent property surveys and registries often makes it difficult to acquire title documents for land.

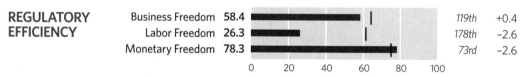

		Score		Rank	1-Year Change
GOVERNMENT SIZE	Fiscal Freedom	96.0		9th	−0.2
	Government Spending	81.9		42nd	−7.1

Paraguay's top individual and corporate income tax rates are 10 percent. Other taxes include a value-added tax and a property tax. Overall tax revenues are equal to 14.3 percent of domestic income. Public spending equals 24.6 percent of domestic production, and public debt is equivalent to 15 percent of gross domestic product.

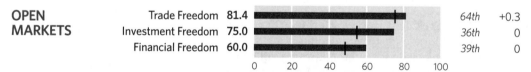

		Score		Rank	1-Year Change
REGULATORY EFFICIENCY	Business Freedom	58.4		119th	+0.4
	Labor Freedom	26.3		178th	−2.6
	Monetary Freedom	78.3		73rd	−2.6

There is no minimum capital requirement, but starting a business takes over a month, and obtaining necessary permits takes more than 130 days on average. The labor market lacks flexibility, hurting job growth. In 2014, labor unions blocked partial privatization and renovation of the airport and water treatment plants and construction of badly needed toll roads to neighboring countries.

		Score		Rank	1-Year Change
OPEN MARKETS	Trade Freedom	81.4		64th	+0.3
	Investment Freedom	75.0		36th	0
	Financial Freedom	60.0		39th	0

The average tariff rate is 4.3 percent. Domestic companies are favored in government procurement bids. Foreign and domestic investors are generally treated equally under the law, and investors may repatriate profits. Banking remains relatively sound and dominates the financial system. Financial intermediation continues to be low, and most lending is short-term. The capital market is not fully developed.

Long-Term Score Change (since 1995)

RULE OF LAW		GOVERNMENT SIZE		REGULATORY EFFICIENCY		OPEN MARKETS	
Property Rights	−20.0	Fiscal Freedom	+5.9	Business Freedom	−11.6	Trade Freedom	+23.0
Freedom from Corruption	+14.0	Government Spending	−9.6	Labor Freedom	−1.8	Investment Freedom	−15.0
				Monetary Freedom	+15.2	Financial Freedom	−10.0

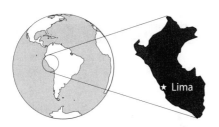

PERU

Economic Freedom Score

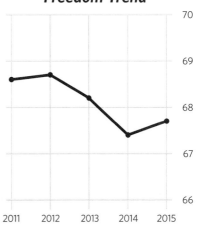

50

25   75

Least
free   0   100   Most
free

67.7

World Rank: 47   **Regional Rank: 8**

Peru's economic freedom score is 67.7, making its economy the 47th freest in the 2015 *Index*. Its score is 0.3 point better than last year, with improvements in freedom from corruption, labor freedom, and monetary freedom outweighing declines in business freedom, the management of government spending, and fiscal freedom. Peru is ranked 8th out of 29 countries in the South and Central America/Caribbean region, and its overall score is above the world average.

Despite rapid growth and a more business-friendly government, economic freedom in Peru has declined by 0.9 point since 2011. Scores have fallen in four of the 10 factors, including fiscal freedom, the management of government spending, business freedom, and labor freedom.

Reforms, openness to international trade, and burgeoning tourism and mining industries have facilitated rapid growth in the past. Numerous free trade agreements have helped provide a catalyst for domestic reforms and to build institutions, but underlying structures remain weak. The judiciary is vulnerable to political interference, and corruption remains pervasive.

BACKGROUND: Economic liberalization begun under former President Alberto Fujimori in the 1990s and continued by successive administrations, including that of current President Ollanta Humala of the leftist Peruvian Nationalist Party, has attracted significant foreign investment and lifted millions out of poverty. Humala, who once led a failed military coup against Fujimori, ran for office on a platform of more state intervention in the economy but has governed moderately and has respected the rule of law. Significant natural resources include gold, copper, and silver. Whether the economy can withstand a commodity-price downturn remains a source of concern. Less than 30 percent of Peruvians now live below the poverty line, and economic growth has been well above the Latin American average. The U.S.–Peru Free Trade Agreement has expanded trade and employment. Peru has entered into numerous other free trade agreements and is a founding member of the Pacific Alliance.

Freedom Trend

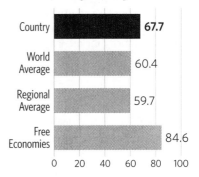

70

69

68

67

66

2011   2012   2013   2014   2015

Country Comparisons

Country — 67.7
World Average — 60.4
Regional Average — 59.7
Free Economies — 84.6

0   20   40   60   80   100

Quick Facts

Population: 30.9 million
GDP (PPP): $344.2 billion
5.0% growth in 2013
5-year compound annual growth 5.5%
$11,124 per capita
Unemployment: 3.8%
Inflation (CPI): 2.8%
FDI Inflow: $10.2 billion
Public Debt: 19.6% of GDP

2013 data unless otherwise noted.
Data compiled as of September 2014.

How Do We Measure Economic Freedom?
See page 475 for an explanation of the methodology
or visit the *Index* Web site at *heritage.org/index.*

THE TEN ECONOMIC FREEDOMS

		Score	■ Country	| World Average	Rank	1-Year Change
RULE OF LAW	Property Rights	40.0			70th	0
	Freedom from Corruption	38.0			83rd	+4.0

Very poor institutions open the door to illegal activities, especially in rural areas. Corruption in the security forces, the judiciary, customs agencies, and ports facilitates shipments of cocaine and other contraband. Abuses of intellectual property rights remain commonplace, enforcement is patchy and slow, and punishments are often disproportionately lax. The dysfunctional judiciary is widely distrusted and prone to corruption scandals.

		Score		Rank	1-Year Change
GOVERNMENT SIZE	Fiscal Freedom	78.6		99th	–0.5
	Government Spending	88.5		17th	–0.6

Peru's top individual and corporate income tax rates are 30 percent. Other taxes include a value-added tax and a financial transactions tax. Total tax revenue amounts to 18.5 percent of the domestic economy, and government spending is equivalent to 19.6 percent of domestic production. Public debt is equal to 20 percent of gross domestic product.

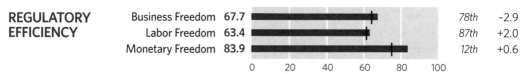

		Score		Rank	1-Year Change
REGULATORY EFFICIENCY	Business Freedom	67.7		78th	–2.9
	Labor Freedom	63.4		87th	+2.0
	Monetary Freedom	83.9		12th	+0.6

With no minimum capital required, it now takes six procedures to start a business, but completing licensing requirements remains burdensome, still taking over five months on average. Employment regulations continue to evolve, with more flexibility gradually being introduced into the labor market. The government subsidizes electricity and automotive and cooking fuels.

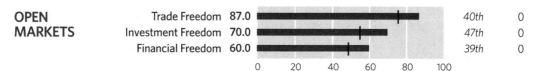

		Score		Rank	1-Year Change
OPEN MARKETS	Trade Freedom	87.0		40th	0
	Investment Freedom	70.0		47th	0
	Financial Freedom	60.0		39th	0

Peru's average tariff rate is 1.5 percent. Trade barriers have been reduced through the Pacific Alliance, but imports of used clothing and cars are restricted. Foreign investors generally receive national treatment, but there are sectoral limits. The financial sector has undergone gradual modernization. Credit to the private sector has increased steadily, and foreign ownership in the financial sector is growing.

Long-Term Score Change (since 1995)

RULE OF LAW		GOVERNMENT SIZE		REGULATORY EFFICIENCY		OPEN MARKETS	
Property Rights	–10.0	Fiscal Freedom	–2.5	Business Freedom	+12.7	Trade Freedom	+36.0
Freedom from Corruption	+28.0	Government Spending	–1.0	Labor Freedom	+17.5	Investment Freedom	0
				Monetary Freedom	+48.0	Financial Freedom	–10.0

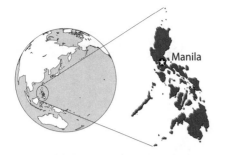

PHILIPPINES

Economic Freedom Score

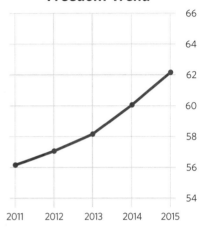

62.2

Least free 0 — 25 — 50 — 75 — 100 Most free

World Rank: 76   **Regional Rank: 13**

The Philippines' economic freedom score is 62.2, making its economy the 76th freest in the 2015 *Index*. Its score has increased by 2.1 points since last year, with notable improvements in financial freedom, freedom from corruption, and labor freedom outweighing declines in business freedom and the management of public spending. The Philippines ranks 13th out of 42 countries in the Asia–Pacific region, and its overall score is above the world and regional averages.

Registering one of the 10 best score improvements in the 2015 *Index*, the Philippines has charted an upward trajectory of economic freedom for the past five years, further advancing into the "moderately free" category. Wide-ranging reforms to address structural weaknesses and improve overall economic competitiveness have put greater emphasis on improving regulatory efficiency, enhancing regional competitiveness, and liberalizing the banking sector. Demonstrating a high level of resilience and overcoming the devastating impact of the massive typhoon that ripped through the central part of the country, the Philippine economy has recorded an average growth rate exceeding 5 percent over the past half-decade.

Despite notable progress since 2011, however, lingering institutional challenges will require a deeper commitment to reform. Corruption continues to be a serious cause for concern, jeopardizing prospects for long-term economic development. The inefficient judiciary, which remains susceptible to political interference, does not provide effective protection for property rights or strong and transparent enforcement of the law.

BACKGROUND: The Philippines' diverse population, speaking more than 80 languages and dialects, is spread over 7,000 islands in the Western Pacific. Democracy was restored in 1986 after two decades of autocratic rule. President Benigno Aquino III took office in 2010 with a mandate to root out corruption. While agriculture is still a significant part of the economy, industrial production in areas like electronics, apparel, and shipbuilding has been growing rapidly. Remittances from overseas workers are equivalent to more than 10 percent of GDP.

Freedom Trend

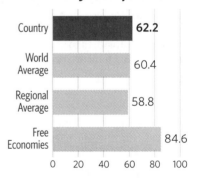

Country Comparisons

Country	62.2
World Average	60.4
Regional Average	58.8
Free Economies	84.6

0 20 40 60 80 100

Quick Facts

Population: 97.5 million
GDP (PPP): $456.4 billion
7.2% growth in 2013
5-year compound annual growth 5.2%
$4,682 per capita
Unemployment: 7.3%
Inflation (CPI): 2.9%
FDI Inflow: $3.9 billion
Public Debt: 38.3% of GDP

2013 data unless otherwise noted.
Data compiled as of September 2014.

How Do We Measure Economic Freedom?
See page 475 for an explanation of the methodology or visit the *Index* Web site at *heritage.org/index.*

THE TEN ECONOMIC FREEDOMS

		Score	■ Country	| World Average	Rank	1-Year Change
RULE OF LAW	Property Rights	30.0			94th	0
	Freedom from Corruption	36.0			95th	+9.9

Corruption, state plunder, cronyism, and a culture of impunity remained in the spotlight in 2014 as numerous instances of malfeasance were exposed. Several senators, for example, were arrested on charges of embezzlement of billions of pesos from the Priority Development Assistance Fund. Judicial independence has traditionally been strong, but the rule of law is generally weak.

		Score			Rank	1-Year Change
GOVERNMENT SIZE	Fiscal Freedom	79.1			94th	−0.1
	Government Spending	89.3			13th	−3.0

The top individual income tax rate is 32 percent, and the top corporate tax rate is 30 percent. Other taxes include a value-added tax and environmental taxes. The overall tax burden equals 12.9 percent of domestic income. Public expenditures are equivalent to 18.9 percent of the domestic economy, and public debt equals 38 percent of gross domestic product.

		Score			Rank	1-Year Change
REGULATORY EFFICIENCY	Business Freedom	55.3			131st	−4.6
	Labor Freedom	58.2			107th	+8.5
	Monetary Freedom	78.8			66th	+0.8

Incorporating a business takes 16 procedures and 34 days. Completing licensing requirements remains time-consuming, taking about three months on average. The labor market remains structurally rigid, with varying degrees of flexibility across economic sectors and regions of the country. Subsidies to state-owned and state-controlled corporations in the power, food, health care, and agriculture sectors were reduced in 2014.

		Score			Rank	1-Year Change
OPEN MARKETS	Trade Freedom	75.4			99th	−0.1
	Investment Freedom	60.0			81st	0
	Financial Freedom	60.0			39th	+10.0

The average tariff rate is 4.8 percent. Domestic companies are favored in government procurement bids. Rice producers are subsidized and protected from competition. Foreign investment in several sectors is restricted. The financial system continues to undergo modernization and liberalization. A new law removing all limits on foreign participation in the banking sector was implemented in 2014.

Long-Term Score Change (since 1995)

RULE OF LAW		GOVERNMENT SIZE		REGULATORY EFFICIENCY		OPEN MARKETS	
Property Rights	−20.0	Fiscal Freedom	+5.9	Business Freedom	+0.3	Trade Freedom	+33.4
Freedom from Corruption	+26.0	Government Spending	+0.9	Labor Freedom	+4.8	Investment Freedom	+10.0
				Monetary Freedom	+2.1	Financial Freedom	+10.0

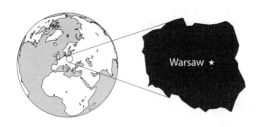

POLAND

Economic Freedom Score

Least free 0   Most free 100

68.6

Poland's economic freedom score is 68.6, making its economy the 42nd freest in the 2015 *Index*. Its score is 1.6 points better than last year, driven by improvements in half of the 10 economic freedoms, especially freedom from corruption, fiscal freedom, the management of government spending, and monetary freedom. Poland is ranked 19th out of 43 countries in the Europe region, and its overall score is above the world average.

Over the past five years, Poland's economic freedom score has advanced by 4.5 points, the largest improvement in the region. Gains in eight of the 10 economic freedoms include double-digit strides in financial freedom and freedom from corruption. In the 2015 *Index*, Poland has recorded its highest economic freedom score ever.

While Poland's transition to a market-based economy has accelerated, some structural foundations still need reinforcement. The labor market remains rigid, and business regulations still lag behind standards in some Western and Northern European countries. Enforcement of the rule of law is hindered by delays in the court system. Membership in the European Union helps to ease trade restrictions and attract investment, and openness to capital contributes to a budding financial sector.

BACKGROUND: Poland joined NATO in 1999 and the European Union in 2004. Prime Minister Donald Tusk of the center-right Civic Platform party was re-elected in October 2011. In 2014, his government survived a vote of no confidence after secret audio tapings of Foreign Minister Radek Sikorski sparked a political scandal. With a flexible exchange rate, an IMF credit line, access to international markets, and healthy economic policies, Poland was the only country in Europe to experience economic growth during the 2009 credit crisis. Low investment rates in agriculture have made Poland uncompetitive in food production, but the automotive, pharmaceutical, aviation, steel, and machinery sectors have made it one of the EU's strongest economic performers. The private sector now accounts for two-thirds of GDP.

Freedom Trend

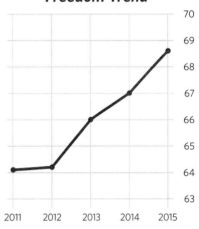

Country Comparisons

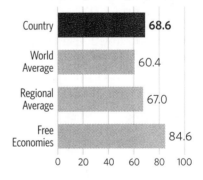

Country	68.6
World Average	60.4
Regional Average	67.0
Free Economies	84.6

Quick Facts

Population: 38.5 million
GDP (PPP): $817.5 billion
1.6% growth in 2013
5-year compound annual growth 2.7%
$21,214 per capita
Unemployment: 10.4%
Inflation (CPI): 0.9%
FDI Inflow: –$6.0 billion
Public Debt: 57.5% of GDP

2013 data unless otherwise noted.
Data compiled as of September 2014.

How Do We Measure Economic Freedom?
See page 475 for an explanation of the methodology
or visit the *Index* Web site at *heritage.org/index*.

THE TEN ECONOMIC FREEDOMS

	Score	Country | World Average	Rank	1-Year Change
RULE OF LAW				
Property Rights	60.0		41st	0
Freedom from Corruption	60.0		37th	+5.2

Slow progress in improving the transparency and accountability of public administration continues to hamper efforts to combat corruption. The legal system protects rights to acquire and dispose of property, and the judiciary is independent, but the courts are notorious for delays in adjudicating cases. Slow action on corruption investigations has prompted concerns that prosecutors are subject to political pressure.

GOVERNMENT SIZE				
Fiscal Freedom	82.1		66th	+6.0
Government Spending	47.1		137th	+3.9

Poland's top individual income tax rate is 32 percent, and its top corporate tax rate is 19 percent. Other taxes include a value-added tax and a property tax. Overall tax revenue amounts to 20.1 percent of domestic income. Public expenditures equal 42 percent of domestic production, and public debt is equivalent to 57 percent of gross domestic product.

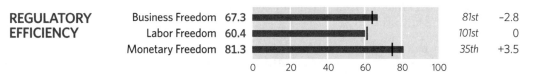

REGULATORY EFFICIENCY				
Business Freedom	67.3		81st	−2.8
Labor Freedom	60.4		101st	0
Monetary Freedom	81.3		35th	+3.5

Despite measures to further streamline start-up procedures and facilitate private-sector development, it still takes about a month to launch a business, although the cost of completing licensing requirements is now significantly lower. Relatively stringent labor codes continue to hinder job growth. The government plans to cut renewable energy subsidies by $780 million in 2015 to reduce power costs.

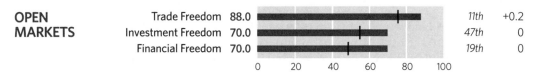

OPEN MARKETS				
Trade Freedom	88.0		11th	+0.2
Investment Freedom	70.0		47th	0
Financial Freedom	70.0		19th	0

EU members have a 1.0 percent average tariff rate. Although some non-tariff barriers exist, the EU is relatively open to external trade. Poland generally treats foreign and domestic investors equally under the law. The financial sector consists mainly of private banks, although the government continues to retain some ownership in the banking sector. Capital markets are expanding.

Long-Term Score Change (since 1995)

RULE OF LAW		GOVERNMENT SIZE		REGULATORY EFFICIENCY		OPEN MARKETS	
Property Rights	+10.0	Fiscal Freedom	+31.1	Business Freedom	−2.7	Trade Freedom	+31.0
Freedom from Corruption	+10.0	Government Spending	+37.5	Labor Freedom	+0.4	Investment Freedom	0
				Monetary Freedom	+32.6	Financial Freedom	+20.0

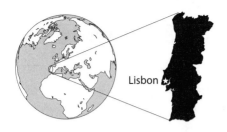

Lisbon

PORTUGAL

Economic Freedom Score

50
25   75
Least   Most
free 0   100 free

65.3

Portugal's economic freedom score is 65.3, making its economy the 64th freest in the 2015 *Index*. Its score has improved by 1.8 points since last year, with improvements in seven of the 10 economic freedoms led by labor freedom, monetary freedom, and business freedom. Portugal is ranked 30th out of 43 countries in the Europe region, and its overall score is above the world average.

A difficult external environment and a domestic banking crisis have not prevented Portugal from advancing its economic freedom. Over the past five years, it has gained 1.3 points and moved up five spots in the rankings. Improvements in five of the 10 factors have been led by a notable easing of business and labor regulations.

Portugal still lags behind other European countries in many areas. Government spending accounts for over half of the domestic economy, and bailouts of financial firms have severely strained government finances. Rigid labor regulations prevent the market from adjusting efficiently to changes in labor demand. The rule of law is generally respected, but budgeting problems have led to backlogs in the court system.

BACKGROUND: Portugal joined the European Union in 1986 and the eurozone in 2002. A sovereign debt crisis in 2011 threatened to sink the economy. Pedro Passos Coelho's center-right Social Democrats defeated Prime Minister Jose Socrates's Socialist Party in the 2011 general elections. In May 2011, Portugal accepted a €78 billion European Union–International Monetary Fund bailout plan that included demands for structural reforms that would reduce public debt and increase incentives for private investment. In 2014, the country's highest court blocked the government from making the public spending cuts required to receive the last installment of the bailout. The economy is based primarily on services and industrial production. Some state enterprises have been privatized. Overall unemployment decreased from 2013 to the first quarter of 2014 but remains well above pre-crisis levels.

Freedom Trend

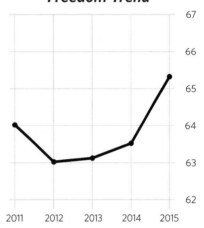

67

66

65

64

63

62

2011   2012   2013   2014   2015

Country Comparisons

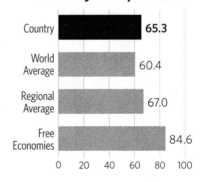

Country **65.3**

World
Average 60.4

Regional
Average 67.0

Free
Economies 84.6

0   20   40   60   80   100

Quick Facts

Population: 10.6 million
GDP (PPP): $244.8 billion
–1.4% growth in 2013
5-year compound annual growth –1.4%
$23,068 per capita
Unemployment: 16.9%
Inflation (CPI): 0.4%
FDI Inflow: $3.1 billion
Public Debt: 128.8% of GDP

2013 data unless otherwise noted.
Data compiled as of September 2014.

THE TEN ECONOMIC FREEDOMS

		Score		Rank	1-Year Change
RULE OF LAW	Property Rights	70.0		30th	0
	Freedom from Corruption	62.0		33rd	+0.9

In 2013, the OECD expressed concern over Portugal's reluctance to crack down on foreign bribery, particularly in regard to its former colonies Brazil, Angola, and Mozambique. Since 2001, Portugal had officially acknowledged only 15 bribery allegations, and there had been no prosecutions. The judiciary is constitutionally independent, but staff shortages and inefficiency contribute to a considerable backlog of pending trials.

		Score		Rank	1-Year Change
GOVERNMENT SIZE	Fiscal Freedom	61.1		166th	+1.0
	Government Spending	28.8		162nd	+2.0

Portugal's top individual income tax rate is 48 percent, and its top corporate tax rate is 23 percent (small and medium-sized enterprises pay a lower rate). Other taxes include a value-added tax. Total tax revenue equals 32.5 percent of domestic production. Public expenditures amount to 48.7 percent of the domestic economy, and public debt is equal to about 130 percent of GDP.

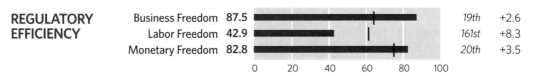

		Score		Rank	1-Year Change
REGULATORY EFFICIENCY	Business Freedom	87.5		19th	+2.6
	Labor Freedom	42.9		161st	+8.3
	Monetary Freedom	82.8		20th	+3.5

Rules regarding the formation of private enterprises are now more straightforward. There is no minimum capital requirement for launching a business, which now takes less than five days and three procedures on average. Measures to reduce severance payments and revise the unemployment insurance system have been implemented. The state maintains a generous mortgage subsidy program to encourage homeownership.

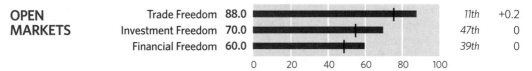

		Score		Rank	1-Year Change
OPEN MARKETS	Trade Freedom	88.0		11th	+0.2
	Investment Freedom	70.0		47th	0
	Financial Freedom	60.0		39th	0

EU members have a 1.0 percent average tariff rate. Although some non-tariff barriers exist, the EU is relatively open to external trade. The government screens foreign investment in several sectors. The overall financial system has endured uncertainty without significant disruption, but banking continues to be under considerable strain, highly dependent on liquidity support from the European Central Bank.

Long-Term Score Change (since 1995)

RULE OF LAW		GOVERNMENT SIZE		REGULATORY EFFICIENCY		OPEN MARKETS	
Property Rights	0	Fiscal Freedom	+0.6	Business Freedom	+17.5	Trade Freedom	+10.2
Freedom from Corruption	-8.0	Government Spending	-7.2	Labor Freedom	+1.7	Investment Freedom	+20.0
				Monetary Freedom	+5.1	Financial Freedom	+10.0

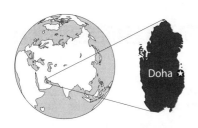

Doha ★

QATAR

Economic Freedom Score

Least free 0

Most free 100

70.8

Qatar's economic freedom score is 70.8, making its economy the 32nd freest in the 2015 *Index*. Its score has declined by 0.4 point since last year, with improvements in trade freedom and labor freedom outweighed by declines in five of the 10 economic freedoms including freedom from corruption, monetary freedom, and business freedom. Qatar is ranked 3rd out of 15 countries in the Middle East/North Africa region, and its overall score is above the world average.

With vast oil and gas reserves, Qatar enjoys one of the world's highest standards of living. Efforts to diversify the economy and reduce reliance on the energy sector have been only moderately successful. The oil and gas industries still contribute about half of GDP. Building on open-market policies, the government is trying to position Qatar as a future logistics and financial hub.

Efforts to advance economic freedom have been notable, but momentum has flagged. Respect for the rule of law is tainted by allegations of corruption surrounding a 2022 World Cup bid. The rigid regulatory environment inhibits the growth of small and medium-size enterprises.

BACKGROUND: The Al-Thani family has ruled Qatar since independence from Great Britain in 1971. Sheikh Tamim bin Hamad Al-Thani, in power since 2013, has focused on domestic issues such as improving infrastructure and providing better health care and educational institutions. Qatar has 25 billion barrels of proven oil reserves and the world's third-largest natural gas reserves. Oil and gas account for about 85 percent of export revenues and more than 50 percent of GDP. Qatar has permitted extensive foreign investment in its natural gas industry and is the world's largest exporter of liquefied natural gas. With one of the world's highest per capita incomes and almost no poverty, Qatar has largely avoided the instability generated by the Arab Spring uprisings, but it has come under fire for its alleged support of radical groups.

Freedom Trend

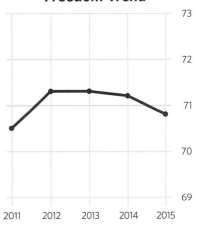

Country Comparisons

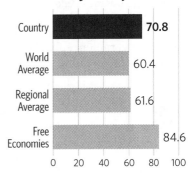

Country	70.8
World Average	60.4
Regional Average	61.6
Free Economies	84.6

Quick Facts

Population: 2.0 million

GDP (PPP): $199.6 billion

6.1% growth in 2013

5-year compound annual growth 10.7%

$98,814 per capita

Unemployment: 0.6%

Inflation (CPI): 3.1%

FDI Inflow: –$840.4 million

Public Debt: 34.2% of GDP

2013 data unless otherwise noted.
Data compiled as of September 2014.

THE TEN ECONOMIC FREEDOMS

		Score	■ Country | World Average	Rank	1-Year Change
RULE OF LAW	Property Rights	70.0		30th	0
	Freedom from Corruption	68.0		28th	-4.4

Although critics cite a lack of transparency in government procurement, Qatar's anti-corruption record is among the best in the Middle East. The rule of law is respected. The legal system, however, has been biased against foreign businesses. The judiciary is susceptible to political influence and can be bureaucratic. Foreigners are generally not allowed to own property.

		Score		Rank	1-Year Change
GOVERNMENT SIZE	Fiscal Freedom	99.7		2nd	-0.2
	Government Spending	71.9		79th	-0.2

Qatar has no individual income tax. The corporate tax rate is a flat 10 percent (the rate for companies in the oil and gas sector is 35 percent). Other taxes include customs duties. Overall tax revenue amounts to 5.1 percent of domestic output. Government expenditures equal 30.6 percent of domestic production, and public debt equals 34 percent of gross domestic product.

		Score		Rank	1-Year Change
REGULATORY EFFICIENCY	Business Freedom	70.5		66th	-1.2
	Labor Freedom	71.2		54th	+1.2
	Monetary Freedom	79.7		59th	-1.5

Forming a business takes eight procedures, and the minimum capital required exceeds half the level of average annual income. Obtaining necessary permits remains relatively time-consuming. The non-salary cost of employing a worker is moderate, but the labor market lacks flexibility. Government subsidies are very high: The IMF estimates that pre-tax energy subsidies alone exceed spending on health and education.

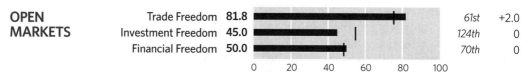

		Score		Rank	1-Year Change
OPEN MARKETS	Trade Freedom	81.8		61st	+2.0
	Investment Freedom	45.0		124th	0
	Financial Freedom	50.0		70th	0

Qatar's average tariff rate is 4.1 percent. Non-tariff barriers are low, but some lines of imports face special import procedures, and others are prohibited. In most cases, foreign investment in a business is capped at 49 percent. The modernized and expanded financial sector is attracting more foreign firms, but the government retains considerable ownership. The capital market continues to grow.

Long-Term Score Change (since 1999)

RULE OF LAW		GOVERNMENT SIZE		REGULATORY EFFICIENCY		OPEN MARKETS	
Property Rights	+20.0	Fiscal Freedom	+12.2	Business Freedom	+15.5	Trade Freedom	+6.8
Freedom from Corruption	-22.0	Government Spending	+24.1	Labor Freedom	+11.2	Investment Freedom	-5.0
				Monetary Freedom	+7.0	Financial Freedom	+20.0

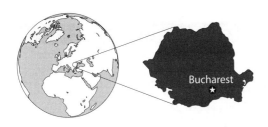

ROMANIA

Economic Freedom Score

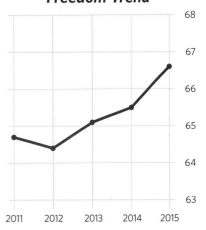

50

25   75

Least free 0   100 Most free

66.6

World Rank: **57**   Regional Rank: **27**

Romania's economic freedom score is 66.6, making its economy the 57th freest in the 2015 *Index*. Its score is 1.1 points better than last year, reflecting improvements in freedom from corruption, labor freedom, and the management of government spending that outweigh a decline in business freedom. Romania is ranked 27th out of 43 countries in the Europe region, and its overall score is higher than the world average.

With a steady five-year increase in economic freedom, Romania joins a growing trend in Eastern Europe. Since 2011, economic freedom in Romania has improved by nearly 2.0 points. Advances in six of the 10 economic freedoms include particularly impressive gains in reducing corruption and loosening labor regulations. In the 2015 *Index*, Romania has achieved its highest economic freedom score ever.

However, even with these improvements and membership in the European Union, Romania's status as a transitional economy is still apparent. Judicial independence is precarious, and the government has struggled to meet EU anti-corruption requirements. Despite progress, the business environment remains inefficient, a remnant of the country's Communist past.

BACKGROUND: Romania's transition to a free-market economy began with the adoption of its new constitution in 1991. In the post–Cold War period, Romania developed closer ties with Western Europe and was accepted into NATO in 2004 and the EU in 2007. President Traian Basescu has served since 2004 and has survived multiple impeachment attempts. After years of growth, Romania experienced a deep recession as a result of the 2008 global financial crisis. Modest growth has resumed, and the government has made progress in reducing the public debt and budget deficit. Privatization of major state corporations has contributed materially to private-sector growth. In addition to its strategic position on the Black Sea, Romania has extensive natural resources, a productive agriculture sector, and the potential for strong growth in industry and tourism.

Freedom Trend

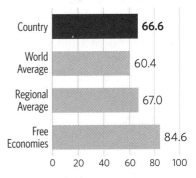

Country Comparisons

Country	**66.6**
World Average	60.4
Regional Average	67.0
Free Economies	84.6

0   20   40   60   80   100

Quick Facts

Population: 21.3 million
GDP (PPP): $285.1 billion
3.5% growth in 2013
5-year compound annual growth -0.3%
$13,396 per capita
Unemployment: 7.4%
Inflation (CPI): 4.0%
FDI Inflow: $3.6 billion
Public Debt: 39.3% of GDP

2013 data unless otherwise noted.
Data compiled as of September 2014.

How Do We Measure Economic Freedom?
See page 475 for an explanation of the methodology
or visit the *Index* Web site at *heritage.org/index.*

THE TEN ECONOMIC FREEDOMS

		Score		Rank	1-Year Change
RULE OF LAW	Property Rights	40.0		70th	0
	Freedom from Corruption	43.0		69th	+5.3

Despite some improvement, corruption remains a serious problem. According to the European Commission, there is a lack of "best practices for public procurement," and the "competent administrative bodies do not apply effective controls to detect conflict of interest and corruption." The courts continue to suffer from such chronic problems as corruption, political influence, staffing shortages, and inefficient resource allocation.

		Score		Rank	1-Year Change
GOVERNMENT SIZE	Fiscal Freedom	86.9		38th	-0.1
	Government Spending	62.3		102nd	+3.1

Romania's top individual and corporate income tax rates are 16 percent. Other taxes include a value-added tax and environmental taxes. The overall tax burden is equal to 28.2 percent of gross domestic product, and government expenditures amount to 35.4 percent of domestic production. Public debt is equivalent to 39 percent of the domestic economy.

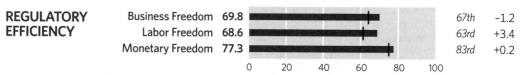

		Score		Rank	1-Year Change
REGULATORY EFFICIENCY	Business Freedom	69.8		67th	-1.2
	Labor Freedom	68.6		63rd	+3.4
	Monetary Freedom	77.3		83rd	+0.2

Launching a business takes five procedures and slightly more than a week on average, but efficient bankruptcy procedures and rules have not been fully implemented. Labor regulations remain rigid, although there have been amendments to improve the labor code's flexibility. The government listed privatization and market liberalization as major priorities for 2014 but took no action to end distorting subsidies.

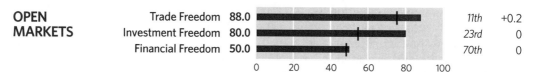

		Score		Rank	1-Year Change
OPEN MARKETS	Trade Freedom	88.0		11th	+0.2
	Investment Freedom	80.0		23rd	0
	Financial Freedom	50.0		70th	0

EU members have a 1.0 percent average tariff rate. Although some non-tariff barriers exist, the EU is relatively open to external trade. Despite bureaucratic challenges, Romania does not generally discriminate against foreign investment. Overall, the financial sector has coped well with the effects of the economic downturn. Banking supervision has been enhanced, but the level of nonperforming loans remains high.

Long-Term Score Change (since 1995)

RULE OF LAW		GOVERNMENT SIZE		REGULATORY EFFICIENCY		OPEN MARKETS	
Property Rights	+10.0	Fiscal Freedom	+47.5	Business Freedom	+14.8	Trade Freedom	+9.0
Freedom from Corruption	+33.0	Government Spending	+10.1	Labor Freedom	+13.1	Investment Freedom	+10.0
				Monetary Freedom	+77.3	Financial Freedom	0

RUSSIA

Economic Freedom Score

World Rank: 143   **Regional Rank: 41**

Russia's economic freedom score is 52.1, making its economy the 143rd freest in the 2015 *Index*. Its score has improved by 0.2 point since last year, with gains in business freedom, freedom from corruption, and labor freedom largely offset by declines in monetary freedom, property rights, and the management of government spending. Russia is ranked 41st out of 43 countries in the Europe region, and its overall score is below the world average.

Despite increased political and economic isolation and falling gas prices, Russia's economic freedom score has increased by 1.6 points since 2011, with gains in half of the 10 economic freedoms led by a particularly notable improvement in business freedom. Significant declines in financial freedom and property rights have held back overall progress.

The foundations of economic freedom in Russia remain weak. Apart from connections with Europe, Russia remains relatively closed to trade and investment. The government screens foreign investment, and subsidized state-owned businesses limit competition and market opportunities. Corruption and respect for property rights have improved little since the fall of Communism. The business environment is constrained by suffocating bureaucracy and a rigid labor market.

BACKGROUND: Former President and Prime Minister Vladimir Putin was re-elected president in March 2012 on the heels of hotly disputed December 2011 Duma elections. Under Putin's leadership, Russia illegally annexed Ukraine's Autonomous Republic of Crimea early in 2014. Moscow's support of Russian separatists in Ukraine has led to capital outflows and targeted sanctions by the United States and European Union. Russia's Gazprom cut gas supplies to Ukraine after violence between Ukrainians and Russian separatists increased in the eastern region of the country. The Russian economy remains heavily dependent on gas exports. Russia became a member of the World Trade Organization in August 2012, but its bid to join the Organisation for Economic Co-operation and Development has been postponed due to its recent actions in Ukraine.

Freedom Trend

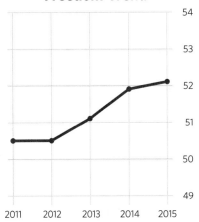

Country Comparisons

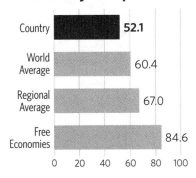

Quick Facts

Population: 142.9 million
GDP (PPP): $2.6 trillion
1.3% growth in 2013
5-year compound annual growth 1.0%
$17,884 per capita
Unemployment: 5.8%
Inflation (CPI): 6.8%
FDI Inflow: $79.3 billion
Public Debt: 13.4% of GDP

2013 data unless otherwise noted.
Data compiled as of September 2014.

How Do We Measure Economic Freedom?
See page 475 for an explanation of the methodology
or visit the *Index* Web site at *heritage.org/index.*

369

THE TEN ECONOMIC FREEDOMS

| | Score | Country | World Average | Rank | 1-Year Change |

RULE OF LAW
Property Rights 20.0 — 138th −5.0
Freedom from Corruption 28.0 — 132nd +5.9

Corruption is rampant. Small elites control most of the nation's assets, and state institutions have been corroded. Anti-corruption campaigns are used to ensure elite loyalty and undermine political opponents. The rule of law is not uniform across the country, and the judiciary is vulnerable to political pressure and inconsistent in applying the law. Protection of private property rights is weak.

GOVERNMENT SIZE
Fiscal Freedom 86.1 — 44th +0.5
Government Spending 57.8 — 119th −3.7

Russia's top individual income tax rate is 13 percent, and its top corporate tax rate is 20 percent. Other taxes include a value-added tax and an environmental tax. The overall tax burden equals 28.7 percent of domestic income. Government expenditures amount to 37.5 percent of domestic production, and public debt is equal to 13 percent of gross domestic product.

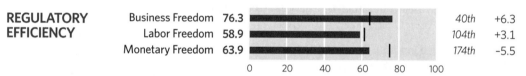

REGULATORY EFFICIENCY
Business Freedom 76.3 — 40th +6.3
Labor Freedom 58.9 — 104th +3.1
Monetary Freedom 63.9 — 174th −5.5

Bureaucratic obstacles and inconsistent enforcement of regulations continue to suppress the private sector. Although forming a business can take less than four procedures on average, completing licensing requirements still takes over 200 days. The outmoded labor code limits employment growth. The government uses extensive subsidies, state-owned companies, export taxes on petroleum products, and other means to influence prices.

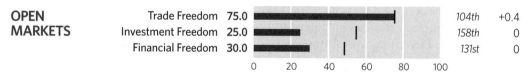

OPEN MARKETS
Trade Freedom 75.0 — 104th +0.4
Investment Freedom 25.0 — 158th 0
Financial Freedom 30.0 — 131st 0

Russia's average tariff rate is 5.0 percent. Informal barriers further interfere with trade. The government can discriminate against foreign investment, and investment in several sectors of the economy is restricted. The financial sector remains subject to considerable state interference. The government retains some ownership in the banking sector, and the central bank has become a single financial market regulator.

Long-Term Score Change (since 1995)

RULE OF LAW		GOVERNMENT SIZE		REGULATORY EFFICIENCY		OPEN MARKETS	
Property Rights	−30.0	Fiscal Freedom	+10.6	Business Freedom	−8.7	Trade Freedom	+23.0
Freedom from Corruption	+18.0	Government Spending	−9.3	Labor Freedom	−2.9	Investment Freedom	−45.0
				Monetary Freedom	+63.9	Financial Freedom	−20.0

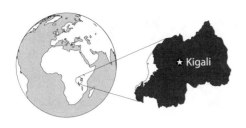

★ Kigali

RWANDA

Economic Freedom Score

50

25   75

Least   Most
free   0   100 free

64.8

| World Rank: **65** | Regional Rank: **4** |

Rwanda's economic freedom score is 64.8, making its economy the 65th freest in the 2015 *Index*. Its score remains essentially the same as last year's, with improvements in half of the 10 economic freedoms, including freedom from corruption and trade freedom, undermined by a significant decline in business freedom. Rwanda is ranked 4th out of 46 countries in the Sub-Saharan Africa region, and its score exceeds the world average.

Over the past five years, economic freedom in Rwanda has advanced by 2.1 points, led by 20-point and 15-point improvements in freedom from corruption and investment freedom, respectively. Efforts to reform the economy have contributed to sustained economic growth and poverty reduction.

However, the government's reform efforts have not yet fully restored the institutions and structures previously undermined by political unrest and civil war. An increasingly authoritarian president has restricted judicial independence. Meanwhile, corruption continues to undermine public trust. An underdeveloped financial system leads to a high cost of financing and discourages many of Rwanda's citizens from opening formal bank accounts.

BACKGROUND: Paul Kagame's Tutsi-led Rwandan Patriotic Front (RPF) seized power in July 1994 in the wake of the state-sponsored genocidal slaughter of an estimated 800,000 Tutsis. Kagame was elected president in 2000 and re-elected in August 2010 amid allegations of fraud, intimidation, and violence. His RPF won a resounding victory in the September 2013 parliamentary elections. In July 2012, the U.N. accused Kagame of supporting the M23 rebels in the Democratic Republic of Congo. The U.S., the Netherlands, and Germany subsequently suspended aid. In 2014, the DRC and Rwanda deployed troops to their shared border in response to cross-border violence. The economy is still recovering from the genocide and civil war. Rwanda remains highly dependent on foreign aid and has a goal of transforming its economy from agriculture-based to service-oriented by 2020.

Freedom Trend

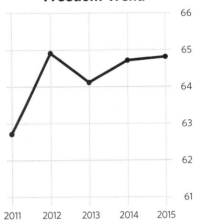

Country Comparisons

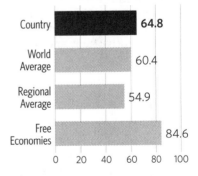

Quick Facts

Population: 10.6 million
GDP (PPP): $16.4 billion
5.0% growth in 2013
5-year compound annual growth 6.9%
$1,538 per capita
Unemployment: 0.6%
Inflation (CPI): 4.2%
FDI Inflow: $110.8 million
Public Debt: 29.4% of GDP

2013 data unless otherwise noted.
Data compiled as of September 2014.

How Do We Measure Economic Freedom?
See page 475 for an explanation of the methodology
or visit the *Index* Web site at *heritage.org/index.*

THE TEN ECONOMIC FREEDOMS

		Score			Rank	1-Year Change
RULE OF LAW	Property Rights	30.0			94th	0
	Freedom from Corruption	53.0			48th	+6.1

Measures to foster a better business environment and improve government transparency and accountability have helped to limit corruption, though graft remains a problem. Recent improvements in the judicial system include improved training and revisions of the legal code, but the judiciary has yet to secure full independence from the executive. A nationwide land registration program is being implemented.

		Score			Rank	1-Year Change
GOVERNMENT SIZE	Fiscal Freedom	80.2			82nd	-0.1
	Government Spending	79.2			49th	+1.0

Rwanda's top individual and corporate income tax rates are 30 percent. Other taxes include a value-added tax and a property transfer tax. Total tax revenue amounts to 13.6 percent of domestic output, and government expenditures are equal to 26.3 percent of domestic production. Public debt is equivalent to 29 percent of gross domestic product.

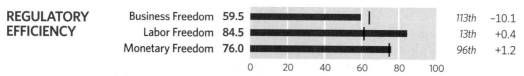

		Score			Rank	1-Year Change
REGULATORY EFFICIENCY	Business Freedom	59.5			113th	-10.1
	Labor Freedom	84.5			13th	+0.4
	Monetary Freedom	76.0			96th	+1.2

Incorporating a business takes eight procedures and about a week on average, with no minimum capital required, but regulatory reform has slowed. Labor regulations are more flexible, but a more vibrant formal labor market has yet to develop. The state sets maximum prices for automotive fuels and subsidizes power for the 20 percent of the population with access to electricity.

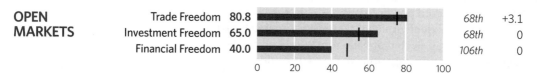

		Score			Rank	1-Year Change
OPEN MARKETS	Trade Freedom	80.8			68th	+3.1
	Investment Freedom	65.0			68th	0
	Financial Freedom	40.0			106th	0

Rwanda's average tariff rate is 4.6 percent. Non-tariff barriers are relatively low. There are concerns that an "abandoned property" law enacted in 2014 may make it easier for the government to expropriate property. Financial markets consist mainly of banks, which have been expanding their services. The capital market continues to grow, but the cost of financing remains relatively high.

Long-Term Score Change (since 1997)

RULE OF LAW		GOVERNMENT SIZE		REGULATORY EFFICIENCY		OPEN MARKETS	
Property Rights	+20.0	Fiscal Freedom	+12.3	Business Freedom	+19.5	Trade Freedom	+46.8
Freedom from Corruption	+43.0	Government Spending	-13.0	Labor Freedom	+26.5	Investment Freedom	+35.0
				Monetary Freedom	+25.2	Financial Freedom	+30.0

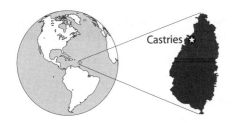

SAINT LUCIA

Economic Freedom Score

50
25   75

Least free 0   100 Most free

70.2

World Rank: 35   **Regional Rank: 3**

Saint Lucia's economic freedom score is 70.2, making its economy the 35th freest in the 2015 *Index*. Its score has decreased by 0.5 point since last year, reflecting considerable declines in business freedom and labor freedom that outweigh modest improvements in five other economic freedoms. Saint Lucia is ranked 3rd out of 29 countries in the South and Central America/Caribbean region, and its overall score is above the world average.

Saint Lucia's successful tourism industry depends in part on the country's commitment to economic freedom and a competitive business environment. Over the past five years, advances in five of the 10 economic freedoms, including a particularly large advance in investment freedom, have been more than offset by sizeable declines in the control of government spending, business freedom, and labor freedom. If this downward trend is not reversed, Saint Lucia could fall into the "moderately free" category.

There is plenty of room for policy improvements. With high tariffs, Saint Lucia remains relatively closed to international trade, and new laws require some approval for investments. Financial freedom is far less than some other Caribbean islands provide.

BACKGROUND: In late 2011, former Prime Minister Kenny D. Anthony and his Saint Lucia Labour Party defeated Prime Minister Stephenson King's more business-friendly United Workers Party. Saint Lucia is a member of the Community of Latin American and Caribbean States (CELAC) and the Caribbean Community (CARICOM) and home to the Organization of Eastern Caribbean States. The economy depends primarily on tourism (65 percent of GDP), banana production, and a diversified light manufacturing sector. An educated workforce and reliable infrastructure and port facilities attract foreign investment in tourism, petroleum storage, and transshipment. A decline in tourism that began during the recession in 2009, fluctuations in banana prices, and reduced European Union banana trade preferences have forced greater economic diversification in cocoa, mangos, and avocados. Violent crime threatens the tourism industry.

Freedom Trend

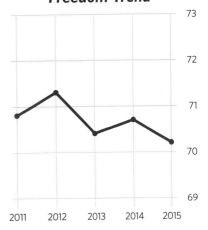

73

72

71

70

69

2011   2012   2013   2014   2015

Country Comparisons

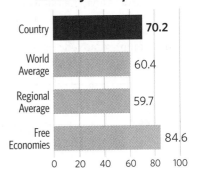

Country — 70.2
World Average — 60.4
Regional Average — 59.7
Free Economies — 84.6

0   20   40   60   80   100

Quick Facts

Population: 0.2 million
GDP (PPP): $2.1 billion
–1.5% growth in 2013
5-year compound annual growth –0.4%
$12,730 per capita
Unemployment: n/a
Inflation (CPI): 1.5%
FDI Inflow: $87.9 million
Public Debt: 79.8% of GDP

2013 data unless otherwise noted.
Data compiled as of September 2014.

How Do We Measure Economic Freedom?
See page 475 for an explanation of the methodology
or visit the *Index* Web site at *heritage.org/index*.

THE TEN ECONOMIC FREEDOMS

		Score		Rank	1-Year Change
RULE OF LAW	Property Rights	70.0		30th	0
	Freedom from Corruption	71.0		22nd	+0.4

Legend: ■ Country | World Average

Saint Lucia has low levels of corruption, although the prime minister was criticized in 2013 for having signed an allegedly unlawful contract with a Texas-based oil exploration company. Access to information is legally guaranteed, and government officials are required to report their financial assets annually to the Integrity Commission. The judicial system is independent and conducts generally fair public trials.

		Score		Rank	1-Year Change
GOVERNMENT SIZE	Fiscal Freedom	77.7		105th	+2.0
	Government Spending	65.8		96th	+2.2

The top individual and corporate income tax rates are 30 percent. Other taxes include a tax on consumption and a property transfer tax. The overall tax burden is equal to 20.8 percent of domestic income. Government spending is equivalent to 33.8 percent of gross domestic product, and public debt equals approximately 80 percent of the size of the economy.

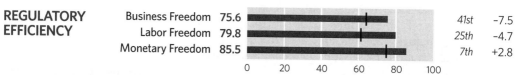

		Score		Rank	1-Year Change
REGULATORY EFFICIENCY	Business Freedom	75.6		41st	–7.5
	Labor Freedom	79.8		25th	–4.7
	Monetary Freedom	85.5		7th	+2.8

The pace of reform has slowed, but business start-up procedures remain relatively straightforward, with no minimum capital required. A well-functioning labor market has not been fully developed, and much of the labor force is employed in agriculture and tourism. In 2014, the government removed sugar subsidies altogether and increased state-controlled fuel prices to reduce budgetary pressures.

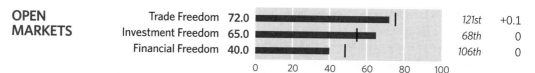

		Score		Rank	1-Year Change
OPEN MARKETS	Trade Freedom	72.0		121st	+0.1
	Investment Freedom	65.0		68th	0
	Financial Freedom	40.0		106th	0

Saint Lucia's average tariff rate is 9.0 percent. Some agricultural imports face additional barriers. The government screens new foreign investment, and investment in some sectors of the economy is restricted. The developing financial system is dominated by banking. Credit to the private sector has been expanding slowly, but a rise in the number of nonperforming loans deters new lending.

Long-Term Score Change (since 2009)

RULE OF LAW		GOVERNMENT SIZE		REGULATORY EFFICIENCY		OPEN MARKETS	
Property Rights	0	Fiscal Freedom	+3.7	Business Freedom	–12.1	Trade Freedom	0
Freedom from Corruption	+3.0	Government Spending	–2.7	Labor Freedom	–3.0	Investment Freedom	+25.0
				Monetary Freedom	+0.4	Financial Freedom	0

SAINT VINCENT AND THE GRENADINES

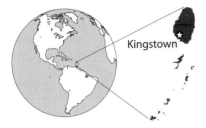

Kingstown

Economic Freedom Score

Least free 0

Most free 100

68.0

World Rank: 44   **Regional Rank: 6**

Saint Vincent and the Grenadines' economic freedom score is 68.0, making its economy the 44th freest in the 2015 *Index*. Its score is 1.0 point higher than last year, with improvements in half of the 10 economic freedoms, led by investment freedom, the management of government spending, and monetary freedom, that outweigh a decline in business freedom. Saint Vincent and the Grenadines is ranked 6th out of 29 countries in the South and Central America/Caribbean region, and its score is above the world and regional averages.

Over the past five years, economic freedom in Saint Vincent and the Grenadines has advanced by 1.1 points, a result of increases in five of the 10 economic freedoms. Leading the way have been impressive gains in both government spending and investment freedom, each of which has advanced by double digits.

Despite duty-free access to the U.S. market, Saint Vincent and the Grenadines' trade and investment regimes remain relatively closed. High tariff rates discourage imports and protect inefficient domestic businesses. Licensing is required for businesses with majority foreign ownership. The economy is vulnerable to global price fluctuations, particularly prices of petroleum products, and drug-related corruption and money-laundering charges have held back development of the islands' legitimate financial sector.

BACKGROUND: Prime Minister Ralph Gonsalves' Unity Labour Party retained a slim majority in the December 2010 parliamentary elections. Saint Vincent and the Grenadines is a parliamentary democracy. It is a member of the Caribbean Community (CARICOM) and the Organization of Eastern Caribbean States. The export sector benefits from the Caribbean Basin Initiative, which provides duty-free access to the U.S. market. Agriculture and tourism employ a significant portion of the workforce, but high formal-sector unemployment has caused many to emigrate. Public debt has been growing, and weak recovery in the tourism and construction sectors has limited economic growth.

Freedom Trend

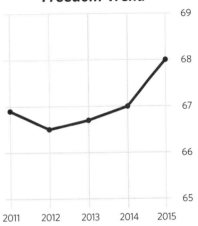

Country Comparisons

Country	68.0
World Average	60.4
Regional Average	59.7
Free Economies	84.6

Quick Facts

Population: 0.1 million
GDP (PPP): $1.3 billion
2.1% growth in 2013
5-year compound annual growth –0.1%
$12,207 per capita
Unemployment: n/a
Inflation (CPI): 0.9%
FDI Inflow: $126.8 million
Public Debt: 76.4% of GDP

2013 data unless otherwise noted.
Data compiled as of September 2014.

How Do We Measure Economic Freedom?
See page 475 for an explanation of the methodology or visit the *Index* Web site at *heritage.org/index*.

THE TEN ECONOMIC FREEDOMS

	Score	Rank	1-Year Change
RULE OF LAW			
Property Rights	70.0	30th	0
Freedom from Corruption	62.0	33rd	+0.9

The rule of law remains strong for the region, and corruption is not pervasive. There have been some allegations of money laundering through Saint Vincent banks and drug-related corruption within the government and police, but the government has taken action to prosecute such crimes. The relatively independent and efficient judicial system is based on British common law.

	Score	Rank	1-Year Change
GOVERNMENT SIZE			
Fiscal Freedom	73.3	125th	-0.4
Government Spending	75.3	66th	+2.9

The top individual and corporate income tax rates are 32.5 percent. Other taxes include a value-added tax and a property tax. The overall tax burden amounts to 23 percent of domestic production. Government expenditures are equal to 28.7 percent of the domestic economy, and public debt is equivalent to approximately 76 percent of gross domestic product.

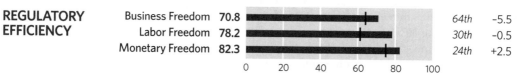

	Score	Rank	1-Year Change
REGULATORY EFFICIENCY			
Business Freedom	70.8	64th	-5.5
Labor Freedom	78.2	30th	-0.5
Monetary Freedom	82.3	24th	+2.5

Establishing a business is generally not burdensome or costly. There is no minimum capital requirement, and it takes seven procedures to start a business, but licensing procedures can be time-consuming. Labor regulations are flexible, but application of labor laws is uneven. Subsidy programs benefit agricultural products such as bananas and state-owned enterprises such as a coconut water bottling plant.

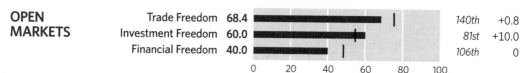

	Score	Rank	1-Year Change
OPEN MARKETS			
Trade Freedom	68.4	140th	+0.8
Investment Freedom	60.0	81st	+10.0
Financial Freedom	40.0	106th	0

Saint Vincent and the Grenadines' average tariff rate is 10.8 percent. Agricultural imports face relatively high tariffs. Foreign and domestic investors are generally treated equally under the law. The financial sector is underdeveloped and dominated by banks. A considerable portion of the population does not use the formal banking sector, and access to financing is limited for potential entrepreneurs.

Long-Term Score Change (since 2009)

RULE OF LAW		GOVERNMENT SIZE		REGULATORY EFFICIENCY		OPEN MARKETS	
Property Rights	0	Fiscal Freedom	+8.6	Business Freedom	-7.4	Trade Freedom	-5.2
Freedom from Corruption	+1.0	Government Spending	+14.4	Labor Freedom	-0.3	Investment Freedom	+20.0
				Monetary Freedom	+6.7	Financial Freedom	0

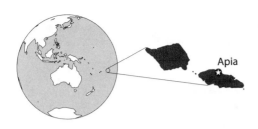

Apia

SAMOA

Economic Freedom Score

25 — 50 — 75

Least free 0 .... 100 Most free

61.9

World Rank: 78   **Regional Rank: 14**

Samoa's economic freedom score is 61.9, making its economy the 78th freest in the 2015 *Index*. Its score has increased by 0.8 point since last year, with considerable gains in monetary freedom and the management of government spending outweighing a decline in labor freedom. Samoa is ranked 14th out of 42 countries in the Asia–Pacific region, and its overall score is above the world and regional averages.

Samoa's efforts to expand its manufacturing sector, open the economy to global investment and financial flows, and encourage tourism correspond to an improvement in its economic freedom, which has risen by 1.3 points over the past five years. Gains in five of the 10 economic freedoms have been led by a 25-point improvement in investment freedom. Following a short drop into the "mostly unfree" category in 2013, Samoa has firmly re-established itself as "moderately free."

Nevertheless, key structural and institutional problems persist. Despite a common-law legal system, the property rights regime is poorly laid out and ineffectively enforced. The government is responsible for much economic activity, and international aid to government services helps to fund a broad range of subsidies. Further gains will be needed to make Samoa an attractive destination for foreign investment.

BACKGROUND: Samoa is a small South Pacific archipelago with a population of less than 200,000. Independent since 1962, it is now a multi-party democracy dominated politically by the Human Rights Protection Party (HRPP). A few politicians were found guilty of bribery in the 2011 parliamentary elections, but the HRPP remains in power. The economy is based on fishing, agriculture, and tourism. Remittances from Samoans working abroad account for about 24 percent of national income. A sizable tsunami in 2009 killed over 200 people and significantly damaged infrastructure and property. To facilitate better trade with Australia and New Zealand, Samoa officially moved west of the International Date Line in 2011.

Freedom Trend

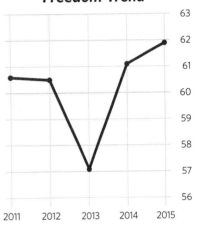

Country Comparisons

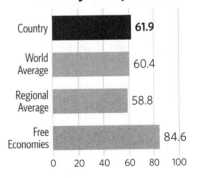

Quick Facts

Population: 0.2 million
GDP (PPP): $1.1 billion
–0.3% growth in 2013
5-year compound annual growth –0.2%
$6,210 per capita
Unemployment: n/a
Inflation (CPI): –0.2%
FDI Inflow: $28.0 million
Public Debt: 58.2% of GDP (2012)

2013 data unless otherwise noted.
Data compiled as of September 2014.

THE TEN ECONOMIC FREEDOMS

		Score			Rank	1-Year Change
RULE OF LAW	Property Rights	60.0			41st	0
	Freedom from Corruption	38.0			83rd	0

The Finance Minister was forced to resign in 2014 over alleged mismanagement of government finances. The judiciary is independent and upholds the right to a fair trial, but a well-functioning legal framework for land ownership and enforcement of property rights is not firmly in place. More than 80 percent of the land is owned by extended families represented by their chiefs.

					Rank	Change
GOVERNMENT SIZE	Fiscal Freedom	80.2			81st	+0.3
	Government Spending	46.5			139th	+4.3

The top individual and corporate income tax rates are 27 percent. Other taxes include a value-added tax and an excise tax. The overall tax burden equals 22.9 percent of the domestic economy. Public expenditures are equal to 42.2 percent of domestic production, and government debt is equivalent to approximately 58 percent of gross domestic product.

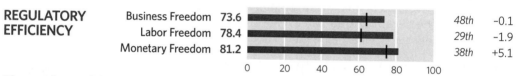

					Rank	Change
REGULATORY EFFICIENCY	Business Freedom	73.6			48th	-0.1
	Labor Freedom	78.4			29th	-1.9
	Monetary Freedom	81.2			38th	+5.1

The regulatory framework generally supports entrepreneurial activity, but application of the commercial codes is not always straightforward. Completing licensing requirements takes 18 procedures and over two months on average. A well-functioning modern labor market is not fully developed, and informal labor activity remains substantial. The government increased subsidies for fuel and health care in 2014.

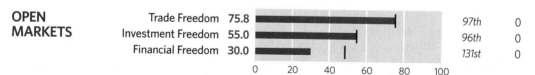

					Rank	Change
OPEN MARKETS	Trade Freedom	75.8			97th	0
	Investment Freedom	55.0			96th	0
	Financial Freedom	30.0			131st	0

Samoa's average tariff rate is 7.1 percent. Foreign investment in several sectors of the economy is capped. The small financial sector is rudimentary. Despite some progress, scarce access to banking and financial services continues to keep much of the population outside of the formal banking sector. Reflecting the lack of financial efficiency and depth, capital markets are poorly developed.

Long-Term Score Change (since 1996)

RULE OF LAW		GOVERNMENT SIZE		REGULATORY EFFICIENCY		OPEN MARKETS	
Property Rights	+10.0	Fiscal Freedom	+15.7	Business Freedom	+3.6	Trade Freedom	+75.8
Freedom from Corruption	-32.0	Government Spending	+44.3	Labor Freedom	-1.8	Investment Freedom	+5.0
				Monetary Freedom	+9.2	Financial Freedom	-20.0

SÃO TOMÉ AND PRÍNCIPE

São Tomé

Economic Freedom Score

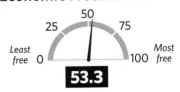

25   50   75

Least free 0   100 Most free

53.3

São Tomé and Príncipe's economic freedom score is 53.3, making its economy the 136th freest in the 2015 *Index*. Its score has increased by 4.5 points from last year, reflecting impressive improvements in seven of the 10 economic freedoms related to regulatory efficiency, the management of public finance, and the rule of law. São Tomé and Príncipe has recorded the largest score improvement of any country graded in the 2015 *Index*, yet it is still ranked 29th out of 46 countries in the Sub-Saharan Africa region, and its score is below the world average.

This year's gains in economic freedom have erased losses recorded in 2013. An improvement of 3.8 points since 2011 has been led by a gain of over 30 points in business freedom, moving São Tomé and Príncipe out of the "repressed" category.

Despite these improvements, however, economic freedom is not firmly established. Rampant corruption is exacerbated by oil exploration and development aid. The government dominates the domestic economy, and the bureaucracy hinders business formation and labor market efficiency. Efforts to attract capital for oil exploration have not translated into a well-crafted investment regime, hindering chances for development of a competitive financial system.

BACKGROUND: Manual Pinto da Costa, who served as president for 15 years following independence from Portugal in 1975, returned to office in 2011.Under São Tomé and Príncipe's democratic constitution, the president shares power with a prime minister who requires the confidence of the parliament to retain power. In 2012, Prime Minister Patrice Trovoada won legislative elections, but he received a vote of no confidence and was replaced by current Prime Minister Gabriel Costa. São Tomé's economy, one of Africa's smallest, is agriculture-based and highly vulnerable to external shocks. São Tomé remains dependent on foreign assistance. Oil production is expected to begin in late 2015, but both São Tomé and Nigeria claim unexploited offshore oil fields.

Freedom Trend

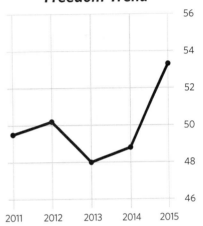

2011   2012   2013   2014   2015

Country Comparisons

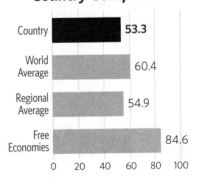

Country	53.3
World Average	60.4
Regional Average	54.9
Free Economies	84.6

0   20   40   60   80   100

Quick Facts

Population: 0.2 million
GDP (PPP): $0.4 billion
4.0% growth in 2013
5-year compound annual growth 4.3%
$2,194 per capita
Unemployment: n/a
Inflation (CPI): 8.1%
FDI Inflow: $30.0 million
Public Debt: 85.3% of GDP

2013 data unless otherwise noted.
Data compiled as of September 2014.

How Do We Measure Economic Freedom?
See page 475 for an explanation of the methodology
or visit the *Index* Web site at *heritage.org/index*.

THE TEN ECONOMIC FREEDOMS

		Score		Rank	1-Year Change
RULE OF LAW	Property Rights	25.0		124th	+5.0
	Freedom from Corruption	42.0		72nd	+9.5

Although the government has undertaken numerous reforms (e.g., an August 2013 anti–money laundering law), development aid and offshore oil exploration have fueled corruption among the ruling elite. Bribery, embezzlement, and mismanagement of public funds are regarded as endemic. The judiciary is independent but weak, underfunded, understaffed, inefficient, and susceptible to political influence. Property rights are not protected effectively.

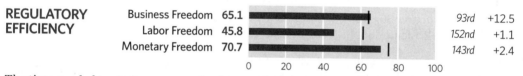

		Score		Rank	1-Year Change
GOVERNMENT SIZE	Fiscal Freedom	87.8		33rd	+0.9
	Government Spending	41.4		149th	+13.5

The top individual income tax rate is 13 percent, and the top corporate tax rate is 25 percent. Other taxes include a sales tax and a dividend tax. Overall tax revenues equal approximately 14 percent of gross domestic product. Government spending equals 44.2 percent of domestic production, and public debt is equivalent to 85 percent of the economy.

		Score		Rank	1-Year Change
REGULATORY EFFICIENCY	Business Freedom	65.1		93rd	+12.5
	Labor Freedom	45.8		152nd	+1.1
	Monetary Freedom	70.7		143rd	+2.4

The time needed to start a company has been reduced to four days, and licensing requirements have been simplified. In the absence of a well-functioning labor market, informal labor activity remains significant. The government stated its intention to cut fuel and power subsidies and fix problems in the state-owned water and electricity firms in 2014 but took no action.

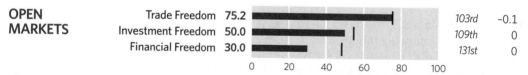

		Score		Rank	1-Year Change
OPEN MARKETS	Trade Freedom	75.2		103rd	-0.1
	Investment Freedom	50.0		109th	0
	Financial Freedom	30.0		131st	0

The average tariff rate for São Tomé and Principe, a member of the Economic Community of Central African States, was 7.4 percent as of 2008. Pork imports are not allowed. Foreign investment generally receives national treatment. The underdeveloped financial sector, consisting of eight firms, does not provide adequate access to banking services for a large portion of the population.

Long-Term Score Change (since 2009)

RULE OF LAW		GOVERNMENT SIZE		REGULATORY EFFICIENCY		OPEN MARKETS	
Property Rights	-5.0	Fiscal Freedom	+12.8	Business Freedom	+20.0	Trade Freedom	+15.2
Freedom from Corruption	+15.0	Government Spending	+19.4	Labor Freedom	-2.2	Investment Freedom	+10.0
				Monetary Freedom	+9.3	Financial Freedom	0

SAUDI ARABIA

★ Riyadh

Economic Freedom Score

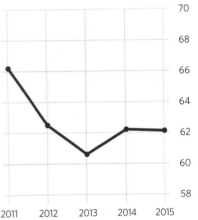

50
25   75
Least   Most
free 0   100 free

62.1

World Rank: **77**   Regional Rank: **8**

Saudi Arabia's economic freedom score is 62.1, making its economy the 77th freest in the 2015 *Index*. Its score is essentially unchanged since last year, with improvements in trade freedom and freedom from corruption offset by declines in labor freedom, business freedom, and the management of public spending. Saudi Arabia is ranked 8th out of 15 countries in the Middle East/North Africa region, and its overall score remains above the world average.

Only one of Saudi Arabia's economic freedom scores has increased over the past five years. Since 2011, a drop of 4.1 points has been led by decreases in five of the 10 economic freedoms, with notable declines of 12 points in government spending and 20 points in business freedom. This has set Saudi Arabia's economy apart from the economies of some of its more freedom-minded Persian Gulf neighbors.

These trends undermine an already uneven institutional and structural economic framework. Government spending and taxation remain relatively well-maintained, with oil profits contributing well over two-thirds of government revenues. However, the rule of law remains weakly enforced, and the judiciary is strongly influenced by the royal family. A closed economy and investment regime limit technology transfers and the investment needed for economic diversification.

BACKGROUND: Saudi Arabia is an absolute monarchy ruled by King Abdallah bin Abdul Aziz Al Saud. Pro-reform Arab Spring demonstrations in 2011 drew few crowds outside of eastern Saudi Arabia, where the Shia minority population is concentrated. Most of the Sunni majority appeared to be satisfied with increased economic handouts and the king's promise of greater political participation. Saudi Arabia is the world's largest oil exporter and dominates the Organization of Petroleum Exporting Countries. Oil revenues account for about 90 percent of export earnings and about 80 percent of government revenues. Saudi Arabia joined the World Trade Organization in 2005 as part of an effort to promote foreign investment and economic diversification.

Freedom Trend

70
68
66
64
62
60
58

2011   2012   2013   2014   2015

Country Comparisons

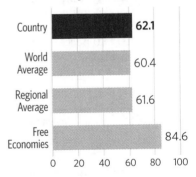

Country **62.1**
World Average 60.4
Regional Average 61.6
Free Economies 84.6

0   20   40   60   80   100

Quick Facts

Population: 30.0 million
GDP (PPP): $937.2 billion
3.8% growth in 2013
5-year compound annual growth 5.5%
$31,245 per capita
Unemployment: 5.5%
Inflation (CPI): 3.5%
FDI Inflow: $9.3 billion
Public Debt: 2.7% of GDP

2013 data unless otherwise noted.
Data compiled as of September 2014.

How Do We Measure Economic Freedom?
See page 475 for an explanation of the methodology
or visit the *Index* Web site at *heritage.org/index.*

THE TEN ECONOMIC FREEDOMS

	Score		Rank	1-Year Change
RULE OF LAW	Property Rights	40.0	70th	0
	Freedom from Corruption	46.0	63rd	+2.3

The public is aware of schemes by which oil wealth is systematically appropriated by members of the royal family (e.g., payments to "facilitators," which are often seen as required to conduct business). The slow and non-transparent judiciary is not independent and must coordinate its decisions with the executive branch. Laws protecting private property are subject to Islamic practices.

	Score		Rank	1-Year Change
GOVERNMENT SIZE	Fiscal Freedom	99.7	3rd	0
	Government Spending	61.9	103rd	−1.2

Saudi nationals and citizens of Gulf Cooperation Council countries pay no income taxes, but net worth is subject to a 2.5 percent religious tax. Foreigners pay income taxes, and non-Saudi companies pay a 20 percent corporate tax. Tax revenue equals 3.7 percent of domestic income, and public spending amounts to 35.7 percent of domestic output. Public debt equals approximately 3 percent of GDP.

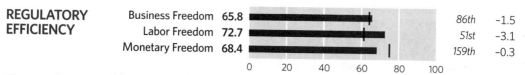

	Score		Rank	1-Year Change
REGULATORY EFFICIENCY	Business Freedom	65.8	86th	−1.5
	Labor Freedom	72.7	51st	−3.1
	Monetary Freedom	68.4	159th	−0.3

The regulatory framework is relatively sound. With no minimum capital required, starting a business takes nine procedures, but licensing requirements are time-consuming. There is no mandated minimum wage, but wage increases have exceeded labor productivity. Subsidies cover nearly 80 percent of the retail cost of electricity and fuel—one of the world's biggest such schemes.

	Score		Rank	1-Year Change
OPEN MARKETS	Trade Freedom	76.4	93rd	+2.4
	Investment Freedom	40.0	131st	0
	Financial Freedom	50.0	70th	0

Saudi Arabia's average tariff rate is 4.3 percent. Government procurement processes favor domestic businesses. Foreign investment in many sectors of the economy is restricted. The government retains considerable ownership in the financial sector, but licensing requirements for foreign investment have gradually been eased. Foreign financial firms have established a strong presence in the local investment banking and brokerage sector.

Long-Term Score Change (since 1996)

RULE OF LAW		GOVERNMENT SIZE		REGULATORY EFFICIENCY		OPEN MARKETS	
Property Rights	−50.0	Fiscal Freedom	+0.3	Business Freedom	−19.2	Trade Freedom	+17.4
Freedom from Corruption	−24.0	Government Spending	+15.6	Labor Freedom	−12.5	Investment Freedom	+10.0
				Monetary Freedom	−16.5	Financial Freedom	0

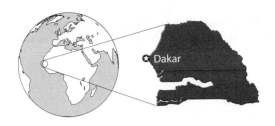

SENEGAL

Economic Freedom Score

57.8

25 — 50 — 75
Least free 0 ... 100 Most free

World Rank: 106   **Regional Rank: 16**

Senegal's economic freedom score is 57.8, making its economy the 106th freest in the 2015 *Index*. Its score has increased by 2.4 points since last year, driven by improvements in half of the 10 economic freedoms, including freedom from corruption, business freedom, and fiscal freedom, that outweigh declines in labor freedom and the management of government spending. Senegal is ranked 16th out of 46 countries in the Sub-Saharan Africa region, and its score is below the world average.

After four years of little progress, economic freedom in Senegal has advanced by 2.1 points since 2011, and the country has recorded the fourth highest score improvement of any country graded in the 2015 *Index*.

However, the Senegalese economy remains "mostly unfree." Senegal's economic freedom remains suppressed by weak rule of law and a poor regulatory environment. The judiciary lacks the resources to prevent corruption and move cases efficiently. Registering a business is expensive, and the rigid labor code confines many to informal employment.

BACKGROUND: Former President Abdoulaye Wade amended Senegal's constitution over a dozen times to augment executive power and weaken the opposition, but his run for a third term ended in his defeat by Macky Sall in March 2012. In September 2012, lawmakers voted to abolish the Senate and the vice presidency to save money for disaster management. Sall appointed Aminata Touré prime minister in 2013. After more than 30 years of conflict between the government and southern separatists, the rebel leader of the Movement of Democratic Forces of Casamance declared a unilateral cease-fire in May 2014. Economic reforms have proceeded slowly. Some 75 percent of the workforce is engaged in agriculture or fishing. High formal-sector unemployment is a major factor in high rates of emigration to Europe. Senegal remains heavily dependent on foreign aid and has suffered from the 2014 Ebola virus outbreak in West Africa.

Freedom Trend

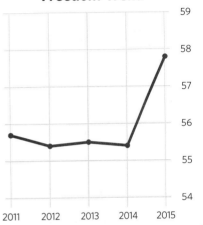

Country Comparisons

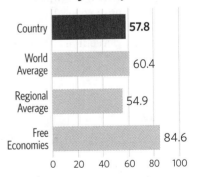

Country	57.8
World Average	60.4
Regional Average	54.9
Free Economies	84.6

Quick Facts

Population: 14.1 million
GDP (PPP): $27.7 billion
4.0% growth in 2013
5-year compound annual growth 3.2%
$1,958 per capita
Unemployment: 9.9%
Inflation (CPI): 0.8%
FDI Inflow: $298.3 million
Public Debt: 45.9% of GDP

2013 data unless otherwise noted.
Data compiled as of September 2014.

How Do We Measure Economic Freedom?
See page 475 for an explanation of the methodology
or visit the *Index* Web site at *heritage.org/index*.

THE TEN ECONOMIC FREEDOMS

		Score	Country	World Average	Rank	1-Year Change

RULE OF LAW

Property Rights 40.0 — 70th — 0
Freedom from Corruption 41.0 — 77th — +11.5

Despite steps to fight corruption, there still are few checks and balances. Several large-scale scandals have involved government construction contracts, but high-ranking officials remain largely unaccountable, and there have been few bribery or corruption convictions. The judiciary is independent but under-resourced and subject to external influences. Property titling procedures are uneven across the country.

GOVERNMENT SIZE

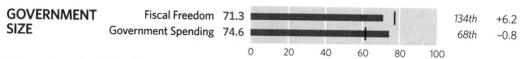

Fiscal Freedom 71.3 — 134th — +6.2
Government Spending 74.6 — 68th — -0.8

Senegal's top individual income tax rate has been lowered to 40 percent, but its top corporate tax rate has increased to 30 percent. Other taxes include a value-added tax and an insurance tax. Tax revenue equals 19.2 percent of domestic income, and government spending is equal to 29.1 percent of domestic output. Public debt equals 46 percent of GDP.

REGULATORY EFFICIENCY

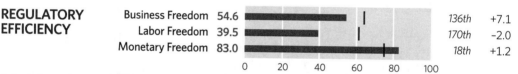

Business Freedom 54.6 — 136th — +7.1
Labor Freedom 39.5 — 170th — -2.0
Monetary Freedom 83.0 — 18th — +1.2

Administrative procedures have been streamlined, and the minimum capital required has been reduced, but the overall cost of launching a business remains high. The underdeveloped labor market still traps much of the labor force in informal economic activity. Electricity subsidies exceed 2.5 percent of GDP, reflecting prices that are about 40 percent below production costs.

OPEN MARKETS

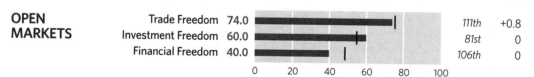

Trade Freedom 74.0 — 111th — +0.8
Investment Freedom 60.0 — 81st — 0
Financial Freedom 40.0 — 106th — 0

Senegal's average tariff rate is 8.0 percent. Non-tariff barriers restrict some agricultural imports. The government does not typically discriminate against foreign investment but may screen new investment. With 19 banks and two financial institutions, the financial sector is underdeveloped and dominated by foreign banks. The capital market remains rudimentary, and few firms have access to credit.

Long-Term Score Change (since 1996)

RULE OF LAW		GOVERNMENT SIZE		REGULATORY EFFICIENCY		OPEN MARKETS	
Property Rights	-30.0	Fiscal Freedom	+10.6	Business Freedom	-0.4	Trade Freedom	+29.0
Freedom from Corruption	-9.0	Government Spending	-12.4	Labor Freedom	-4.2	Investment Freedom	+10.0
				Monetary Freedom	+27.2	Financial Freedom	-10.0

SERBIA

Economic Freedom Score

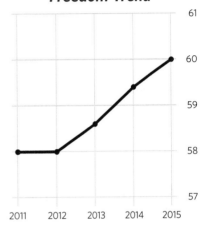

60.0

S erbia's economic freedom score is 60.0, making its economy the 90th freest in the 2015 *Index*. Its score is up by 0.6 point from last year, reflecting improvements in five of the 10 economic freedoms, including freedom from corruption, property rights, and monetary freedom, that outweigh a large deterioration in the control of government spending. Serbia is ranked 37th out of 43 countries in the Europe region, and its overall score is below the world and regional averages.

Reaching the "moderately free" category for the first time, Serbia has made substantive institutional improvements in its transition to a more market-driven economy. Over the past five years, its economic freedom has risen by 2.0 points. Gains have occurred in six of the 10 economic freedoms, with investment freedom, freedom from corruption, and monetary freedom highlighting the upward trend.

Serbia's ongoing transition to a more open and dynamic market economy will continue to require a sustained commitment to deep institutional and structural reforms. Corruption remains widespread, and the judicial system's lack of independence and transparency continues to undermine the rule of law and investors' confidence in the economy.

BACKGROUND: Serbia signed a Stability and Association Agreement with the European Union in 2008 and applied for membership in 2009. Accession talks were contingent on the arrest of wartime leader Ratko Mladic, who was apprehended in May 2011. An agreement between Serbia and Kosovo normalized relations in April 2013. The center-right Progressive Party won the early parliamentary elections in March 2014, making Aleksandar Vucic prime minister. Floods in the Balkans severely affected Serbian infrastructure in 2014 and hampered growth. Vucic continues to reform the budget and move toward an increasingly privatized economy and EU membership. Serbia's economy has attracted significant investment in manufacturing and services as it has integrated into the international economic system. However, growth remains sluggish, and unemployment is high.

Freedom Trend

Country Comparisons

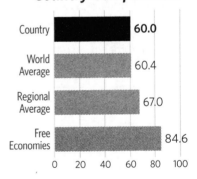

Quick Facts

Population: 7.2 million
GDP (PPP): $81.1 billion
2.5% growth in 2013
5-year compound annual growth 0.0%
$11,269 per capita
Unemployment: 22.6%
Inflation (CPI): 7.7%
FDI Inflow: $1.4 billion
Public Debt: 65.8% of GDP

2013 data unless otherwise noted.
Data compiled as of September 2014.

How Do We Measure Economic Freedom?
See page 475 for an explanation of the methodology
or visit the *Index* Web site at *heritage.org/index*.

385

THE TEN ECONOMIC FREEDOMS

		Score		Rank	1-Year Change
RULE OF LAW	Property Rights	45.0		66th	+5.0
	Freedom from Corruption	42.0		72nd	+8.0

Since 2013, the government has adopted an anti-corruption action plan, prosecuted several high-profile corruption cases, and made progress in combating organized crime and criminal networks, but corruption remains a serious concern. Despite a reform strategy that seeks to improve independence, competence, and efficiency, the courts remain vulnerable to political influence. Enforcement of property rights can be extremely slow.

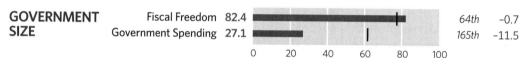

		Score		Rank	1-Year Change
GOVERNMENT SIZE	Fiscal Freedom	82.4		64th	–0.7
	Government Spending	27.1		165th	–11.5

Serbia's top individual and corporate income tax rates are 15 percent. Other taxes include a value-added tax and a property tax. The overall tax burden amounts to 36.2 percent of domestic output. Public expenditures equal 49.3 percent of domestic production, and public debt is equivalent to 66 percent of gross domestic product.

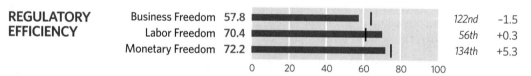

		Score		Rank	1-Year Change
REGULATORY EFFICIENCY	Business Freedom	57.8		122nd	–1.5
	Labor Freedom	70.4		56th	+0.3
	Monetary Freedom	72.2		134th	+5.3

Despite some progress, regulatory efficiency is weak. Launching a business takes slightly less than a week on average, but licensing requirements are time-consuming. Labor regulations are relatively flexible but not enforced effectively. To secure a loan from the IMF, the government abolished incentive payments to foreign investors and cut other discretionary subsidies for about 200 loss-making state firms.

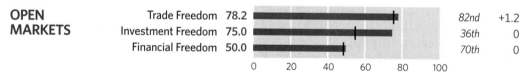

		Score		Rank	1-Year Change
OPEN MARKETS	Trade Freedom	78.2		82nd	+1.2
	Investment Freedom	75.0		36th	0
	Financial Freedom	50.0		70th	0

The average tariff rate is 5.9 percent, and efforts are being made to reduce trade barriers in order to join the WTO. Legal barriers to international trade and investment have been reduced. Foreign investment generally receives national treatment. Banking is largely stable, although two state-owned banks failed in 2013. Nonperforming loans amount to around 20 percent of total loans.

Long-Term Score Change (since 2009)

RULE OF LAW		GOVERNMENT SIZE		REGULATORY EFFICIENCY		OPEN MARKETS	
Property Rights	+5.0	Fiscal Freedom	–3.5	Business Freedom	+1.8	Trade Freedom	+0.2
Freedom from Corruption	+8.0	Government Spending	–19.2	Labor Freedom	+0.4	Investment Freedom	+35.0
				Monetary Freedom	+6.4	Financial Freedom	0

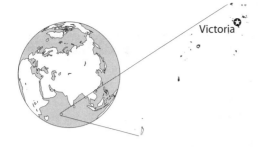
Victoria

SEYCHELLES

Economic Freedom Score

25   50   75

Least free 0   100 Most free

57.5

World Rank: **114**	Regional Rank: **20**

Seychelles' economic freedom score is 57.5, making its economy the 114th freest in the 2015 *Index*. Its score has increased by 1.3 points since last year, with declines in labor freedom and the management of government spending outweighed by considerable improvements in trade freedom and freedom from corruption that have enabled the island economy to achieve its highest economic freedom score ever. Seychelles is ranked 20th among 46 countries in the Sub-Saharan Africa region.

Seychelles has posted the fourth best record for advancing economic freedom over the past half-decade. Since 2011, Seychelles has increased its economic freedom score by 6.1 points, with scores advancing in eight of the 10 economic freedoms. Most impressively, economic freedom has not declined in any of the factors. Led by monetary stabilization and robust trade reforms, Seychelles has propelled itself to the upper tier of the "mostly unfree" category.

Seychelles' recent reform success has helped to improve a weak and uncompetitive economic framework. Despite recent improvements in government accounts, however, Seychelles was forced to accept an IMF loan in 2011 to handle its overall debt and spending levels, and the economy remains one of the most closed in the world, reducing competition and holding back investment. A restrictive business environment and strict labor regulations limit business formation and formal employment.

BACKGROUND: The People's Progressive Front has ruled Seychelles since 1977, when France Albert René seized power in a bloodless coup. In 2004, René ceded power to Vice President James Michel. Michel was elected to a third five-year term in May 2011. Seychelles enjoys a relatively stable economic environment as a high-middle-income country with a lucrative fishing and tourism industry. Piracy remains a significant threat off the coast of Seychelles. In early 2013, tropical cyclone Felleng brought torrential rain, flooding, and landslides that destroyed hundreds of houses.

Freedom Trend

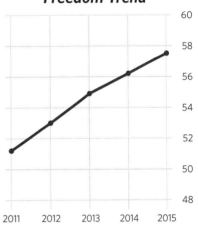

60

58

56

54

52

50

48

2011   2012   2013   2014   2015

Country Comparisons

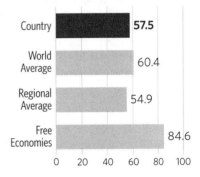

Country	57.5
World Average	60.4
Regional Average	54.9
Free Economies	84.6

0   20   40   60   80   100

Quick Facts

Population: 0.1 million
GDP (PPP): $2.5 billion
3.6% growth in 2013
5-year compound annual growth 3.8%
$26,492 per capita
Unemployment: n/a
Inflation (CPI): 4.3%
FDI Inflow: $177.6 million
Public Debt: 62.0% of GDP

2013 data unless otherwise noted.
Data compiled as of September 2014.

How Do We Measure Economic Freedom?
See page 475 for an explanation of the methodology or visit the *Index* Web site at *heritage.org/index*.

THE TEN ECONOMIC FREEDOMS

		Score		Rank	1-Year Change
RULE OF LAW	Property Rights	50.0		56th	0
	Freedom from Corruption	54.0		46th	+5.5

Corruption and extensive drug trafficking and money-laundering continue to plague the archipelago. Concerns over government corruption have focused on a lack of transparency in the privatization and allocation of government-owned land as well as dysfunction in government finances, illegal procedures, and embezzlement. Judges generally decide cases fairly but face interference in high-level economic and political cases.

		Score		Rank	1-Year Change
GOVERNMENT SIZE	Fiscal Freedom	79.8		87th	+3.0
	Government Spending	59.4		117th	−2.4

The top individual income tax rate is 15 percent, and the top corporate tax rate is 33 percent. Other taxes include a vehicle tax, a tax on interest, and a new value-added tax. Overall tax revenues equal 26.6 percent of domestic income, and government expenditures amount to 36.8 of percent domestic production. Public debt is equivalent to 62 percent of GDP.

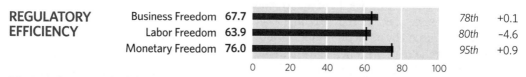

		Score		Rank	1-Year Change
REGULATORY EFFICIENCY	Business Freedom	67.7		78th	+0.1
	Labor Freedom	63.9		80th	−4.6
	Monetary Freedom	76.0		95th	+0.9

The requirements for incorporating a business have been simplified, but regulatory inefficiency and lack of transparency still hamper the regulatory environment. The labor market remains inefficient, and the public sector is the main source of employment. Inflation stabilized at a low level in 2013, aided by exchange rate strength, and the state rebalanced utility prices to cut implicit subsidies.

		Score		Rank	1-Year Change
OPEN MARKETS	Trade Freedom	44.0		179th	+10.6
	Investment Freedom	50.0		109th	0
	Financial Freedom	30.0		131st	0

The average tariff rate was 28.3 percent as of 2007. Reliance on tariff revenues has declined but remains relatively high. Foreign investors can repatriate profits. Foreign investment in many sectors is restricted. The financial sector, dominated by banks, offers offshore services. The government owns two of the largest banks. The capital market is evolving, and there is a stock exchange.

Long-Term Score Change (since 2009)

RULE OF LAW		GOVERNMENT SIZE		REGULATORY EFFICIENCY		OPEN MARKETS	
Property Rights	0	Fiscal Freedom	+6.0	Business Freedom	+2.2	Trade Freedom	+15.6
Freedom from Corruption	+9.0	Government Spending	+59.4	Labor Freedom	+6.8	Investment Freedom	0
				Monetary Freedom	−2.1	Financial Freedom	0

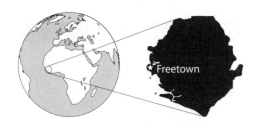
★ Freetown

SIERRA LEONE

Economic Freedom Score

51.7

Sierra Leone's economic freedom score is 51.7, making its economy the 147th freest in the 2015 *Index*. Its score has increased by 1.2 points since last year, with improvements in labor freedom, freedom from corruption, and the control of government spending outweighing deteriorations in property rights and business freedom. Sierra Leone is ranked 36th out of 46 countries in the Sub-Saharan Africa region, and its overall score is below the world average.

Advances in the past two years have lifted Sierra Leone out of the "repressed" category for the first time since 1996. Over the past five years, economic freedom in Sierra Leone has advanced by 2.1 points, led by improvements in half of the 10 economic freedoms, including trade freedom and investment freedom.

Years of civil war, disease, and political unrest have left property rights either nonexistent or poorly established, with no land-titling system. The poor entrepreneurial environment is exacerbated by underdeveloped capital markets and restrictions on trade and investment. Strict labor market regulations undermine efforts to improve formal employment and prosperity.

BACKGROUND: In 2002, Sierra Leone emerged from a decade of civil war that displaced more than 2 million people. Opposition candidate Ernest Bai Koroma, elected president in 2007 in the first peaceful transition of power since independence from Britain in 1961, was re-elected in 2012. Despite some institutional progress since the end of the civil war, living standards remain very low. According to the U.N.'s Human Development Index, which measures things like infant mortality, literacy, and life expectancy, Sierra Leone ranks 177th out of 187 countries. Infrastructure is inadequate, corruption is pervasive, and the population is mostly poor. Mining is the primary industry. Mineral exports are the principal foreign exchange source, with gem-quality diamonds accounting for nearly half of exports and high rates of economic growth. In 2014, West Africa's Ebola virus spread to Sierra Leone.

Freedom Trend

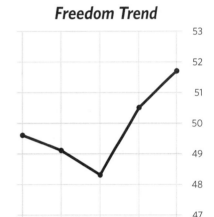

Country Comparisons

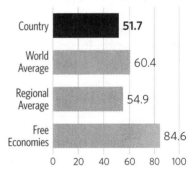

Quick Facts

Population: 6.1 million
GDP (PPP): $9.4 billion
16.3% growth in 2013
5-year compound annual growth 9.1%
$1,542 per capita
Unemployment: 3.2%
Inflation (CPI): 9.8%
FDI Inflow: $579.1 million
Public Debt: 32.6% of GDP

2013 data unless otherwise noted.
Data compiled as of September 2014.

How Do We Measure Economic Freedom?
See page 475 for an explanation of the methodology
or visit the *Index* Web site at *heritage.org/index*.

THE TEN ECONOMIC FREEDOMS

		Score		Rank	1-Year Change
RULE OF LAW	Property Rights	10.0		165th	−5.0
	Freedom from Corruption	30.0		121st	+5.4

Corruption remains rampant throughout government and the economy, with high-profile allegations of corruption against bankers, police officers, and government officials and long-standing accounting irregularities that led to a one-year suspension in 2013 from the Extractive Industries Transparency Initiative. There is no land titling system, and judicial corruption is significant. Traditional tribal justice systems prevail in rural areas.

		Score		Rank	1-Year Change
GOVERNMENT SIZE	Fiscal Freedom	80.8		75th	+0.1
	Government Spending	87.5		22nd	+1.8

Sierra Leone's top individual and corporate income tax rates are 30 percent. Other taxes include a goods and services tax and a tax on interest. The overall tax burden is equivalent to 11.1 percent of domestic output, and government expenditures equal 20.4 percent of GDP. Public debt equals approximately 33 percent of gross domestic product.

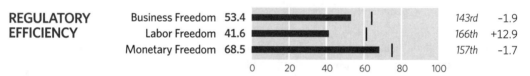

		Score		Rank	1-Year Change
REGULATORY EFFICIENCY	Business Freedom	53.4		143rd	−1.9
	Labor Freedom	41.6		166th	+12.9
	Monetary Freedom	68.5		157th	−1.7

The procedure for establishing a business has been simplified, but licensing requirements remain burdensome. Rudimentary labor regulations have little impact, as much of the labor force is employed in the informal sector. Consumer price inflation has receded to single digits, underpinned by increased food supply, but the government still subsidizes electricity production, health care, and education.

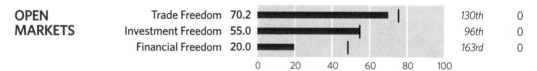

		Score		Rank	1-Year Change
OPEN MARKETS	Trade Freedom	70.2		130th	0
	Investment Freedom	55.0		96th	0
	Financial Freedom	20.0		163rd	0

Sierra Leone's average tariff rate is 9.9 percent. The government is working to modernize customs procedures in order to facilitate trade. Sierra Leone does not allow foreign investors to own land. Modernization and strengthening of the banking sector, defunct during the civil war, is ongoing. A small stock exchange has been in operation since 2007.

Long-Term Score Change (since 1995)

RULE OF LAW		GOVERNMENT SIZE		REGULATORY EFFICIENCY		OPEN MARKETS	
Property Rights	−40.0	Fiscal Freedom	+29.1	Business Freedom	−16.6	Trade Freedom	+25.2
Freedom from Corruption	+20.0	Government Spending	−4.0	Labor Freedom	+9.1	Investment Freedom	+5.0
				Monetary Freedom	+18.6	Financial Freedom	−10.0

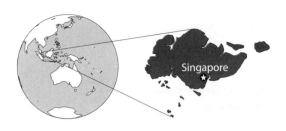

SINGAPORE

Economic Freedom Score

Least free 0 — Most free 100

89.4

World Rank: 2   **Regional Rank: 2**

Singapore's economic freedom score is 89.4, making its economy the 2nd freest in the 2015 *Index*. Its score is unchanged from last year, with gains in the management of government spending, monetary freedom, and labor freedom offset by a slightly lower score for freedom from corruption. Only 0.2 point behind Hong Kong, Singapore ranks 2nd out of 42 countries in the Asia–Pacific region.

Already benefiting from one of the world's highest levels of economic freedom, Singapore has reinforced its commitment to continued reform. Over the past five years, the small city economy has advanced its economic freedom by 2.1 points, the largest score increase among the 10 freest economies. Sustained efforts to build a world-class financial center and further open its market to global commerce have led to advances in four of the 10 economic freedoms, including financial freedom and investment freedom.

A highly educated and motivated workforce has added to the economy's dynamism and resilience, reinforcing Singapore's innovative capacity. Singaporean society has a low tolerance for corruption, and the effective rule of law strongly undergirds all aspects of economic development. More work to reduce the state's involvement in key sectors will be necessary to realize continued advances in economic freedom.

BACKGROUND: Singapore is a nominally democratic state that has been ruled by the People's Action Party (PAP) since independence in 1965. The PAP won 81 out of 87 seats in the legislature in the May 2011 elections, although its percentage of the vote (just over 60 percent) was the lowest in history. The opposition won another seat in 2013 during a special election. Certain civil liberties, such as freedom of assembly and freedom of speech, remain restricted, but the PAP has embraced economic liberalization and international trade. Singapore is one of the world's most prosperous nations. Its economy is dominated by services, but the country is also a major manufacturer of electronics and chemicals.

Freedom Trend

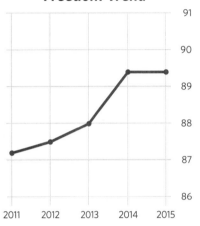

Country Comparisons

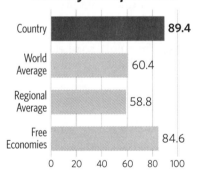

Quick Facts

Population: 5.4 million
GDP (PPP): $348.7 billion
4.1% growth in 2013
5-year compound annual growth 5.2%
$64,584 per capita
Unemployment: 3.1%
Inflation (CPI): 2.4%
FDI Inflow: $63.8 billion
Public Debt: 103.8% of GDP

2013 data unless otherwise noted.
Data compiled as of September 2014.

How Do We Measure Economic Freedom?
See page 475 for an explanation of the methodology
or visit the *Index* Web site at *heritage.org/index*.

THE TEN ECONOMIC FREEDOMS

		Score		Rank	1-Year Change
RULE OF LAW	Property Rights	90.0		3rd	0
	Freedom from Corruption	86.0		5th	–5.9

Singapore has traditionally been lauded for its lack of corruption. As in most countries, there are ongoing concerns over issues of transparency and the power of deeply entrenched groups. Political speech is regulated, inhibiting organized pressure for policy changes. Contracts are secure, there is no expropriation, and commercial courts function well. Singapore has one of Asia's best intellectual property regimes.

		Score		Rank	1-Year Change
GOVERNMENT SIZE	Fiscal Freedom	91.2		26th	0
	Government Spending	93.8		4th	+2.6

The top individual income tax rate is 20 percent, and the top corporate tax rate is 17 percent. Other taxes include a value-added tax and a tax on property. The overall tax burden equals 14 percent of domestic production. Government expenditures are equivalent to 14.4 percent of the domestic economy, and public debt equals 104 percent of gross domestic product.

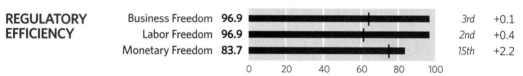

		Score		Rank	1-Year Change
REGULATORY EFFICIENCY	Business Freedom	96.9		3rd	+0.1
	Labor Freedom	96.9		2nd	+0.4
	Monetary Freedom	83.7		15th	+2.2

Singapore's regulatory framework is one of the world's most efficient. Starting a business takes three days, and required procedures are straightforward. No minimum wage is enforced, but wage adjustments are guided by the National Wage Council. The state funds housing, education, transport, and health care subsidy programs and influences other prices through regulations and state-linked enterprises.

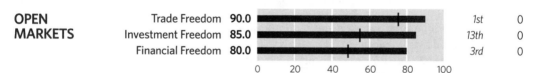

		Score		Rank	1-Year Change
OPEN MARKETS	Trade Freedom	90.0		1st	0
	Investment Freedom	85.0		13th	0
	Financial Freedom	80.0		3rd	0

The average tariff rate is 0 percent. Imports of chewing gum and "objectionable" publications are restricted, and some service industries face barriers. Foreign investment is welcomed, but investment in several sectors is restricted. The banking-dominated financial system is well supported by liquid capital markets. As of 2014, 119 of 124 banks were foreign. The state retains some ownership in the financial sector.

Long-Term Score Change (since 1995)

RULE OF LAW		GOVERNMENT SIZE		REGULATORY EFFICIENCY		OPEN MARKETS	
Property Rights	0	Fiscal Freedom	+10.4	Business Freedom	–3.1	Trade Freedom	+7.0
Freedom from Corruption	–4.0	Government Spending	+5.7	Labor Freedom	–1.3	Investment Freedom	–5.0
				Monetary Freedom	–1.5	Financial Freedom	+10.0

Bratislava

SLOVAKIA

Economic Freedom Score

Least free 0   100 Most free

67.2

Slovakia's economic freedom score is 67.2, making its economy the 50th freest in the 2015 *Index*. Its score has increased by 0.8 point from last year, with improvements in freedom from corruption, business freedom, and labor freedom outweighing declines in monetary freedom and the management of government spending. Slovakia is ranked 22nd out of 43 countries in the Europe region, and its overall score is higher than the world average.

Economic freedom has not fared as well in Slovakia as it has in other Eastern European countries in recent years. In fact, over the past five years, economic freedom in Slovakia has declined by 2.3 points. Score declines have been concentrated largely in the fiscal and regulatory spheres, led by drops of 8.0 points in the control of government spending and labor freedom.

Slovakia's basic economic environment still needs improvement. The rule of law is weak, allowing corruption to flourish, and there is a lack of transparency in the government and state-owned sector. Despite some progress, business regulations remain inefficient, and labor market rigidity has prolonged the downside of business cycles. The financial crisis and the weak regional environment have undermined public finances. The government's long-term commitment to economic freedom must be renewed to boost prosperity and competition.

BACKGROUND: After Slovakia gained independence in 1993, market reforms made it one of Europe's most attractive destinations for capital. Slovakia entered the European Union in 2004 and has been part of the eurozone since 2009. Andrej Kiska was elected president in 2014 and reappointed Robert Fico, who had been serving since 2012, as prime minister. Fico has enacted new measures aimed at reducing tax evasion and fraud. In 2014, there were divisions within the government about the role of NATO and the correct response to the crisis in Ukraine.

Freedom Trend

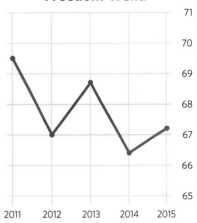

Country Comparisons

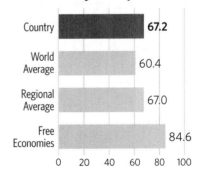

Quick Facts

Population: 5.4 million
GDP (PPP): $133.1 billion
0.9% growth in 2013
5-year compound annual growth 1.0%
$24,605 per capita
Unemployment: 14.0%
Inflation (CPI): 1.5%
FDI Inflow: $591.0 million
Public Debt: 54.9% of GDP

2013 data unless otherwise noted.
Data compiled as of September 2014.

THE TEN ECONOMIC FREEDOMS

		Score		Rank	1-Year Change
RULE OF LAW	Property Rights	50.0		56th	0
	Freedom from Corruption	47.0		61st	+5.2

Corruption is significant, notably in public procurement and health care. Many state-owned companies do not publish even basic information. The constitution provides for an independent judiciary, but notwithstanding some reforms, the court system continues to be burdened by corruption, intimidation of judges, and a significant backlog of cases. Secured interests in property and contractual rights are enforced.

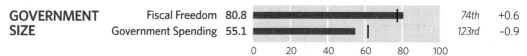

		Score		Rank	1-Year Change
GOVERNMENT SIZE	Fiscal Freedom	80.8		74th	+0.6
	Government Spending	55.1		123rd	−0.9

Slovakia's top individual income tax rate is 25 percent, and its top corporate tax rate has been reduced to 22 percent. Other taxes include a value-added tax and a property tax. Tax revenues equal approximately 28.5 percent of domestic income. Public expenditures amount to 38.7 percent of gross domestic production, and government debt equals 55 percent of GDP.

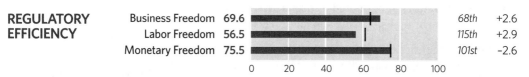

		Score		Rank	1-Year Change
REGULATORY EFFICIENCY	Business Freedom	69.6		68th	+2.6
	Labor Freedom	56.5		115th	+2.9
	Monetary Freedom	75.5		101st	−2.6

Despite progress in streamlining the process for launching a business, other time-consuming requirements reduce the efficiency of the regulatory system. Rigid labor regulations hamper dynamic employment growth. In 2013, the government adopted the new EU agricultural policy for 2014–2020 that will reduce per hectare subsidies for large farms but increase them for smaller ones.

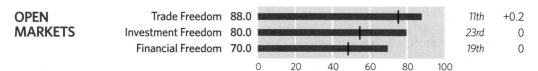

		Score		Rank	1-Year Change
OPEN MARKETS	Trade Freedom	88.0		11th	+0.2
	Investment Freedom	80.0		23rd	0
	Financial Freedom	70.0		19th	0

EU members have a 1.0 percent average tariff rate. Although some non-tariff barriers exist, the EU is relatively open to external trade. Slovakia generally treats foreign and domestic investment equally under the law. The relatively well-regulated financial market continues to grow. The predominantly foreign-owned banking sector is well capitalized, but the recently doubled bank levy discourages dynamic lending.

Long-Term Score Change (since 1995)

RULE OF LAW		GOVERNMENT SIZE		REGULATORY EFFICIENCY		OPEN MARKETS	
Property Rights	−20.0	Fiscal Freedom	+23.1	Business Freedom	−15.4	Trade Freedom	+13.0
Freedom from Corruption	−3.0	Government Spending	+32.8	Labor Freedom	−19.2	Investment Freedom	+10.0
				Monetary Freedom	+12.2	Financial Freedom	+20.0

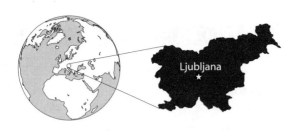

Ljubljana ★

SLOVENIA

Economic Freedom Score

50
25   75
Least free 0   100 Most free

60.3

World Rank: 88   **Regional Rank: 36**

Slovenia's economic freedom score is 60.3, making its economy the 88th freest in the 2015 *Index*. Its score has decreased by 2.4 points since last year, reflecting a combined decline in the management of public spending, business freedom, and freedom from corruption that dwarfs improvements in labor freedom and monetary freedom. Slovenia is ranked 36th out of 43 countries in the Europe region, and its overall score is just below the world average.

Over the past five years, economic freedom in Slovenia has fallen by 4.3 points, the biggest decline in Europe other than in Greece and Cyprus. A decline of more than 40 points in the control of government spending has led to a deterioration of fiscal soundness that has pushed Slovenia close to losing its status as a "moderately free" economy.

Slovenia's rising government spending and failure to privatize industries after its transition from Communism underline its structural problems. The labor market remains rigid despite reform efforts, and the lack of overall regulatory efficiency limits private-sector growth. While property rights are respected, the level of perceived corruption has increased.

BACKGROUND: The government of Slovenian Democratic Party Prime Minister Janez Janša collapsed in February 2013. Janša was subsequently convicted of corruption and began serving a two-year prison sentence in June 2014. In July 2014, Miro Cerar's new SMC party won a plurality of seats in parliament with about 35 percent of the popular vote. Privatizations and efforts to reduce the public sector have been slowed by instability. The government still controls about half of the economy. A government bailout of over €3 billion went to banks carrying bad loans in December 2013. Slovenia joined the European Union and NATO in 2004, adopted the euro in 2007, and joined the Organisation for Economic Co-operation and Development in 2010. The country has excellent infrastructure and an educated workforce.

Freedom Trend

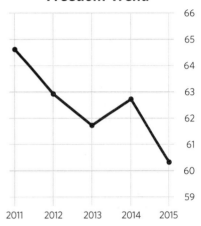

66
65
64
63
62
61
60
59

2011   2012   2013   2014   2015

Country Comparisons

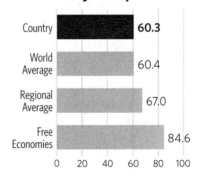

Country	**60.3**
World Average	60.4
Regional Average	67.0
Free Economies	84.6

0   20   40   60   80   100

Quick Facts

Population: 2.1 million
GDP (PPP): $57.4 billion
-1.1% growth in 2013
5-year compound annual growth -2.0%
$27,900 per capita
Unemployment: 10.6%
Inflation (CPI): 1.6%
FDI Inflow: -$678.6 million
Public Debt: 73.0% of GDP

2013 data unless otherwise noted.
Data compiled as of September 2014.

How Do We Measure Economic Freedom?
See page 475 for an explanation of the methodology or visit the *Index* Web site at *heritage.org/index*.

THE TEN ECONOMIC FREEDOMS

		Score		Rank	1-Year Change
RULE OF LAW	Property Rights	60.0		41st	0
	Freedom from Corruption	57.0		42nd	-4.0

Corruption, while less extensive than in some other Central European countries, remains a problem, usually involving conflicts of interest and contracting links between government officials and private businesses. The judicial system is sound and transparent but remains comparatively inefficient, understaffed, and plagued by a large case backlog. Private property rights are constitutionally guaranteed, but enforcement is slow.

		Score		Rank	1-Year Change
GOVERNMENT SIZE	Fiscal Freedom	58.1		169th	-0.8
	Government Spending	0.0		176th	-22.6

Slovenia's top individual income tax rate is 50 percent, and its corporate tax rate has increased to 17 percent. Other taxes include a value-added tax and a property transfer tax. The overall tax burden equals 37.4 percent of the domestic economy. Public expenditures amount to 59.4 percent of domestic income, and government debt is equal to 73 percent of GDP.

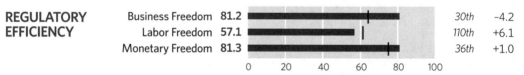

		Score		Rank	1-Year Change
REGULATORY EFFICIENCY	Business Freedom	81.2		30th	-4.2
	Labor Freedom	57.1		110th	+6.1
	Monetary Freedom	81.3		36th	+1.0

The overall regulatory framework has undergone a series of reforms aimed at facilitating entrepreneurial activity, but the pace of reform has slowed. A labor market reform in 2013 has reduced the costs of hiring and layoffs. The IMF urged the government to cut numerous subsidies and transfers, but renewable energy subsidies were increased by over 30 percent.

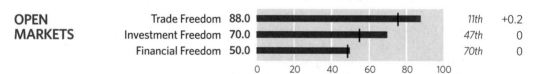

		Score		Rank	1-Year Change
OPEN MARKETS	Trade Freedom	88.0		11th	+0.2
	Investment Freedom	70.0		47th	0
	Financial Freedom	50.0		70th	0

EU members have a 1.0 percent average tariff rate. Although some non-tariff barriers exist, the EU is relatively open to external trade. Slovenia generally treats foreign and domestic investors equally. With economic stagnation continuing, nonperforming loans have increased and undermine overall banking soundness. The state continues to retain ownership in the banking sector.

Long-Term Score Change (since 1996)

RULE OF LAW		GOVERNMENT SIZE		REGULATORY EFFICIENCY		OPEN MARKETS	
Property Rights	+30.0	Fiscal Freedom	-11.2	Business Freedom	+11.2	Trade Freedom	+29.0
Freedom from Corruption	+27.0	Government Spending	-34.6	Labor Freedom	+16.8	Investment Freedom	+40.0
				Monetary Freedom	+20.8	Financial Freedom	-20.0

SOLOMON ISLANDS

Honiara

Economic Freedom Score

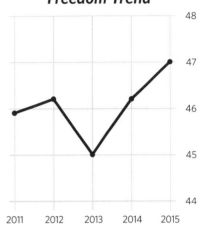

Least free 0

25 50 75

Most free 100

47.0

T he Solomon Islands' economic freedom score is 47.0, making its economy the 159th freest in the 2015 *Index*. Its score is up by 0.8 point from last year, reflecting gains in the management of government spending, labor freedom, and business freedom that outweigh losses in monetary freedom and fiscal freedom. The Solomon Islands is ranked 36th out of 42 countries in the Asia–Pacific region. Although it has registered its highest economic freedom score ever in the 2015 *Index*, its overall score continues to be far below the world average.

Failure to fully embrace the principles of economic freedom has exacerbated poverty and undermined sustained development on the Solomon Islands. However, over the past five years, economic freedom in the island economy has advanced by 1.1 points. Efforts to open the economy to trade and investment have more than offset declines in the fiscal environment and freedom from corruption.

Nevertheless, the trade and investment environment remains weak. Trade restrictions are present on exports and imports, and the government screens foreign investment. The independence of the judicial system is threatened by corruption and political meddling. The government controls more than half of the domestic economy.

BACKGROUND: The Solomon Islands is a parliamentary democracy and one of Asia's poorest nations. Danny Philip's election as prime minister in 2010 stabilized a chaotic political environment, but allegations of corruption forced Philip to resign in 2011 rather than face a motion of no confidence. Gordon Darcy Lilo won the next election, held shortly thereafter. In recent years, Australia has had to intervene several times to defuse ethnic conflict, which holds back economic development. Australia, the European Union, Japan, New Zealand, and Taiwan provide significant financial aid. Most of the population lives in rural communities, and three-fourths of the workforce is engaged in subsistence farming and fishing. Growth depends largely on logging and timber exports.

Freedom Trend

(graph values: 2011 ≈ 46, 2012 ≈ 46.5, 2013 = 45, 2014 ≈ 46.5, 2015 = 47; y-axis 44 to 48)

Country Comparisons

Country	47.0
World Average	60.4
Regional Average	58.8
Free Economies	84.6

0 20 40 60 80 100

Quick Facts

Population: 0.6 million
GDP (PPP): $1.9 billion
2.9% growth in 2013
5-year compound annual growth 4.2%
$3,455 per capita
Unemployment: 3.9%
Inflation (CPI): 6.1%
FDI Inflow: $105.3 million
Public Debt: 14.6% of GDP

2013 data unless otherwise noted.
Data compiled as of September 2014.

How Do We Measure Economic Freedom?
See page 475 for an explanation of the methodology
or visit the *Index* Web site at *heritage.org/index*.

THE TEN ECONOMIC FREEDOMS

		Score	■ Country	World Average	Rank	1-Year Change

RULE OF LAW

Property Rights 30.0 — 94th 0
Freedom from Corruption 25.0 — 149th 0

Corruption is pervasive, and public offices are seen as opportunities for personal enrichment. Many current and former lawmakers have faced corruption charges. Threats against judges and prosecutors have weakened the judicial system's independence and rigor. Judges and prosecutors have been implicated in scandals relating to corruption and abuse of power. Land ownership is reserved for Solomon Islanders.

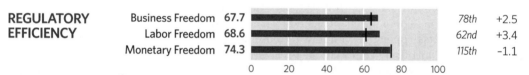

GOVERNMENT SIZE

Fiscal Freedom 61.1 — 167th −0.3
Government Spending 25.7 — 167th +4.4

The Solomon Islands' top individual income tax rate is 40 percent, and its top corporate tax rate is 30 percent. Other taxes include a property tax and a sales tax. The overall tax burden amounts to 37.3 percent of the domestic economy. Government spending equals 49.8 percent of domestic output, and public debt is equivalent to 15 percent of gross domestic product.

REGULATORY EFFICIENCY

Business Freedom 67.7 — 78th +2.5
Labor Freedom 68.6 — 62nd +3.4
Monetary Freedom 74.3 — 115th −1.1

Implementation of a simplified registration process has improved the business environment but only marginally. The regulatory process continues to be undermined by uneven enforcement of existing laws. The labor market is underdeveloped, and informal labor activity remains substantial. About one-third of total public spending subsidizes infrastructure development projects, many of them funded by international donors.

OPEN MARKETS

Trade Freedom 73.0 — 113th 0
Investment Freedom 15.0 — 168th 0
Financial Freedom 30.0 — 131st 0

The Solomon Islands' average tariff rate is 8.5 percent. Some natural resources are subject to export taxes. Foreign investment is screened, and investment in many sectors is restricted. A small number of banks dominate the underdeveloped financial sector. The level of financial intermediation remains low, and access to credit for small and medium-sized companies remains very limited.

Long-Term Score Change (since 2009)

RULE OF LAW		GOVERNMENT SIZE		REGULATORY EFFICIENCY		OPEN MARKETS	
Property Rights	0	Fiscal Freedom	−7.8	Business Freedom	+0.5	Trade Freedom	+6.6
Freedom from Corruption	−3.0	Government Spending	+25.7	Labor Freedom	−7.7	Investment Freedom	−5.0
				Monetary Freedom	+0.8	Financial Freedom	0

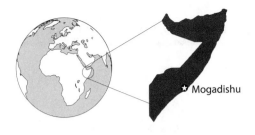

SOMALIA

World Rank: Not Ranked   Regional Rank: Not Ranked

Economic Freedom Score

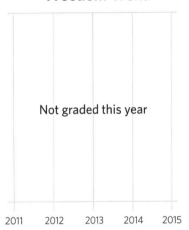

This economy is not graded

S omalia's economic freedom remains unrated due to a severe lack of reliable data caused by ongoing political instability. The last time Somalia was fully graded and ranked was in the 2000 *Index* when it received a score of only 27.8.

Violence and political unrest have prevented Somalia from developing a coherent and coordinated domestic marketplace. The central government controls only part of the country, and formal economic activity is largely relegated to urban areas like Mogadishu. Progress toward economic normalization is continuing as the government takes back more land from the rebels.

Lack of central authority makes the rule of law inconsistent and fragmented, with different militias, authorities, and tribes applying varying legal frameworks. Traditional customs, like Sharia law, have become more entrenched. Corruption remains high, and a lack of transparency and formal book-keeping means that government revenues are easily embezzled. Establishment of government control and security will be vital for fostering broad-based economic freedom based on consistent rules and regulations.

BACKGROUND: Somalia has been in chaos since the collapse of the Siad Barre regime in 1991 and the subsequent civil war. When a U.N. humanitarian mission's mandate ended in 1995, the transitional government was forced to rely on the African Union's peacekeeping mission to protect civilians. A provisional constitution was passed in August 2012, and Hassan Sheikh Mohamud was elected president in September. The Islamist terrorist organization al-Shabaab remains a potent threat. There was an upsurge in attacks by maritime pirates off the coast in 2013 and 2014. Somalia's GDP and living standards are among the lowest in the world. The population is dependent on foreign aid. Economic growth is slowly expanding beyond Mogadishu, which has been recovering since al-Shabaab retreated to rural areas in 2011. In September 2014, the leader of al-Shabaab, Ahmed Abdi Godane, was killed in a U.S. airstrike; he was replaced by Ahmed Omar.

Freedom Trend

Not graded this year

2011   2012   2013   2014   2015

Country Comparisons

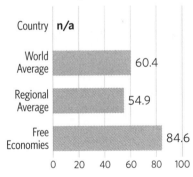

Country	n/a
World Average	60.4
Regional Average	54.9
Free Economies	84.6

Quick Facts

Population: 10.4 million
GDP (PPP): $5.9 billion (2010)
2.6% growth in 2010
5-year compound annual growth n/a
$600 per capita (2010)
Unemployment: n/a
Inflation (CPI): n/a
FDI Inflow: n/a
Public Debt: n/a

2013 data unless otherwise noted.
Data compiled as of September 2014.

THE TEN ECONOMIC FREEDOMS

		Score	■ Country | World Average	Rank	1-Year Change
RULE OF LAW	Property Rights	n/a		—	n/a
	Freedom from Corruption	8.0		182nd	+3.0

Somalia is tied with North Korea and Afghanistan for last place among 177 countries in Transparency International's 2013 Corruption Perceptions Index. According to a 2013 U.N. Monitoring Group report, government officials used the central bank as a "slush fund," with an average of 80 percent of withdrawals made for private purposes. There is no functioning national judicial system.

		Score		Rank	1-Year Change
GOVERNMENT SIZE	Fiscal Freedom	n/a		—	n/a
	Government Spending	n/a		—	n/a

Somalia's central government lacks the ability to administer taxes or provide basic services effectively. Little effective fiscal policy exists, although some duties and taxes are collected. Most government expenditures are financed through aid. Warlords and militias continue to collect levies from the population, particularly in the south of the country.

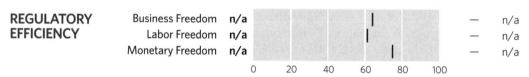

		Score		Rank	1-Year Change
REGULATORY EFFICIENCY	Business Freedom	n/a		—	n/a
	Labor Freedom	n/a		—	n/a
	Monetary Freedom	n/a		—	n/a

Institutional shortcomings, including absence of the rule of law, severely impede any meaningful and sustained economic activity. A functioning formal labor market is nearly absent, and much of the labor force is employed in the informal sector. Despite almost nonexistent national governance, the informal agricultural, financial, and telecommunications sectors have prospered without subsidies.

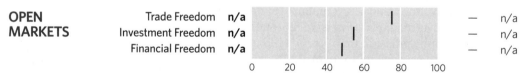

		Score		Rank	1-Year Change
OPEN MARKETS	Trade Freedom	n/a		—	n/a
	Investment Freedom	n/a		—	n/a
	Financial Freedom	n/a		—	n/a

Violence in Somalia has deterred international trade and investment flows. Political instability, an outmoded regulatory environment, and inadequate infrastructure continue to suppress development of the financial sector, which has been under reconstruction following the civil war. A large portion of the population remains outside of the formal banking sector, and access to credit remains severely inadequate.

Long-Term Score Change: n/a

RULE OF LAW		GOVERNMENT SIZE		REGULATORY EFFICIENCY		OPEN MARKETS	
Property Rights	n/a	Fiscal Freedom	n/a	Business Freedom	n/a	Trade Freedom	n/a
Freedom from Corruption	n/a	Government Spending		Labor Freedom	n/a	Investment Freedom	n/a
				Monetary Freedom	n/a	Financial Freedom	n/a

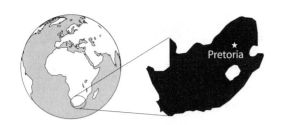

SOUTH AFRICA

Economic Freedom Score

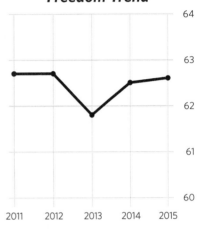

Least free 0

Most free 100

62.6

South Africa's economic freedom score is 62.6, making its economy the 72nd freest in the 2015 *Index*. Its score is essentially unchanged from last year, with a 0.1-point gain reflecting improvements in labor freedom, fiscal freedom, trade freedom, and freedom from corruption that are largely offset by declines in investment freedom, business freedom, and the management of government spending. South Africa is ranked 6th out of 46 countries in the Sub-Saharan Africa region, and its overall score is higher than the world and regional averages.

South Africa's large domestic market and natural resource base make it a promising candidate for economic freedom–led growth. However, recent labor unrest and falling commodity prices have undermined growth and tarnished the economy's investment reputation.

More committed structural and institutional reform is needed. Pervasive corruption jeopardizes the rule of law. Rigid labor market regulations and the inefficient regulatory framework perpetuate high unemployment and underemployment. Non-tariff barriers constrict gains from global trade. The regionally significant financial sector has been helped by deregulation and remains a model for further reforms.

BACKGROUND: Jacob Zuma of the African National Congress was elected president by the National Assembly in 2009 and re-elected by an ANC-dominated parliament for another five years in May 2014. The ANC has directed politics since the end of apartheid in 1994. South Africa is sub-Saharan Africa's second-largest economy and one of the world's largest producers and exporters of gold and platinum. Mining, services, manufacturing, and agriculture rival similar sectors in the developed world. Many South Africans are poor, and the country has high formal-sector unemployment and crime, low-quality public education, and a lack of access to infrastructure and basic services. Strikes by miners in 2014 brought platinum mining to a halt. In June 2014, Zuma and the ANC announced a National Development Plan that was claimed would stimulate economic growth using a market-based, long-term strategy.

Freedom Trend

Country Comparisons

Country	**62.6**
World Average	60.4
Regional Average	54.9
Free Economies	84.6

0   20   40   60   80   100

Quick Facts

Population: 53.0 million
GDP (PPP): $596.5 billion
1.9% growth in 2013
5-year compound annual growth 1.9%
$11,269 per capita
Unemployment: 25.3%
Inflation (CPI): 5.8%
FDI Inflow: $8.2 billion
Public Debt: 45.2% of GDP

2013 data unless otherwise noted.
Data compiled as of September 2014.

How Do We Measure Economic Freedom?
See page 475 for an explanation of the methodology
or visit the *Index* Web site at *heritage.org/index*.

THE TEN ECONOMIC FREEDOMS

		Score		Rank	1-Year Change
RULE OF LAW	Property Rights	50.0		56th	0
	Freedom from Corruption	42.0		72nd	+0.4

Notwithstanding more than 700 charges of fraud and corruption controversially dropped before his first election in 2009, President Zuma was re-elected in 2014. Public procurement is often politically driven and opaque, and enforcement of anti-corruption statutes is inadequate. Although judicial and prosecutorial independence is under political pressure, property rights are relatively well protected. Contracts are generally secure.

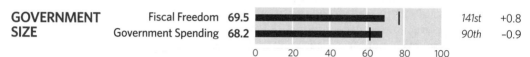

		Score		Rank	1-Year Change
GOVERNMENT SIZE	Fiscal Freedom	69.5		141st	+0.8
	Government Spending	68.2		90th	-0.9

The top individual income tax rate is 40 percent, and the top corporate tax rate is 28 percent. Other taxes include a value-added tax and a capital gains tax. The overall tax burden equals 25.8 percent of domestic income. Public expenditures amount to 32.6 percent of domestic production, and government debt equals 45 percent of gross domestic product.

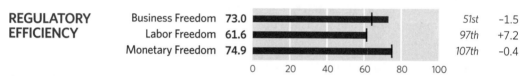

		Score		Rank	1-Year Change
REGULATORY EFFICIENCY	Business Freedom	73.0		51st	-1.5
	Labor Freedom	61.6		97th	+7.2
	Monetary Freedom	74.9		107th	-0.4

With no minimum capital required, it takes five procedures and 19 days to launch a company. Completing licensing requirements still takes more than a month on average. Labor regulations are not applied effectively, and the labor market lacks flexibility. The government has eliminated price controls on all but a few items such as gasoline, coal, and paraffin.

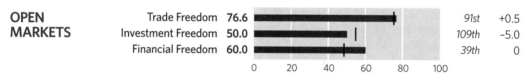

		Score		Rank	1-Year Change
OPEN MARKETS	Trade Freedom	76.6		91st	+0.5
	Investment Freedom	50.0		109th	-5.0
	Financial Freedom	60.0		39th	0

South Africa's average tariff rate is 4.2 percent. Government procurement favors domestic firms. The government cancelled bilateral investment treaties with Germany, Spain, and several other countries in 2013. The financial system has undergone modernization, and banking has been resilient and sound. Four big banks account for over 80 percent of banking-sector assets. The capital market is well developed.

Long-Term Score Change (since 1995)

RULE OF LAW		GOVERNMENT SIZE		REGULATORY EFFICIENCY		OPEN MARKETS	
Property Rights	0	Fiscal Freedom	+8.4	Business Freedom	-12.0	Trade Freedom	+33.6
Freedom from Corruption	-8.0	Government Spending	+4.9	Labor Freedom	+2.9	Investment Freedom	-20.0
				Monetary Freedom	+1.1	Financial Freedom	+10.0

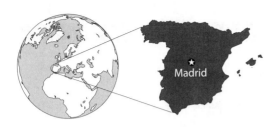

Madrid

SPAIN

Economic Freedom Score

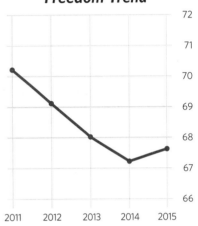

Least free 0   100 Most free

67.6

World Rank: 49   **Regional Rank: 21**

Spain's economic freedom score is 67.6, making its economy the 49th freest in the 2015 *Index*. Its score has increased by 0.4 point since last year, reflecting improvements in six of the 10 economic freedoms, driven by investment freedom, monetary freedom, and the management of government spending, that outweigh declines in freedom from corruption and fiscal freedom. Spain is ranked 21st out of 43 countries in the Europe region, and its overall score is above the world average.

Over the past five years, a 2.6-point drop in economic freedom has pushed Spain's economy into the "moderately free" category. Deteriorations in six of the 10 economic freedoms have been led by declines in the management of government spending and financial freedom.

Nevertheless, Spain's most recent uptick in economic freedom reverses three straight years of declines. The rule of law is respected, and export growth is encouraged by an open trade and investment framework.

BACKGROUND: In 2008, Spain's housing sector was highly leveraged, and the bursting of the housing bubble led in part to the recession beginning in 2009 and saddled banks with bad debt. Responses by the Spanish Socialist Workers Party, then in power, made the situation worse. Mariano Rajoy's conservative Popular Party won the November 2011 election and introduced the largest budget deficit-reduction plan in Spain's history, including crucial structural and labor reforms. In 2012, the EU bailed out Spain's banking sector with a €41 billion loan. However, Rajoy's government has dismissed recent warnings that more government austerity measures are needed and has demurred from tackling pension reform. Upcoming elections make further reforms unlikely until at least 2016. In the first quarter of 2014, Spain experienced its largest GDP increase since the 2008 recession. However, debt rose to over 90 percent of GDP in 2013. Spain's unemployment rate has declined slightly to about 25 percent, and youth unemployment hovers around 55 percent.

Freedom Trend

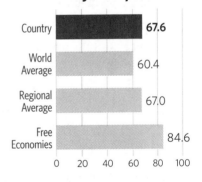

Country Comparisons

Country	67.6
World Average	60.4
Regional Average	67.0
Free Economies	84.6

0   20   40   60   80   100

Quick Facts

Population: 46.6 million
GDP (PPP): $1.4 trillion
–1.2% growth in 2013
5-year compound annual growth –1.4%
$29,851 per capita
Unemployment: 26.7%
Inflation (CPI): 1.5%
FDI Inflow: $39.2 billion
Public Debt: 93.9% of GDP

2013 data unless otherwise noted.
Data compiled as of September 2014.

How Do We Measure Economic Freedom?
See page 475 for an explanation of the methodology
or visit the *Index* Web site at *heritage.org/index*.

THE TEN ECONOMIC FREEDOMS

		Score	■ Country | World Average	Rank	1-Year Change
RULE OF LAW	Property Rights	70.0		30th	0
	Freedom from Corruption	59.0		39th	–3.6

A wave of scandals exposed systematic corruption within the political class during the years of easy credit and economic boom and caused a severe erosion of institutional credibility. The judicial system is slow-moving and somewhat politicized, limiting redress for firms that have had contractual obligations breached. Protection of intellectual property meets or exceeds EU standards.

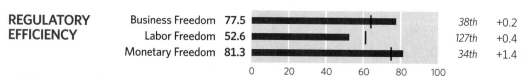

		Score		Rank	1-Year Change
GOVERNMENT SIZE	Fiscal Freedom	53.1		172nd	–0.9
	Government Spending	39.8		153rd	+1.1

Spain's top individual income tax rate is 52 percent, and its top corporate tax rate is 30 percent. Other taxes include a value-added tax and a capital gains tax. The overall tax burden equals 32.9 percent of gross domestic product. Government expenditures amount to 44.8 percent of domestic production, and public debt equals 94 percent of domestic output.

		Score		Rank	1-Year Change
REGULATORY EFFICIENCY	Business Freedom	77.5		38th	+0.2
	Labor Freedom	52.6		127th	+0.4
	Monetary Freedom	81.3		34th	+1.4

Procedures for establishing a business have been streamlined, and licensing requirements have been reduced. Bankruptcy proceedings are fairly straightforward. Labor market reforms have made it less costly to dismiss a permanent worker. Spain subsidizes fuel for high-seas fishing fleets, but a 2013 clean energy bill cut renewable-energy subsidies and capped the earnings of existing renewable-power plants.

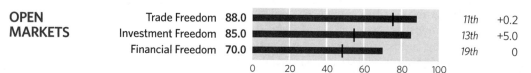

		Score		Rank	1-Year Change
OPEN MARKETS	Trade Freedom	88.0		11th	+0.2
	Investment Freedom	85.0		13th	+5.0
	Financial Freedom	70.0		19th	0

EU members have a 1.0 percent average tariff rate. Although some non-tariff barriers exist, the EU is relatively open to external trade. Like other EU member states, Spain generally treats foreign and domestic investors equally. Banking has experienced deep restructuring and a notable turnaround. The number of *cajas* (savings banks) has declined after several rounds of consolidation.

Long-Term Score Change (since 1995)

RULE OF LAW		GOVERNMENT SIZE		REGULATORY EFFICIENCY		OPEN MARKETS	
Property Rights	0	Fiscal Freedom	+7.9	Business Freedom	+7.5	Trade Freedom	+10.2
Freedom from Corruption	+9.0	Government Spending	+3.0	Labor Freedom	+3.8	Investment Freedom	+15.0
				Monetary Freedom	+5.5	Financial Freedom	0

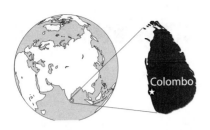

SRI LANKA

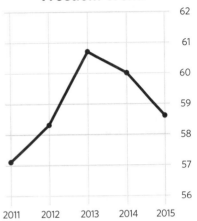

World Rank: 101   **Regional Rank: 21**

Sri Lanka's economic freedom score is 58.6, making its economy the 101st freest in the 2015 *Index*. Its score has decreased by 1.4 points since last year, with modest gains in freedom from corruption and the management of government spending outweighed by declines in half of the 10 economic freedoms, including investment freedom, property rights, and trade freedom. Sri Lanka is ranked 21st out of 42 countries in the Asia–Pacific region, and its score is just below the world and regional averages.

The return to relative political stability has precipitated a rise in Sri Lanka's economic freedom. Over the past five years, economic freedom on the island has advanced by 1.5 points, with improvements in half of the 10 factors led by double-digit gains in fiscal freedom.

Overall, however, the foundations of economic freedom remain weak. Property rights are hard to enforce because of fraud, and a weak judiciary fails to mediate disputes effectively. Government industrial policies distort trade and shelter domestic industry from competition. The central bank is not fully independent, raising the fear of inflation and monetized government deficits.

BACKGROUND: In May 2009, the Sri Lankan military defeated the rebel Liberation Tigers of Tamil Eelam (LTTE), ending a 26-year civil war and contributing to President Mahinda Rajapakse's April 2010 re-election. In March 2014, the U.N. Human Rights Council adopted a resolution mandating a comprehensive investigation into human rights violations by both the government and the rebels. In September 2013, for the first time in 25 years, Sri Lanka held elections for its Northern Provincial Council, a step that can be seen as an effort to begin addressing grievances of the Tamil community. Agriculture, apparel, and tourism are the main economic sectors. Sri Lanka depends heavily on foreign assistance and remittances from workers abroad, primarily in the Middle East. China has become a significant lender for infrastructure projects.

Freedom Trend

(chart showing values: 2011: 57, 2012: 58.3, 2013: 60.7, 2014: 60, 2015: 58.6)

2011 2012 2013 2014 2015

Country Comparisons

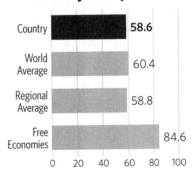

Country	58.6
World Average	60.4
Regional Average	58.8
Free Economies	84.6

0   20   40   60   80   100

Quick Facts

Population: 20.8 million
GDP (PPP): $136.0 billion
7.3% growth in 2013
5-year compound annual growth 6.7%
$6,531 per capita
Unemployment: 4.2%
Inflation (CPI): 6.9%
FDI Inflow: $915.6 million
Public Debt: 78.3% of GDP

2013 data unless otherwise noted.
Data compiled as of September 2014.

How Do We Measure Economic Freedom?
See page 475 for an explanation of the methodology
or visit the *Index* Web site at *heritage.org/index*.

THE TEN ECONOMIC FREEDOMS

		Score	Country	World Average	Rank	1-Year Change
RULE OF LAW	Property Rights	35.0			87th	–5.0
	Freedom from Corruption	37.0			92nd	+3.6

The government's populist rhetoric and harsh treatment of critics since 2013 have raised concerns about the erosion of democratic institutions. Some observers charge that the president's authoritarian rule (he and his family control approximately 70 percent of the national budget) has led to a lack of transparent and inclusive policy formulation. Judicial independence has weakened significantly.

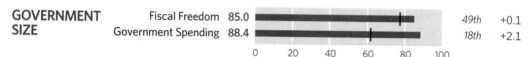

				Rank	1-Year Change
GOVERNMENT SIZE	Fiscal Freedom	85.0		49th	+0.1
	Government Spending	88.4		18th	+2.1

Sri Lanka's top individual income tax rate is 24 percent, and its top corporate tax rate is 28 percent. Other taxes include a value-added tax. Overall tax revenue equals 12 percent of domestic production. Public expenditures account for 19.7 percent of the domestic economy, and government debt is equivalent to approximately 80 percent of gross domestic product.

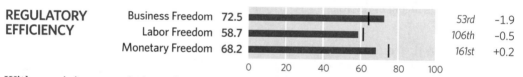

				Rank	1-Year Change
REGULATORY EFFICIENCY	Business Freedom	72.5		53rd	–1.9
	Labor Freedom	58.7		106th	–0.5
	Monetary Freedom	68.2		161st	+0.2

With no minimum capital required, launching a business takes nine procedures and less than a week. The cost of completing licensing requirements has been reduced, but it still takes more than five months on average. Labor regulations are rigid, though enforcement can be lax. An extensive system of price controls and subsidies distorts most sectors of the economy.

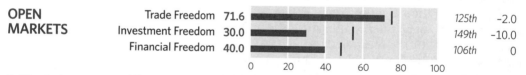

				Rank	1-Year Change
OPEN MARKETS	Trade Freedom	71.6		125th	–2.0
	Investment Freedom	30.0		149th	–10.0
	Financial Freedom	40.0		106th	0

Sri Lanka's average tariff rate is 6.7 percent. Imports are further impeded by government policies designed to promote import substitution and agricultural self-sufficiency. Investment levels in several sectors of the economy are capped. Despite some improvement, nonperforming loans remain a problem. The state continues to influence the allocation of credit, and the non-banking financial sector remains underdeveloped.

Long-Term Score Change (since 1995)

RULE OF LAW		GOVERNMENT SIZE		REGULATORY EFFICIENCY		OPEN MARKETS	
Property Rights	–15.0	Fiscal Freedom	+20.7	Business Freedom	+2.5	Trade Freedom	+17.4
Freedom from Corruption	+7.0	Government Spending	+10.1	Labor Freedom	–8.9	Investment Freedom	–20.0
				Monetary Freedom	–10.2	Financial Freedom	–30.0

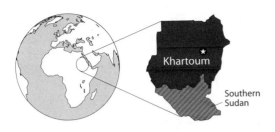

Khartoum

Southern
Sudan

SUDAN

Economic Freedom Score

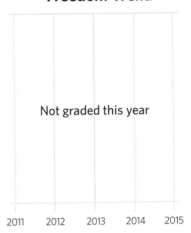

This economy is not graded

Sudan's economic freedom remains unrated due to the lack of reliable data. Those facets of economic freedom for which data are available have been individually scored. The last time Sudan was fully graded and ranked was in the 2000 *Index*, when it received a score of 47.2.

Civil war, political conflict, and unrest have undermined the development of a stable society ready for sustained economic growth. Although the petroleum sector provides some economic stability and foreign exchange earnings, other parts of the economy are underdeveloped and face serious structural and institutional headwinds. Continued conflict with rebels and South Sudan promotes uncertainty and undermines investor confidence.

Further diversification of the economy is undermined by poor governance and inefficient regulations. A large informal economy remains trapped by business regulations that inhibit registration and a rigid labor market that discourages formal hiring. High tariffs discourage imports and protect domestic industry, while investment remains largely reserved for the hydrocarbon sector.

BACKGROUND: Omar Hassan al-Bashir, who came to power in a 1989 military coup and still rules the country, faces two international arrest warrants on charges of genocide in the conflict in Western Darfur, where over 2 million people were displaced and over 200,000 killed. In October 2013, 30 members of al-Bashir's National Congress Party broke away and formed a new opposition party. Cross-border violence, political instability, poor infrastructure, weak property rights, and corruption hinder development. Export growth, other than with respect to oil, is largely stagnant, and 80 percent of the workforce is employed in agriculture. Following the secession of South Sudan in 2011, Sudan lost two-thirds of its oil revenue to the South. Subject to multiple comprehensive sanctions, Sudan has begun austerity measures to reduce government spending. Reports of an upsurge of violence in Darfur have raised concerns.

Freedom Trend

Not graded this year

2011   2012   2013   2014   2015

Country Comparisons

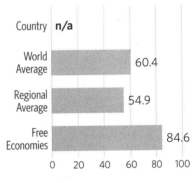

Country	n/a
World Average	60.4
Regional Average	54.9
Free Economies	84.6

0   20   40   60   80   100

Quick Facts

Population: 34.4 million
GDP (PPP): $90.5 billion
3.4% growth in 2013
5-year compound annual growth 1.3%
$2,631 per capita
Unemployment: 15.3%
Inflation (CPI): 36.5%
FDI Inflow: $3.1 billion
Public Debt: 90.9% of GDP

2013 data unless otherwise noted.
Data compiled as of September 2014.

How Do We Measure Economic Freedom?
See page 475 for an explanation of the methodology
or visit the *Index* Web site at *heritage.org/index*.

THE TEN ECONOMIC FREEDOMS

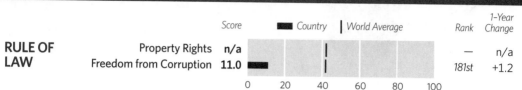

		Score		Rank	1-Year Change
RULE OF LAW	Property Rights	n/a		—	n/a
	Freedom from Corruption	11.0		181st	+1.2

Sudan is considered one of the world's most corrupt countries. Power and resources are concentrated in and around Khartoum, leaving outlying states impoverished. Members of the ruling party control the national economy and use their wealth to buy political support. There is little respect for private property, and the legal framework is severely hampered by years of political conflict.

		Score		Rank	1-Year Change
GOVERNMENT SIZE	Fiscal Freedom	86.4		42nd	+1.3
	Government Spending	94.5		2nd	+4.2

Sudan's top individual income tax rate is now 10 percent. The top corporate tax rate is 35 percent for the oil and gas sector. Other taxes include a value-added tax and a capital gains tax. The total tax burden is 5.7 percent of domestic income. Public expenditures are equivalent to 13.6 percent of domestic output, and public debt equals 91 percent of GDP.

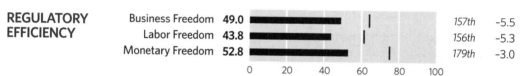

		Score		Rank	1-Year Change
REGULATORY EFFICIENCY	Business Freedom	49.0		157th	-5.5
	Labor Freedom	43.8		156th	-5.3
	Monetary Freedom	52.8		179th	-3.0

Political instability, a poor regulatory environment, and inadequate infrastructure significantly deter business formation and operation. The labor market is dominated by the agricultural sector and informal hiring practices. Violent protests in September 2013 against dramatic cuts in fuel subsidies prompted the state to reduce some subsidies to investors to free more revenue for social services.

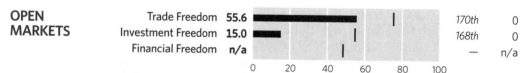

		Score		Rank	1-Year Change
OPEN MARKETS	Trade Freedom	55.6		170th	0
	Investment Freedom	15.0		168th	0
	Financial Freedom	n/a		—	n/a

Sudan's average tariff rate is 14.7 percent. International trade and investment flows are impeded by regional instability. The underdeveloped financial system is dominated by banks that practice Islamic banking, which prevents banks from charging interest. The government is heavily involved in the system, and the banking penetration rate is very low and uneven across the country.

Long-Term Score Change: n/a

RULE OF LAW		GOVERNMENT SIZE		REGULATORY EFFICIENCY		OPEN MARKETS	
Property Rights	n/a	Fiscal Freedom	n/a	Business Freedom	n/a	Trade Freedom	n/a
Freedom from Corruption	n/a	Government Spending	n/a	Labor Freedom	n/a	Investment Freedom	n/a
				Monetary Freedom	n/a	Financial Freedom	n/a

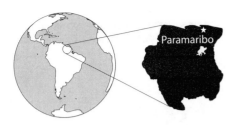

SURINAME

Economic Freedom Score

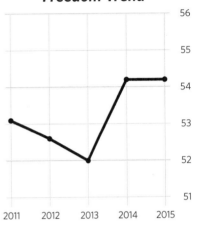

Least free 0

Most free 100

54.2

World Rank: **129**   Regional Rank: **23**

Suriname's economic freedom score is 54.2, making its economy the 129th freest in the 2015 *Index*. Its score remains the same as last year, with improvements in half of the 10 economic freedoms, including monetary freedom and freedom from corruption, offset by declines in property rights and the management of government spending. Suriname is ranked 23rd out of 29 countries in the South and Central America/Caribbean region, and its overall score is lower than the regional average.

Over the past five years, Suriname's overall economic freedom score has risen by 1.1 points, with advances in half of the 10 economic freedoms. Large gains in investment freedom have been offset by declines in the control of government spending and property rights.

Despite an export-oriented economy focused on commodity and mineral trade, Suriname has yet to benefit fully from global trade and investment. High tariff rates protect domestic businesses from competition, and regulatory inefficiency often impedes overseas investment. The rule of law is undermined by a growing domestic drug trade that encourages corruption.

BACKGROUND: In 2010, former dictator and convicted narco-trafficker Desire "Dési" Bouterse of the National Democratic Party was re-elected president for a five year term. Bouterse first took power in 1980 when he led the "Sergeants Coup" that overthrew the civilian government and installed a military regime that ruled until 1987. In 2012, Suriname's legislature gave him amnesty for the 1982 murders of 15 prominent young Surinamese men who had criticized the military dictatorship. In 2013, Bouterse's son Dino was arrested in Panama and extradited to New York, where he pleaded guilty in 2014 to charges of drug-trafficking and providing material support to a terrorist organization. Suriname remains one of South America's poorest and least-developed countries. The economy is dominated by exports of natural resources, especially alumina, oil, and gold, which are subject to boom-and-bust price fluctuations.

Freedom Trend

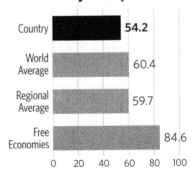

Country Comparisons

Country	54.2
World Average	60.4
Regional Average	59.7
Free Economies	84.6

Quick Facts

Population: 0.5 million
GDP (PPP): $7.2 billion
4.7% growth in 2013
5-year compound annual growth 4.4%
$13,116 per capita
Unemployment: 12.4%
Inflation (CPI): 1.9%
FDI Inflow: $112.8 million
Public Debt: 29.2% of GDP

2013 data unless otherwise noted.
Data compiled as of September 2014.

How Do We Measure Economic Freedom?
See page 475 for an explanation of the methodology or visit the *Index* Web site at *heritage.org/index.*

THE TEN ECONOMIC FREEDOMS

	Score		Rank	1-Year Change
RULE OF LAW				
Property Rights	35.0		87th	−5.0
Freedom from Corruption	36.0		95th	+3.1

Organized crime and drug networks undermine governance and the judicial system. Corruption is most pervasive in government procurement, license issuance, land policy, and taxation. In 2013, despite a pledge to do so, the government did not establish a constitutional court to review the revised amnesty law's constitutionality. The judiciary is susceptible to political influence. Property rights are not well protected.

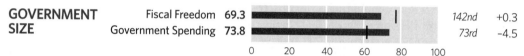

	Score		Rank	1-Year Change
GOVERNMENT SIZE				
Fiscal Freedom	69.3		142nd	+0.3
Government Spending	73.8		73rd	−4.5

The top individual income tax rate is 38 percent, and the top corporate tax rate is 36 percent. Other taxes include a property tax, a tax on dividends, and an excise tax. The overall tax burden equals 18.3 percent of domestic output. Public expenditures amount to 29.5 percent of the domestic economy, and government debt equals 29 percent of GDP.

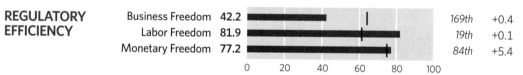

	Score		Rank	1-Year Change
REGULATORY EFFICIENCY				
Business Freedom	42.2		169th	+0.4
Labor Freedom	81.9		19th	+0.1
Monetary Freedom	77.2		84th	+5.4

Incorporating a business takes six procedures and 10 days, with no minimum capital required, but licensing takes more than 200 days on average. Although labor codes are favorable to flexibility, an efficient labor market has not been developed, and informal activity remains substantial. The government supports state-owned utility companies through a complicated web of cross subsidies and transfers.

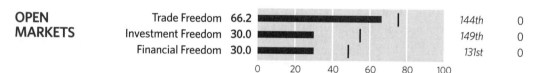

	Score		Rank	1-Year Change
OPEN MARKETS				
Trade Freedom	66.2		144th	0
Investment Freedom	30.0		149th	0
Financial Freedom	30.0		131st	0

Suriname's average tariff rate is 11.9 percent. Imports of used cars are restricted, and foreign firms may face barriers when bidding for government contracts. The government reviews new foreign investment. The financial system is underdeveloped, and credit decisions are subject to state influence. Reflecting the system's lack of depth and efficiency, the capital market remains rudimentary.

Long-Term Score Change (since 1996)

RULE OF LAW		GOVERNMENT SIZE		REGULATORY EFFICIENCY		OPEN MARKETS	
Property Rights	−15.0	Fiscal Freedom	+19.8	Business Freedom	−27.8	Trade Freedom	+41.2
Freedom from Corruption	+26.0	Government Spending	+28.0	Labor Freedom	−3.9	Investment Freedom	−20.0
				Monetary Freedom	+77.2	Financial Freedom	0

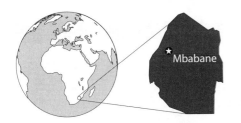

SWAZILAND

Economic Freedom Score

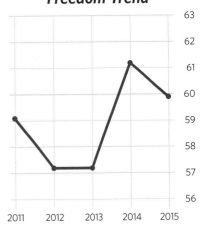

25 50 75

Least free 0   100 Most free

59.9

World Rank: 91   **Regional Rank: 8**

Swaziland's economic freedom score is 59.9, making its economy the 91st freest in the 2015 *Index*. Its score is down by 1.3 points from last year, with improvements in freedom from corruption, fiscal freedom, and monetary freedom offset by deteriorations in five of the 10 economic freedoms, including a 10-point drop in investment freedom. Swaziland is ranked 8th out of 46 countries in the Sub-Saharan Africa region, and its overall score is just above the world average.

Swaziland's economy has risen briefly to "moderately free" in recent years only to fall back to "mostly unfree." Nonetheless, over the past five years, its economic freedom has advanced by 0.8 point, with a 9.0-point increase in the fiscal freedom score offset by declines in three of the 10 economic freedoms, including business freedom and trade freedom.

Swaziland has not fully embraced the principles of economic freedom. Rule of law remains weak and ineffective. A dual judicial system can rule based on either customary laws or European laws. The inefficient business environment discourages formal business formation. Recent success in the apparel industry, however, has been a testament to Swaziland's slowly opening economy.

BACKGROUND: King Mswati III rules Africa's last monarchy. September 2013 parliamentary elections were disputed because candidates were handpicked by the king. Banned political parties have called for greater democracy and limits on the king's power. In June 2014, as a result of crackdowns on peaceful demonstrations and lack of protection of workers' rights, the U.S. disqualified Swaziland from receiving the market-access benefits available under the African Growth and Opportunity Act. Swaziland's currency is pegged to the South African rand, and South Africa is its largest trading partner. The soft-drink concentrate, textile, and cane sugar industries are the leading export earners and largest private-sector manufacturers. Coal and diamonds are also exported. Fiscal profligacy and the high HIV/AIDS rate undermine development.

Freedom Trend

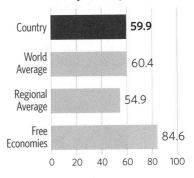

Country Comparisons

Country	59.9
World Average	60.4
Regional Average	54.9
Free Economies	84.6

0 20 40 60 80 100

Quick Facts

Population: 1.1 million
GDP (PPP): $6.8 billion
2.8% growth in 2013
5-year compound annual growth 1.4%
$6,218 per capita
Unemployment: 22.9%
Inflation (CPI): 5.6%
FDI Inflow: $67.0 million
Public Debt: 18.8% of GDP

2013 data unless otherwise noted.
Data compiled as of September 2014.

How Do We Measure Economic Freedom?
See page 475 for an explanation of the methodology
or visit the *Index* Web site at *heritage.org/index.*

THE TEN ECONOMIC FREEDOMS

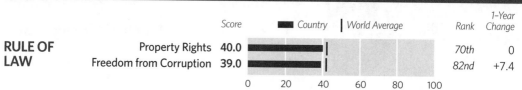

		Score	Rank	1-Year Change
RULE OF LAW	Property Rights	40.0	70th	0
	Freedom from Corruption	39.0	82nd	+7.4

Government corruption was widely blamed for contributing to Swaziland's financial crisis. The dual judicial system includes courts based on Roman–Dutch law and traditional courts using customary law. The judiciary is independent in most civil cases, though the king has ultimate judicial powers, and the royal family and government often refuse to respect rulings with which they disagree.

		Score	Rank	1-Year Change
GOVERNMENT SIZE	Fiscal Freedom	76.4	112th	+1.7
	Government Spending	68.6	89th	-2.3

Swaziland's top individual income tax rate is 33 percent, and its top corporate rate is down to 27.5 percent. Other taxes include a fuel and sales tax. Overall tax revenue amounts to 22.7 percent of domestic income, and government expenditures are equivalent to 32.4 percent of domestic output. Government debt equals 19 percent of gross domestic product.

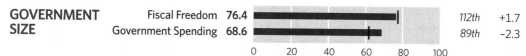

		Score	Rank	1-Year Change
REGULATORY EFFICIENCY	Business Freedom	60.5	109th	-3.7
	Labor Freedom	69.3	58th	-2.4
	Monetary Freedom	73.9	123rd	+1.6

Many regulatory requirements increase the overall cost of entrepreneurial activity. It still takes about a month to establish a business. Labor regulations are not enforced effectively, and there is no efficient countrywide labor market. A large share of the workforce is employed in the informal sector. The state continues to influence prices through numerous state-owned enterprises and utilities.

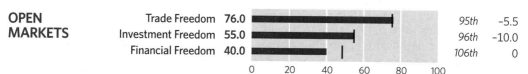

		Score	Rank	1-Year Change
OPEN MARKETS	Trade Freedom	76.0	95th	-5.5
	Investment Freedom	55.0	96th	-10.0
	Financial Freedom	40.0	106th	0

The average tariff rate is 7.0 percent. Informal barriers further impede trade. Foreign investment is allowed in most sectors of the economy. The underdeveloped financial system is closely linked to South Africa. Three commercial banks owned by South African institutions account for over 80 percent of total assets. The capital market is nascent, and the stock market is largely inactive.

Long-Term Score Change (since 1995)

RULE OF LAW		GOVERNMENT SIZE		REGULATORY EFFICIENCY		OPEN MARKETS	
Property Rights	-30.0	Fiscal Freedom	+12.9	Business Freedom	-9.5	Trade Freedom	+18.0
Freedom from Corruption	-11.0	Government Spending	-0.7	Labor Freedom	+0.1	Investment Freedom	-15.0
				Monetary Freedom	+4.6	Financial Freedom	-10.0

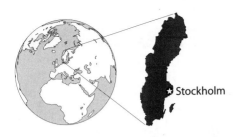
Stockholm

SWEDEN

Economic Freedom Score

50
25   75
Least
free 0   100
Most
free

72.7

World Rank: 23   **Regional Rank: 12**

Sweden's economic freedom score is 72.7, making its economy the 23rd freest in the 2015 *Index*. Its score has decreased by 0.4 point since last year, with improvements in four of the 10 economic freedoms outweighed by deteriorations in freedom from corruption, business freedom, and the management of government spending. Sweden is ranked 12th out of 43 countries in the Europe region, and its overall score is above the world and regional averages.

Despite its well-established welfare state and large government budget, Sweden has made marginal changes to improve its economic freedom and competitiveness. Over the past five years, economic freedom in Sweden has advanced by 0.8 point with gains in five of the 10 economic freedoms, including fiscal freedom, the management of government spending, monetary freedom, trade freedom, and investment freedom.

Sweden's high-performing economy has built its success on openness to global trade and investment. Reforms over the past two decades reduced the role of government and introduced market mechanisms that set the foundations for today's competitive economy. Sweden's business freedom score is one of the highest in the world. Fiscal responsibility remains central to the new government's policy proposals, but plans to reverse some of the previous government's tax cuts in order to fund higher spending could hurt growth.

BACKGROUND: Sweden joined the European Union in 1995 but rejected adoption of the euro in 2003. The public remains opposed to eurozone membership. The economic downturn in 2009 led to a slight increase in unemployment, but unemployment levels appeared to be stabilizing in 2014. A general election was held in September 2014. After difficult negotiations, a new center-left coalition government consisting of the Social Democratic Party and the Green Party took office. Banks are well capitalized, and Sweden has weathered the financial crisis relatively well. Sweden's economy is export-oriented; principal exports include automobiles, telecommunications products, construction equipment, and other investment goods.

Freedom Trend

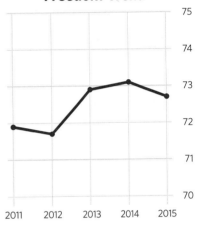

75
74
73
72
71
70
2011   2012   2013   2014   2015

Country Comparisons

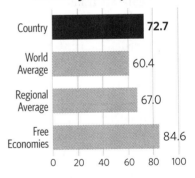

Country — **72.7**
World Average — 60.4
Regional Average — 67.0
Free Economies — 84.6

0   20   40   60   80   100

Quick Facts

Population: 9.6 million
GDP (PPP): $396.8 billion
1.5% growth in 2013
5-year compound annual growth 1.3%
$41,188 per capita
Unemployment: 8.0%
Inflation (CPI): 0.0%
FDI Inflow: $8.1 billion
Public Debt: 41.4% of GDP

2013 data unless otherwise noted.
Data compiled as of September 2014.

How Do We Measure Economic Freedom?
See page 475 for an explanation of the methodology
or visit the *Index* Web site at *heritage.org/index*.

THE TEN ECONOMIC FREEDOMS

		Score		Rank	1-Year Change
RULE OF LAW	Property Rights	90.0		3rd	0
	Freedom from Corruption	89.0		3rd	-3.3

Sweden is ranked 3rd out of 177 countries in Transparency International's 2013 Corruption Perceptions Index. Effective anti-corruption measures discourage bribery of public officials and uphold government integrity. The rule of law is well maintained. The judicial system operates independently and impartially, with consistent application of laws. Property rights and contract enforcement are very secure.

		Score		Rank	1-Year Change
GOVERNMENT SIZE	Fiscal Freedom	43.0		179th	+0.1
	Government Spending	19.2		171st	-2.2

Sweden's top individual income tax rate is 57 percent, and its top corporate tax rate is 22 percent. Other taxes include a value-added tax and a capital gains tax. The overall tax burden equals approximately 44.3 percent of the domestic economy. Public expenditures account for 51.9 percent of domestic output, and government debt is equal to 49 percent of gross domestic product.

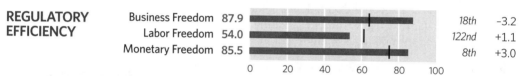

		Score		Rank	1-Year Change
REGULATORY EFFICIENCY	Business Freedom	87.9		18th	-3.2
	Labor Freedom	54.0		122nd	+1.1
	Monetary Freedom	85.5		8th	+3.0

The regulatory framework facilitates entrepreneurial activity, allowing efficient business formation. The government generally takes a hands-off approach in sectors dominated by small businesses. The labor market is dynamic, although the non-salary cost of hiring a worker is high. Sweden has continued to lead the fight to eliminate all European Union farm subsidies while also limiting green energy support.

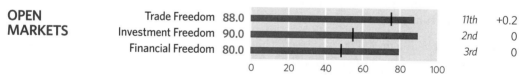

		Score		Rank	1-Year Change
OPEN MARKETS	Trade Freedom	88.0		11th	+0.2
	Investment Freedom	90.0		2nd	0
	Financial Freedom	80.0		3rd	0

EU members have a 1.0 percent average tariff rate. Although some non-tariff barriers exist, the EU is relatively open to external trade. Sweden generally treats foreign and domestic investors equally. The number of state-owned enterprises is relatively large. The modern and efficient financial system provides a wide range of financing instruments for foreign and domestic investors. Banks remain well-capitalized.

Long-Term Score Change (since 1995)

RULE OF LAW		GOVERNMENT SIZE		REGULATORY EFFICIENCY		OPEN MARKETS	
Property Rights	+20.0	Fiscal Freedom	-1.0	Business Freedom	+17.9	Trade Freedom	+11.0
Freedom from Corruption	-1.0	Government Spending	+19.2	Labor Freedom	-11.2	Investment Freedom	+20.0
				Monetary Freedom	+4.0	Financial Freedom	+30.0

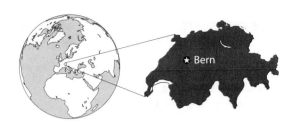

SWITZERLAND

Economic Freedom Score

25 50 75

Least free 0

Most free 100

80.5

S witzerland's economic freedom score is 80.5, making its economy the 5th freest in the 2015 *Index*. Its score has decreased by 1.1 points since last year, with modest improvements in business freedom, fiscal freedom, and monetary freedom overwhelmed by a large decline in labor freedom and smaller declines in freedom from corruption and the management of government spending. Switzerland is ranked 1st out of 43 countries in the Europe region.

Switzerland has enjoyed economically "free" status since 2010. With an economy that benefits from sound fundamentals that include monetary stability, low public debt, and a vibrant employment market, the Swiss economy has weathered the global economic uncertainty well.

Switzerland continues to be a regional leader in economic freedom. Efficient and transparent regulations underpin an efficient business environment and support diversified economic growth. Openness to global trade and investment is firmly institutionalized, buttressed by a dynamic financial sector and a well-functioning independent judiciary. Switzerland has a strong tradition of reliable protection of property rights, and the legal system is transparent and evenly applied. Effective anti-corruption measures are in force.

BACKGROUND: Switzerland's federal system of government disperses power widely, and executive authority is exercised collectively by the seven-member Federal Council. Switzerland has a long tradition of openness to the world but jealously guards its independence and neutrality. It did not join the United Nations until 2002, and two referenda on membership in the European Union have failed by wide margins. Membership in the European Economic Area was rejected by referendum in 1992. Switzerland is one of the world's richest and most investment-friendly countries. It has a well-developed financial services industry. In addition to banking, the economy relies heavily on precision manufacturing, metals, pharmaceuticals, chemicals, and electronics.

Freedom Trend

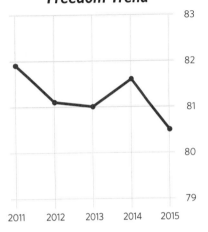

Country Comparisons

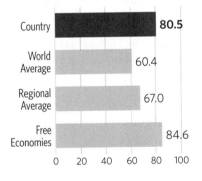

Quick Facts

Population: 8.0 million
GDP (PPP): $371.6 billion
2.0% growth in 2013
5-year compound annual growth 1.2%
$46,430 per capita
Unemployment: 4.4%
Inflation (CPI): -0.2%
FDI Inflow: -$5.3 billion
Public Debt: 49.4% of GDP

2013 data unless otherwise noted.
Data compiled as of September 2014.

How Do We Measure Economic Freedom?
See page 475 for an explanation of the methodology
or visit the *Index* Web site at *heritage.org/index*.

THE TEN ECONOMIC FREEDOMS

		Score	■ Country | World Average	Rank	1-Year Change
RULE OF LAW	Property Rights	90.0		3rd	0
	Freedom from Corruption	85.0		7th	-3.1

Switzerland was ranked 7th out of 177 countries in Transparency International's 2013 Corruption Perceptions Index. Protection of property rights is strongly enforced, and an independent and fair judicial system is institutionalized throughout the economy. Commercial and bankruptcy laws are applied consistently and efficiently. Intellectual property rights are respected and enforced.

GOVERNMENT SIZE	Fiscal Freedom	70.3		137th	+1.4
	Government Spending	65.1		98th	-0.6

Switzerland's tax system operates mostly on the cantonal level. The top effective federal income tax rate is 11.5 percent, and the combined rate can be over 40 percent. The federal corporate tax rate is 8.5 percent, but the combined rate can reach 24 percent. The tax burden is equal to 28.2 percent of the economy, and public expenditures are equivalent to 34.1 percent of domestic production. Public debt equals 50 percent of GDP.

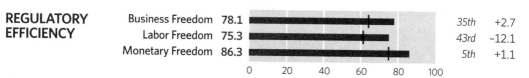

REGULATORY EFFICIENCY	Business Freedom	78.1		35th	+2.7
	Labor Freedom	75.3		43rd	-12.1
	Monetary Freedom	86.3		5th	+1.1

The competitive regulatory framework promotes business formation and operational efficiency. With no minimum capital required, starting a business involves six procedures. Labor regulations are still relatively flexible. Proportionately, Switzerland's agricultural subsidies are among the highest in the world and dampen innovation in agriculture, but the government did cut solar subsidies by 10 percent in 2014.

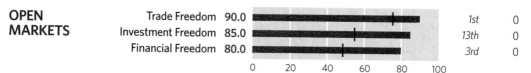

OPEN MARKETS	Trade Freedom	90.0		1st	0
	Investment Freedom	85.0		13th	0
	Financial Freedom	80.0		3rd	0

Switzerland has a 0 percent average tariff rate and is a member of the European Free Trade Association. Agricultural subsidies are significant. Foreign and domestic investments are generally treated equally. The highly competitive and well-developed financial sector offers a wide range of financial services and encourages entrepreneurial activity. Banking regulations are sensible, and lending practices are prudent.

Long-Term Score Change (since 1996)

RULE OF LAW		GOVERNMENT SIZE		REGULATORY EFFICIENCY		OPEN MARKETS	
Property Rights	+20.0	Fiscal Freedom	-7.7	Business Freedom	+8.1	Trade Freedom	+12.0
Freedom from Corruption	-5.0	Government Spending	+11.7	Labor Freedom	-1.9	Investment Freedom	-5.0
				Monetary Freedom	-5.3	Financial Freedom	+10.0

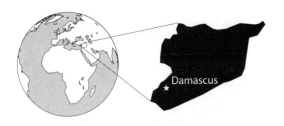

SYRIA

Economic Freedom Score

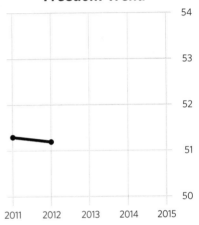

25   50   75

Least free 0

Most free 100

This economy is not graded

Grading of Syria's overall economic freedom remains suspended in the 2015 *Index* due to the political turmoil that has led to civil war and a significant deterioration in the quality of publicly available economic statistics. Facets of economic freedom for which data are still available have been individually scored. As a "mostly unfree" economy with a score of 51.2, Syria was ranked fourth lowest in the Middle East/North Africa region when it was last graded in the 2012 *Index*.

Civil war has left Syria's economy in ruins. The government does not control portions of the major cities, and the war has killed nearly 200,000 people and displaced millions. The rule of law has been ravaged by extrajudicial killings, kidnappings, and torture. Inflation has grown as the Syrian pound has become an unreliable medium of exchange.

The little formal economic activity that continues is impeded by weak structural and institutional foundations. The president, his cabinet, and close family members dominate many of the major economic sectors. Rampant corruption has destroyed any entrepreneurial dynamism. Continuing conflict limits trade and investment, and currency controls limit the free flow of capital.

BACKGROUND: The Assad family's iron grip on Syria, which it has ruled since Hafez al-Assad's military coup in 1970, faces serious challenges. Bashar al-Assad, who succeeded his father in 2000, has failed to deliver on promises to reform Syria's socialist economy and ease political repression. Arab Spring protests in 2011 were met with brutal crackdowns. By 2012, the uprising against Assad had spiraled into a sectarian civil war with Sunni-dominated rebels pitted against the Alawite-dominated regime. By mid-2014, the terrorist group Islamic State of Iraq and Syria (ISIS) had gained control of much of the northern half of the country. The conflict has triggered a severe economic recession. Before the conflict, Syria's economy was hobbled by a large state bureaucracy, falling oil production, rising budget deficits, and inflation.

Freedom Trend

54

53

52

51

50

2011   2012   2013   2014   2015

Country Comparisons

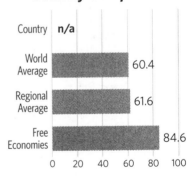

Country	n/a
World Average	60.4
Regional Average	61.6
Free Economies	84.6

0   20   40   60   80   100

Quick Facts

Population: 19.1 million
GDP (PPP): $70.0 billion
–20.6% growth in 2013
5-year compound annual growth n/a
$3,640 per capita
Unemployment: n/a
Inflation (CPI): 89.6%
FDI Inflow: n/a
Public Debt: n/a

2013 data unless otherwise noted.
Data compiled as of September 2014.

THE TEN ECONOMIC FREEDOMS

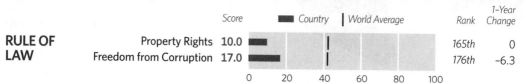

		Score		Rank	1-Year Change

RULE OF LAW

	Score	Rank	1-Year Change
Property Rights	10.0	165th	0
Freedom from Corruption	17.0	176th	-6.3

Even before the armed conflict and ongoing disintegration of Syria, government institutions lacked public accountability and were plagued by corruption. Members of the ruling family and their inner circle are said to own and control a major portion of the economy. Corruption is also present in rebel-held areas on a smaller scale. The judiciary is neither transparent nor independent.

GOVERNMENT SIZE

	Score	Rank	1-Year Change
Fiscal Freedom	n/a	—	n/a
Government Spending	n/a	—	n/a

Syria's top individual income tax rate is 22 percent, and its top corporate tax rate is 28 percent. Other taxes include a tax on inheritance and a property tax. Ongoing civil conflict has rendered fiscal policy and tax administration (if any) opaque. It has been reported that budget deficits have been on the rise.

REGULATORY EFFICIENCY

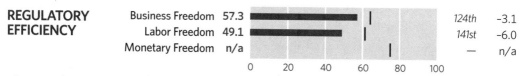

	Score	Rank	1-Year Change
Business Freedom	57.3	124th	-3.1
Labor Freedom	49.1	141st	-6.0
Monetary Freedom	n/a	—	n/a

The repressive business environment, severely impaired by the ongoing civil war and uncertainty, suppresses entrepreneurial activity and prolongs economic stagnation. The labor market is heavily state-controlled and undermined by instability. The Assad regime spent 45 percent of its 2014 budget on subsidies and attempted to "suppress" the inflation rate, which is one of the world's highest, with price controls.

OPEN MARKETS

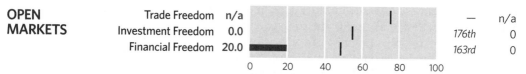

	Score	Rank	1-Year Change
Trade Freedom	n/a	—	n/a
Investment Freedom	0.0	176th	0
Financial Freedom	20.0	163rd	0

Syria has a 6.1 percent average tariff rate, and foreign investment is subject to government screening. The ongoing political turmoil is a major deterrent to international trade and investment, and the financial system has been under significant strain. The stock market has been running out of monetary resources, and bank deposits have dwindled, especially with capital fleeing the country.

Long-Term Score Change: n/a

RULE OF LAW		GOVERNMENT SIZE		REGULATORY EFFICIENCY		OPEN MARKETS	
Property Rights	n/a	Fiscal Freedom	n/a	Business Freedom	n/a	Trade Freedom	n/a
Freedom from Corruption	n/a	Government Spending	n/a	Labor Freedom	n/a	Investment Freedom	n/a
				Monetary Freedom	n/a	Financial Freedom	n/a

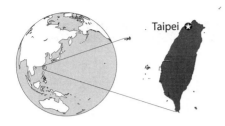
Taipei

TAIWAN

Economic Freedom Score

75.1

Taiwan's economic freedom score is 75.1, making its economy the 14th freest in the 2015 *Index*. Its score is up by 1.2 points from last year, with improvements in seven of the 10 economic freedoms led by investment freedom, the control of government spending, and labor freedom. Taiwan is ranked 5th out of 42 economies in the Asia–Pacific region, and its overall score is well above the world average.

Prudent macroeconomic policy within a stable legal and monetary environment has been the key to rising levels of economic freedom over the past five years. Commitment to structural reforms and openness to global commerce have enabled Taiwan to advance far into the "mostly free" category. Recording uninterrupted years of growth in economic freedom since 2009, Taiwan has achieved its highest score ever in the 2015 *Index*.

Taiwan's export-driven, dynamic economy benefits from a well-functioning legal framework and a tradition of private-sector entrepreneurship. The efficient business environment is facilitated by a competitively low corporate tax rate and the elimination of minimum capital requirements for incorporating a company. Despite progress, however, a relatively high level of perceived corruption and a rigid labor market still restrain Taiwan's overall economic freedom.

BACKGROUND: Taiwan is a dynamic multi-party democracy, and its economy is one of the richest in Asia. President Ma Ying-jeou, re-elected in 2012 on a platform that promised economic revitalization, has relaxed cross-Strait barriers with the People's Republic of China and negotiated a multi-stage formal economic agreement with Beijing. Taiwan is excluded from membership in the United Nations, other international organizations, and a variety of free trade arrangements as part of Beijing's efforts to pressure it into unification. Although internal opposition to engaging with China is considerable because of fears that sovereignty will be lost, recent economic arrangements bind the island much closer to the PRC. The government's possible ratification of a Trade in Services Agreement with China is controversial.

Freedom Trend

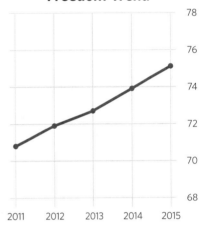

Country Comparisons

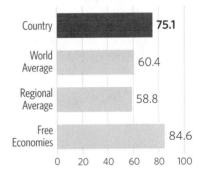

Country	75.1
World Average	60.4
Regional Average	58.8
Free Economies	84.6

Quick Facts

Population: 23.4 million
GDP (PPP): $929.5 billion
2.1% growth in 2013
5-year compound annual growth 3.3%
$39,767 per capita
Unemployment: 4.1%
Inflation (CPI): 0.8%
FDI Inflow: $3.7 billion
Public Debt: 41.0% of GDP

2013 data unless otherwise noted.
Data compiled as of September 2014.

How Do We Measure Economic Freedom?
See page 475 for an explanation of the methodology
or visit the *Index* Web site at *heritage.org/index.*

THE TEN ECONOMIC FREEDOMS

		Score		Rank	1-Year Change
RULE OF LAW	Property Rights	70.0		30th	0
	Freedom from Corruption	61.0		35th	+1.3

Though less pervasive than in the past, connections remain between politics and big business, and corruption is still a problem. In June 2014, a senior local official was indicted for accepting bribes from a construction company. The judiciary is independent, and the court system is free of political interference. Property rights are generally protected, and the judiciary enforces contracts effectively.

		Score		Rank	Change
GOVERNMENT SIZE	Fiscal Freedom	80.4		77th	+0.1
	Government Spending	87.1		26th	+2.4

Taiwan's top individual income tax rate is 40 percent, and its top corporate tax rate is 17 percent. Other taxes include a value-added tax and a tax on interest. The overall tax burden is equal to 8.7 percent of domestic income. Government spending amounts to 20.7 percent of the domestic economy, and public debt equals 41 percent of gross domestic product.

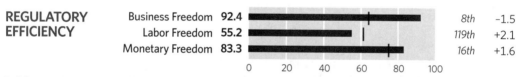

		Score		Rank	Change
REGULATORY EFFICIENCY	Business Freedom	92.4		8th	−1.5
	Labor Freedom	55.2		119th	+2.1
	Monetary Freedom	83.3		16th	+1.6

With no minimum capital required, it takes three procedures to incorporate a company. Bankruptcy proceedings are straightforward. However, completing licensing requirements remains relatively time-consuming. Labor mobility is impeded in the rigid labor market. Prices are market-determined for the most part, but the government does influence some prices and controls prices for electricity and pharmaceutical products.

		Score		Rank	Change
OPEN MARKETS	Trade Freedom	86.4		43rd	+0.6
	Investment Freedom	75.0		36th	+5.0
	Financial Freedom	60.0		39th	0

The average tariff rate is 1.8 percent. Tariff-rate quotas restrict many agricultural imports. The government screens new investments. Investment in some sectors is restricted. The evolving financial sector provides a wide range of financial instruments and services, and the state has stepped back from its previously dominant role. Liberalization has progressed, but the foreign bank presence remains relatively small.

Long-Term Score Change (since 1995)

RULE OF LAW		GOVERNMENT SIZE		REGULATORY EFFICIENCY		OPEN MARKETS	
Property Rights	−20.0	Fiscal Freedom	+6.3	Business Freedom	+7.4	Trade Freedom	+11.2
Freedom from Corruption	−29.0	Government Spending	+17.2	Labor Freedom	+9.1	Investment Freedom	+25.0
				Monetary Freedom	−0.1	Financial Freedom	+10.0

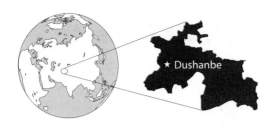
★ Dushanbe

TAJIKISTAN

Economic Freedom Score

50
25   75
Least free 0   100 Most free

52.7

Tajikistan's economic freedom score is 52.7, making its economy the 140th freest in the 2015 *Index*. Its score is up by 0.7 point since last year, with improvements in six of the 10 economic freedoms, including business freedom, the control of government spending, and freedom from corruption, offsetting a large decline in financial freedom. Tajikistan is ranked 31st out of 42 countries in the Asia–Pacific region, and its overall score is lower than the world average.

Tajikistan's relatively stable overall level of economic freedom in recent years masks large score declines in financial freedom and labor freedom that offset more modest gains in other areas. Over the past five years, economic freedom in Tajikistan has declined by 0.8 point, with losses in four of the 10 economic freedoms.

A five-year civil war destroyed much of Tajikistan's economic infrastructure and institutions. The rule of law is extremely weak, and the president's family dominates key positions in government and business. Poverty is rampant, and inefficient business regulations inhibit individuals from lifting themselves from poverty. The trade environment limits investment and the transfer of productive technologies.

BACKGROUND: The 1992–1997 civil war between an Islamist/democratic coalition and the ruling Communists severely damaged an already weak economy and caused a sharp decline in industrial and agricultural production. Emomali Rahmon, president since 1994 and re-elected to another seven-year term in November 2013 in an election that was neither free nor fair, controls all three branches of government. Corruption, Islamic terrorism, and narco-trafficking are endemic. Most Tajiks survive by working in the underground economy. Relations with neighboring Uzbekistan are strained. Government abuses of human rights are widespread. Tajikistan is heavily dependent on revenues from aluminum and cotton exports. The illegal drug trade and remittances from migrant workers, primarily in Russia, account for over 45 percent of GDP. Tajikistan became a member of the World Trade Organization in 2013.

Freedom Trend

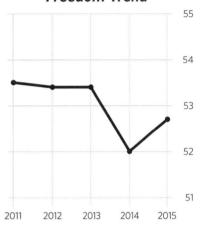

55

54

53

52

51

2011   2012   2013   2014   2015

Country Comparisons

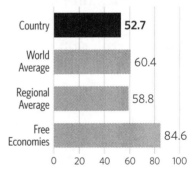

Country — 52.7
World Average — 60.4
Regional Average — 58.8
Free Economies — 84.6

0   20   40   60   80   100

Quick Facts

Population: 8.1 million
GDP (PPP): $19.1 billion
7.4% growth in 2013
5-year compound annual growth 6.5%
$2,354 per capita
Unemployment: 10.8%
Inflation (CPI): 5.0%
FDI Inflow: $107.8 million
Public Debt: 29.2% of GDP

2013 data unless otherwise noted.
Data compiled as of September 2014.

THE TEN ECONOMIC FREEDOMS

		Score		Rank	1-Year Change
RULE OF LAW	Property Rights	20.0		138th	0
	Freedom from Corruption	22.0		161st	+2.6

Corruption is pervasive. Patronage networks are central to political life. At least two of President Rahmon's children hold senior government posts, and various family members reportedly maintain extensive business interests in the country. The judiciary lacks independence. Many judges are poorly trained and inexperienced, and bribery is reportedly widespread. Under Tajik law, all land belongs to the state.

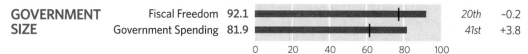

		Score		Rank	Change
GOVERNMENT SIZE	Fiscal Freedom	92.1		20th	-0.2
	Government Spending	81.9		41st	+3.8

The top individual income tax rate is 13 percent, and the top corporate tax rate is 15 percent. Some companies, including foreign entities, pay different rates. Other taxes include a value-added tax and a sales tax. The overall tax burden is equal to 19.9 percent of domestic production. Government spending equals 24.6 percent of domestic output, and public debt equals 29 percent of GDP.

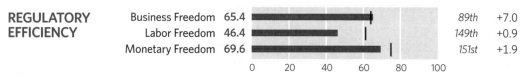

		Score		Rank	Change
REGULATORY EFFICIENCY	Business Freedom	65.4		89th	+7.0
	Labor Freedom	46.4		149th	+0.9
	Monetary Freedom	69.6		151st	+1.9

The business environment has improved with implementation of more simplified business registration in recent years, but entrepreneurial activity remains seriously hampered by inconsistent bureaucracy. The labor market remains underdeveloped. The government influences prices through regulation and large subsidies to numerous state-owned and state trading enterprises. Nearly half of the recipients of social protection subsidies are "non-poor."

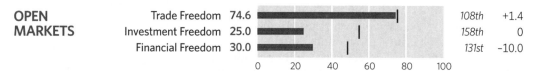

		Score		Rank	Change
OPEN MARKETS	Trade Freedom	74.6		108th	+1.4
	Investment Freedom	25.0		158th	0
	Financial Freedom	30.0		131st	-10.0

Tajikistan's average tariff rate is 5.2 percent. Goods may face delays clearing customs, and it is expensive to import products into the country. Foreign investors may not own land, and proposed new investments may be subject to review by government agencies. Financial-sector assets have grown rapidly, but continuing state interference seriously handicaps private-sector development.

Long-Term Score Change (since 1998)

RULE OF LAW		GOVERNMENT SIZE		REGULATORY EFFICIENCY		OPEN MARKETS	
Property Rights	-10.0	Fiscal Freedom	+34.6	Business Freedom	+10.4	Trade Freedom	+6.2
Freedom from Corruption	+12.0	Government Spending	-7.4	Labor Freedom	-13.9	Investment Freedom	-5.0
				Monetary Freedom	+69.6	Financial Freedom	0

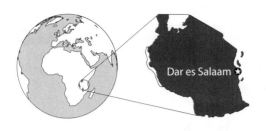

TANZANIA

Economic Freedom Score

50

25   75

Least free   0

Most free   100

57.5

Tanzania's economic freedom score is 57.5, making its economy the 109th freest in the 2015 *Index*. Its score has decreased by 0.3 point since last year due to declines in trade freedom and business freedom that outweigh improvements in half of the 10 economic freedoms, including freedom from corruption and monetary freedom. Tanzania is ranked 17th out of 46 countries in the Sub-Saharan Africa region, and its overall score is lower than the world average.

Productive economic growth in recent years has helped to promote prosperity, but widespread poverty still plagues an economy that lacks fundamental aspects of economic freedom. A greater commitment to structural and institutional reforms is needed to create an efficient entrepreneurial environment and open markets.

Tanzania lacks an effective rule of law. Corruption remains pervasive and has been especially noticeable in energy and mining, which have experienced rapid growth in recent years. Business and labor regulations remain stringent and prohibitively difficult for new job-creating activities. Entrepreneurs find it hard to register businesses legally, and the formal labor market's barriers to entry inhibit full employment. Efforts to open the economy have experienced some success, but government bureaucracy still delays some investment.

BACKGROUND: President Jakaya Kikwete was elected in December 2005 and re-elected in October 2010. Kikwete's Chama Cha Mapinduzi party has been in power since the emergence of multi-party politics in 1961. The adoption of a limited number of market-based policies has stimulated moderate growth, but property rights are still uncertain, and corruption is endemic. Tanzania also has a high HIV/AIDS rate and poor infrastructure. Foreign investments have led to improvements in efficiency. A 50-year border dispute with Malawi recently resurfaced when Malawi gave a British firm exploration rights for oil in Lake Malawi. Tanzania hosts more than half a million refugees, mainly from the Democratic Republic of Congo and Burundi, and is a transit point for both human and drug trafficking.

Freedom Trend

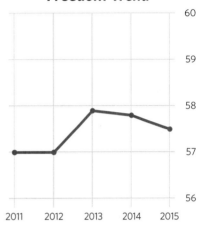

2011	2012	2013	2014	2015

Country Comparisons

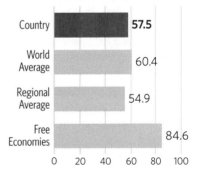

Country	57.5
World Average	60.4
Regional Average	54.9
Free Economies	84.6

Quick Facts

Population: 46.3 million
GDP (PPP): $79.4 billion
7.0% growth in 2013
5-year compound annual growth 6.7%
$1,715 per capita
Unemployment: 3.5%
Inflation (CPI): 7.9%
FDI Inflow: $1.9 billion
Public Debt: 41.0% of GDP

2013 data unless otherwise noted.
Data compiled as of September 2014.

How Do We Measure Economic Freedom?
See page 475 for an explanation of the methodology
or visit the *Index* Web site at *heritage.org/index*.

THE TEN ECONOMIC FREEDOMS

		Score	Country	World Average	Rank	1-Year Change
RULE OF LAW	Property Rights	30.0			94th	0
	Freedom from Corruption	33.0			113th	+4.2

Corruption is pervasive in all aspects of political and commercial life, but especially in the energy and natural resources sectors. Tanzania's judiciary remains under political influence and suffers from underfunding and corruption, in part due to increasing problems stemming from narcotics trafficking. Complex land laws have been accompanied by a high incidence of land disputes.

		Score		Rank	1-Year Change
GOVERNMENT SIZE	Fiscal Freedom	79.9		85th	+0.2
	Government Spending	79.3		48th	+1.0

Tanzania's top individual and corporate income tax rates are 30 percent. Other taxes include a value-added tax and a sales tax. The tax burden amounts to 14.4 percent of domestic production. Public spending is equal to 26.3 percent of the domestic economy, and government debt has reached 41 percent of gross domestic product.

		Score		Rank	1-Year Change
REGULATORY EFFICIENCY	Business Freedom	45.0		164th	–2.0
	Labor Freedom	61.4		99th	+0.3
	Monetary Freedom	69.7		150th	+3.7

The business environment remains hampered by a lack of efficiency. Requirements for launching a business are not time-consuming, but licensing remains costly. Labor regulations are not modern and flexible enough to support a vibrant labor market. In late 2013, in line with IMF recommendations, the government curbed power subsidies and raised electricity tariffs to sustain growth and ease fiscal pressures.

		Score		Rank	1-Year Change
OPEN MARKETS	Trade Freedom	67.0		143rd	–9.8
	Investment Freedom	60.0		81st	0
	Financial Freedom	50.0		70th	0

The average tariff rate is 11.5 percent. Imports may face customs delays. All land is the property of the government. The small financial sector remains shallow, dominated by commercial banks. Banking is relatively sound, but the rate of banking penetration across the country remains low. A stock exchange has been in operation, but the capital market remains underdeveloped.

Long-Term Score Change (since 1995)

RULE OF LAW		GOVERNMENT SIZE		REGULATORY EFFICIENCY		OPEN MARKETS	
Property Rights	–20.0	Fiscal Freedom	+2.1	Business Freedom	–10.0	Trade Freedom	+13.2
Freedom from Corruption	+3.0	Government Spending	–11.3	Labor Freedom	+13.5	Investment Freedom	+10.0
				Monetary Freedom	+11.2	Financial Freedom	0

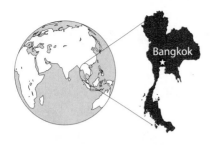

★ Bangkok

THAILAND

Economic Freedom Score

25   50   75

Least free 0   Most free 100

62.4

Thailand's economic freedom score is 62.4, making its economy the 75th freest in the 2015 *Index*. Its score has decreased by 0.9 point since last year, with deteriorations in financial freedom, property rights, and the control of government spending outweighing small improvements in six of the 10 economic freedoms, including labor freedom, fiscal freedom, and freedom from corruption. Thailand is ranked 12th out of 42 countries in the Asia–Pacific region, and its overall score is higher than the world and regional averages.

Thailand's economic freedom score has declined for three years in a row. Since 2011, economic freedom in Thailand has fallen by 2.3 points. Score declines in a majority of the 10 economic freedoms have been led by double-digit declines in investment freedom and labor freedom and a nearly double-digit drop in the control of government spending.

Political unrest and conflict between rural and urban voters have led to increased perceptions of corruption and an unsteady investment climate. A growing foreign automobile manufacturing industry provides evidence of the benefits of increasing economic openness, but the business environment for small entrepreneurs remains difficult due to inefficient business and labor regulations.

BACKGROUND: Thailand has experienced 19 military coups since becoming a constitutional monarchy in 1932. The government returned to democratic civilian control in December 2007, but political turmoil continues. In the July 2011 parliamentary elections, Pheu Thai, the opposition party of exiled leader Thaksin Shinawatra, won an outright majority, and Shinawatra's sister, Yingluck Shinawatra, became prime minister. In spring 2014, Yingluck Shinawatra was ousted from power in a military coup led by Army General Prayuth Chan-Ocha. Elections are not expected until October 2015. Since the coup, freedom of speech and freedom of association have been severely restricted, and leading politicians have been placed under house arrest. About 40 percent of the population is engaged in agriculture, but a thriving manufacturing sector contributes significantly to the economy.

Freedom Trend

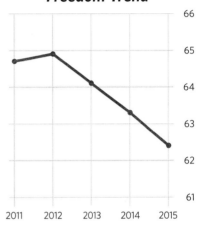

66

65

64

63

62

61

2011 2012 2013 2014 2015

Country Comparisons

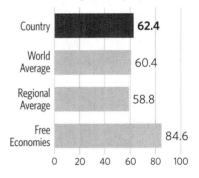

Country	62.4
World Average	60.4
Regional Average	58.8
Free Economies	84.6

0   20   40   60   80   100

Quick Facts

Population: 68.2 million
GDP (PPP): $673.7 billion
2.9% growth in 2013
5-year compound annual growth 2.9%
$9,875 per capita
Unemployment: 0.8%
Inflation (CPI): 2.2%
FDI Inflow: $12.9 billion
Public Debt: 45.3% of GDP

2013 data unless otherwise noted.
Data compiled as of September 2014.

How Do We Measure Economic Freedom?
See page 475 for an explanation of the methodology
or visit the *Index* Web site at *heritage.org/index.*

THE TEN ECONOMIC FREEDOMS

	Score	Rank	1-Year Change
RULE OF LAW			
Property Rights	40.0	70th	–5.0
Freedom from Corruption	35.0	103rd	+1.4

Corruption and graft are widespread at all levels of government and society amid unprecedented levels of political instability. Before a May 2014 military coup replaced the democratically elected government, the independent judiciary had been generally effective in enforcing property and contractual rights but remained vulnerable to political interference. Private property has generally been protected, but the legal process is slow.

	Score	Rank	1-Year Change
GOVERNMENT SIZE			
Fiscal Freedom	81.5	69th	+1.8
Government Spending	81.4	44th	–2.2

Thailand's top individual income tax rate has been reduced from 37 percent to 35 percent. The top corporate tax rate is 20 percent. Other taxes include a value-added tax and a property tax. Overall tax revenues equates to 15 percent of the domestic economy. Government spending amounts to 24.9 percent of domestic production, and public debt equals 45 percent of gross domestic product.

	Score	Rank	1-Year Change
REGULATORY EFFICIENCY			
Business Freedom	72.5	53rd	+1.1
Labor Freedom	63.5	86th	+1.9
Monetary Freedom	69.9	147th	+1.3

Forming a business takes almost a month, but no minimum capital is required. Licensing requirements remain onerous. Reform of the relatively rigid labor market has lagged. The new military government imposed price controls and expanded its power over state-owned enterprises (e.g., in the utility, energy, telecommunications, banking, agriculture, and transport sectors) that account for more than 40 percent of GDP.

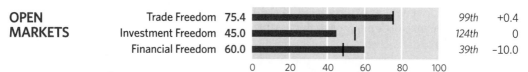

	Score	Rank	1-Year Change
OPEN MARKETS			
Trade Freedom	75.4	99th	+0.4
Investment Freedom	45.0	124th	0
Financial Freedom	60.0	39th	–10.0

Thailand's average tariff rate is 4.9 percent. Tariffs on agricultural imports are especially high. The government restricts foreign investment in many sectors of the economy. The financial system is under strain caused by political instability. Revisions in the Foreign Business Act, intended to open capital markets further to foreign investors, have been largely cosmetic. The banking sector remains relatively stable.

Long-Term Score Change (since 1995)

RULE OF LAW		GOVERNMENT SIZE		REGULATORY EFFICIENCY		OPEN MARKETS	
Property Rights	–50.0	Fiscal Freedom	+6.9	Business Freedom	+2.5	Trade Freedom	+9.0
Freedom from Corruption	–35.0	Government Spending	–11.4	Labor Freedom	–13.3	Investment Freedom	–5.0
				Monetary Freedom	–7.8	Financial Freedom	+10.0

TIMOR-LESTE

Dili

Economic Freedom Score

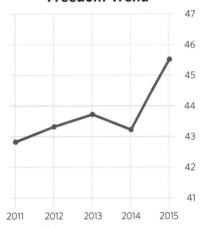

Least free 0 — 25 — 50 — 75 — 100 Most free

45.5

World Rank: **167**   Regional Rank: **40**

Timor-Leste's economic freedom score is 45.5, making its economy the 167th freest in the 2015 *Index*. Its score has increased by 2.3 points from last year, with improvements in trade freedom, business freedom, and freedom from corruption that more than offset declines in labor freedom and investment freedom. Timor-Leste is ranked 40th out of 42 countries in the Asia–Pacific region, and its overall score is well below the world and regional averages.

Timor-Leste remains one of the world's least economically free countries. Its economic freedom has increased by 2.7 points over the past five years, but improvements have come from such a low base that economic activity remains suppressed. Efforts to spur investment and increase regulatory efficiency have led gains in four of the 10 economic freedoms.

Economic institutions and infrastructure remain weak. Residual instability following violence surrounding independence from Indonesia has slowed or even prevented much economic reform. The rule of law is weakly respected, and vast oil and gas reserves encourage corruption and nepotism. Timor-Leste's trade freedom is among the worst in the world, and a slow-moving bureaucracy hampers investment that could diversify the economy.

BACKGROUND: The Democratic Republic of Timor-Leste became independent in 2002, and successive governments have struggled to pacify the country. Revolutionary leader Xanana Gusmao, its first president, has been prime minister since 2007 but has stated his intention to step down at the end of 2014. Economic liberalization has mostly stalled, and the economy depends heavily on foreign aid. Infrastructure is very poor, and corruption is pervasive. The economy remains primarily agricultural. Oil and gas profits account for more than 95 percent of government revenue. The government deposits all oil income in a Petroleum Fund that is not counted as part of GDP but is reflected in government revenue figures. In 2011, with Indonesia's support, Timor-Leste applied for membership in the Association of Southeast Asian Nations.

Freedom Trend

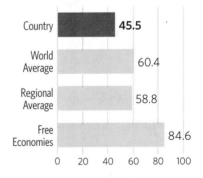

2011   2012   2013   2014   2015

Country Comparisons

Country	**45.5**
World Average	60.4
Regional Average	58.8
Free Economies	84.6

0   20   40   60   80   100

Quick Facts

Population: 1.2 million
GDP (PPP): $25.8 billion
8.4% growth in 2013
5-year compound annual growth 10.4%
$21,705 per capita
Unemployment: 4.5%
Inflation (CPI): 10.6%
FDI Inflow: $19.8 million
Public Debt: 0.0% of GDP

2013 data unless otherwise noted.
Data compiled as of September 2014.

How Do We Measure Economic Freedom?
See page 475 for an explanation of the methodology
or visit the *Index* Web site at *heritage.org/index*.

427

THE TEN ECONOMIC FREEDOMS

		Score	■ Country	World Average	Rank	1-Year Change

RULE OF LAW
Property Rights 20.0 — 138th — 0
Freedom from Corruption 30.0 — 121st — +4.6

President Taur Matan Rauk reportedly has said that corruption exists at all levels in society. Increasing allegations of petty corruption against the police force and a perception that government contracts generally go to those with the right connections have raised concerns about endemic public-sector corruption. Rule of law is weak. Land reform remains an unresolved and contentious issue.

GOVERNMENT SIZE
Fiscal Freedom 64.7 — 157th — 0
Government Spending 0.0 — 176th — 0

Timor-Leste's top individual and corporate income tax rates are 10 percent. Other taxes include a sales tax. The majority of tax revenue, which is equal to 69.1 percent of gross domestic product, comes from offshore oil and gas production in the Timor Sea. Government expenditures are equivalent to 86.4 percent of domestic production.

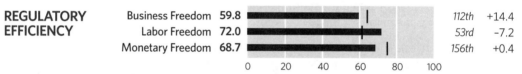

REGULATORY EFFICIENCY
Business Freedom 59.8 — 112th — +14.4
Labor Freedom 72.0 — 53rd — –7.2
Monetary Freedom 68.7 — 156th — +0.4

The regulatory environment remains burdensome and costly. The minimum capital required to establish a business still costs more than the level of average annual income. The public sector accounts for around half of non-agricultural employment, and the formal labor market remains underdeveloped. The government uses its substantial oil revenues to fund large subsidy programs for food, power, and fuel.

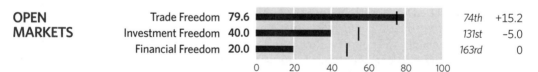

OPEN MARKETS
Trade Freedom 79.6 — 74th — +15.2
Investment Freedom 40.0 — 131st — –5.0
Financial Freedom 20.0 — 163rd — 0

The simple average tariff rate for Timor-Leste was 6.0 percent as of 2007. New foreign investment is subject to government screening. The investment environment is significantly limited by inadequate institutional capacity, complex licensing requirements, and poor infrastructure. The financial sector is very small and underdeveloped. Less than 2 percent of the population has access to financial services.

Long-Term Score Change (since 2009)

RULE OF LAW		GOVERNMENT SIZE		REGULATORY EFFICIENCY		OPEN MARKETS	
Property Rights	0	Fiscal Freedom	0	Business Freedom	+12.8	Trade Freedom	+6.6
Freedom from Corruption	+4.0	Government Spending	–84.0	Labor Freedom	+6.0	Investment Freedom	+10.0
				Monetary Freedom	–5.4	Financial Freedom	0

TOGO

★ Lomé

Economic Freedom Score

25   50   75

Least   0   100   Most
free   free

53.0

ogo's economic freedom score is 53.0, making its economy the 138th freest in the 2015 *Index*. Its score is up by 3.1 points from last year, reflecting improvements in six of the 10 economic freedoms, including investment freedom, business freedom, freedom from corruption, and trade freedom. Togo is ranked 30th out of 46 countries in the Sub-Saharan Africa region, and its overall score is well below the world and regional averages.

Steady improvements in economic freedom have boosted Togo from the "repressed" category for the first time, and it has recorded its highest score ever in the 2015 *Index*. Over the past five years, economic freedom in Togo has advanced by 3.9 points, with relatively broad-based improvements led by gains of 25 points in investment freedom and 15 points in business freedom.

Togo has one of West Africa's largest natural harbors, but its institutional framework is not fully consistent with the freer standards expected in the international marketplace. The rule of law remains weakly enforced, and corruption is prevalent. Rigid and inefficient business regulations encourage the use of graft to expedite bureaucratic delays.

BACKGROUND: The military appointed Faure Gnassingbé to the presidency in 2005 following the death of his father. Faced with sanctions by the Economic Community of West African States and the African Union, he stepped down two months later and called for an election, which he won despite electoral irregularities. Gnassingbé was re-elected in 2010, and his Union of Forces for Change won a majority of seats in flawed parliamentary elections in 2013. Togo is the world's fourth-largest producer of phosphate. Cocoa, coffee, and cotton generate about 40 percent of export earnings. With West Africa's only deep-water port, its secure territorial waters have become a relatively safe zone for international shippers amid the regional surge in maritime piracy. Togo remains dependent on foreign assistance and continues to work on International Monetary Fund–designed reforms.

Freedom Trend

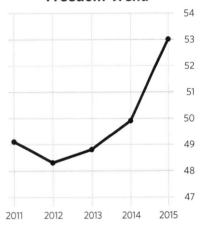

2011   2012   2013   2014   2015

Country Comparisons

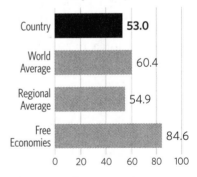

Country	53.0
World Average	60.4
Regional Average	54.9
Free Economies	84.6

0   20   40   60   80   100

Quick Facts

Population: 6.8 million
GDP (PPP): $7.4 billion
5.6% growth in 2013
5-year compound annual growth 4.8%
$1,084 per capita
Unemployment: 8.5%
Inflation (CPI): 2.0%
FDI Inflow: $84.2 million
Public Debt: 43.3% of GDP

2013 data unless otherwise noted.
Data compiled as of September 2014.

How Do We Measure Economic Freedom?
See page 475 for an explanation of the methodology
or visit the *Index* Web site at *heritage.org/index.*

THE TEN ECONOMIC FREEDOMS

		Score				Rank	1-Year Change

RULE OF LAW

	Score		Rank	1-Year Change
Property Rights	30.0		94th	0
Freedom from Corruption	29.0		127th	+5.2

Although the government has taken some steps to reduce graft, it is still common practice to provide cash or other gifts to expedite business transactions and shorten delays for obtaining registrations, permits, and licenses. The judicial system lacks resources and is heavily influenced by the presidency. Private property is not well protected, and enforcement of contracts is difficult.

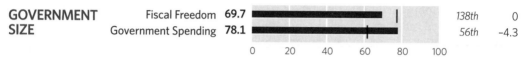

GOVERNMENT SIZE

	Score		Rank	1-Year Change
Fiscal Freedom	69.7		138th	0
Government Spending	78.1		56th	-4.3

Togo's top individual income tax rate is 45 percent, and its top corporate tax rate is 27 percent. Other taxes include a value-added tax and a property tax. The overall tax burden equals 16.5 percent of the domestic economy, and government expenditures amount to 27 percent of domestic production. Public debt is equivalent to 43 percent of gross domestic product.

REGULATORY EFFICIENCY

	Score		Rank	1-Year Change
Business Freedom	51.9		148th	+8.6
Labor Freedom	43.4		158th	+0.6
Monetary Freedom	80.4		49th	+1.1

Togo lags behind other developing countries in easing regulatory constraints. The process for launching a business has been streamlined, but getting necessary licenses takes over five months. The labor market remains underdeveloped, and the informal sector employs much of the workforce. In 2013, the IMF recommended that Togo reduce fuel subsidies to allow for higher social and infrastructure spending.

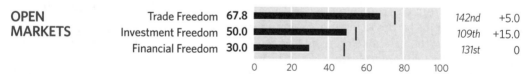

OPEN MARKETS

	Score		Rank	1-Year Change
Trade Freedom	67.8		142nd	+5.0
Investment Freedom	50.0		109th	+15.0
Financial Freedom	30.0		131st	0

The average tariff rate is 11.1 percent. Togo adopted a new customs code in 2014 and is implementing a single window to facilitate trade. Foreign and domestic investors are generally treated equally under the investment code. The underdeveloped legal infrastructure impedes the development of a modern financial sector. Much of the population operates outside of the formal banking sector.

Long-Term Score Change (since 1999)

RULE OF LAW		GOVERNMENT SIZE		REGULATORY EFFICIENCY		OPEN MARKETS	
Property Rights	0	Fiscal Freedom	-7.7	Business Freedom	+11.9	Trade Freedom	+4.8
Freedom from Corruption	+19.0	Government Spending	-8.5	Labor Freedom	-3.5	Investment Freedom	+20.0
				Monetary Freedom	+13.5	Financial Freedom	0

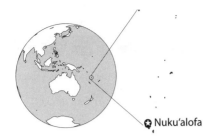

● Nuku'alofa

TONGA

Economic Freedom Score

Least free 0   Most free 100

59.3

Tonga's economic freedom score is 59.3, making its economy the 95th freest in the 2015 *Index*. Its score is 1.1 points better than last year, with improvements in investment freedom, the control of government spending, and monetary freedom outweighing declines in trade freedom and business freedom. Tonga is ranked 18th out of 42 countries in the Asia–Pacific region, and its score is below the world average.

Tonga is relatively well developed compared to some of its South Pacific island neighbors. Underpinned by a relatively open trading environment, it has cultivated agricultural exports to boost incomes and lower poverty. These improvements are reflected in Tonga's overall economic freedom score, which has advanced by 3.5 points since 2011. Gains in half of the 10 factors have been led by large improvements in trade and investment freedom. In the 2015 *Index*, Tonga has recorded its highest score ever.

Despite these gains, however, Tonga's economic framework is still weak, and the government relies heavily on foreign aid to balance the books. While the judicial system is based on British common law and relatively independent, judicial procedures are inefficient. Corruption is pervasive, and nepotism and favoritism benefit the elite and royals. Investment is limited and screened by the government, limiting non-aid–based financial flows.

BACKGROUND: The island Kingdom of Tonga, the South Pacific's last Polynesian monarchy, has been independent since 1970. The royal family, hereditary nobles, and a few other landholders control politics. Tonga held its first elections in November 2010 under its newly formed constitutional monarchy. The Friendly Islands Democratic Party won a plurality in parliament, and Lord Siale'ataonga Tu'ivakano became Tonga's first elected prime minister. Tonga boasts a 99 percent literacy rate, although more than half of the population lives abroad, mostly in New Zealand. Agriculture is the principal productive sector of the economy, and remittances from abroad are the primary source of income.

Freedom Trend

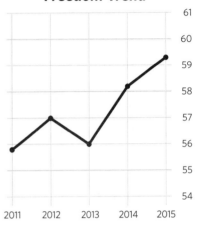

2011   2012   2013   2014   2015

Country Comparisons

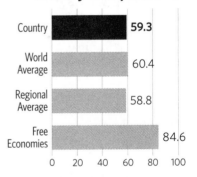

Country	59.3
World Average	60.4
Regional Average	58.8
Free Economies	84.6

0   20   40   60   80   100

Quick Facts

Population: 0.1 million
GDP (PPP): $0.8 billion
1.0% growth in 2013
5-year compound annual growth 2.0%
$8,168 per capita
Unemployment: n/a
Inflation (CPI): 3.2%
FDI Inflow: $11.6 million
Public Debt: 40.8% of GDP

2013 data unless otherwise noted.
Data compiled as of September 2014.

THE TEN ECONOMIC FREEDOMS

		Score		Rank	1-Year Change
RULE OF LAW	Property Rights	20.0		138th	0
	Freedom from Corruption	28.6		131st	0

Corruption is widespread, with royals, nobles, and their top associates allegedly having used state assets for personal benefit, and transparency and accountability are lacking. An Anti-Corruption Commission established in 2007 lacks power and resources to operate. The judiciary is generally independent, but a shortage of judges has caused long case backlogs. Property rights are uncertain, and enforcement is weak.

		Score		Rank	1-Year Change
GOVERNMENT SIZE	Fiscal Freedom	87.2		35th	+0.5
	Government Spending	79.0		50th	+4.2

The top individual income tax rate is 20 percent, and the top corporate tax rate is 25 percent. Other taxes include a sales tax and a tax on interest. The total tax burden amounts to 15.9 percent of domestic production. Government expenditures equal 26.4 percent of domestic output, and public debt is equivalent to 40.8 percent of gross domestic product.

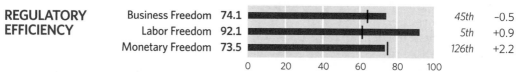

		Score		Rank	1-Year Change
REGULATORY EFFICIENCY	Business Freedom	74.1		45th	−0.5
	Labor Freedom	92.1		5th	+0.9
	Monetary Freedom	73.5		126th	+2.2

Launching a company takes four procedures, and no minimum capital is required. The regulatory framework generally supports entrepreneurial activity, but application of the commercial codes is not always straightforward. A well-functioning modern labor market is not fully developed. The government influences prices through subsidies for electricity and to loss-making state-owned enterprises.

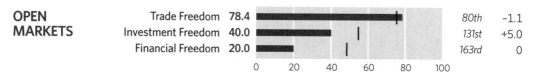

		Score		Rank	1-Year Change
OPEN MARKETS	Trade Freedom	78.4		80th	−1.1
	Investment Freedom	40.0		131st	+5.0
	Financial Freedom	20.0		163rd	0

Tonga's average tariff rate is 5.8 percent. Foreign investment in some sectors of the economy is prohibited. The government screens new foreign investment. In the absence of a modern and efficient financial system, much of the population has no access to financial services. Nonperforming loans remain a problem in the banking system. Capital markets are almost nonexistent.

Long-Term Score Change (since 2009)

RULE OF LAW		GOVERNMENT SIZE		REGULATORY EFFICIENCY		OPEN MARKETS	
Property Rights	0	Fiscal Freedom	+4.7	Business Freedom	−4.9	Trade Freedom	+22.4
Freedom from Corruption	+11.6	Government Spending	+21.0	Labor Freedom	−7.3	Investment Freedom	0
				Monetary Freedom	+4.6	Financial Freedom	0

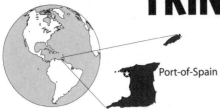

TRINIDAD AND TOBAGO

Port-of-Spain

Economic Freedom Score

25   50   75

Least free 0   100 Most free

64.1

Trinidad and Tobago's economic freedom score is 64.1, making its economy the 67th freest in the 2015 *Index*. Its score is 1.4 points higher than last year, with gains in the management of government spending, business freedom, and freedom from corruption outweighing a loss in fiscal freedom. Trinidad and Tobago is ranked 13th out of 29 countries in the South and Central America/Caribbean region, and its score is above the world average.

Trinidad and Tobago has become one of the most prosperous countries in the Caribbean Basin. Endowed with hydrocarbon reserves, the island group has been struggling against slow growth and an uptick in violence in recent years. Despite this year's gain, economic freedom in Trinidad and Tobago has declined since 2001 by 2.4 points, largely reflecting falling scores in financial freedom, government spending, and fiscal freedom.

Drug-related violence undermines the rule of law, and corruption has infiltrated the police force and increases the daily cost of living. The regulatory environment remains relatively inefficient. The economy is fairly open to trade and investment. The financial system is undergoing modernization in response to the recent financial upheaval and government bailouts.

BACKGROUND: Trinidad and Tobago is one of the Caribbean's richest nations, with hydrocarbons accounting for more than 40 percent of GDP and 80 percent of exports. Oil production has declined over the past decade as the country has focused on natural gas, but the government is providing fiscal incentives for investments in onshore and deep-water acreage to boost oil reserves. Prime Minister Kamla Persad-Bissessar has remained popular since her election in 2010 but has had to contend with a surge in drug-related corruption and violent crime. A Heritage and Stabilisation Fund was established in 2007 to provide a countercyclical backstop for government accounts when global energy prices fall. Financial services and construction have been among the strongest non-energy subsectors. Tourism has the potential for significant growth.

Freedom Trend

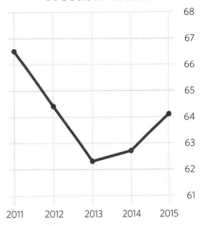

Country Comparisons

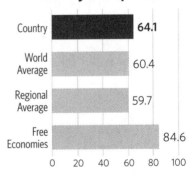

Country	**64.1**
World Average	60.4
Regional Average	59.7
Free Economies	84.6

0   20   40   60   80   100

Quick Facts

Population: 1.3 million
GDP (PPP): $27.5 billion
1.6% growth in 2013
5-year compound annual growth –0.8%
$20,438 per capita
Unemployment: 6.6%
Inflation (CPI): 5.2%
FDI Inflow: $1.7 billion
Public Debt: 30.6% of GDP

2013 data unless otherwise noted.
Data compiled as of September 2014.

THE TEN ECONOMIC FREEDOMS

		Score		Rank	1-Year Change
RULE OF LAW	Property Rights	50.0		56th	0
	Freedom from Corruption	38.0		83rd	+4.0

Corruption, much of it drug-related, diverts resources and damages the rule of law. Narcotics-related corruption in the police force is endemic. The judicial branch is independent but subject to some political pressure and corruption. Rising rates of crime and very high levels of violent crime have produced long delays in the court system. Property rights are well protected.

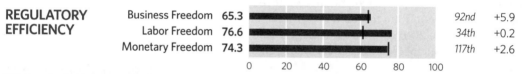

		Score		Rank	1-Year Change
GOVERNMENT SIZE	Fiscal Freedom	79.0		96th	–5.8
	Government Spending	69.3		87th	+6.8

Trinidad and Tobago's top individual and top corporate income tax rates are 25 percent. Other taxes include a value-added tax and a property tax. Tax revenue amounts to about 29.2 percent of the domestic economy. Government spending, supported partly by hydrocarbon revenues, equals approximately 32 percent of domestic production. Public debt equals 31 percent of gross domestic product.

		Score		Rank	1-Year Change
REGULATORY EFFICIENCY	Business Freedom	65.3		92nd	+5.9
	Labor Freedom	76.6		34th	+0.2
	Monetary Freedom	74.3		117th	+2.6

With no minimum capital required, it takes about 12 days to start a company, but licensing requirements remain time-consuming. The relatively flexible labor market facilitates the matching of supply and demand in the labor market. The government's 2013–2014 budget proposal included large subsidies for natural gas, education, and the environment, but it also reduced the national fuel subsidy.

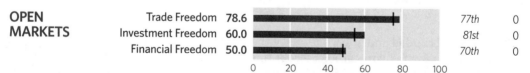

		Score		Rank	1-Year Change
OPEN MARKETS	Trade Freedom	78.6		77th	0
	Investment Freedom	60.0		81st	0
	Financial Freedom	50.0		70th	0

Trinidad and Tobago's average tariff rate is 5.7 percent. Cars and many agricultural goods require import licenses. Over 40 companies are 100 percent state-owned. The financial system has regained its stability after strain caused by the collapse of a large financial group. State influence is not substantial, and banking remains relatively well capitalized, with the number of nonperforming loans declining.

Long-Term Score Change (since 1996)

RULE OF LAW		GOVERNMENT SIZE		REGULATORY EFFICIENCY		OPEN MARKETS	
Property Rights	–40.0	Fiscal Freedom	+14.5	Business Freedom	–4.7	Trade Freedom	+43.6
Freedom from Corruption	–12.0	Government Spending	–8.2	Labor Freedom	–2.4	Investment Freedom	–30.0
				Monetary Freedom	–1.6	Financial Freedom	–20.0

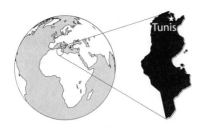
Tunis

TUNISIA

Economic Freedom Score

25   **50**   75

Least free 0   100 Most free

57.7

Tunisia's economic freedom score is 57.7, making its economy the 107th freest in the 2015 *Index*. Its score is 0.4 point higher than last year, with improvements in the control of government spending, freedom from corruption, and business freedom largely offset by declines in labor freedom and monetary freedom. Tunisia is ranked 11th out of 15 countries in the Middle East/North Africa region.

Tunisia's transition to a more open and inclusive economy has been hurt by political instability and indecisiveness in implementing critical reforms. Over the past five years, economic freedom in Tunisia has declined by 0.8 point, with deteriorations in four of the 10 economic freedoms, including property rights, the control of government spending, and monetary freedom.

Inconsistent rule of law and regulatory inefficiency weaken Tunisia's fragile economic framework. Years of corruption under the Ben Ali regime instilled a culture of nepotism and cronyism that prevented much-needed market liberalization. Following through on structural and institutional reforms will be critical to the success of Tunisia's ongoing transition to a functioning market economy.

BACKGROUND: Tunisia, birthplace of the Arab Spring, ousted President Zine al-Abidine Ben Ali in January 2011. Shortly thereafter, the formerly banned Islamist Ennahda Party won the largest number of seats in the National Constituent Assembly. The Ennahda government stepped aside in 2014 following the ratification of a new constitution in January, and an interim technocratic government was installed, led by Interim Prime Minister Mehdi Jomaa. The Nidaa Tounes party headed by Béji Caïd Essebsi won the most seats in parliamentary elections in late 2014. Tunisia's diverse economy is based on manufacturing, tourism, agriculture, and mining. An association agreement with the European Union has helped to create jobs and modernize the economy, but the EU economic slowdown has depressed demand for Tunisian-made goods. Salafi Islamist violence has undermined foreign investment and tourism. Political stability is also threatened by high formal-sector unemployment.

Freedom Trend

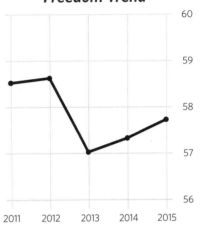

Country Comparisons

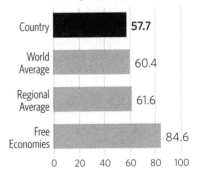

Country	57.7
World Average	60.4
Regional Average	61.6
Free Economies	84.6

Quick Facts

Population: 10.9 million
GDP (PPP): $108.4 billion
2.7% growth in 2013
5-year compound annual growth 2.1%
$9,932 per capita
Unemployment: 17.5%
Inflation (CPI): 6.1%
FDI Inflow: $1.1 billion
Public Debt: 44.4% of GDP

2013 data unless otherwise noted.
Data compiled as of September 2014.

THE TEN ECONOMIC FREEDOMS

		Score	■ Country	| World Average	Rank	1–Year Change
RULE OF LAW	Property Rights	40.0			70th	0
	Freedom from Corruption	41.0			77th	+1.8

Tunisia's handling of commercial disputes is fairly efficient by regional standards, but only slow progress has been made in reforming the judiciary. A majority of citizens say that corruption has increased during the past two years as the breakdown of authority has encouraged graft at lower levels of government and in law enforcement. Property rights are not protected effectively.

		Score			Rank	1-Year Change
GOVERNMENT SIZE	Fiscal Freedom	74.3			119th	0
	Government Spending	70.8			82nd	+7.0

Tunisia's top individual income tax rate is 35 percent, and its top corporate tax rate is 30 percent. Other taxes include a value-added tax and a property tax. The overall tax burden equals 21 percent of domestic output. Government expenditures amount to 31.2 percent of gross domestic product, and public debt equals 44 percent of the domestic economy.

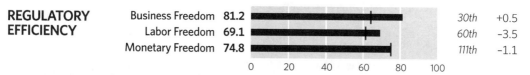

		Score			Rank	1-Year Change
REGULATORY EFFICIENCY	Business Freedom	81.2			30th	+0.5
	Labor Freedom	69.1			60th	–3.5
	Monetary Freedom	74.8			111th	–1.1

Previous regulatory reforms have proven to be largely cosmetic, failing to create momentum for entrepreneurial growth. In the absence of a well-functioning labor market, informal labor persists in many sectors. The state decreased subsidies for bread, sugar, and other basic materials in 2014 but ultimately reversed an effort to raise subsidized gasoline prices to reduce the fiscal deficit.

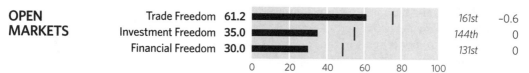

		Score			Rank	1-Year Change
OPEN MARKETS	Trade Freedom	61.2			161st	–0.6
	Investment Freedom	35.0			144th	0
	Financial Freedom	30.0			131st	0

Tunisia's average tariff rate is 14.4 percent. Some agricultural imports face additional barriers. In most cases, foreign investment is capped by the government. Foreign investors may not own agricultural land. The financial sector is weak, fragmented, and dominated by the government. Financing options for start-ups and small and medium-sized companies remain very limited, with capital markets underdeveloped.

Long-Term Score Change (since 1995)

RULE OF LAW		GOVERNMENT SIZE		REGULATORY EFFICIENCY		OPEN MARKETS	
Property Rights	–10.0	Fiscal Freedom	+4.6	Business Freedom	–3.8	Trade Freedom	+15.8
Freedom from Corruption	–9.0	Government Spending	+1.7	Labor Freedom	+6.4	Investment Freedom	–35.0
				Monetary Freedom	–6.3	Financial Freedom	–20.0

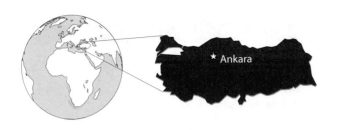

TURKEY

Economic Freedom Score

Least free 0   100 Most free

63.2

| World Rank: **70** | Regional Rank: **32** |

Turkey's economic freedom score is 63.2, making its economy the 70th freest in the 2015 *Index*. Its score has decreased by 1.7 points since last year, with declines in five of the 10 economic freedoms, including labor freedom, business freedom, the control of government spending, and property rights, outweighing improvements in freedom from corruption and investment freedom. Turkey is ranked 32nd out of 43 countries in the Europe region, and its overall score is higher than the world average.

Turkey's economic freedom score has declined by 1.0 point since 2011. A 26-point decline in the management of government spending has offset a double-digit gain in financial freedom. Scores for five other economic freedoms, including business freedom and property rights, have also dropped.

Turkey's commitment to economic freedom is vital given its position as an important emerging market. Its economic freedom rests on relatively stable but fragile foundations. The judiciary is subject to government influence, and corruption charges have reached high-level officials close to the government. While the economy is open and boasts a burgeoning manufacturing sector, regulatory inefficiencies and a rigid labor market hinder business formation and full employment, undermining more vibrant private-sector growth.

BACKGROUND: Turkey is a constitutionally secular republic, but Prime Minister Recep Tayyip Erdogan's Justice and Development Party is pushing an Islamist agenda and eroding Turkey's Euro–Atlantic connections. Large-scale protests resulting from unpopular government decisions continued sporadically in 2014. Economic modernization is progressing despite clashes with the media and the slow pace of judicial reform. Turkey has been a member of NATO since 1952. The European Union granted Turkey candidate status in 1999, but there is strong opposition from France, Germany, and Austria. Turkey's dispute with Cyprus has also delayed negotiations. Turkey's economy has been growing steadily for the past decade and weathered the 2008 global financial crisis relatively well. Principal exports include foodstuffs, textiles, clothing, iron, and steel.

Freedom Trend

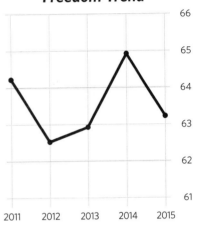

Country Comparisons

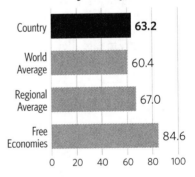

Quick Facts

Population: 76.5 million
GDP (PPP): $1.2 trillion
4.3% growth in 2013
5-year compound annual growth 3.8%
$15,353 per capita
Unemployment: 9.9%
Inflation (CPI): 7.5%
FDI Inflow: $12.9 billion
Public Debt: 35.8% of GDP

2013 data unless otherwise noted.
Data compiled as of September 2014.

How Do We Measure Economic Freedom?
See page 475 for an explanation of the methodology
or visit the *Index* Web site at *heritage.org/index*.

THE TEN ECONOMIC FREEDOMS

		Score			Rank	1-Year Change
RULE OF LAW	Property Rights	45.0			66th	−5.0
	Freedom from Corruption	50.0			52nd	+6.0

Corruption, cronyism, and nepotism persist in government and daily life. An October 2013 report noted weaknesses related to transparency, with government ministries refusing to hand over information to the Court of Accounts and pressuring the court to alter its reports on corruption. The judiciary is only nominally independent. Property rights are generally enforced, but the courts are slow.

				Rank	1-Year Change
GOVERNMENT SIZE	Fiscal Freedom	76.1		113th	−1.4
	Government Spending	57.6		120th	−5.9

The top individual income tax rate is 35 percent, and the top corporate tax rate is 20 percent. Other taxes include a value-added tax and an environment tax. Tax revenues account for approximately 27.7 percent of the domestic economy. Government expenditures equal 37.6 percent of domestic production, and public debt is equivalent to 36 percent of gross domestic product.

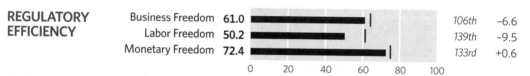

				Rank	1-Year Change
REGULATORY EFFICIENCY	Business Freedom	61.0		106th	−6.6
	Labor Freedom	50.2		139th	−9.5
	Monetary Freedom	72.4		133rd	+0.6

The regulatory framework remains cumbersome. There is a minimum capital requirement for incorporating a business, and licensing requirements consume over five months on average. The labor market lacks flexibility and hinders dynamic job growth. The state introduced a subsidy program intended to nearly double agricultural crop production by 2023 and maintains subsidies for fuel, electricity, and health care.

				Rank	1-Year Change
OPEN MARKETS	Trade Freedom	84.6		53rd	+0.1
	Investment Freedom	75.0		36th	+5.0
	Financial Freedom	60.0		39th	0

Turkey's average tariff rate is 2.7 percent. Government procurement may favor domestic firms. Turkey, while generally very open to foreign investment, restricts investment in some sectors. The evolving financial sector remains dominated by the concentrated banking sector, in which the 10 largest banks account for over 80 percent of total lending. The number of nonperforming loans has increased.

Long-Term Score Change (since 1995)

RULE OF LAW		GOVERNMENT SIZE		REGULATORY EFFICIENCY		OPEN MARKETS	
Property Rights	−25.0	Fiscal Freedom	+31.6	Business Freedom	−24.0	Trade Freedom	+9.8
Freedom from Corruption	+40.0	Government Spending	−5.7	Labor Freedom	+9.5	Investment Freedom	+5.0
				Monetary Freedom	+34.2	Financial Freedom	−10.0

TURKMENISTAN

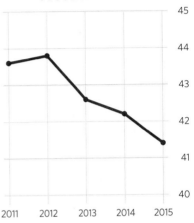

Economic Freedom Score

25　50　75

Least free　0

Most free　100

41.4

Turkmenistan's economic freedom score is 41.4, making its economy the 172nd freest in the 2015 *Index*. Its score has declined by 0.8 point since last year, with improvements in freedom from corruption, trade freedom, and the control of government spending outweighed by a combined decline in labor freedom, monetary freedom, and fiscal freedom. Turkmenistan is ranked 41st out of 42 countries in the Asia–Pacific region, and its overall score is significantly lower than the world and regional averages.

Turkmenistan is one of the world's most closed and most centralized countries. Apart from natural gas exports, it engages little with the outside world, and a large proportion of its society lives in poverty. Since 2011, economic freedom in Turkmenistan has declined by 2.2 points, reflecting a further worsening of already strict labor rules and increasing inflation.

Turkmenistan ranks last in the world for its investment regime, and state-owned enterprises dominate much of the domestic economy and formal sector. The executive controls all three branches of government, making judicial independence impossible. Corruption and nepotism limit the economic prospects of those who are not well connected.

BACKGROUND: In 2012, President Gurbanguly Berdymukhammedov was re-elected to a second five-year term with 97 percent of the vote in elections that international observers regarded as flawed. The presidency tightly controls all three branches of government, the economy, social services, and the mass media. Berdymukhammedov's policies are somewhat more open than those of his predecessor, President-for-Life Saparmurad Niyazov, but the government still tends toward isolationism. Most statistics on Turkmenistan's inefficient and highly corrupt economy are state secrets. Turkmenistan has intensive agriculture in irrigated oases, sizeable oil resources, and the world's fifth largest natural gas reserves. Berdymukhammedov has encouraged some foreign investment in the energy sector, especially from Russia, China, and Iran. Turkmenistan's gas currently accounts for around one-sixth of China's total gas consumption, with Russia the next biggest buyer.

Freedom Trend

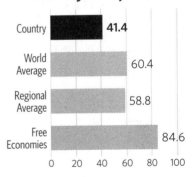

2011　2012　2013　2014　2015

Country Comparisons

Country　41.4

World Average　60.4

Regional Average　58.8

Free Economies　84.6

0　20　40　60　80　100

Quick Facts

Population: 5.7 million

GDP (PPP): $54.2 billion

10.2% growth in 2013

5-year compound annual growth 10.2%

$9,510 per capita

Unemployment: 10.7%

Inflation (CPI): 6.6%

FDI Inflow: $3.1 billion

Public Debt: 20.6% of GDP

How Do We Measure Economic Freedom?
See page 475 for an explanation of the methodology or visit the *Index* Web site at *heritage.org/index*.

2013 data unless otherwise noted.
Data compiled as of September 2014.

THE TEN ECONOMIC FREEDOMS

		Score			Rank	1-Year Change

RULE OF LAW

	Score		Rank	1-Year Change
Property Rights	5.0		179th	0
Freedom from Corruption	17.0		176th	+3.6

Corruption is widespread, and public officials often bribe their way into their positions. The president appoints and removes judges without legislative review. The legal system does not enforce contracts and property rights effectively. Laws are poorly developed, and judges are poorly trained and open to bribery. All land is owned by the government, and other ownership rights are limited.

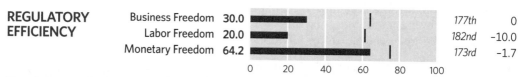

GOVERNMENT SIZE

	Score		Rank	1-Year Change
Fiscal Freedom	94.0		12th	-1.2
Government Spending	93.5		5th	+0.5

The top individual income tax rate is 10 percent. The top corporate tax rate is 8 percent (other entities pay 20 percent under the petroleum law). Other taxes include a value-added tax and a property tax. The tax burden equals 21 percent of domestic output. Government spending amounts to approximately 15 percent of domestic production, and public debt equals 21 percent of GDP.

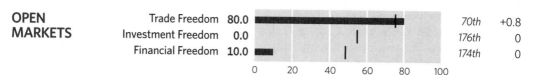

REGULATORY EFFICIENCY

	Score		Rank	1-Year Change
Business Freedom	30.0		177th	0
Labor Freedom	20.0		182nd	-10.0
Monetary Freedom	64.2		173rd	-1.7

Regulatory codes are outmoded, and cutting through red tape often requires personal relations with government officials. The public sector provides most jobs, but the informal sector remains an important source of employment. Although some fuel subsidies were scrapped in 2014, subsidies as a percentage of GDP are still among the world's highest. Natural gas is free to citizens.

OPEN MARKETS

	Score		Rank	1-Year Change
Trade Freedom	80.0		70th	+0.8
Investment Freedom	0.0		176th	0
Financial Freedom	10.0		174th	0

There are no general tariffs on most imports, but the excise tax system is biased against imports. Imports face customs delays, and government procurement favors domestic firms. Foreign investors face several regulatory and bureaucratic hurdles. Foreign exchange accounts and all international transfers require state approval. The financial system is heavily government-controlled, with loans typically directed to state-owned enterprises.

Long-Term Score Change (since 1998)

RULE OF LAW		GOVERNMENT SIZE		REGULATORY EFFICIENCY		OPEN MARKETS	
Property Rights	-25.0	Fiscal Freedom	+37.8	Business Freedom	-25.0	Trade Freedom	+40.0
Freedom from Corruption	+7.0	Government Spending	+9.4	Labor Freedom	-10.0	Investment Freedom	-30.0
				Monetary Freedom	+64.2	Financial Freedom	0

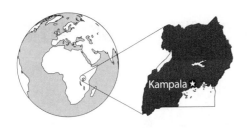

UGANDA

Economic Freedom Score

25   50   75

Least free 0 .... 100 Most free

59.7

World Rank: 92   **Regional Rank: 9**

Uganda's economic freedom score is 59.7, making its economy the 92nd freest in the 2015 *Index*. Its score has decreased by 0.2 point since last year, with improvements in half of the 10 economic freedoms, including monetary freedom and freedom from corruption, outweighed by declines in fiscal freedom and property rights. Uganda is ranked 9th out of 46 countries in the Sub-Saharan Africa region, and its overall score is below the world average.

Once a model for reform and a favored investment destination, Uganda has recorded a decline of 2.0 points in economic freedom over the past five years as the momentum for reform has slowed. This diminishment has occurred in six of the 10 economic freedoms, including a 20-point decline in financial freedom. A 15-point improvement in the investment regime is one bright spot.

Uganda has mostly recovered from its past civil and political unrest, but moderate reforms have not been enough to put the economy on the path to sustainable growth. The executive exerts serious influence on the judiciary, and foreign aid has been frozen in recent years due to corruption allegations. The business environment impedes the formation of new businesses, and most of the largely impoverished and agricultural population works in the informal sector.

BACKGROUND: President Yoweri Museveni, who seized power in a military coup in 1986, was elected to a fourth term in 2011. Museveni has been accused of aiding rebels in the Democratic Republic of Congo. Limited market reforms have produced more than a decade of relatively strong economic growth. Uganda has substantial natural resources, including copper, gold, and newly discovered oil. Infrastructure projects in the transport and energy sectors have increased domestic demand and stimulated growth. Instability in South Sudan, Uganda's main export partner, threatens to destabilize the economy. Uganda continues to play an important role in peacekeeping operations in Somalia and in the fight against terrorism.

Freedom Trend

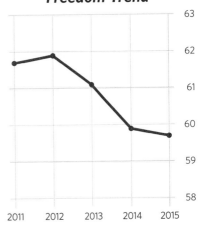

2011   2012   2013   2014   2015

Country Comparisons

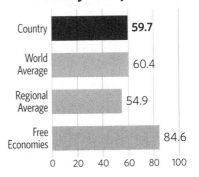

Country	59.7
World Average	60.4
Regional Average	54.9
Free Economies	84.6

0   20   40   60   80   100

Quick Facts

Population: 36.8 million
GDP (PPP): $54.6 billion
6.0% growth in 2013
5-year compound annual growth 5.1%
$1,484 per capita
Unemployment: 3.8%
Inflation (CPI): 5.4%
FDI Inflow: $1.1 billion
Public Debt: 33.9% of GDP

2013 data unless otherwise noted.
Data compiled as of September 2014.

How Do We Measure Economic Freedom?
See page 475 for an explanation of the methodology
or visit the *Index* Web site at *heritage.org/index*.

THE TEN ECONOMIC FREEDOMS

		Score	Country	World Average	Rank	1-Year Change
RULE OF LAW	Property Rights	25.0			124th	-5.0
	Freedom from Corruption	26.0			145th	+2.2

Uganda has laws and institutions tasked with combating corruption, but enforcement is very weak. In 2013, government harassment of anti-corruption activists increased, and the Constitutional Court suspended the Anti-Corruption Court. The rule of law is weak. Land disputes in northern Uganda escalated in 2014, often due to the absence of title deeds in areas where customary tenure is still common.

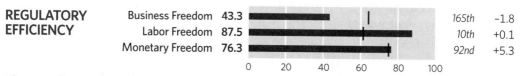

		Score			Rank	1-Year Change
GOVERNMENT SIZE	Fiscal Freedom	73.3			124th	-5.8
	Government Spending	89.0			15th	+1.7

Uganda's top individual income tax rate has increased from 30 percent to 40 percent. The top corporate tax rate is 30 percent. Other taxes include a value-added tax and a property tax. Overall tax revenues equal 13.1 percent of the domestic economy. Government expenditures are equivalent to 19.1 percent of domestic production, and public debt equals 36 percent of GDP.

		Score			Rank	1-Year Change
REGULATORY EFFICIENCY	Business Freedom	43.3			165th	-1.8
	Labor Freedom	87.5			10th	+0.1
	Monetary Freedom	76.3			92nd	+5.3

The overall regulatory framework has undergone a series of reforms, but the pace of reform has slowed. Despite some progress, the labor market lacks dynamism because of lingering rigidities. A large informal sector persists. Inflation was low in 2014, with monetary stability relatively well maintained, and the government embarked on a four-year project to improve the targeting of electricity subsidies.

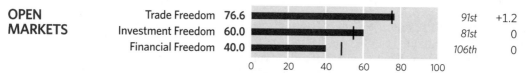

		Score			Rank	1-Year Change
OPEN MARKETS	Trade Freedom	76.6			91st	+1.2
	Investment Freedom	60.0			81st	0
	Financial Freedom	40.0			106th	0

Uganda's average tariff rate is 6.7 percent. Importing goods can be time-consuming. The Uganda Investment Authority has implemented a one-stop shop to facilitate foreign direct investment. The small financial markets are dominated by commercial banks and regulated by the central bank. The economy is still largely cash-based, and the limited availability of financing options precludes more vibrant private-sector development.

Long-Term Score Change (since 1995)

RULE OF LAW		GOVERNMENT SIZE		REGULATORY EFFICIENCY		OPEN MARKETS	
Property Rights	-25.0	Fiscal Freedom	-8.2	Business Freedom	-26.7	Trade Freedom	+18.8
Freedom from Corruption	-4.0	Government Spending	-0.6	Labor Freedom	-0.4	Investment Freedom	-10.0
				Monetary Freedom	+9.2	Financial Freedom	-10.0

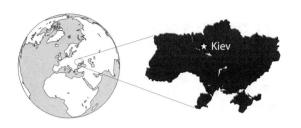
★ Kiev

UKRAINE

Economic Freedom Score

25   50   75

Least free   0   100   Most free

46.9

Ukraine's economic freedom score is 46.9, making its economy the 162nd freest in the 2015 *Index*. Its score is 2.4 points lower than last year, reflecting declines in eight of the 10 economic freedoms with especially grave deteriorations in property rights, the management of government spending, and investment freedom. Ukraine is ranked last out of 43 countries in the Europe region, and its overall score is lower than the world average.

Ukraine has registered the second largest score decline of any country graded in the 2015 *Index*. Previously, its economic freedom had advanced by 1.1 points, with improvements in half of the 10 economic freedoms driven largely by gains in business freedom and monetary freedom.

Ukraine's economy remains "repressed." The rule of law is particularly weak. The investment regime remains closed, with foreign investment competing with large state-owned enterprises. A rigid labor market and bureaucratic business regulations inhibit the development of a dynamic private sector.

BACKGROUND: Ukraine gained independence after the collapse of the Soviet Union in 1991. In February 2014, President Victor Yanukovych was ousted by pro-Euro–Atlantic members of parliament after he used security forces to crack down on popular protests against his attempt to tighten ties with Russia. Petro Poroshenko was elected to replace him in May 2014. After Yanukovych was unseated, Russia illegally annexed the Autonomous Republic of Crimea, and pro-Russian separatists increased their efforts to destabilize the eastern part of the country. In 2014, Ukraine accepted $30 billion in aid from the IMF, World Bank, EU, and other bilateral donors. Ukraine has signed an Association Agreement with the EU that includes Deep and Comprehensive Free Trade Area (DCFTA) accords. Ukraine has well-developed agricultural and industrial sectors, but dependence on steel exports and natural gas imports makes it vulnerable to global financial turmoil and Russian pressure. Ukraine joined the World Trade Organization in 2008 and the EU's Eastern Partnership in 2009.

Freedom Trend

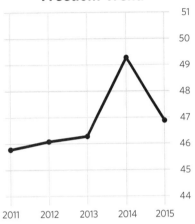

2011   2012   2013   2014   2015

Country Comparisons

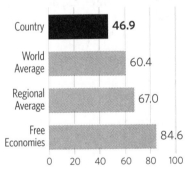

Country	46.9
World Average	60.4
Regional Average	67.0
Free Economies	84.6

0   20   40   60   80   100

Quick Facts

Population: 45.4 million
GDP (PPP): $336.8 billion
0.1% growth in 2013
5-year compound annual growth –1.3%
$7,423 per capita
Unemployment: 7.9%
Inflation (CPI): –0.3%
FDI Inflow: $3.8 billion
Public Debt: 41.0% of GDP

2013 data unless otherwise noted.
Data compiled as of September 2014.

How Do We Measure Economic Freedom?
See page 475 for an explanation of the methodology
or visit the *Index* Web site at *heritage.org/index.*

THE TEN ECONOMIC FREEDOMS

		Score	Country	World Average	Rank	1-Year Change
RULE OF LAW	Property Rights	20.0			138th	−10.0
	Freedom from Corruption	25.0			149th	+3.1

Pro-Western Ukrainians hoped their 2014 Euromaidan revolution would dismantle the oligarchic politics and deeply rooted cronyism that allowed business owners to amass wealth by exploiting their access to those in power rather than through efficient management, but that corrupt system is still largely in place under the Poroshenko government. The judiciary remains weak, and contracts may not be well enforced.

		Score		Rank	Change
GOVERNMENT SIZE	Fiscal Freedom	78.7		97th	−0.4
	Government Spending	28.0		163rd	−9.5

Ukraine's top individual income tax rate is 17 percent, and the top corporate tax rate is 18 percent. Other taxes include a value-added tax and a property tax. The total tax burden equals 38.9 percent of domestic income. Government spending amounts to 49 percent of GDP, and public debt equals 41 percent of domestic output. The IMF is helping to bolster public finances.

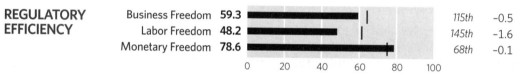

		Score		Rank	Change
REGULATORY EFFICIENCY	Business Freedom	59.3		115th	−0.5
	Labor Freedom	48.2		145th	−1.6
	Monetary Freedom	78.6		68th	−0.1

Complexity often creates uncertainty in commercial transactions. The business start-up process has been streamlined, but completing licensing requirements is still time-consuming. Modern and efficient bankruptcy procedures are not in place. The labor code is outmoded and lacks flexibility. Massive and price-skewing government subsidies (7 percent of GDP on natural gas subsidies alone) have caused deep economic distortions.

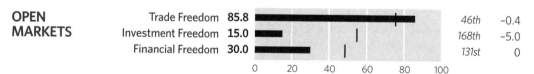

		Score		Rank	Change
OPEN MARKETS	Trade Freedom	85.8		46th	−0.4
	Investment Freedom	15.0		168th	−5.0
	Financial Freedom	30.0		131st	0

Ukraine's average tariff rate is 2.1 percent. Trade and investment flows have been disrupted as a result of disputes with Russia. Foreign investors may not purchase agricultural land. Bureaucratic requirements deter much-needed growth in private investment. The primarily cash-based economy suffers from a lack of sufficient capitalization. Nonperforming loans continue to be a drag on the banking system.

Long-Term Score Change (since 1995)

RULE OF LAW		GOVERNMENT SIZE		REGULATORY EFFICIENCY		OPEN MARKETS	
Property Rights	−10.0	Fiscal Freedom	+16.9	Business Freedom	+4.3	Trade Freedom	+30.8
Freedom from Corruption	+15.0	Government Spending	−19.1	Labor Freedom	−7.6	Investment Freedom	−35.0
				Monetary Freedom	+78.6	Financial Freedom	−20.0

UNITED ARAB EMIRATES

Abu Dhabi

World Rank: **25**   Regional Rank: **2**

Economic Freedom Score

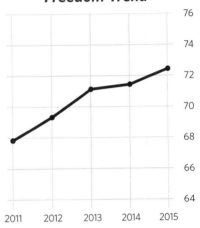

50
25   75
Least
free 0   100 Most
free

72.4

The United Arab Emirates' economic freedom score is 72.4, making its economy the 25th freest in the 2015 *Index*. Its score has increased by 1.0 point since last year, driven by improvements in investment freedom, the management of government spending, and freedom from corruption that outweigh a small combined decline in monetary freedom, trade freedom, and fiscal freedom. The UAE is ranked 2nd out of 15 countries in the Middle East/North Africa region, and its overall score is higher than the world and regional averages.

Over the past five years, economic freedom in the UAE has advanced by 4.6 points, the region's largest increase. Score improvements in seven of the 10 economic freedoms have been led by sizeable gains in the regulatory environment and monetary freedom.

Improved economic freedom has corresponded with moderate levels of growth. Economic reforms have cemented the UAE's position as a commercial, financial, and logistical Persian Gulf hub. However, institutional reforms have not been comprehensive. The perceived level of corruption has declined, but the relatively inefficient judicial system remains vulnerable to political influence.

BACKGROUND: The United Arab Emirates is a federation of seven monarchies: Abu Dhabi, Ajman, Dubai, Fujairah, Ras Al-Khaimah, Sharjah, and Umm al-Qaiwain. The government responded to the Arab Spring protests with a $1.6 billion program to improve the infrastructure in the poorer northern emirates and by expanding the number of people allowed to vote in September 2011 elections for the Federal National Council. The UAE clamped down on Internet activism in 2012 and imprisoned 68 Islamists for allegedly attempting to seize power in 2013. Abu Dhabi accounts for about 90 percent of oil production; Dubai is the center of finance, commerce, transportation, and tourism. Free trade zones that permit 100 percent foreign ownership with zero taxation help to diversify the economy. Oil and gas exports account for roughly 80 percent of government revenues.

Freedom Trend

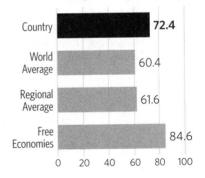

76

74

72

70

68

66

64

2011   2012   2013   2014   2015

Country Comparisons

Country — **72.4**
World Average — 60.4
Regional Average — 61.6
Free Economies — 84.6

0   20   40   60   80   100

Quick Facts

Population: 9.0 million
GDP (PPP): $272.0 billion
4.8% growth in 2013
5-year compound annual growth 1.9%
$30,122 per capita
Unemployment: 3.8%
Inflation (CPI): 1.1%
FDI Inflow: $10.5 billion
Public Debt: 12.3% of GDP

2013 data unless otherwise noted.
Data compiled as of September 2014.

How Do We Measure Economic Freedom?
See page 475 for an explanation of the methodology
or visit the *Index* Web site at *heritage.org/index*.

THE TEN ECONOMIC FREEDOMS

	Score		Rank	1-Year Change
		Country ▮ World Average ▏		

RULE OF LAW

	Score		Rank	1-Year Change
Property Rights	55.0		50th	0
Freedom from Corruption	69.0		26th	+2.6

Although the UAE is considered one of the Middle East's least corrupt countries, most decisions of any significance are made by the ruling families of the various emirates. The judiciary is not independent, and the political leadership reviews court rulings, but the rule of law is generally well maintained. All land in Abu Dhabi, largest of the seven emirates, is government-owned.

GOVERNMENT SIZE

	Score		Rank	1-Year Change
Fiscal Freedom	99.5		4th	-0.1
Government Spending	85.8		30th	+2.7

The UAE has no federal-level individual or corporate income taxes. Some emirates apply corporate taxes for different business entities. There are few other taxes. Overall tax revenues are equal to 7.2 percent of domestic income. Government spending, supported by significant oil and gas revenues, amounts to 21.8 percent of domestic output, and government debt equal to 12 percent of gross domestic product.

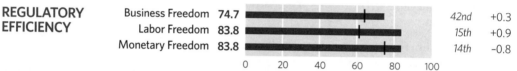

REGULATORY EFFICIENCY

	Score		Rank	1-Year Change
Business Freedom	74.7		42nd	+0.3
Labor Freedom	83.8		15th	+0.9
Monetary Freedom	83.8		14th	-0.8

Regulatory efficiency has improved. With no minimum capital required, establishing a business involves six procedures. Licensing has been streamlined and is less costly. The non-salary cost of employing a worker is moderate, and labor codes generally facilitate labor market efficiency. The government plans to reduce fuel and power subsidies to help limit energy consumption and imports of natural gas.

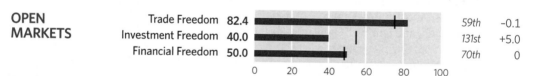

OPEN MARKETS

	Score		Rank	1-Year Change
Trade Freedom	82.4		59th	-0.1
Investment Freedom	40.0		131st	+5.0
Financial Freedom	50.0		70th	0

The UAE's average tariff rate is 3.8 percent. Foreign firms are disadvantaged in government procurement. In general, foreign investment in UAE companies is capped at 49 percent. The competitive and modern financial sector provides a full range of services, although the state's presence remains considerable. Capital markets are open and vibrant, with a number of foreign firms in operation.

Long-Term Score Change (since 1996)

RULE OF LAW		GOVERNMENT SIZE		REGULATORY EFFICIENCY		OPEN MARKETS	
Property Rights	-35.0	Fiscal Freedom	-0.4	Business Freedom	-10.3	Trade Freedom	+5.4
Freedom from Corruption	-21.0	Government Spending	+38.7	Labor Freedom	+9.5	Investment Freedom	+10.0
				Monetary Freedom	+8.6	Financial Freedom	0

UNITED KINGDOM

World Rank: 13   **Regional Rank: 5**

Economic Freedom Score

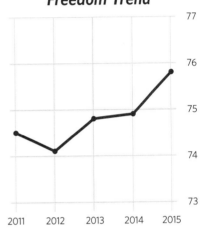

25   50   75

Least free 0   Most free 100

75.8

The United Kingdom's economic freedom score is 75.8, making its economy the 13th freest in the 2015 *Index*. Its score has increased by 0.9 point since last year, reflecting improvements in half of the 10 economic freedoms, including fiscal freedom and labor freedom, that outweigh declines in business freedom and freedom from corruption. The U.K. is ranked 5th out of 43 countries in the Europe region, and its overall score is above the world and regional averages.

Over the past five years, economic freedom in the U.K. has advanced by 1.3 points. Led by a sizeable improvement stemming from corporate tax rate cuts in recent years, score improvements have occurred in four of the 10 economic freedoms, including fiscal freedom and property rights.

Historically a champion of economic freedom in Europe, the United Kingdom has developed its economy based on a strong rule of law, an open trading environment, and one of the world's most advanced financial sectors. A relatively liberal labor market by European standards complements one of the world's most efficient business environments. Large government spending, which still takes up nearly half of the domestic economy, has consumed resources that could have enabled additional private-sector growth.

BACKGROUND: Following the market reforms instituted by Prime Minister Margaret Thatcher in the 1980s, Britain experienced steady economic growth throughout the 1990s, but government spending grew significantly under successive Labour governments. Since 2010, Prime Minister David Cameron's Conservative–Liberal Democrat coalition government has made government austerity the core of its economic policy. Last year, the U.K. experienced its strongest growth since 2007. In 2014, the GDP surpassed pre-crisis levels due to bullish performances by its three main sectors: services, manufacturing, and construction. Unemployment is at a five-year low, and retail sales are robust. Euro-skepticism is on the rise in the U.K., and the United Kingdom Independence Party won the most seats in the 2014 European Parliament elections.

Freedom Trend

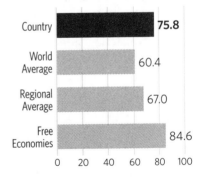

77

76

75

74

73

2011   2012   2013   2014   2015

Country Comparisons

Country **75.8**

World Average 60.4

Regional Average 67.0

Free Economies 84.6

0   20   40   60   80   100

Quick Facts

Population: 64.1 million
GDP (PPP): $2.4 trillion
1.8% growth in 2013
5-year compound annual growth –0.1%
$37,307 per capita
Unemployment: 7.5%
Inflation (CPI): 2.6%
FDI Inflow: $37.1 billion
Public Debt: 90.1% of GDP

2013 data unless otherwise noted.
Data compiled as of September 2014.

How Do We Measure Economic Freedom?
See page 475 for an explanation of the methodology or visit the *Index* Web site at *heritage.org/index.*

THE TEN ECONOMIC FREEDOMS

	Score		Rank	1-Year Change
RULE OF LAW				
Property Rights	90.0		3rd	0
Freedom from Corruption	76.0		14th	-0.4

Corruption is not pervasive, although a few high-profile scandals have damaged political reputations in both major parties. The 2011 Bribery Act is considered one of the world's most sweeping anti-bribery laws. Rule of law is well established within an independent legal framework. Private property rights and contracts are secure, and the court system is efficient. Protection of intellectual property rights is effective.

	Score		Rank	1-Year Change
GOVERNMENT SIZE				
Fiscal Freedom	62.9		162nd	+6.3
Government Spending	30.3		161st	+0.8

The top individual income tax rate is now 45 percent, and the top corporate tax rate is now 21 percent. Other taxes include a value-added tax and an environment tax. The overall tax burden equals 35.2 percent of the domestic economy. Public expenditures amount to 48.2 percent of domestic output, and government debt equals 90 percent of gross domestic product.

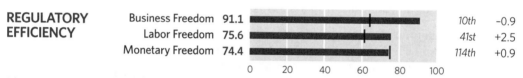

	Score		Rank	1-Year Change
REGULATORY EFFICIENCY				
Business Freedom	91.1		10th	-0.9
Labor Freedom	75.6		41st	+2.5
Monetary Freedom	74.4		114th	+0.9

The regulatory environment is transparent. With no minimum capital required, starting a business takes six procedures and less than a week. Bankruptcy proceedings are straightforward. The labor market is relatively efficient, and non-salary costs are moderate. Inflation has fallen rapidly, reflecting the end of administered price increases, and the government has pledged to end subsidies for onshore wind farms.

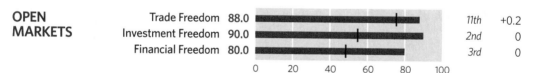

	Score		Rank	1-Year Change
OPEN MARKETS				
Trade Freedom	88.0		11th	+0.2
Investment Freedom	90.0		2nd	0
Financial Freedom	80.0		3rd	0

EU members have a 1.0 percent average tariff rate. Although some non-tariff barriers exist, the EU is relatively open to external trade. The U.K. generally treats foreign and domestic investors equally. The government still holds substantial stakes in the banking sector but is trying to sell its shares. A bank levy applied to both domestic and foreign banks has been in place.

Long-Term Score Change (since 1995)

RULE OF LAW		GOVERNMENT SIZE		REGULATORY EFFICIENCY		OPEN MARKETS	
Property Rights	0	Fiscal Freedom	+1.6	Business Freedom	-8.9	Trade Freedom	+10.2
Freedom from Corruption	-14.0	Government Spending	-7.0	Labor Freedom	-3.4	Investment Freedom	+20.0
				Monetary Freedom	-10.6	Financial Freedom	-10.0

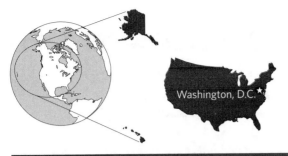

UNITED STATES

Economic Freedom Score

76.2

| World Rank: **12** | Regional Rank: **2** |

The United States' economic freedom score is 76.2, making its economy the 12th freest in the 2015 *Index*. Its score is 0.7 point higher than last year, with modest gains in six of the 10 economic freedoms, including control of government spending, outweighing a slight decline in business freedom.

Although the precipitous downward spiral in U.S. economic freedom since 2008 has come to a halt in the 2015 *Index*, a 1.6-point decline in overall economic freedom over the past five years reflects broad-based deteriorations in key policy areas, particularly those related to upholding the rule of law and limited government. Continuing to trail such comparable economies as Australia, New Zealand, Switzerland, and Canada, America has been ranked "mostly free" since 2010.

The anemic post-recession recovery has been characterized by slow growth, high unemployment, a decrease in the number of Americans seeking work, and great uncertainty that has held back investment. Increased tax and regulatory burdens, aggravated by favoritism toward entrenched interests, have undercut America's historically dynamic entrepreneurial growth.

BACKGROUND: President Barack Obama's second-term efforts to expand government spending and regulation have been thwarted to some extent by Republican Party opposition in Congress. Economic policy leadership has devolved by default to the Federal Reserve, whose attempts to use monetary policy to stimulate economic activity have not restored robust growth. Implementation of the 2010 health care law, which has reduced competition in most health insurance markets, remains a drag on job creation and full-time employment. Overall, the U.S. economy continues to underperform, despite a private sector–led energy boom that has made the U.S. the world's largest producer of oil and natural gas. The weak economic recovery and uncertain responses to foreign policy challenges, particularly in the Middle East, in Ukraine, and along the southern U.S. border, have contributed to a loss of support for the President and his party and Republican majorities in both chambers of Congress as a result of 2014 midterm elections.

How Do We Measure Economic Freedom?
See page 475 for an explanation of the methodology or visit the *Index* Web site at *heritage.org/index.*

Freedom Trend

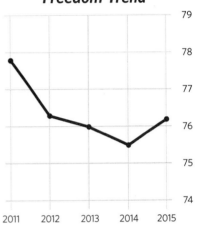

Country Comparisons

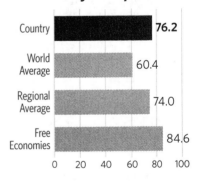

Country	76.2
World Average	60.4
Regional Average	74.0
Free Economies	84.6

Quick Facts

Population: 316.4 million
GDP (PPP): $16.8 trillion
1.9% growth in 2013
5-year compound annual growth 1.2%
$53,101 per capita
Unemployment: 5.9% (September 2014)
Inflation (CPI): 1.5%
FDI Inflow: $187.5 billion
Public Debt: 104.5% of GDP

2013 data unless otherwise noted.
Data compiled as of September 2014.

THE TEN ECONOMIC FREEDOMS

	Score		Rank	1-Year Change
RULE OF LAW	Property Rights	80.0	20th	0
	Freedom from Corruption	73.0	19th	+1.0

Corruption in government and the political process remains a concern. High levels of government spending and the expansion and complexity of the government's regulatory agenda have increased opportunities for political favoritism and cronyism. The judiciary functions independently. Protection of property rights has been uneven, with instances of regulatory overreach by the executive branch requiring court adjudication.

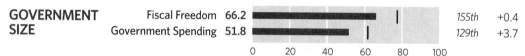

	Score		Rank	1-Year Change
GOVERNMENT SIZE	Fiscal Freedom	66.2	155th	+0.4
	Government Spending	51.8	129th	+3.7

The top individual income tax rate is 39.6 percent, and the top corporate tax rate remains among the world's highest at 35 percent. Other taxes include a capital gains tax and excise taxes. Tax revenue is equal to 24.3 percent of gross domestic product, and government spending is well over one-third of GDP. Public debt exceeds the value of the economy's annual production.

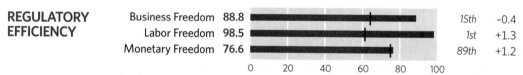

	Score		Rank	1-Year Change
REGULATORY EFFICIENCY	Business Freedom	88.8	15th	−0.4
	Labor Freedom	98.5	1st	+1.3
	Monetary Freedom	76.6	89th	+1.2

The regulatory burden has been mounting. Since 2009, over 150 new major regulations have been imposed at an annual cost of more than $70 billion. As of 2014, 125 new regulations were in the pipeline. The labor market, primarily regulated at the state level, remains flexible. Subsidies for agriculture, health care, and renewable energy have bred economic distortions.

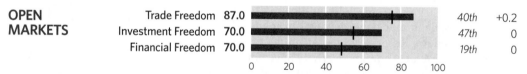

	Score		Rank	1-Year Change
OPEN MARKETS	Trade Freedom	87.0	40th	+0.2
	Investment Freedom	70.0	47th	0
	Financial Freedom	70.0	19th	0

The average tariff rate is 1.5 percent. Tariffs on clothing are high, sugar imports face tariff-rate quotas, and petroleum and liquefied natural gas exports are restricted. Foreign investment in some sectors is capped. The financial market is well developed, but the 2010 Dodd–Frank Act has instituted more federal regulation, socializing the cost of financial risk-taking and increasing the likelihood of future financial crises and bailouts.

Long-Term Score Change (since 1995)

RULE OF LAW		GOVERNMENT SIZE		REGULATORY EFFICIENCY		OPEN MARKETS	
Property Rights	−10.0	Fiscal Freedom	+1.4	Business Freedom	+3.8	Trade Freedom	+8.6
Freedom from Corruption	−17.0	Government Spending	−6.0	Labor Freedom	+3.1	Investment Freedom	0
				Monetary Freedom	−7.2	Financial Freedom	0

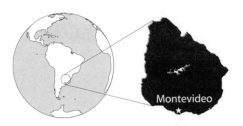
Montevideo

URUGUAY

Economic Freedom Score

50

25   75

Least   Most
free   0   100   free

68.6

Uruguay's economic freedom score is 68.6, making its economy the 43rd freest in the 2015 *Index*. Its score has decreased by 0.7 point since last year, with declines in six of the 10 economic freedoms, including labor freedom and the management of government spending, outweighing an improvement in freedom from corruption. Uruguay is ranked 5th out of 29 countries in the South and Central America/Caribbean region, and its overall score is above the world average.

Over the past five years, economic freedom in Uruguay has declined by 1.4 points, with losses in half of the 10 economic freedoms. A double-digit improvement in business freedom has been more than offset by declines in labor freedom and the control of government spending.

Uruguay has a history of economic openness and relies on international markets for its agricultural exports. A liberal labor market, strong rule of law, and prudent government size distinguish Uruguay from neighboring Brazil and Peru. Economic reforms have largely turned around an economy that sought IMF help for its fiscal problems in the early 2000s. More sustained efforts are needed to rein in growing government spending and fix an increasingly rigid labor market.

BACKGROUND: Former leftist guerrilla Jose Mujica was elected president in 2009. After strong growth in 2010 and 2011, the economy has slowed. Trade has been hurt by commercial restrictions in Argentina. State involvement in the economy is substantial, and deregulation is needed in telecommunications, energy, and public utilities. Crime and violence are increasing, and drug trafficking is a problem in urban areas. Uruguay is a founding member of MERCOSUR and signed a Trade and Investment Framework Agreement with the United States in 2007. The economy is still based largely on exports of commodities like milk, beef, rice, and wool. Despite excellent banking services, including branches of some of the world's largest banks, an information-sharing agreement with Argentina has reduced consumer confidence in Uruguay as a safe haven for assets.

Freedom Trend

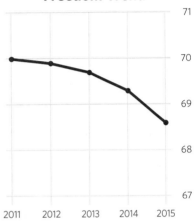

71

70

69

68

67

2011   2012   2013   2014   2015

Country Comparisons

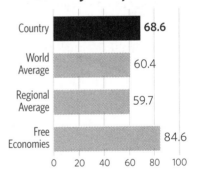

Country   **68.6**

World
Average   60.4

Regional
Average   59.7

Free
Economies   84.6

0   20   40   60   80   100

Quick Facts

Population: 3.4 million
GDP (PPP): $56.7 billion
4.2% growth in 2013
5-year compound annual growth 5.1%
$16,723 per capita
Unemployment: 6.3%
Inflation (CPI): 8.6%
FDI Inflow: $2.8 billion
Public Debt: 59.4% of GDP

2013 data unless otherwise noted.
Data compiled as of September 2014.

How Do We Measure Economic Freedom?
See page 475 for an explanation of the methodology
or visit the *Index* Web site at *heritage.org/index*.

THE TEN ECONOMIC FREEDOMS

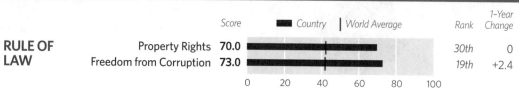

		Score		Rank	1-Year Change
RULE OF LAW	Property Rights	70.0		30th	0
	Freedom from Corruption	73.0		19th	+2.4

Corruption is low by regional standards, and by 2013, government institutions had established a fairly strong record of accountability to the electorate. The Transparency Law criminalizes a broad range of potential abuses of power by officeholders. The judiciary is relatively independent, but the court system remains severely backlogged. Private property is generally secure, expropriation is unlikely, and contracts are enforced.

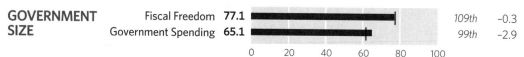

		Score		Rank	1-Year Change
GOVERNMENT SIZE	Fiscal Freedom	77.1		109th	-0.3
	Government Spending	65.1		99th	-2.9

The top individual income tax rate is 30 percent, and the top corporate tax rate is 25 percent. Other taxes include a value-added tax and a capital gains tax. The overall tax burden amounts to 27.6 percent of gross domestic product. Government spending equals 34.1 percent of domestic output, and public debt equals approximately 60 percent of the domestic economy.

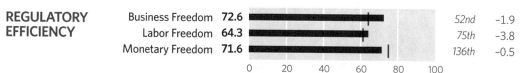

		Score		Rank	1-Year Change
REGULATORY EFFICIENCY	Business Freedom	72.6		52nd	-1.9
	Labor Freedom	64.3		75th	-3.8
	Monetary Freedom	71.6		136th	-0.5

With no minimum capital required, incorporating a business takes five procedures and less than a week, but licensing requirements are still time-consuming. Although the non-salary cost of hiring a worker is moderate, the labor market remains relatively rigid. The state resorted to unsustainable measures (e.g., a supermarket price freeze agreement) in early 2014 to prevent inflation from rising above 10 percent.

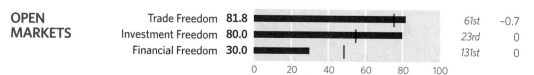

		Score		Rank	1-Year Change
OPEN MARKETS	Trade Freedom	81.8		61st	-0.7
	Investment Freedom	80.0		23rd	0
	Financial Freedom	30.0		131st	0

The average tariff rate is 4.1 percent. Uruguay, a member of the MERCOSUR Common Market, requires import licenses for some goods. Foreign and domestic investors are generally treated equally under the law. The financial system has become more stable, but significant state presence continues in many parts of the system including the banking sector. Government-owned commercial banks pose systemic vulnerabilities.

Long-Term Score Change (since 1995)

RULE OF LAW		GOVERNMENT SIZE		REGULATORY EFFICIENCY		OPEN MARKETS	
Property Rights	+20.0	Fiscal Freedom	-7.5	Business Freedom	+2.6	Trade Freedom	+18.8
Freedom from Corruption	+23.0	Government Spending	-14.5	Labor Freedom	-11.6	Investment Freedom	+10.0
				Monetary Freedom	+26.4	Financial Freedom	-20.0

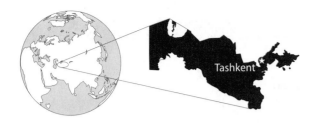

UZBEKISTAN

Economic Freedom Score

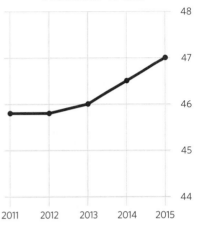

47.0

Uzbekistan's economic freedom score is 47.0, making its economy the 160th freest in the 2015 *Index*. Its score is up by 0.5 point from last year, with improvements in trade freedom, freedom from corruption, and labor freedom outweighing declines in the management of government spending and business freedom. Uzbekistan is ranked 37th out of 42 countries in the Asia–Pacific region, and its overall score is much lower than the world average.

A stagnant economic reform environment over the past five years has turned more positive recently, but gains have not been strong enough to propel the economy out of the "repressed" category. Since 2011, economic freedom in Uzbekistan has increased by 1.2 points, with modest improvements in business freedom, labor freedom, monetary freedom, and trade freedom.

Despite sustained rapid growth on the back of high commodity prices and relative stability, the underlying foundations of Uzbekistan's economy are weak. The rule of law is weakly enforced, a holdover from the Soviet past. Investment is restricted in many industries, and financial markets are shallow, preventing the capital accumulation necessary for sustained growth. The state-owned banks and industries tend to respond to the government's political priorities.

BACKGROUND: Uzbekistan has one of the world's most repressive governments. President Islam Karimov, in power since the late 1980s, has hinted that he may seek re-election in 2015. Karimov rose through the ranks of the Soviet-era State Planning Committee (Gosplan) and remains wedded to a command economy, which discourages foreign investment. Uzbekistan is dry and landlocked; 11 percent of the land is cultivated in irrigated river valleys. More than 60 percent of the population lives in densely populated rural communities. Production of cotton and grain has relied on overuse of agrochemicals and has depleted water supplies. Much of the agricultural land is degraded, and the Aral Sea and certain rivers are half dry. Uzbekistan is heavily dependent on natural gas, oil, gold, and uranium exports.

Freedom Trend

Country Comparisons

Country	47.0
World Average	60.4
Regional Average	58.8
Free Economies	84.6

Quick Facts

Population: 30.2 million
GDP (PPP): $113.8 billion
8.0% growth in 2013
5-year compound annual growth 8.2%
$3,762 per capita
Unemployment: 10.8%
Inflation (CPI): 11.2%
FDI Inflow: $1.1 billion
Public Debt: 8.6% of GDP

2013 data unless otherwise noted.
Data compiled as of September 2014.

How Do We Measure Economic Freedom?
See page 475 for an explanation of the methodology
or visit the *Index* Web site at *heritage.org/index*.

THE TEN ECONOMIC FREEDOMS

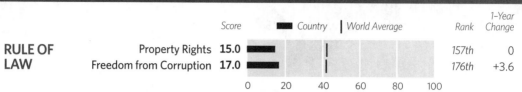

		Score		Rank	1-Year Change
RULE OF LAW	Property Rights	15.0		157th	0
	Freedom from Corruption	17.0		176th	+3.6

The president appoints all judges and can remove them at any time. Court procedures fall short of international standards, and powerful figures can expropriate property with impunity. Corruption is rampant. Property ownership, although generally respected by local and central authorities, can be subverted by the government. There is no general system for registration of liens on chattel property.

		Score		Rank	1-Year Change
GOVERNMENT SIZE	Fiscal Freedom	90.2		30th	-0.1
	Government Spending	67.3		94th	-3.1

Uzbekistan's top individual income tax rate is 22 percent, and its top corporate tax rate is 9 percent. Other taxes include a value-added tax and a property tax. The overall tax burden equals 20.3 percent of domestic income. Public spending is equivalent to 33 percent of domestic production, and government debt equals approximately 9 percent of gross domestic product.

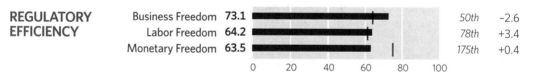

		Score		Rank	1-Year Change
REGULATORY EFFICIENCY	Business Freedom	73.1		50th	-2.6
	Labor Freedom	64.2		78th	+3.4
	Monetary Freedom	63.5		175th	+0.4

The regulatory system lacks clarity and consistent enforcement, injecting considerable uncertainty into business decision-making. The start-up process has been streamlined, but licensing requirements remain time-consuming. The labor market lacks flexibility, and employment in the informal sector is substantial. The state administers the prices of many basic staples, such as petroleum products, natural gas, utilities, and bread.

		Score		Rank	1-Year Change
OPEN MARKETS	Trade Freedom	69.8		134th	+3.7
	Investment Freedom	0.0		176th	0
	Financial Freedom	10.0		174th	0

Uzbekistan's average tariff rate is 5.1 percent. Uzbekistan is not yet a member of the WTO. The government screens foreign investment. Foreign investors may not purchase land. The financial sector is subject to heavy state intervention. Along with the high costs of financing, the banking sector's limited capacity for financial intermediation is a key barrier to private-sector development.

Long-Term Score Change (since 1998)

RULE OF LAW		GOVERNMENT SIZE		REGULATORY EFFICIENCY		OPEN MARKETS	
Property Rights	-15.0	Fiscal Freedom	+32.8	Business Freedom	+33.1	Trade Freedom	+19.8
Freedom from Corruption	+7.0	Government Spending	+10.8	Labor Freedom	-2.9	Investment Freedom	-30.0
				Monetary Freedom	+63.5	Financial Freedom	0

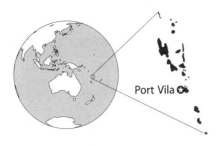

Port Vila ⊛

VANUATU

Economic Freedom Score

Least free　0

Most free　100

61.1

Vanuatu's economic freedom score is 61.1, making its economy the 84th freest in the 2015 *Index*. Its score is 1.6 points better than last year, with a substantial improvement in trade freedom outweighing a combined decline in labor freedom and business freedom. Vanuatu is ranked 16th out of 42 countries in the Asia–Pacific region, and its overall score is above the world and regional averages.

With few natural resources and an isolated geography, Vanuatu has increasingly embraced economic freedom to drive growth. Over the past five years, its economic freedom has advanced by 4.4 points, reflecting advances in six of the 10 economic freedoms. Recording its highest economic freedom score ever in the 2015 *Index*, Vanuatu has become a "moderately free" economy for the first time since it was initially graded in 2009.

Despite notable progress, more structural and institutional reforms remain critical to spurring sustained growth and long-term economic development. Rule of law, based on British common law, remains unevenly enforced, and corruption is widespread. Despite its size and isolation, the economy is largely closed to the outside world, with lingering non-tariff barriers and restricted investment.

BACKGROUND: The South Pacific island Republic of Vanuatu achieved independence in 1980 and is today a parliamentary democracy that remains divided between its English-speaking and French-speaking citizens. In the 2012 elections, 18 parties won seats in the legislature, with the Vanua'aku Pati party winning the most seats at eight. Sato Kilman served as prime minister until being forced to resign in March 2013. The legislature subsequently elected Moana Carcasses Kalosil of the Green Confederation party as prime minister. In late May 2014, parliament ousted Carcasses through a vote of no confidence, bringing Joe Natuman to power as prime minister. The economy is dominated by tourism and agriculture, and over 80 percent of the population is involved in farming, which accounts for roughly 20 percent of GDP.

Freedom Trend

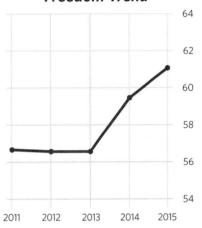

Country Comparisons

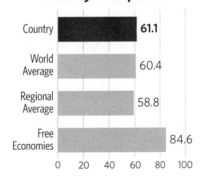

Country	61.1
World Average	60.4
Regional Average	58.8
Free Economies	84.6

Quick Facts

Population: 0.3 million
GDP (PPP): $1.3 billion
2.8% growth in 2013
5-year compound annual growth 2.1%
$4,718 per capita
Unemployment: n/a
Inflation (CPI): 1.3%
FDI Inflow: $34.8 million
Public Debt: 20.4% of GDP

2013 data unless otherwise noted.
Data compiled as of September 2014.

THE TEN ECONOMIC FREEDOMS

		Score		Rank	1-Year Change
RULE OF LAW	Property Rights	40.0		70th	0
	Freedom from Corruption	33.5		112th	0

Thirty years of debilitating corruption have had widespread damaging effects on Vanuatu's development. This corruption manifests itself in many ways, including political cronyism, "islandism," and nepotism; settlement of costly and fabricated "deeds of release" lawsuits against the government; and passport sales. The largely independent judiciary lacks the resources to hire and retain qualified judges and prosecutors.

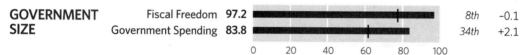

		Score		Rank	1-Year Change
GOVERNMENT SIZE	Fiscal Freedom	97.2		8th	-0.1
	Government Spending	83.8		34th	+2.1

Vanuatu has no individual or corporate income taxes. Most tax revenue comes from a value-added tax and import duties. The overall tax burden is equal to about 16.6 percent of the domestic economy. Government spending is equivalent to approximately 23.2 percent of the domestic economy, and public debt equals 20 percent of gross domestic product.

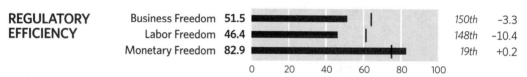

		Score		Rank	1-Year Change
REGULATORY EFFICIENCY	Business Freedom	51.5		150th	-3.3
	Labor Freedom	46.4		148th	-10.4
	Monetary Freedom	82.9		19th	+0.2

No minimum capital is required, but starting a business takes more than a month, and licensing remains onerous. Labor codes are rigid and outmoded, and the formal labor market is not fully developed. Fiscal and monetary policies have kept deficits, sovereign debt, and inflation low, but a bloated public sector crowds out funding needed to improve health care, education, and infrastructure.

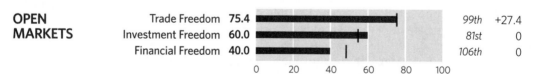

		Score		Rank	1-Year Change
OPEN MARKETS	Trade Freedom	75.4		99th	+27.4
	Investment Freedom	60.0		81st	0
	Financial Freedom	40.0		106th	0

Vanuatu's average tariff rate is 4.8 percent. Investment in some sectors is restricted, and foreign investors may not own land. Inadequate infrastructure and heavy state involvement deter long-term investment. The financial system remains rudimentary and subject to state interference. Access to financing is still poor, and less than 15 percent of rural adults have access to formal banking services.

Long-Term Score Change (since 2009)

RULE OF LAW		GOVERNMENT SIZE		REGULATORY EFFICIENCY		OPEN MARKETS	
Property Rights	0	Fiscal Freedom	+1.9	Business Freedom	-17.5	Trade Freedom	+12.4
Freedom from Corruption	+2.5	Government Spending	-0.2	Labor Freedom	-6.2	Investment Freedom	+30.0
				Monetary Freedom	+4.2	Financial Freedom	0

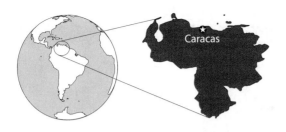

Caracas

VENEZUELA

Economic Freedom Score

50

25   75

Least free 0   100 Most free

34.3

World Rank: 176   **Regional Rank: 28**

Venezuela's economic freedom score is 34.3, making its economy the 176th freest in the 2015 *Index*. Its score has decreased by 2.0 points since last year, reflecting declines in half of the 10 economic freedoms including labor freedom, monetary freedom, investment freedom, and business freedom. Venezuela is ranked 28th out of 29 countries in the South and Central America/Caribbean region, and its overall score is far below the world and regional averages.

Over the past five years, economic freedom in Venezuela has declined by 3.3 points, primarily due to deteriorations in the management of government spending, labor freedom, business freedom, and investment freedom. Recording the fifth largest score drop of any country graded, Venezuela has registered its lowest economic freedom score ever in the 2015 *Index*.

Venezuela's economic collapse has been preceded by blatant disregard for the basic foundations of the rule of law and limited government. The administration of Nicolás Maduro has pushed government finances to the brink despite some of the world's largest petroleum reserves. Price controls and import barriers have expanded the informal sector. With monetary stability severely eroded by high inflation, the livelihood of the poor and middle class has deteriorated severely.

BACKGROUND: In 2014, 15 years after the "21st-century socialist revolution" began, Venezuela was rocked by antigovernment student-led protests in which over 40 Venezuelans were killed, many by government security forces or their proxies. Hugo Chávez's legacy of free-spending social programs and socialist economic policies has led to skyrocketing inflation. There have been significant reductions in civil liberties and economic freedom. Under Chávez's successor, Nicolás Maduro, the economy has collapsed, and personal security is at an all-time low. In mid-2014, Venezuela announced plans to raise the retail price of gasoline, currently the lowest in the world at 5 cents a gallon, but such reforms fall far short of what is needed to ameliorate an unsustainable financial and political situation.

Freedom Trend

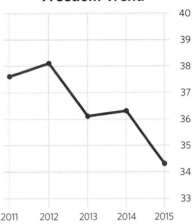

40

39

38

37

36

35

34

33

2011 2012 2013 2014 2015

Country Comparisons

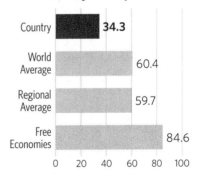

Country **34.3**

World Average 60.4

Regional Average 59.7

Free Economies 84.6

0   20   40   60   80   100

Quick Facts

Population: 30.0 million
GDP (PPP): $407.9 billion
1.0% growth in 2013
5-year compound annual growth 1.2%
$13,605 per capita
Unemployment: 7.6%
Inflation (CPI): 40.7%
FDI Inflow: $7.0 billion
Public Debt: 49.8% of GDP

2013 data unless otherwise noted.
Data compiled as of September 2014.

How Do We Measure Economic Freedom?
See page 475 for an explanation of the methodology or visit the *Index* Web site at *heritage.org/index*.

THE TEN ECONOMIC FREEDOMS

	Score		Rank	1-Year Change
RULE OF LAW	Property Rights	5.0	179th	0
	Freedom from Corruption	20.0	168th	+3.5

Political power is concentrated in the executive, with many opportunities for corruption. Capital controls, for example, allow officials to purchase U.S. dollars at a fixed peg and then sell them on the black market for as much as a 1,100 percent profit. The government has expropriated nearly 1,300 businesses since 2002. The dysfunctional judiciary is completely controlled by the executive.

	Score		Rank	1-Year Change
GOVERNMENT SIZE	Fiscal Freedom	75.0	117th	-0.3
	Government Spending	52.0	127th	+0.2

Venezuela's top individual and corporate income tax rates are 34 percent. Other taxes include a value-added tax. The overall tax burden amounts to 13.6 percent of the domestic economy. Government expenditures, bolstered by oil revenues, are equivalent to 40 percent of domestic production, and public debt is equal to 50 percent of the domestic economy.

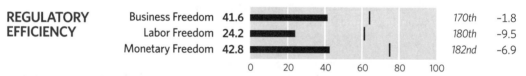

	Score		Rank	1-Year Change
REGULATORY EFFICIENCY	Business Freedom	41.6	170th	-1.8
	Labor Freedom	24.2	180th	-9.5
	Monetary Freedom	42.8	182nd	-6.9

The overall freedom to engage in entrepreneurial activity is constrained by government control and inconsistent enforcement of regulations. Most contracts are awarded without competition. The labor market remains stagnant and controlled by the state. President Maduro has used dictatorial emergency decree powers to fight rampant inflation with price controls instead of addressing such causes as money printing and a fixed currency.

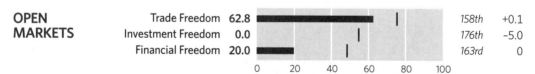

	Score		Rank	1-Year Change
OPEN MARKETS	Trade Freedom	62.8	158th	+0.1
	Investment Freedom	0.0	176th	-5.0
	Financial Freedom	20.0	163rd	0

Venezuela's average tariff rate is 8.6 percent. Non-tariff barriers limit competition from foreign companies and agricultural producers. Private investment remains hampered by state interference in the economy, and hostility to foreign investment, coupled with threats of expropriation, persists. The financial sector is tightly controlled by the state and often allocates credit based on political expediency.

Long-Term Score Change (since 1995)

RULE OF LAW		GOVERNMENT SIZE		REGULATORY EFFICIENCY		OPEN MARKETS	
Property Rights	-45.0	Fiscal Freedom	-5.0	Business Freedom	-43.4	Trade Freedom	-2.2
Freedom from Corruption	+10.0	Government Spending	-24.1	Labor Freedom	-8.1	Investment Freedom	-50.0
				Monetary Freedom	-9.2	Financial Freedom	-50.0

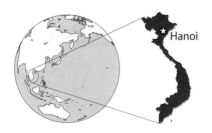

Hanoi

VIETNAM

Economic Freedom Score

25   50   75

Least free 0   100 Most free

51.7

Vietnam's economic freedom score is 51.7, making its economy the 148th freest in the 2015 *Index*. Its score has increased by almost 1.0 point since last year, with improvements in the control of government spending, freedom from corruption, and monetary freedom outweighing declines in labor freedom and business freedom. Vietnam is ranked 32nd out of 42 countries in the Asia–Pacific region. Although the Vietnamese economy has achieved its highest economic freedom score ever in the 2015 Index, its overall score continues to be lower than the world and regional averages.

Vietnam's rapidly expanding links to the global marketplace have failed to materialize into a comprehensive program of economic reform. Over the past five years, economic freedom in Vietnam has stagnated, with advances over the past year mitigating three years of deteriorating scores. A worrying expansion of inflation has undercut potential gains from advances in trade freedom.

A member of the Trans-Pacific Partnership talks, Vietnam has steadily opened its market and reduced other tariff and non-tariff barriers. However, other factors of economic freedom remain less entrenched. The ruling Communist Party controls the judiciary, corruption and bribery are common, and the government lacks transparency. The government's suspicion of private business is reflected in inefficient business regulations. State-owned enterprises dominate many economic sectors.

BACKGROUND: The Socialist Republic of Vietnam remains a Communist dictatorship characterized by political repression and an absence of civil liberties. Economic liberalization began in 1986 with its *doi moi* reforms, and Vietnam joined the World Trade Organization in 2007. In 2012, Prime Minister Nguyen Tan Dung acknowledged mismanagement of the Vietnamese economy and affirmed his commitment to reforming the state sector, but the Vietnamese are still waiting for action. Vietnam's economy is driven primarily by tourism and exports. Inflation is a problem, and the country has struggled to attract investment in the absence of a transparent legal and regulatory system.

Freedom Trend

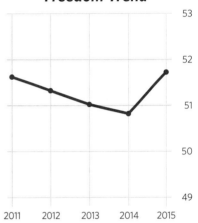

53

52

51

50

49

2011   2012   2013   2014   2015

Country Comparisons

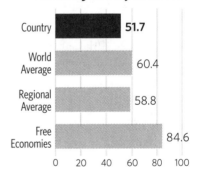

Country	51.7
World Average	60.4
Regional Average	58.8
Free Economies	84.6

0   20   40   60   80   100

Quick Facts

Population: 89.7 million
GDP (PPP): $359.8 billion
5.4% growth in 2013
5-year compound annual growth 5.7%
$4,012 per capita
Unemployment: 1.9%
Inflation (CPI): 6.6%
FDI Inflow: $8.9 billion
Public Debt: 55.0% of GDP

2013 data unless otherwise noted.
Data compiled as of September 2014.

THE TEN ECONOMIC FREEDOMS

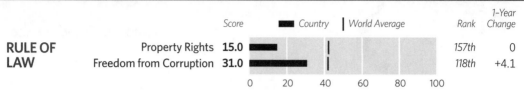

		Score		Rank	1-Year Change
RULE OF LAW	Property Rights	15.0		157th	0
	Freedom from Corruption	31.0		118th	+4.1

Corruption blights all levels of the Vietnamese government and judiciary. Factionalism and bureaucratic rivalries, nepotism and vast corruption within the Communist Party of Vietnam, and a general lack of accountability ensure that many agencies are run as fiefdoms, perpetuating the culture of payoffs. Private property rights are not strongly respected, and resolution of disputes can take years.

		Score		Rank	1-Year Change
GOVERNMENT SIZE	Fiscal Freedom	79.1		95th	+2.1
	Government Spending	77.1		60th	+5.7

Vietnam's top individual income tax rate is 35 percent, and its top corporate tax rate is 22 percent. Other taxes include a value-added tax and a property tax. Overall tax revenue equals 19.6 percent of the domestic economy, and government spending amounts to 27.6 percent of domestic production. Public debt is equivalent to 55 percent of gross domestic product.

		Score		Rank	1-Year Change
REGULATORY EFFICIENCY	Business Freedom	61.5		103rd	-0.5
	Labor Freedom	62.9		91st	-5.4
	Monetary Freedom	66.8		165th	+3.2

Despite ongoing reform efforts, the regulatory framework lacks efficiency. No minimum capital is required to start a business, but the process still takes over a month, and licensing requirements remain time-consuming. The labor market remains rigid, and informal labor activity is considerable. Although inflation has moderated, the state continues to influence prices though controls and state-owned and state-subsidized firms.

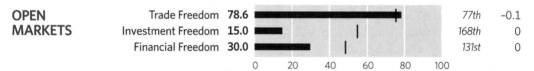

		Score		Rank	1-Year Change
OPEN MARKETS	Trade Freedom	78.6		77th	-0.1
	Investment Freedom	15.0		168th	0
	Financial Freedom	30.0		131st	0

Vietnam's average tariff rate is 5.7 percent. Tariff-rate quotas affect imports of goods like eggs and sugar. The government screens new foreign investment and restricts investment in some sectors. Directed lending by state-owned commercial banks has been scaled back in recent years. Foreign equity in domestic banks remains capped at 30 percent, but it can be higher for weak banks.

Long-Term Score Change (since 1995)

RULE OF LAW		GOVERNMENT SIZE		REGULATORY EFFICIENCY		OPEN MARKETS	
Property Rights	+5.0	Fiscal Freedom	+10.3	Business Freedom	+21.5	Trade Freedom	+34.0
Freedom from Corruption	+21.0	Government Spending	-10.0	Labor Freedom	-1.2	Investment Freedom	-15.0
				Monetary Freedom	+11.6	Financial Freedom	0

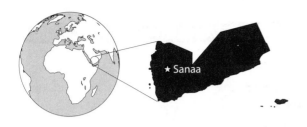

YEMEN

Economic Freedom Score

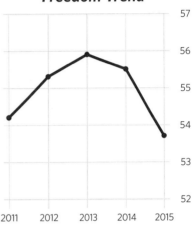

25   50   75

Least free   0   100   Most free

53.7

Yemen's economic freedom score is 53.7, making its economy the 133rd freest in the 2015 *Index*. Its score is 1.8 points lower than last year, with declines in five of the 10 economic freedoms, led by the control of government spending, business freedom, and trade freedom, outweighing improvements in monetary freedom and labor freedom. Yemen is ranked 13th out of 15 countries in the Middle East/North Africa region, and its overall score is lower than the world and regional averages.

Civil unrest and terrorism-related violence have undermined economic growth. Overall, Yemen's economic freedom has declined by 0.5 point since 2011, primarily due to double-digit drops in business freedom and monetary freedom. Yemen has registered the eighth largest score decline of any country graded in the 2015 *Index*.

These declines undermine an already weak economic system. Government corruption is standard. The judiciary is semi-independent, but government weakness makes enforcing the law difficult. The economy is open to trade, but the investment regime remains closed. An underdeveloped financial sector and strict business regulations make it difficult to form and finance new ventures.

BACKGROUND: Yemen is one of the Arab world's poorest countries. Secessionists, unruly tribes, and Islamist extremists oppose its relatively moderate foreign policy and cooperation with the United States against al-Qaeda. President Ali Abdullah Saleh, forced to resign in 2011 in a deal brokered by the Gulf Cooperation Council, transferred power to Vice President Abd Rabbuh Mansur al-Hadi after a February 2012 election. The next reforms are supposed to include a constitution, a constitutional referendum, and national elections. The government initiated an economic reform program in 2006, but declining oil production, terrorism, kidnappings, clashes between Sunni and Shia Muslims, tribal rivalries, a strong al-Qaeda presence, and water shortages have undermined foreign investment, tourism, and economic growth. Yemen relies heavily on foreign aid. Economic prospects will depend on progress on the political and security fronts and implementation of critical reforms.

Freedom Trend

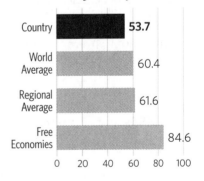

2011   2012   2013   2014   2015

Country Comparisons

Country	**53.7**
World Average	60.4
Regional Average	61.6
Free Economies	84.6

0   20   40   60   80   100

Quick Facts

Population: 26.7 million
GDP (PPP): $61.8 billion
4.4% growth in 2013
5-year compound annual growth 0.9%
$2,316 per capita
Unemployment: 17.2%
Inflation (CPI): 11.1%
FDI Inflow: –$133.6 million
Public Debt: 49.9% of GDP

2013 data unless otherwise noted.
Data compiled as of September 2014.

THE TEN ECONOMIC FREEDOMS

		Score	Country	World Average	Rank	1-Year Change
RULE OF LAW	Property Rights	30.0			94th	0
	Freedom from Corruption	18.0			175th	-1.4

The government has yet to fully tackle the pervasive network of corruption and patronage built up over 30 years under former President Ali Abdullah Saleh. Auditing and investigative bodies are not sufficiently independent of executive authorities. The judiciary is nominally independent, but it is susceptible to interference from the executive branch. Authorities have a poor record of enforcing judicial rulings.

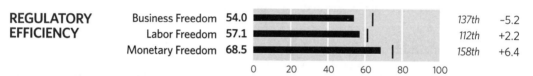

		Score			Rank	1-Year Change
GOVERNMENT SIZE	Fiscal Freedom	91.5			23rd	-0.2
	Government Spending	59.9			114th	-15.0

The top individual income tax rate is 20 percent, and the top corporate tax rate is 20 percent. Other taxes include a general sales tax and a property tax. The overall tax burden equals 7 percent of gross domestic product. Public expenditures amount to 36.6 percent of domestic production, and government debt is equivalent to 51 percent of the domestic economy.

		Score			Rank	1-Year Change
REGULATORY EFFICIENCY	Business Freedom	54.0			137th	-5.2
	Labor Freedom	57.1			112th	+2.2
	Monetary Freedom	68.5			158th	+6.4

The regulatory efficiency needed for more vibrant private-sector development is not institutionalized. While there is no minimum capital requirement, starting a business takes over a month on average. The rigid labor market perpetuates high unemployment and underemployment. In 2014, government efforts to reduce energy subsidies, which are very high and a major drain on the budget, sparked violent protests.

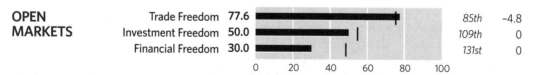

		Score			Rank	1-Year Change
OPEN MARKETS	Trade Freedom	77.6			85th	-4.8
	Investment Freedom	50.0			109th	0
	Financial Freedom	30.0			131st	0

Yemen's average tariff rate is 6.2 percent. Yemen joined the WTO in 2014. Courts do not resolve business disputes in a timely manner. The underdeveloped financial system is dominated by banks and subject to state influence. Nonperforming loans burden the banking sector. Obtaining credit for entrepreneurial activity remains difficult. The capital market is rudimentary, with no stock exchange in place.

Long-Term Score Change (since 1995)

RULE OF LAW		GOVERNMENT SIZE		REGULATORY EFFICIENCY		OPEN MARKETS	
Property Rights	0	Fiscal Freedom	+13.3	Business Freedom	-16.0	Trade Freedom	+32.6
Freedom from Corruption	+8.0	Government Spending	-13.5	Labor Freedom	-19.7	Investment Freedom	-20.0
				Monetary Freedom	+26.7	Financial Freedom	0

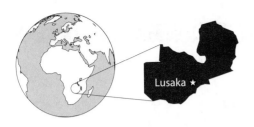

Lusaka ★

ZAMBIA

Economic Freedom Score

25   **50**   75

Least free 0   Most free 100

58.7

Zambia's economic freedom score is 58.7, making its economy the 100th freest in the 2015 *Index*. Its score is down by 1.7 points from last year due to deteriorations in half of the 10 economic freedoms, including trade freedom, business freedom, investment freedom, and the control of government spending, that outweigh improvement in freedom from corruption. Zambia is ranked 12th out of 46 countries in the Sub-Saharan Africa region, and its overall score is below the world average.

Over the past five years, Zambia's commodity-linked economy has grown, but policymakers have done little to boost overall economic freedom. Bursts of reform have been followed by declines. Led by score decreases in labor freedom and trade freedom, Zambia's overall economic freedom has declined by 1.0 point since 2011.

A sharp decline in economic freedom over the past year has returned the economy to the "mostly unfree" category. The rule of law is weak, and corruption is pervasive. The trading regime is relatively open, but an inefficient court system undermines Zambia's attractiveness to investors.

BACKGROUND: In 2011, Michael Sata of the Patriotic Front was elected president after 20 years of rule by the Movement for Multiparty Democracy. In April 2012, Zambia released the first draft of a new constitution that included press freedoms, decentralized government, a bill of rights, and a 50 percent-plus-1-vote requirement to win the presidency. The final draft, due to be released in November 2013, was suppressed by the government but leaked in early 2014 by a citizen watchdog group. Parliament still has not voted on it. Zambia has experienced a decade of rapid economic growth driven primarily by mining. It is Africa's largest copper producer. Recent increases in copper prices have boosted trade revenues and attracted foreign investment, particularly from China. The influx of Chinese workers has caused tensions between Zambians and the Chinese community. High rates of HIV/AIDS and unemployment contribute to high poverty rates.

Freedom Trend

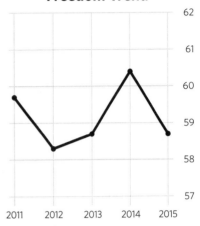

62

61

60

59

58

57

2011   2012   2013   2014   2015

Country Comparisons

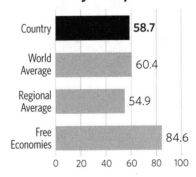

Country	58.7
World Average	60.4
Regional Average	54.9
Free Economies	84.6

0   20   40   60   80   100

Quick Facts

Population: 14.5 million
GDP (PPP): $25.5 billion
6.0% growth in 2013
5-year compound annual growth 6.8%
$1,754 per capita
Unemployment: 13.2%
Inflation (CPI): 7.0%
FDI Inflow: $1.8 billion
Public Debt: 35.1% of GDP

2013 data unless otherwise noted.
Data compiled as of September 2014.

How Do We Measure Economic Freedom?
See page 475 for an explanation of the methodology
or visit the *Index* Web site at *heritage.org/index.*

THE TEN ECONOMIC FREEDOMS

	Score	Country	World Average	Rank	1-Year Change

RULE OF LAW

	Score		Rank	1-Year Change
Property Rights	30.0		94th	0
Freedom from Corruption	38.0		83rd	+6.7

Corruption is perceived as widespread, although the government has taken some steps to fight graft. The rule of law remains uneven across the country. The judicial system suffers from inefficiency, government influence, and a lack of resources. Contract enforcement is weak, and courts are relatively inexperienced in commercial litigation. The government lacks the capacity to enforce intellectual property rights laws effectively.

GOVERNMENT SIZE

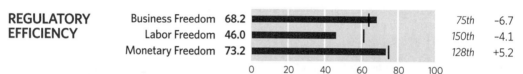

	Score		Rank	1-Year Change
Fiscal Freedom	71.9		131st	+0.1
Government Spending	78.0		57th	-4.9

Zambia's top individual and corporate income tax rates are 35 percent. Other taxes include a value-added tax and a property tax. Total tax revenue is equivalent to 19.1 percent of domestic income, and public expenditures have reached 27.1 percent of domestic output. Public debt is equal to 35 percent of gross domestic product.

REGULATORY EFFICIENCY

	Score		Rank	1-Year Change
Business Freedom	68.2		75th	-6.7
Labor Freedom	46.0		150th	-4.1
Monetary Freedom	73.2		128th	+5.2

The regulatory environment is still not conducive to entrepreneurial activity. No minimum capital is required to start a business, but requirements for commercial licenses are time-consuming. Labor codes are not applied consistently, and workers are often hired on a short-term basis. The central bank tightened monetary policy in 2013 to curb inflationary pressure from cuts in fuel and agricultural subsidies.

OPEN MARKETS

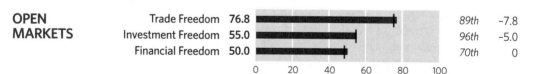

	Score		Rank	1-Year Change
Trade Freedom	76.8		89th	-7.8
Investment Freedom	55.0		96th	-5.0
Financial Freedom	50.0		70th	0

Zambia's average tariff rate is 4.1 percent. Agricultural imports may face additional barriers. The government screens new foreign investment, but in general, it treats foreign and domestic investment equally. The financial system is dominated by banking. Zambia has a relatively advanced banking regime, and financial intermediation and credit to the private sector continue to expand.

Long-Term Score Change (since 1995)

RULE OF LAW		GOVERNMENT SIZE		REGULATORY EFFICIENCY		OPEN MARKETS	
Property Rights	-20.0	Fiscal Freedom	-0.5	Business Freedom	+13.2	Trade Freedom	+15.6
Freedom from Corruption	+8.0	Government Spending	+3.2	Labor Freedom	-6.6	Investment Freedom	-15.0
				Monetary Freedom	+61.0	Financial Freedom	-20.0

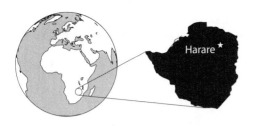

ZIMBABWE

Economic Freedom Score

25   50   75

Least free 0   100 Most free

37.6

World Rank: 175   **Regional Rank: 46**

Zimbabwe's economic freedom score is 37.6, making its economy the 175th freest in the 2015 *Index*. Its score has increased by 2.1 points from last year, driven by a particularly large gain in the control of government spending and improvements in six other economic freedoms including trade freedom and fiscal freedom. Nonetheless, Zimbabwe is ranked last out of 46 countries in Sub-Saharan Africa, and its overall score remains far below the world and regional averages.

After near economic collapse in the late 2000s, Zimbabwe has experienced five consecutive years of improvements in economic freedom. Over the past five years, economic freedom in Zimbabwe has improved by 15.5 points, the largest improvement of any nation. The biggest score gains have been in monetary freedom and the control of government spending. A move to dollarize the economy has brought the hyperinflation of 2008 and 2009 under control.

Nevertheless, Zimbabwe remains one of the world's least free economies. President Robert Mugabe's government is corrupt and inefficient. The labor market is one of the most restricted in the world, and business licensing forces most workers to seek employment in the informal sector. The violent seizure of land has underscored poor government land reform policies and upset investor confidence in a once-vibrant agricultural sector.

BACKGROUND: When it became independent in 1965, Zimbabwe had a diversified economy, well-developed infrastructure, and an advanced financial sector. It is now one of Africa's poorest countries. In July 2013, President Robert Mugabe of the Zimbabwe African National Union–Patriotic Front was re-elected to his seventh five-year term, and his party won three-quarters of the seats in parliament in a peaceful but flawed election. In March 2013, voters approved a new constitution that would roll back presidential power. After decades of corruption and mismanagement, Zimbabwe now faces a cash crisis and declining support from China. In 2014, poor harvests left 2.2 million people in need of food assistance.

Freedom Trend

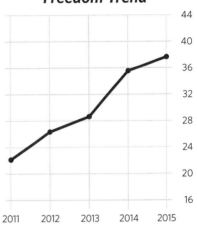

44

40

36

32

28

24

20

16

2011   2012   2013   2014   2015

Country Comparisons

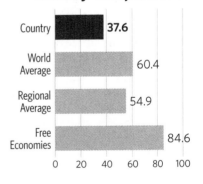

Country	37.6
World Average	60.4
Regional Average	54.9
Free Economies	84.6

0   20   40   60   80   100

Quick Facts

Population: 13.1 million
GDP (PPP): $10.3 billion
3.0% growth in 2013
5-year compound annual growth 8.9%
$788 per capita
Unemployment: 5.5%
Inflation (CPI): 1.6%
FDI Inflow: $400.0 million
Public Debt: 54.7% of GDP

2013 data unless otherwise noted.
Data compiled as of September 2014.

How Do We Measure Economic Freedom?
See page 475 for an explanation of the methodology
or visit the *Index* Web site at *heritage.org/index*.

THE TEN ECONOMIC FREEDOMS

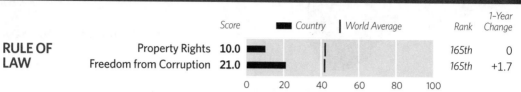

	Score	Rank	1-Year Change
RULE OF LAW — Property Rights	10.0	165th	0
Freedom from Corruption	21.0	165th	+1.7

Corruption remains endemic. Civil servants may make unpredictable demands for unofficial payments for a variety of "services." Pressure from the executive branch has substantially eroded judicial independence. The government has repeatedly violated property rights. Its land reform program, characterized by chaos and violence, badly damaged commercial farming.

	Score	Rank	1-Year Change
GOVERNMENT SIZE — Fiscal Freedom	66.6	153rd	+3.3
Government Spending	74.2	70th	+10.2

The top individual income tax rate is 46.4 percent, and the top corporate tax rate is 25 percent. Other taxes include a value-added tax and a capital gains tax. Overall tax revenue equals approximately 26.3 percent of domestic income, and government spending is equal to 29.3 percent of gross domestic product. Public debt amounts to 55 percent of domestic output.

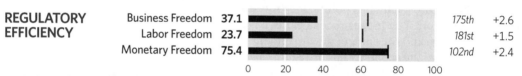

	Score	Rank	1-Year Change
REGULATORY EFFICIENCY — Business Freedom	37.1	175th	+2.6
Labor Freedom	23.7	181st	+1.5
Monetary Freedom	75.4	102nd	+2.4

The regulatory framework remains costly and time-consuming. Incorporating a business costs more than the level of average annual income, and completing licensing requirements takes over 400 days. The formal labor market remains rudimentary. Dollarization, instituted in 2009 to end hyperinflation, now raises the specter of deflation as the U.S. dollar strengthens and the government continues to delay meaningful structural reforms.

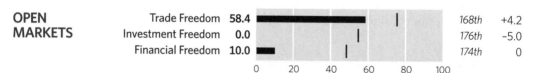

	Score	Rank	1-Year Change
OPEN MARKETS — Trade Freedom	58.4	168th	+4.2
Investment Freedom	0.0	176th	−5.0
Financial Freedom	10.0	174th	0

Zimbabwe's average tariff rate is 13.3 percent. Imports may face significant delays. Foreign ownership levels are capped by the government, and numerous state-owned enterprises distort the economy. The small, bank-dominated financial system is vulnerable to state interference. Nonperforming loans have risen to over 15 percent of total loans. Much of the population remains outside of the formal banking sector.

Long-Term Score Change (since 1995)

RULE OF LAW		GOVERNMENT SIZE		REGULATORY EFFICIENCY		OPEN MARKETS	
Property Rights	−40.0	Fiscal Freedom	+16.5	Business Freedom	−17.9	Trade Freedom	+6.6
Freedom from Corruption	−9.0	Government Spending	+8.9	Labor Freedom	−19.1	Investment Freedom	−30.0
				Monetary Freedom	+20.7	Financial Freedom	−40.0

Appendix

Index of Economic Freedom Scores, 1995–2015

Country	1995	1996	1997	1998	1999	2000	2001	2002	2003	2004	2005	2006	2007	2008	2009	2010	2011	2012	2013	2014	2015
Afghanistan	-	-	-	-	-	-	-	-	-	-	-	-	-	-	-	-	-	-	-	-	-
Albania	49.7	53.8	54.8	53.9	53.4	53.6	56.6	56.8	56.8	58.5	57.8	60.3	61.4	62.4	63.7	66.0	64.0	65.1	65.2	66.9	65.7
Algeria	55.7	54.5	54.9	55.8	57.2	56.8	57.3	61.0	57.7	58.1	53.2	55.7	55.4	56.2	56.6	56.9	52.4	51.0	49.6	50.8	48.9
Angola	27.4	24.4	24.2	24.9	23.7	24.3	-	-	-	-	-	43.5	44.7	46.9	47.0	48.4	46.2	46.7	47.3	47.7	47.9
Argentina	68.0	74.7	73.3	70.9	70.6	70.0	68.6	65.7	56.3	53.9	51.7	53.4	54.0	54.2	52.3	51.2	51.7	48.0	46.7	44.6	44.1
Armenia	-	42.2	46.7	49.6	56.4	63.0	66.4	68.0	67.3	70.3	69.8	70.6	68.6	69.9	69.9	69.2	69.7	68.8	69.4	68.9	67.1
Australia	74.1	74.0	75.5	75.6	76.4	77.1	77.4	77.3	77.4	77.9	79.0	79.9	81.1	82.2	82.6	82.6	82.5	83.1	82.6	82.0	81.4
Austria	70.0	68.9	65.2	65.4	64.0	68.4	68.1	67.4	67.6	67.6	68.8	71.1	71.6	71.4	71.2	71.6	71.9	70.3	71.8	72.4	71.2
Azerbaijan	-	-	34.0	43.1	47.4	49.8	50.3	53.3	54.1	53.4	54.4	53.2	54.6	55.3	58.0	58.8	59.7	58.9	59.7	61.3	61.0
The Bahamas	71.8	74.0	74.5	74.5	74.7	73.9	74.8	74.4	73.5	72.1	72.6	72.3	72.0	71.1	70.3	67.3	68.0	68.0	70.1	69.8	68.7
Bahrain	76.2	76.4	76.1	75.6	75.2	75.7	75.9	75.6	76.3	75.1	71.2	71.6	71.2	72.2	74.8	76.3	77.7	75.2	75.5	75.1	73.4
Bangladesh	40.9	51.1	49.9	52.0	50.0	48.9	51.2	51.9	49.3	50.0	47.5	52.9	46.7	44.2	47.5	51.1	53.0	53.2	52.6	54.1	53.9
Barbados	-	62.3	64.5	67.9	66.7	69.5	71.5	73.6	71.3	69.4	70.1	71.9	70.0	71.3	71.5	68.3	68.5	69.0	69.3	68.3	67.9
Belarus	40.4	38.7	39.8	38.0	35.4	41.3	38.0	39.0	39.7	43.1	46.7	47.5	47.0	45.3	45.0	48.7	47.9	49.0	48.0	50.1	49.8
Belgium	-	66.0	64.6	64.7	62.9	63.5	63.8	67.6	68.1	68.7	69.0	71.8	72.5	71.7	72.1	70.1	70.2	69.0	69.2	69.9	68.8
Belize	62.9	61.6	64.3	59.1	60.7	63.3	65.9	65.6	63.5	62.8	64.5	64.7	63.3	63.0	63.0	61.5	63.8	61.9	57.3	56.7	56.8
Benin	-	54.5	61.3	61.7	60.6	61.5	60.1	57.3	54.9	54.6	52.3	54.0	55.1	55.2	55.4	55.4	56.0	55.7	57.6	57.1	58.8
Bhutan	-	-	-	-	-	-	-	-	-	-	-	-	-	-	57.7	57.0	57.6	56.6	55.0	56.7	57.4
Bolivia	56.8	65.2	65.1	68.8	65.6	65.0	68.0	65.1	64.3	64.5	58.4	57.8	54.2	53.1	53.6	49.4	50.0	50.2	47.9	48.4	46.8
Bosnia and Herzegovina	-	-	-	29.4	29.4	45.1	36.6	37.4	40.6	44.7	48.8	55.6	54.4	53.9	53.1	56.2	57.5	57.3	57.3	58.4	59.0
Botswana	56.8	61.6	59.1	62.8	62.9	65.8	66.8	66.2	68.6	69.9	69.3	68.8	68.1	68.2	69.7	70.3	68.8	69.6	70.6	72.0	69.8
Brazil	51.4	48.1	52.6	52.3	61.3	61.1	61.9	61.5	63.4	62.0	61.7	60.9	56.2	56.2	56.7	55.6	56.3	57.9	57.7	56.9	56.6
Brunei	-	-	-	-	-	-	-	-	-	-	-	-	-	-	-	-	-	-	-	69.0	68.9
Bulgaria	50.0	48.6	47.6	45.7	46.2	47.3	51.9	57.1	57.0	59.2	62.3	64.1	62.7	63.7	64.6	62.3	64.9	64.7	65.0	65.7	66.8
Burkina Faso	-	49.4	54.0	54.5	55.0	55.7	56.7	58.8	58.9	58.0	56.6	55.8	55.1	55.7	59.5	59.4	60.6	60.6	59.9	58.9	58.6
Burma	-	45.1	45.4	45.7	46.4	47.9	46.1	45.5	44.9	43.6	40.5	40.0	41.0	39.5	37.7	36.7	37.8	38.7	39.2	46.5	46.9
Burundi	-	-	45.4	44.7	41.1	42.6	-	-	-	-	-	48.7	46.9	46.2	48.8	47.5	49.6	48.1	49.0	51.4	53.7
Cabo Verde	-	49.7	47.7	48.0	50.7	51.9	56.3	57.6	56.1	58.1	57.8	58.6	56.5	57.9	61.3	61.8	64.6	63.5	63.7	66.1	66.4

Index of Economic Freedom Scores, 1995–2015

Country	1995	1996	1997	1998	1999	2000	2001	2002	2003	2004	2005	2006	2007	2008	2009	2010	2011	2012	2013	2014	2015
Cambodia	-	-	52.8	59.8	59.9	59.3	59.6	60.7	63.7	61.1	60.0	56.7	55.9	55.9	56.6	56.6	57.9	57.6	58.5	57.4	57.5
Cameroon	51.3	45.7	44.6	48.0	50.3	49.9	53.3	52.8	52.7	52.3	53.0	54.6	55.6	54.3	53.0	52.3	51.8	51.8	52.3	52.6	51.9
Canada	69.4	70.3	67.9	68.5	69.3	70.5	71.2	74.6	74.8	75.3	75.8	77.4	78.0	80.2	80.5	80.4	80.8	79.9	79.4	80.2	79.1
Central African Republic	-	-	-	-	-	-	-	59.8	60.0	57.5	56.5	54.2	50.6	48.6	48.3	48.4	49.3	50.3	50.4	46.7	45.9
Chad	-	-	45.1	46.6	47.2	46.8	46.4	49.2	52.6	53.1	52.1	50.0	50.1	47.8	47.5	47.5	45.3	44.8	45.2	44.5	45.9
Chile	71.2	72.6	75.9	74.9	74.1	74.7	75.1	77.8	76.0	76.9	77.8	78.0	77.7	78.6	78.3	77.2	77.4	78.3	79.0	78.7	78.5
China	52.0	51.3	51.7	53.1	54.8	56.4	52.6	52.8	52.6	52.5	53.7	53.6	52.0	53.1	53.2	51.0	52.0	51.2	51.9	52.5	52.7
Colombia	64.5	64.3	66.4	65.5	65.3	63.3	65.6	64.2	64.2	61.2	59.6	60.4	59.9	62.2	62.3	65.5	68.0	68.0	69.6	70.7	71.7
Comoros	-	-	-	-	-	-	-	-	-	-	-	-	-	-	43.3	44.9	43.8	45.7	47.5	51.4	52.1
Congo, Dem. Rep. of	41.4	39.5	39.5	40.6	34.0	34.8	-	-	-	-	-	-	-	-	42.8	41.4	40.7	41.1	39.6	40.6	45.0
Congo, Rep. of	-	40.3	42.2	33.8	41.6	40.6	44.3	45.3	47.7	45.9	46.2	43.8	44.4	45.3	45.4	43.2	43.6	43.8	43.5	43.7	42.7
Costa Rica	68.0	66.4	65.6	65.6	67.4	68.4	67.6	67.5	67.0	66.4	66.1	65.9	64.0	64.2	66.4	65.9	67.3	68.0	67.0	66.9	67.2
Côte d'Ivoire	53.4	49.9	50.5	51.3	51.7	50.2	54.8	57.3	56.7	57.8	56.6	56.2	54.9	53.9	55.0	54.1	55.4	54.3	54.1	57.7	58.5
Croatia	-	48.0	46.7	51.7	53.1	53.6	50.7	51.1	53.3	53.1	51.9	53.6	53.4	54.1	55.1	59.2	61.1	60.9	61.3	60.4	61.5
Cuba	27.8	27.8	27.8	28.2	29.7	31.3	31.6	32.4	35.1	34.4	35.5	29.3	28.6	27.5	27.9	26.7	27.7	28.3	28.5	28.7	29.6
Cyprus	-	67.7	67.9	68.2	67.8	67.2	71.0	73.0	73.3	74.1	71.9	71.8	71.7	71.3	70.8	70.9	73.3	71.8	69.0	67.6	67.9
Czech Republic	67.8	68.1	68.8	68.4	69.7	68.6	70.2	66.5	67.5	67.0	64.6	66.4	67.4	68.1	69.4	69.8	70.4	69.9	70.9	72.2	72.5
Denmark	-	67.3	67.5	67.5	68.1	68.3	68.3	71.1	73.2	72.4	75.3	75.4	77.0	79.2	79.6	77.9	78.6	76.2	76.1	76.1	76.3
Djibouti	-	-	54.5	55.9	57.1	55.1	58.3	57.8	55.7	55.6	55.2	53.2	52.4	51.2	51.3	51.0	54.5	53.9	53.9	55.9	57.5
Dominica	-	-	-	-	-	-	-	-	-	-	-	-	-	-	62.6	63.2	63.3	61.6	63.9	65.2	66.1
Dominican Republic	55.8	58.1	53.5	58.1	58.1	59.0	59.1	58.6	57.8	54.6	55.1	56.3	56.8	57.7	59.2	60.3	60.0	60.2	59.7	61.3	61.0
Ecuador	57.7	60.1	61.0	62.8	62.9	59.8	55.1	53.1	54.1	54.4	52.9	54.6	55.3	55.2	52.5	49.3	47.1	48.3	46.9	48.0	49.2
Egypt	45.7	52.0	54.5	55.8	58.0	51.7	51.5	54.1	55.3	55.5	55.8	53.2	54.4	58.5	58.0	59.0	59.1	57.9	54.8	52.9	55.2
El Salvador	69.1	70.1	70.5	70.2	75.1	76.3	73.0	73.0	71.5	71.2	71.5	69.6	68.9	68.5	69.8	69.9	68.8	68.7	66.7	66.2	65.7
Equatorial Guinea	-	-	-	-	45.1	45.6	47.9	46.4	53.1	53.3	53.3	51.5	53.2	51.6	51.3	48.6	47.5	42.8	42.3	44.4	40.4

Index of Economic Freedom Scores, 1995–2015

Country	1995	1996	1997	1998	1999	2000	2001	2002	2003	2004	2005	2006	2007	2008	2009	2010	2011	2012	2013	2014	2015
Eritrea	-	-	-	-	-	-	-	-	-	-	-	-	-	-	38.5	35.3	36.7	36.2	36.3	38.5	38.9
Estonia	65.2	65.4	69.1	72.5	73.8	69.9	76.1	77.6	77.7	77.4	75.2	74.9	78.0	77.9	76.4	74.7	75.2	73.2	75.3	75.9	76.8
Ethiopia	42.6	45.9	48.1	49.2	46.7	50.2	48.9	49.8	48.8	54.5	51.1	50.9	53.6	52.5	53.0	51.2	50.5	52.0	49.4	50.0	51.5
Fiji	54.7	57.4	58.0	58.2	58.4	57.8	53.7	53.9	54.7	58.0	58.2	58.4	60.8	61.8	61.0	60.3	60.4	57.3	57.2	58.7	59.0
Finland	-	63.7	65.2	63.5	63.9	64.3	69.7	73.6	73.7	73.4	71.0	72.9	74.0	74.6	74.5	73.8	74.0	72.3	74.0	73.4	73.4
France	64.4	63.7	59.1	58.9	59.1	57.4	58.0	58.0	59.2	60.9	60.5	61.1	62.1	64.7	63.3	64.2	64.6	63.2	64.1	63.5	62.5
Gabon	57.5	55.7	58.8	59.2	60.5	58.2	55.0	58.0	58.7	57.1	54.8	56.1	54.8	54.2	55.0	55.4	56.7	56.4	57.8	57.8	58.3
The Gambia	-	-	52.9	53.4	52.1	52.7	56.6	57.7	56.3	55.3	56.5	57.3	57.7	56.9	55.8	55.1	57.4	58.8	58.8	59.5	57.5
Georgia	-	44.1	46.5	47.9	52.5	54.3	58.3	56.7	58.6	58.9	57.1	64.5	69.3	69.2	69.8	70.4	70.4	69.4	72.2	72.6	73.0
Germany	69.8	69.1	67.5	64.3	65.6	65.7	69.5	70.4	69.7	69.5	68.1	70.8	70.8	70.6	70.5	71.1	71.8	71.0	72.8	73.4	73.8
Ghana	55.6	57.7	56.7	57.0	57.9	58.1	58.0	57.2	58.2	59.1	56.5	55.6	57.6	57.0	58.1	60.2	59.4	60.7	61.3	64.2	63.0
Greece	61.2	60.5	59.6	60.6	61.0	58.1	63.4	59.1	58.8	59.1	59.0	60.1	58.7	60.6	60.8	62.7	60.3	55.4	55.4	55.7	54.0
Guatemala	62.0	63.7	65.7	65.8	66.2	64.3	65.1	62.3	62.3	59.6	59.5	59.1	60.5	59.8	59.4	61.0	61.9	60.9	60.0	61.2	60.4
Guinea	59.4	58.5	52.9	61.0	59.4	58.2	58.4	52.9	54.6	56.1	57.4	52.8	54.5	52.8	51.0	51.8	51.7	50.8	51.2	53.5	52.1
Guinea-Bissau	-	-	-	-	33.5	34.7	42.5	42.3	43.1	42.6	46.0	46.5	46.1	44.4	45.4	43.6	46.5	50.1	51.1	51.3	52.1
Guyana	45.7	50.1	53.2	52.7	53.3	52.4	53.3	54.3	50.3	53.0	56.5	56.6	53.7	48.8	48.4	48.4	49.4	51.3	53.8	55.7	52.0
Haiti	43.0	41.0	45.8	45.7	45.9	45.7	47.1	47.9	50.6	51.2	48.4	49.2	51.4	49.0	50.5	50.8	52.1	50.7	48.1	48.9	55.5
Honduras	57.0	56.6	56.0	56.2	56.7	57.6	57.0	58.7	60.4	55.3	55.3	57.4	59.1	58.9	58.7	58.3	58.6	58.8	58.4	57.1	57.4
Hong Kong	88.6	90.5	88.6	88.0	88.5	89.5	89.9	89.4	89.8	90.0	89.5	88.6	89.9	89.7	90.0	89.7	89.7	89.9	89.3	90.1	89.6
Hungary	55.2	56.8	55.3	56.9	59.6	64.4	65.6	64.5	63.0	62.7	63.5	65.0	64.8	67.6	66.8	66.1	66.6	67.1	67.3	67.0	66.8
Iceland	-	-	70.5	71.2	71.4	74.0	73.4	73.1	73.5	72.1	76.6	75.8	76.0	75.8	75.9	73.7	68.2	70.9	72.1	72.4	72.0
India	45.1	47.4	49.7	49.7	50.2	47.4	49.0	51.2	51.2	51.5	54.2	52.2	53.9	54.1	54.4	53.8	54.6	54.6	55.2	55.7	54.6
Indonesia	54.9	61.0	62.0	63.4	61.5	55.2	52.5	54.8	55.8	52.1	52.9	51.9	53.2	53.2	53.4	55.5	56.0	56.4	56.9	58.5	58.1
Iran	-	36.1	34.5	36.0	36.8	36.1	35.9	36.4	43.2	42.8	50.5	45.0	45.0	45.0	44.6	43.4	42.1	42.3	43.2	40.3	41.8
Iraq	-	17.2	17.2	17.2	17.2	17.2	17.2	15.6	-	-	-	-	-	-	-	-	-	-	-	-	-
Ireland	68.5	68.5	72.6	73.7	74.6	76.1	81.2	80.5	80.9	80.3	80.8	82.2	82.6	82.5	82.2	81.3	78.7	76.9	75.7	76.2	76.6
Israel	61.5	62.0	62.7	68.0	68.3	65.5	66.1	66.9	62.7	61.4	62.6	64.4	64.8	66.3	67.6	67.7	68.5	67.8	66.9	68.4	70.5
Italy	61.2	60.8	58.1	59.1	61.6	61.9	63.0	63.6	64.3	64.2	64.9	62.0	62.8	62.6	61.4	62.7	60.3	58.8	60.6	60.9	61.7

Index of Economic Freedom Scores, 1995-2015

Country	1995	1996	1997	1998	1999	2000	2001	2002	2003	2004	2005	2006	2007	2008	2009	2010	2011	2012	2013	2014	2015
Jamaica	64.4	66.7	67.7	67.1	64.7	65.5	63.7	61.7	67.0	66.7	67.0	66.4	65.5	65.7	65.2	65.5	65.7	65.1	66.8	66.7	67.7
Japan	75.0	72.6	70.3	70.2	69.1	70.7	70.9	66.7	67.6	64.3	67.3	73.3	72.7	73.0	72.8	72.9	72.8	71.6	71.8	72.4	73.3
Jordan	62.7	60.8	63.6	66.8	67.4	67.5	68.3	66.2	65.3	66.1	66.7	63.7	64.5	64.1	65.4	66.1	68.9	69.9	70.4	69.2	69.3
Kazakhstan	-	-	-	41.7	47.3	50.4	51.8	52.4	52.3	49.7	53.9	60.2	59.6	61.1	60.1	61.0	62.1	63.6	63.0	63.7	63.3
Kenya	54.5	56.4	60.1	58.4	58.2	59.7	57.6	58.2	58.6	57.7	57.9	59.7	59.6	59.3	58.7	57.5	57.4	57.5	55.9	57.1	55.6
Kiribati	-	-	-	-	-	-	-	-	-	-	-	-	-	-	45.7	43.7	44.8	46.9	45.9	46.3	46.4
North Korea	8.9	8.9	8.9	8.9	8.9	8.9	8.9	8.9	8.9	8.9	8.0	4.0	3.0	3.0	2.0	1.0	1.0	1.0	1.5	1.0	1.3
South Korea	72.0	73.0	69.8	73.3	69.7	69.7	69.1	69.5	68.3	67.8	66.4	67.5	67.8	68.6	68.1	69.9	69.8	69.9	70.3	71.2	71.5
Kosovo	-	-	-	-	-	-	-	-	-	-	-	-	-	-	-	-	-	-	-	-	-
Kuwait	-	66.1	64.8	66.3	69.5	69.7	68.2	65.4	66.7	63.6	64.6	66.5	66.4	68.1	65.6	67.7	64.9	62.5	63.1	62.3	62.5
Kyrgyz Republic	-	-	-	51.8	54.8	55.7	53.7	51.7	56.8	58.0	56.6	61.0	60.2	61.1	61.8	61.3	61.1	60.2	59.6	61.1	61.3
Laos	-	38.5	35.1	35.2	35.2	36.8	33.5	36.8	41.0	42.0	44.4	47.5	50.3	50.3	50.4	51.1	51.3	50.0	50.1	51.2	51.4
Latvia	-	55.0	62.4	63.4	64.2	63.4	66.4	65.0	66.0	67.4	66.3	66.9	67.9	68.3	66.6	66.2	65.8	65.2	66.5	68.7	69.7
Lebanon	-	63.2	63.9	59.0	59.1	56.1	61.0	57.1	56.7	56.9	57.2	57.5	60.4	60.0	58.1	59.5	60.1	60.1	59.5	59.4	59.3
Lesotho	-	47.0	47.2	48.4	48.2	48.4	50.6	48.9	52.0	50.3	53.9	54.7	53.2	52.1	49.7	48.1	47.5	46.6	47.9	49.5	49.6
Liberia	-	-	-	-	-	-	-	-	-	-	-	-	-	-	-	-	-	-	-	-	-
Libya	-	31.7	28.9	32.0	32.3	34.7	34.0	35.4	34.6	31.5	32.8	33.2	37.0	38.7	43.5	40.2	38.6	35.9	-	52.4	52.7
Liechtenstein	-	-	-	-	-	-	-	-	-	-	-	-	-	-	-	n/a	n/a	N/A	-	-	-
Lithuania	-	49.7	57.3	59.4	61.5	61.9	65.5	66.1	69.7	72.4	70.5	71.8	71.5	70.9	70.0	70.3	71.3	71.5	72.1	73.0	74.7
Luxembourg	-	72.5	72.8	72.7	72.4	76.4	80.1	79.4	79.9	78.9	76.3	75.3	74.6	74.7	75.2	75.4	76.2	74.5	74.2	74.2	73.2
Macau	-	-	-	-	-	-	-	-	-	-	-	-	-	-	72.0	72.5	73.1	71.8	71.7	71.3	70.3
Macedonia	51.6	-	-	-	-	-	-	58.0	60.1	56.8	56.1	59.2	60.6	61.1	61.2	65.7	66.0	68.5	68.2	68.6	67.1
Madagascar	-	52.2	53.8	51.8	52.8	54.4	53.9	56.8	62.8	60.9	63.1	61.0	61.1	62.4	62.2	63.2	61.2	62.4	62.0	61.7	61.7
Malawi	54.7	56.2	53.4	54.1	54.0	57.4	56.2	56.9	53.2	53.6	53.6	55.4	52.9	52.7	53.7	54.1	55.8	56.4	55.3	55.4	54.8
Malaysia	71.9	69.9	66.8	68.2	68.9	66.0	60.2	60.1	61.1	59.9	61.9	61.6	63.8	63.9	64.6	64.8	66.3	66.4	66.1	69.6	70.8
Maldives	-	-	-	-	-	-	-	-	-	-	-	-	-	-	51.3	49.0	48.3	49.2	49.0	51.0	53.4
Mali	52.4	57.0	56.4	57.3	58.4	60.3	60.1	61.1	58.6	56.6	57.3	54.1	54.7	55.6	55.6	55.6	56.3	55.8	56.4	55.5	56.4
Malta	56.3	55.8	57.9	61.2	59.3	58.3	62.9	62.2	61.1	63.3	68.9	67.3	66.1	66.0	66.1	67.2	65.7	67.0	67.5	66.4	66.5

Index of Economic Freedom Scores, 1995–2015

Country	1995	1996	1997	1998	1999	2000	2001	2002	2003	2004	2005	2006	2007	2008	2009	2010	2011	2012	2013	2014	2015
Mauritania	-	45.5	47.0	43.7	42.8	46.0	48.5	52.5	59.0	61.8	59.4	55.7	53.6	55.2	53.9	52.0	52.1	53.0	52.3	53.2	53.3
Mauritius	-	-	-	-	68.5	67.2	66.4	67.7	64.4	64.3	67.2	67.4	69.4	72.6	74.3	76.3	76.2	77.0	76.9	76.5	76.4
Mexico	63.1	61.2	57.1	57.9	58.5	59.3	60.6	63.0	65.3	66.0	65.2	64.7	66.0	66.2	65.8	68.3	67.8	65.3	67.0	66.8	66.4
Micronesia	-	-	-	-	-	-	-	-	-	-	-	-	-	-	51.7	50.6	50.3	50.7	50.1	49.8	49.6
Moldova	33.0	52.5	48.9	53.5	56.1	59.6	54.9	57.4	60.0	57.1	57.4	58.0	58.7	57.9	54.9	53.7	55.7	54.4	55.5	57.3	57.5
Mongolia	47.8	47.4	52.9	57.3	58.6	58.5	56.0	56.7	57.7	56.5	59.7	62.4	60.3	63.6	62.8	60.0	59.5	61.5	61.7	58.9	59.2
Montenegro	-	-	-	-	-	-	-	46.6	43.5	-	-	-	-	-	58.2	63.6	62.5	62.5	62.6	63.6	64.7
Morocco	62.8	64.3	64.7	61.1	63.8	63.2	63.9	59.0	57.8	56.7	52.2	51.5	56.4	55.6	57.7	59.2	59.6	60.2	59.6	58.3	60.1
Mozambique	45.5	48.4	44.0	43.0	48.9	52.2	59.2	57.7	58.6	57.2	54.6	51.9	54.7	55.4	55.7	56.0	56.8	57.1	55.0	55.0	54.8
Namibia	-	-	61.6	66.1	66.1	66.7	64.8	65.1	67.3	62.4	61.4	60.7	63.5	61.4	62.4	62.2	62.7	61.9	60.3	59.4	59.6
Nepal	-	50.3	53.6	53.5	53.1	51.3	51.6	52.3	51.5	51.2	51.4	53.7	54.4	54.1	53.2	52.7	50.1	50.2	50.4	50.1	51.3
The Netherlands	-	69.7	70.4	69.2	70.2	70.4	73.0	75.1	74.6	74.5	72.9	75.4	75.5	77.4	77.0	75.0	74.7	73.3	73.5	74.2	73.7
New Zealand	-	78.1	79.0	79.2	81.7	80.9	81.1	80.7	81.1	81.5	82.3	82.0	81.4	80.7	82.0	82.1	82.3	82.1	81.4	81.2	82.1
Nicaragua	42.5	54.1	53.3	53.8	54.0	56.9	58.0	61.1	62.6	61.4	62.5	63.8	62.7	60.8	59.8	58.3	58.8	57.9	56.6	58.4	57.6
Niger	-	45.8	46.6	47.5	48.6	45.9	48.9	48.2	54.2	54.6	54.1	52.5	53.2	52.9	53.8	52.9	54.3	54.3	53.9	55.1	54.6
Nigeria	47.3	47.4	52.8	52.3	55.7	53.1	49.6	50.9	49.5	49.2	48.4	48.7	55.6	55.1	55.1	56.8	56.7	56.3	55.1	54.3	55.6
Norway	-	65.4	65.1	68.0	68.6	70.1	67.1	67.4	67.2	66.2	64.5	67.9	67.9	68.6	70.2	69.4	70.3	68.8	70.5	70.9	71.8
Oman	70.2	65.4	64.5	64.9	64.9	64.1	67.7	64.0	64.6	66.9	66.5	63.7	65.8	67.3	67.0	67.7	69.8	67.9	68.1	67.4	66.7
Pakistan	57.6	58.4	56.0	53.2	53.0	56.4	56.0	55.8	55.0	54.9	53.3	57.9	57.2	55.6	57.0	55.2	55.1	54.7	55.1	55.2	55.6
Panama	71.6	71.8	72.4	72.6	72.6	71.6	70.6	68.5	68.4	65.3	64.3	65.6	64.6	64.7	64.7	64.8	64.9	65.2	62.5	63.4	64.1
Papua New Guinea	-	58.6	56.7	55.2	56.3	55.8	57.2	-	-	-	-	-	-	-	54.8	53.5	52.6	53.8	53.6	53.9	53.1
Paraguay	65.9	67.1	67.3	65.2	63.7	64.0	60.3	59.6	58.2	56.7	53.4	55.6	58.3	60.0	61.0	61.3	62.3	61.8	61.1	62.0	61.1
Peru	56.9	62.5	63.8	65.0	69.2	68.7	69.6	64.8	64.6	64.7	61.3	60.5	62.7	63.8	64.6	67.6	68.6	68.7	68.2	67.4	67.7
The Philippines	55.0	60.2	62.2	62.8	61.9	62.5	60.9	60.7	61.3	59.1	54.7	56.3	56.0	56.0	56.8	56.3	56.2	57.1	58.2	60.1	62.2
Poland	50.7	57.8	56.8	59.2	59.6	60.0	61.8	65.0	61.8	58.7	59.6	59.3	58.1	60.3	60.3	63.2	64.1	64.2	66.0	67.0	68.6
Portugal	62.4	64.5	63.6	65.0	65.6	65.5	66.0	65.4	64.9	64.9	62.4	62.9	64.0	63.9	64.9	64.4	64.0	63.0	63.1	63.5	65.3
Qatar	-	-	-	-	62.0	62.0	60.0	61.9	65.9	66.5	63.5	62.4	62.9	62.2	65.8	69.0	70.5	71.3	71.3	71.2	70.8
Romania	42.9	46.2	50.8	54.4	50.1	52.1	50.0	48.7	50.6	50.0	52.1	58.2	61.2	61.7	63.2	64.2	64.7	64.4	65.1	65.5	66.6

Index of Economic Freedom Scores, 1995–2015

Country	1995	1996	1997	1998	1999	2000	2001	2002	2003	2004	2005	2006	2007	2008	2009	2010	2011	2012	2013	2014	2015
Russia	51.1	51.6	48.6	52.8	54.5	51.8	49.8	48.7	50.8	52.8	51.3	52.4	52.2	49.8	50.8	50.3	50.5	50.5	51.1	51.9	52.1
Rwanda	-	-	38.3	39.1	39.8	42.3	45.4	50.4	47.8	53.3	51.7	52.8	52.4	54.2	54.2	59.1	62.7	64.9	64.1	64.7	64.8
Saint Lucia	-	-	-	-	-	-	-	-	-	-	-	-	-	-	68.8	70.5	70.8	71.3	70.4	70.7	70.2
Saint Vincent and the Grenadines	-	-	-	-	-	-	-	-	-	-	-	-	-	-	64.3	66.9	66.9	66.5	66.7	67.0	68.0
Samoa	-	47.6	51.5	49.9	58.7	60.8	63.1	-	-	-	-	-	-	-	59.5	60.4	60.6	60.5	57.1	61.1	61.9
São Tomé and Príncipe	-	-	-	-	-	-	-	-	-	-	-	-	-	-	43.8	48.8	49.5	50.2	48.0	48.8	53.3
Saudi Arabia	-	68.3	68.7	69.3	65.5	66.5	62.2	65.3	63.2	60.4	63.0	63.0	60.9	62.5	64.3	64.1	66.2	62.5	60.6	62.2	62.1
Senegal	-	58.2	58.1	59.7	60.6	58.9	58.7	58.6	58.1	58.9	57.9	56.2	58.1	58.3	56.3	54.6	55.7	55.4	55.5	55.4	57.8
Serbia	-	-	-	-	-	-	-	46.6	43.5	-	-	-	-	-	56.6	56.9	58.0	58.0	58.6	59.4	60.0
Seychelles	-	-	-	-	-	-	-	-	-	-	-	-	-	-	47.8	47.9	51.2	53.0	54.9	56.2	57.5
Sierra Leone	49.8	52.3	45.0	47.7	47.2	44.2	-	-	42.2	43.6	44.8	45.2	47.0	48.3	47.8	47.9	49.6	49.1	48.3	50.5	51.7
Singapore	86.3	86.5	87.3	87.0	86.9	87.7	87.8	87.4	88.2	88.9	88.6	88.0	87.1	87.3	87.1	86.1	87.2	87.5	88.0	89.4	89.4
Slovak Republic	60.4	57.6	55.5	57.5	54.2	53.8	58.5	59.8	59.0	64.6	66.8	69.8	69.6	70.0	69.4	69.7	69.5	67.0	68.7	66.4	67.2
Slovenia	-	50.4	55.6	60.7	61.3	58.3	61.8	57.8	57.7	59.2	59.6	61.9	59.6	60.2	62.9	64.7	64.6	62.9	61.7	62.7	60.3
Solomon Islands	-	-	-	-	-	-	-	-	-	-	-	-	-	-	46.0	42.9	45.9	46.2	45.0	46.2	47.0
Somalia	-	25.6	25.6	27.8	27.8	27.8	-	-	-	-	-	-	-	-	-	-	-	-	-	-	-
South Africa	60.7	62.5	63.2	64.3	63.3	63.7	63.8	64.0	67.1	66.3	62.9	63.7	63.5	63.4	63.8	62.8	62.7	62.7	61.8	62.5	62.6
Spain	62.8	59.6	59.6	62.6	65.1	65.9	68.1	68.8	68.8	68.9	67.0	68.2	69.2	69.1	70.1	69.6	70.2	69.1	68.0	67.2	67.6
Sri Lanka	60.6	62.5	65.5	64.6	64.0	63.2	66.0	64.0	62.5	61.6	61.0	58.7	59.4	58.4	56.0	54.6	57.1	58.3	60.7	60.0	58.6
Sudan	39.4	39.2	39.9	38.3	39.6	47.2	-	-	-	-	-	-	-	-	-	-	-	-	-	-	-
Suriname	-	36.7	35.9	39.9	40.1	45.8	44.3	48.0	46.9	47.9	51.9	55.1	54.8	54.3	54.1	52.5	53.1	52.6	52.0	54.2	54.2
Swaziland	63.3	58.6	59.4	62.0	62.1	62.6	63.6	60.9	59.6	58.6	59.4	61.4	60.1	58.4	59.1	57.4	59.1	57.2	57.2	61.2	59.9
Sweden	61.4	61.8	63.3	64.0	64.2	65.1	66.6	70.8	70.0	70.1	69.8	70.9	69.3	70.8	70.5	72.4	71.9	71.7	72.9	73.1	72.7
Switzerland	-	76.8	78.6	79.0	79.1	76.8	76.0	79.3	79.0	79.5	79.3	78.9	78.0	79.5	79.4	81.1	81.9	81.1	81.0	81.6	80.5

Index of Economic Freedom Scores, 1995–2015

Country	1995	1996	1997	1998	1999	2000	2001	2002	2003	2004	2005	2006	2007	2008	2009	2010	2011	2012	2013	2014	2015
Syria	-	42.3	43.0	42.2	39.0	37.2	36.6	36.3	41.3	40.6	46.3	51.2	48.3	47.2	51.3	49.4	51.3	51.2	-	-	-
Taiwan	74.2	74.1	70.0	70.4	71.5	72.5	72.8	71.3	71.7	69.6	71.3	69.7	69.4	70.3	69.5	70.4	70.8	71.9	72.7	73.9	75.1
Tajikistan	-	-	-	41.1	41.2	44.8	46.8	47.3	46.5	48.7	50.4	52.6	53.6	54.4	54.6	53.0	53.5	53.4	53.4	52.0	52.7
Tanzania	57.3	57.5	59.3	59.6	60.0	56.0	54.9	58.3	56.9	60.1	56.3	58.5	56.8	56.5	58.3	58.3	57.0	57.0	57.9	57.8	57.5
Thailand	71.3	71.0	66.1	67.3	66.9	66.6	68.9	69.1	65.8	63.7	62.5	63.3	63.5	62.3	63.0	64.1	64.7	64.9	64.1	63.3	62.4
Timor-Leste	-	-	-	-	-	-	-	-	-	-	-	-	-	-	50.5	45.8	42.8	43.3	43.7	43.2	45.5
Togo	-	-	-	-	48.2	46.4	45.3	45.2	46.8	47.0	48.2	47.3	49.7	48.9	48.7	47.1	49.1	48.3	48.8	49.9	53.0
Tonga	-	-	-	-	-	-	-	-	-	-	-	-	-	-	54.1	53.4	55.8	57.0	56.0	58.2	59.3
Trinidad and Tobago	-	69.2	71.3	72.0	72.4	74.5	71.8	70.1	68.8	71.3	71.5	70.4	70.6	69.5	68.0	65.7	66.5	64.4	62.3	62.7	64.1
Tunisia	63.4	63.9	63.8	63.9	61.1	61.3	60.8	60.2	58.1	58.4	55.4	57.5	60.3	60.1	58.0	58.9	58.5	58.6	57.0	57.3	57.7
Turkey	58.4	56.7	60.8	60.9	59.2	63.4	60.6	54.2	51.9	52.8	50.6	57.0	57.4	59.9	61.6	63.8	64.2	62.5	62.9	64.9	63.2
Turkmenistan	-	-	-	35.0	36.1	37.6	41.8	43.2	51.3	50.7	47.6	43.8	43.0	43.4	44.2	42.5	43.6	43.8	42.6	42.2	41.4
Uganda	62.9	66.2	66.6	64.7	64.8	58.2	60.4	61.0	60.1	64.1	62.9	63.9	63.1	63.8	63.5	62.2	61.7	61.9	61.1	59.9	59.7
Ukraine	39.9	40.6	43.5	40.4	43.7	47.8	48.5	48.2	51.1	53.7	55.8	54.4	51.5	51.0	48.8	46.4	45.8	46.1	46.3	49.3	46.9
United Arab Emirates	-	71.6	71.9	72.2	71.5	74.2	74.9	73.6	73.4	67.2	65.2	62.2	62.6	62.6	64.7	67.3	67.8	69.3	71.1	71.4	72.4
United Kingdom	77.9	76.4	76.4	76.5	76.2	77.3	77.6	78.5	77.5	77.7	79.2	80.4	79.9	79.4	79.0	76.5	74.5	74.1	74.8	74.9	75.8
United States	76.7	76.7	75.6	75.4	75.5	76.4	79.1	78.4	78.2	78.7	79.9	81.2	81.2	81.0	80.7	78.0	77.8	76.3	76.0	75.5	76.2
Uruguay	62.5	63.7	67.5	68.6	68.5	69.3	70.7	68.7	69.8	66.7	66.9	65.3	68.4	67.9	69.1	69.8	70.0	69.9	69.7	69.3	68.6
Uzbekistan	-	-	-	31.5	33.8	38.1	38.2	38.5	38.3	39.1	45.8	48.7	51.5	51.9	50.5	47.5	45.8	45.8	46.0	46.5	47.0
Vanuatu	-	-	-	-	-	-	-	-	-	-	-	-	-	-	58.4	56.4	56.7	56.6	56.6	59.5	61.1
Venezuela	59.8	54.5	52.8	54.0	56.1	57.4	54.6	54.7	54.8	46.7	45.2	44.6	47.9	44.7	39.9	37.1	37.6	38.1	36.1	36.3	34.3
Vietnam	41.7	40.2	38.6	40.4	42.7	43.7	44.3	45.6	46.2	46.1	48.1	50.5	49.8	50.4	51.0	49.8	51.6	51.3	51.0	50.8	51.7
Yemen	49.8	49.6	48.4	46.1	43.3	44.5	44.3	48.6	50.3	50.5	53.8	52.6	54.1	53.8	56.9	54.4	54.2	55.3	55.9	55.5	53.7
Zambia	55.1	59.6	62.1	62.7	64.2	62.8	59.5	59.6	55.3	54.9	55.0	56.8	56.2	56.2	56.6	58.0	59.7	58.3	58.7	60.4	58.7
Zimbabwe	48.5	46.7	48.0	44.6	47.2	48.7	38.8	36.7	36.7	34.4	35.2	33.5	32.0	29.5	22.7	21.4	22.1	26.3	28.6	35.5	37.6

Methodology

The *Index of Economic Freedom* focuses on four key aspects of the economic environment over which governments typically exercise policy control:

- **Rule of law,**
- **Government size,**
- **Regulatory efficiency,** and
- **Market openness.**

In assessing conditions in these four categories, the *Index* measures 10 specific components of economic freedom, each of which is graded on a scale from 0 to 100. Scores on these 10 components of economic freedom, which are calculated from a number of sub-variables, are equally weighted and averaged to produce an overall economic freedom score for each economy.

The following sections provide detailed descriptions of the formulas and methodology used to compute the scores for each of the 10 components of economic freedom.

RULE OF LAW

Property Rights

The property rights component is a qualitative assessment of the extent to which a country's legal framework allows individuals to freely accumulate private property, secured by clear laws that are enforced effectively by the government. It measures the degree to which a country's laws protect private property rights and the extent to which those laws are respected. It also assesses the likelihood that private property will be expropriated by the state and analyzes the independence of the judiciary, the existence of corruption within the judiciary, and the ability of individuals and businesses to enforce contracts.

The more effective the legal protection of property, the higher a country's score. Similarly, the greater the chances of government expropriation of property or the less independent the judiciary, the lower a country's score.

Each country's property rights score is assessed according to the following criteria:

- **100**—Private property is guaranteed by the government. The court system enforces contracts efficiently and quickly. The justice system punishes those who unlawfully confiscate private property. There is no corruption or expropriation.
- **90**—Private property is guaranteed by the government. The court system enforces contracts efficiently. The justice system punishes those who unlawfully confiscate private property. Corruption is nearly nonexistent, and expropriation is highly unlikely.
- **80**—Private property is guaranteed by the government. The court system enforces contracts efficiently but with some delays. Corruption is minimal, and expropriation is highly unlikely.
- **70**—Private property is guaranteed by the government. The court system is subject to delays and lax in enforcing contracts. Corruption is possible but rare, and expropriation is unlikely.
- **60**—Enforcement of property rights is lax and subject to delays. Corruption is possible but rare, and the judiciary may be influenced by other branches of government. Expropriation is unlikely.
- **50**—The court system is inefficient and subject to delays. Corruption may be present, and the judiciary may be influenced by other branches of government. Expropriation is possible but rare.
- **40**—The court system is highly inefficient, and delays are so long that they deter resort to the court system. Corruption is present, and the judiciary is influenced by other branches of government. Expropriation is possible.
- **30**—Property ownership is weakly protected. The court system is highly inefficient. Corruption is extensive, and the judiciary is strongly influenced by other branches of government. Expropriation is possible.
- **20**—Private property is weakly protected. The court system is so inefficient and corrupt that outside settlement and arbitration is the norm. Property rights are difficult to enforce. Judicial corruption is extensive. Expropriation is common.
- **10**—Private property is rarely protected, and almost all property belongs to the state. The country is in such chaos (for example, because of ongoing war) that protection of property is almost impossible to enforce. The judiciary is so corrupt that property is not protected effectively. Expropriation is common.
- **0**—Private property is outlawed, and all property belongs to the state. People do not have the right to sue others and do not have access to the courts. Corruption is endemic.

An intermediate score such as 75 or 45 may be assigned to countries whose property rights fall between two adjacent categories.

Sources. Unless otherwise noted, the *Index* relies on the following sources for information on property rights, in order of priority: Economist Intelligence Unit, *ViewsWire*; Freedom House, *Freedom in the World*, 2011–2014; U.S. Department of Commerce, *Country Commercial Guide*, 2011–2014; U.S. Department of State, *Investment Climate Statements*, 2011–2014; U.S. Department of State, *Country Reports on Human Rights Practices*, 2010–2013; and various news and magazine articles.

Freedom from Corruption

Corruption erodes economic freedom by introducing insecurity and uncertainty into economic relations. It also reduces economic vitality by increasing costs and shifting resources into unproductive activities.

The score for this component is derived directly from Transparency International's Corruption Perceptions Index (CPI), which measures the level of perceived corruption in 177 countries.

For countries that are not covered in the CPI, the freedom from corruption score is determined by using the qualitative information from internationally recognized and reliable sources.[1] This procedure considers the extent to which corruption prevails in a country.

Sources. Unless otherwise noted, the *Index* relies on the following sources for information on informal market activities, in order of priority: Transparency International, *Corruption Perceptions Index*, 2011–2013; U.S. Department of Commerce, *Country Commercial Guide*, 2011–2014; U.S. Department of State, *Investment Climate Statements*, 2011–2014; Economist Intelligence Unit, *ViewsWire* and *Risk Briefing*; Freedom House, *Freedom in the World*, 2011–2014; Office of the U.S. Trade Representative, *2014 National Trade Estimate Report on Foreign Trade Barriers*; various news and magazine articles; and official government publications of each country.

GOVERNMENT SIZE

Fiscal Freedom

The fiscal freedom component is a composite measure of the burden of taxes that reflects both marginal tax rates and the overall level of taxation, including direct and indirect taxes imposed by all levels of government, as a percentage of GDP. The component score is derived from three quantitative sub-factors:

- The top marginal tax rate on individual income,
- The top marginal tax rate on corporate income, and
- The total tax burden as a percentage of GDP.

Each of these numerical variables is weighted equally as one-third of the component score. This equal weighting allows a country to achieve a score as high as 67 based on two of the factors even if it receives a score of 0 on the third.

Fiscal freedom scores are calculated with a quadratic cost function to reflect the diminishing revenue returns from very high rates of taxation. The data for each sub-factor are converted to a 100-point scale using the following equation:

$$\text{Fiscal Freedom}_{ij} = 100 - \alpha \, (\text{Factor}_{ij})^2$$

where Fiscal Freedom$_{ij}$ represents the fiscal freedom in country i for factor j; Factor$_{ij}$ represents the value (a percentage expressed on a scale of 0 to 100) in country i for factor j; and α is a coefficient set equal to 0.03. The minimum score for each sub-factor is zero, which is not represented in the printed equation but was utilized because it means that no single high tax burden will make the other two sub-factors irrelevant.

As an example, in the 2015 *Index*, Mauritius has a flat rate of 15 percent for both individual and corporate tax rates, which yields a score of 93.3 for each of the two factors. Mauritius's overall tax burden as a portion of GDP is 18.9 percent, yielding a tax burden factor score of 89.7. When the three factors are averaged together, Mauritius's overall fiscal freedom score becomes 92.1.

Sources. Unless otherwise noted, the *Index* relies on the following sources for information on tax rate data, in order of priority: Deloitte, *International Tax and Business Guide Highlights*; International Monetary Fund, *Staff Country Report*, "Selected Issues and Statistical Appendix," and *Staff Country Report*, "Article IV Consultation," 2011–2014; PricewaterhouseCoopers, *Worldwide Tax Summaries*, 2011–2014; countries' investment agencies; other government authorities (embassy confirmations and/or the country's treasury or tax authority); and Economist Intelligence Unit, *Country Commerce*, 2010–2014.

For information on tax burden as a percentage of GDP, the primary sources are Organisation for Economic Co-operation and Development data; Eurostat, Government Finance Statistics data; African Development Bank and Organisation for Economic Co-operation and Development, *African Economic Outlook 2014*; International Monetary Fund, *Staff Country Report*, "Selected Issues," and *Staff*

Country Report, "Article IV Consultation," 2011–2014; Asian Development Bank, *Key Indicators for Asia and the Pacific*, 2011–2014; United Nations Economic Commission for Latin America, Economic Survey of Latin America and the Caribbean, 2011–2014; and individual contacts from government agencies and multinational organizations such as the IMF and the World Bank.

Government Spending

The government spending component captures the burden imposed by government expenditures, which includes consumption by the state and all transfer payments related to various entitlement programs.

No attempt has been made to identify an optimal level of government spending. The ideal level will vary from country to country, depending on factors that range from culture to geography to level of economic development. However, government spending becomes an unavoidable burden at some point as government grows in scope and size, resulting in both misallocation of resources and loss of economic efficiency. Volumes of research have shown that excessive government spending that causes chronic budget deficits and the accumulation of public debt is one of the most serious drags on economic dynamism.

The *Index* methodology treats zero government spending as the benchmark. As a result, underdeveloped countries, particularly those with little government capacity, may receive artificially high scores. However, such governments, which can provide few if any public goods, are likely to receive low scores on some of the other components of economic freedom (such as property rights, financial freedom, and investment freedom) that measure aspects of government effectiveness.

Government spending has a major impact on economic freedom, but it is just one of many important components. The scale for scoring government spending is non-linear, which means that government spending that is close to zero is lightly penalized, while levels of government spending that exceed 30 percent of GDP lead to much worse scores in a quadratic fashion (for example, doubling spending yields four times less freedom). Only extraordinarily large levels of government spending—for example, over 58 percent of GDP—receive a score of zero.

The equation used for computing a country's government spending score is:

$$GE_i = 100 - \alpha \, (Expenditures_i)^2$$

where GE_i represents the government expenditure score in country i; $Expenditures_i$ represents the total amount of government spending at all levels as a portion of GDP (between 0 and 100); and α is a coefficient to control for variation among scores (set at 0.03). The minimum component score is zero.

In most cases, the *Index* uses general government expenditure data that include all levels of government such as federal, state, and local. In cases where data on general government spending are not available, data on central government expenditures are used instead.

Sources. Unless otherwise noted, the *Index* relies on the following sources for information on government intervention in the economy, in order of priority: Organisation for Economic Co-operation and Development data; Eurostat data; African Development Bank and Organisation for Economic Co-operation and Development, *African Economic Outlook 2014*; International Monetary Fund, *Staff Country Report*, "Selected Issues and Statistical Appendix," *Staff Country Report*, "Article IV Consultation," 2011–2014, and *World Economic Outlook Database 2014*; Asian Development Bank, *Key Indicators for Asia and the Pacific*, 2011–2014; African Development Bank, *The ADB Statistics Pocketbook 2014*; official government publications of each country; and United Nations Economic Commission for Latin America, *Economic Survey of Latin America and the Caribbean*, 2011–2014.

REGULATORY EFFICIENCY

Business Freedom

Business freedom is an overall indicator of the efficiency of government regulation of business. The quantitative score is derived from an array of measurements of the ease of starting, operating, and closing a business.

The business freedom score for each country is a number between 0 and 100, with 100 indicating the freest business environment. The score is based on 10 sub-factors, all weighted equally, using data from the World Bank's *Doing Business* report:

- Starting a business—procedures (number);
- Starting a business—time (days);
- Starting a business—cost (% of income per capita);
- Starting a business—minimum capital (% of income per capita);
- Obtaining a license—procedures (number);[2]
- Obtaining a license—time (days);
- Obtaining a license—cost (% of income per capita);
- Closing a business—time (years);
- Closing a business—cost (% of estate); and
- Closing a business—recovery rate (cents on the dollar).[3]

Each of these sub-factors is converted to a scale of 0 to 100, after which the average of the converted values is computed. The result represents the country's business freedom score in comparison to those of other countries. Even if a country requires the highest number of procedures for starting a business, which yields a score of zero in that factor, it could still receive a score as high as 90 based on scores in the other nine factors. Canada, for instance, receives scores of 100 in nine of these 10 factors, but the 14 licensing procedures required by the government equate to a score of 64.5 for that factor.

Each sub-factor is converted to a scale of 0 to 100 using the following equation:

$$\text{Factor Score}_i = 50 \ \text{factor}_{average}/\text{factor}_i$$

which is based on the ratio of the country data for each sub-factor relative to the world average, multiplied by 50. For example, on average worldwide, it takes 18 procedures to get necessary licenses. Canada's 14 licensing procedures are a factor value that is better than the average, resulting in a ratio of 1.29. That ratio multiplied by 50 equals the final factor score of 64.5.

For the six countries that are not covered by the World Bank's *Doing Business* report, business freedom is scored by analyzing business regulations based on qualitative information from reliable and internationally recognized sources.[4]

Sources. Unless otherwise noted, the *Index* relies on the following sources in determining business freedom scores, in order of priority: World Bank, *Doing Business 2015*; Economist Intelligence Unit, *Country Commerce*, 2011–2014; U.S. Department of Commerce, *Country Commercial Guide*, 2011–2014; and official government publications of each country.

Labor Freedom

The labor freedom component is a quantitative measure that considers various aspects of the legal and regulatory framework of a country's labor market, including regulations concerning minimum wages, laws inhibiting layoffs, severance requirements, and measurable regulatory restraints on hiring and hours worked.

Six quantitative sub-factors are equally weighted, with each counted as one-sixth of the labor freedom component:[5]

- Ratio of minimum wage to the average value added per worker,
- Hindrance to hiring additional workers,
- Rigidity of hours,
- Difficulty of firing redundant employees,
- Legally mandated notice period, and
- Mandatory severance pay.

Based on data collected in connection with the World Bank's *Doing Business* report, these sub-factors specifically examine labor regulations that affect "the hiring and redundancy of workers and the rigidity of working hours."[6]

In constructing the labor freedom score, each of the six sub-factors is converted to a scale of 0 to 100 based on the following equation:

$$\text{Factor Score}_i = 50 \times \text{factor}_{average}/\text{factor}_i$$

where country *i* data are calculated relative to the world average and then multiplied by 50. The six sub-factor scores are then averaged for each country, yielding a labor freedom score in comparison to other countries.

The simple average of the converted values for the six sub-factors is computed for the country's overall labor freedom score. Even if a country had the worst rigidity of hours in the world with a zero score for that sub-factor, it could still get a score as high as 83.3 based on the other five sub-factors.

For the six countries that are not covered by the World Bank's *Doing Business* report, the labor freedom component is scored by looking at labor market flexibility based on qualitative information from other reliable and internationally recognized sources.[7]

Sources. Unless otherwise noted, the *Index* relies on the following sources for data on labor freedom, in order of priority: World Bank, *Doing Business 2015*; Economist Intelligence Unit, *Country Commerce*, 2011–2014; U.S. Department of Commerce, *Country Commercial Guide*, 2011–2014; and official government publications of each country.

Monetary Freedom

Monetary freedom combines a measure of price stability with an assessment of price controls. Both inflation and price controls distort market activity. Price stability without microeconomic intervention is the ideal state for the free market.

The score for the monetary freedom component is based on two sub-factors:

- The weighted average inflation rate for the most recent three years and
- Price controls.

The weighted average inflation rate for the most recent three years serves as the primary input into an equation that generates the base score for monetary freedom. The extent of price controls is then assessed as a penalty deduction of up to 20 points from the base score. The two equations used to convert inflation rates into the final monetary freedom score are:

$$\text{Weighted Avg. Inflation}_i = \theta_1 \text{ Inflation}_{it} + \theta_2 \text{Inflation}_{it-1} + \theta_3 \text{ Inflation}_{it-2}$$

$$\text{Monetary Freedom}_i = 100 - \alpha \sqrt{\text{Weighted Avg. Inflation}_i} - \text{PC penalty}_i$$

where θ_1 through θ_3 (thetas 1–3) represent three numbers that sum to 1 and are exponentially smaller in sequence (in this case, values of 0.665, 0.245, and 0.090, respectively); Inflation_{it} is the absolute value of the annual inflation rate in country i during year t as measured by the Consumer Price Index; α represents a coefficient that stabilizes the variance of scores; and the price control (PC) penalty is an assigned value of 0–20 penalty points based on the extent of price controls.

The convex (square root) functional form was chosen to create separation among countries with low inflation rates. A concave functional form would essentially treat all hyperinflations as equally bad, whether they were 100 percent price increases annually or 100,000 percent, whereas the square root provides much more gradation. The α coefficient is set to equal 6.333, which converts a 10 percent inflation rate into a freedom score of 80.0 and a 2 percent inflation rate into a score of 91.0.

Sources. Unless otherwise noted, the *Index* relies on the following sources for data on monetary policy, in order of priority: International Monetary Fund, *International Financial Statistics Online*; International Monetary Fund, *World Economic Outlook*, 2014, and *Staff Country Report*, "Article IV Consultation," 2011–2014; Economist Intelligence Unit, *ViewsWire*; U.S. Energy Information Administration (EIA), *Country Analysis Briefs*; various country reports and blogs by the World Bank; various news and magazine articles; and official government publications of each country.

OPEN MARKETS

Trade Freedom

Trade freedom is a composite measure of the extent of tariff and non-tariff barriers that affect imports and exports of goods and services. The trade freedom score is based on two inputs:

- The trade-weighted average tariff rate and
- Non-tariff barriers (NTBs).

Different imports entering a country can, and often do, face different tariffs. The weighted average tariff uses weights for each tariff based on the share of imports for each good. Weighted average tariffs are a purely quantitative measure and account for the calculation of the base trade freedom score using the following equation:

$$\text{Trade Freedom}_i = (((\text{Tariff}_{max} - \text{Tariff}_i)/(\text{Tariff}_{max} - \text{Tariff}_{min})) * 100) - \text{NTB}_i$$

where Trade Freedom_i represents the trade freedom in country i; Tariff_{max} and Tariff_{min} represent the upper and lower bounds for tariff rates (%); and Tariff_i represents the weighted average tariff rate (%) in country i. The minimum tariff is naturally zero percent, and the upper bound was set as 50 percent. An NTB penalty is then subtracted from the base score. The penalty of 5, 10, 15, or 20 points is assigned according to the following scale:

- **20**—NTBs are used extensively across many goods and services and/or act to impede a significant amount of international trade.
- **15**—NTBs are widespread across many goods and services and/or act to impede a majority of potential international trade.
- **10**—NTBs are used to protect certain goods and services and impede some international trade.
- **5**—NTBs are uncommon, protecting few goods and services, and/or have very limited impact on international trade.
- **0**—NTBs are not used to limit international trade.

We determine the extent of NTBs in a country's trade policy regime using both qualitative and quantitative information. Restrictive rules that hinder trade vary widely, and their overlapping and shifting nature makes their complexity difficult to gauge. The categories of NTBs considered in our penalty include:

- **Quantity restrictions**—import quotas; export limitations; voluntary export restraints; import–export embargoes and bans; countertrade, etc.
- **Price restrictions**—antidumping duties; countervailing duties; border tax adjustments; variable levies/tariff rate quotas.
- **Regulatory restrictions**—licensing; domestic content and mixing requirements; sanitary and phytosanitary standards (SPSs); safety and industrial standards regulations; packaging, labeling, and trademark regulations; advertising and media regulations.
- **Customs restrictions**—advance deposit requirements; customs valuation procedures; customs classification procedures; customs clearance procedures.
- **Direct government intervention**—subsidies and other aid; government industrial policies; government-financed research and other technology policies; competition policies; government procurement policies; state trading, government monopolies, and exclusive franchises.

As an example, Brazil received a trade freedom score of 69.6. By itself, Brazil's weighted average tariff of 7.7 percent would have yielded a score of 84.6, but the existence of NTBs in Brazil reduced its score by 15 points.

Gathering tariff statistics to make a consistent cross-country comparison is a challenging task. Unlike data on inflation, for instance, some countries do not report their weighted average tariff rate or simple average tariff rate every year.

To preserve consistency in grading the trade freedom component, the *Index* uses the most recently reported weighted average tariff rate for a country from our primary source. If another reliable source reports more updated information on the country's tariff rate, this fact is noted, and the grading of this component may be reviewed if there is strong evidence that the most recently reported weighted average tariff rate is outdated.

The World Bank publishes the most comprehensive and consistent information on weighted average applied tariff rates. When the weighted average applied tariff rate is not available, the *Index* uses the country's average applied tariff rate; and when the country's average applied tariff rate is not available, the weighted average or the simple average of most favored nation (MFN) tariff rates is used.[8] In the very few cases where data on duties and customs revenues are not available, data on international trade taxes or an estimated effective tariff rate are used instead. In all cases, an effort is made to clarify the type of data used in the corresponding write-up for the trade freedom component.

Sources. Unless otherwise noted, the *Index* relies on the following sources to determine scores for trade policy, in order of priority: World Bank, *World Development Indicators 2014*; World Trade Organization, *Trade Policy Review*, 1995–2014; Office of the U.S. Trade Representative, *2014 National Trade Estimate Report on Foreign Trade Barriers*; World Bank, *Doing Business 2013* and *Doing Business 2014*; U.S. Department of Commerce, *Country Commercial Guide*, 2009–2014; Economist Intelligence Unit, *Country Commerce*, 2014; World Economic Forum, *The Global Enabling Trade Report 2014*; and official government publications of each country.

Investment Freedom

In an economically free country, there would be no constraints on the flow of investment capital. Individuals and firms would be allowed to move their resources into and out of specific activities, both internally and across the country's borders, without restriction. Such an ideal country would receive a score of 100 on the investment freedom component of the *Index*.

In practice, however, most countries have a variety of restrictions on investment. Some have different rules for foreign and domestic investment; some restrict access to foreign exchange; some impose restrictions on payments, transfers, and capital transactions; in some, certain industries are closed to foreign investment.

The *Index* evaluates a variety of regulatory restrictions that are typically imposed on investment. Points, as indicated below, are deducted from the ideal score of 100 for each of the restrictions found in a country's investment regime. It is not necessary for a government to impose all of the listed restrictions at the maximum level to effectively eliminate investment freedom. Those few governments that impose so many restrictions that they total more than 100 points in deductions have had their scores set at zero.

Investment restrictions:

National treatment of foreign investment
- No national treatment, prescreening — 25 points deducted
- Some national treatment, some prescreening — 15 points deducted
- Some national treatment or prescreening — 5 points deducted

Foreign investment code
- No transparency and burdensome bureaucracy — 20 points deducted
- Inefficient policy implementation and bureaucracy — 10 points deducted
- Some investment laws and practices non-transparent or inefficiently implemented — 5 points deducted

Restrictions on land ownership
- All real estate purchases restricted — 15 points deducted
- No foreign purchases of real estate — 10 points deducted
- Some restrictions on purchases of real estate — 5 points deducted

Sectoral investment restrictions
- Multiple sectors restricted — 20 points deducted
- Few sectors restricted — 10 points deducted
- One or two sectors restricted — 5 points deducted

Expropriation of investments without fair compensation
- Common with no legal recourse — 25 points deducted
- Common with some legal recourse — 15 points deducted
- Uncommon but occurs — 5 points deducted

Foreign exchange controls
- No access by foreigners or residents — 25 points deducted
- Access available but heavily restricted — 15 points deducted
- Access available with few restrictions — 5 points deducted

Capital controls

• No repatriation of profits; all transactions require government approval	25 points deducted
• Inward and outward capital movements require approval and face some restrictions	15 points deducted
• Most transfers approved with some restrictions	5 points deducted

Up to an additional 20 points may be deducted for security problems, a lack of basic investment infrastructure, or other government policies that indirectly burden the investment process and limit investment freedom.

Sources. Unless otherwise noted, the *Index* relies on the following sources for data on capital flows and foreign investment, in order of priority: official government publications of each country; U.S. Department of State, *Investment Climate Statements 2014*; Economist Intelligence Unit, *Country Commerce*, 2011–2014; Office of the U.S. Trade Representative, *2014 National Trade Estimate Report on Foreign Trade Barriers*; World Bank, *Investing Across Borders, 2012*; Organisation for Economic Co-operation and Development, *Services Trade Restrictiveness Index*; and U.S. Department of Commerce, *Country Commercial Guide*, 2011–2014.

Financial Freedom

Financial freedom is an indicator of banking efficiency as well as a measure of independence from government control and interference in the financial sector. State ownership of banks and other financial institutions such as insurers and capital markets reduces competition and generally lowers the level of access to credit.

In an ideal banking and financing environment where a minimum level of government interference exists, independent central bank supervision and regulation of financial institutions are limited to enforcing contractual obligations and preventing fraud. Credit is allocated on market terms, and the government does not own financial institutions. Financial institutions provide various types of financial services to individuals and companies. Banks are free to extend credit, accept deposits, and conduct operations in foreign currencies. Foreign financial institutions operate freely and are treated the same as domestic institutions.

The *Index* scores an economy's financial freedom by looking at five broad areas:

- The extent of government regulation of financial services,
- The degree of state intervention in banks and other financial firms through direct and indirect ownership,
- Government influence on the allocation of credit,
- The extent of financial and capital market development, and
- Openness to foreign competition.

These five areas are considered to assess an economy's overall level of financial freedom that ensures easy and effective access to financing opportunities for people and businesses in the economy. An overall score on a scale of 0 to 100 is given to an economy's financial freedom through deductions from the ideal score of 100.

- **100—Negligible government interference.**
- **90—Minimal government interference.** Regulation of financial institutions is minimal but may extend beyond enforcing contractual obligations and preventing fraud.

- **80—Nominal government interference.** Government ownership of financial institutions is a small share of overall sector assets. Financial institutions face almost no restrictions on their ability to offer financial services.
- **70—Limited government interference.** Credit allocation is influenced by the government, and private allocation of credit faces almost no restrictions. Government ownership of financial institutions is sizeable. Foreign financial institutions are subject to few restrictions.
- **60—Moderate government interference.** Banking and financial regulations are somewhat burdensome. The government exercises ownership and control of financial institutions with a significant share of overall sector assets. The ability of financial institutions to offer financial services is subject to some restrictions.
- **50—Considerable government interference.** Credit allocation is significantly influenced by the government, and private allocation of credit faces significant barriers. The ability of financial institutions to offer financial services is subject to significant restrictions. Foreign financial institutions are subject to some restrictions.
- **40—Strong government interference.** The central bank is subject to government influence, its supervision of financial institutions is heavy-handed, and its ability to enforce contracts and prevent fraud is weak. The government exercises active ownership and control of financial institutions with a large minority share of overall sector assets.
- **30—Extensive government interference.** Credit allocation is extensively influenced by the government. The government owns or controls a majority of financial institutions or is in a dominant position. Financial institutions are heavily restricted, and bank formation faces significant barriers. Foreign financial institutions are subject to significant restrictions.
- **20—Heavy government interference.** The central bank is not independent, and its supervision of financial institutions is repressive. Foreign financial institutions are discouraged or highly constrained.
- **10—Near repressive.** Credit allocation is controlled by the government. Bank formation is restricted. Foreign financial institutions are prohibited.
- **0—Repressive.** Supervision and regulation are designed to prevent private financial institutions. Private financial institutions are nonexistent.

Sources. Unless otherwise noted, the *Index* relies on the following sources for data on banking and finance, in order of priority: Economist Intelligence Unit, *Country Commerce* and *Financial Services*, 2011–2014; International Monetary Fund, *Staff Country Report*, "Selected Issues," and *Staff Country Report*, "Article IV Consultation," 2010–2014; Organisation for Economic Co-operation and Development, *Economic Survey*; official government publications of each country; U.S. Department of Commerce, *Country Commercial Guide*, 2011–2014; Office of the U.S. Trade Representative, *2014 National Trade Estimate Report on Foreign Trade Barriers*; U.S. Department of State, *Investment Climate Statements*, 2011–2014; World Bank, *World Development Indicators 2014*; and various news and magazine articles on banking and finance.

GENERAL METHODOLOGICAL ISSUES

Period of Study. For the current *Index of Economic Freedom*, scores are generally based on data for the period covering the second half of 2013 through the first half of 2014. To the extent possible, the information considered for each variable was current as of June 30, 2014. It is important to understand, however, that some component scores are based on historical information. For example, the monetary freedom component uses a three-year weighted average rate of inflation from January 1, 2011, to December 31, 2013.

Equal Weight. In the *Index of Economic Freedom*, the 10 components of economic freedom are equally weighted so that the overall score will not be biased toward any one component or policy direction. It is clear that the 10 economic freedoms interact, but the exact mechanisms of this interaction are not clearly definable: Is a minimum threshold for each one essential? Is it possible for one to maximize if others are minimized? Are they dependent or exclusive, complements or supplements?

These are valid questions, but they are beyond the scope of our fundamental mission. The purpose of the *Index* is to reflect the economic and entrepreneurial environment in every country studied in as balanced a way as possible. The *Index* has never been designed specifically to explain economic growth or any other dependent variable; that is ably done by researchers elsewhere. The raw data for each component are provided so that others can study, weight, and integrate as they see fit.

Using the Most Currently Available Information. Analyzing economic freedom annually enables the *Index* to include the most recent information as it becomes available country by country. A data cutoff date is used so that all countries are treated fairly. As described above, the period of study for the current year's *Index* considers all information as of the last day of June of the previous year (in this case, June 30, 2014). Any new legislative changes or policy actions effective after that date have no positive or negative impact on scores or rankings.[9]

ENDNOTES

1. The following countries are not covered by the 2013 CPI: Belize, Fiji, Kiribati, Liechtenstein, Macau, Maldives, Micronesia, Samoa, Solomon Islands, Tonga, and Vanuatu. In addition, in 2012, Transparency International adopted a new CPI methodology and indicated that country scores computed with its revised methodology should not be considered directly comparable to scores for previous years. To accommodate the CPI revision, the 2014 *Index* adopted a transitional methodology to phase in the change. As detailed in the methodology chapter of the 2014 *Index of Economic Freedom*, the 2014 *Index* used an average of current and previous years' scores to lessen the abruptness of any score changes and maintain as much comparability as possible. That transitional adjustment has served its purpose and is no longer needed. The 2015 *Index* thus directly reports the current CPI scores where they are available. Because of these changes, the reader is urged to use caution in comparing corruption scores over time.

2. Obtaining a license indicates necessary procedures, time, and cost in getting construction permits.

3. The recovery rate is a function of time and cost. However, the business freedom component uses all three sub-variables to emphasize closing a business, starting a business, and dealing with licenses equally.

4. The six countries that are not covered by the World Bank's *Doing Business* study are Burma, Cuba, North Korea, Libya, Macau, and Turkmenistan. The methodology for business freedom dates from the 2006 *Index* because of the limited availability of quantitative data before that date. For the 1995 through 2005 editions, we used a subjective assessment with a score of 1–5. Those earlier scores have been converted by means of a simple formula to make them comparable. Top scores were converted to 100, the next best to 85, and so on. This conversion formula is different from the one used for other subjective factors, but it is unique because those other factors are not bridging to a new, data-driven methodology.

5. The labor freedom assessment in the 2009 *Index* expanded its factors to six from the four used in previous editions. This refinement was applied equally to past editions' labor freedom scores to maintain consistency. The assessment of labor freedom dates from the 2005 *Index* because of the limited availability of quantitative data before that time.

6. For more detailed information on the data, see "Employing Workers" in World Bank, *Doing Business*, http://www.doingbusiness.org/MethodologySurveys/EmployingWorkers.aspx. Reporting only raw data, the *Doing Business 2011* study discontinued all of the sub-indices of Employing Workers: the difficulty of hiring index, the rigidity of hours index, and the difficulty of redundancy index. For the labor freedom component of the 2014 *Index*, the three indices were reconstructed by *Index* authors according to the methodology used previously by the *Doing Business* study.

7. See note 4.

8. MFN is now referred to as permanent normal trade relations (PNTR).

9. Occasionally, because the *Index* is published several months after the cutoff date for evaluation, more recent economic events cannot be factored into the scores. In the past, such occurrences have been uncommon and isolated to one region of the world. The Asian financial crisis, for example, erupted at the end of 1997 just as the 1998 *Index* was going to print. The policy changes in response to that crisis, therefore, were not considered in that year's scoring, but they were included in the next year's scores. Similarly, this year, the impact of government policies and more recently available macroeconomic statistics since the second half of 2014 have not affected the rankings for the 2015 *Index* but almost certainly will show up in scores for the next edition.

Major Works Cited

The 2015 *Index of Economic Freedom* relies on data from multiple internationally recognized sources to present a representation of economic freedom in each country that is as comprehensive, impartial, and accurate as possible. The following sources provided the primary information for analyzing and scoring the 10 components of economic freedom. In addition, the authors and analysts used supporting documentation and information from various government agencies and sites on the Internet, news reports and journal articles, and official responses to inquiries. All statistical and other information received from government sources was verified with independent, credible third-party sources.

African Development Bank, *Statistics Pocketbook 2014*; available at http://www.afdb.org/en/documents/publications/afdb-statistics-pocket-book/.

African Development Bank and Organisation for Economic Co-operation and Development, *African Economic Outlook 2014*; available at http://www.africaneconomicoutlook.org/en/.

African Financial Markets Initiative, *Country Profiles*; available at http://www.africanbondmarkets.org/en/country-profiles/.

Asian Development Bank, *Asian Development Outlook 2014: Asian Development Outlook*; available at http://www.adb.org/publications/asian-development-outlook-2014-fiscal-policy-inclusive-growth.

——, Key Indicators for Asia and the Pacific 2014; available at http://www.adb.org/publications/key-indicators-asia-and-pacific-2014.

Country statistical agencies, central banks, and ministries of finance, economy, and trade; available at http://unstats.un.org/unsd/methods/inter-natlinks/sd_natstat.asp; http://www.census.gov/aboutus/stat_int.html; and http://www.bis.org/cbanks.htm.

Deloitte, International Tax and Business Guide, *Country Highlights*; available at http://www.deloitte.com/view/en_PG/pg/insights-ideas/itbg/index.htm.

Economist Intelligence Unit, Ltd., *Country Commerce*, London, U.K., 2010–2014.

——, *Country Finance*, London, U.K., 2010–2014.

——, *Country Report*, London, U.K., 2010–2014.

European Bank for Reconstruction and Development, *Country Strategies*, 2010–2014; available at http://www.ebrd.com/pages/country.shtml.

European Commission, Eurostat, *European Statistics*; available at http://epp.eurostat.ec.europa.eu/portal/page/portal/statistics/themes.

International Monetary Fund, *Article IV Consultation Staff Reports*, various countries, Washington, D.C., 2010–2014; available at http://www.imf.org/external/ns/cs.aspx?id=51.

——, *Country Information*; available at http://www.imf.org/external/country/index.htm.

——, *Selected Issues and Statistical Appendix*, various countries, Washington, D.C., 2010–2014.

——, World Economic Outlook Database, April 2014; available at http://www.imf.org/external/pubs/ft/weo/2014/01/weodata/index.aspx.

Low Tax Network, various countries; available at http://www.lowtax.net.

Organisation for Economic Co-operation and Development, *OECD Economic Outlook*, No. 94 (May 2014); available at http://www.keepeek.com/Digital-Asset-Management/oecd/economics/oecd-economic-outlook-volume-2014-issue-1_eco_outlook-v2014-1-en#page1.

——, *OECD Factbook 2014*; available at http://www.oecd.org/publications/factbook/.

——, *OECD Statistics Portal*; available at http://stats.oecd.org/source/.

——, OECD Web site; available at www.oecd.org/home.

PricewaterhouseCoopers, *Worldwide Tax Summaries*; available with registration at http://www.pwc.com/gx/en/tax/corporate-tax/worldwide-tax-summaries/taxsummaries.jhtml.

Transparency International, *The Corruption Perceptions Index*, Berlin, Germany, 2000–2013; available at http://www.transparency.org/cpi2013/.

United Nations Conference on Trade and Development, *World Investment Report 2014: Investing in the SDGs: An Action Plan*; available at http://unctad.org/en/pages/PublicationWebflyer.aspx?publicationid=937.

United States Central Intelligence Agency, *The World Factbook 2014*; available at https://www.cia.gov/library/publications/the-world-factbook/index.html.

United States Department of Commerce, *Country Commercial Guides*, Washington, D.C., 2010–2014; available at http://www.buyusainfo.net/adsearch.cfm?search_type=int&loadnav=no.

United States Department of State, *Country Reports on Human Rights Practices for 2013*, released by the Bureau of Democracy, Human Rights, and Labor, February 2014; available at http://www.state.gov/j/drl/rls/hrrpt/humanrightsreport/index.htm#wrapper.

——, *Investment Climate Statements: 2010–2014*, released by the Bureau of Economic and Business Affairs; available at http://www.state.gov/e/eb/rls/othr/ics/.

United States Trade Representative, Office of the, *2014 National Trade Estimate Report on Foreign Trade Barriers*, Washington, D.C., 2014; available at http://www.ustr.gov/about-us/press-office/reports-and-publications/2014-NTE-Report.

World Bank, *World Bank World Development Indicators Online*, Washington, D.C., 2014; available at http://data.worldbank.org/data-catalog/world-development-indicators.

——, *Country Briefs and Trade-at-a-Glance (TAAG) Tables*, Washington, D.C., available at http://web.worldbank.org/WBSITE/EXTERNAL/TOPICS/TRADE/0,,contentMDK:22421950~pagePK:148956~piPK:216618~theSitePK:239071,00.html.

——, *Doing Business*, 2005–2015; available at www.doingbusiness.org.

World Trade Organization, *Trade Policy Reviews*, 1996–2014; available at http://www.wto.org/english/tratop_e/tpr_e/tpr_e.htm.

Our International Partners

Institute of Economic Affairs

2 Lord North Street,
Westminster
London, SW1P 3LB
United Kingdom

Phone: +44-20-7799-8900
Fax: +44-20-7799-2137
E-mail: iea@iea.org.uk
Website: www.iea.org.uk/

ADRIATIC INSTITUTE
FOR PUBLIC POLICY

Adriatic Institute for Public Policy

Markovici 15, Srdoci
51000 Rijeka, Croatia

Phone: +385-51-626-582
E-mail:
AdriaticIPP@aol.com
Website:
www.adriaticinstitute.org

Istituto Bruno Leoni

Istituto Bruno Leoni

Piazza Cavour 3
10123 Torino
Italy

Phone: +39 (011) 1978 1215
Fax: +39 (011) 1978 1216
E-mail: info@brunoleoni.it
Website: www.brunoleoni.it/

F. A. Hayek
Foundation

Nadácia F. A. Hayeka Bratislava

Jašíkova 6
Bratislava
Slovakia
821 03

Phone: +421-2-48-291-585
Fax: +421-2-48-291-243
E-mail: hayek@hayek.sk
Website: www.hayek.sk

IME
Institute for Market Economics

Institute for Market Economics

Bulgaria
1000 Sofia
10 Patriarh Evtimii Blvd., fl.2

Phone: +359-2-952-62-66
E-mail: mail@ime.bg
Website: http://ime.bg/en/

Lithuanian
Free
Market
Institute

Lithuanian Free Market Institute

3A Šeimyniškių St.
LT-09312 Vilnius
Lithuania

Phone: +370-5-250 0280
E-mail: LFMI@freema.org
Website: http://en.llri.lt/

Fundación Libertad

Mitre 170
2000 Rosario Sta Fe Rep. Arg.

Teléfono: ++54 341 4105000
Email:
prensa@libertad.org.ar
Página Web:
http://www.libertad.org.ar

Fundación Libertad y Desarrollo

Pedro de Villagra 2265,
Vitacura

Teléfono: ++ (56-2) 377-4800
Email: lyd@lyd.com
Página Web:
http://www.lyd.com

Instituto de Ciencia Política (ICP)

Calle 70 No. 7A-29
Bogotá

Teléfono: (+571) 317 7979
Email: info@icpcolombia.org
Página Web:
http://www.icpcolombia.org

Fundación para el Análisis y los Estudios Sociales (FAES)

C/ María de Molina 40 –
6ª planta
28006 – Madrid

Teléfono: +++34 91 576 6857
Email: fundacionfaes
@fundacionfaes.org
Página Web:
http://www.fundacionfaes.org

Centro de Investigaciones Sobre la Libre Empresa, A.C.

Camelia 329 Col. Florida C.P.
01030 México D.F.

Teléfono: +++56.62.42.50
Teléfono: +++ 56.62.45.00
Email: instituto@cisle.org.mx
Página Web:
http://www.cisle.org.mx/

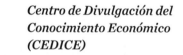

Centro de Investigación y Estudios Legales (CITEL)

Coronel Portillo No 521
San Isidro, Lima 27

Teléfono: ++511-222-3286
Email: info@citel.org
Página Web: www.citel.org

Centro de Divulgación del Conocimiento Económico (CEDICE)

Av. Andrés Eloy Blanco (Este
2)
Edificio Cámara de comercio
de Caracas, Nivel Auditorio
Los Caobos, Caracas

Teléfono: ++58 212 571 3357
Página Web:
www.cedice.org.ve

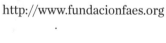